Lecture Notes in Computer Science 13517

Gabriele Meiselwitz · Abbas Moallem ·
Panayiotis Zaphiris · Andri Ioannou ·
Robert A. Sottilare · Jessica Schwarz ·
Xiaowen Fang (Eds.)

HCI International 2022 – Late Breaking Papers

Interaction in New Media, Learning and Games

24th International Conference on Human-Computer Interaction
HCII 2022, Virtual Event, June 26 – July 1, 2022
Proceedings

 Springer

Editors
Gabriele Meiselwitz
Computer and Information Sciences
Towson University
Towson, MD, USA

Panayiotis Zaphiris 🆔
Department of Multimedia and Graphic Arts
Cyprus University of Technology
Limassol, Cyprus

Robert A. Sottilare
Soar Technology, Inc.
Orlando, FL, USA

Xiaowen Fang
DePaul University
Chicago, IL, USA

Abbas Moallem
San Jose State University
San Jose, CA, USA

Andri Ioannou 🆔
Cyprus University of Technology
Limassol, Cyprus

Research Center on Interactive Media, Smart
Systems and Emerging Technologies
(CYENS)
Limassol, Cyprus

Jessica Schwarz
MMS
Fraunhofer FKIE
Wachtberg, Nordrhein-Westfalen, Germany

ISSN 0302-9743 ISSN 1611-3349 (electronic)
Lecture Notes in Computer Science
ISBN 978-3-031-22130-9 ISBN 978-3-031-22131-6 (eBook)
https://doi.org/10.1007/978-3-031-22131-6

This Springer imprint is published by the registered company Springer Nature Switzerland AG
The registered company address is: Gewerbestrasse 11, 6330 Cham, Switzerland

Foreword

Human-computer interaction (HCI) is acquiring an ever-increasing scientific and industrial importance, as well as having more impact on people's everyday life, as an ever-growing number of human activities are progressively moving from the physical to the digital world. This process, which has been ongoing for some time now, has been dramatically accelerated by the COVID-19 pandemic. The HCI International (HCII) conference series, held yearly, aims to respond to the compelling need to advance the exchange of knowledge and research and development efforts on the human aspects of design and use of computing systems.

The 24th International Conference on Human-Computer Interaction, HCI International 2022 (HCII 2022), was planned to be held at the Gothia Towers Hotel and Swedish Exhibition & Congress Centre, Göteborg, Sweden, during June 26 to July 1, 2022. Due to the COVID-19 pandemic and with everyone's health and safety in mind, HCII 2022 was organized and run as a virtual conference. It incorporated the 21 thematic areas and affiliated conferences listed on the following page.

A total of 5583 individuals from academia, research institutes, industry, and governmental agencies from 88 countries submitted contributions, and 1276 papers and 275 posters were included in the proceedings that were published just before the start of the conference. Additionally, 296 papers and 181 posters are included in the volumes of the proceedings published after the conference, as "Late Breaking Work". The contributions thoroughly cover the entire field of human-computer interaction, addressing major advances in knowledge and effective use of computers in a variety of application areas. These papers provide academics, researchers, engineers, scientists, practitioners, and students with state-of-the-art information on the most recent advances in HCI. The volumes constituting the full set of the HCII 2022 conference proceedings are listed in the following pages.

I would like to thank the Program Board Chairs and the members of the Program Boards of all thematic areas and affiliated conferences for their contribution and support towards the highest scientific quality and overall success of the HCI International 2022 conference; they have helped in so many ways, including session organization, paper reviewing (single-blind review process, with a minimum of two reviews per submission) and, more generally, acting as good-will ambassadors for the HCII conference.

This conference would not have been possible without the continuous and unwavering support and advice of Gavriel Salvendy, Founder, General Chair Emeritus, and Scientific Advisor. For his outstanding efforts, I would like to express my appreciation to Abbas Moallem, Communications Chair and Editor of HCI International News.

July 2022   Constantine Stephanidis

HCI International 2022 Thematic Areas and Affiliated Conferences

Thematic Areas

- HCI: Human-Computer Interaction
- HIMI: Human Interface and the Management of Information

Affiliated Conferences

- EPCE: 19th International Conference on Engineering Psychology and Cognitive Ergonomics
- AC: 16th International Conference on Augmented Cognition
- UAHCI: 16th International Conference on Universal Access in Human-Computer Interaction
- CCD: 14th International Conference on Cross-Cultural Design
- SCSM: 14th International Conference on Social Computing and Social Media
- VAMR: 14th International Conference on Virtual, Augmented and Mixed Reality
- DHM: 13th International Conference on Digital Human Modeling and Applications in Health, Safety, Ergonomics and Risk Management
- DUXU: 11th International Conference on Design, User Experience and Usability
- C&C: 10th International Conference on Culture and Computing
- DAPI: 10th International Conference on Distributed, Ambient and Pervasive Interactions
- HCIBGO: 9th International Conference on HCI in Business, Government and Organizations
- LCT: 9th International Conference on Learning and Collaboration Technologies
- ITAP: 8th International Conference on Human Aspects of IT for the Aged Population
- AIS: 4th International Conference on Adaptive Instructional Systems
- HCI-CPT: 4th International Conference on HCI for Cybersecurity, Privacy and Trust
- HCI-Games: 4th International Conference on HCI in Games
- MobiTAS: 4th International Conference on HCI in Mobility, Transport and Automotive Systems
- AI-HCI: 3rd International Conference on Artificial Intelligence in HCI
- MOBILE: 3rd International Conference on Design, Operation and Evaluation of Mobile Communications

Conference Proceedings – Full List of Volumes

http://2022.hci.international/proceedings

24th International Conference on Human-Computer Interaction (HCII 2022)

The full list with the Program Board Chairs and the members of the Program Boards of all thematic areas and affiliated conferences is available online at:

http://www.hci.international/board-members-2022.php

HCI International 2023

The 25th International Conference on Human-Computer Interaction, HCI International 2023, will be held jointly with the affiliated conferences at the AC Bella Sky Hotel and Bella Center, Copenhagen, Denmark, 23–28 July 2023. It will cover a broad spectrum of themes related to human-computer interaction, including theoretical issues, methods, tools, processes, and case studies in HCI design, as well as novel interaction techniques, interfaces, and applications. The proceedings will be published by Springer. More information will be available on the conference website: http://2023.hci.international/.

General Chair
Constantine Stephanidis
University of Crete and ICS-FORTH
Heraklion, Crete, Greece
Email: general_chair@hcii2023.org

http://2023.hci.international/

Contents

Online and Adaptive Learning

Interaction in New Media

Hints of Advertising Digital Literacy: Fragments of Media Discourses

Karine Berthelot-Guiet[(⊠)]

CELSA Sorbonne Université, Paris, France
karine.berthelot-guiet@sorbonne-universite.fr

Abstract. This paper aims to continue a reflection already started several years ago on the installation and development of digital literacy and advertising culture by the public. We intend to explore how online and offline media, platforms, and social networks have contributed and still contribute to the actualization of digital advertising literacy by producing and disseminating, in various ways, content informing about new forms of advertising, the advertising nature of some speeches and/or by giving a choice to refuse some forms of advertising. At the same time, our results lead us to note, despite legislation, the capacity to reinvent itself and to persist of advertising systems as problematic as dark patterns.

Keywords: Advertising · Dark patterns · Advertising literacy

1 Introduction: Communication Studies Approaches to Advertising Digital Literacy

This paper aims to continue a reflection already started several years ago on the installation and development of digital literacy and advertising culture by the public. We intend to explore how online and offline media, platforms, and social networks have contributed and still contribute to the actualization of digital advertising literacy by producing and disseminating, in various ways, content informing about new forms of advertising, the advertising nature of some speeches and/or by giving a choice to refuse some forms of advertising.

Different corpora are used to address different cases without claiming to be exhaustive. We will work on the basis of a sociosemiotic method. Thus, we will explore, mainly in the French context, how press magazines have presented over time the monetization of spaces on the web such as blogs, influencers, algorithms, dark patterns, etc. Then, since French law now requires websites to ask for the user's permission to use cookies, authorization interfaces are also forms of explanation that ought to be analyzed.

1.1 Defining Advertising Literacy

In the course of our research, our reflection focused on the question of advertising literacy in general, within the framework of a kind of retrospective inquiry. We proposed

G. Meiselwitz et al. (Eds.): HCII 2022, LNCS 13517, pp. 3–15, 2022.
https://doi.org/10.1007/978-3-031-22131-6_1

a theoretical positioning that enables to think of self-taught literacy [1], by a daily company with advertising, not necessarily linked to education and state intervention. Our approach to literacy does not correspond to the notions of competence and recognition deficits that are most of the time linked to it. Thus, contrary to UNESCO and the media literacy perspective [2], we do not look for ways to empower the public, mostly seen as composed of children and adolescents, to defend itself from advertising influence. This specific definition of advertising literacy builds on a long tradition of research that has established advertising as a powerful means of psychological and behavioral manipulation in the service of capitalism.

The academic analysis of advertising manipulation fed a suspicious point of view applied to mass media productions, such as the educational vision of literacy. It has to be linked to the tradition of critical analysis of advertising that gives the most negative role to advertising in its effects [4–9]. Advertising is then supposed to be a powerful means of acting on the crowds since the receivers of advertising are supposed to be passive, inactive, receiving the messages and reacting mechanically to them. This type of theoretical approach ignores individual or collective intelligence in front of the advertising, which is all about manipulation and false needs.

This perspective is based in particular on the writings of Tchakhotine [3], who demonstrates how the techniques of advertising persuasion, such as psychological conditioning under the effect of the repetition and scanning of slogans, have served Hitler's propaganda. In a different theoretical perspective, the works of the main researchers of the Frankfurt School [4–7] take up the idea of a mechanical, psychological influence of advertising, capable of creating, in poor and uneducated people, false needs. At the same time, from an economic point of view, its cost prevents small producers from entering the market. Thus, advertising is necessary to the development of mass culture and mass consumption. In synergy with the media, it manipulates the consumers to embrace the standards of mass culture and allows companies to absorb production surpluses by creating artificial or false needs. This theoretical perspective on advertising justifies the need to educate from the youngest age to the recognition and understanding of the stakes of advertising messages to ensure resistance to manipulation.

However, UNESCO's proposals do not take into consideration a common critical activity of the receptors that occurs, especially when mass media production tends to be manipulative [10]. Thanks to the reception analysis research, we postulate that advertising can be treated by receivers in the way they treat other media productions since it is mass-produced and supposedly manipulative. Moreover, It requires a critical activity of the receivers, which will be all the stronger that the messages are openly manipulative. The meaning of media products is not fixed and predetermined; it varies from one cultural sphere to another, which is corroborated by semiotics that establishes the polysemy of media and advertising messages. Their meaning results from the interpretation of those who receive the message according to the cultural, sociological, and a part of individual context; it results from a permanent negotiation of signs as a process of co-production [12].

Building on this open conception of "reception," we propose to think about media and advertising literacy as a gradual acquisition of knowledge and control of the codes rather than conceiving literacy as a material and method of self-defense. To do this, we relied on the work of Hoggart [11] and the analysis proposed by Jeanneret [13]. Hoggart is part of the cultural studies, which are based on the principle that mass communications, through media and audiences, are linked to broader social and cultural practices. Culture is seen as a process of production of meaning instead of a set of reference works. Hoggart defines literacy as the mastery of codes more often acquired through experience and socially valued skills than through education. It is not at all circumscribed to lecture and writing and relies on a distance in which resides the quality of popular know-how. In other words [13], literacy is the ability of a person to recognize and identify documents and their statuses even with floating attention and poor concentration. It enables, thanks to a double implementation of practical and critical adjustment, the ability to have an evaluative view. But distanciation does not end adhesion.

Jeanneret links literacy and advertising, describing the situation of advertising in France in the 1980s. The public of advertising bore expectations. Therefore, it enabled solicitation, provocation, and collective complicity. Advertising messages can be staggered or aberrant, staging public adhesions and rejections. These ads seek the reaction and interpretative activity of audiences. Practical and critical adjustment regarding advertising is exploited and traps media culture in return.

Therefore, we eventually define advertising literacy through this alternative approach: how people build, about advertising, knowledge, reading, interpretative, critical, and commenting skills. Overall, this means exploring how advertising audiences build and implement a culture of the domain, and this for several centuries for some European countries and the USA.

1.2 Pre-digital Advertising Literacy

Contemporary forms of advertising literacy are deeply linked to the historical transformations of advertising forms and formats [14]. They forged the ability of the public to analyze and take some distance. As well, the history of reactions and criticism against advertising discourse is necessary to understand contemporary advertising literacy its oblique and defiant receptions [15]. We shall concentrate on the example of France.

The advertising poster is one of the oldest advertising media. It is still an advertising medium of importance today. Overtime came the stabilization of different forms of advertising posters in sizes, formats, and organizations. These formats constrain advertising while making it recognizable: some elements are expected, and some of them are almost mandatory. This phenomenon is also noticeable in press advertisements that rely on what one can call canonical formats. In fact, the seniority of the presence of advertisements in the press allowed the sedimentation of the forms in formats.

Thus, formats impose themselves and transform the billboard or the press ad into stereotypes in the typographic sense of the term, that is to say, a fixed form, which programs the reading and shapes the messages "according to the imperatives of a prefabricated model" [16]. This is precisely what allows the emergence of advertising literacy. The long frequentation of formats, by impregnation more than by education, allows the public, at a glance, to recognize that it is an advertisement. In this case, "the form informs" [17], it enables and even empowers people to be aware of its nature and choose to look at it or not. In other advertising media such as cinema, radio, and television, classical advertising relies also on formats and is, at the same time, regulated by strong forms of delimitation that can be a short intermission in movie theatres, a change in tone and frequency of voice on the radio, and a dedicated opening and ending with a jingle of the advertising broadcasting on French television.

Through this approach of classical advertising media, we managed to think, from a theoretical point of view, an advertising literacy, with a theoretical positioning that enables us to think of self-taught literacy, not necessarily linked to education and governmental intervention, by a daily company with advertising. We can understand how people develop advertising literacy through different means, people being in control and/or capable of distancing from advertising codes from one media to another. How is it working on the web?

2 An Advertising Digital Literacy

2.1 A History of Web Advertising

Insofar as advertising on the web appeared at least 25 years ago, it seems useful, before tackling the question of digital literacy of advertising, to return, in a "historical" approach, to the forms of advertising that have appeared and evolved during this quarter-century [1; 15].

Advertising on the Internet started officially in 1994, as a banner on an American website; it very quickly became a new pole of importance for brand communication and a major growth relay for advertising agencies. A banner involves the integration of an ad into a web page to attract traffic to the advertiser's website. As early as 1995, the Yahoo! site included advertising. In 1996, the first advertising banner was launched in France. The same year, the Interactive Advertising Bureau was created in the United States and gave standards (Banners, Buttons, Leaderboards, Billboards, Square, Skyscraper, Pop-ups).

In 1998, Hewlett Packard proposed the first interactive advertising, and systems for tracking "advertising efficiency" were designed. In 2000, the first cell phone advertising was launched in Finland, and the "pop up" format appeared as well as "flash" and "rich media." The standards of online advertising started to be fixed. Thus, formats continue to evolve under the impetus of new computer systems. Thanks to an agreement with Yahoo!, Google became the leader of the online advertising market at that time.

In 2008, banners and sponsored links were the most common, but new possibilities emerged: blogs, online games, sites like Second Life, community sites, cell phone advertising. An advertising literacy has begun all along these 15 years, despite the continuous launch of different formats. It was known and addressed by the professionals who qualify it as banner blindness [18]. That's why online advertising professionals have been looking for other ways to advertise or promote brands.

This was the period when what professionals now call "brand content" and the notion of "conversation" with brands appeared on the advertising market. As early as 2006, in France, Publicis CEO used the term, in 2007, Havas put it forward and, in 2008, Publicis presented the idea in its annual report [15]. The idea of the emergence of a new communication paradigm is widely put forward by advertisers. Indeed, under the impetus of a few American consultants, the marketing and commercial communication world will experience a massive conversion to the virtues of conversation [19], thought of as a sort of communication panacea, adorned with all the qualities that advertising does not have, a pacified, egalitarian communication that would put brands and consumers on the same hierarchical level. Under the combined action of all kinds of agencies, brands will therefore fervently start producing Facebook pages, Twitter accounts, and others, even if they did not always know why or even really had something to say.

As early as 1999, several Anglo-Saxon consultants published a text called the *Clue Train Manifesto*, which today is given as the starting point for brand conversation. This text links conversation to an ancient state of society, prior to the industrial era when selling was the simple conclusion of a conversation between people in a place called a market. From this ideal and consensual vision, the authors conclude that: "markets are conversations."The paper then states that this type of exchange disappeared in the industrial era until the appearance of the Internet. We can say that, in the talks of professionals, the conversation is a "de-hierarchicalized horizontality" that allows recharacterizing content production, participative, co-production, and co-creation in advertising [19].

Subsequently, and in parallel, online advertising underwent a major transformation with the rise of platforms and algorithms for the recommendation and characterization of browsing. This is why thinking about the digital literacy of advertising has become a sort of priority in order to understand how, in the context of accelerated production of formats, literacy can be constituted and operate.

2.2   Fragments of an Advertising Digital Literacy?

In the course of our research, we first questioned the presupposition of the existence of digital advertising literacy at work in the new advertising proposals of brands and communication agencies. The communicational productions that we have analyzed in terms of unadvertising and hyperadvertising [19] are based on figures bypassing the knowledge/recognition of the formats of advertising in order to circumvent it or to use it.

We focused on advertising and, more broadly, on brand discourses on the web since brands tend to try to reach and take advantage of all web spaces. As a matter of fact, it is easy to notice that discourses promoting brands pervade the web, whether it is in dedicated websites, paid space in web media, online presence on "forums," and social media such as Facebook, Instagram, Twitter, Snapchat, and so on. Some of them are what we can call classical advertising occurring on paid media spaces. They also mix with web media discourses in all kinds of hybridizations that appeared in the last decade due to a rising criticism against traditional advertising as too present and obviously seeking selling. The kind of communicational uncertainty linked to the Internet as a system and its blurring effect on the identification of the enunciator tends to emphasize the phenomenon. This kind of jamming should be positive for brands since it enables their display and minimize bypass, thanks to contents (texts and images) presenting a cultural interest, whether it be as entertainment or information.

This explains why contemporary marketing, advertising, and branding professionals are so willing and eager to shape brand discourses with social and/or aesthetic appearances as different as possible from regular, classic advertising. Thus, advertising, in the traditional sense of the term, which openly presents itself as such, still exists on the web, particularly in environments where the audience is thought to be "captured" because it wants to access content, as is often the case on YouTube or on social media and online shopping platforms.

Since 2005, communication professionals have questioned the capacity of traditional advertising formats to stay efficient, arguing about the global saturation of usual media advertising spaces or the mistrust and even the rejection of "consumers" towards advertising. This, combined with the emergence of new broadcasting possibilities essentially via the web (the so-called "social" networks, Youtube, brand sites, influential bloggers, etc.), opened up possibilities of new horizons such as "conversation," "brand content," or "native advertising." [19].

These new formats do not seem to be able to confuse the perception of the receivers for long, and traces of the development of literacy quickly appear. On this question, we conducted a study on the Facebook fan-pages of a French and an American brand (Oasis and M&Ms), allowed us to show that the participants and subscribers to these pages are aware of the advertising quality of the posts proposed by the brands and of the status of professional advertisers of those who participate and write, on behalf of the brand, these exchanges.

The M&M's and OasisBeFruit Facebook pages are advertising productions where brands are omnipresent with discursive content very strongly linked to their advertising discourse on traditional media. The advertising show is obvious, and the participants describe the "authors" of these messages as marketing and advertising professionals. The advertising nature of these brand communications attracts participants who are willing to voluntarily receive, several times a week, advertising content from brands they have chosen. We cannot know if all of them are consumers and/or buyers of these brands, but it is certain that they are voluntary consumers of their advertising discourse, their signs.

This consumption of the brand's signs is accompanied by an evaluation by the same public of the advertising quality of the messages produced with aesthetic, narrative, or even strategic judgment capacities as to what can be considered as good advertising for a specific brand [1]. The advertising show is accompanied by the development of an amateurish criticism that takes roots in an advertising culture. Thus, audiences interact with brands on social media in ways that are informed and consented. In a more agonistic way, the general public understood quickly that the presence of brands on social networks enables them to express easily, with a broad audience, criticisms, or complaints about brands. Thus, for some brands, social networks have become a place for a new kind of crisis communication that can be described as "permanent.".

Algorithms add to the system as newcomers in advertising with actual possibilities and a long tail of imaginary, including surveillance or objectivity. Computer systems and algorithms have been developed, refined, and expressly designed to facilitate the identification of "consumers" as they navigate and supposedly allow the production and broadcasting of a tailor-made advertising message. On this aspect of digital advertising literacy, we conducted exploration on how the cohabitation, on the web, of different forms of advertisings allowed by the algorithmic calculations, ended up with forms of communication closer to the hype and the race to the promotion than to a refinement of advertising [20].

Some of it is related to the recurring need to ensure an audience for "non-advertising" productions of brands. It is, in fact, very likely that only people who are already "fans" of a brand will easily find the short films and all the other messages on social networks. They are already subscribers. The probability that other Internet users will come across these productions "by chance" or even "by algorithms" is much lower. Paradoxically, it is then regularly the good old advertising in traditional offline media which is chosen using its capacity to make known, public, and promote. This is what we qualify as "return of the repressed." [20] As a result, classic advertising productions intend to direct the public towards brands' online communication productions and not towards their products or services, as is normally the case. The message retains a classic and expected advertising form and additional content online, with its URL; the message is a classic "teasing" advertising, giving access to a part of the message, long enough to entice and make the viewer watch the rest of it; the message takes the advertising form of a classic movie poster, thus consecrating the message's spectacular form.

The intensive use of algorithms in almost all areas of the web paves the way for a massive presence of advertising wherever we go. This intense advertising presence is all the more a contemporary form of hype, a bludgeoning that comes as the results of the calculations carried out. It brings us to face the same advertisements or the same types of products, which introduces repetition and monotony that can be counterproductive. The more you spend time online, the more the sensation of ad hype occurs and imposes itself everywhere, whether you are on Google, Safari, influencer sites, sales sites, health forums, media sites, apps, Facebook, Instagram, TikTok, Pinterest, etc. Advertising, reduced to sales by redirecting to commercial platforms, is repeated, returning to the idea that repetition is the key to influence. This causes the discomfort of navigation, to which is added the idea of being denied any form of free will in favor of messages that are more of the order of pure promotion. Even adblockers are not enough to stop this.

The advertising hype is, in essence, obvious. This is not the case for another form of advertising, usually called "Native advertising," [19] particularly prevalent on the web, which raises ethical issues since it intends to mislead the web user on the nature of the message. This low profile or rather disguised advertising insertion is usually melted in the publishing spaces, and it mimics digital media discourses. It is specially made to deceive, looking like the rest of the website and matching the tone of the place. Some of it looks like journalistic writings, and the idea is based on the fact that, caught up in his reading, the Internet user will not question the origin of what he reads.

The desire to produce an advertising message that blends into the journalistic environment to the point of deceiving its nature is not new. In France, under the name "réclame," this kind of message was very common in the newspaper at the end of the 19th century and beginning of the 20th century when the French advertising self-regulatory association led a campaign called "truth in advertising" to rid French advertising of advertisements that gave it a very bad image with both advertisers and the public. Indeed, a certain number of financial malpractices followed by the ruin of small and large savers as well as health problems caused by pseudo-pharmaceutical products had exposed these practices, which were then perceived as dishonest. Aware of the problem, the press leaders also wanted this moralization of the advertising activity [15; 1].

This kind of luring process is supposedly forbidden in most countries, but new kinds of communication forms and formats constantly appear on the web, especially on the different kinds of platforms. Thus, it is very difficult to identify the blurrings between advertising and regular messages. The contemporary French advertising self-regulation authority pointed out as soon as 2014 that there was a need to clarify the nature of the issuer in order for the public to be able to make the difference between advertising and press on the web [15].

3   Media Denunciations of Digital Advertising Manipulations

We start now a new step in the exploration of forms of digital advertising literacy. We will explore how online and offline media, platforms, and social networks have contributed and still contribute to the actualization of digital advertising literacy by producing and disseminating, in various ways, content informing about new forms of advertising and the advertising nature of some speeches. We will try to understand how it can be supported by legislative decisions that impose explanatory discourse empowering web users to refuse advertising and, moreover, to understand the underground side of online advertising.

Different corpora are used to address different cases without claiming to be exhaustive. We will work on the basis of a sociosemiotic method. Thus, we will explore, mainly in the French context, how press magazines have presented over time the monetization of spaces on the web: blogs, influencers, algorithms, dark patterns, etc. Then, since French law now requires websites to ask for the user's permission to use cookies, authorization interfaces are new forms of explanation to be analyzed.

3.1   Inform and Explain/Alert and Denounce

Denouncing advertising through the press is not new in France. However, between the 1950s and 2000, it was the responsibility of the specialized press published by consumer protection association [15]. These associations appeared, in France, during the 1950s, such as the Union fédérale des consommateurs (1951) and the Organisation générale des consommateurs (1959). The State-supported, these associations by granting them and creating the Comité national de la consommation (National Consumer Committee) (1961) and then the Institut national de la consommation (INC) (1966). The associations focused their actions on two main areas: removing anything that might hinder free competition and guaranteeing consumer information. They published periodicals: *Que Choisir?* was edited by the UFC in 1951 and *50 Millions de consommateurs* by the INC from 1969. They wanted to challenge the monopoly of information, attacking advertising. Their main goal was to elaborate a judgment device allowing consumers to sort out advertising messages respecting their interest, that is to say, not misleading and valid from an informative point of view.

After this few decades, the question of the criticism of advertising and brands in the French press is constantly developing since the beginning of the 2000s. The French population has a strong tradition regarding the criticism of advertising which encountered fully the international movement of questioning both advertising and brands. The turn of the millennium saw the dual release, in 2000, of the French novel *99 francs* by the soon-to-be ex-advertiser Frédéric Beigbeder and, in 2001, of the international essay *No logo: The Tyranny of Bra*nds by Naomi Klein. The press wrote a lot about these books both because they were successful but also because it enabled newspapers and magazines, largely financed by advertising, to develop more easily a critical discourse towards the brands which were their advertisers, undercover of reporting on social news. In 2009, the same type of media treatment was reserved for the French animated film Logorama, which hijacked several thousand logos of major international brands to form both its setting and its characters. This short movie won numerous awards (Cannes, Oscar, César), which ensured its wide distribution and comments in the news.

These productions would not have had such an impact if they had not been widely reported in the French and international press: newspapers, television, and radio and were relayed by actions. Anyone who walked the corridors of the Paris subway in the autumn of 2003 was able to notice, in certain stations, strange advertising posters that had been damaged, scratched out, "graffitied" with black marker. It was the result of collective actions, organized and programmed by the RAP movement (Resistance to advertising aggression) in the framework of "commando" actions called "Stop Pub." Some of them were arrested and tried after the complaint filed by the RATP and the advertising agency Metrobus for "damage to equipment."

The arrest and the trial were immediately identified and highlighted by the media. The messages left on the posters pointed out, in particular, a degrading image of the woman and the absence of respect for the ecology. The aim of the action of the anti-advertising commandos was to denounce this degradation and accuse advertising of being a vector of cultural, aesthetic, linguistic, and social evils. Overall, advertising was accused of trying to deceive its receivers/consumers by resorting to forms of communication that are not straightforward. And all of this was fully explained in newspapers, TV, and radio news on a national level. It should be noted that in 2022, it is usual to see billboards "commented" or "degraded" in the subway because they are sexist, promote meat, a company that treats its employees badly, or simply because it is an advertisement.

We will now analyze the contemporary media treatment of the issues raised by online advertising and everything related to it. Our approach being a first exploration, we will reduce it to the analysis of a circumscribed case, that of the treatment by the French press of the question of "dark patterns." We choose them because they are still not well known by the non-professional public, they are the object of a precise period of appearance in the French media, and there is an international study carried out on the online media coverage of the question in English which will allow, as much as possible, a comparison. In English as well as in French, most articles emphasize the negative valence attached to the notion of "dark patterns" and recall that the notion, its first description, definition, and typology were proposed in 2010 by Harry Brignull, a digital interface design specialist. Dark patterns appeared in media between 2016 and 2018 since former employees of GAFAM started to denounce these practices because they "have gone too far,", especially in the creation of an "attention economy".

Since 2015, 27 articles on "black patterns" have been published in the French national press, 9 in professional publications, and 18 in general public publications. Leading newspapers such as Le Monde, Le Figaro, and La Croix have addressed the issue several times. The analysis of their titles and subtitles immediately indicates the negative critical judgment that is at work and the will to denounce: the analysis of their titles and subtitles immediately indicates the negative critical judgment that is at work and the will to denounce; the vocabulary is very explicit: deceive, manipulate, abuse, trap, hell, dark side, trick, spoil, etc. are the common terms to describe "dark patterns" and encourage the public to be suspicious. The very name "dark patterns" and its definition also endorses this warning role since dark patterns are explained as "are deceptive elements that are intentionally crafted to make the users do actions that they wouldn't do otherwise. Those patterns are designed to benefit certain stakeholders, not the user" [21]. Made to deceive, widespread in all spaces of the web and taking multiple forms, sometimes difficult to detect even for a sharp analyst, dark patterns are a kind of challenge for consumer protection. Their journalistic treatment in France, most of the time, denounces their abuses and their will to deceive, but it is difficult to give them the means to recognize them. The papers often end with tedious lists presenting some of the different possible dark patterns. The will to give the general public the means to guard against "dark patterns" or to use them consciously is therefore difficult to implement.

Internationally, the study conducted on the online media treatment of "dark patterns" gives results similar to ours [22] This paper ends with the fact that "dark patterns can be described according to three criteria: the strategic purpose of the pattern, the popularity among the media and how harmful is considered."In our review of the French press, we noticed, in the press related to the communication, marketing, and design professions, that "dark patterns" are treated in two ways: either they are described for their interest, as useful techniques in the field, or they are questioned for ethical issues, specifically in "Le Journal du Net," a pure player publication that depicts itself as "the reference site for executives in companies." Ethical issues appear slowly, on a small scale, and in a publication that is not really aimed at the professionals who produce dark patterns.

The ethical questions linked to dark patterns are, however, very strong, especially since they are present almost everywhere on the web. This has been noticed and legally taken care of by some countries: On the dedicated website, the European Union presents its law, its implications, and above all, the uncompromising choices it makes.

3.2   Ordinary Manual of Digital Advertising: Cookies Instructions for Use

The ethical questions linked to dark patterns are, however, very strong, especially since they are present almost everywhere on the web. This has been noticed and legally taken care of by some countries: "some dark patterns are regulated in some parts of the world through legislation like the General Data Protection Regulation in European Union" [22]. On the dedicated website, the European Union presents this law, its implications, and above all, the uncompromising choices it makes: the GPRD is presented as the "toughest privacy and security law in the world. Though it was drafted and passed by the European Union (EU), it imposes obligations onto organizations anywhere, so long as they target or collect data related to people in the EU" [gdpr.eu.] Europe has chosen to strongly emphasize its commitment to securing private data, especially when more and more people share personal data on the web. It came into force on May 25, 2018.

In France, RGPD is a continuation of the Data Protection Act of 1978, establishing rules on the collection and use of data on French territory. It was designed to reinforce the rights of individuals, to make the actors process data more responsible, and to give credibility to the regulation thanks to reinforced cooperation between data protection authorities. Personal data are described by the CNIL (National Commission for Information Technology and Civil Liberties) as "any information relating to an identified or identifiable individual," [cnil.fr] whether it be direct identification (name, first name, etc.) or indirect identification (identifier, number, etc.). Every operation involving personal data is referred to as personal data processing, as keeping a file of customers, updating a file of suppliers. Under the GDPR, cookies that are not strictly necessary for the basic operation of a website should only be authorized if users first give explicit consent.

The deadline for websites and mobile applications to comply with the tracking rules was on March 31, 2021. Since then, Internet users must be clearly informed that their data are tracked and for which purposes. RGPD and CNIL websites specify that all the uses related to cookies must be presented to the users before entering the websites, platform, or application, and they must make a choice. They also define two levels of information to preserve what they name "clarity and conciseness": the first level is an initial description limited to a brief presentation of the purposes of cookies, and the second level of information is a more detailed description.

They state that refusing cookies should be as simple as accepting them and, most of all, that Internet users must consent to the deposit of cookies by clear positive action, such as clicking on "I accept" in a cookie banner. For once in the French legal system, silence, as in simply continuing browsing, does not mean approval; on the contrary, it should be taken as a refusal. In this respect, no tracker not essential to the functioning of the service should be deposited on the user's device. The precisions and impositions of use that are made lead users to have to give a form of informed consent to the information provided by the system each time they arrive on a new site, platform or application. As a result, most web content must provide both levels of information and produce, each in its own way, little guides comparable to the well-known books "for dummies": cookies for dummies.

However, between the rule and its implementation, dark patterns can still occur. As the purpose of this paper is not to denounce the "bad boys," we will not quote the names of the concerned sites; we will only describe and analyze the interfaces. The first difficulty encountered appears as soon as one arrives on these sites, in the areas that the law explicitly addresses. Indeed, the choices of agreement and refusal are not always put on the same level. By any interpretation of the law, it is most of the time the choices of agreement in all things and request for additional information (Learn more button) that are put on the same level. The proposal to "continue without accepting" is sometimes put in another font size, sometimes another font, and/or another color in another place; you have to look for it, it means one knows that it exists and have some perseverance. Indeed, the choices of agreement and refusal are not always put on the same level.

The consequence of this organization is either to confuse the visitor who can then go to the quickest "accept all" selection or decide to get more information in order to make an enlightened choice. He is then potentially exposed to proposals that fall under the dark pattern techniques. In some cases, cookies and trackers are presented in large groups, with an explanation for each one and a clarification of what is essential to the functioning of the site and the fate that may be reserved for others. The user can then select the types of cookies that he accepts and those that he refuses.

Other presentations are more confusing. Indeed, the list of cookies, with some explanations, is present, but it seems infinite, quite destined to divert even the most courageous from a complete reading. Without coercion, the list does the work of undermining to bring the site visitor back to a conducive behavior, i.e., choosing the "accept all" button.

4 Conclusion: The web is not for free

In conclusion, we would like to untangle a little more the ways in which applications and platforms enter, towards some recalcitrant Internet users facing the choice of the "accept all." When it comes to a media platform, the user is brutally brought back to a reality he sometimes wishes not to see: the web is not free. If access to many sites may seem free, it is because they welcome advertising in its most classic forms as well as in the form of dark patterns. When the user of a website, platform, or media application starts browsing, in accordance with the RGPD rule, he/she is first offered to accept everything, to request more information, and, at another point of the screen, to refuse everything. Clicking on the latter then leads her/him to another screen that, this time, offers to subscribe or return to the question of accepting cookies and other trackers.

This interface shatters the mythology of the gratuity of the web, well-anchored because it goes back to the beginning of the network [23]. It reminds the Internet user of a truth that exists for most of the media and that was, in 2004, recalled crudely but with a form of sincerity, by the former chairman and CEO of the French television group TF1, Patrick Le Lay, during an interview in which he declared: "What we sell to Coca-Cola is available human brain time." Refusing to agree to donate available "brain time" requires agreeing to pay for the media content one wishes to consult; in some cases, the logic of financing the media through advertising is briefly explained.

Facing this imaginary of the web, rooted in utopian beginnings, and curiously maintained despite the heavy presence of advertising, the new regulations lead the online media to remind very directly that the refusal of cookies deprives them of the money of advertising financing by "proposing" to the recalcitrant Internet user to take a subscription sometimes for a few euros because it is temporary and most often higher. In these cases, the choice not to pay leads to backtracking to eventually accept cookies, which considerably delays the consultation. Anyway, the darks patterns are still there at the end of the road to "punish" the Internet user by leaving him only two choices "pay" or "accept everything," closing the access to "learn more," which allowed a choice of cookies. Paradoxically, as is often the case in the field of advertising, the profession turns around the constraint and manages to reintroduce dark patterns into the very system that should protect web users from them.

References

1. Berthelot-Guiet, K.: The digital advertising call: an archeology ok advertising literacy. In: Meiselwitz, G. (ed.) Participation, User Experience, Consumer Experience, and Applica-tions of Social Computing - 12th International Conference, SCSM 2020, HCII 2020, pp. 278–294, Springer, Cham (2020). https://doi.org/10.1007/978-3-030-49576-3_21

2. Malmelin, N.: What is Advertising Literacy? Exploring the Dimensions of Advertising Literacy. J. Visual Literacy **29**(2), 129–142 (2010)
3. Tchakhotine, S.: The Rape of the Masses; the Psychology of Totalitarian Political Propaganda, London, George Routledge, (1940, 2007)
4. Adorno, T., Horkheimer, M.: Dialectic of Enlightenment. Verso, Milano (1997)
5. Habermas, J.: The structural transformation of the public sphere: an inquiry into a category of bourgeois society. MIT Press, Cambridge (1989)
6. Marcuse, H.: One-Dimensional Man, London, Routledge (1964–2006)
7. Galbraith, J.K.: Economic Development in Perspective. Harvard University Press, Cambridge (1962)
8. Packard, V.: The Hidden Persuaders. Longmans, Green and Co, London (1957)
9. Ewen, S.: Captains of Consciousness: Advertising and the Social Roots of the Consumer Culture. McGraw-Hill Professional, New York (1977)
10. Katz, E., Liebes, T.: Interacting with "Dallas": cross-cultural readings of American TV. Can. J. Commun. **1**, 41–66 (1990)
11. Hoggart, R.: The Uses of Literacy. Aspects of Working-Class Life, [1957], London, Penguin Books (1990)
12. Eco, U.: La Structure Absente, Introduction à la recherche sémiotique, Paris, Mercure de France (1972)
13. Jeanneret, Y.: Critique de la Trivialité. Les Médiations de la Communication, Enjeu de Pouvoir, Le Havre, Editions Non Standard (2014)
14. Martin, M.: Histoire de la publicité en France. Presses Universtaires de Paris Ouest, Nanterre (2012)
15. Berthelot-Guiet, K.: 80 ans d'autorégulation publicitaire, In: Avis à la publicité, Wolton, D., (ed). Paris: Cherche-midi (2015)
16. Amossy, R.: Les idées reçues: sémiologie du stéréotype. Nathan, Paris (1991)
17. Souchier, E., Candel, E., Gomez Mejia, G.: Le numérique comme écriture Paris, Armand Colin (2019)
18. Benway, J.-P., Lane, D.M.: Banner Blindness: Web Searchers Often Miss 'Obvious' Links, Internet Technical Group, Rice University (1998)
19. Marti, C., BerthelotGuiet, K.: Advertising or not advertising: representations and expressions of advertising digital literacy on social media. In: Meiselwitz, G. (ed.) HCII 2019. LNCS, vol. 11579, pp. 417–433. Springer, Cham (2019). https://doi.org/10.1007/978-3-030-21905-5_32
20. BerthelotGuiet, K.: Advertising on the web: soft narration or hard promotion. In: Meiselwitz, G. (ed.) HCII 2021. LNCS, vol. 12775, pp. 41–53. Springer, Cham (2021). https://doi.org/10.1007/978-3-030-77685-5_4
21. Ducato, R., Marique, E. Come to the Dark Side: We Have Patterns. Choice Architecture and Design for (Un) Informed Consent. Choice Architecture and Design for (Un) Informed Consent, 1 July 2018
22. Cara, C.: Dark patterns in the medias; a systematic review. Network Intell. Stud. VII **14**, 105–113 (2019)
23. Flichy, P.: The Internet Imaginaire. The MIT Press, Cambridge (2008)

Geolocation Detection Approaches for User Discussion Analysis in Twitter

Ivan Blekanov$^{(\boxtimes)}$ (iD), Alexey Maksimov, Dmitry Nepiyushchikh,
and Svetlana S. Bodrunova (iD)

St. Petersburg State University, 199034 St. Petersburg, Russia
{i.blekanov,s.bodrunova}@spbu.ru

Abstract. In this research, the authors consider methods for identifying geodata of users of social networks within user discussions. The knowledge of user geolocation data makes it possible to analyze the spread of discussion among users of different countries. Authors do not try to determine the exact geolocation, but rather the country where the users are located. The problem of getting country-level user location data lies in the fact that a high percentage of users do not state their location correctly, either mentioning it in humorous ways or even not stating it at all. There are various methods of obtaining data about the location of users. Among them, there are text-based methods, methods based on the analysis of the context, and methods based on the topology of the user graph. In this paper, we make a special emphasis on a method that allows to reveal geodata of users who specified their geodata incorrectly or did not specify it at all. In order to test our method, we use Twitter datasets.

We propose several approaches to resolve the issues stated above. The paper highlights three approaches: the naïve approach, the naïve approach using natural language processing (NLP), and the graph approach, which is glossary-based and determines the number of outgoing connections. We have introduced two measures in order to evaluate the proposed approaches. Recall-GEO and Precision-GEO that are described throughout the paper. The accuracy of UserGraph method is finally evaluated using the metrics above.

Keywords: Social network analysis · Geolocation detection · Twitter users discussion · Open street map service · Name entity recognition model · User graph analysis

1 Introduction

Social media services on the Internet, such as microblogs offered by social media platforms such as Twitter, have demonstrated a phenomenal growth in the amount of users. This growth has sparked interest in using the data provided by these platforms to extract various kinds of information, such as, for example, the geographical location of users. The data obtained can be used to provide users with personalized services, such as relevant news, advertising, marketing and other content. Knowledge about the geolocation

G. Meiselwitz et al. (Eds.): HCII 2022, LNCS 13517, pp. 16–29, 2022.
https://doi.org/10.1007/978-3-031-22131-6_2

of users can allow researchers to analyze global social events in terms of which segments of the population they have influence on and what kind of influence there is. With over 300 million monthly active Twitter accounts in various geographical locations, the short messages they generate form a huge dataset that can be analyzed to extract such geographical information.

Twitter allows its users to specify their own geographical location. Location information is entered manually by the user or updated using GPS (but this function is activated only by small percentage of users [6] of the network). Consequently, geolocation data may be missing or incorrect for most users. There are several types of problems when using geolocation data, which are set and updated manually by users:

- Limited access to the Twitter API. The only tool for obtaining information about the geolocation of users is the official Twitter API service. Unfortunately, since 2021, access to this service is opened exclusively on a paid basis.
- Incorrect user data. Users may enter incorrect or fictitious geographical location data. For example, a user can enter "Mars, Kowalski crater" as a geo-position. Also, users can use geographical locations that do not exist at all, for example, "Krypton".
- Data ambiguity. Some users ambiguously indicate geolocation information. For example, "cosmopolitan, but from Moscow". It is difficult to process such a string with a naive approach, since there is a lot of unnecessary information in it;
- Lack of user geodata.

2 Related Works

Various approaches are used to solve the problem of the availability of information about the geolocation of users. They can be divided into 3 classes:

1. Methods based on the text content of the message.
2. Methods based on connections in the social graph of users.
3. Methods based on the context of user messages.

2.1 Methods Based on the Text Content of the Message

This class of methods includes approaches that use information about dialects, which are aimed at finding and using special words to determine the geolocation of users. Obviously, not all words indicate geolocation. Therefore, only local words should be used, i.e. words that are used by users living in the same territory and indicating their geolocation.

According to statistics, local words that can be used to identify a geo-location are much less common in the text than the usual frequently used words. Methods of identifying local words without a teacher are aimed at calculating statistical indicators. So, using the idea of the Inverse Document Frequency (IDF) indicator [1, 2, 12] propose Inverse Location Frequency (ILF) and Inverse City Frequency (ICF), respectively, to measure the locality of words. Usage of such idea minimizes the use and spread of local words by increasing the values of ILF and ICF. Authors [4] applied a number of heuristic rules to select local words. In the research [5], the authors propose a comparison of statistical methods based on information theory and heuristic methods for selecting local words.

Methods of identifying local words with a teacher are also considered in a number of studies. In studies [6], the problem of searching for local words was considered as a classification problem. First, the authors construct the geographical distribution of each word using a spatial variation model presented by authors in [7]. The spatial variation model assumes that each word has a geographical center, a central frequency and a coefficient of variance. The probability of using a word together with the distance to the center is proportional to the central frequency. Then the authors manually marked up 19178 words from the dictionary into local and non-local ones. As a result, a trained classifier was obtained, which the authors applied to the rest of the words from the marked-up list. The authors of the article [8] applied the above method and achieved satisfactory results for a set of Twitter messages in Korean.

After identifying local words, the next problem is to use them to predict the geolocation of users. Most researchers propose probabilistic models for constructing the distribution of users by geolocation, using the textual context of their messages, and then concretize the model for forecasting [6]. Another approach is based on highlighting local words of a special type in the message text, such words are the names of places. Authors [9] noticed that the probability of mentioning place names in messages can be both natural and depend on geolocation, and be random. Thus, the authors make a two-level assessment based on the Bernoulli distribution of randomness or regularity of mentioning the name of a place to determine geolocation and a polynomial distribution to estimate the probability of publishing a message with the name of a place from each geolocation.

In several studies, classification methods are used to detect and predict the location of users. Researchers consider user statistics on the use of local words in communications as signs, and various geolocations as classification labels. B. Hecht et al. [11] choose 10,000 words with the highest CALGARI scores as local words. Then users are represented as 10000-dimensional vectors with the values of the frequencies of terms, which are fed into the naive Bayesian classifier for training and predicting the geolocation of users. Similarly, Rahimi et al. [10] apply logistic regression to TF-IDF vectors of users. Instead of using local words as features, the authors add constraints using L1-regularization. In [4, 12] authors apply a hierarchical ensemble of algorithms to train ensembles of two-level classifiers to determine a geo-location with varying degrees of detail, such as a city, state, or time zone.

There are also studies in which approaches based on information analysis are used to determine the geolocation of users. In this case, locations are treated as pseudo-documents consisting of tweets from all users living in this location. Considering the pseudo-document of the user whose geolocation needs to be predicted, the most similar pseudo-documents are issued as the results of forecasting. In particular, [13] represent geolocation in the form of a grid. The authors evaluate the language model for each grid with its pseudo-document. In other studies [15], the authors use the Kullback-Leibler distance as a measure of similarity between geolocation pseudo-documents and user pseudo-documents. In their subsequent work [14], the authors use adaptive networks.

In addition to traditional methods, some papers also explore deep learning models for predicting user geolocation. Continuing their previous work [16, 17] authors propose a more complex model. The authors organize the Twitter user's messages in chronological order and apply a sequential RNN model for encoding. Thanks to the attention mechanism, it is possible to get a general idea of the message, which contains important and necessary information. A similar process can also be applied to context, i.e. to the description of the geodata of the message and the time zone. Then the combination of the three representations is passed to the softmax layer to determine the geolocation of the user. In [18] authors use a multilayer perceptron (MLP) with one hidden layer to classify user geolocation. The authors use the representation of the user's message in the form of an L2-normalized bag of words as input. The output is a predefined discretized region generated either by a k-d tree or by a k-means algorithm.

2.2 Methods Based on Links in the Social Graph of Users

In addition to generating content, users of social networks, in particular Twitter, perform other interesting activities, the analysis of which helps to reveal hidden patterns that have a positive impact on the definition of geolocation of users. Such activities include, for example, the subscription of some users to the accounts of others, the establishment of friendly relations between users, the reaction of some users to the published content of others through tools built into the social network, such as "likes", reposts and comments. Like the content of user messages, users' social relationships on social networks can also indicate their geo-location.

Such relationships are described in sociology by the concept of "homophilia", which indicates the tendency of individuals to be more likely to come into contact with people similar to them. Considering this concept in the context of the task of detecting the geolocation of users, the user's location most likely coincides with the geolocation of most of his friends. Authors [1] suggested that the more friends a user has in a particular place, the higher is the probability that the user is in the same location. [19] use a similar approach, except that they consider only mutual friendship. All the methods mentioned above implicitly assume that friendly relations between users on a social network implies friendship in real life and, consequently, a small distance between the geolocations of friends. However, this may be far from the truth. In studies [20], the authors found that a couple of friends live within 10 km with a probability of 83% if their mutual friends make up more than half of the entire list of their friends. The probability is reduced to 2.4% if the number of common friends is 10%. This means that a strong friendship based on the total number of users' friends can better indicate friendship in real life and positively influence the proximity of their geolocations.

In social networks, mention is another type of user interaction. When users mention each other in a discussion, it is assumed that such users have similar interests. Information about this type of friendship is very useful for determining the geo-positions of users. McGee et al. [21] conducted an analysis of 104214 users living in the USA. The authors found out that in addition to mutual friendship based on subscriptions, mentions and conversations of users also indicate a small distance between their geolocations. In his next paper, McGee et al. [22] confirmed their observations by examining a more extensive data set. Other observations were also noted:

1) if the user's subscriber account is closed, i.e. other users need permission to subscribe to this account, then these two users are located close to each other;
2) accounts of local news sources are located in the same location with their subscribers.

Considering geographical proximity to be directly related to social proximity [22] trained a decision tree to compare social proximity between different users to ten quantiles. As well as [21, 22], Compton et al. in [23] also use information about the mention of users in the text content of the message. The authors build a graph of user mentions and identify unknown locations so that users mentioning each other are close to each other. In studies [24], authors also consider mutual mentions of users as friendships. Rahimi et al. in [10] argue that mutual mentions are too rare to be useful. The authors consider the mention by one user of another as an undirected edge in the graph.

2.3 Methods Based on the Context of User Messages

Authors [4, 12] take into account the time of publication of the tweet, the values of which are presented in GMT format in the dataset under consideration. After dividing the day into time intervals of equal length, users are considered as distributions of the publication time of their messages. Then, when using the classifier, the shifts of distributions caused by the difference in time zones are also taken into account. In other studies [25] authors use a probabilistic model based on the time distribution of geographical labels of text messages to estimate the location of the user's home and workplace. The method is based on the authors' observation that the publication of messages by the user during non-working hours (for example, in the evening) is most likely to occur from the "home" geolocation, while the publication of posts during working hours is most likely to occur from the working location. Authors [30] also use geotags in their work, but note the publication activity of users in several locations at once. The authors first cluster geotags, and then define the group with the largest number of posts as a "home' geolocation. The geometric median of all points in the "home cluster" is taken as the coordinates of the "home" geolocation.

2.4 Summary

Thus, different methods of analysis and forecasting are used to detect the geolocation of users. More accurate geolocation detection models are based on combined approaches using both the text content of user messages and information about the structural interaction of users. The use of such a number of diverse content parameters has a positive effect on the accuracy of detection, however, it negatively affects the speed of calculations, and in some cases, the inability to use individual parts of the content due to the privacy settings of the user's profile in the social network. The speed problem is especially sensitive when processing user discussions in social networks within the framework of real events, where the volume of discussion can vary greatly even over a short period of analysis (from tens of thousands of users to several million). Therefore, as part of the implementation of the current stage, exceptionally fast methods of detecting user geolocation were considered.

3 Our Approach for User Geolocation Detection in Twitter Discussions

To implement our software solution for determining geolocation, a micro-service architecture was chosen, which allows us to present each stage of data processing as a separate service. This approach ensures the modularity of the system, which makes it possible to distribute tasks more efficiently and structure work on the solution.

To solve the problem of accessibility of information about the geolocation of users, it was decided to evaluate the geographical position of a Twitter user at the level of him belonging to the country. The following types of information were used as source data:

- information specified by the user on his personal Twitter page in a special localization field. It contains text string of limited length.
- information about the structural interaction of users of the discussion with each other through built-in tools (such as "likes", reposts, comments). This discussion information is presented in the form of a user-oriented web graph described in the hidden communities search section.

3.1 Discussion Processing

The discussion processing consists of several stages:

1. Obtaining the geolocation information specified by the user in accordance with his unique name. This information was collected and processed using a search robot developed previously for working with Twitter data.
2. Processing of the received information with a naive OSM or naïve approach (Open Street Maps API). With the help of the search robot in the previous step, text information was extracted from a special location field for each user of the discussion. The received list of text strings with a potential geolocation name at this stage is verified using the program API of the non-commercial web mapping project Open Street Maps (OSM), Nominatim in particular. It is a tool for searching OSM data by name and address of a geographical location. Nominatim accepts a string with the name of the object as input and, in case of successful verification, returns a JSON containing the two-letter code of the country in which the object is located. The resulting code is further reduced to the standard form in ISO 3 with the help of a dependency dictionary. It is important to note that each processed string is saved to the database in order to minimize the frequency of API requests in case it has multiple occurrences.
3. Improving the results of the previous step by using named entity recognition methods "naïve + NER". As noted in the review, in real life, users more often enter their location randomly, without any particular pattern, which leads to the fact that this data cannot be processed using just OSM Nominatim. Let's take "I'm from St. Petersburg" as an example of a string. Processing this string using the API will return an error. However, OSM Nominatim returns a correct result 'ru' for the "Saint Petersburg" string. This problem of geodata noise is solved using Named Entity Recognition methods (hereinafter referred to as NER). The python spaCy library was considered

as a ready implementation of NER for this project. NER allows not only to define named entities, but also to assign them to one of the following labels:

a) LOC (Location) - the name of the location (city, country, region, etc.);
b) ORG (Organization) - the name of the organization;
c) PER (Person) - first name, last name, etc.;
d) MISC (Miscellaneous entities) - other various names (holidays, nationalities, products, works of art, etc.).

Pipeline of text processing in the case of spaCy is Transition-based NER. This architecture is described in the article [3]. The idea is as follows. We have a buffer of words in a sentence and an array of state words (initially empty). We also have operations on states: shift, reduce, out. Under these conditions, the task of NER is to predict the next operation. Matthew Honnibal, the creator of Explosion AI, one of the creators of spaCy, identifies four stages in named entity recognition algorithm:

- Embedding - vectorization of document words;
- Encoding - reduction of vectors obtained at the first stage to a matrix, where each row represents a layer in the context of the sentence under consideration;
- Vectorization (attend) - bringing the sentence matrix obtained during the second stage to the form of a vector for further processing;
- Prediction - classification of words in a sentence according to the received sentence vector.

As a result of the processing described above, we will get the source text with the labels of the recognized named entities. The LOC label is of particular interest for our task. It allows you to highlight geolocation in the user's noisy text. Thus, at this stage, the NER method is applied to the geolocation field. It searches for a word in the noisy text indicating geolocation, which is subsequently fed to OSM Nominatim.

4. Determination of the remaining geolocations using the user discussion graph "naïve+NER+UserGraph". The user graph was constructed according to the methodology proposed in the article [26]. As a result of data processing at stage 2) and 3), two types of fields remain unprocessed at this stage:
- fields that do not contain information about the user's geolocation;
- empty/unfilled fields.

At this stage, information about the structural interaction of users in the discussion is taken into account. Using the glossary method, we assign users the geolocations that are most frequent among the participants of the discussion they mostly interact with. This approach does not allow to determine the true geolocation of the user, however, it reveals the probability of him choosing the side that he adheres to and quotes. Ideally, this approach calculates geolocation for each user of the discussion. However, it is important to note that the geolocation of some users may not be recognized in the following cases:

- the case of complete isolation of the vertex of the user web graph (when the user generated content but did not interact with other users);

- the case of partial isolation of the vertex of the user web graph (when the user has only one outgoing connection with another user);
- the case of mixed interaction of a vertex with two or more vertices (when the user has an equal number of outgoing connections with 2 (or more) users with different geolocations);
- the case of a vertex being connected exclusively with unidentified vertices (when the user does not have direct connections with identified vertices).

3.2 Datasets and Evaluation Measures

To evaluate the efficiency of the proposed approaches in relation to the task of determining the geolocation of users, several datasets of conflictual public discussions in Twitter were selected. These cases were collected from Twitter and studied by the authors in their previous papers [27]-[29]. The datasets of varying volumes were chosen to test the methods. The sample cases include the following datasets of different volumes:

A. a small user discussion (up to 10 thousand nodes) is a case of "Biryulevo", which consists of tweets published on 17–31.10.2013 during the acute phase of unrest in the Moscow district of Western Biryulevo. Initially, it contains 11,429 users and 1,016 user connections. After excluding vertices with full, partial isolation and mixed vertices, there were 8670 users left.
B. medium-sized user discussion (up to 50 thousand nodes) - the "Keln" case contains data collected from 01 to 31.01.2016 as part of the discussion of mass attacks on women in Keln on the eve of 2016. Initially, it contained 40117 users and 98508 user links. After excluding vertices with full, partial isolation and mixed vertices, there were 30641 users left.
C. large user discussion (up to 200 thousand nodes) - the "Ferguson" case contains data from August 22 to 31, 2014 on riots in Ferguson provoked by the murder of an 18-year-old teenager by a policeman. Initially, it contained 169,676 users and 325,369 user connections. After excluding vertices with full, partial isolation and mixed vertices, 122779 users remained.
D. extra-large user discussion (more than 500 thousand nodes) - the case of "Charlie Hebdo" was retrieved for the period from January 7 to January 10, 2015 by collecting a response to a terrorist attack on the editorial office of Charlie Hebdo magazine. Initially, it contained 719503 users and 981131 user connections. After excluding vertices with full, partial isolation and mixed vertices, there were 580,580 users left.

We have introduced two measures in order to evaluate the proposed approaches. Recall-GEO (the number of users with determined geolocation divided by the total number of users) is used for all three methods, and the second one, Precision-GEO (the number users with properly detected geolocation divided by the total number of users with determined geolocation) is used for the UserGraph approach only.

A Recall-GEO completeness measure was used:

$$Recall - GEO = \frac{number\ of\ users\ with\ identified\ geolocation}{total\ number\ of\ users\ of\ the\ discussion}$$

To evaluate the accuracy of the graph algorithm, the following algorithm was used:

1. Users were selected from real datasets, the ones who correctly indicated their geo-location, where the correctness was checked by OSM. As noted above, there is 55–59% of the total number of such users ().
2. The algorithm is first run on a data set with all the geolocations defined in the previous stages;
3. Users with complete and partial isolation were removed from the obtained subsample of data.
4. The resulting subsample was divided into a training and a test sample in a percentage ratio of 80% and 20%, respectively. The graph algorithm was run on a training sample, and the geolocation of users was calculated on a test sample.
5. The results obtained are evaluated using the Precision-GEO accuracy measure:

$$Precision - GEO = \frac{number\ of\ correct\ solutions}{total\ number\ of\ solutions}$$

3.3 Evaluation Results

The Table 1 shows that in all 4 real discussions, 55–59% of all users indicate their geolocation on their personal page. It is not difficult to notice that the proposed method of detecting the geolocation of users based on the recognition of named entities NER adds 7–12% to the naive OSM approach. The graph method gives an increase of about 33% on top of OSM on average and about 21% on top of NER.

Table 1. Recall-GEO measures values for four datasets

Methods	Biryulevo	Keln	Ferguson	Charlie Hebdo
Total amount of users	8670	30641	122779	580580
naïve	0,56	0,55	0,59	0,59
naïve + NER	0,60	0,61	0,65	0,66
naïve + NER + UserGraph	0,74	0,74	0,78	0,79

As a result of applying the Precision-GEO estimate described above on real user discussions, the following values were obtained (Table 2):

Table 2. Precision-GEO measures values for four datasets

Measure	Biryulevo	Keln	Ferguson	Charlie Hebdo
Precision-GEO	0.72	0.7	0.75	0.72

The table shows that with its simplicity and high speed of operation, this method shows good accuracy (about 72% on average).

4 Geolocation Detection Results for Real Datasets

As a result of using the "naïve + NER + UserGraph" algorithm, the following distribution of real discussions was obtained for the top 10 most active countries:

The table shows that users of the United States are the most active users in all discussions, not taking users of the country where the event directly occurred into account.

To visualize the results, a web application was implemented that allows to display the activity of users from different countries on a dynamic heat map based on a list of unique discussion user names (Figs. 1, 2, 3 and 4). To implement the Front-end part of the visualization software component, the JavaScript language was used together with the React JS library. The backend was implemented in python using the Flask library.

Fig. 1. Biryulevo dataset heat map

Fig. 2. Keln dataset heat map

Fig. 3. Ferguson dataset heat map

The "naïve+NER+UserGraph" algorithm developed as a result of the study is capable of determining geolocation for users of discussions in social networks who have indicated information about themselves, as well as predicting geolocation for users without such information.

Fig. 4. «Charlie Hebdo» case heat map

5 Conclusion

As a result, authors developed three algorithms "naïve", "naïve+NER" and "naïve+NER+UserGraph", which were tested on 4 real user discussions in Twitter social network of different volumes: small size (up to 10 thousand nodes) - "Biryu-lyovo", medium size (up to 50 thousand nodes) - "Keln", large size (up to 200 thousand nodes) – "Ferguson", extra large size (more than 500 thousand nodes) – "Charlie Hebdo".

As a result of the experiment, it was revealed that the *Recall-GEO* measure of the approaches proposed by the authors was quite satisfying: 57%, 63% and 76% for naïve, "naïve+NER" and "naïve+NER+UserGraph" approaches on average, respectively. In particular, the naïve approach allows to determine the geolocation of 57% of users. NER allows you to refine other 7% to 12% for cases when the users specified their geolocation with errors. The graph method allows one to determine location for another 20–23% of users on top of NER. The latter approach works in cases when the users did not specify their geolocation at all.

Then, we have evaluated the accuracy of the UserGraph method comparing the results of the graph method with the results of other approaches. The final *Precision-GEO* of the UserGraph method turned out to be 72% on average for the 4 datasets. Taking the simplicity of the latter approach and its decent speed, the evaluated precision value is considered to be good, especially for large-scale discussions.

Acknowledgements. This research has been supported in full by Russian Science Foundation, project 21–18-00454 (2021–2023).

References

1. Ren, K., Zhang, S., Lin, H.: Where are you settling down: geo-locating twitter users based on tweets and social networks. In: Hou, Y., Nie, J.-Y., Sun, L., Wang, B., Zhang, P. (eds.) AIRS 2012. LNCS, vol. 7675, pp. 150–161. Springer, Heidelberg (2012). https://doi.org/10.1007/978-3-642-35341-3_13

2. Han, B., Cook, P., Baldwin, T.: Geolocation prediction in social media data by finding location indicative words. In: Proceedings of the Conference on Computing Linguistics: Technical, Papers, pp. 1045–1062 (2012)
3. Dai, X., Karimi, S., Hachey, B., Paris, C.: An effective transition-based model for discontinuous NER. In: Proceedings of the 58th Annual Meeting of the Association for Computational Linguistics, pp. 5860–5870 (2020)
4. Mahmud, J., Nichols, J., Drews, C.: Where is this tweet from? inferring home locations of twitter users. In: Proceedings of the International Conference on Weblogs Social Media, pp. 511–514 (2012)
5. Han, B., Cook, P., Baldwin, T.: Text-based twitter user geolocation prediction. J. Artif. Intell. Res. **49**(1), 451–500 (2014)
6. Cheng, Z., Caverlee, J., Lee, K.: You are where you tweet: a content-based approach to geolocating twitter users. In: Proceedings of the ACM Conference on Information Knowledge Management, pp. 759–768 (2010)
7. Backstrom, L., Kleinberg, J., Kumar, R., Novak, J.: Spatial variation in search engine queries. In: Proceedings of the Conference on World Wide Web, pp. 357–366 (2008)
8. Ryoo, K., Moon, S.: Inferring twitter user locations with 10 km accuracy. In: Proceedings of the World Wide Web Conference on Companion Volume, pp. 643–648 (2014)
9. Li, R., Wang, S., Chang, K.C.-C.: Multiple location profiling for users and relationships from social network and content. Proc. VLDB Endowment **5**(11), 1603–1614 (2012). in Proc. Conf. Human Factors Comput. Syst., pp. 237–246, 2011
10. Rahimi, A., Vu, D., Cohn, T., Baldwin, T.: Exploiting text and network context for geolocation of social media users. In: Proceedings of the Conference of the North American Chapter of the Association for Computational Linguistics: Human Language Technologies, pp. 1362–1367 (2015)
11. Hecht, B., Hong, L., Suh, B., Chi, E.H.: Tweets from justin bieber's heart: the dynamics of the location field in user profiles. In: CHI '11: Proceedings of the SIGCHI Conference on Human Factors in Computing Systems, pp. 237–246 (2011)
12. Mahmud, J., Nichols, J., Drews, C.: Home location identification of twitter users. ACM Trans. Intell. Syst. Technol. **5** (3), 47:1–47:21 (2014)
13. Wing, B.P., Baldridge, J.: Simple supervised document geolocation with geodesic grids. In: Proceedings of the Annual Meeting Association Computing Linguistics: Human Language Technology, pp. 955–964 (2011)
14. Wing, B., Baldridge, J.: Hierarchical discriminative classification for text-based geolocation. In: Proceedings of the Conference on Empirical Methods Natural Language Process, pp. 336–348 (2014)
15. Roller, S., Speriosu, M., Rallapalli, S., Wing, B., Baldridge, J.: Supervised text-based geolocation using language models on an adaptive grid. In: Proceedings of the Joint Conference on Empirical Methods Natural Language Processing Computing Natural Language Learning, pp. 1500–1510 (2012)
16. Miura, Y., Taniguchi, M., Taniguchi, T., Ohkuma, T.: A simple scalable neural networks based model for geolocation prediction in twitter. In: Proceedings of the Workshop Noisy User-Generated Text, pp. 235–239 (2016)
17. Miura, Y., Taniguchi, M., Taniguchi, T., Ohkuma, T.: Unifying text, metadata, and user network representations with a neural network for geolocation prediction. In: Proceedings of the Annual Meeting Association Computing Linguistics, pp. 1260–1272 (2017)
18. Rahimi, A., Cohn, T., Baldwin, T.: A neural model for user geolocation and lexical dialectology. In: Proceedings of the Annual Meeting Association Computing Linguistics, Volume 2: Short Papers, pp. 209–216 (2017)
19. Davis Jr., C.A., Pappa, G.L., de Oliveira, D.R.R., de L Arcanjo, F.: Inferring the location of twitter messages based on user relationships. Trans. GIS, **15**(6), 735–751 (2011)

20. Kong, L., Liu, Z., Huang, Y.: SPOT: locating social media users based on social network context. Proc. VLDB Endowment **7**(13), 1681–1684 (2014)
21. McGee, J., Caverlee, J.A., Cheng, Z.: A geographic study of tie strength in social media. In: Proceedings of the ACM Conference on Information Knowledge Management, pp. 2333–2336, 2011
22. McGee, J., Caverlee, J., Cheng, Z.: Location prediction in social media based on tie strength. In: Proceedings of the ACM Conference on Information Knowledge Management, pp. 459–468 (2013)
23. Compton, R., Jurgens, D., Allen, D.: Geotagging one hundred million twitter accounts with total variation minimization. In: Proceedings of the IEEE International Conference on Big Data, pp. 393–401 (2014)
24. Jurgens, D.: That's what friends are for: Inferring location in online social media platforms based on social relationships. In: Proceedings of the International Conference on Weblogs Social Media, pp. 273–282 (2013)
25. Efstathiades, H., Antoniades, D., Pallis, G., Dikaiakos, M.D.: Identification of key locations based on online social network activity. In: Proceedings of the IEEE/ACM Conference on Advanced Social Network Analysis Mining, pp. 218–225 (2015)
26. Blekanov, I., Bodrunova, S.S., Akhmetov, A.: Detection of hidden communities in twitter discussions of varying volumes. Future Internet. **13**(11), 295–311 (2021)
27. Bodrunova, S.S., Litvinenko, A.A., Blekanov, I.S.: Please follow us: media roles in twitter discussions in the United States, Germany, France, and Russia. Journal. Pract. Routledge **12**(2), 177–203 (2018). https://doi.org/10.1080/17512786.2017.1394208
28. Bodrunova, S.S., Blekanov, I.S.: Power laws in ad hoc conflictual discussions on twitter. In: Alexandrov, D.A., Boukhanovsky, A.V., Chugunov, A.V., Kabanov, Y., Koltsova, O. (eds.) DTGS 2018. CCIS, vol. 859, pp. 67–82. Springer, Cham (2018). https://doi.org/10.1007/978-3-030-02846-6_6
29. Bodrunova, S.S., Blekanov, I., Smoliarova, A., Litvinenko, A.: Beyond left and right: real-world political polarization in twitter discussions on inter-ethnic conflicts. Media Commun. **7**(3), 119–132 (2019). https://doi.org/10.17645/mac.v7i3.1934
30. Poulston, A., Stevenson, M., Bontcheva, K.: Hyperlocal home location identification of twitter profiles. In: Proceedings of the 28th ACM Conference on Hypertext and Social Media (HT 2017), pp. 45–54. ACM. https://doi.org/10.1145/3078714.3078719, 2017

Portraits of a Killer: Visual Expressions of Patient/Parent Expertise on Social Media
The Case of Glioblastoma on Instagram

Juliette Charbonneaux[✉] and Karine Berthelot-Guiet

GRIPIC, CELSA, Sorbonne University, Paris, France
juliette.charbonneaux@sorbonne-universite.fr

Abstract. This paper aims to investigate the search for online information and support for rare cancer patients and their families, focusing on a very specific type of cancer, glioblastoma. Glioblastoma is a rare brain cancer more than often diagnosed at a late stage, with a very poor prognosis and huge and disabling neurological impairments at the time of identification of the disease. Therefore, the analysis deals with the means of expression of the patients' families and not of the patient's themselves and on focuses on the understanding of their using of pictures, specially on a very specific platform: Instagram. Through the semio-communicational analysis of the french Instagram account #glioblastome, which includes 472 images and their captions, the study aims to understand how, in the case of glioblastoma, the mediation of digital writing and picturing can promote the recognition of the parent as a potential expert in this disease characterized by its rarity.

Keywords: Cancer · Instagram · Picture · Portrait · Representation · Science

1 Introduction

In the unprecedented context of the pandemic and its communicational corollaries, the "infodemic" and fake news, this paper aims to investigate the search for online information and support for rare cancer patients and their families. By mobilizing the tools of content, discourse and semiotic analysis, we question the on-line construction of the "expert parent" figure, focusing on a very specific type of cancer: glioblastoma. Glioblastoma is a rare brain cancer more than often diagnosed at a late stage, with a very poor prognosis and huge and disabling neurological impairments at the time of identification of the disease. Therefore, the analysis conducted focuses on the means of expression of the patients' families and not of the patients' themselves.

After highlighting in a previous research the federating role that a digital space such as online forums could play [5], we now wish to analyze the way in which "photographic sharing", which is today "at the heart of amateur practices" [10], can also take part in the construction of "emotional online communities" [13]. For this, we choose to focus on a specific social media platform - Instagram - and raise the following research questions: How does the use of Instagram help the families and close relatives find support? How

© Springer Nature Switzerland AG 2022
G. Meiselwitz et al. (Eds.): HCII 2022, LNCS 13517, pp. 30–40, 2022.
https://doi.org/10.1007/978-3-031-22131-6_3

does the use of images of the disease allow them to create a bond, between them but also within the family group? What role does the image play in the apprehension of the disease?

"Intentional and conventional, our symbolic images freeze our history in a few agreed-upon figures," writes Lambert [14]. They are, as Marion would say, mediagenic: "they correspond to the narratives that we want to produce with what happens to us and all events, they manufacture our news, they find in media screens of predilection. They are easily exported and make their visual slogans slam in the winds of our battlefields".

In this perspective, this paper aims to grasp the apparently paradoxical mediagenic encounter between a device that promotes images and an illness characterized by its share of invisibility. The paradox between hypervisibility and non-visible disabilities and will be addressed here. How do patients' parents deal with this communication challenge? What type of images provides access to a better understanding of the disease? How does this publication process create new visual stereotypes that coexist with scientific imagery and even use it?

Through the semio-communicational analysis of the French Instagram results to the query #glioblastome in its search engine: that gathers 472 images and their captions, this research aims to understand how, in the case of glioblastoma, the mediation of digital visual representation and writing can promote the recognition of the parent as potential experts in certain aspects of this disease characterized by its rarity.

2 Scientific Images

2.1 Instagram and Images: Collecting a Collection About Glioblastoma

When querying "glioblastoma" on Instagram, the most populated response, i.e., with the most results, is #glioblastoma. This result is not insignificant insofar as it precedes the name of the disease with a typographic sign called "hashtag" which, in a short time, has become, along with the @, one of the star signs of what we can call digital culture: "this sign, which is based on the use of the alphanumeric keyboard cross (#), has become a reference and a nodal point of the net culture. Its occurrences are moreover diffuse, from the universes of practices of contemporary computerized media (implemented by Twitter, it unfolds on Facebook and flourishes on Instagram)" [7].

This result indicates that many users of Instagram France have chosen to address the issue of glioblastoma according to the rules of the web and, by the same token, to inform other users, whether they are looking for information or to share their experiences. This "#glioblastoma" says that the producer of the post wishes that its image-text message can be easily found and it is a promise of community of information which can be of very different nature. It is also a sign of the contemporaneity of the participants to the accumulation of images and posts around the glioblastoma. They seek to make community even in its most contemporary forms and this puts at a distance the supposed or sometimes denounced vacuity of the practices on social networks. As Candel puts it, hashtag, which is definitely a social object has too main meanings:

- It appears as a tool for mobilization be it highly visible, on a political level or more diffuse, but very present, in the composition of aggregates, movements,

– It is also loaded with ideologies and representations, values.

What do we see once we've chosen #glioblastome? The usual presentation of results on the Instagram application of a cell phone is a mosaic of images. To access the text, you have to click on each image. Thus, the mosaic is our first link with the persons, institutions, associations that choose to speak out openly about this cancer, visibly willing, thanks to the # sign to be identified as such and have other people, institutions and associations see that and eventually click and find more about what they have to say. Instagram is the location of the connection and it stages a specific and dedicated sociability.

The search page mosaic makes it possible to gather and, at the same, start to distinguish between users and each image representing a profile a whole universe of representation and discourse about glioblastoma gathered and summarized by Instagram and, at the same time, the differences, yet serial, emerging. Therefore, the presentation image is all the more important as it is the first and often the only image shared with an audience. This is linked to the idea of conscription (written together or gathering writing and images) as defined by Gomez-Mejia [11] "[it] refers to seeing one's name written with other names. The devices of the contemporary Web multiply the conscriptions of names and effigies of Internet users within automatically generated lists and mosaics and promote the possibility of seeing one's name written with a third-party actor partner in search of clientele and audience".

The image mosaic is also important for other effects of meaning it induces. This modality of visual enunciation produces an effect of densification of the thematic and/or information which is given as a multiple whole so vast that it cannot be embraced by a single glance on the device and requires the use of scrolling to reveal its extent, reinterpreted in wealth. The mosaic is a universe and diversity, a claim to completeness and a focus on eclecticism. The mosaic form gives us to think by the "juxtaposition of glances on even more numerous events" that it is only a link of an underlying richness and abundance but promised [18].

2.2   The Medical Image, Portrait of the Glioblastoma?

Let's go back to the results page on Instagram from the query #glioblastoma. What do we see? First, on the left, a "profile" image, in a circle that contrasts well with all the rectangular shapes of the "buttons" and square pictures; then, a numerical indication saying that there are more than one hundred publications with an emphasis on the number transcribed "+ of 100" in bold letters. Then a blue button proposing the subscription to this #glioblastoma.

Since #glioblastoma collects all publications that include this hashtag, the profile picture goes to the last contributor, i.e. the most recent. At the time of writing, this account is called "la nature aux pattes" (nature on legs), which is a play on the word "naturopathe". Although #cancer and #glioblastoma are associated with it, the link is not salient. The image itself is a sheet of white paper on which is printed a simplified image of a mid-sun with rays, with the text "as the sun we always rise" and a name that we can assume is that of the author.

In the mosaic itself, as the Instagram interface wants in these latest changes, a small video is proposed first, it presents a blonde woman, smiling and wearing a T-shirt "wonder woman". The profile picture comes next, then four images representing a member of the medical staff or research or an image from medical imaging equipment. In addition, there are two portraits: one of the woman in the video in a different outfit and a black and white photographic portrait of a brown child who appears to be 4 years old. At the top right of this portrait appears a gray ribbon similar in shape to the red ribbons worn to fight AIDS.

Half of the images are therefore related to the medical world and they tell us that glioblastoma is part of this universe. We are typically in the case, described by Jeanneret [12], when the presence of the scientific image goes out of the closed scientific community. This implies selecting images that are meaningful both for those who put them into circulation and for those who will receive them, while producing a discourse that is based on scientific quality. As Jeanneret writes: "The scientific image concerns, by deliberate diffusion or by capillarity, the whole of society - in particular of a society like ours, where scientific rationality and technical efficiency play a decisive role."

He then describes the main categories of images that allow us to know that "we are dealing with science". The first category provides iconography and he gives the French Encyclopedia linked to the Enlightenment period as a good example of this aspect. The illustrations show "the structure of a salt mine", or try "to make visible the movement of the planets". These are illustrative challenges and "the occasion to create new techniques of representation, to renew the illustrative material"; it is also, necessarily, "a way to modify our glance on the objects".

On this category, the pictures of an X-ray or the results of another imaging system of the brain of a patient suffering from glioblastoma makes it possible to visualize the white spot of the tumor and its regression. It is the case in one image of the corpus presenting, in the mosaic, a composite mosaic image representing 3 images of a brain which one thinks to be the same one and making possible to see, by a system of dating added by the author of the composition, the regression of a white spot which one supposes to be the tumor. It should be noted that the understanding of this image is based on the assumption that the receivers will be sufficiently familiar with this type of medical image to recognize that it is a brain and that they will understand, as a result, that there is an anomaly in progress. It is thus an acculturation through the media and/or the experience of the disease that is defined.

The second image of this type in our corpus is more complex to understand. It represents a system of turquoise spots and fushia filaments on a black background. Its use thus presupposes that the receptors are able to recognize an image created by a very powerful microscope then worked and colored to make appear the various elements. We can think that it could be a cancerous cell linked to the glioblastoma. However, this is not specified, so we can conclude that this image is rather the detonation of an overall connotation which would be "the high scientific technicality and its mastery".

According to Jeanneret, the second category of scientific images gathers the didactic images and they often put in scene the scientists in their activity. It is for us the case here. One of the images presents a woman in a white coat in front of a bench carrying medical equipment and a screen; the other one presents a surgeon from behind obviously operating on the brain of a patient. The figure of the caregiver is mixed with those of the scholar, the knower and the researcher.

With these portrait-representations of the disease and the researchers and doctors who fight it, coexist portraits of the patients and their relatives that we will now explore.

3 Parents as Portraitists

The observation of the collection of images configured by the architext of Instagram around the "#glioblastoma" shows, alongside scientific images, the importance of photographs relating to the expression of an affective relationship, between patients and their loved ones. These photographs are thus akin to portraits which, as Adeline Wrona writes, "the interest lies in the unveiling of the link [21]. "The portrait, she further advances, according to the narratives reporting the mythical birth of painting, proposes a figuration of the living to anticipate its disappearance, or conversely, of the disappeared to preserve its memory among the living" [21].The uses made of Instagram only reinforce this trait and testify to its durability in the sense that we find there, centuries apart, these two figurative tendencies.

3.1 Holding on to the Living

Reviewing the pictures proposed on "#glioblastoma" leads to stop on scenes and motifs that could seem incongruous in the sense that they oppose to the mortal sentence, brought by the initial diagnosis, the representation of shared moments that deeply connote the joy of living-together. Some photographs give us the opportunity to contemplate what Barthes designated as "another proof of the phantasmatic force of Living Together": "living well" together, cohabiting well; what is most fascinating in others, what one can be most jealous of: successful couples, groups, even families. It is the myth (the lure?) in its pure state: good novelistic material (there would be no families if there were not some successful ones!) [3].

The reunited and successful family is therefore also a good subject for Instagram, especially, it seems, when added the unifying weight of the ordeal to overcome. The case of the account of a woman named Carole, c.a.r.o.l.e.l.i.f.e, whose pseudonym underlines the lively character she wants to give to her publications. These consist of documenting the joys of family life, alongside her mother, who has glioblastoma, on different occasions. According to Adeline Wrona, "the occasions of journalistic portraiture thus designate the moments of social life that motivate the figure of an individual distinguished by his or her role in the public space" [21]. In the case of Carol's account, the family portrait opportunities carry a double social dimension that symbolically pulls her mother out of the isolation to which the illness may have condemned her. On the one hand, they inscribe the individual life in that of a first circle, composed of the children, the sister but also the parents of the sick person. Carole systematically details, in the posts accompanying the images, the composition of the group and insists on the pleasure of being together.

A picture of her, sprawled out on a couch, snuggled up against her mother and grandparents, all smiling, is accompanied by the following text: "You don't choose your family, but I love mine like crazy! Cracking up and laughing in selfie mode and #rockyourlifebaby! My grandparents are huge, at 86 and worth all the gold in the world! My mom and aunt are #sorock and we say #fuck to #glioblastoma and #lupus by the way! So I wish you the same crazy family as me! Laughing your ass off! Keep a rocking spirit for the rest of your lives! Laughing to keep illness at bay! Because we will always win by laughing 😂. Love you 💙#famille #familia #famillesanchez #lossanchez #som ossanchez #fuckingcancer #rockyourlife #smile #happy #hapiness #tropdelove #tropde lovedeouf #coeuraveclesdoigts #jenrigoleencore #mercipourcemoment #tropouf".

On the other hand, these moments of life gain in potential social recognition because of their inclusion in calendars of occasions that can broaden the circle of those concerned. A first calendar is the one corresponding to the countdown of the months that have passed since the diagnosis and that become, through the celebration in images orchestrated by Carole, as many months gained over the disease. On April 22, 2018, she thus posts a portrait of her mother and herself, accompanied by the following words: "Happy sunday! Very nice day under the sun and shared with my family. My mom who was discovered with a grade IV glioblastoma 1 year ago and is fighting every day! 1 year that everything is going well and I hope that it continues for years to come! I love you mom".

Bernard Lamizet draws the attention on "the importance of the dating, of the temporal scansion, in the narrative of the represented event". It is about, he adds, "a kind of horizon of temporal reference: a horizon which makes the social time readable and intelligible" [15]. Through the writing of dating, the singular history of Carole and her mother is inscribed in a time that is no longer only individual but collective, since it is potentially common to all those who live and experience the passage of this cancer. The boundaries of this collective time are further stretched when Carol seizes social occasions that are not related to the illness but, on the contrary, to ritual family celebrations. This is the case for the birthdays of family members, her brother's wedding or Mother's Day, for which various family portraits are published, whose caption contributes, once again, to the meaning "still alive! Under a double portrait, captioned "Mother & Daughter 💋, Carole thus wishes a "Happy Birthday to my mom and all moms", followed by these "#s": #happymothersday #fetedesmeres #motherday #mereanddaughter #mumanddaughter #mummy #mum #love #happy #smile #smilealavie #loveunconditional #family #raybansunglasses #girlsinblack #incognito #retourdescheveux #glioblastome #fuckingcancer.

This example demonstrates how Instagram re-enacts the "paradox" identified by Anne Beyaert-Geslin about reportage photography, namely that "by becoming a textuality, the present of experience becomes past, but the photo is also a way of making the past remain in the field of presence, of not "passing it on" [6]. The property of this paradox, according to her, is also to "generate an affective effect". By this type of family photographs, the parents thus try to keep present the living-together, under an affective form that comes to reinforce the recurrent presence of another visual pattern.

3.2 Touched for the Very Last Time

In *La Chambre claire*, Barthes, quoting Baudelaire, evokes "the emphatic truth of gesture in the great circumstances of life" [2]. The analysis of the account "#glioblastoma" reveals the presence in images of a particular gesture, that consisting for the author of the photograph to hold closely the hand of the patient in his own. This gesture is all the more emphatic as it connotes the desire to hold the person, literally and figuratively, as if to prevent him from tipping over into the beyond. At the semiotic level, the effect of emphasis of this gesture is encouraged by the conjunction of two processes: the framing and the anchoring operated by the work of the caption, in commentary.

The various photographs of this type resemble each other in that they seem to proceed from the same intention, that of guiding the attention towards the joined hands. In her analysis of reportage photographs, Anne Beyaert-Geslin exposes that with the notion of framing, the metaphor of the tightening becomes particularly enlightening: "the press photo frames the event closely, the faces and the bodies closely to adopt this tightened pattern (weak extent and strong intensity) that we recognize from one horror photograph to another. Such an adjustment to the body of the model responds to a rhetorical concern. It allows us to enter into the intimate distance in order to capture the expression of the faces and restore the often paroxysmal affect of the event" [6]. We are dealing here with a similar configuration since the framing operates a tightening on the hands alone, detached from the bodies to which they belong. However, this narrowing allows us to perceive a detail that is highly significant: the hospital bed on which they are resting, which serves as a metonymic reminder of the reason for this gesture of support, which is itself metonymic, since it is part of a longer process, which is also taking place outside the hospital. In some cases, the connotative effects of the bed are reinforced by the presence of a second detail, also highlighted by the framing, namely the presence of the hospital identification bracelet. The gesture portrait then becomes a "stigmatized image", "this "image that has the particularity of being produced right in the flesh" and that "displaces the inscription of the photograph towards the body itself"[6]. "The stigma then becomes an autonomous narrative of the event (…). Through it, the body-witness now embodies the event. It carries it and it shows it", writes Anne Beyaert-Geslin. Here, the body, represented by the hand, comes to tell the struggle against the disease, a struggle all the more tragic as it is desperate as the texts accompanying these images give us to read, a posteriori.

It is there the second effect of emphasis operated by the images of hands. It is there that appears in all its power the anchoring function of the text, as identified by Barthes (Barthes, 1964). Indeed, in these precise cases, it is from the legend and from it alone, that can come the understanding that we are dealing, in front of the image, with a "that will be and that has been", with a "future anterior of which death is the stake" [2]. "You left soothed and surrounded by love, and during what was to be our last moment together, I couldn't help but take this picture. It illustrates the bond we had, indestructible", writes Anne Sophie Labourdette addressing her recently deceased father. The motif of the joined hands thus becomes emphatic because it is designated in the caption as a metonymic signifier of the very end of life, qualified a posteriori by the various authors who exhibit it, as the last opportunity to make a link. Debo 82200 evokes for example "the last moments when I could touch you" about the photograph of her hand in the one of her father, published on January 17, 2021. The owner of the account Dailyaboutclo mentioned for her part on September 24, about her father, his "last breath surrounded by (his) loved ones, Jules and me…".

In a diachronic study on the motif of the hand in art, Arlette Sérullaz and Edward Vignot wrote: "With the hand, man can grasp and manipulate objects. With the hand, he also has a means of expression, in complement or in replacement of the word. From the hand, whose lines are different according to each individual and evolve throughout his life, the human being expresses his existence in the world and his relationship to the other", [19]. The analysis of the photographs of hands on #glioblastoma clearly shows the persistence of this imaginary of the hand which allows the relatives of the patients to signify their support and their attachment to a dialogical relationship which can continue, in these digital spaces, beyond death.

4   Remember the Dead

"It is not the past that obsesses us, it is the images of the past." Georg Steiner.

Returning to Barthes' work on photography, Anne Beyaert-Geslin recalls that, for the author, "emphasis is a force for cohesion" and adds that it is also "this gain in presence that marks the mind" [6]. We saw in the previous section how much the images of #glioblastoma helped us to understand the cohesion between the patients and their loved ones, and now we need to examine how they also ensure a "gain in presence", after the death, which allows the parents to express their emotions and attachment. We then find what Barthes wrote about the power of photography: "Photography does not remind me of the past (there is nothing Proustian about a photo). The effect it produces on me is not to restore what is abolished (by time, distance), but to attest that what I see, has indeed been. Photography has something to do with Resurrection" [2]. In the case studied, two types of images take on this role: the self-portrait or "selfie" and the portrait of the disappeared.

4.1   One-Self(ie) for Others

In her work on the portrait form, Adeline Wrona draws a connection between "the work of publishing images of oneself authorized by the sites of networking", and Foucault's description "of the game of glances implemented by the writing of correspondence": "To write, he exposes, is thus to "show oneself", to make one's own face appear to the other" [21]. Instagram can therefore be seen as a renewed modality of this "making oneself seen." In the case studied here, this logic is split, in the sense that showing one's face, through a selfie, allows the poster to put himself or herself in relation to both the generalized other that is the one of the subscribers and to the missing person. This is what debo 82 200, whose father died of glioblastoma, does. She posts on #glioblastoma several self-portraits that fit the stereotypical aesthetic canons now well established on Instagram: smooth face, prim look, a slight smile on the lips… She seems to have worked to look good and, were it not for the commentary, it would be impossible to guess that it may be a portrait of grief. On December 31, 2021, she posts a selfie on which appears her face, slightly tilted, embellished with a mention "beautiful naturally", affixed under the lower eyelids, and another wishing "good weekend to everyone". The text states, "I wish you all a happy holiday season 😊😊😊enjoy your loved ones for me there will always be the lack of my daddy the 6th year still without him 😔😔😔😔#fete #nouvelan #papa #glioblastome 🖤🖤

A few months earlier, in August 2021, she had already published an image of her only face, accompanied by the following text: "Positive thoughts but alsoi negative…. Lots of questions but one thing is for sure I'm getting little by little to what I wanted to do professional level little by little ♥♥♥A lack of you dad so much emptiness without you but know that I continue what you would have been proud of…. I am and will remain proud of you for all that you have fought and all that you have had to endure both at home with mom! And in the hospital… I love you and will always love you, you will always be with me 😊#me #dad #fierce #hospital #ash #caregiver #love #glioblastoma".

We can see from this example how intertwined the narrative of the self and the narrative of the other are, as if one could not stand without the other. The individual, put in series in this "flow of identity images which tries to tame time by a multiplication and a potentially daily fragmentation of the self" [9], becomes collective. It is a "Monumental act" drawn up by the scripting parent to his or her ill parent, "the act that makes one recognize"[4] and which is enriched by another form of portraiture.

4.2 Obituary Portrait

The portraits of individuals are not limited, indeed, to the form "selfie", one also meets photographs representing, contrary to what was observed above, the life in the past. One finds there what Marin names the "primitive of the representation as effect: to present the absent one, as what returned was the same one and sometimes better, more intense, stronger than if it was the same one" [16]. Indeed, the snapshots of the departed show cheerful characters, full of life, and Instagram then offers, again, an extension to the obituary logic analyzed by Adeline Wrona around the journalistic portrait. "In journalistic matters," she writes, "the portraits of the departed, too, tell of the living, not the dead; the obituary offers portraits that capture the intersection between an individual existence and the collective time of living together"[21]. This is evidenced by the small narrative, written by raphael homat to accompany a photograph in which his brother-in-law appears all smiles, on a beach, shirtless, standing, in water up to mid-thigh, seemingly ready to leave the ocean after the joys of a good swim. "Everything goes too fast sometimes! Last Christmas I shared some oysters and board games with Francky, my brother-in-law. In the spring, he learned that he had a brain tumor. In the summer he left us".

We can see it in this example: on Instagram, the dead of glioblastoma are not "illustrious" people whose representation "reinforces the coherence of the community of readers" [21] but people recognized for their role in another community, that of the family. The missing individual then becomes collective because of his inscription, through the commentary texts, in the life of this group and in its memory. Pf fams thus publishes on September 11, 2020 a photograph of a woman, her mother, sitting with a baby, her daughter, on a beach, in a soft ray of sunshine. She writes next to it, in caption, the following words: 2 years since her light left us. To all the wonderful women she was and will remain. Mom ♥, grandmother, wife, friend, daughter, sister, teacher, traveler,… I have a thought today for all those who fight for life, and those who support them. #love #cancer #glioblastoma.

These portraits of the deceased thus show the adoption, by relatives, of an "allegorical posture" that "adapts in a media context the ancient forms of homage; the individual then becomes a place of memory" [21]. And, insofar as "memory is life" [17], the deceased person is revived during the time of publication, and all the more so when it is accompanied by a text in which the publishing parent will address him or her directly. "You will always be a fighter, a warrior, a mother, a sister, a golden cousin... Dédé will take care of you up there. This world, our family once again loses an extraordinary person 😔My thoughts are with your children, our family... Towards mom and dad... I loved you I love you I will love you nénétte... ", thus writes Cyndella 05 on November 14, 2015, to the attention of his sister Sandra.

Once again, the text illuminates the reading of the image, here that of a young woman well alive holding a young child in her arms, and, as Marin states "iconic powers become discursive forces to be sent back to their object of origin - absent" [16]. For it is indeed the force of discourse that the scribblers come to seek, in the hope, no doubt, of finding there another force, that of continuing to live with the absence. In this perspective, the use of Instragram by the relatives of glioblastoma patients appears, like digital forums, as a "technique of the self", a notion of Michel Foucault taken up by Alexandre Coutant [8] which allows "individuals to perform, alone or with the help of others, a certain number of operations on their body and soul, their thoughts, their conduct, their mode of being".

5 Conclusion

About portraits in the digital regime, Adeline Wrona writes that "these systems of figuration exploit relations based on contiguity, more than on the relation of inclusion: individuals make sense in their reciprocal vicinity, according to principles of sometimes incongruous gathering" [21]. In the case of #glioblastoma, the representation of the disease, of the illness and of the way of living it is thus composed by the incongruous contiguity between images connoting science, on the one hand, and others the deepest intimacy.

These images, profane, acquire a testimonial value when they enter the dynamics of sharing specific to Instagram. Mediagenic, these images are also "mnemonic" (Lambert, 2013, 70), in the sense that they allow loved ones to rekindle a treasured relationship, attested to by the "it has been" of the photograph [2].

This visual set composes a global representation that oscillates between the form of the "memento vivere" and that of the "memento mori", that "is addressed to the spectator understood as belonging to the human race: it is about a collective totality, a you indicating the humanity" [9].

Indeed, in the case studied, the relationship narrative takes on an exemplary value and erects a Family Monument that can enter the circle of stories experienced by other users of this account [5], through the game of repartee and open discussion in the comments. This is how "digital affects" are expressed, understood as "an ability to feel or to make people feel emotions". Fanny George and Virginie Julliard add in this respect: "The uses of signs charged with an emotional value participate in the construction of enunciative positions (of subjectivations). (...) The same way of signifying an emotion can suggest the existence of an "emotional community"[13].

It is the inscription in this type of "community" that the relatives of patients seem to come to seek on # glioblastoma. However, we must not lose sight of the fact that subjectivation, apparently favored by the use of Instagram, remains deeply constrained by the specificities of this device, whose "editorial architext imposes itself as an authoritative framework of enunciation" [21]. Thus, it is a highly normalized subjectivation in which the represented as representatives tend to be "crushed as mere numbers in a series" [21].

References

1. Barthes, R.: Rhétorique de l'image. Communications (4), 40–51 (1964)
2. Barthes, R.: La Chambre claire. Notes sur la photographie. Gallimard, Paris (1980)
3. Barthes, R.: Comment Vivre-Ensemble. Cours et séminaires au Collège de France (1976–1977). Seuil, Paris (2002)
4. Barthes, R.: Le Journal de deuil. Seuil, Paris (2009)
5. Berthelot-Guiet, K., Charbonneaux, J.: Vers une entraide numérique intergénérationnelle? Le cas du Glioblastome sur les forums de discussion en ligne. In: Revue française des sciences de l'information et de la communication (2020). https://doi.org/10.4000/rfsic.8642. http://journals.openedition.org/rfsic/8642
6. Beyaert-Geslin, A.: L'image ressassée. Photo de presse et photo d'art. Commun. Langages (147), 119–135 (2006)
7. Candel, E., Escande-Gauquié, P., Naivin, B. (ed.): Comprendre la culture numérique. Dunod, Paris (2019)
8. Coutant, A.: Des techniques de soi ambivalentes. Hermès, La Revue (59), 53–58 (2011)
9. D'Armenio, E.: Les influenceurs et l'économie des identités sur le web. In: Badir, S., Servais, C. (eds.) Médiations visibles et invisibles. Essais critiques sur les dispositifs médiatiques contemporains, pp. 33–70. Academia, Louvain-la-Neuve (2021)
10. Escande-Gauquié, P., Jeanne-Perrier, V.: Le partage photographique: le régime performatif de la photo. Commun. Langages (194), 21–27 (2017)
11. Gomez-Mejia, G.: Les fabriques de soi? Indentités et industrie sur le web. MKF, Paris (2016)
12. Jeanneret, Y.: Les images de la science. Commun. et langages (99), 54–73 (1994)
13. Julliard, V., Georges, F.: Produire le mort: Pratiques d'écriture et travail émotionnel des deuilleurs et des deuilleuses sur Facebook. Réseaux 210, 89–116 (2018)
14. Lambert, F.: Je sais bien mais quand même. Éditions Non Standard, Saint-Romain de Colbosc (2013)
15. Lamizet, B.: Sémiotique de l'événement. Hermès Lavoisier, Paris (2006)
16. Marin, L.: Du pouvoir de l'image. Seuil, Paris (1993)
17. Nora, P.(dir.): Les Lieux de mémoire. Tome 1: La République. Gallimard, Paris (1984)
18. Ruellan, D.: Le journalisme ou le professionnalisme du flou, Grenoble, Presses de l'Université de Grenoble (2007)
19. Sérullaz, A., Vignot, E.: La Main dans l'art. Citadelles & Mazenod, Paris (2010)
20. Souchier, E., Candel, E., Gomez-Mejia, G.: Le numérique comme écriture. Armand Colin, Paris (2019)
21. Wrona, A.: Face au portrait. De Sainte-Beuve à Facebook. Hermann, Paris (2012)

The Research on User Use of Social Media in China Mobile Based on Self-image Construction

Lingxi Chen[1] , Linda Huang[2]([⊠]) , and Xinyao Wang[2]

[1] Hunan University, Changsha University of Science and Technology, Changsha, China
[2] Changsha University of Science & Technology, Changsha, China
huanglinda@csust.edu.cn

Abstract. With the development of "intelligent" society, smart terminals have been used in many occasions of daily life. Smart phones have become an extension of people, which is an indispensable medium that people connect with each other and the society. Currently, among the 274 million elderly mobile phone users in China, 134 million are elderly smartphone users. Nearly 140 million seniors are connected to the Internet through smartphones. Through an online questionnaire survey on smartphone use experience for young-old, this paper attempts to investigate the actual needs and difficulties of young-old in the use of smartphones, and the preference of this group for the age-appropriate design of mobile phones. Based on the 500 valid samples of the survey, we found that the young-old tend to actively learn the use of mobile phones, but the current smartphone APPs does not take into account the special need of the young-old, and the adaptability of the touch-screen experience. We suggest that it's necessary to consider the need of the old users in terms of functions, interfaces, menu settings, so as to improve the willingness of the old to use mobile APPS and improve the effect of human-computer interaction.

Keywords: Aged-appropriate design · Smartphone APPs · Young-old

1 Introduction

With the development of Internet and the popularity of mobile devices, social media has become an important platform for online interaction. On August 27, 2021, China Internet Network Information Center published the 48th Statistical Report on China's Internet Development. As shown in the report, by June 2021, the number of Internet users in China had reached 1.011 billion, with an Internet penetration rate of 71.6%. The number of mobile Internet users was 1.007 billion, an increase of 20.92 million compared with December 2020 and 99.6% of Internet users accessed the Internet via mobile devices. A total 1 billion Internet users makes China one of the most vast and vigorous digital society. Mobile social media, as an instant messenger, takes the advantage of the rapid development of media technology. Users who communicate with mobile social media account for a vast majority of the social interaction, almost dwarfing the traditional face-to-face communication in real life. Using the mobile social media to present, express and construct ourselves has become a new type of lifestyle.

© Springer Nature Switzerland AG 2022
G. Meiselwitz et al. (Eds.): HCII 2022, LNCS 13517, pp. 41–51, 2022.
https://doi.org/10.1007/978-3-031-22131-6_4

1.1 Research Object

Chinese mobile social media users based on self-image construction.

1.2 Research Method

Questionnaire Survey. Questionnaire-based survey is universal in experience research. The researchers conducted a questionnaire survey on personal account image and usage on WJX.cn through online social media like Weblog, WeChat and Tencent QQ. 880 questionnaires were collected and 803 were valid. Among interviewees, 434 (54.05%) were males and 369 were females (45.59%), ageing from 10 to 45.

Interview. In response to the collected questionnaires, the researcher formulated correspondent interview outline and conducted in-depth communication with respondents of different genders and ages via online video or phone calls. With the specific situation learned as a supplement to the questionnaire survey, the research will be more comprehensive and the conclusions drawn will be more objective.

The Analysis Method of Mathematical Statistics. Based on the questionnaire and interview, professional statistic software was used to analyze and draw a conclusion.

2 Core Concepts

2.1 Self-image

Self-image was early and commonly seen in social psychology. It was first conceptualized by James W, an American psychologist. Self consists of 2 elements and 2 sub-systems: self-concept of a general perception of one's own nature, characteristic (the personal viewpoint we adopt towards ourselves; self-image) and self-awareness and self-consciousness that constitute self-concept (viewpoint other adopts on us; self-image constructor). Under this circumstance, people in a certain social environment, rather than passively react to it, always attempt to influence the surrounding environment in order to establish a favorable self-image to realize their goals. The manipulation of the environment starts with the manipulation of oneself. They continuously regulate and control the information presented to others, particularly information about themselves. This regulation and control of behavior sometimes is either conscious or unconscious. The theory of regulating and controlling social information and personal information can be traced back to the early symbolic interaction theory as well.

The above-mentioned were then fully developed and expanded in the theory of impression management (or self-presentation) put forward by Goffman (1951, 1971). He pointed out: when individuals appear in other's presence, there are always some certain reasons motivating them to convey a self-image that is in their personal interests. …life is a show, and society is a stage. Everyone strives to create an image appropriate for the current social situation and ensure that they are viewed positively by others.

Although Goffman's theory was criticized for downgrading internal psychological factors of individuals, it blazed trail for the subsequent social psychological studies on self and self-presentation.

In modern society, people's display on mobile social media is a process of self-image construction and self-presentation. We present, express and construct ourselves through texts, pictures and videos on social medias, thus forming an online self-image.

2.2 Mobile Social Media

Social media refers to the content production and exchange platform on the Internet that facilitates the sharing of opinions, understandings, experience and ideas based on user relationship. On the current stage, it is mainly composed of social network sites, Weblog, WeChat, Blog, BBS and Podcast. Mobile social media are platforms for network information generation and exchange with mobile media represented by mobile phone and PAD, which has now become the primary medium for social interaction. Mobile social media bring different people into different relationship groups to form different types of virtual communities. The time and space boundaries between people's work and life are increasingly blurred. It brought changes to the traditional media ecology and at the same time shaped the unique cultural characteristics of mobile social media.

3   Research Results and Analysis

3.1 Analysis of Basic Usage of Mobile Social Media

Time and Number of Mobile Social Media Usage. The survey reveals that with the development of mobile Internet, most people have been using mobile social media for a long time. Mobile social media plays an important role in interpersonal communication. 420 users, more than half of the surveyed, have been using social media over four years (Fig. 1).

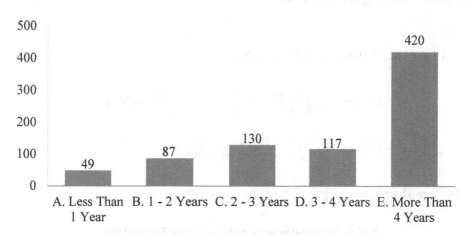

Fig. 1. Years of mobile Social Media usage

More than 90% users use two or more social media, about 30% of them more than 3, which explains that with the revolution of technology and the emergence of new social media, people are more likely to choose more platforms for their social interaction and communication, instead of being limited by one single mobile social media. Social interaction in cyberspace then becomes more complicated (Fig. 2).

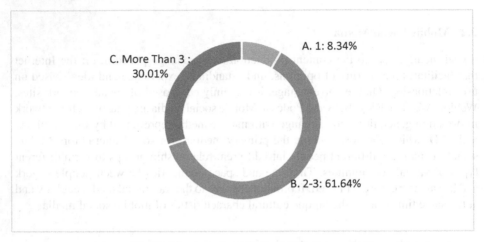

Fig. 2. Number of mobile Social Media usage

Average Time Spent Daily on Social Media and Update Frequency. If online social products are designed to satisfy the need of communication and interaction between individuals, mobile Internet can realize users' need in an even more fragmented time and context. Nearly half of the interviewees used social media for an average of 1–3 h per day; 204 people (25.4%) for 3–5 h; 15.57% of users less than 1 h; and 113 people even more than 5 h per day (Fig. 3).

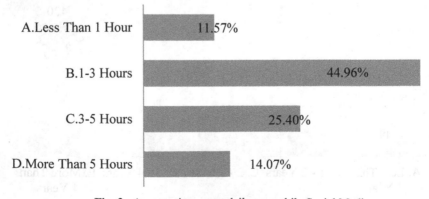

Fig. 3. Average time spent daily on mobile Social Media

The update frequency of social media indicates the degree of users' self-presentation towards their friends and the construction of their self-image. In general, the more frequent one updates his social media, the more information will be displayed. As shown in Fig. 4, only 15.19% of the interviewees update once or several times a day, 24.78% of users update once or twice a week. They update comparatively more frequent on social media; Nearly half of the surveyed interviewees do not update frequently, basically do not update or update only 1–2 times in a few months. It shows that despite the demand for mobile social media is increasing and people are willing to spend time using them, not all users are accustomed to presenting themselves and sharing life on social media with a high frequency.

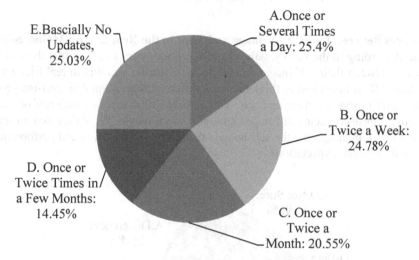

Fig. 4. Average time spent daily on mobile Social Media

Ways of Publishing on Social Media. The virtual interactive space formed by mobile social media is a platform integrating texts, pictures, videos and links. Users can present content in different ways according to their preferences. The survey found that the combination of text and picture is the most commonly used way to publish a post, accounting for nearly 80%, with 622 people choosing this option. Text and picture can display the original state of life more intuitively and vividly and help users to better express their feelings. In addition, pure text is still favored by many users, and the simplicity and subtlety of text still has its unique communication effect in the age of social media (Fig. 5).

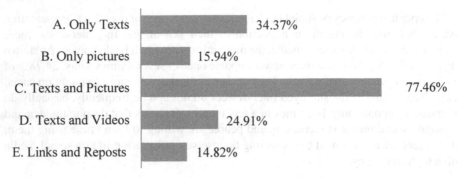

Fig. 5. Ways of publishing on social media

Differences Between Users' Self-image and That in the Real Life on Mobile Social Media. According to the survey, only 17.68% of interviewees believe that there is no difference between their self-image on mobile social media and that in real life, while more than 70% of interviewees think there are differences between their self-image on mobile social media and their real self. This indicates that the vast majority of users consciously construct their self-image on mobile social media. What they demonstrate is not the real self-image, but the self-image falsified by modification and performance in line with personal expectations.

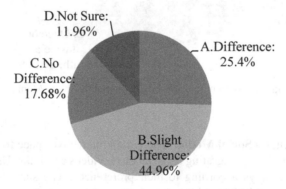

Fig. 6. The differences between users' self-image and that in real life on mobile Social Media

Differences Between Other People's Image on Mobile Social Media and That in the Real Life. As social media is a venue for people to interact with each other, not only can users choose on the media their image to construct and display, but also they can see the image of their counterparts. As shown in Fig. 7, 639 out of all the interviewees, accounting for nearly 80%, believe there are differences between other people's image on the social media and that in the real life, while less than 1 percent thinks otherwise.

Through the comparison of Figs. 6 and 7, one fourth of the users deny difference between the social media image and the real one, while 7.85% of the users stand the same for others. There are more interviewees thinking that there are differences for other people on social media and in real life than those who thinking the same for themselves. In the context, it is found that most users do not believe that others' images are real on social media since they have been delicately constructed and displayed. While the users respond that their image is not completely real either, they believe there is less element of falsification.

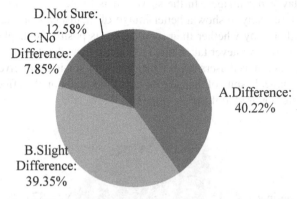

Fig. 7. Users viewing differences between other people's image on mobile Social Media and that in the real life

3.2   Ways to Construct Users' Self-image on Mobil Social Media

Self-expression as Priority of Self-image Display. Social media, since its emergence, has enriched the contents and ways of people's self-expression in the public space, with contents mainly from life. As shown in Fig. 8, 60% of interviewees share their emotions and views as the contents of self-expression, followed by those who share their daily

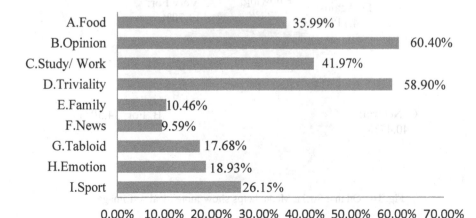

Fig. 8. Different posts on mobile Social Media

chores and triviality, and those who share respectively their study and work, delicious food and travel, and sports and competitions. These are all emotional expression and personal views that have been prioritized in the self-image construction.

Idealized Self-image as Focus of Self-image Display. People in their life hope to leave a positive impression on others. When it comes to the Internet social interaction, the users also tend to display better images. In the survey, it is found that almost three fourths of the users are more likely to show a better image of themselves on the social media, 13.2% are not bothered by whether their own image is positively displayed and even 12.3% claim that they have never taken this factor into consideration (Fig. 9), whereas nearly 50% of the interviewed users believe that social media is conducive to presenting a more ideal self-image. In spite of that, 40.5% cast their doubt on the effect of the social media and 4.1% are opposed to the view (Fig. 10).

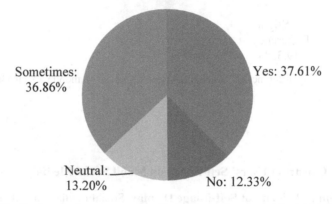

Fig. 9. On whether users tend to display better images on Social Media

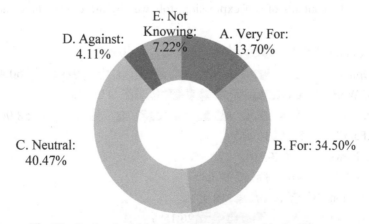

Fig. 10. On that Social Media helps show more ideal self images

4 Conclusion and Suggestions

4.1 Conclusion

(1) Users are emotional satisfied by expressing themselves on social media.
The survey has found that almost 60% of the users think that the social media is for expressing their emotions and reliving their emotional burdens, which may explain that more than what they have done in the real life, people tend to speak more emotionally on the social media and resort to more radical ways to do that on the Internet. This is to a certain degree attributable to the phenomenon that people's will and opportunities to express themselves are deprived of with or without any intent in the real life. On the contrary, social media has left the users with infinite space, where they can exchange with their friends some emotions and views which otherwise are only transmitted in a limited or blocked from being spread offline, and those that they share online find their way to being seen, liked, reposted and commented on. Therefore, the users make an attempt to gain a sense of emotional satisfaction and fulfillment by constructing their own self-image based on such theatrical behaviour or displaying their skills.

(2) Users obtain others' recognition and followers by sharing their life moments on mobile social media.
According to the statistics based on the survey, most of the users choose to share their life stories, with more than 70 percent of interviewees are for the view that social media is for recording and sharing the stories of their life. 50.44 percent of the interviewees claim that the reason they use mobile social media is to show themselves and by sharing everything related to their life and displaying their skills to support, deepen or adjust their perception of their self-evaluation, public expectation, accumulated experience, present situation, and hope for future by being engaged in interaction with or without any intent to construct a complete, harmonious, and ideal self-image.

(3) Users construct their own self-image on mobile social media to maintain personal relationship and expand social interaction.
As a platform for content generation and opinion exchange, mobile social media has also been regarded by the users as a venue for social interaction. Most users in a certain community may not have communication to exchange their emotions on a regular basis, but they are able to learn something about others' life and engage themselves in the social interaction through their sharing one the social media. The statistics of the survey indicate that more than 50 percent of the interviewees believe that social media is used to maintain and develop their real-life interpersonal relationship while 43.83 percent attribute their using social media partly to that their surrounded people are all involved in the media use. The contents upgraded on the mobile social media serve as a real-time complement of the users' real-life images, and the information spread helps shape a round self-image so that friends on the Internet know better about the users themselves. For strangers, however, pieces of information on the social media also foster a preliminary image of the person who releases them.

4.2 Suggestions

(1) Users should not construct their self-image on mobile social media in an over theatrical manner; otherwise, it would distance them from others. When it comes to interpersonal interaction on the social media, basic theatrical tactics include the choice of the profile photo, the name, the motto, the mode of communication and the content displayed. If some windows for online display are accessible in a limited scope and based on demand, it is not helpful to deepen interaction and mutual understanding when users choose over delicate self-images since some falsified elements in them tend to drive a wedge among the users.

(2) The self-image construction on mobile social media should comply with users' authenticity; otherwise it would hamper self-recognition and lead to loss of online trust. The authenticity may be compromised by the virtual self-image in online social interaction and the complicated overplay may blur privacy boundaries, contributing to distortion of self-recognition and anxiety of impression management. Therefore, it is suggested that social media not be seen as a theatre to fabricate and attain the persona through continuous glossing over a self-image or even constructing an imaginary image, which otherwise may exert a toll on the real life.

(3) Users should not be over indulged in interaction on mobile social media to stay free from fatigue of social interaction. On the social media, the users are prompted by vanity and self-expectation to construct an ideal self-image, the maintenance of which, however, demands constant generation and sharing of related contents. Under such circumstances, the users have to review their self-image and live a theatric life and they will plunge into pressure and anxiety of slackening in image management and exposing the authentic self when they do not upgrade the related contents. Any individual user would therefore get confused about the present situation and the self-image, leading to the fatigue of social interaction.

(4) Users should have their privacy protected when constructing their own self-image on mobile social media. Every piece of information, including pictures and videos posted by the users to show themselves, have publicly exposed their life on the Internet, but such over exposure has already uncovered personal information in the public.

The limitation of the study is that the conclusion is not applicable to senior people. The survey covers people of all ages but since the majority of them are middle-aged and young people with little understanding of the senior, the conclusion in essence represents the attitudes of the former two groups towards the self-image construction on mobile social media. In the follow-up studies, the surveyed population distribution among all age groups will be managed to reveal the situations of the users' self-image construction on mobile social media across the board.

References

1. Erving, G.: The Presentation of Self in Everyday Life. Zhejiang People's Publishing House, Hangzhou (2021)
2. Junrui, W.: Self-presentation and expression: on university students' "Clocking in Study" at the WeChat moment. New Media Res. 6(12), 87–88 (2020)

3. Duanmengrong, H.J.: Social Media fatigue and self-image in internet social interaction under WeChat over communication. Mod. Commun. **2020**(2) (2020)
4. Lan, P.: Connection and anti-connection: the swing of internet rules. Chin. J. J. Commun. **41**(2), 20–37 (2019)
5. Huang, L.V., Liu, S.: Presenting an ideal self on Weibo: the effects of narcissism and self-presentation valence on uses and gratifications. Front. Psychol. **11**, 1–6 (2020)
6. Eriksson, G., Fitzgerald, R.: Web-TV as a backstage activity: emerging forms of audience address in the post-broadcast era. Text. Talk. **39**(1), 1–14 (2018)

Gender and Culture Differences in Perception of Deceptive Video Filter Use

Susan C. Herring(✉) ⓘ, Meredith Dedema ⓘ, Enrique Rodriguez ⓘ, and Leo Yang ⓘ

Indiana University, Bloomington, IN 47405, USA
{herring,fndedema,enrodri,leoyang}@indiana.edu

Abstract. This study investigates how Augmented Reality (AR) beauty filters affect perception of the motives and trustworthiness of a stranger in online social interaction. One-on-one Zoom interviews were conducted with 44 video filter users from five different cultural backgrounds – China, India, South Korea, Spain, and the US – about their reactions to a hypothetical scenario intended to represent a deceptive use of beauty filters. The findings of quantitative and qualitative thematic analysis suggest that beauty filter use does not strongly affect assessments of trustworthiness among young video filter users, and that it is likely to be interpreted in different – and perhaps naïve – ways, such as a lack of self-confidence. Women express more compassion and understanding toward the "deceptive" stranger, while men express more negative judgment and distrust. Culture differences do not fall neatly along East-West lines, but rather vary for different themes. The findings contrast with evidence of actual risk of deception in online environments, particularly risk to women, who are more often targets of online dating deception.

Keywords: Augmented reality · Beauty filter · Trust

1 Introduction

It has recently become possible to modify one's own and other peoples' appearance in recorded videos and video chat using facial filters, augmented reality 3-D animations overlaid dynamically on the image of the face. Filters are enormously popular among young people on social media (Chua and Chang 2016) and are rapidly gaining in popularity on video conferencing platforms such as Zoom. While filters can promote playful enjoyment, boost self-confidence, and facilitate identity exploration (e.g., Javornik et al. 2022), they also raise ethical concerns. The effects produced by face-transforming filters, such as those that change the user's gender or age, overlap with those of deepfake videos and can be used to deceive, as for example in online dating site scams.[1] Beauty enhancement filters raise concerns about unrealistic beauty standards and increasing body dissatisfaction (e.g., Lyu et al. 2021) and can also be deceptive, for example, if

---

[1] https://slate.com/technology/2021/09/deepfake-video-scams.html, last accessed 2022/05/26.

© Springer Nature Switzerland AG 2022
G. Meiselwitz et al. (Eds.): HCII 2022, LNCS 13517, pp. 52–72, 2022.
https://doi.org/10.1007/978-3-031-22131-6_5

used to lure or entrap others.[2] More generally, difficult-to-detect filter use can exacerbate uncertainty and doubt in online interactions and promote a culture of skepticism or 'disbelief as default' (Gregory 2019).

This study investigates how beauty filters affect the perception of the motives and trustworthiness of strangers in online social interaction through interviewing video filter users about their reactions to a hypothetical scenario intended to represent a deceptive use of beauty filters. Specifically, we ask: How does the use of a beauty filter that significantly changes one's appearance affect trust in social interaction? Do participants' answers to this questions vary according to their gender and cultural background?

2 Literature Review

2.1 Augmented Reality Filters

Augmented reality (AR) filters have become extremely popular with the general public in recent years, transforming the landscape of online communication (Fribourg et al. 2021). Some AR technologies are dedicated to improving the consumer experience; for example, by allowing consumers to virtually try on products such as virtual sunglasses (Yim and Park 2019) and digital fashion (Xue et al. 2021). Other filters are intended for entertainment or for use on social media platforms. Filter effects can generally be situated along a spectrum of change from subtle beautification to cartoonification to grotesque distortion; some filters change the user's gender or age; others exchange the user's face with the face of another person. TikTok, for example, offers a wide range of facial modifications, from beauty enhancement to unrealistic distortions (Li 2021). Some appearance enhancement apps that are popular in Asia even add filters directly to the camera of the user's phone, such that any video recorded from the phone is automatically filtered, thereby extending filter use beyond social media.[3] The increasingly normalized use of filters raises issues of authenticity and the potential for misrepresentation. Javornik et al. (2022) identified "ideal self-presentation," "transformed self-presentation," and "social interactions" as motivations for AR face filter use on Instagram. However, there is little research as yet on the social outcomes of video filter use. Most studies of online self-presentation focus either on photographs or selfies (e.g., Chae 2017) or textual communication (e.g., Walther 1996).

2.2 Filters and Self-concept

AR filters serve as an important tool for online activities related to body satisfaction and self-esteem (Yu and Lee 2020). Studies of teenage girls have found that using appearance-enhancing filters can boost the users' mood and self-confidence, and that girls with low self-esteem or negative body image use filters more and engage in more self-promotion online (Lee et al. 2014). Similarly, in a Korean study, Chae (2017) found that individuals

---

[2] https://timesofindia.indiatimes.com/blogs/voices/india-becoming-sextortion-capital-of-the-world/, last accessed 2022/05/26.

[3] https://www.insider.com/samsung-phones-default-beauty-mode-camera-airbrush-2016-6?amp, last accessed 2022/05/26.

use filters on their selfies because of their desire for a more ideal online self-presentation. However, discrepancies between the appearance of the digitally beautified self and the actual self can lower self-esteem and exacerbate body dysmorphia (Kleemans et al. 2018). Plastic surgeons report that increasing numbers of young people of both sexes are requesting surgeries to alter their physical face to look like a filtered face from their social media feed.[4] A Chinese study found that young women's selfie-filtering behavior increased their willingness to consider cosmetic surgery when mediated by body surveillance and body shame (Lyu et al. 2021). Girls and young women are especially susceptible to societal pressures to look attractive; they are also the most active users of beauty filters (Dhir et al. 2016). Most of the studies cited here were conducted in Asia, where filter use is more widespread than in the West (Madan et al. 2018). In the present study, we interviewed filter users from Asia and the West, and our analysis controls for interviewee gender.

2.3   Online Deception

Lying is a common behavior in daily life and is especially ubiquitous online. Technology and online settings allow for more deception (Keyes 2004) as a result of the interplay between users and the technical affordances of the medium in which they are communicating, the meticulous control they have over their self-presentation strategies (Walther 1996), and the psychological rewards that might lead users to lie to present themselves more positively (Hancock and Guillory 2015). Of particular interest here are private interactions over video-mediated communication, including those in the context of online dating (Drouin et al. 2016; Toma and Hancock 2010). Dating and friendship-seeking sites are typically oriented to the possibility of meeting offline, so in theory, online daters should present themselves truthfully. Nevertheless, in one study, 51% of online daters admitted to misrepresenting themselves (Whitty 2008).

Women are more likely to lie about their physical characteristics (Lo et al., 2013), while men most often lie about their relationship status, goals, and height (Schmitz et al. 2013). Relatedly, less attractive individuals are more likely to engage in deception in their online dating profiles (i.e., via enhanced photographs and physical characteristics), suggesting a strong connection between self-presentation strategies, perceived attractiveness, and deception in the online realm (Toma and Hancock 2010).

One study found that nine out of 16 female college students interviewed had experienced catfishing, and four out of 16 had been targets of online impersonation involving fake or heavily photoshopped pictures (Simmons and Lee 2020). Another study found that 16% of European online daters had encountered scammers (Buchanan and Whitty 2014). "Catfishing," an activity involving the creation of a fake online profile for deceptive purposes (Harris 2013), is common in online dating contexts. Women are more likely to be targets and men are more likely to perpetrate this form of deception (Mosley et al. 2020). The motives behind catfishing may not always be entirely criminal or malicious, however. For instance, people might misrepresent themselves due to loneliness, dissatisfaction with physical traits, or for sexual identity exploration (Santi 2019). Nonetheless,

---

[4] https://people.com/health/snapchat-dysmorphia-plastic-surgery-trend/,   last   accessed 2022/05/26.

victims of catfishing can be exposed to severe physical, psychological, and financial harm (Koch 2017; Santi 2019). Public awareness of these behaviors in the United States has been raised through the popular TV show "Catfishing." However, there are no laws tailored to criminalize catfishing in the US (Santi 2019). Catfishing victims can also be found in other countries, including China (Huang et al. 2015), India (Kaur and Iyer 2021), and Korea (Kim 2015).

Increasingly, online dating scammers are using deepfake videos to fool their victims into believing that they are interacting with a desirable potential sexual or romantic partner.[5] The effects of deepfake videos overlap with those of face-transforming filters, particularly filters where the user swaps their face with that of another person (Westerlund 2019). Filters can also be used to perpetuate deception and fraud, as illustrated by the case of a beautiful young Chinese vlogger who was revealed to be an unattractive 58-year-old woman when her filter failed due to a technical glitch. Outrage followed this revelation, particularly since the "beautiful" vlogger had been soliciting cash gifts from her followers.[6] Thus online self-presentation strategies can have real-life consequences if the online self does not match the users' actual self, resulting, for example, in a breakdown of trust (Whitty and Buchanan 2016).

2.4 Trust

Schoorman et al. (2007) define trust as someone's perceptions about an individual's ability, benevolence, and integrity. In their model of trust behavior, ability refers to the individual's perceived skills and knowledge, benevolence accounts for how much someone perceives others' intentions to be good-natured, and integrity denotes others' personal and moral principles. While these three categories can be strengthened in face-to-face interaction via behavioral and emotional cues, they can be undermined by deceptive behaviors, as described above. There can also be real-life consequences for trusting others, especially when those individuals prove to be untrustworthy. Social psychology research has identified gender differences regarding trust behavior: Women are less likely to lose trust and also more likely to restore trust after being the target of a transgression than men are (Haselhuhn et al. 2015). Moreover, there is a relationship between trust and attractiveness. Women are more likely to perceive attractive men as more trustworthy based on their profile picture, while men tend to find attractive women's profile pictures less trustworthy (McGloin and Denes 2018). In this study we focus on the relationship between gender and perceived trustworthiness in a hypothetical scenario in which attractiveness is presumed to be enhanced through the use of video beauty filters.

---

[5] https://slate.com/technology/2021/09/deepfake-video-scams.html; https://www.freepressjou rnal.in/mumbai/sextortion-25-year-old-man-from-mumbai-gets-blackmailed-over-a-fake-video-clip. last accessed 2022/05/26.

[6] https://www.bbc.com/news/blogs-trending-49151042, last accessed 2022/05/26.

3 Methods

3.1 Data Collection

Data for this study were collected through two means, an online screener survey and one-on-one interviews. The online survey was designed to screen and recruit participants who use video filters; it also asked about use of different social media platforms and use of different types of filters. A recruitment message containing a link to the screener was sent out via several electronic mailing lists at a large university in the midwestern United States and posted on the researchers' social media accounts. To qualify for participation in the interview study, individuals had to be 18 or older, able to participate in a spoken interview in English, and be from China, India, South Korea, Spain, or the US. We focused on these countries for three main reasons. First, they represent broad cultural differences between the East and the West, and filter differences along this axis can be expected, since filters are more widespread in Asia than the West. Second, the selection allows us to explore differences within the two broad cultures. India, although part of Asia, differs culturally from East Asia, and there are cultural differences between Spain and the US. Finally, the members of our research team have first-hand knowledge of these cultures. This study received Institutional Review Board approval from the authors' university.

We conducted one-on-one, semi-structured interviews with survey respondents who met our requirements, all of whom were familiar with video filter use on social media and who were video filter users themselves. Forty-four participants were interviewed from five different cultural backgrounds, as summarized in Table 1. All but five of the interviewees were residing in the US at the time of the interviews (3 were in South Korea, and 2 were in Spain), and most were students. The interviewees ranged in age from 19 to 38; 64% are female, 32% are male, one identified as non-binary, and one interviewee declined to provide their gender. The interviewees reported using video filters on Instagram, Snapchat, TikTok, Zoom, Kakao Talk, and other social media platforms.

Table 1. Gender and cultural background of interview participants.

	China	India	South Korea	Spain	USA	Total
Female	8	4	5	4	7	28
Male	1	5	2	1	5	14
Other	1	0	0	0	1	2
Total	10	9	7	5	13	44

The semi-structured interviews lasted 45–60 min and were conducted and recorded over Zoom. The 45-item interview protocol included questions about participants' use of filters, the effects of filter use on their self-concept, and their perceptions of others' filter usage in social interaction. This study focuses on responses to a subset of the interview questions involving beauty filters, including comments made about motivations for beauty filter use, their effects on perceived authenticity and deception, and perceptions of frequency of filter use by others. These responses are described in aggregate as background for an in-depth, quantitative analysis of interviewee responses to the following two-part hypothetical question:

a. If you were to meet someone in person whom you previously chatted with exclusively over video online, and you found out that their face looked very different from their videos, how would you feel about them? Why?
b. Would you feel differently if it was a potential romantic partner? Why?

3.2 Data Analysis

The interviews were transcribed by Zoom and manually checked for accuracy. A thematic content analysis approach was used to code the transcripts (Vaismoradi et al. 2013). Some themes were informed by the wording of the hypothetical question (i.e., *emotional reaction* and *action taken in response*). Other themes emerged from the data using a grounded theory approach (Glaser 2002) and an iterative coding process. This involved discussion among the four authors until consensus on the themes was reached. We ended up with seven themes, which we coded independently for each part of the hypothetical question. In addition, we coded for whether the interviewee said they would respond differently to a potential romantic partner. The resulting codebook (variables and values) can be seen in Tables 2 and 3 in Sect. 4.2. After training, each author coded part of the data, then all four authors together checked a random sample of more than half the data to confirm the consistency of the coding.

3.3 Research Questions

In this study we address two research questions:

RQ1: How does the use of beauty filters affect trust in social interaction with a stranger?

RQ2: Do participants' answers to this question vary according to their gender and cultural background?

This is an exploratory study; no specific hypotheses are advanced. However, based on the literature reviewed in the previous sections, we expected to find gender differences in trust and in attitudes toward beauty filter use.

4 Findings

4.1 Beauty Filter Use

Most participants, except for some males and the nonbinary participant, reported that they use video beauty filters, explaining that they employ such filters to subtly enhance their natural appearance. The interviewees perceived beauty filter use to be prevalent in video mediated communication, estimating that a majority of social media users, 60% to 90% on average, use filters to enhance their appearance. Young people and females were generally thought to use beauty filters the most.

4.2 Responses to the Hypothetical Question

We asked each interviewee, "How would you feel if you found that someone you'd been video chatting with online was using a filter all along and looked very different when you met them in person?" The interviewees overwhelmingly interpreted this question as referring to beauty enhancement filters. Responses to the hypothetical scenario varied according to gender and culture. The gender breakdown is presented quantitatively and discussed qualitatively, and the cultural differences are discussed qualitatively, due to the small numbers of participants in some of the culture groups.

Gender Differences. The results for each thematic variable broken down by gender are presented in Tables 2 and 3.

Overall, women more often than men expressed disappointment, compassion, understanding, respect, and speculated about (lack of) self-confidence, and more women (initially) said they would proceed normally. Men attributed dishonesty as the motive more, were more distrustful, and expressed indifference and mixed judgments more than women did. These overall patterns are illustrated in the following quotes.

1) S_06(F): If I'm meeting for a date or something, I would feel *disappointed*. I would say, like, that person's a bit superficial, but, if it's … for friendship or something, I would say, "okay". It wouldn't upset me if it's like, if that person doesn't like to post their authentic face because *maybe something's going on with their self-esteem, and it has to be treated, and we cannot judge that, because it's like, the more you judge, the more they're gonna hide themselves from society. So I wouldn't judge them.*
2) I_16(M): [I'd be] *angry*. If they don't have a good reason for using the filter, then I would end it there. I don't know what a good reason would be for using the filter with a potential romantic partner, and not letting him or her know that you are using a filter. So that's basically *deceiving*. You are practically *lying* to me even before we have met. So why would I continue the relationship if they can lie about such small things.

Most participants said their response would be different if the other (henceforth, O) was a potential romantic partner. Women said 'slightly' different more, and men said 'strongly' different more (Fig. 1).

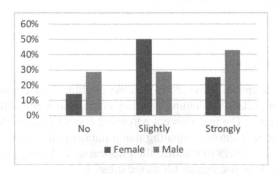

Fig. 1. Would your answer be different if it was a potential romantic partner?

Table 2. Responses to initial question (Part a.).

Variable	Values	Females N = 28	Males N = 14	Other N = 2	All N = 44
Motive for O's presumably deceptive use of filters	1) Dishonesty	7 (23)	7 (39)	0 (0)	14 (27)
	2) Self-confidence	11 (35)	4 (22)	1 (50)	16 (31)
	3) Other	5 (16)	4 (22)	0 (0)	9 (18)
	4) Didn't mention	8 (26)	3 (17)	1 (50)	12 (24)
	Total	31 (100)	18 (100)	2 (100)	51 (100)
Reaction to O presumably being less attractive in real life	1) Disappointed	5 (18)	0 (0)	0 (0)	5 (11)
	2) Don't care	2 (7)	0 (0)	1 (50)	3 (11)
	3) It's expected	2 (7)	0 (0)	0 (2)	2 (5)
	4) Didn't mention	19 (68)	14 (100)	1 (50)	34 (77)
	Total	28 (100)	14 (100)	2 (100)	44 (100)
Respectful of O's choice to use filters	1) Yes	10 (36)	4 (29)	1 (50)	15 (34)
	2) No	6 (21)	2 (14)	0 (0)	8 (18)
	3) Neutral/mixed	5 (18)	6 (43)	0 (0)	11 (25)
	4) Didn't mention	7 (25)	2 (14)	1 (50)	10 (23)
	Total	28 (100)	14 (100)	2 (100)	44 (100)
Emotional reaction to O's presumably deceptive self-presentation	1) Cheated/betrayed	8 (29)	2 (13)	0 (0)	10 (22)
	2) Disappointed	3 (11)	1 (7)	0 (0)	4 (9)
	3) Sad	2 (7)	0 (0)	0 (0)	2 (4)
	4) Surprised	3 (11)	3 (20)	0 (0)	6 (13)
	5) Indifferent	3 (11)	2 (13)	0 (0)	5 (11)
	6) Other	6 (21)	7 (47)	1 (50)	14 (31)
	7) Didn't mention	3 (11)	0 (0)	1 (50)	4 (9)
	Total	28 (100)	15 (100)	2 (100)	45 (100)
Attitude toward O	1) Compassionate	4 (13)	0 (0)	0 (0)	4 (9)
	2) Understanding	6 (20)	2 (13)	1 (50)	9 (19)
	3) Indifferent	4 (13)	3 (20)	0 (0)	7 (15)
	4) Mixed	2 (7)	5 (33)	0 (0)	7 (15)
	5) Judgmental	13 (43)	5 (33)	1 (50)	19 (40)
	6) Didn't mention	1 (3)	0 (0)	0 (0)	1 (2)
	Total	30 (100)	15 (100)	2 (100)	47 (100)
Would you still trust O?	1) Yes	4 (14)	3 (21)	0 (0)	7 (16)

(*continued*)

Table 2. (*continued*)

Variable	Values	Females N = 28	Males N = 14	Other N = 2	All N = 44
	2) No	4 (14)	4 (19)	1 (50)	9 (20)
	3) Mixed/neutral	0 (0)	1 (7)	0 (0)	1 (2)
	4) Didn't mention	20 (71)	6 (43)	1 (50)	27 (61)
	Total	28 (100)	14 (100)	2 (100)	44 (100)
Action taken in response	1) Proceed normally	5 (18)	1 (7)	0 (0)	6 (14)
	2) Say something	3 (11)	1 (7)	1 (50)	5 (11)
	3) Cut off contact	2 (7)	1 (7)	0 (0)	3 (7)
	4) Seek other qualities	0 (0)	1 (7)	0 (0)	1 (2)
	6) Didn't mention	18 (64)	10 (71)	1 (50)	29 (66)
	Total	28 (100)	14 (100)	2 (100)	44 (100)
Response differs if a potential romantic partner	1) No	4 (14)	4 (29)	1 (50)	9 (20)
	2) Yes, slightly	14 (50)	4 (29)	1 (50)	19 (43)
	3) Yes, strongly	7 (50)	6 (43)	0 (0)	13 (30)
	4) Didn't mention	3 (11)	0 (0)	0 (0)	3 (7)
	Total	28 (100)	14 (100)	2 (100)	44 (100)

Table 3. Responses to question about potential romantic partner (Part b.).

Variable	Values	Females N = 28	Males N = 14	Other N = 2	All N = 44
Motive for O's presumably deceptive use of filters	1) Dishonesty	5 (18)	5 (36)	0 (0)	10 (23)
	2) Self-confidence	11 (36)	1 (7)	1 (50)	13 (30)
	3) Other	1 (4)	0 (0)	0 (0)	1 (2)
	4) Didn't mention	11 (39)	8 (57)	1 (50)	20 (45)
	Total	28 (100)	14 (100)	2 (100)	44 (100)
Reaction to O presumably being less attractive in real life	1) Disappointed	12 (43)	4 (29)	0 (0)	16 (36)
	2) Don't care	2 (7)	0 (0)	0 (0)	2 (5)
	3) It's expected	1 (4)	0 (0)	0 (0)	2 (2)
	4) Didn't mention	13 (46)	10 (71)	2 (100)	25 (57)
	Total	28 (100)	14 (100)	2 (100)	44 (100)

(*continued*)

Table 3. (*continued*)

Variable	Values	Females N = 28	Males N = 14	Other N = 2	All N = 44
Respectful of O's choice to use filters	1) Yes	3 (11)	1 (7)	0 (0)	4 (9)
	2) No	5 (18)	6 (43)	0 (0)	11 (25)
	3) Neutral/mixed	10 (36)	1 (7)	0 (0)	11 (25)
	4) Didn't mention	10 (36)	6 (43)	2 (100)	18 (41)
	Total	28 (100)	14 (100)	2 (100)	44 (100)
Emotional reaction to O's presumably deceptive self-presentation	1) Cheated/betrayed	7 (24)	6 (43)	0 (0)	13 (29)
	2) Disappointed	7 (24)	2 (14)	0 (0)	9 (20)
	3) Sad	2 (7)	0 (0)	0 (0)	2 (4)
	4) Disrespected	0 (0)	2 (14)	0 (0)	2 (4)
	5) Other	8 (28)	2 (14)	0 (0)	10 (22)
	6) Didn't mention	5 (17)	2 (14)	2 (100)	9 (20)
	Total	29 (100)	14 (100)	2 (100)	44 (100)
Attitude toward O	1) Compassionate	2 (7)	1 (7)	0 (0)	3 (6)
	2) Understanding	10 (33)	0 (0)	1 (50)	11 (23)
	3) Indifferent	1 (3)	1 (7)	0 (0)	2 (4)
	4) Mixed	2 (7)	2 (13)	0 (0)	4 (9)
	5) Judgmental	14 (47)	10 (67)	0 (0)	24 (51)
	6) Didn't mention	1 (3)	1 (7)	1 (50)	3 (6)
	Total	30 (100)	15 (100)	2 (100)	47 (100)
Would you still trust O?	1) Yes	4 (14)	1 (7)	0 (0)	5 (11)
	2) No	20 (71)	3 (21)	0 (0)	7 (16)
	3) Didn't mention	4 (14)	10 (71)	2 (100)	32 (72)
	Total	28 (100)	14 (100)	2 (100)	44 (100)
Action taken in response	1) Proceed normally	0 (0)	0 (0)	0 (0)	0 (0)
	2) Say something	1 (4)	1 (7)	0 (0)	2 (5)
	3) Cut off contact	9 (32)	3 (21)	0 (0)	12 (27)
	4) Seek other qualities	2 (7)	1 (7)	0 (0)	3 (7)
	6) Didn't mention	16 (57)	9 (64)	2 (100)	27 (61)
	Total	28 (100)	14 (100)	2 (100)	44 (100)

In comparing the reponses to the first and the second parts of the question (Tables 2 and 3), it can be seen that men's responses differ more than women's. Men mention (lack of) self-confidence as a motive less, a lack of respect more, feeling cheated more (and other feelings less), more negative judgment, and less trust. Women are more disappointed and more understanding, but say they will cut off contact more often (for reasons of character/lack of self-esteem) when thinking of a potential romantic partner. These differences are highlighted in what follows for each theme that emerged from the content analysis. Quotes by the interviewees are provided, as well as figures that compare the responses of females and males to the two parts of the hypothetical question. (The figures exclude the two 'other' gender participants and the N/A responses for the sake of clarity).

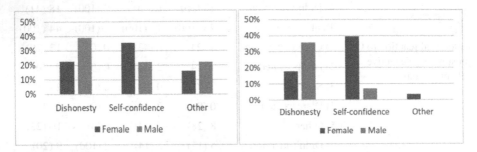

Fig. 2. Motivation in initial and potential romantic partner responses.

Figures 2a and 2b show the distribution of responses by females and males relating to the theme of **motivation**.

When speculating about the hypothetical other's (O's) motivations, a surprisingly high number of participants attribute a lack of self-confidence to O. This is especially true for women, as illustrated in quote 1) above and quotes 3) and 4) below.

3) C_02(F): I may be curious why they are using filters at the moment even though they use it before. And I may feel, *she is not very confident or he's not very confident,* and that he wants the filter at the moment.

4) SK_06(F): I understand them. I think I could think that *they are not confident enough in their appearances* and that's why they use video filters. I do it sometimes.

Mentions of self-confidence and seeking to understand O's motives decrease for males when considering a potential romantic interest. Both genders, especially men, also characterize O's behavior as dishonest or deceptive, as in quote 2). Thinking that O is deceptive is not incompatible with seeking to understand what personal or psychological issues might motivate O's behavior, however, as illustrated in quote 5):

5) US_31(F): That's *catfishing*, and I'm against that. I mean I probably wouldn't just like, rule them out as a person, like if I really like their personality and this was like coming out of something that was like *a deep insecurity*? I mean I don't love being *lied to,* and I do think that's *lying.* But you know I don't think that's like the worst thing in the world.

The second theme, **attractiveness,** is mentioned more by women and mentioned more overall for romantic relationships, as shown in Figs. 3a and 3b.

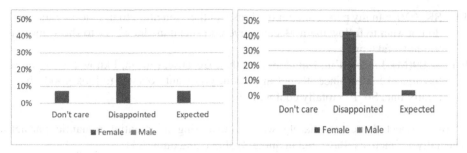

Fig. 3. Attractiveness in initial and potential romantic partner responses.

Disappointment is expressed most often in mentions of attractiveness, as illustrated in quotes 6)–8) below.

6) SK_12(F): I think agreeing to meet an online person in the real world is all about physical appearances. His looks are the only real thing I know about him. The online relationship is built on physical appearances. The chats we have online is meaningless until we actually meet in person and experience things together. So I would communicate with someone online for his looks but if he doesn't look like that? it's a lie? a fake? Then I wouldn't want to meet him. I would run away.

7) C_04(F): So, normally, they will look very good online. And then, like in real life would not be that attractive, so I will be disappointed. If that's the case, I'll be disappointed. Yeah.

8) SK_13(M): I would be a little disappointed, but that wouldn't affect the relationship much. There are a lot of other things besides the looks. I would be a little disappointed at first, as long as she doesn't look totally different, I would still try to get to know her better.

   Interviewer: What if she looks VERY different?

   SK_13(M): Then I will be VERY disappointed.

Responses relating to the theme of **respect** are shown in Figs. 4a and 4b.

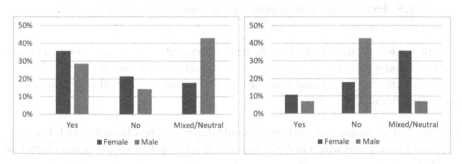

Fig. 4. Respect in initial and potential romantic partner responses.

A surprising number of interviewees indicated that they would respect O's choice to use a filter (quote 10), despite many of them finding the behavior deceptive, as in 9).

9) SK_02(F): In my personal opinion, I respect their intention to use video filter, but I do not want to follow them. Because even on social media we try to show our real life not a fake one.

10) C_09(M): I mean, I'm, I'm okay with that. Because, I mean, I know that if you're having, like, a … since it's not in person, you want yourself to look good, that's totally fine. So, I'm totally cool with that.

But respect decreases sharply when considering a potential romantic partner, especially for men, as illustrated in quote 2) above and quote 11).

11) US_27(M): I think if it was a potential romantic partner I'd feel kind of *led on*, or like *catfished*, in a sense, *lied to*. Obviously, maybe if it was such a drastic difference, I was expecting this person to look like this, but then they actually looked like this, I don't think I'd want to pursue a relationship with them anymore. It just shows that like they're, to me, like they're not confident in themselves and that I was just *deceived*.

Our hypothetical scenario asked the interviewees specifically about their **emotional reactions** (How would you feel?). Women's and men's responses are summarized in Figs. 5a and 5b.

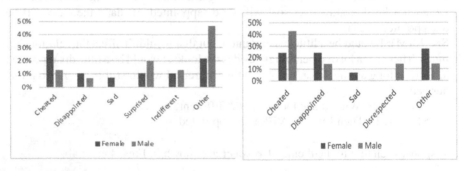

Fig. 5. Emotional reactions in initial and potential romantic partner responses.

Both genders say they would feel cheated or deceived, while more women than men would feel disappointed, especially in a romantic relationship (see quote 6). Men feel much more cheated in romantic relationships and mention fewer other feelings, as in quotes 2), 11), and 13).

12) US_18(F): I would feel catfished. I would definitely feel cheated, which I think is one of the reasons why it makes it so that I don't want to use misleading filters like that.

13) SK_11(M): I wouldn't be too emotionally invested if it was a guy, but if it is a romantic partner, I would feel betrayed. It will be difficult to maintain the relationship.

Regarding **attitude** toward O, as Figs. 6a and 6b show, the women were more compassionate and understanding than the men; see quotes 1), 4), and 14), although the women were also more judgmental initially (quote 15). But men were more judgmental if it concerned a potential romantic relationship (quotes 2 and 11).

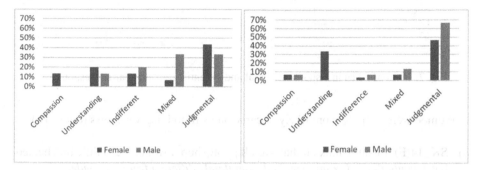

Fig. 6. Attitude and judgment in initial and potential romantic partner responses.

14) C_10(F): Depends on my relationship with them. If I'm not dating any of them, I don't really care. Cuz like I understand it's kind of a common thing right now. And in my mind, I'll go like "oh poor girl, another one who doesn't feel comfortable with her face". But only in my head, I won't say anything. I just wish them the best. Hope they can make peace of [sic] their facial appearance in the future.

15) I_10(F): I would definitely feel deceived, and, because, they, like, put in something that was completely different, especially if it was like a romantic relationship, and the relationship kind of matters for looks too, then I would feel completely deceived of them, like, kind of, they are trying to portray someone they are not, and I might ... not go follow with it, not because of how they look, but because they won't, like, comfortably show their true selves.

Some interviewees mentioned **actions** they would take in response to the hypothetical scenario; see Figs. 7a and 7b.

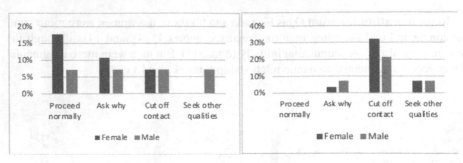

Fig. 7. Actions taken in response in initial and potential romantic partner responses.

Women were initially more likely to carry on as if nothing was amiss (quote 16).

16) SK_14(F): I would think oh that was all photoshop. I would feel a little bit cheated but *I wouldn't tell her that you look completely different from your video.*

No one mentioned doing this with a potential romantic partner, though. Both genders indicated they would 'cut off contact' more in that case, especially women (quotes 13, 15, 17).

17) I_20(F): If it's somebody that I would like to date then I would feel much more betrayed than somebody I just want to be friends with. And I would just consider that oh, they feel more confident and happy by using a filter so it's not my space to comment on them, but I would be taken aback, I would be thrown off. *I would likely not engage with them more.*

Finally, the gender breakdown for **trust** is given in Figs. 8a and 8b.

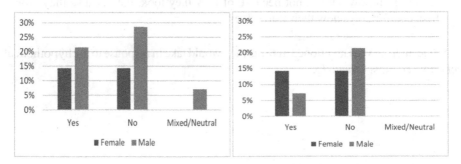

Fig. 8. Trust in initial and potential romantic partner responses.

Although we expected the hypothetical scenario to elicit reactions of distrust, mentions of trust or distrust were relatively infrequent overall. Some occurred only when prompted by a question about trust from the interviewer. Overall, male interviewees more often expressed distrust of O (quotes 18 and 19), and positive expressions of trust decreased sharply, from 21% to 7%, for men in a potential romantic relationship.

18) US_16(M): If it was someone I had, like, a personal connection with in any way, it might be kind of a red flag just because it's like, "oh, well, they're not showing who they really are", like it kind of gives that idea of, like, "is everything they're talking about truthful?", and it goes down that rabbit hole.

19) SK_11(M): I would be skeptical if I were to have a business relationship with that person because he might be deceiving.

Interviewer: So you would distrust that person

SK_11(M): Yes. I wouldn't take it for granted that he is a distrustful person, but I will be suspicious.

Surprisingly, however, several interviewees of both genders said that they would still trust O, despite finding O's behavior deceptive (as reported above).

20) Interviewer: Would you trust them?

S_08(F): Yeah. I would trust them, I would just think that this thing ... makes them feel more reassured, and that's the reason why they use the video filter, but I would trust them. I judge honesty by different standards.

21) SK_14(F): yeah [I would trust him], its just about his appearance that he lied about so I don't think that relates to his actual personality, yeah.

22) Interviewer: What does it mean to be disappointed? Does it mean you can't trust her anymore?

SK_13(M): I won't distrust her. Like I said, the looks are not everything I am looking for in a relationship. I would be disappointed in her looks but that doesn't mean I will be disappointed in her personality. So I'll try to get to know her.

Cultural Differences. Some patterns in the inteviewee responses appear to be related to culture. For example, Indian and US participants most often attributed the motivation for O's deceptive video filter use to dishonesty (quotes 2 & 11). In contrast, South Korean and Spanish interviewees, who were mostly females, more often associated O's use of video filters with a lack of self-confidence (quotes 2 & 4). Chinese participants often did not offer any motivation for O's video filter use. A very different picture emerges in the case of a potential romantic partner. South Korean participants mentioned dishonesty as a possible motivation more than self-confidence (quote 6), while US participants attributed O's behavior to a lack of self-confidence more. The Chinese and Indian interviewees often did not mention potential motivations for using filters in this hypothetical scenario. Participants were more likely to be disappointed about O's attractiveness if O was a potential romantic partner, with Koreans and Chinese emphasizing the importance of attractiveness more and expressing the most disappointment (quotes 6-8). Regarding respect for O's choice to use a beauty filter, South Korean (quote 9) and Spanish (quote 1) participants expressed the most respect, whereas Indians expressed the least respect (quote 2). US participants had mixed responses, and Chinese interviewees often did not mention respect. However, in the hypothetical situation involving a potential romantic partner, none of the participants from China, India, or the US, and only a few of the Spanish interviewees, mentioned respecting O's choice.

The emotional reactions mentioned by Indian and US participants mostly related to feeling cheated and betrayed (quotes 2 & 12), while Spanish interviewees mostly showed disappointment (quote 1). For a potential romantic partner, negative feelings associated with dishonesty (i.e., feeling betrayed) were most common overall, and Chinese, South Korean, and American participants also mentioned being more disappointed (quotes 7 & 8). Overall, in terms of attitudes towards O's use of a video filter, participants were more judgmental than compassionate. Americans and Indians were the most judgmental (quotes 11 & 15), followed by South Korean, Chinese, and Spanish interviewees. Chinese participants were the most understanding overall (quote 14), while Spanish interviewees were the most compassionate (quote 1); both cultural groups were predominantly females. When responding to a potential romantic partner, US and Chinese participants were the most understanding, although Americans also expressed judgmental attitudes in this hypothetical situation (quotes 11 & 12). In terms of actions they would take in response to O's deceptive use of a video filter, US and Spanish participants mentioned confronting O about the discrepancy between O's filtered and real self, while Chinese and South Korean participants would say nothing and proceed normally. We hypothesize that this could be due to a cultural difference regarding conflict avoidance in Asian cultures (Leung et al. 2002). Finally, mentions of trust were infrequent overall. Interestingly, US participants mentioned a lack of trust more often initially (quote 18), but if O was a potential romantic partner, they expressed less distrust. Overall, however, participants were less trusting of O when O was a potential romantic interest.

5   Discussion

In this study we asked, "How does the use of beauty filters affect trust in social interaction with a stranger?" and "Do participants' answers to this question vary according to their gender and cultural background?".

With respect to the first question, the responses to our hypothetical scenario suggest that beauty filter use does not strongly affect assessments of untrustworthiness among young video filter users, and that it is likely to be interpreted in different – and perhaps naïve – ways, especially by women. The female participants sought to understand – and sometimes sympathized with – the "deceptive" filter users' motivations in terms of body image and self-esteem. This finding is consistent with past research findings that women have more compassion than men toward others (López et al. 2018). When women expressed a negative emotional reaction, it was often disappointment that O lacked self-confidence, was not honest, or was not as physically attractive as initially advertised, especially if O was a potential romantic partner.

In contrast, male participants more often responded with negative judgment and distrust, especially toward potential romantic partners. However, only a few interviewees, most of them men (e.g., quote 18), indicated that they would be suspicious of O's motives more generally. Other men said that they might be surprised but would not care, because "it's [O's] choice" to present themselves as they please.

The scenario presented in our interview study is not only hypothetical. Our findings contrast with evidence of actual risk of deception in online environments, particularly risk to women, who are more often targets of online dating deception (Mosley et al. 2020). Romance fraud, for example, is on the rise since the Covid-19 lockdown in 2020. Fraudsters sometimes groom their victims for months to establish trust, and they increasingly make use of video communication to do so.[7] Victims have been defrauded of money, and some have experienced online sexual abuse (Buchanan and Whitty 2014). The risks associated with online dating can transition to the offline world, including rape and murder (Santi 2019). Males, too, have been victimized by sextortion schemes that involve scammers misrepresenting themselves as attractive women online. In one tragic recent case in the US, a 17-year old boy who was being blackmailed after sharing nude photos with a "young girl" committed suicide rather than face the shame of exposure.[8] As filter use becomes increasingly normalized, awareness of these risks needs to be raised among young internet users.

With respect to the second question, some cultural differences were observed, although these should be interpreted with caution, because the numbers of interviewees in some of the culture groups are small. The Indian and US interviewees were most likely to attribute O's behavior to dishonesty, although the US participants also attributed it to lack of self-confidence if O was a potential romantic partner. Overall, Spanish and South Korean participants were the most respectful towards O's beauty filter use, whereas Indian and US interviewees were the most judgmental. There is likely an interaction here with the gender findings, in that the Spanish and South Korean participants are mostly females, while about half of the Indian and US interviewees are males. Finally, the female Spanish participants were the most compassionate of all the demographic groups, although the Chinese interviewees showed the most understanding of O's possible reasons for using a deceptive video filter with a potential romantic partner. These findings suggest that the broad distinction between East and West is insufficient to explain cultural differences in perceptions of trustworthiness in video filter use; rather, the histories of individual cultures (e.g., their experiences with cases of deceptive filter and deepfake use) and the demographics of individuals within those cultures should also be taken into account.

6   Conclusion

We have presented what we believe is the first cross-cultural study of video filter use. Our findings indicate that beauty filters are considered normal and acceptable by young social media users, and most users say that they employ such filters only to subtly enhance their natural appearance. However, in response to a hypothetical situation where a stranger used enhancement filters that significantly changed their appearance in private video interactions, participants attributed the discrepancy between the filtered and the

---

[7] https://www.which.co.uk/news/article/online-dating-fraud-up-40-through-pandemic-aKHlv5 M09iYX, accessed 2022/05/27.

[8] https://www.weau.com/2022/05/24/high-school-senior-dies-by-suicide-after-falling-victim-online-sextortion-family-says/, accessed 2022/05/27.

real appearance to motives such as dishonesty and lack of self-confidence. Gender and culture-related differences were evident in their responses.

Despite many of our participants explicitly mentioning deception as the motivation for O's use of video filters and judging it negatively, most participants did not seem inclined to distrust O. This suggests that for young social media users, beauty filter use does not strongly affect assessments of trustworthiness in private interactions over video. However, this lack of distrust could render young adults susceptible to becoming targets of online fraud or abuse, a possibility that is especially concerning as regards women, who tend to trust more than men and to trust attractive men more than less attractive men (Haselhuhn et al. 2015; McGloin and Denes 2018).

A limitation of this study is that we only interviewed active video filters users; the perceptions of non-users, who might also be vulnerable to deception, were not taken into account. Also, we did not interview children or teenagers, the most vulnerable age groups. A second limitation is that this exploratory study reports on a sample of participants that is relatively small and culturally unbalanced, especially for Spain and Korea. Moreover, some of the latter participants were located in their home countries rather than the US. While their responses might be more culturally authentic, their experiences differ from those of the majority of interviewees. Finally, there is an imbalance in the ratio of male to female participants in some culture groups. A larger, more balanced interview population is desirable for future studies.

Meanwhile, the future outlook for filter use is increasing tolerance and acceptance of beauty filters. As beauty filter use becomes more expected and normalized, more people will use them to enhance their appearance online. The filters themselves will also become more sophisticated; some, such as the Chinese app Meitu, already have the ability to virtually modify the bone structure of the user's face. Finally, we foresee a time when social media filters and deepfake apps, already similar in some of their effects, will converge and become functionally indistinguishable, raising further challenges for identifying deception in online interaction.

References

Buchanan, T., Whitty, M.T.: The online dating romance scam: causes and consequences of victimhood. Psychol. Crime Law **20**(3), 261–283 (2014)

Chae, J.: Virtual makeover: Selfie-taking and social media use increase selfie-editing frequency through social comparison. Comput. Hum. Behav. **66**, 370–376 (2017)

Chua, T.H.H., Chang, L.: Follow me and like my beautiful selfies: Singapore teenage girls' engagement in self-presentation and peer comparison on social media. Comput. Hum. Behav. **55**, 190–197 (2016)

Dhir, A., Pallesen, S., Torsheim, T., Andreassen, C.S.: Do age and gender differences exist in selfie-related behaviours? Comput. Hum. Behav. **63**, 549–555 (2016)

Drouin, M., Miller, D., Wehle, S.M., Hernandez, E.: Why do people lie online? Because everyone lies on the internet. Comput. Hum. Behav. **64**, 134–142 (2016)

Fribourg, R., Peillard, E., Mcdonnell, R.: Mirror, mirror on my phone: Investigating dimensions of self-face perception induced by augmented reality filters. In: Marchal, M., Ventura, J., Olivier, A.H., Wang, L., Radkwski, R. (eds.) 2021 IEEE INTERNATIONAL SYMPOSIUM ON MIXED AND AUGMENTED REALITY (ISMAR), pp. 470–478. IEEE Computer Society, Los Alamitos, CA (2021)

Glaser, B.G.: Conceptualization: on theory and theorizing using grounded theory. Int. J. Qual. Methods **1**(2), 23–38 (2002)

Gregory, S.: Cameras everywhere revisited: how digital technologies and social media aid and inhibit human rights documentation and advocacy. J. Human Rights Pract. **11**(2), 373–392 (2019)

Hancock, J.T., Guillory, J.: Deception with technology. In: Sundar, S. (ed.) The Handbook of the Psychology of Communication Technology, pp. 270–289 (2015)

Harris, A.: Who coined the term catfish? Slate, 18 January 2013. https://slate.com/culture/2013/01/catfish-meaning-and-definition-term-for-online-hoaxes-has-a-surprisingly-long-history.html. Accessed 27 May 2022

Haselhuhn, M.P., Kennedy, J.A., Kray, L.J., Van Zant, A.B., Schweitzer, M.E.: Gender differences in trust dynamics: women trust more than men following a trust violation. J. Exp. Soc. Psychol. **56**, 104–109 (2015)

Huang, J.M., Stringhini, G., Yong, P.: Quit playing games with my heart: Understanding online dating scams. In: Almgren, M., Gulisano, V., Maggi, F. (eds.) Detection of Intrusions and Malware, and Vulnerability Assessment. LNCS, vol. 9148, pp. 216–236. Springer, Cham (2015). https://doi.org/10.1007/978-3-319-20550-2_12

Javornik, A., et al.: 'What lies behind the filter?' Uncovering the motivations for using augmented reality (AR) face filters on social media and their effect on well-being. Comput. Hum. Behav. **128**, 107–126 (2022)

Kaur, G., Iyer, S.: Digital crimes on Indian online dating platforms during Covid-19: Impact on women. Int. J. Law Manag. Human. **4**(4), 1277–1291 (2021)

Keyes, R.: The Post-Truth Era: Dishonesty and Deception in Contemporary Life. St. Martin's Publishing Group, New York (2004)

Kim, J.H.: Technique for identifying cyber crime using clue. J. Korea Inst. Inf. Secur. Cryptol. **25**(4), 767–780 (2015)

Kleemans, M., Daalmans, S., Carbaat, I., Anschütz, D.: Picture perfect: the direct effect of manipulated Instagram photos on body image in adolescent girls. Media Psychol. **21**(1), 93–110 (2018)

Koch, C.M.: To catch a catfish: a statutory solution for victims of online impersonation. Univ. Colorado Law Rev. **88**(1), 233–280 (2017)

Lee, H.R., Lee, H.E., Choi, J., Kim, J.H., Han, H.L.: Social media use, body image, and psychological well-being: a cross-cultural comparison of Korea and the United States. J. Health Commun. **19**(12), 1343–1358 (2014)

Leung, K., Koch, P.T., Lu, L.: A dualistic model of harmony and its implications for conflict management in Asia. Asia Pacific J. Manage. **19**(2), 201–220 (2002)

López, A., Sanderman, R., Ranchor, A.V., Schroevers, M.J.: Compassion for others and self-compassion: levels, correlates, and relationship with psychological well-being. Mindfulness **9**(1), 325–331 (2018)

Li, Y.: Research on user behavior of beauty filters in Tik Tok app: taking college students as an example. Master's thesis, Southwest University, China (2021)

Lo, S.K., Hsieh, A.Y., Chiu, Y.P.: Contradictory deceptive behavior in online dating. Comput. Hum. Behav. **29**(4), 1755–1762 (2013)

Lyu, Z., Jiao, Y., Zheng, P., Zhong, J.: Why do selfies increase young women's willingness to consider cosmetic surgery in China? The mediating roles of body surveillance and body shame. J. Health Psychol. **27**(5), 1205–1217 (2021)

Madan, S., Basu, S., Ng, S., Ching Lim, E.A.: Impact of culture on the pursuit of beauty: Evidence from five countries. J. Int. Mark. **26**(4), 54–68 (2018)

McGloin, R., Denes, A.: Too hot to trust: examining the relationship between attractiveness, trustworthiness, and desire to date in online dating. New Media Soc. **20**(3), 919–936 (2018)

Mosley, M.A., Lancaster, M., Parker, M.L., Campbell, K.: Adult attachment and online dating deception: a theory modernized. Sexual Relationsh. Therapy. **35**(2), 227–243 (2020)

Santi, A.: "Catfishing": a comparative analysis of US v. Canadian Catfishing laws & their limitations. S. Ill. ULJ. **44**, 75–104 (2019)

Schmitz, A., Zillmann, D., Blossfeld, H.P.: Do women pick up lies before men? The association between gender, deception patterns, and detection modes in online dating. Online J. Commun. Med. Technol. **3**(3), 52 (2013)

Schoorman, F.D., Mayer, R.C., Davis, J.H.: An integrative model of organizational trust: past, present, and future. Acad. Manag. Rev. **32**(2), 344–354 (2007)

Simmons, M., Lee, J.S.: Catfishing: a look into online dating and impersonation. In: Meiselwitz, G. (ed.) Social Computing and Social Media. Design, Ethics, User Behavior, and Social Network Analysis. LNCS, vol. 12194, pp. 349–358. Springer, Cham (2020). https://doi.org/10.1007/978-3-030-49570-1_24

Toma, C.L., Hancock, J.T.: Looks and lies: the role of physical attractiveness in online dating self-presentation and deception. Commun. Res. **37**(3), 335–351 (2010)

Vaismoradi, M., Turunen, H., Bondas, T.: Content analysis and thematic analysis: Implications for conducting a qualitative descriptive study. Nurs. Health Sci. **15**(3), 398–405 (2013)

Walther, J.B.: Computer-mediated communication: impersonal, interpersonal, and hyperpersonal interaction. Commun. Res. **23**(1), 3–43 (1996)

Westerlund, M.: The emergence of deepfake technology: a review. Technol. Innov. Manag. Rev. **9**(11), 39–52 (2019)

Whitty, M.T.: Revealing the 'real' me, searching for the 'actual' you: presentations of self on an internet dating site. Comput. Hum. Behav. **24**(4), 1707–1723 (2008)

Whitty, M.T., Buchanan, T.: The online dating romance scam: the psychological impact on victims–both financial and non-financial. Criminol. Crim. Just. **16**(2), 176–194 (2016)

Xue, L., Parker, C.J., Hart, C.A.: How to design effective AR retail apps. In: Claudia, M., tomDieck, M., Jung, T.H., Louriro, S.M.C. (eds.) Augmented Reality and Virtual Reality. PI, pp. 3–16. Springer, Cham (2021). https://doi.org/10.1007/978-3-030-68086-2_1

Yim, M.Y.-C., Park, S.-Y.: "I am not satisfied with my body, so I like augmented reality (AR)": consumer responses to AR-based product presentations. J. Bus. Res. **100**, 581–589 (2019)

Yu, H., Lee, M.: Effects of the virtual makeup using beauty makeup applications on mood, body satisfaction, and self-esteem among female university students. J. Korean Soc. Cloth. Textiles **44**(4), 727–738 (2020)

Research on Experience Design of Social Reading Platforms Based on Social Presence Theory

Yingying Li and Hong Chen[✉]

School of Art Design and Media, East China University of Science and Technology, Xuhui District, No. 130, Meilong Road, Shanghai, People's Republic of China
engoy2008@163.com

Abstract. With the development of the Internet, digital reading is becoming more and more popular. The change of reading media strongly affected users' reading behavior. In the Era of Web 3.0, the sociality of reading has been amplified by the Internet. A social reading model with readers as the core and emphasis on sharing, interaction and dissemination came into being. This paper introduces social Presence theory to study how to enhance the perception among users on platforms, thereby improving the user experience of social reading. Firstly, through literature research, we subdivided the social presence on social reading platforms into conscious social presence, emotional social presence, and cognitive social presence. We extracted the design elements of social reading platforms which might lead to high social presence then. By card sorting, design elements were grouped. Finally, we proposed an experience model of social reading platforms which explains the relationship between social presence and user experience as a reference for the interaction design of social reading platforms in the future.

Keywords: Social Presence · Social reading · User experience

1 Research Background

With the popularity of mobile Internet, people's reading behavior has changed dramatically. From paper books to Kindle ink screens to digital reading, people have more choices. Digital reading is welcomed by users because of its high degree of personalization, rich content, and other advantages. In 2020, the contact rate of digital reading (online reading, mobile phone reading, e-reader reading, iPad reading, etc.) among Chinese adults was 79.4%. Digital reading has become an important way for many readers to obtain information and knowledge. [1] The number of digital readers in China is growing, and various media are integrating and complementing each other. Reading is entertainment, and reading and social interaction are deeply integrated.

In the Era of Web 3.0, the sociality of reading is amplified by the Internet and various social reading platforms. With readers as the core, the social reading model that emphasizes sharing, interaction and dissemination arises at the historic moment. However, in digital reading, social communication transmits information through digital media.

© Springer Nature Switzerland AG 2022
G. Meiselwitz et al. (Eds.): HCII 2022, LNCS 13517, pp. 73–80, 2022.
https://doi.org/10.1007/978-3-031-22131-6_6

Compared with reading discussion, information and emotion between users inevitably suffer certain loss in transmission, thus affecting user experience.

At present, China's research on social reading mainly focuses on social reading theory, social reading intention, social reading behavior and social reading practice. However, the research on user experience in social reading is insufficient, so this paper focuses on the experience design of online reading community. This paper discusses how to reduce the sense of distance brought by media through design and make interactive experience more vivid, to improve users' social reading experience.

2   Social Presence and User Experience in Reading Communities

2.1   Social Presence Theory

The theory of social presence was first proposed by Short et al. in 1976. They believe that social presence refers to the degree to which a person is regarded as a "real person" and the perceived degree of connection with others in the process of communication through media, which is a media attribute [2]. Tu believes that social presence occurs in the media environment and relates to people's awareness of others [6]. Social presence is not only supported by media, but also a psychological perception, which is affected by both technical and social factors [3].

Social presence was first proposed and applied in the field of communication. With the development of the Internet, the boundaries of various fields are constantly broken, and integrated with each other. Therefore, social presence theory has been gradually applied to more fields related to communication and social interaction, such as online learning, telemedicine and so on. Wang Han et al. applied social presence to the research of digital reading, and explored the influencing factors and causes of users' pan-recreational reading [4]. Ji Dan et al. proposed through research that social presence mediated by satisfaction has a positive impact on users' reading behavior [5]. In a study of user experience in commercial communities, Wang divides social presence into three types: cognitive social presence, emotional social presence and conscious social presence, which provides references for the study of this paper [6].

2.2   User Experience

In 1982, Steve Jobs and Hartmut Eslinger established the value of "user-centered, design-centered" for Apple. Don Norman and Jakob Nielsen firstly put forward that user experience encompasses all aspects of the end-user's interaction with the company, its services, and its products [7]. The core of user experience design is to consider the overall user experience from the user's point of view. Typical methods of user experience design include user journey map, card taxonomy, etc. With the development of Internet products, more and more attention has been paid to user experience. Good user experience can bring users a pleasant feeling, thus improving satisfaction and turning ordinary users into loyal users.

2.3 The Relationship Between Social Presence and Reading Community Experience

Reading, as a kind of dialogue, first takes place between individuals and texts, and then extends to texts and readers. The reading experience is inherently social. Personal interpretations are shaped and consolidated by constant discussion with other readers. The social reading mode supported by the reading community is a new digital reading mode with readers as the center and social relations as the link. Social reading mode emphasizes sharing, interaction and communication, pays more attention to user experience advocates user creation of content, attaches importance to joint communication and profit, and realizes infinite amplification of reading value on the basis of multi-directional interaction.

Compared with the traditional reading mode, the reading experience generated in the process of social reading is more complex and diverse. Li et al. summarized the reading experience under the new technology environment into aesthetic experience, emotional experience, thinking experience and other traditional reading experience, value experience, social experience, immersion experience and other dimensions. Moreover, from the perspective of experience level, value experience, social experience and thinking experience are the development products of aesthetic experience and emotional experience as general experience. On this basis, immersion experience is finally achieved, namely the peak of experience [8]. Currently, there are few studies on the specific formation patterns and design strategies of user experience in online reading communities under new technologies and media.

Social presence theory mainly studies the cognitive feelings of users when they communicate and interact with others through the Internet and other media. Many studies have shown that social presence has a positive impact on immersive experience, useful perception, etc. One of the biggest differences between a reading community and a traditional reading or purely digital document reading tool is the emphasis on the interaction of multiple readers. The impact of socializing through reading between users on the experience is a key part of user experience research in reading communities. It can be concluded that the two research scenarios match each other. Therefore, this paper analyzes the influence of design elements in reading community on user experience from the perspective of social presence, and then comes to the experience design strategy of online reading community.

3 Read Community Experience Elements from the Perspective of Social Presence

3.1 Extraction of User Experience Elements of Social Reading

In order to study the influence mechanism of social presence and social reading experience, this paper subdivides users' social presence in online reading community into conscious social presence, emotional social presence, and cognitive social presence, and respectively explores the design elements. To ensure that the design elements in the design model are verified in real design practice, the discussion takes "WeRead", a typical online reading community, as a case study.

"WeRead" is a reading software based on WeChat relationship chain which is popular in China. The slogan "make reading no longer lonely" reflects its product positioning for social reading. Through the operation of the reading community, WeRead promotes the interaction between readers, thus creating a warm and not lonely reading experience.

We recruited 8 WeRead users as interview subjects. We discussed and recorded their social reading experience and related experience on the platform. And pull out the relevant experience elements Including user profile pictures, comments, likes and so on.

Then, three users were invited to classify the elements together with us through the card sorting. All the elements were divided into three groups, and the following table was obtained (see Table 1).

Table 1. Design elements on social reading platforms

Original elements	Element groups	Social presence
Avatar, nickname, gender, region tag, personality signature……	Users' identity elements	Conscious social presence
Comments, likes, Dynamic effect……	Reading interaction elements	Emotional social presence
Graphic links, context, Browsing path……	Reading situation elements	Cognitive social presence

3.2 Conscious Social Presence and Reading Community Experience Elements

Conscious social presence refers to that readers are aware of other social participants' virtual presence and feel their social influence in the process of reading community experience. Good design can make users aware of the real existence of the users behind them when facing other user accounts in the community, instead of a bunch of cold digital information or robots.

Take WeRead as an example, there will be other users' identities exposed before, during and after reading. The display of user identity mainly includes avatar, nickname, gender, region tag and personality signature. WeRead also transfers the original social relations in WeChat and sets the label "WeChat friends", which greatly reduces the cognitive cost of friend identity. This was followed by the number of hours spent reading, likes and followers. Reading duration can reflect the richness of reading experience and indirectly reflect reading thinking ability. The number of likes and followers can reflect her reading appreciation ability through social influence. Meanwhile, it can reflect social influence, arouse the group consciousness of users, and attract users' attention more.

The sense of social presence of consciousness mainly affects readers' feelings of trust and companionship. When recommending books, the app will recommend books based on social connections, and mark the information that "your friends are reading" for the recommended books, to improve the credibility of the recommendation through the influence of friends. After clicking, you can see the reading information of the reading users. The number of reading users has changed from a number to real users or even some friends, which enhances the user's sense of trust in the system recommendation. In the reading page and operation interface state, you can see the total number of readers of the current book, that is, the number of book friends. Click to see the details of the book friends, their reading progress. This streamlined way of presentation can provide the right sense of conscious presence and bring people a sense of company.

3.3 Emotional Social Presence and Reading Community Experience Elements

Emotional social presence refers to the reader's emotional relationship with others in society and the ability to empathize with others emotionally. Emotional relationships are often generated in behavioral interactions, especially interactive rituals that can stimulate users' personal emotional energy [9]. On the WeRead interface, there is a heart-shaped "like" button after each chapter of a book, which allows users to express their liking for the chapter. Through the display of the number of likes, you can feel the reading mood of other users. All users who like the same chapter have the same focus, i.e., the content of the current paragraph; Readers can share their love of the content, and the interaction is private enough that only those who read the book can participate in it, perfect for an interactive ritual that inspires more intense user emotion. After clicking the "like" button, the interface will not only display the simulation of heartbeat pattern dynamic effect, but also users can feel a short vibration, truly simulate the joy of reading when meeting friends. Vivid and diverse design elements provide conditions for the generation of emotional presence.

Emotional social presence mainly affects readers' emotional experience, social experience, and achievement experience. In the process of praising each other to express the recognition and love of each other's views is itself a kind of emotional transmission. Strong emotional resonance can generate a sense of self-identity, enhance self-confidence, achieve a good emotional experience and gain a sense of belonging to the group which contributes to nice social experience. In addition, the number of likes from others represents the attention and respect of others, expanding personal social influence and feeling self-worth, users can get strong achievement experience.

3.4 Cognitive Social Presence and Reading Community Experience Elements

Cognitive social presence means that in the reading community, users can understand others' views on things and comprehensively judge others' emotional, cognitive, and behavioral tendencies [10]. Cognition is characterized by situational relevance. Situational cognition regards systems -- people, others, society, and natural environment -- as a co-existing whole, which together constitute the vision of cognitive meaning. In the process of reading on WeRead, users can underline their thoughts and see other readers' comments on the current snippet. Multiple readers can post their thoughts on the same clip or reply to or like a comment. Since all comments are based on the same paragraph context, the interactive communication is in a unified and specific reading context, making the user's interaction with the content discussion more targeted and easier to understand. The posting and sharing of readers' thought will also be automatically accompanied by a text location link to the source of the thought, so that visitors can quickly locate the context in which the author post the idea to read. The users in WeRead are also divided into circles, such as mystery reasoning circles, social observer circles and so on. Circles help users find people with the same interests and similar knowledge background, to better reach tacit understanding in the process of communication, identify with each other's values, carry out smooth exchange of views, and obtain a high sense of cognitive presence.

Cognitive social presence mainly affects readers' emotional experience, thinking experience, achievement experience and social experience. When users find people who share the same values with them, they can "like", "comment" or even "follow" them as friends, quickly establishing intimate psychological connections and feeling like friends at first sight. The published ideas are praised and paid attention by other users. After receiving their attention, users' needs for social recognition are satisfied and achievement experience is achieved. Behaviors such as taking notes, communicating, and sharing, commenting, and forwarding further visualize the emotions and thoughts in reading, deepen the reading experience, and help readers enjoy high-quality reading experience. The expression and communication of ideas enhance the thinking experience.

4 The Construction of an Interaction Design Model

It is concluded that the elements of identity design can increase users' trust in book recommendation and companionship in the reading process, which are mediated by conscious social presence. The elements of interactive design such as interface animation, interactive rituals, can externalize the user's internal emotions, form resonance among users, stimulate users' stronger personal emotional energy to achieve a high emotional presence. The emotional identity that people gain in their interpersonal interactions promotes social influence and a sense of accomplishment. The elements of situational design build a social context in reading which reduces the cognitive cost of users to other people's views, makes it easier for users to understand each other, and gain deep reflection in the high cognitive presence. When each basic experience is built compelling,

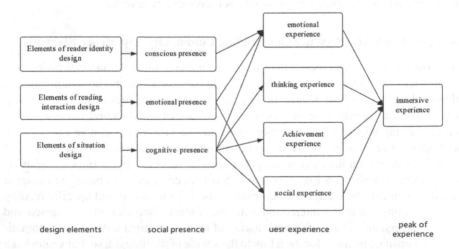

Fig. 1. The experience model of social reading platforms

the immersive experience will be brought into being which is the peak of experience (Fig. 1).

5 Design Strategies for Social Reading Platform

Finally, we put forward reference suggestions for the experience design of future reading communities from the perspective of practical application:

- Focus on the interactive design between user and reading platform, user, and user. Organize interactive groups around reading content and reading interest, design natural and easy interaction, and improve the timeliness and vividness of interaction, to strengthen user engagement.
- Intensify the emotional design of a social reading platform. Using the design method of emotion metaphor build interactive way for users to improve the emotional expression and create emotional resonance between the user, create a pleasant reading atmosphere, to enhance the sense of intimacy and companionship in the reading community, and enhance users' sense of belonging to the community platform.
- Focus on the segmentation of reading and social situations in the design. Before reading, users search for books in a large amount of information and pay attention to experience such as efficiency and trust. When reading, thinking, and accompanying experience are more critical. In the evaluation and expression process after reading, users focus on interaction, social influence, and achievement experience. Design according to specific situations can provide users with more precise services and promote a virtuous cycle of experience in all links.
- Actively apply innovative media that contain more social clues, such as AR technology and video interactive technology, to expand the social presence from a technical perspective, and explore more possibilities of the social reading platform.

6 Conclusion and Prospect

From the perspective of social presence, this paper takes WeRead app as an example to study the mechanism by which specific design elements in the reading community influence user experience through social presence. This study constructs user experience model of online social reading platform. Combined with the future development trend, this paper puts forward constructive suggestions for the experience design of reading community from four aspects: interactive design, emotional design, situational design and combining technological innovation design.

The innovation of this paper is the introduction of the social presence theory to the social reading media. Recognizing the socialized characteristics of reading behavior in the Internet environment, this paper studies users' reading experience from the perspective of socializing social attributes, and innovatively introduces social existence theory, which is a novel research approach.

in the future, Further research is needed in the following aspects. (1) The sample number of user studies is small, and all of them are from China, so its applicability to the global scale needs to be verified. (2) The research on the design of anti-addiction is limited to qualitative research, and future research can include qualitative research to make the model more accurate.

References

1. 2020 China Mobile Reading Industry Report [EB/OL]. https://tech.sina.com.cn/roll/2020-10-14/doc-iiznezxr5809828.shtml. 21 July 2021
2. Short, J., Williams, E., Christie, B.: The Social Psychology of Telecommunications. Wiley, London (1976)
3. Tu, C.H.: The measurement of social presence in an online learning environment. Int. J. E-learn. 1(2), 34–45 (2002)
4. Wang, H., Zhong, L., Yang, Y.: Research on the influencing factors of users' entertainment reading in social media environment. Inf. Sci. 36(10), 116–121 (2018). https://doi.org/10.13833/j.issn.1007-7634.2018.10.021
5. Dan, J., Wu, L.: A study on the Relationship between reading behavior and online community presence. Librar. Inf. Work. 60(02), 42–46+58 (2016). https://doi.org/10.13266/j.issn.0252-3116.2016.02.006
6. Wang, Y.F., Jiang, X.: Research on experience design of community e-commerce platform from the perspective of social presence. Pack. Eng. 41(14), 222–227 (2020). https://doi.org/10.19554/j.cnki.1001-3563.2020.14.034
7. Norman, D., Miller, J., Henderson, A.: What you see, some of what's in the future, and how we go about doing it: HI at Apple Computer. In: Conference Companion on Human Factors in Computing Systems (CHI 1995). Association for Computing Machinery, New York, NY, USA, 155 (1995). https://doi.org/10.1145/223355.223477
8. Li, G., Fan, S.: Research on the composition of reading experience. Librar. Tribune. 40(01), 19–28 (2020)
9. Yihan, L.: Study on the Interactive ceremony of Douban Group. Audio-visual 10, 124–125 (2021). https://doi.org/10.19395/j.cnki.1674-246x.2021.10.054
10. Sheng, X., Li, H.: Situated cognition. Sci. Res. 05, 806–811 (2007). https://doi.org/10.16192/j.cnki.1003-2053.2007.05.003

e-Participation as Mediated Ecosystem? A Case Study on Municipalities of St. Petersburg, Russia

Yuri Misnikov[1] and Olga Filatova[1,2]

[1] ITMO University, Kronverksky Pr. 49, Bldg. A, St. Petersburg 197101, Russia
k636711@kansai-u.ac.jp
[2] St. Petersburg State University, Universitetskaya Emb., St. Petersburg 199034, Russia
o.filatova@spbu.ru

Abstract. The paper presents the findings of an exploratory empirical study of the e-participation infrastructure available in St. Petersburg municipalities from the media ecosystem perspective. We argue that in order to obtain deeper insights into the evolution of participatory services provided via digital means, there is a need to take a stronger account of the underlying media properties – both in technology and social practice terms – that embed and host e-participation services. While no evidence has been found that e-participation practices have matured enough to form a holistic ecosystem environment of citizen engagement at the municipal level, the media ecology approach applied in this research as a central theoretical frame might have a potential to better explain some of the findings. These are consistent with broader global trends, such as the dominance of information provision and the lack of such more interactive forms of empowerment as cooperation, consultation, participation in policy making that lag significantly behind across municipalities globally. We also have found that the population size of municipalities does not influence the range of available e-participation services.

Keywords: e-Participation · e-Democracy · Media ecology · Mediated participation · Municipality · Ecosystem

1 Introduction

The research presented in this paper is a follow-up to the earlier exploratory study undertaken by the authors of e-participation services viewed from the municipal ecosystem perspective [1]. The meaning of e-participation as a social and political practice envisaged by participatory democracy advocates and designed by software engineers as technological constructs greatly varies in form and purpose. As a rule, it is viewed as a stand-alone tool, a platform, an instrument intended to be used by the public, government officials, businesses. For example, e-petition sites and e-participation portals are the most visible (in the literal sense) examples of such tools focusing on national and regional (city) audiences. Sometimes they take a shape of mega-systems spanning across national borders (e.g., Change.org). e-Participation is also present at the local government level, however to which extent these are distinguishable from electronic administrative (e-government) services is less clear. The empirics collected for the construction of the

© Springer Nature Switzerland AG 2022
G. Meiselwitz et al. (Eds.): HCII 2022, LNCS 13517, pp. 81–96, 2022.
https://doi.org/10.1007/978-3-031-22131-6_7

popular e-participation index published by the UN e-Government Surveys do not look below the select number of big city portals offering citizen engagement opportunities [2].

As we argued in our previous research, it is worth studying e-participation more closely at the grassroots governance level paying attention to the type of media that host e-participation tools beyond web technologies. We proposed that in order to do so, it might be productive to invoke the Marshall McLuhan's media ecology concept [3] to overcome the epistemic limitations imposed by focusing on the tool itself and ignoring the medium it is embedded in. This approach intends to unlock the benefits of ecological thinking and start looking not only at individual tools but also at the relationships between them as much systemically as possible. Applying the ecosystem concept to media ecology amends its metaphorical interpretation proposed by Neil Postman [4] into a more tangible concept that can be described and tested empirically. Another methodological proposition is to strengthen the notion of media ecology by enriching it with the idea of information ecology to expand its applicatory scope and reach out to the local micro contexts where disparate actors and technologies coevolve and cohabitate in mutual dependence as a form of e-democracy from below [5, 6].

In this paper we provide a further rationale why to apply the media ecosystem approach and demonstrate it by examining e-participation services in all 111 municipalities of St. Petersburg in Russia, a home of over 5 million people. First, we take a closer look at the media ecology literature, followed by presenting the empirical case study and describing the methodology used to analyze e-participation services at the municipal level. The paper concludes by discussing the outcome of such analysis. In line with the quantitative research philosophy, we intended to conduct the study in a replicable manner so as anyone could reproduce the research by investigating any other municipalities elsewhere.

While there was a goal to characterize each municipality in terms of its e-participation infrastructure, a complementary objective was added to construct an imaginary, generalized image of, as it were, an average municipality within main population groups and thus to understand better whether there should be specific strategies to build e-participation services depending on municipality size.

2 What Do We Know and What Don't About Mediated Participation?

2.1 The Media Ecology Dimension

When examining the latest e-participation research, we are especially interested in understanding the role of the media as a specific medium in the original McLuhanian ecological sense; that is, the moment when the medium, as well as its assemblages, becomes a holistic media environment in which participatory forms, processes and structures evolve together. Kate Milberry [7] argues that the notion of media "refers to communication technologies" as specific forms of communication (and includes other non-technological communication forms), whereas the term ecology draws "upon systems theory and cybernetics" to understand "the integration, interdependence, and dynamism of media and technology in human affairs". From this perspective, she defines the concept of media ecology "…as the study of complex communication systems as environments, media ecology has emerged as a metadiscipline that seeks integrated and holistic accounts of the consequences wrought by the collision of technology, culture, and consciousness". Coleman et al. [8, p. 4] highlight the integrative potential of the media ecology theoretical framework to explain the ways in which citizens and their communities are communicatively integrate with one another through, for example, the news ecologies in community context. On the other hand, when looking from the e-participation angle – centered on the citizens interested to influence policymaking in general and the well-being of the communities they live in particular – we are interested in the media ecology potential to exercise social control and change as a way of community integration.

The systemic side of the ecology notion that resonates with e-participation is the diverse unity of its parts, relationships, experiences that coevolve together as a unique system. This approach helps imagine municipalities as unique administrative, governance and ecological systems interested in communicative interactions between authorities and citizens. Yet there is a scarce knowledge to understand to which extent these mediated participatory environments are indeed systemic. Or, put it differently, which communication mediums are represented at the municipal level and whether these are interrelated to realize their systemic potential to mediate social and political participation?

2.2 e-Participation Dimension

e-Participation as a research domain in relation to decision-making in government continues to significantly expand – a growth trend discovered a decade earlier [9]. A recent systemic literature review undertaken by Malte Steinbacha et al. [10] reveals knowledge gaps concerning the efficacy of e-participation in public administrations. One major gap is weak institutionalization, which is the last phase of e-participation diffusion as a "routinized activity within an organization" [10, p. 63]. Another important under-researched area is the meso- and micro-level – the level of organizations (and their units) and the individual level of managers, respectively. Little evidence is available about studying the institutionalization of e-participation at the grassroots level of public office.

We have undertaken a search for the most recent and cited work published during 2019–2021 in academic journals by applying the following keywords on Web of Science: "e-participation" (Topic) OR "electronic participation" (Topic) OR "digital participation" (Topic) OR "virtual participation" (Topic) OR "e-democracy" (Topic) OR "electronic democracy" (Topic) OR "digital democracy" (All Fields) OR "virtual democracy" (All Fields) OR "participatory democracy" (All Fields). As a result, 505 journal articles were found that have been cited 1,399 times (the average citations per item was 2.77). The search intentionally omitted such keywords as "media ecology", "municipality", "ecosystem" (and the like that stem from the media ecological perspective) to understand whether the latter dimensions were integral to the original e-participation research design.

The analysis of the papers' titles reveals that the terms 'e-participation" and "e-democracy" are featured in 201 articles, while as many as 336 include the word "media"; however, almost all of them were associated with social media. Neither the role of the media type, nor the ecosystem approach have been included into research agenda. Interest in research agenda in the field of "municipal/municipality" and "local government" is less pronounced, with 75 articles found. Little evidence has emerged about the institutionalization of e-participation at the local government level of public office. Overall, the academic scholarship on the municipal governance level is found to be fragmented describing experiences and lessons learned from a handful of countries, such as the United States [11–18], Spain [19], Israel [20], Austria [21], Turkey [22] the Netherlands [23], Italy [24], Finland [25].

The keyword "mobile" featured in just 28 papers, whereas "messenger" and "media ecology" were absent altogether, i.e., the research into the mobile medium (represented by messaging applications and platforms designed for the use on smartphones) is far less prominent, although smartphone have become central to the media use in general, especially among young people [26–28]. Likewise, the terms "ecology" and "ecosystem" featured in only 35 articles, which means that researching e-participation from the systemic media ecology point of view seems to generate little attention.

The research of the local government websites usually looks at the tools that enable three most accepted parameters of e-participation through the e-Participation Index (EPI) comprising (i) e-information (electronic information provision), (ii) e-consultation (electronic consultations) and (iii) e-decision making (electronic participation in public policies) decision-making [2]. There are other e-participation metrics that address other features of public participation to emphasize more strongly the empowerment aspect, such as Citizen Web Empowerment Index (CWEI) [29] designed specifically to assess e-participation at the municipal level. In addition to the above three parameters, CWEI introduces the Web 2.0 tools and strategies (WTS) metrics to better understand better how municipalities communicate with its citizens through six criteria: blog/forum; chat; social networking tools; mobile services; Web TV; and open government data strategy [30]. This is a significantly richer assessment metrics including the mobile media services that, as mentioned above, are becoming increasingly fundamental for government-citizens communication.

3 Methodology

3.1 Underlying Research Assumptions

The main goal is to acquire empirical evidence about e-participation from the media ecology viewpoint at the municipal level. The research's working assumptions presume that the municipal authorities most typically do have concrete plans, motivation (whatever genuine it might be) and resources to design and implement e-participation tools to engage with citizens. The literature – as argued above – provides numerous accounts that the adoption of new technologies (say, the Web 2.0 interactive technology including social media) has reached the local level. However, we don't know to which extent the technology adoption process has matured enough to create a holistic e-participation infrastructure in technical, social, human terms as a media ecosystem, when its different components complement one another. Otherwise speaking, the question is whether municipalities not only deploy e-participation tools within their governance mandate but do it systemically to embed them in medium type that is capable to generate as much of participation efficacy as possible. We also don't know to which extent e-participation practice depends on or includes into account other e-participation instruments available above the municipal levels, such as city-wide, regional, or national ones. Finally, it is not clear what type of media is a preferred choice when providing e-participation opportunities for local residents.

3.2 Case Study

The case study includes all municipalities of St. Petersburg, Russia. The city's territory is divided into 111 intra-city municipalities – officially named as municipal formations – comprising 81 municipal city districts, 9 cities and 21 semi-urban settlements. See a full list of the examined municipalities in Appendix A. Each municipality was studied to identify all the available e-participation resources visible to end-users also considering the underlying media type including its status, namely: (i) official resources deployed by municipal authorities, (ii) public resources deployed by non-governmental organizations, and (iii) personal resources deployed by private persons. In addition, we distinguish three forms of e-participation technologies: (a) the form of Internet sites (Web technologies); (b) the form of pages on social networking sites (social media); and (c) the form of mobile applications (messenger platforms/applications).

All empirical data were collected in a manner that this research methodologically could be replicated to study any other municipalities in any country.

3.3 e-Participation Services

We call the municipal e-participation tools (instruments, platforms) as 'services' due to the understanding that in many cases citizen engagement technically is part of the broader plans to provide electronic administrative services. This means that it can be any technically implemented tool for communication and interaction between the authorities and residents; it can be a channel or a chat in the form of a mobile application, a menu section of a website, a discussion group on a social network, a poll, a streaming service, a voting procedure, etc. Particular attention was paid to the study of the sections of the menu of the municipal websites containing specific services aimed at communication and interaction with residents. From this perspective, each section/subsection of the menu was considered as a stand-alone service of information provision, consultation, cooperation, decision-making; for example, the presence of a page in social networks was considered as a separate service. Mobile application services were evaluated in a similar way.

To categorize e-participation services, we have adopted the methodology adopted by the United Nations EPI index consisting of information services (e-information); public consultation services as an opportunity to discuss local problems in the form of public consultations and hearings (e-consultation); services of direct participation in decision-making, such as voting (e-decisions). Using as a base, we have modified this classification scheme in two ways: (a) to turn e-consultation into e-cooperation by including in it other forms of two-way interactive participatory activities, and (b) to add one more service of public deliberation (e-deliberation) as an essential aspect of participatory (deliberative) democracy.

3.4 Municipality Size

Given the diversity of the municipal structure and composition of a such a big city as St. Petersburg, we have undertaken an additional analysis to determine whether there is any regularity between the number of inhabitants and the number of e-participation services available in individual municipalities. The following six population groups were used to account for the municipality size:

- over 100 thousand inhabitants
- 50–100 thousand inhabitants
- 25–50 thousand inhabitants
- 10–25 thousand inhabitants
- 5–10 thousand inhabitants
- less than 5 thousand inhabitants.

It seemed essential to have a closer look at the impact of municipality size since the smaller municipalities possess usually less technical, financial and human resources to develop e-participation services. In this context, the intention was to understand whether or not the larger – and potentially richer – municipalities create more holistic e-participation environments that could be considered the mediated e-participation ecosystems. It was also assumed that smaller municipalities presumably having less resources would have access to the e-participation services deployed at the city-wide or national level. Therefore, to look for any regularities each size group was averaged to come up with an imaginary typified municipality specific to each population grouping, which was accompanied by the similar process of averaging the available e-participation services identified in the group.

3.5 Research Questions

The study attempts to answer the following research questions:

1. What types of media technologies are dominant at the municipal level to embed e-participation services?
2. What types of e-participation services prevail at the municipal level depending on the medium type and the respective resource status?
3. Does the municipality size influence the number of employed e-participation services?
4. Does the collected evidence suggest the availability of e-participation ecosystem in some form?

4 Results

4.1 e-Participation Media Resources by Type and Status

There are 475 media resources were available in 111 St. Petersburg municipalities at the beginning of 2022 (Table 1).

Table 1. Number of media resources available in St. Petersburg municipalities.

Media type	Media status		
	Official	Public	Personal
Websites	110	15	0
Social media pages	129	104	5
Mobile apps	105	7	1
Total	344	126	6

Figure 1 and Fig. 2 below show how the media resources are distributed by their type and status across all municipalities.

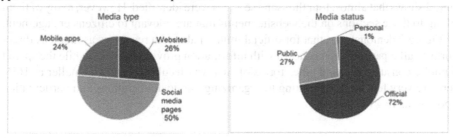

Fig. 1. Distribution of media resources by type.

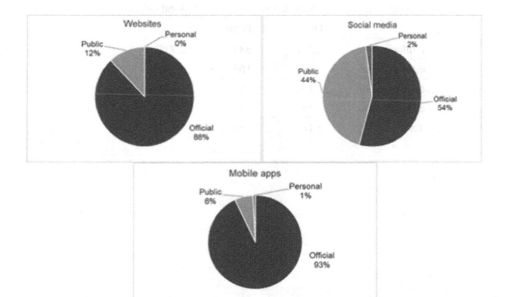

Fig. 2. Distribution of media resources by status.

The social media pages are the main media type available at the municipal level accounting for half of all resources available, with websites and mobile applications constituting the other half in equal proportions (26% and 24% respectively). When it comes to the media status, the ownership of municipal authorities dominates in the category of websites and mobile applications by a large margin comprising around nine-tens of all resources. The monopoly of local governments drops to 54% on social media, where the role of unofficial pages raises substantially reaching 44%. There are few websites (12%) and mobile apps (6%) not owned by municipalities.

4.2 e-Participation Services by Media Status

The collection of data pertinent to each group of four e-participation services for technical reasons was limited to the official and public media resources excluding personal ones. Table 2 shows that almost four thousand services were identified. However, many of them belong to those sections on the website menus that are relevant to citizens engagement.

Figure 3 demonstrates that for official municipal media resources as much as three-fourth of all e-participation concern with information provision (74%), while the spread of public consultations and other forms of two-way feedback is much smaller at 16%; there are very few services relating to organizing public deliberations and participation if policy making (5% each).

Table 2. Number of e-participation services by media status.

Service	Media status		Total services
	Official	Public	
e-Information	2,351	384	2,735
e-Cooperation	497	163	660
e-Deliberation	169	85	254
e-Decisions	167	18	185
Total	3,184	650	3,834

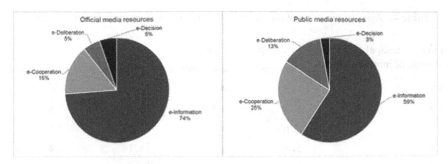

Fig. 3. Distribution of e-participation services by media status.

For public resources, the role of the interactive forms of public engagement, both consultations and deliberation, is more important thanks largely to the prevalence of social media that, as mentioned earlier, is the underlying media resource used by the public. Yet providing information still dominates (59%).

4.3 E-Participation Services by Municipality Size

Table 3 presents the total number of e-participation services by major population groups.

Table 3. Number of e-participation services by population size.

Population size			Number of municipalities	Total services	Service groups			
Population groups (in thousands)	Average municipality size (inhabitants per population group)	Total inhabitants			e-Information	e-Cooperation	e-Deliberation	e-Decisions
>100	123,297	986,378	8	252	196	35	16	5
50–100	68,707	3,229,228	47	1,318	977	207	67	67
25–50	42,425	933,351	22	689	475	120	38	56
10–25	18,388	275,820	15	436	327	68	20	21
5–10	7,656	30,623	4	142	102	16	13	11
<5	2,009	30,137	15	381	293	55	20	13
Total		5,485,537	111	3218	2,370	501	174	173

While these data are illustrative in its own right, one of the major methodological approaches implemented in this study was to construct an imaginative typical municipality depending on the number of its inhabitants and thus create an opportunity for comparison across other cities and countries. Table 4 below contain such averaged information.

These averaged data point at the relatively small number of e-participation services available per one averaged municipality and small differences as to the municipality

Table 4. Averaged number of e-participation services by average municipality size.

Average municipality size (in thousands of inhabitants)	e-Participation service			
	e-Information	e-Cooperation	e-Deliberation	e-Decisions
123.3	24.5	4.4	2.0	0.6
68.7	20.8	5.5	1.4	2.5
42.4	21.6	5.5	1.7	2.5
18.4	21.8	4.5	1.3	1.4
7.7	25.5	4.0	3.3	2.8
2.0	19.5	3.7	1.3	0.9

size. Figure 4 confirms that the number of services is not much dependent of the number of inhabitants.

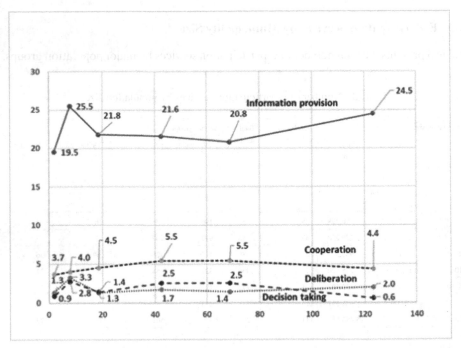

Fig. 4. Distribution of e-participation services (vertical axis, in numbers) by the averaged population size of municipalities (horizontal axis, in thousands of inhabitants).

5 Discussion and Conclusions

As argued above, providing information from municipalities to its inhabitants as an e-participation service clearly dominates over other services; that trend does not change substantially with the increase of the municipality size. Moreover, if anything, the proportions between different groups of e-participation does not change in any visible way either. As a rule, e-Information is represented on average by 20–25 services, most of which are hosted by the municipal websites and social media. The role of mobile applications is not important as yet. The number of other services does not exceed five (this is the case for e-Cooperation), whilst e-Deliberation and e-Decisions vary typically between one and three services. These trends are in line with other research across a diverse set of countries where a similarly designed research has been undertaken, as described in Sect. 2. For instance, Costopoulou et al. [31] applied the CWEI approach to assess the websites of 325 Greek municipalities in terms of e-participation progress in 2017–2018. The research reveals that while 60% of the municipalities are present on social media, only 7% of them use mobile channels. Overall, the results show that the use of Web 2.0 tools, e-consultation services and e-decision have made slower progress in comparison to the better developed information provision services, with "…only a handful of online tools are used for collecting citizens' opinions (e.g., chat and social media)" that enhance citizens' trust in local government [31, p. 323].

Other works provide similar evidence arguing that the implementation of e-participation platforms by local governments to involve citizens in consultation and decision-making processes remains a challenging task, when "municipalities largely use their websites to inform citizens on on-going decision-making processes, thereby strengthening the traditional representative democracy rather than deepening the democratic involvement of citizens" [25, p. 3]. Reddick and Norris [18, p. 468] echo these findings arguing that "e-participation is a more complicated process that needs further empirical investigation" to understand the reasons why only about one-third of the surveyed 684 U.S. local governments implemented three e-participation activities, while half of them implemented just one, usually of the one-way nature transmitting information from government to citizens.

Another major finding of our research relates to the media aspect of e-participation. The gathered evidence reveals a strong domination of the official municipal websites remaining the main single-entry point to most of the e-participation opportunities, particularly as far as information provision is concerned. Yet the role of social media is stronger when it comes of interactive services. This is especially relevant to public resources implemented outside the official municipal e-participation infrastructure. There is one issue that needs to be further clarified, namely: some of the public resources available on social media are in fact 'sponsored' or encouraged by municipal officials which is rather typical for such undemocratic regimes that today's Russia represents.[1] If this is the case, then the dominance of the official resources would be even stronger across the media type. This finding corroborates with global findings described in the UN e-Government Surveys. For example, it was found that 72% of services aimed at filing complaints or

---

[1] It should be noted that the amendments to the Russia's constitution of 2020 have de-facto eliminated self-governance at the local level, including municipalities.

sharing opinions with local governments are implemented via city portals [2]; fewer than half of the cities surveyed (43%) provide information on public meetings of the city or municipal council, while just 28% of the portals provide calendar announcements or postings of upcoming online consultations such as voting forums, surveys or polls. This study has found that direct participation in decision-making is the least available service typically represented on average at most by one or two services, which means that in many municipalities such a service is simply unavailable. The UN data also point at the fact that only 17% of the surveyed city portals offer online voting tools or systems to facilitate people's involvement in local government decision-making. It is reasonable to assume that residents of even small municipalities have access to services provided at the higher administrative level of governance. However, whether this is the case needs further research and clarification.

In the light of the above findings, the answers to the research questions could answered as follows:

RQ 1: What types of media technologies are dominant at the municipal level to embed e-participation services?

- Answer: Firstly, these are the traditional municipal websites, and, secondly, social media.

RQ 2: What types of e-participation services prevail at the municipal level depending on the medium type and the respective resource status?

- Answer: Information provision leads with a large margin, followed by far less available e-cooperation and e-deliberation services, and especially e-decision ones; the latter are typically hosted by social media, often outside official municipal resources.

RQ3: Does the municipality size influence the number of employed e-participation services?

- Answer: The size has marginal impact on the availability and scope of e-participation services.

RQ4: Does the collected evidence suggest the availability of e-participation ecosystem in some form?

- Answer: There is little credible evidence that municipalities have built technologically and socially mature mediated e-participation infrastructures that could be considered as holistic ecosystems of citizen engagement and empowerment; however, this issue needs additional clarification in the next phase of the research to better understand whether planning and designing e-participation accounts for the benefits arising from specific types of the host media.

Acknowledgment. The research has been supported by the Russian Science Foundation (RSF) as part of a project № 22–18-00364 «Institutional transformation of e-participation governance in Russia: a study of regional peculiarities».

Appendices

A.1 List of Municipalities

Administrative-territorial status and the number of inhabitants in St. Petersburg municipalities (as of 2021).

Village Serovo village - 281	Obukhov district - 53,374
Settlement Ushkovo settlement -701	Moskovskaya Zastava District - 53,640
Village Smolyachkovo village - 773	Polyustrovo district - 54,842
Village Komarovo village - 1300	Bolshaya Okhta district - 56,397
Village Tyarlevo village - 1319	Volkovskoye municipal district - 56,917
Settlement Petro-Slavyanka settlement - 1390	Uritsk district - 57,726
Settlement Solnechnoye settlement -1586	Vladimirsky district district - 57,768
Settlement Saperny settlement - 1611	Knyazhevo district - 59,737
Settlement Molodyozhnoe settlement - 1702	Krasnoe Selo city - 60,029
Village Ust-Izhora village - 1999	Lanskoe district - 60,510
Settlement Beloostrov settlement - 2301	Rzhevka district - 60,639
Village Alexandrovskaya village - 2728	Island of the Decembrists district - 61,163
Village Repino village - 2968	Piskarevka District - 62,241
Village Lisiy Nos village - 4653	Sosnovaya Polyana district - 64,461
Lakhta-Olgino district - 4825	No. 15 district - 64,663
Levashovo Settlement - 5559	No. 72 district - 64,868
Palace District district - 6761	Rybatskoe district - 65.174
Settlement Pesochny settlement - 9030	Sosnovskoye district - 67,425
Settlement Pontoon settlement – 9273	Southwest district - 67,582
Sea Gate district - 10,140	Okkervil district - 67,770
No. 78 District - 10,873	Sergievskoe district - 67,803
Village of Strelna village - 14,696	People's District - 68,121
Zelenogorsk city - 15,208	Gagarinsky District - 68,531
Ligovka-Yamskaya district - 16,194	Nevsky District district - 69,984
Pavlovsk city - 17,223	No. 54 District - 70,158
Vvedensky District - 18,888	Dachnoe district - 71.145
Kronverkskoe District - 19,559	Prometheus district - 73,296
Aptekarsky Island District - 19,828	Citizen district - 73,528
Posadsky District - 20,300	Ulyanka district - 74,066
Okrug Petrovsky district - 20,793	Finlandsky district district - 74,424

(*continued*)

(continued)

Sennoy district district - 21,954	Balkan district - 74,639
Admiralteisky District district - 22,710	Smolninskoe district - 75,417
Semyonovsky district - 23,223	No. 21 district - 78,268
Yekateringofsky istrict - 24,231	Pravoberezhny District -78,445
Izmailovskoye district - 26,306	Zvezdnoe district - 80,503
Chkalovsk district - 26,363	Pargolovo settlement - 81,033
Settlement Metallostroy settlement - 30,895	Svetlanovskoe district - 84,256
Ivanovsky district - 31,479	Peterhof city - 84,930
Narva District district - 31,574	Georgievsky district - 86,666
Vasilyevsky district - 32,763	South Primorsky district - 91,319
Gorelovo district - 33,437	Komendantsky airfield district - 91,736
Nevskaya Zastava district - 33,818	Novoizmailovskoye district - 92,848
Marine District - 34,722	Shushary village - 95,155
Harbor District - 35,997	Ozero Dolgoe district - 101,876
Konstantinovskoye district - 38,332	Academic district - 106,782
Kolomna district - 38,534	Shuvalovo-Ozerki district - 111,347
Krasnenkaya Rechka district - 40,432	Pushkin city - 112,978
No. 7 district - 40,595	Yuntolovo district -117,031
Municipality Sampsonievsky district - 41,411	Powder District - 136.234
Lomonosov city - 43,029	Kolpino city -149,766
	No. 65 District -150,364
Sestroretsk city - 43,060	Total: 5,384,342
Foundry District district - 43,886	
Kronstadt city - 44,353	
Avtovo District - 44,456	
Malaya Okhta District - 47,509	
Kolomyagi District - 49,105	
Kupchino district - 50,403	
No. 75 district - 50,892	
Pulkovo Meridian district - 51,500	
Northern district - 53,336	

References

1. Misnikov, Y., Filatova, O., Trutnev, D.: Empirical modeling of e-participation services as media ecosystems. In: Meiselwitz, G. (ed.) HCII 2021. LNCS, vol. 12774, pp. 87–104. Springer, Cham (2021). https://doi.org/10.1007/978-3-030-77626-8_6
2. UN E-government survey. https://publicadministration.un.org/en/research/un-e-government-surveys. Accessed 02 Feb 2022
3. McLuhan, M.: Understanding media: the extensions of man. In: Gordon, W.T. (ed.) Critical edn. (2003). (Original work published in 1964)
4. Postman, N.: The reformed English curriculum. In: Eurich, A.C. (ed.) High School 1980: The Shape of the Future in American Secondary Education, pp. 160–168. Pitman, New York (1970)
5. Nardi, B., O'Day, V.: Information Ecologies: Using Technology with Heart. MIT Press, Cambridge (2000)

6. Coleman, S., Blumler, J.G.: The Internet and Democratic Citizenship: Theory, Practice and Policy. Cambridge University Press, Cambridge (2009)
7. Milberry, K.: Media Ecology, Oxford Bibliographies (2012). https://www.oxfordbibliogra phies.com/view/document/obo-9780199756841/obo-9780199756841-0054.xml#obo-978 0199756841-0054-bibItem-0007. Accessed 12 Apr 2022
8. Coleman, S., et al.: The Mediated City: The News in a Post-industrial Context. Zed Books Ltd., London (2016). https://doi.org/10.5040/9781350251113. Accessed 12 Apr 2022
9. Susha, I., Grönlund, Å.: eParticipation research: systematizing the field. Govern. Inf. Q. **29**(3), 373–82, (2012). https://doi.org/10.1016/j.giq.2011.11.005
10. Steinbacha, M., Siewekeb, J., Süßa, S.: E-participation on the local level? A census survey approach for researching its implementation. J. Inf. Technol. Polit. **17**(1), 12–32 (2020)
11. Carriages, T.: Critical Factors in an Electronic Democracy: a Study of Municipal Managers. Electron. J. e-Govern. **6**(1), 23–30 (2008)
12. Carrizales, T.: Functions of E-government: a study of municipal practices. State Local Govern. Rev. **40**, 12–26 (2008)
13. Aikins, S.K., Dale, K.: Are public officials obstacles to citizen-centered E-government? An examination of municipal administrators' motivations and actions. State Local Govern. Rev. **42**(2), 87–103 (2010)
14. Scott, J.K.: E the people: do U.S. municipal government web sites support public involvement? Public Adm. Rev. **66**(3), 341–53 (2006)
15. Shen, C.-W., Chu, S.-H.: Web 2.0 and social networking services in municipal emergency management: a study of US cities. J. Univ. Comput. Sci. **20**(15), 1995–2004 (2014)
16. Ganapati, S., Reddick, C.G.: The use of ICT for open government in U.S. municipalities: perceptions of chief administrative officers. Public Perform. Manag. Rev. **37**(3), 365–87 (2014). https://doi.org/10.2753/Pmr1530-9576370302
17. Royo, S., Yetano, A.: "Crowdsourcing" as a tool for e-participation: two experiences regarding CO2 emissions at municipal level. Electron. Commer. Res. **15**(3), 323–48 (2015). https://doi.org/10.1007/s10660-015-9183-6
18. Reddick, C., Norris, D.F.: E-participation in local governments. Transf. Govern. People Process Policy **7**(4), 453–476 (2013). http://dx.doi.org/10.1108/TG-02-2013-0008
19. Karamagioli, E., Koulolias, V.: Challenges and barriers in implementing e-participation tools. One year of experience from implementing Gov2demoss in 64 municipalities in Spain. Int. J. Electron. Govern. **1**(4), 434–51 (2008). https://doi.org/10.1504/IJEG.2008.022070
20. Lev-On, A., Steinfeld, N.: Local engagement online: municipal Facebook pages as hubs of interaction. Govern. Inf. Q. **32**(3), 299–307 (2015). https://doi.org/10.1016/j.giq.2015.05.007
21. Höchtl, J., Parycek, P., Sachs, M.: E-participation readiness of Austrian municipalities. Transf. Govern.: People Process Policy **5**(1), 32–44 (2011). https://doi.org/10.1108/175061611111 14635
22. Sobaci, M.Z., Eryigit, K.Y.: Determinants of E-democracy adoption in Turkish municipalities: an analysis for spatial diffusion effect. Local Govern. Stud. **41**(3), 445–69 (2015). https://doi.org/10.1080/03003930.2014.995296
23. van Veenstra, A.F., Janssen, M., Boon, A.: Measure to improve: a study of eParticipation in Frontrunner Dutch municipalities. In: Tambouris, E., Macintosh, A., de Bruijn, H. (eds.) ePart 2011. LNCS, vol. 6847, pp. 157–168. Springer, Heidelberg (2011). https://doi.org/10.1007/978-3-642-23333-3_14
24. Capineri, C., Calvino, C., Romano, A.: Citizens and institutions as information prosumers. The case study of Italian municipalities on Twitter. Int. J. Spat. Data Infrastruct. Res. **10**, 1–26 (2015). https://doi.org/10.2902/1725-0463.2015.10.art1
25. Christensen, H.S.: Broadening democratic participation? An exploratory study of e-democracy in 188 Finnish municipalities. Scand. J. Public Adm. **17**(3), 3–21 (2013)

26. Lee, D., Menda, Y.P., Peristeras, V., Price, D.: The WAVE platform: utilising argument visualisation, social networking and web 2.0 technologies for eParticipation. Int. J. E-Serv. Mob. Appl. **3**(3), 69–85 (2010). https://doi.org/10.4018/978-1-4666-2654-6.ch015

27. de Reuver, M., Stefan Stein, S., Hampe, J.F.: From eParticipation to mobile participation: designing a service platform and business model for mobile participation. Inf. Polity: Int. J. Govern. Democracy Inf. Age **18**(1), 57–73 (2013)

28. Kalogeropoulos, A., Fletcher, R., Nielsen, K.: News brand attribution in distributed environments: do people know where they get their news? New Media Soc. **21**(3), 583–601 (2019)

29. Buccoliero, L., Bellio, E.: Citizens web empowerment in European municipalities. J. E-Govern. **33**(4), 225–236 (2010)

30. Naranjo-Zolotova, M., Oliveira, T., Casteleyn, S., Iranic, Z.: Continuous usage of e-participation: the role of the sense of virtual community. Gov. Inf. Q. **36**(3), 536–545 (2019)

31. Costopoulou, C., Ntaliani, M., Ntalianis, F.: Evolution of e-participation in Greek local government. Inf. Polity **26**(3), 311–325 (2021). https://doi.org/10.3233/IP-190174

Sports Journalism: Its Global Future in the Age of Digital Media

Olga Monteiro Da Silva[1], Ricardo G. Lugo[2]([⊠]), Richard Lenton[1], and Andrea M. Firth[1]

[1] University Campus of Football Business, Global Institute of Sport, Wembley Stadium, Wembley, London, England
[2] Health, Welfare and Organization, Østfold University College, Halden, Norway
Ricardo.g.Lugo@ntnu.no

Abstract. This study considers the possible future outcomes and developments of sports journalism in the age of digital media. A group of sports journalists from different countries around the world rationalised their points of view, in relation to the economy and sustainability of their profession in the digital era, alongside the digital changes they have faced during their careers. Despite having disclosed their personal opinions, several significant and strong correlations were found in almost all aspects. The sports journalists emphasise more advantages than disadvantages of digital media in their daily lives, and, despite recognising that the sector is in crisis, they believe that it will be possible to overcome it by producing creative content and increasing online interaction with consumers. Financially, the majority agree that they will have to put aside old advertisement practices and introduce new premium versions and paid content. Despite some disagreements in thoughts, it is concluded that to survive they will undoubtedly have to adapt to the online platforms and develop features that keep pace with the advancement of the digital world.

Keywords: Sports journalism · Digital · Technology introduction

1 Introduction

Over the past decade, the use of the internet has continuously grown, becoming one of the main outlets of information today (Parganas et al. 2015). This has allowed for social media channels to prosper, allowing a reach of 2.6 billion active users in 2018 (Statista 2019). With its increase in popularity, these networks are now used, not only by football fans, players, and teams to communicate with each other, but also by journalists to disseminate sport related news. One of the biggest changes to sport journalism during the beginning of this digitalisation, was how accessible information became to the public. Information can now be published 24/7, allowing journalists not only to report flash news, but also to keep up with a multitude of games, updating the audience with results and movements minute by minute.

© Springer Nature Switzerland AG 2022
G. Meiselwitz et al. (Eds.): HCII 2022, LNCS 13517, pp. 97–114, 2022.
https://doi.org/10.1007/978-3-031-22131-6_8

1.1 World Wide Web Adaptation

The internet has already overtaken the print industry as the number one media source for consumers (Kian et al. 2011). When looking for sporting information, consumers use the internet more regularly than buying newspapers. In the past decade, new technologies have evolved and presented numerous challenges to the conventional journalism channels (Hayes et al. 2007), as the media environment has been continuously changing, mostly due to the new technologies' insurgency (Sheffer and Schultz 2010). The problem lies in the fact that online sports journalism does not only work as a fundamental complementary part of the newspaper, but it also represents itself as its direct competitor. Moritz (2015) found that sports journalism during the digital age lives in the "now", so everything needs to be fast and momentary, giving the journalists a different routine of gathering, reporting and then problem solving (Mortiz 2015). The digital age has reinforced the tendency to publish the news first, and only to check afterwards its veracity, as there is little time to do this initially. This type of 'tabloid' journalism, is considered one of the greatest problems sports and general journalism has faced (Chen et al. n.d.). Tabloid journalism goes against some ethical guidelines of the profession, especially in matters when dealing with the truth by often generating fake news. Fake news is seen as one of the major problems in modern journalism, and the best solution to this problem is the creation of an automated tool that flags clickbait's sensationalist news Chen, Conroy, and Rubin (n.d.).

Online sports journalists operate within a pressurized environment, mostly because even though traditional media channels and newspapers are institutionalised, the online press community is still working on establishing official organisations, rules, and appropriate practices (Mortiz 2015). New technologies affect the journalism industry in four different ways: their content, how they produce their content, the physical organisation within the newsroom and the relationship amongst themselves, other organisations and their consumers (Pavik 2010). Contrary views of the ways journalists have changed include the belief that journalists have stopped interacting with colleagues, became more sedentary whilst using technological mediation, skype meetings, online conventions, and virtual information shares (Batista, n.d.). Similarly, sources and content has changed due to the World Wide Web providing an efficient way of finding content. Consequently, consultation of websites is now part of journalist's daily work routine. A contrary view is that digitalisation improved the journalist's skills, making them multifaceted (George 2008). A single journalist can now record, photograph, edit, present and report, as the digital world gave them the tools and the urgency to learn and apply those abilities.

Another important factor when looking into the new media environment, is that the consumers have changed. These new readers are called "couch readers", passive content receivers, accessing information from their home, smartphone and any other digital devices. They force traditional news outlets to be more concerned and aware of their preferences (Kawamoto 2003). (Kawamoto 2003). It is crucial to understand what online fans' new relationship with sports is, to understand their expectations about journalism today (Mortiz 2015).

The internet has helped greatly with blurring the gap between the consumer and broadcasting outlets. The World Wide Web has opened new doors for sports lovers to watch their games, such as IPTV, Web TV, Internet TV, Mobile TV, which offers consumers the same services, for more reasonable prices than normal cable television. It is acknowledged that IPTV is considered by many as a "media market issue", as its consumers perceive it to be the same as traditional broadcasting TV, when it represents an alternative way of disintegrating it (Hutchins and Rowe 2012). Consequently, it is difficult today to sell news and information, since the internet proposes alternative methods of information consumption with free online streams, for example, weakening the financial system of any sports communication company (Fletcher 2020).

1.2 Sports Journalism and Social Media

Social media gives sports journalism a flood of simultaneous advantages and disadvantages. The relationship between social media and sporting journalism is "competitive, integrative, and complementary" (Nölleke et al. 2016). This view, suggest that the journalists believe these new social media tools are helpful, as almost all the interviewed journalists perceived sport media official pages as "beneficial new sources" (Nölleke et al. 2016). Social media brought consumers closer to their desired source of information (their clubs or favourite player or sport), decreasing more and more the need for an intermediary, the journalist (Murray 2013). Today, consumers can usually get easy access to the information they want, directly from the source. There is no longer a need to wait for someone to present news, they can easily search for information online, whenever they want. This presents a threat to the print sports journalist industry, as the print industry publishes information that is already know hours, sometimes even days ago – for example, a match result (Sheffer and Schultz 2010).

Breaking news. With the online news outlets, content has become accessible immediately, resulting in print newspapers, unable to produce breaking news. Social media has played a core role in providing information to the online world, since it is the heart of the sharing process (Sheffer and Schultz 2010). Even though this study admits that social media may present a threat to the printed press, it also argues that these same online channels can and should help the journalist to connect with the audience. Interacting with audiences allows for a better understanding of consumer behaviour, which is the key for the success of any company.

Twitter is the best social network for delivering sports content, especially football, as it is estimated that more than 41% of all tweets are in relation to this industry (Parganas et al. 2015). The best usage a sports journalist can have from Twitter is to look at its network as a communication channel with the consumers. It has become a useful resource for acquiring information (Ketterer et al. 2013) whilst also engaging with fans (Sheffer and Schultz 2010). Despite still having some disadvantages, it remains a positive and useful tool for the sports journalists.

The Sporting Journalism Business Economy in the Digital Era

Nowadays, consumers have easy and free access to all sources of information online, creating a major problem for the online sports journalism economy. A study from the Reuters Institute Digital News Report, in 2017, (Fig. 1) shows that 54% of the interviewees were not willing to pay for news, across all markets (including football), because they have access to online news freely – with more than 25% saying that online news is not worth paying for (Fletcher 2020).

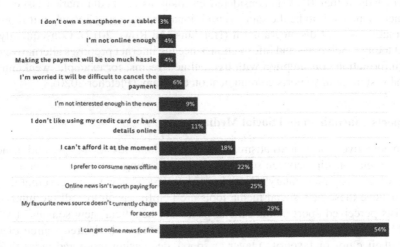

Fig. 1. Reasons for not paying online news (YouGov Research Methods 2017).

In a previous study, Barthel (2015) had already predicted subscriptions in decline, forcing newsrooms to depend on online advertising. The problem of online advertisement payment is in the way which revenue is measured, usually by the page views, or in other words, the number of clicks on a links – this explains the rise of tabloids and clickbait news. This demonstrates desperate measures of finding new ways to finance online journalism.

To improve the sustainability of the industry, f the creation of a paywall might be the solution for this digital problem (Myllylahti's 2012). A paywall is a blocking way of not allowing consumers to access certain data without paying a subscription (Wang 2011). This incorporates Newman's (2018) ideology that to overcome the online newspaper crisis, publishers need to include in their business strategy subscription plans more actively.

The reason why the current study has been undertaken is that, despite previous studies acknowledging that digital transformations existent in sports journalism, with the emerge of social media, such studies are mostly about the business itself, neglecting the journalist's point of view and personal experiences. Therefore, existing research has so far focused on the institutional perspective, rather than the humane standpoint of the journalist. By examining the lived experiences of journalists, the current study aims to understand how digitalisation impacts journalists professionally. It seeks to understand the potential solutions for sports journalism, which will enable it to survive economically and sustainably in this digital age.

2 Methodology and Framework

This research aims to understand the development and adaptation of sports journalism in the digital era and comprehend where its continuous evolution will take it. To support the theory of adaptation and continuous development, there are two theoretical frameworks in this study: *The Theory of Digital Darwinism* and *Digital transformation of Social Theory*. Both reflect on how the society is changing through the digital era.

Digital Darwinism purports that, in a world with an inherent technology dependence, whoever fails to keep up with this development will be left behind (Goodwin 2018). This theory shapes the understanding of mistakes sports journalism have made resulting in crisis within the industry and how technologically may help negate this crisis. It examines whether digital adaptation is the path to a more successful business. According to Vollmer (2009), consumers became prosumers, and for businesses to thrive in this digital era they must acknowledge the vital significance these individuals truly represent. This theory purports that it is necessary to create detailed insights exclusively towards their consumers' behaviour, thus offering a competitive advantage over other companies. It is no longer a question of what the best product is, or content, in this case, but how this is presented to the consumers, and where they lay their business strategy off and online. They call it "the survival of the smartest" (Kreutzer and Land 2013); for newspapers this means one with better content, better news, and that's more truthful, may, according to this theory, be overtaken by a newspaper whose content is not so good but instead, has adapted their strategy to this new era, and has a better knowledge of its consumers and delivers a better use of the internet as well as having greater digital understanding.

Digital Transformation of Social Theory underpins understanding of the changes that sports journalism faces as the digital transformation continues to change its working practices and environments. This theory purports that to d remain relevant, journalism must undergo transformation.

This is a phenomenological study aiming to understand the sports journalists' personal experiences of the digital adaptation of their profession and how they reflect on the transformations within the industry and their understanding of the future of journalism. Sports journalists from all over the world were interviewed to understand their experiences of technological change within the industry and investigate views on what they believed could be improved in the future. T

Qualitative inductive methodology was used to rigorously analyse participant responses, whilst understanding the journalists' perspectives of the digital evolution which have led to changes within their profession.

2.1 Procedure

Semi-structured interviews were conducted and recorded via Skype, lasting around 40 min each. The participants' identity is protected with a confidentiality clause, so pseudonyms were used to facilitate their interviews analysis. The names were randomly selected in a UK name generator website (https://www.name-generator.org.uk) in the option of "10 random first names". To avoid misleading conclusions, there are no ethnicity or race suggestions or indications in the present names, as they were chosen randomly.

After some rapport building questions unrelated to the nature of the study, participants discussed how the digitalisation of their profession changed their careers, whether the new technologies helped them, or not, as sports journalists, and if the consumers had changed over time. It was also important to recognise their definition of a journalist, and if they believed society misperceived the concept. Lastly, they shared their future perspective for sports journalism and their opinion on how they can thrive in this era, sustainably. The transcription manually transcribed verbatim, from the recording and then, thematically analysed based on Braun and Clarke's (2006) six stage process. Firstly, the transcriptions were read several times to become familiar with their content. Initial codes were generated based on participants personal experiences that influenced their opinions of digital journalism. Codes were then grouped into initial themes, which were then reviewed. After reviewing the following themes emerged; crisis in sport journalism, journalist definition, shared emotions, World Wide Web media channels insufficiencies, reforms, need for professionalization, social media networks and internet, consumer transformation (see Fig. 2-page x).

Sample and Data Collection

The sample for this study comprehends journalists who currently work or have worked as sports journalists between the years 2000 and 2020. The study includes journalists from all around the world, specifically England, Portugal, Brazil, and Spain, allowing a broad analysis of the differences between countries, giving this study a wider perspective. Participants were drawn from the researcher's personal contacts and the snowball sampling technique was applied to encourage other sports journalists to take part in this study. The participation of the study was entirely voluntary and without any financial or other incentives. The journalists who took part in this research work for different media outlets – television, radio, and newspapers – this is because each industry may offer different perspectives. Regardless of the outlet, sports journalism cannot escape digitalisation and for that, it is important to understand whether the technology helps them to play their part. The different roles the participants have in sports journalism allowed the researcher to study and understand the singular standpoints of sporting journalists from the diverse branches of the profession itself, conceding a wider and global evaluation, rather than a unilateral view.

The participants' ages range between 25 and 56, averaging at 34 years of age, and are from four different countries: Spain, Portugal, Brazil, and England. All the candidates represent diversity, allowing a wider range of opinion, as different ages, active roles, countries, and years of experience help deliver a more truthful and not biased result (Table 1).

Table 1. Participants information

Participant[a]	Years of experience	Current job	Previous profession	Number of companies they simultaneously work for
Zach	25	Editor, Reporter and Radio Host	Reporter; Broadcasting Journalist	4

(continued)

Table 1. (*continued*)

Participant[a]	Years of experience	Current job	Previous profession	Number of companies they simultaneously work for
Lia	4	Unemployed	Pivot; Press Officer; Producer; Football Coach	–
Meghan	6	News Anchor and Editor	Radio Producer; Reporter	2
Ralph	7 ½	News Anchor and Commentator	Reporter; Editor	3
Sam	15	Columnist	–	2
Hailey	10	Reporter and Online Content Producer	–	2
John	23	Producer and Reporter	Tv Editing; Journalist Coordinator	3
Peter	22	Online Writing and Editor	Reporter and	2
Anne	5	Tv Journalist Coordinator	–	–
Kate	6	Reporter and Commentator	–	–
Louis	12	Columnist	Online Writing Support	2
Carl	15	Senior Producer and Reporter	Producer; Broadcasting Journalist	4
Jo	22	Senior Editor	Reporter; Producer; Broadcasting Assistant	–

[a]To protect the participants' personal information, all the above names are fictional, generically generated at: https://www.name-generator.org.uk.

3   Results

This chapter presents the overall results of the qualitative inductive analysis of the formerly conducted 13 semi-structured interviews described in chapters three and four. The researcher identified the codes and generated the subsequent themes (Fig. 2).

Throughout the coding and interactive process, the emerged themes were: Crisis in Sporting Journalism; Lack of Job Opportunities; Sporting newspaper Endurance;

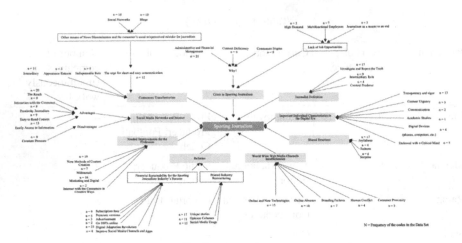

Fig. 2. Thematic map.

Shared Emotions about Work Experiences; World Wide Web Media Channels Insufficiencies; Consumers Transformation; Important Individual Characteristics in the Digital Era; Social Media Networks and Internet Advantages and Disadvantages; Needed Improvements for the Profession; Journalist Definition; Financial Sustainability for the Sporting Journalism Industry's Success; Printed Industry Reform; and Other means of News Dissemination and the Consumer's Usual Misperceived Mistake for Journalism. In these results, the opinions and insights of the sports journalists are shown in relation to the current situation that their profession is facing, and their personal circumstances will also depict what they believe should be the future improvements in the industry.

During the interviews, journalists referred to the fact that their profession is currently facing a major crisis which has eventually led to a lack of job opportunities. Despite agreeing regarding the crisis, when asked about the reasons for it, some answers varied. Figure 3 describes the main justifications the interviewees gave for the industry crisis, and it represents the percentages of times those reasonings were mentioned in the Data Set. All the participants agreed that the crisis was financial, nine included flaws in sharing and writing content as a part of the problem, and four considered the consumers changing as an obstacle to the financial development of the profession.

To overcome this crisis, the interviewees have pointed out some necessary improvements to the sports journalist area (Fig. 4). Most of the suggested changes are directly connected with the digital world, as the figure below presents, including interacting with consumers through creative ways (online contests, giveaways, etc.), hiring more millennials to work in their facilities (since they usually are the most knowledgeable about this digital world) are the ones most frequently commented on throughout the interviews, as well as having a stake in the company's digital-oriented marketing teams, and creating new methods of content creation, different from conventional ones.

With the world's increased usage of the internet, the sports journalists who have witnessed these two different eras (on and offline) and, of course, dealt with some changes in their working methods, have presented some differences from the printed industry

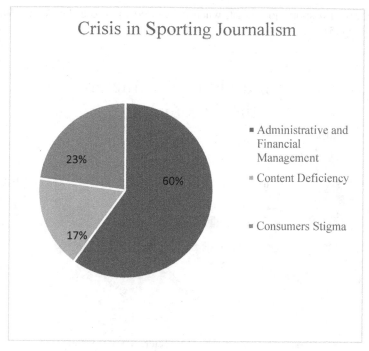

Fig. 3. Reasons for the crisis in sporting journalism.

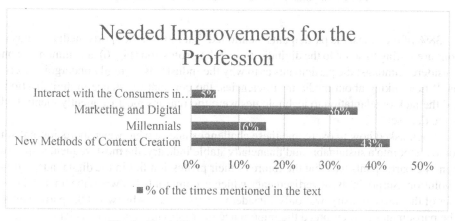

Fig. 4. Needed improvements for the profession.

to the digital world. They talked about advantages and disadvantages of the online world according to their own personal experiences and how this revolution changed their consumers' behaviour. The participants mostly pointed out advantages of digital, always emphasising how it facilitated them in different points of their profession – only one negative was mentioned. This digitalisation also triggered some changes in the main characteristics of a sports journalist, when compared to before the World Wide Web revolution (Fig. 5).

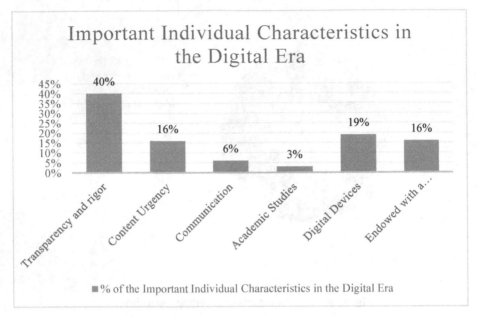

Fig. 5. Important individual characteristics in the digital.

38% of the times, the participants mentioned that most of the sports media organisations are failing to adapt to the digitalisation of the profession (Fig. 6), a common reason considered amongst the participants as to why the industry is currently undergoing a crisis. When talking about media insufficiencies, the constant resistance in digitalisation, and the lack of adaptation to technologies were the reasons most frequently mentioned in the data set.

When asked how to overcome these challenges and in what ways sports journalism could adapt into a sustainable and financially stable industry, the most frequent response from the participants was that the future of their profession lies in the digital adaptation revolution. Surprisingly, advertisements, which is commonly known as the financial rescuer of the news industry, was only considered as the solution by two of the participants. The participants also enforced the importance of improving apps and social media networks, as well as recommending premium subscriptions as an economic support. Two of the participants trusts that the future for some organisations lies in the full conversion to the online world, whilst some believe that the printed era will never come to an end (Fig. 7). Participants also suggested developments for the written industry, focusing mainly on the creation of their own personalised content, with opinion columns for example, yet still retaining a connectedness to online, sharing different content through their social media accounts (Fig. 8).

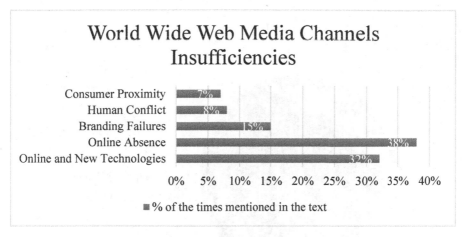

Fig. 6. World Wide Web media channels insufficiencies.

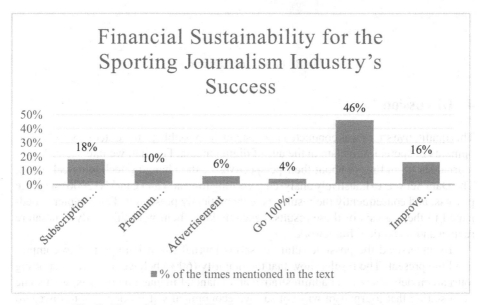

Fig. 7. Financial sustainability for the sporting journalism industry's.

Lastly, participants agreed on how digitalisation gave birth to new and innovative means of news dissemination, often leading consumers to confusion as to what a journalist really is. For that reason, the participants have defined what the most important characteristics of a journalist should be and mentioned Bloggs and Social Media Channels as new forms of news' sharing that have entered modern society, which confuses consumers in their understanding of who is the professional and who is not.

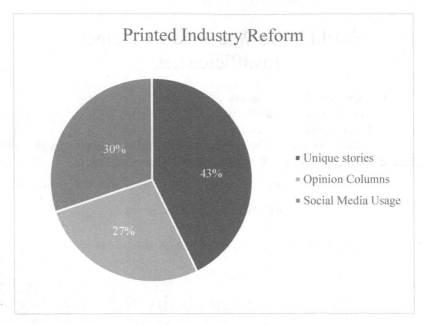

Fig. 8. Printed industry reforms.

4   Discussion

This qualitative study was conducted understand the possible future outcomes and developments of sports journalism in the age of digital media. For that, we interviewed sport journalists to find more about their perspectives of the changing technological world. The Data Set was exhaustively analysed according to Braun and Clark's (2006) six stage process, and consequently the results were thematically presented. This chapter is dedicated to the analysis of these results, benchmarking them with this study's literature review and theoretical framework.

To understand the possible future of sports journalism, it is important to comprehend the present. The results show that the majority (60%) believe the current sporting journalism deficiency is an administrative and financial management crisis, with some even stating that journalism will not survive economically if it continues to disregard online and not look for new sustainable ways to finance it, Peter says "(…) the online sector is starting to become a financial problem". According to Fletcher (2020), people are not willing to pay for news, creating a financial gap in the journalism industry. This economic deficiency influences the money flow in the profession, impacting job opportunities. This issue is considered relevant by 54% of the participants, mainly due to the growing need for journalists to work in multi-functions, as Meghan says, "now we don't need to hire one editor, one journalist and one content producer, often one person can do these three jobs". Another important reason, mentioned 23% of the time, was the constant use of the sports media industry to achieve other means, such as becoming a television celebrity. As Zack states, "some individuals, who don't like this profession, study this because they see it as a means to achieve fame", taking the place of many journalists who really love what they do. Also, according to Knight (2008) blogging has changed communication in the online space, forcing journalism to redefine itself before society. As Meghan stated, "communication is for all, but journalism is not". When talking about which organisations make readers most confused about what journalism really is, 61% of the sports journalists mentioned that social media channels, like Instagram and Twitter, are often confused with methods of journalism as well-known people give their opinions, 39% of the participants stated that blogging was the reason for confusion and 2 participants disagreed, stating that consumers are not confused about what is journalism and what it's not.

The internet has made the spread of news faster (Boyle 2017), and consequently accustomed people to want everything by the minute. According to more than 80% of the participants, this urgency for content was born with the internet development. Prior to digitalisation, consumers were used to waiting until the next day or even the next week to have access to information. Vollmer (2009) called the new digital era consumers as prosumers. This is undoubtedly in line with Ralph's thoughts that "consumers are now part of the content (…)", as he believes sports journalists cannot live without the sports lovers. The consumers being part of the content, and importance some interviewed journalists believe they should represent to the companies, is in line with the Digital Transformation of Social Theory, as their model lays on a digitally transformed society, where the companies need to focus on the transformed consumers (Ossewaarde 2019). The concept of couch readers (Kawamoto 2003), passive consumers who desperately want news as easily as possible, was also mentioned by five of the participants. They believe consumers now want, as Zack describes, "direct and short news, through a phone notification".

Journalists also had to change their behaviour to adapt in the digital world. All this study's participants referenced transparency as a main necessary characteristic, highlighting that these are timeless and will forever be important, a Jo says "(…) with rigor, with transparency, always with a lot of humility". These qualities have been used to describe journalists since the dawn of the profession – ethics (Knight 2008), values (Gerlis 2008) and constant search for the truth (George 2008). But with the internet revolution, other characteristics emerged, as being highly connected with digital devices, knowing how technology can help them in their work – "I can use my phone to do a complete report", Zack. Two of the participants mentioned the importance of having a critical mind being the first and foremost important characteristic of a journalist in the digital age, and the capacity of analysing and quickly interpreting and appraising data. Zack even states that to be a good journalist it is important to have critical intellect for every area of their lives. These findings are in line with George's (2008) research, where he prorupts that the journalists have gain several important skills with the digitalisation, enhancing their ability to work, and completely refute Batista's (n.d.) idea of a sedentary journalist that never leaves the newsroom and rarely goes out to investigate news.

With the social media networks' increasing popularity, sports journalists were asked to identify some advantages and disadvantages of this new online as a tool. The most referenced advantage was the reach the internet gives them. Online networking allows a post to reach millions of people simultaneously, with just one click. With more than 2.6 billion active users in 2018 (Statista 2019), and numbers increasing frantically, social media has become the best content sharing channel for sports journalism. "News is dissipated in an incredible way", says Hailey. Social media not only helps the news travel, but also brings people together. As a journalist, Sam believes social media "allows the journalist to connect with the consumers individually". Connecting with the audience gives the reporter a better understanding of consumer behaviour (Sheffer and Schultz 2010), which is important for any company's marketing success. This proximity gives the journalist a way of knowing their audience, and understanding what they want to read, and adapting their content to the reader's needs (Parganas et al. 2015). The most mentioned disadvantage was the constant pressure that the journalist is subjected to, primarily due to consumer demands. One of the participants, made no reference to any negative aspect of the online world.

These results are in line with this study's two theoretical frameworks – The Theory of Digital Darwinism and Digital Transformation of Social Theory – sports journalism is undergoing powerful changes and it's possible if it doesn't adapt, it won't be able to resist. Goodwin (2018) considered that digital adaptation is the only way to achieve success. Starting with the printed industry reforms, 46% of the participants believe it is essential to adapt the content, to prevent the sholveware mistake (Bardoel 2002). Ralph states that the sporting printed industry should focus on opinion columns more than the information itself: "it does not make any sense for newspapers to exclusively publish information about games that happened last night - everyone already knows the results.". He says there is a need to add something that readers still don't know, such as the opinion of influential journalists or a different story with some content attached to the context. Meghan believes the printed industry still needs to have an online presence. Enforcing social media channels and apps is important to get the consumer's attention: "If you are going to make an opinion column with someone important, you have to advertise it, otherwise people will not know about its existence. For that, there's nothing better than social networks", she says. Zack adds that the online should not be used as a single method, but instead, as a supporting tool for the newspaper. As for digital adaptation, Louis said that "online is unavoidable (…)", Carl that "(…) newspapers either adapt, or die." and Peter believes "(…) there will be no way to survive without changing.", supporting the theory of Digital Darwinism.

Financially, and to recover from the present crisis, the participants' opinions differ a little. 69% of the participants suggested that social networking could contribute towards the financial sector. 61% of the responses also proposed that subscription fees could be implemented to gain financial growth. Lastly, Freemiums were also considered as a contribution towards financial gain in the sports journalism sector by 50% of the responses. Myllylahti's (2012) idea of a freemium paywall turns out to be a combination of these two last mentioned options and may be the preferred solution of the interviewees. On the other hand, Fletcher (2020) strongly disagrees with the subscription solution, as he believes people are not willing to pay for news. Like him, only the 2 oldest participants thinks that subscriptions are not the solution, as he was the only one who mentioned advertisement as a potential source of economic revenue, While the eldest participants continuously focus on advertisement, the youngest strongly believes that some institutions will become bankrupt and perish if they do not settle 100% online quote. This may suggest that there could be a relationship between the ages of journalists and their opinions regarding digital adaptations.

There is also the need to restructure the profession, where the majority of sports journalists believe that improving the marketing and digital team is the key to progress in the digital era. Sam and Hailey went even further with this previous idea, saying that hiring millennials could be the solution for this necessary improvement, since they are usually more knowledgeable of the online world – "it is important to have young people in the team, as they have a better understanding of the digital era." – Sam. Some of the interviewees also consider it important to have creative methods to produce and deliver content as well as actively interacting with the consumer. These thoughts are in line with Mortiz's (2015) study, as he sees the online sphere as an opportunity for the journalists to interact with the consumers, focusing on the importance of minimising the gap between the spectator and the journalist.

4.1 Limitations of This Study and Future Research

Although effectiveness has been demonstrated in the project, some limitations should be noted. Firstly, the present abnormal conditions of the coronavirus pandemic occurring throughout 2019–2020 did not allow the researcher to carry out the interviews in person, and of course, limited the access to several key informants. The time limit is also a determining factor, since half a year does not permit an evaluation of abundant information, neither a large sample to analyse. This also means findings cannot be generalised, as the sample size was not exhaustive enough and the study only provides suggestions and not definite solutions. Since people from different parts of the world were interviewed, some have chosen to do the interview in their home language, creating some conflict in the translations.

This present study found some attention-grabbing co-relations that suggest that there are different thoughts between younger and older people. As for future research, it would be interesting to further develop the differences of opinion, regarding the digitalisation, between different ages within the same area of sports journalism. It would be important to understand whether there exist differences between their age, and if it affects their choices and beliefs, and if any of them have more resistance to adapt to the new online media.

5 Conclusion

The purpose of the research is to help sports journalism to move forwards in the digital era. The main objective was to understand the opinions of journalists of different ages and from different parts of the world and gather their thoughts on the current and future adaptation of the profession in relation to online. Clearly the participants are aware of the current crisis affecting their profession, and whilst for the most part they believe this is an economic management failure crisis, others blame the lack of well-produced content and consumers' changing behaviour. Not only the consumers changed, but also journalists. The findings of this study show that all participants agree that the internet improved their skills and abilities, recognising this transformation was mostly due to the immediacy of this digital world.

Most of the participants also admit there are insufficiencies in the communication industry, especially regarding the online platforms' absence and the lack of new technology usage. Their suggestion is to apply some necessary reforms. The most popular proposals were the implementation of new and more modern content creation methods and the development of the company's online marketing and advertising teams. Some other participants suggested the improvement of social interaction with consumers, with things such as online contests and giveaways, and the inclusion of millennials in the working panels.

As for the print industry, participants agree the main change lies in their content, as they must create unique and special content, that somehow differentiates them from online models, and which contribute something which the consumers do not know – such as opinion columns for example. Adapting is a key element that the participants agreed on. Most of the participants also agreed on the importance of online networking, suggesting that printed outlets should be active on their social channels, sharing videos, photos and advertising their renewed and different content to the audience.

Financially, the vast majority of the sports journalists believe the answer lies in subscription plans and premium versions, whilst a small proportion suggest the well-known old method of advertisement. It was found a small link between the ages and the suggestions, as the youngest participant hinted that if some outlets did not change to online 100%, they would perish, whilst the oldest participant believes the paper versions will never disappear and that subscriptions or premiums will never work, due to people being able to overcome the payment and have access to pirated versions, relying on increasing online finances purely through advertisement.

Although the age, occupation and countries vary, this research shows sports journalists' thoughts are well in line with each other's. In their own way, they all believe that the industry needs to adapt to survive, as the theories of Digital Darwinism and Digital Transformation of Social Theory propose. At this point, there is no right answer, but the participants strongly suggest that to thrive, outlets will have to undergo thorough content adaptation and engage with a more frequent use of social networks, apps and websites. The attention to the consumers will have to be greater than it already was, combined with a socially implicit interaction. The print industry will have to reform their content and be more active online. As for the online financial solutions, this study suggests that the best option for the industry is to stop relying on advertising and move towards subscriptions and freemium versions. Most of the interviewed sports journalists do not believe that the written press will end, but that it will have to undergo major changes to survive, agreeing that despite some disadvantages, the internet has helped the sports communication industry more than it could ever harm.

References

Alexander, J.C.: The crisis of journalism reconsidered: cultural power. Fudan J. Hum. Soc. Sci. 8(1), 9–31 (2015). https://doi.org/10.1007/s40647-014-0056-5

Bakker, P.: Aggregation, content farms and huffinization. The rise of low-pay and no-pay journalism (2012)

Bardoel, J.: The internet, journalism and public communication policies. Gazette (Leiden, Netherlands) **64**(5), 501–511 (2002)

Barthel, M.: Newspapers: Fact Sheet (2015). http://www.journalism.org/2015/04/29/newspapers-fact-sheet

Batista, C.: Media & Jornalismo (n.d.)

Bengtsson, M.: How to plan and perform a qualitative study using content analysis. NursingPlus Open **2**, 8–14 (2016)

Boyle, R.: Sports journalism. Digit. J. **5**(5) (2017)

Braun, V., Clarke, V.: Using thematic analysis in psychology. Qual. Res. Psychol. **3**(2) (2006)

Chaffey, D., Ellis-Chadwick, F.: Digital Marketing, 5th edn. (2012)

Chen, Y., Conroy, N., Rubin, V.: Misleading Online Content: Recognizing Clickbait as "False News" (n.d.)

Choak, C.: Asking questions: interviews and evaluations. In: Bradford, S., Cullen, F. (eds.) Research and Research Methods for Youth Practitioners, pp. 90–112. Routledge, London (2012)

Curran, J.: The future of journalism. J. Stud. **11**(4), 464–476 (2010)

Daniels, P., Leyshon, A., Bradshaw, M., Beaverstock, J.: Geographies of the New Economy. Routledge, London (2007)

Digital News Report. Yougov Research Methods (2017). http://www.digitalnewsreport.org/. Accessed 29 July 2020

Duncan, P., Davies, R., Sweney, M.: Children 'Bombarded' With Betting Adverts During World Cup. The Guardian (2018). https://www.theguardian.com/media/2018/jul/15/children-bombarded-with-betting-adverts-during-world-cup. Accessed 29 June 2020

English, P.: Twitter's diffusion in sports journalism: role models, laggards and followers of the social media innovation (2014)

Evans, C.: Analysing Semi-Structured Interviews Using Thematic Analysis: Exploring Voluntary Civic Participation Among Adults. SAGE Publications, Ltd. (2017)

Fletcher, R.: Paying For News. Digital News Report (2020). http://www.digitalnewsreport.org/survey/2017/paying-for-news-2017/. Accessed 29 Apr 2020

George, C.: Who is a journalist? Journal. Stud. **9**(1), 117–131 (2008)

Gerlis, A.: Who is a journalist? Journal. Stud. **9**(1), 132–138 (2008)

Gilpin, K.: From A Giant Job To An Internet Fledgling (Published 1999). Nytimes.com (2020). https://www.nytimes.com/1999/10/27/business/from-a-giant-job-to-an-internet-fledgling.html. Accessed 21 Sept 2020

Goodwin, T.: Digital Darwinism. Kogan Page, London (2018)

Grinyer, A.: The anonymity of research participants: assumptions, ethics and practicalities. Soc. Res. Update (36) (2002)

Bucy, E.: Second generation net news: interactivity and information accessibility in the online environment. Int. J. Media Manag. **6**(1–2), 102–113 (2004)

Hutchins, B., Rowe, D.: Sport Beyond Television. Routledge, Taylor & Francis Group, New York (2012)

Kawamoto, K.: Digital Journalism. Rowman & Littlefield, Lanham (2003)

Ketterer, S., McGuire, J., Murray, R.: Contrasting desired sports journalism skills in a convergent media environment. Commun. Sport **2**(3), 282–298 (2013)

Kian, E., Burden, J., Jr., Shaw, S.: Internet sport bloggers: who are these people and where do they come from? J. Sport Adm. Supervision **3**(1), 30–43 (2011)

Knight, A.: Who is a journalist? Journal. Stud. **9**(1), 117–131 (2008)

Kramp, L., Loosen, W.: The Transformation of Journalism: From Changing Newsroom Cultures to a New Communicative Orientation? (2017)

Kreutzer, R., Land, K.: Digital Darwinism. Springer, Heidelberg (2013)

Loke, A., Ali, F.: Direct conversion radio for digital mobile phones-design issues, status, and trends. IEEE Trans. Microw. Theory Tech. **50**(11), 2422–2435 (2002)

Louise Barriball, K., While, A.: Collecting data using a semi-structured interview: a discussion paper. J. Adv. Nurs. **19**(2), 328–335 (1994)

Maguire, M., Delahunt, B.: Doing a thematic analysis: a practical, step-by-step guide for learning and teaching scholars. AISHE **8**(3) (2017)

Moritz, B.: The story versus the stream: digital media's influence on newspaper sports journalism. Int. J. Sport Commun. **8**(4), 397–410 (2015)

Newman, N.: Journalism, Media, and Technology Trends and Predictions 2018. The Reuters Institute for the Study of Journalism (2018)

Newman, N.: Journalism, Media, and Technology Trends and Predictions 2019 NIC Newman. Digital News Project (2019)

Nölleke, D., Grimmer, C., Horky, T.: News Sources and Follow-Up Communication. Taylor & Francis (2016). https://www.tandfonline.com/doi/abs/10.1080/17512786.2015.1125761. Accessed 29 July 2020

Örnebring, H., Jönsson, A.: Tabloid journalism and the public sphere: a historical perspective on tabloid journalism. Journal. Stud. **5**(3), 283–295 (2004)

Ossewaarde, M.: Digital transformation and the renewal of social theory: unpacking the new fraudulent myths and misplaced metaphors. Technol. Forecast. Soc. Chang. **146**, 24–30 (2019)

Parganas, P., Anagnostopoulos, C., Chadwick, S.: 'You'll never tweet alone': managing sports brands through social media. J. Brand Manag. **22**(7), 551–568 (2015)

Potthast, M., Köpsel, S., Stein, B., Hagen, M.: Clickbait Detection (n.d.)

Rainie, L., Purcell, K.: The Economics of Online News. Pew Research Center: Internet, Science & Tech (2010). https://www.pewresearch.org/internet/2010/03/15/the-economics-of-onl ine-news/. Accessed 23 June 2020

Rich, M., Ginsburg, K.: The reason and rhyme of qualitative research: why, when, and how to use qualitative methods in the study of adolescent health. J. Adolesc. Health **25**(6), 371–378 (1999)

Rivers, W., Schramm, W., Christians, C.: Responsibility in Mass Communication. Harper and Row (1980)

Roth, S., Dahms, H., Welz, F., Cattacin, S.: Print theories of computer societies. Introduction to the digital transformation of social theory. Technol. Forecasting Soc. Change **149**, 119778 (2019)

Scherer, K.: Emotional experience is subject to social and technological change: extrapolating to the future. Soc. Sci. Inf. **40**(1), 125–151 (2001)

Scott, B.: A contemporary history of digital journalism. Telev. New Media **6**(1), 89–126 (2005)

Sheffer, M., Schultz, B.: Paradigm shift or passing fad? Twitter and sports journalism. Int. J. Sport Commun. **3**(4), 472–484 (2010)

Stávková, J., Stejskal, L., Toufarová, Z.: Factors influencing consumer behaviour. Agric. Econ. (Zemědělská ekonomika) **54**(6), 276–284 (2008)

Theil, S.: The Media and Markets: How Systematic Misreporting Inflates Bubbles, Deepens Downturns and Distorts Economic Reality. Shorenstein Center on Media, Politics and Public Policy (2013)

Vollmer, C.: Digital Darwinism (2009). http://geoffroigaron.com/wp-content/uploads/2010/04/Digital_DarwinismMME2010FinalReport.pdf. Accessed 27 Sept 2020

Wang, Y.: Making online pay: the prospect of the paywall in a digital and networked economy. J. Digit. Res. (2011)

Antecedents and Consequences of Information Cocoon Awareness in Short-Form Video APPs: An Information Ecology Perspective

Shanjiao Ren, Lili Liu(✉), Yingfei Zheng, Lingfei Yu, Yufei Hu, and Chuanmin Mi

College of Economics and Management, Nanjing University of Aeronautics and Astronautics, Nanjing, China
{joy9971,lili85,Cmmi}@nuaa.edu.cn

Abstract. As increasingly optimized recommendation technology and increasing average daily time spending on short-from video APPs, users may easily fall into the so-called "information cocoon"(IC). However, little is known about the antecedents and consequences of information cocoon in short-form video APPs. To fill the gap, drawing on the information ecology theory, we develop a model that identifies four predictors of IC awareness, and continuance usage intention as the consequence of IC awareness. An online survey was conducted to collect data from 206 respondents. Smart PLS 3.3 was used to analyze data. Findings reveal that subjective norm, perceived novelty of online recommendations, and alternative attraction are positively associated with IC awareness, while community participation is negatively associated with IC awareness. Besides, IC awareness positively affects users' continuous usage intention. This study extends our knowledge on IC by providing empirical explanations of the combined effect of information people, information, information technology, and information environment.

Keywords: Information cocoon awareness · Short-from video APPs · Information ecology perspective

1 Introduction

In recent years, the number of users of short-form video apps has grown dramatically. By December 2021, the number of Chinese short-form video apps' users has reached 974 million, accounting for 94.5% of entire internet users [6]. Short-form video refers to videos less than five minutes, and are distributed digitally by specific platforms such as Tik Tok [1]. Featuring low-cost and highly spreadable, users have spent ever-increased time on short-form video apps, which allows the short-from videos APPs to accurately capture users' preferences. At present, the personalized recommendation algorithm of the short-from video APPs not only analyzes the type of video that users are interested in, but also continuously collects the length of stay, shielding, retweeting, commenting and other traces of use after users receive personalized recommendations, then constantly adjusts the recommendations to better fulfill consumers' temporary and ever-changing

© Springer Nature Switzerland AG 2022
G. Meiselwitz et al. (Eds.): HCII 2022, LNCS 13517, pp. 115–125, 2022.
https://doi.org/10.1007/978-3-031-22131-6_9

demand or preferences. In this process, users have been in a passive state of receiving information, and gradually fall into the so-called "information cocoon"(IC).

IC is defined as a special "communication universe" where people only choose to hear information that makes them comfortable and pleasant [36]. As Lazarsfeld et al. argue that audiences prefer to be exposed to content that is consistent with or close to their established positions and attitudes, while avoiding content that contradicts or conflicts with them [29]. Meanwhile, according to group polarization theory [37], IC can act as a mechanism to reinforce an existing opinion within a group and, as a result, move the entire group toward more extreme positions. There is growing research interest in the consequences of IC. However, majority of prior studies apply vague and general restatement of Sunstein's theory to descriptively explain IC, in-depth empirical research is scarce. Moreover, while IC has been investigated in network environments[39], prior researches pay particular attention to the IC phenomena in news websites [27], we know little about the influence of IC in other contexts, such as the short-form video APPs.

To fill above research gap, we synthesize the literature pertaining to this topic and conducted an empirical study to investigate the antecedents of IC awareness as well as its impact on user's continuous usage intention. Drawing on Information Ecology Theory [32], this research identifies four elements of information ecology system, namely information people (represented by subjective norm), information (community participation), information technology (perceived novelty of online recommendations) and information environment (alternative attraction), as predictors of information cocoon awareness in short-form video APPs. In conclusion, this study aims to verify how subjective norm, community participation, perceived novelty of online recommendations, and alternative attraction jointly affect IC awareness, which in turn determines continuance usage intention.

2   Theoretical Background

Horton (1978) firstly introduced the Information Ecology by considering the flow relationship of information within an organization from an ecological perspective, which has been continuously enriched by following studies [24]. For instance, Hasenyager (1996) and Davenport (2000) examined the impact of information and communication technologies on an organization's information processes [7, 20], that is, instead of exclusively focusing on technology, considering people and information behavior as additional predictors. Nardi further summarized the characteristics and connotation of information ecology and improved the conception of information ecology as "a system of people, practices, values, and technologies in a particular local environment" [32] (BA Nardi.,1998). Garcia-Marco (2011) state that information systems should be investigated as information ecologies, as a totality in its whole complexity and with all its apparent contradictions [15].

Information ecology perspective has been gradually applied and verified in many research contexts, such as information ecosystems, network environments, e-commerce/e-business, and digital libraries [40]. Huberman (2001) and Shim (2006) empirically demonstrate the influence of information ecology on the legal environment of the worldwide web and the evolution of web portal websites [25, 35]. In addition,

Hawkins (2000) explores the development of digital library on the basis of information ecology [21]; T. Finin (2008) investigates the information ecosystem in social media and online communication [12]; C. Grafton (2006) examines information ecology in e-government [16]. Moreover, information ecology has also been adopted by F.J. Garcia-Marco and J. Miedema (2008) to explain many new media derivations, such as microblog and blog [14].

In light of the Information Ecology Theory, the study recognizes information ecology as an organic entirety of social information function, in which information people transmit and response to information resources with the help of information technology, so as to achieve a balanced state within the information environment. We thus identify four antecedents of IC awareness in short-form video apps, including information people (subjective norm), information (community participation), information technology (perceived novelty of online recommendations) and information environment (alternative attraction).

3   Research Model and Hypotheses

The research model is shown in Fig. 1. Corresponding assumptions are discussed in detail as followings.

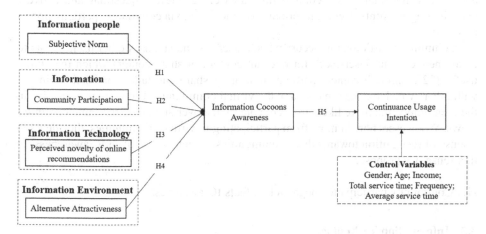

Fig. 1. Research model

3.1   Information People

According to the information ecology theory, information human is the core of information ecosystem, including information producers, organization processors, communication transmitters and users [40]. Subjective norms are often used to measure the influence of society on individual behavior. Therefore, information people are represented by subjective norm in this study.

Subjective norm refers to the perceived social pressure to perform or not to perform the behavior [2]. Individuals will pay more attention to and care about their own life or social circle of people's opinions, and these opinions will also affect the user's behavior and behavior intention to a certain extent. Previous studies have shown that people may choose to perform a behavior, even if they are not favorable toward the behavior or its consequences, if they believe one or more important referents think they should, and they are sufficiently motivated to comply with the referents [38]. In the process of use, connected with the network belt, users will involve in an original social circle or form a new social circle, so the subjective norm possibly has an impact on users' IC awareness. In other words, if one person in a social group could be aware of IC, it is highly likely that others in the group will generate IC awareness as well. Accordingly, we formulate the following hypothesis:

H1. Subjective norm positively affects the IC awareness.

3.2 Information

The theory of information ecology points out that information is equivalent to the central system of information ecology, acting as a link between other factors, which mainly refers to the movement state and change characteristics of information [40]. Users usually share and receive information via commenting, answering relevant questions and actively participating in events. Hence, information is measured via community participation in this study.

Community participation occurs when a user comments, uses other users' posts to create new content. Users seek for relevant content or share content which they think useful [22]. Through content participation, users share and talk about their opinions with others who have the same idea in the virtual community. The more they involve in the community, the more likely they are able to discover and enjoy the same or similar views. When users benefit more from participating in virtual communities, they develop a sense of recognition towards these communities, which will weaken IC awareness. In this sense, we propose:

H2. Community participation negatively affects IC awareness.

3.3 Information Technology

Information technology is an indispensable part of information ecology system which works as an intermediate between information people and information. The video and service provided by Short-form video APPs can be seen as main information technology of this system. The characteristic of recommendation systems directly affects human interaction with the short-form video information system, as well as interactions among users [33]. In this research, we employ perceived novelty of online recommendation system to measure the function of information technology.

Novelty is a measurement of recommendation system which reflects whether the recommended videos are surprising and newfangled enough for specific users and the general community [23]. Considering the inaccuracy of inherent data gathered from algorithm system, it cannot be guaranteed that the recommended videos are novel to users or not [31]. After receiving novel videos, users may find themselves immerse in certain types of information wall for a long time. This new discovery might contradict to their original ideas about certain topics and consequently evoke awareness that they are in the trap of IC. In this sense, we assume:

H3. Perceived novelty of online recommendation positively affects IC awareness.

3.4 Information Environment

Information environment describes how an individual evaluates the relationship between himself and the media, including the evaluation of the relationship between an individual and a specific media, and the individual's attitude towards the media environment [42]. Communication on social media platforms tends to be much more interactive compared to that on traditional media platforms [9]. People can express their own ideas and share their opinions freely and also come across with new and unique pieces of various information frequently via these platforms [28]. Individuals are able to communicate more interactively and these active actions leave various traces of behavior and consumption on the Internet. Various media, enterprises or data companies record the data and use varieties of latest artificial intelligence technologies and algorithms to analyze the traces of actions left by users and then establish a recommendation object model and user interest model to push relevant information or items.

Different types of social media have different directions of personalized recommendations and different behavioral traces of users. Users may participate in various online platforms, rather than only use a particular short-form video APP. Therefore, users who are active in different online platforms, which can provide them with information, have more access to a wide range of information, and the more likely to find themselves wrapped in an IC. Therefore, we argue:

H4. Alternative attraction is positively related to IC awareness.

3.5 IC Awareness and Continuance Usage Intention

Users' awareness will directly affect their sense of experience in a certain environment [4]. The positive awareness is one of the main drivers of users' willingness to use or continue to use a particular service [30]. If users hold the view that the costs like time, energy and emotion spent in a short-video APP are worthwhile, they will be happy to keep using it and introduce it to others.

Meanwhile, according to cognitive dissonance theory, simply avoiding cognitive elements that cause dissonance can be helpful to reduce uncomfortable emotions [11]. In former study, the social media users generally have the propensity to avoid mental discomforts coming from exposure to heterogeneity. In accordance with this finding, it seems to be necessary for social media platforms to provide reinforced homogeneity functions that enable users to reduce their exposure to heterogeneity, such as recommending similar types of content the users, which makes them happily to be trapped in information cocoon [26]. That is, users of short-form video APPs somehow aware that they keep been recommending videos on the same topic (e.g., K pop music videos), yet still would like to continuously watch them and watch more. We thus propose:

H5. IC awareness is positively related to continuance usage Intention.

4 Research Methodology

4.1 Measurements

In order to test above research model and hypotheses, we designed and distributed a survey via Sojump to collect data from Chinese short-form video apps' users. All measurement items were adapted from existing research, and gauged by Seven-point Likert scales that ranged from 1 (strongly disagree) to 7 (strongly agree). We measured subject norm via there items adapted from Ajzen (1991) [2]. Items for measuring community participation were derived from the work of Xu (2015) [41]. Items for perceived novelty of online recommendations were adapted from Matt C (2014) [31]. Items for alternative attraction were adapted from Jones (2000) [26]. Furthermore, items for IC awareness were obtained from Dubois, E., & Blank, G. (2018) [8], while items of continuous usage intention were derived from Bhattacherjee (2001) [3].

After the distribution of questionnaires, 206 valid responses were received. Smart PLS 3.3 was used to analyze data. In terms of the composition of the participants, females consist of 76.7% of respondents. Most participants (96.12%) were between 18 and 25 years old. Among them approximately 90% were students while the rest of them were corporate employees or government workers. Moreover, over 93% of our participants had tertiary education background. Since juveniles and millennials are the main stream users of short-form videos, the composition of our respondents reflects current situation (Table 1).

Table 1. Respondent demographics

Item	Category	Frequency	Ratio (%)
Gender	Male	48	23.30
	Female	158	76.70
Age	<18	1	0.49
	18–25	104	96.12
	26–30	5	2.43
	>30	2	0.97
Education	High school and below	7	3.40
	Associate's degree	6	2.91

(*continued*)

Table 1. (*continued*)

Item	Category	Frequency	Ratio (%)
	Bachelor's degree	173	83.98
	Master's degree	19	9.22
	Doctor's degree and above	1	0.49
Monthly Income (CNY)	≤2000	123	59.71
	2001–5000	68	33.01
	5001–8000	11	5.34
	>8000	4	1.95

4.2 Data Analysis and Results

SmartPLS3.3 was used to analyze data. The reliability was verified by using three criteria suggested by Hair et al. (2006) and Chin (1998) [5, 17]: Cronbach's α should exceed 0.7, construct composite reliabilities (CR) should exceed 0.7, and average variance extracted (AVE) by each construct should exceed 0.5. As shown in Table 2, all Cronbach'sαs were greater than 0.7 and the CR values of all constructs ranged from 0.829 to 0.949. The AVE values ranged from 0.624 to 0.862. These results suggested that all the constructs had adequate reliability [13]. Furthermore, all item loadings exceeded 0.7, indicating adequate convergent validity [13].

In Table 3, the diagonal elements are the square roots of AVE for the constructs. It can be found that all square roots of AVE are greater than any correlation among that construct and other constructs, indicating sufficient validity [13]. In summary, our measurement model has sufficient reliability, convergence validity and discriminant validity.

We employed regression analysis to verify the structural model and results were shown in Fig. 2. First, the findings indicated that IC awareness positively affected users' continuance usage intention ($\beta = 0.384$, $p < 0.001$). Consequently, H5 were supported. Second, subjective norm ($\beta = 0.388$, $p < 0.001$), perceived novelty of online recommendation ($\beta = 0.330$, $p < 0.001$) and alternative attraction ($\beta = 0.149$, $p < 0.05$) were positively associated with IC awareness. Therefore, H1, H3 and H4 were supported. Third, community participation had negative impact on IC awareness ($\beta = -0.165$, $p < 0.05$). Therefore, H2 were supported.

In addition, according to Falk's and Miller's 10% recommended value, 38.4% variance in IC awareness and 35.9% variance of continuance usage intention indicated that the structural model had valid predictive ability [10]. Finally, the results indicated that control variable—usage frequency ($\beta = 0.386$, $p < 0.001$)—significantly affected continuance usage intention.

Table 2. Item means and loadings of reflective construct

Construct	Item Code	Loading	Cronbach's α	CR	AVE
Subjective norm	SUB1	0.795	0.717	0.829	0.624
	SUB2	0.809			
	SUB3	0.775			
Community participation	COM1	0.896	0.884	0.924	0.803
	COM2	0.892			
	COM3	0.900			
Perceived novelty of online recommendation	NOV1	0.863	0.762	0.864	0.679
	NOV2	0.782			
	NOV3	0.825			
Alternative attraction	ALT1	0.881	0.825	0.891	0.731
	ALT2	0.892			
	ALT3	0.789			
Information cocoon awareness	ICA1	0.868	0.837	0.901	0.753
	ICA2	0.843			
	ICA3	0.891			
Continuance usage intention	CON1	0.939	0.920	0.949	0.862
	CON2	0.956			
	CON3	0.888			

Table 3. Discriminant validity

	NOV	SUB	ALT	COM	CON	ICA
NOV	**0.824**					
SUB	0.398	**0.691**				
ALT	0.305	0.216	**0.855**			
COM	0.431	0.210	0.206	**0.896**		
CON	0.484	0.411	−0.033	0.273	**0.928**	
ICA	0466	0.510	0.309	0.088	0.367	**0.868**

Notes: NOV = Perceived novelty of online recommendations; SUB = Subjective norm; ALT, Alternative attraction; COM = Community participation; CON = Continuance usage intention; ICA = Information cocoon awareness. The square root of average variance extracted (AVE) is shown on the diagonal of the correlation matrix.

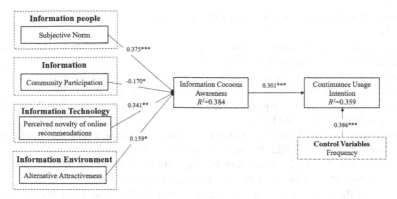

Fig. 2. Structural model

5 Conclusions

This study seeks to develop and test a comprehensive framework that explains the antecedents and consequences of information cocoon awareness in short-form video APPs. Findings indicate that subjective norm, perceived novelty of online recommendations and alternative attraction positively affect IC awareness, while community participation negatively affects IC awareness. Besides, IC awareness positively affect the users' continuous usage intention.

This research is of great significance in various measures. Theoretical implications of this study are three fold: (1) adopt Information Ecology Theory to explore users' information cocoon awareness, thus enriches existing knowledge on information cocoon; (2) carry out this research in the short-form video app context, extends the applicability of Information Ecology Theory; (3) identify and empirically verify the antecedents and consequences of information cocoon awarenesss. Practically, our findings can provide inspiration for the service construction and development of short-form video platforms to better serve users. In addition, the study encourages more users to break the information cocoon and enrich their horizon actively.

There are some limitations in this study. For instance, respondents age and gender were not evenly distributed. In future research, the respondents would be carefully selected with distributive and representative profile and preference. Secondly, we identify four independent variables in our research model, which might fail to fully capture the important determinants of IC. Further research is suggested to consider additional predictors to extend the current study.

Acknowledgment. This study was supported by the Fundamental Research Funds for the Central Universities No. NR2021003 awarded to the second author.

References

1. 36kr Research Center. http://www.199it.com/archives/672181.html. Accessed 25 Nov 2017

2. Ajzen, I.: The theory of planned behavior. Organ. Behav. Hum. Decis. Process. **50**(2), 179–211 (1991)
3. Bhattacherjee, A.: An empirical analysis of the antecedents of electronic commerce service continuance. Decis. Support Syst. **32**(2), 201–214 (2001)
4. Chang, C.C.: Examining users' intention to continue using social network games: a flow experience perspective. Telematics Inform. **30**(4), 311–321 (2013)
5. Chin, W.W.: The partial least squares approach to structural equation modeling. Mod. Methods Bus. Res. **295**(2), 295–336 (1998)
6. China Internet Network Information Center (CINIC). http://www.cnnic.net.cn/hlwfzyj/hlw xzbg/hlwtjbg/202202/P020220407403488048001.pdf. Accessed 25 Feb 2022
7. Davenport, T.H., Prusak, L.: Information Ecology: Mastering the Information and Knowledge Environment. Oxford University Press on Demand, Location (1997)
8. Dubois, E., Blank, G.: The echo chamber is overstated: the moderating effect of political interest and diverse media. Inf. Commun. Soc. **21**(5), 729–745 (2018)
9. Eveland, W.P., Jr.: A "mix of attributes" approach to the study of media effects and new communication technologies. J. Commun. **53**(3), 395–410 (2003)
10. Falk, R.F., Miller, N.B.: A Primer for Soft Modeling. University of Akron Press, Location (1992)
11. Festinger, L.: A Theory of Cognitive Dissonance, 2nd edn. Stanford University Press, Location (1957)
12. Finin, T., Joshi, A., Kolari, P., Java, A., Kale, A., Karandikar, A.: The information ecology of social media and online communities. AI Mag. **29**(3), 77–92 (2008)
13. Fornell, C., Larcker, D.F.: Evaluating structural equation models with unobservable variables and measurement error. J. Mark. Res. **18**(1), 39–50 (1981)
14. García-Marco, F.J.: El libro electrónico y digital en la ecología informacional: avances y retos. El profesional de la información **17**(4), 373–389 (2008)
15. Garcia-Marco, F.J.: Libraries in the digital ecology: reflections and trends. Electron. Libr. **29**(1), 105–120 (2011)
16. Grafton, C.: Book review: the information ecology of e-government. Soc. Sci. Comput. Rev. **24**(1), 132–134 (2006)
17. Hair, J.F., Black, W.C., Babin, B.J., Anderson, R.E., Tatham, R.L.: Multivariate Data Analysis.Prentice Hall, Pearson Prentice Hall, Upper Saddle River (2006)
18. Harris, K.: Information ecology. Int. J. Inf. Manag.: J. Inf. Prof. **9**(4), 289–290 (1989)
19. Hart, W., Albarracín, D., Eagly, A.H., Brechan, I., Lindberg, M.J., Merrill, L.: Feeling validated versus being correct: a meta-analysis of selective exposure to information. Psychol. Bull. **135**(4), 555 (2009)
20. Hasenyager, B.W.: Managing the Information Ecology: A Collaborative Approach to Information Technology Management. Greenwood Publishing Group, Location (1996)
21. Hawkins, B.L.: A view on the ecology of information. In: Marcum, D.B. (ed.) Development of Digital Libraries: An American Perspective, Librarianship and Information Science Contributions, pp. 187–210. Greenwood Press, Westport (2000)
22. Heinonen, K.: Consumer activity in social media: managerial approaches to consumers' social media behavior. J. Consum. Behav. **10**(6), 356–364 (2011)
23. Herlocker, J.L., Konstan, J.A., Terveen, L.G., Riedl, J.T.: Evaluating collaborative filtering recommender systems. ACM Trans. Inf. Syst. (TOIS) **22**(1), 5–53 (2004)
24. Horton, F.W.: Information ecology. J. Syst. Manag. **29**(9), 32–36 (1978)
25. Huberman, B.A.: The Laws of the Web: Patterns in the Ecology of Information. MIT Press, Location (2003)
26. Jeong, M., Zo, H., Lee, C.H., Ceran, Y.: Feeling displeasure from online social media postings: a study using cognitive dissonance theory. Comput. Hum. Behav. **97**, 231–240 (2019)

27. Kobayashi, T., Ikeda, K.I.: Selective exposure in political web browsing: empirical verification of 'cyber-balkanization' in Japan and the USA. Inf. Commun. Soc. **12**(6), 929–953 (2009)
28. Kumar, N.: Facebook for self-empowerment? A study of Facebook adoption in urban India. New Media Soc. **16**(7), 1122–1137 (2014)
29. Lazarsfeld, P., Berelson, B., Gaudet, H.: The People's Choice, 2nd edn. Columbia University Press, Location (1948)
30. Li, W.: The effects of perceived value on users' satisfaction and loyalty towards E-book reading applications. J. Libr. Sci. in China **43**(6), 35–49 (2017)
31. Matt, C., Benlian, A., Hess, T., Weiß, C.: Escaping from the filter bubble? The effects of novelty and serendipity on users' evaluations of online recommendations. In: Thirty Fifth International Conference on Information Systems, Auckland, pp. 1–18 (2014)
32. Nardi, B.A.: Information ecologies. Ref. User Serv. Q. **38**(1), 49–50 (1998)
33. Ren, S., Liu, H.: Research on the theory and application of information ecology at home and abroad. China CIO News (01), 81–83 (2014)
34. Rowland, F.: The filter bubble: what the internet is hiding from you. Portal: Libr. Acad. **11**(4), 1009–1011 (2011)
35. Shim, S., Lee, B.: Evolution of portals and stability of information ecology on the web. In: Proceedings of the 8th International Conference on Electronic Commerce: The New E-commerce: Innovations for Conquering Current Barriers, Obstacles and Limitations to Conducting Successful Business on the Internet, pp. 584–588. ACM, New York (2006)
36. Sunstein, C.R.: Infotopia: How Many Minds Produce Knowledge. Oxford University Press, Location (2006)
37. Sunstein, C.R.: The law of group polarization. University of Chicago Law School, John M. Olin Law & Economics Working Paper (91) (1999)
38. Venkatesh, V., Davis, F.D.: A theoretical extension of the technology acceptance model: four longitudinal field studies. Manag. Sci. **46**(2), 186–204 (2000)
39. Wang, X., Guo, Y., Yang, M., Chen, Y., Zhang, W.: Information ecology research: past, present, and future. Inf. Technol. Manag. **18**(1), 27–39 (2015). https://doi.org/10.1007/s10799-015-0219-3
40. Wang, X., Jing, J., Liu, Y., Zhao, Y.: Empirical research on the construction of information ecological model in E-commerce. Libr. Inf. Serv. **53**(22), 128–132 (2009)
41. Xu, B., Li, D.: An empirical study of the motivations for content contribution and community participation in Wikipedia. Inf. Manag. **52**(3), 275–286 (2015)
42. Yu, X., Wang, J.: A New understanding of the "Information Cocoon". News Writing (03), 65–78 (2022)

Privacy and Data Protection in COVID-19 Contact Tracing Apps: An Analysis from a Socio-Technical System Design Perspective

Michael Roesler[✉] 🆔 and Paul Liston 🆔

Centre for Innovative Human Systems, Trinity College, Dublin, Ireland
roeslerm@tcd.ie

Abstract. This paper examines privacy and data protection concerns of the public in relation to COVID-19 contact tracing apps. In addition, the role played by these concerns in the adoption of contact tracing apps has been investigated. Further emphasis has been directed at the limitations of contact tracing apps that could stem from privacy and data protection accommodations. Regarding socio-technical system design, this paper attempts to identify mechanisms preserving privacy in contact tracing apps. It has been a further research aim to determine factors that assist and hinder adoption.

A mixed methods approach utilising a survey including both qualitatively and quantitatively evaluable questions was employed. Contact tracing apps have been a highly topical subject during the COVID-19 pandemic. This research found that privacy and data protection are indeed important factors in people's decision-making about whether to use a contact tracing app. While certain privacy trade-offs are inevitable when it comes to contact tracing, this research found that a decentralised design approach characterised by full anonymity for users and the largest amount of data possible remaining on the device is best suited to achieve widespread adoption and approval with a privacy-conscious public that is concerned with data protection.

Keywords: Privacy · Data protection · COVID-19 · Contact tracing app

1 Introduction

1.1 Objectives, Justification and Structure of Research

This paper investigates privacy and data protection in COVID-19 contact tracing apps from a socio-technical system design perspective. The fundamental research objective is to examine the privacy and data protection concerns of the public in relation to COVID-19 contact tracing apps. Additionally, the role these concerns play in the practical adoption of contact tracing apps is investigated. further emphasis is directed at the limitations for

© Springer Nature Switzerland AG 2022
G. Meiselwitz et al. (Eds.): HCII 2022, LNCS 13517, pp. 126–141, 2022.
https://doi.org/10.1007/978-3-031-22131-6_10

contact tracing apps that might stem from privacy and data protection considerations. Regarding socio-technical system design, this paper seeks to address mechanisms that can promote privacy in contact tracing apps as well as factors that assist and hinder adoption.

The COVID-19 pandemic has created strong demand for innovative technologies that can help societies cope with the disease and its ramifications (O'LEary 2020). In addition, the pandemic has not only boosted technology-based solutions but also created an opportunity to study the design, functionality, and use of these technologies (Sein 2020). Smartphone contact tracing applications have been introduced since spring 2020 as a technological response to combat the COVID-19 pandemic (HSE 2020). The World Health Organization (WHO 2020) has defined contact tracing as "the process of identifying, assessing, and managing people who have been infected with the covid-19 virus" (para. 1). furthermore, the WHO (2021) has suggested that while digital tools might support COVID-19 contact tracing efforts, ethical considerations regarding privacy, security, accountability and accessibility needed to be taken into account in their development and implementation.

Ethical considerations furthermore play a major role in the successful adoption of this type of app, and are related to the degree of trust and confidence the public has towards the use of the app itself and of the personal data gathered (Ferreti et al. 2020). While many COVID-19 apps target the protection of individual privacy, contact tracing in itself requires the revelation of some otherwise private personal information (Bengio et al. 2020). Digital contact tracing bears inherent privacy risks that can be alleviated but not fully removed through technological solutions (Bengio et al. 2020). COVID-19 contact tracing apps mark an intersection of technology and public health. While they are currently being deployed internationally as a response to the COVID-19 pandemic, their effectiveness and privacy concerns remain issues of great controversy. The socio-technical factors that enable successful digital contact tracing have not been sufficiently analysed in existing literature (cf. Vinuesa et al. 2020). Therefore, the consideration of socio-technical system design in the context of contact tracing apps may enable a broader understanding of the role of privacy and data protection in the adoption. This paper aims to facilitate preliminary insights into how the incorporation of socio-technical thinking into the design of contact tracing apps can foster privacy, data protection, informational autonomy and thereby widespread adoption.

Finally, the often conflict-laden relationship between privacy and information technology (Stanford Encyclopaedia of Philosophy 2019) provides another background for this dissertation. Rich (2021) argued that a lack of trust by the public in the government or large technology companies to collect, store, and use their personal data including health and precise location data had negatively impacted the adoption and thereby diminished the role of contact tracing apps in managing the COVID-19 pandemic in the United States. This paper is directed at investigating and analysing if and which privacy and data protection concerns influence the adoption and consequently effectivity of contact tracing apps.

1.2 Initial Hypotheses

The following three initial hypotheses are based on a preliminary engagement with the subject of this research:

1. Privacy and data protection concerns are crucial factors in the adoption, acceptance and thereby impact, effectivity and overall success of contact tracing apps. The public in western democratic societies values privacy and data protection and would not tolerate far-reaching privacy invasions.
2. Contact tracing apps have the potential to play a role in combating a pandemic such as COVID-19 in conjunction with other public health measures, as one tool out of many.
3. From a socio-technical system design perspective, a decentralised approach that can be largely characterised by user data remaining on the device, is best suited to accommodate a high degree of privacy, data protection and informational self-determination.

2 Literature Review

The following section will introduce the current academic discussion on COVID-19 contact tracing apps regarding (1) their design, functionality, and limitations, (2) privacy and data protection considerations, and (3) adoption.

2.1 Design, Functionality, and Limitations

Generally, a distinction can be made between centralised and decentralised architectures in contact tracing apps (Shubina et al. 2020). While the signal input via Bluetooth is generally the same in both architectures, centralised solutions upload the information to a cloud server in order to compute the likelihood of an infection, whereas in decentralised architectures these processes largely take place on each device (Shubina et al. 2020).

A widely used decentralised approach is the Google/Apple Exposure Notification (GAEN) API (cf. Leith and Farrell 2020). The GAEN API utilises Bluetooth technology as previously depicted sending out a beacon that includes a random identifier. This identifier can be described as a string of random numbers that are not linked to the identity of a user and update every 10 to 20 min. Other phones search for these beacons and send out their own at the same time, constantly receiving, recording and storing the beacons on the device. The system will download a list at least once per day of those keys for the beacons that have been confirmed as belonging to individuals tested positive for COVID-19. Subsequently, every device will verify the list of beacons stored against the downloaded list, and the user will be alerted and advised on steps to take if there is a match between the beacons recorded on the device and the list of positive cases. In case a user is tested positive for COVID-19, they can report that result to a health authority in order for their beacons to be then added to the positive diagnosis list (Google/Apple Google 2020)

Blasimme et al. (2021) investigated European contact tracing apps listing the following common characteristics: a development in public-private partnerships, a voluntariness of use, an implementation of the GAEN API. In fact, they clarified that only the French and Hungarian apps used a centralised architecture, with the French government stating that the protection of the health of the French people was an exclusive responsibility of the state and not of international private corporations (Blasimme et al. 2021).

Kleinman and Merkel (2020) determined five limitations of contact tracing apps, their dependence on the degree of adoption, measurement errors, restrictions in their Bluetooth usage on iOS-based smartphones for apps not using the GAEN API, privacy objections surpassing those tolerated in conventional contact tracing, and the lack of evidence on their effectiveness. Similarly, Elkhodr et al. (2021) were concerned with constraints in digital contact tracing naming a lack of a standardised approach and interoperability between countries as a major drawback. In summary, decentralised contact tracing apps seem to be favoured over centralised architectures.

2.2 Privacy and Data Protection

Mobile operating systems including Android and iOS use permission requests to control access to device capabilities requiring consent from the user in order to limit to which extent personal information can be accessed by apps (cf. Hamed et al. 2016; Hatamian et al. 2017). The most common device capabilities contact tracing apps request access to are Bluetooth (for Bluetooth-based apps), location (for GPS-based apps), notifications (to alert users), exposure notifications (part of GAEN API), motion and activity (to improve location accuracy), and camera (e.g. to scan a QR code to report a positive test result) (cf. Hatamian et al. 2021). With the exception of camera access, those resources are generally required for contact tracing apps to function as intended requiring access to the capabilities they are technologically based on. Regarding permission requests in EU and non-EU contact tracing apps, Hatamian et al. (2021) concluded that location-based apps had shown "privacy-invasive permission access behaviour" (p. 15), and that EU apps generally had a lower privacy risk than non-EU apps.

Based on this introduction on the technical implementation of privacy and data protection within apps through permission requestions, the focus will be on factors and strategies that can reduce privacy and data protection concerns towards contact tracing apps in the following. Abeler et al. (2020) listed data minimisation and proportionality as core characteristics for effective and efficient solutions that protected fundamental rights and met broad acceptance in the public. Similarly, Cho et al. (2020) explained that the willingness of the population for privacy trade-offs needed to be incorporated into the design concluding that privacy-invasive early design choices could have long-lasting consequences in trust and adoption. As a means to increase trust, Fox et al. (2021) advocated for transparency in addressing privacy concerns both before and after roll-out of an app. Furthermore, knowledge of an app and its functionality, benefits and limitations, as well as trust in developers, reduced privacy concerns and improved users' perception of an app's advantages (Meier et al. 2021).

2.3 Adoption

Altmann et al. (2020) found strong support in the public for contact tracing apps acknowledging that at the same time additional research was needed to determine to which degree this public support extended into actual adoption and a potential for pandemic control.

In approaches studying the influence which technology a contact tracing app is based on had on adoption, both Simko et al. (2020) and O'Callaghan et al. (2020) discovered a preference for proximity tracing via Bluetooth over GPS location tracking.

Seto et al. (2021) advocated for a balance between privacy and effectiveness to increase contact tracing app adoption. Whereas the level of privacy of a contact tracing app depended on factors such as voluntariness, the underlying technology, and the degree of data centralisation, these characteristics translated into users' sense of privacy in connection to the norms and values of their society (Seto et al. 2021).

Finally, Zimmermann et al. (2021) highlighted that it was crucial for authorities to clearly communicate the objectives, and the contribution of the particular technology chosen in successfully launching a contact tracing app. Additionally, to overcome privacy concerns as a hurdle for adoption, evaluation and communication of the effectiveness of these apps was needed (Zimmermann et al. 2021).

3 Methods

3.1 Participants/Recruitment

The online survey was initially circulated on 22nd June 2021 via Twitter and LinkedIn. On 2nd July the survey was also circulated to all Trinity College Dublin (TCD) postgraduate students. In total the survey was fully completed by 147 respondents. The intended minimum number of 100 respondents was reached. A circulation within TCD seemed appropriate as it was a reachable and relatively large audience. Furthermore, an attempt at a broader sampling was made through the additional distribution of the survey via social media.

3.2 Materials

The survey was composed with the Qualtrics XM software after being initially developed in a Microsoft Word document. It was intended for the survey to take participants no longer than 10–15 min to complete. The survey is set up of four closed background factor questions, 12 statements utilising a Likert scale, one ranking question, and three open-ended questions. The four closed questions relate to demographic information of the respondents, specifically their country of residence, gender, and age-group, and whether they use a COVID-19 contact tracing app. The participants were also asked to indicate to which extent they agreed or disagreed with each of the 12 statements by ticking the appropriate box. The responses are based on a five-point Likert scale with the options "Strongly disagree", "Somewhat disagree", "Neither agree nor disagree", "Somewhat agree", and "Strongly agree".

The single ranking question requests participants to click and drag the factors "Privacy ", "Data protection", "Anonymity", "Helping fight the pandemic", and "Helping venues reopen" to create an order of importance for their decision to use or not use a contact tracing app. The three open-ended questions looked at the perspectives of the respondents regarding the most important aspects in a contact tracing app for them, additional features or functionalities they would like to see being added to current or future contact tracing apps, and any additional suggestions or comments regarding COVID-19 contact tracing apps they might have. Table 1 below shows the questions participants were asked in the order they appeared in the actual survey.

Table 1. Survey questions.

#	Question	Response type/option
1	**Background factors:**	
I.	Country: In which country do you currently reside? Please select from below drop-down list	Drop-down list with all countries starting with Ireland
II.	Gender: What gender do you identify as? Please select the option that applies to you	Male, Female, Non-binary/other, Prefer not to say
III	Age-group: Which age-group do you belong to? Please tick the option that applies to you	18–25, 26–35, 36–45, 46–55, 56–65, 66 and older
IV.	Contact tracing app use: I am using a COVID-19 contact tracing app such as COVID Tracker Ireland by the HSE. Please tick the option that applies to you. Regardless of which option you choose you will still be able to complete all aspects of the study	Yes/No
2	**Statements:**	Five-point Likert scale
I.	Contact tracing apps have the potential to play a role in combating pandemics such as COVID-19	
II.	Privacy is a crucial aspect in my decision whether to use a COVID-19 contact tracing app	
III.	Data protection is a crucial aspect in my decision whether to use a COVID-19 contact tracing app	
IV.	The use of contact tracing apps should be mandatory during a pandemic	

(*continued*)

Table 1. (*continued*)

#	Question	Response type/option
V	I would be willing to sacrifice privacy in my use of a contact tracing app if it would help fight the pandemic	
VI.	I would be willing to share my location data with government authorities operating a contact tracing app	
VII.	I would only use a contact tracing app that is fully anonymous	
VIII.	I would be more likely to report a positive test result in a contact tracing app if anonymity were guaranteed	
IX.	I would follow the government guidelines were I to receive an alert for a close contact with an infected person from the app	
X.	I would be willing to use an app in order for a government-mandated quarantine to be tracked through the use of my location data	
XI.	I would be willing to use an app to check-in at retail, culture and sports venues (i.e. providing my contact information for the purpose of contact tracing) in order to facilitate the reopening of these establishments	
XII.	I would be willing to use an app storing my vaccination records in order to show this to authorities when travelling abroad	
3	**Ranking question:**	
I.	Please CLICK & DRAG the following factors to create an order of importance for your decision to use or not use a contact tracing app. 1 is the most important factor, 5 is the least important factor	Privacy, Data protection, Anonymity, Helping fight the pandemic, Helping venues reopen
4	**Open questions:**	Free text
I.	What are the most important aspects in a contact tracing app for you?	
II.	Which features and/or functionalities (if any) would you like to see being added to current or future contact tracing apps?	

(*continued*)

Table 1. (*continued*)

#	Question	Response type/option
III.	Do you have any additional suggestions or comments regarding COVID-19 contact tracing apps?	

The survey data was approached with a quantitative and qualitative analysis. While the background factors, Likert scale statements, and the ranking question were analysed quantitatively, the responses to the open questions underwent a qualitative inspection. 20 incomplete surveys were discounted from the analysis as they did not include answers to any questions or only to the background factor questions.

In order to ensure validity and reliability of the survey a pilot study was conducted. Applicability and appropriateness were tested with a small group of course staff including the course director, and the course administrator, and the supervisor of this dissertation. In total 11 responses were received for the pilot study. As the feedback from participants was positive and no issues were reported, no changes on the questionnaire itself were made in the final survey.

Moreover, the quality of the research was ensured by considering the data within the context of the survey and its context in the current pandemic, and the immersion of the researcher into the data, explicitly acknowledging the own biases and experiences of the researcher conducting the research and in professional practice.

4   Results

In the following a selection of the results of the online survey will be presented in sequence of the survey questions. The results are grouped into: (1) demographic factors, (2) Likert scale data, (3) ranking data, and (4) qualitative data.

4.1   Demographic Factors

The reported country of participants is heavily skewed towards Ireland with 120 respondents (82%). A two-third majority of 99 participants reported their gender as female (67%), while 44 respondents indicated their gender was male (30%). The age of participants is centred around the three younger groups. Finally, 92 participants (63%) indicated that they used a COVID-19 contact tracing app, while 55 (37%) responded that they did not.

4.2   Likert Scale Data

The statements with the highest levels of agreement ("Strongly agree" and "Somewhat agree" combined) were regarding willingness to use a vaccination passport, compliance with government guidelines in case of an alert for a close contact, and potential of contact tracing apps to play a role in combating pandemics at over 80% each. In contrast, the statements that received the lowest levels of agreement related to mandatory use of contact tracing apps during a pandemic, and the requirement for a contact tracing app to be fully anonymous for oneself to use it at under 50% each. There were no statements that a majority of respondents disagreed to ("Strongly disagree" and "Somewhat disagree" combined). Results regarding the responses to all statements using a Likert Scale are outlined in Fig. 1.

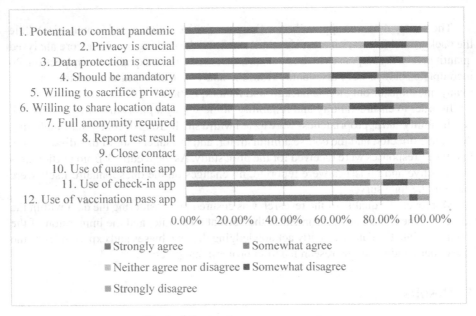

Fig. 1. Likert scale responses overview.

In the following, responses to selected individual statements will be presented. The first statement was in relation to the potential of contact tracing apps to play a role in combating pandemics such as COVID-19; 30% of participants strongly agreed with this statement, while a further 50% somewhat agreed, and 8% neither agreed nor disagreed. 9% somewhat disagreed with the first statement, whereas 3% strongly disagreed.

The second and third statements asked participants to which extent they agreed or disagreed that privacy and data protection respectively were crucial aspects in their decision whether to use a COVID-19 contact tracing app. In relation to privacy 26% of respondents strongly agreed with the statement, 30% somewhat agreed, 18% each neither agreed nor disagreed and somewhat disagreed, while 9% strongly disagreed. Regarding data protection, the distribution of responses has been similar with a majority of respondents either strongly agreeing (35%) or somewhat agreeing (25%) with the statement. 11% neither agreed nor disagreed, whereas 18% somewhat disagreed and 10% strongly disagreed.

The fifth statement the survey delved into the willingness of the participants to sacrifice privacy in their use of a contact tracing app if it helped fight the pandemic. A majority of 62% at least partially agreed with this statement (22% strongly agreed,

40% somewhat agreed), whereas 16% chose the neutral option, and 11% somewhat disagreed and strongly disagreed respectively. Slightly less than half of participants at least partially agreed with the seventh statement that they would only use a contact tracing app that was fully anonymous (19% strongly agreed, 29% somewhat agreed). However, this statement had the highest share of respondents out of all statements that neither agreed nor disagreed at 21%. Almost a third of participants disagreed with the statement to at least some degree (23% somewhat disagreed, 8% strongly disagreed).

The tenth statement dealt with the willingness of participants to use an app to track a government-mandated quarantine using their location data. Out of the final three statements on the use of types of COVID-19-related apps other than contact tracing, this one received the most varied responses with 27% strongly agreeing, 28% somewhat agreeing, 12% neither agreeing nor disagreeing, 20% somewhat disagreeing, and 14% strongly disagreeing. Most participants also showed a willingness to use an app to check-in at retail, culture or sports venues providing their contact information for the purpose of contact tracing to facilitate the reopening of these establishments. Three quarters of respondents either strongly (44%) or somewhat (31%) agreed with the eleventh statement. Meanwhile, 5% proved to be indecisive, while 10% somewhat disagreed and 9% strongly disagreed. The twelfth and final statement on the willingness to use a vaccination passport when travelling abroad saw the largest strong agreement among participants between all statements at 69%. A further 19% somewhat agreed, whereas 4% neither agreed nor disagreed, 3% somewhat disagreed, and 5% strongly disagreed.

Looking at the relationship between background factors and responses to the statements no moderate or strong correlations could be found; correlations were either weak or very weak. However, moderate correlations between the responses to individual statements could be observed in the data set. The assessment that contact tracing apps had the potential to play a role in combating a pandemic was found to be moderately positively correlated with the willingness to sacrifice privacy ($r(145) = .406$, $p < .001$), the willingness to share location data ($r(145) = .413$, $p < .001$), and the willingness to use a check-in app ($r(145) = .404$, $p < .001$). In addition, there was a very strong positive correlation between the assertion that privacy was a crucial aspect in a participant's decision whether to use a contact tracing app and the same statement in relation to data protection ($r(145) = .812$, $p < .001$).

A moderate negative correlation was determined between privacy being crucial and the willingness to sacrifice privacy ($r(145) = -.459$, $p < .001$), and share location data ($r(145) = -.445$, $p < .001$). In contrast, both of the latter statements correlated moderately positively ($r(145) = .448$, $p < .001$ for sacrificing privacy, $r(145) = .503$, $p < .001$ for sharing location data) with the notion that contact tracing apps should be mandatory during a pandemic.. Moreover, a strong positive correlation between the willingness to sacrifice privacy and the willingness to share location data existed ($r(145) = .725$, $p < .001$), while moderate positive correlations of the former with the willingness to use a quarantine tracking app ($r(145) = .583$, $p < .001$) and a check-in app ($r(145) = .477$, $p < .001$) were present.

The sole willingness to use a fully anonymous contact tracing app correlated strongly positively with the compliance with government guidelines in case of a close contact alert ($r(145) = .693$, $p < .001$), and moderately positively with the increased likelihood to report a positive test result if anonymity were guaranteed ($r(145) = .576$, $p < .001$). A moderate positive correlation was also observed between the willingness to use a check-in app and the willingness to use a vaccination passport app ($r(145) = .515$, $p < .001$).

4.3 Ranking Data

In the ranking question participants were tasked with creating an order of importance for their decision to use or not use a contact tracing app with "1" representing the most important factor and "5" being the least important factor from the following factors: privacy, data protection, anonymity, fighting the pandemic, reopening venues. 67% of participants ranked "Helping fight the pandemic" as the most important factor. "Helping venues reopen" was the most often named second most important factor being ranked in this position by almost 40% of respondents. A third of participants rated "Privacy" as the third most important factor in their decision on contact tracing app use. "Anonymity" was most ranked in fourth place with 29% of respondents making this choice. "Helping venues reopen" was ranked as the least important factor by almost 40% of participants, while 38% found "Anonymity" least important.

Table 2 shows that when looking at the mean participants ranked "Helping fight the pandemic" as the most important factor, followed by "Privacy" as the second most important, "Data protection" as the third most important, "Helping venues reopen" as the second least, and "Anonymity" as the least important factor in their decision to use or not use a contact tracing app. While "Anonymity" had the smallest standard deviation, values for "Helping fight the pandemic" were the furthest spread out from the mean which can also be seen in this factor being both most commonly ranked as the second most important and the least important factor.

Table 2. Descriptive statistics for ranking responses

Factor	Mean	Standard Deviation
Privacy	2.78	1.115
Data protection	3.09	1.249
Anonymity	3.92	1.076
Helping fight the pandemic	1.73	1.178
Helping venues reopen	3.48	1.401

Note. N=147, Minimum: 1 ("most important factor"), Maximum: 5 ("least important factor")

4.4 Qualitative Data

A qualitative approach has been taken to identify the themes articulated by the participants in response to the three open questions. The first question asked participants about the most important aspects in contact tracing apps for them.

The most mentioned theme was *fighting or ending the pandemic*. Participants expressed that this was an important aspect in a contact tracing app, while also requesting more information about the efficacy in achieving this purpose. *Privacy* constitutes another theme frequently referred to by respondents, sometimes in combination with the aforementioned theme and the concern of purpose limitation. *Effectiveness* in its core function was named as a crucial characteristic. Several participants stated the importance of *information and statistics* in a contact tracing app. This theme includes the demand for local or regional statistics, frequent updates, and illustrative visualisation. A need for *accuracy* and *safety* was a prominent theme, in some cases linked to *data protection* concerns and *anonymity*. The *ease of use* of a contact tracing app represents another theme articulated by participants. Respondents among other things stressed its relevance for adoption.

The second open question queried which features and/or functionalities (if any) participants would like to see being added to current or future contact tracing apps. The most requested functionality concerns the provision of information and statistics. More precisely, these requests asked for statistics on current case numbers, vaccination uptake, and hospitalisations and deaths on a local, regional, and national level as well as informational content on reopening and safety guidelines, virus variants, symptoms, vaccines, and vaccinations. Moreover, participants requested a vaccination passport feature stressing the importance to display the vaccination status within the app. In addition, a check-in feature to register at retail and hospitality establishments was a popular request among participants. Several respondents suggested a variety of location or map features and functionalities they desired to be included in a contact tracing app. The proposed concepts ranged from maps broadly indicating local infection outbreaks, to tracing the whereabouts of oneself at a given time and potential contacts for one's own reference. Furthermore, features and functionalities aimed at preserving privacy in contact tracing apps were frequently requested by respondents.

The third and last open question asked participants to provide any additional suggestions or comments regarding COVID-19 contact tracing apps. No predominant themes could be identified in relation to this question, but criticism on contact tracing apps in general, the Irish app in particular, or individual perspectives on usage deterrents were present in the responses.

5 Discussion

5.1 Privacy and Data Protection Concerns of the Public

A majority of 56% and 61% of survey participants respectively saw privacy and data protection as important factors in their decision to use or not use a contact tracing app. These results confirm the hypothesis that privacy and data protection concerns were crucial factors in the acceptance and adoption of contact tracing apps. Additionally, the high willingness among participants (62%) to sacrifice privacy in their use of these apps indicates a realistic perspective on the trade-offs intrinsic to contact tracing.

Findings from the qualitative component of the survey indicate that privacy and data protection were important to respondents, but not the most important aspects in contact tracing apps. Fighting the pandemic emerged to be the most important aspect for participants, and informational content the most requested feature or functionality.

5.2 Role of Privacy and Data Protection Concerns in Adoption

A large majority of participants (80%) agreed with the statement that contact tracing apps had the potential to play a role in fighting a pandemic. This corresponds with the hypothesis that contact tracing apps could act a part in combating a pandemic such as COVID-19 if used in conjunction with other public health measures. The large general acceptance of contact tracing apps as a tool in tackling a pandemic coupled with the realistic view on privacy sacrifice mentioned in the previous subsection could be seen as beneficial for adoption.

63% of participants stated they used a contact tracing app. This figure regarding the actual adoption seems relatively high considering the novelty of the technology. The qualitative findings regarding adoption can only be considered as anecdotal evidence, but a distrust in authorities operating the apps, and doubts about the technological validity and effectiveness of the concept seem to outweigh strictly privacy or data protection related concerns as deterrents from contact tracing app use.

5.3 Limitations Due to Privacy and Data Protection Considerations

Another research aim has been to investigate limitations for contact tracing apps that might stem from privacy and data protection considerations. These limitations largely played a role in the self-reflective interview but were also articulated by survey participants. The requirement for an active participation of the population can be seen as the most significant limitation for privacy and data protection preserving contact tracing apps. It is required for users to download and set up the app, report positive test results, and follow government guidelines such as isolating and getting tested in case of a close contact alert.

Other limitations are related to the technology chosen. Bluetooth can be regarded as the technological base most commonly chosen for privacy-preserving contact tracing apps. Inherent limitations include Bluetooth signals being unable to detect external factors such as walls or floors, and the way a phone is kept inside a pocket influencing signal strength. Further limitations lie in the provision of anonymity that makes it impossible to get to know details about a close contact such as where, when, for exactly how long or with whom it occurred.

5.4 Socio-Technical Mechanisms Preserving Privacy and Data Protection

This research sought to identify socio-technical mechanisms that can guarantee privacy and data protection in contact tracing apps as well as factors that assist and hinder adoption. The hypothesis that a decentralised approach, largely characterised by user data remaining on the device, would be best suited to accommodate a high degree of privacy, data protection and informational self-determination held valid throughout the research. The high importance attributed to data protection and privacy by survey participants confirmed that this approach was appropriate to alleviate concerns in the public.

While the choice of a technology that in its character allows for anonymity, data minimisation, and decentralisation has the potential to accommodate privacy concerns, a backend infrastructure resilient to hacks or other attacks could be crucial in mitigating data protection fears articulated. In addition, a well-designed UI and UX emphasising intuitiveness and user guidance could satisfy the survey participants' request for ease of use.

6 Conclusion

This research has lent support to the hypothesis that privacy and data protection concerns are crucial factors in the adoption, acceptance and thereby impact, effectivity and over-all success of contact tracing apps. Findings indicate that the public values high privacy and data protection standards and agrees that contact tracing apps have the potential to play a role in combating a pandemic such as COVID-19. It has been established that a contact tracing app architecture aimed at preserving privacy to the greatest possible extent includes certain limitations. Aspects including anonymity and voluntariness require an active participation of the population and transparent communications from the government operating the app.

Furthermore, technological limitations such as measurement inaccuracies need to be considered. Consequently, contact tracing apps cannot be seen as a solution on their own, but only as one tool in a larger strategy to fight a pandemic. From a socio-technical perspective it has been concluded that a decentralised approach is best suited to accommodate high levels of privacy and data protection while facilitating widespread adoption.

References

Abeler, J., Bäcker, M., Buermeyer, U., Zillessen, H.: COVID-19 contact tracing and data protection can go together. JMIR Mhealth Uhealth 8(4), 1–5 (2020). https://doi.org/10.2196/19359

Altmann, S., et al.: Acceptability of app-based contact tracing for COVID-19: cross-country survey study. JMIR Mhealth Uhealth 8(8) (2020). https://doi.org/10.2196/19857

Bengio, Y., et al.: Inherent privacy limitations of decentralized contact tracing apps. J. Am. Med. Inform. Assoc., 1–3 (2020). https://doi.org/10.1093/jamia/ocaa153

Blasimme, A., Ferretti, A., Vayena, E.: Digital contact tracing against COVID-19 in Europe: Current features and ongoing developments. Front. Digital Health 3(660823), 1 (2021). https://doi.org/10.3389/fdgth.2021.660823

Cho, H., Ippolito, D., Yu, Y.W.: Contact tracing mobile apps for COVID-19: Privacy considerations and related trade-offs. arXiv, 2003(11511), pp. 1–10 (2020). https://arxiv.org/abs/2003.11511

Elkhodr, M., et al.: Technology, privacy, and user opinions of COVID-19 mobile apps for contact tracing: Systematic search and content analysis. J. Med. Internet Res. 23(2), 1–17 (2021). https://doi.org/10.2196/23467

Ferreti, L., et al.: Quantifying SARS-CoV-2 transmission suggests epidemic control with digital contact tracing. Science 368(6491), 1–7 (2020). https://doi.org/10.1126/science.abb6936

Fox, G., Clohessy, T., van der Werff, L., Rosati, P., Lynn, T.: Exploring the competing influences of privacy concerns and positive beliefs on citizen acceptance of contact tracing mobile applications. Comput. Hum. Behav. **121** (2021). Doi: https://doi.org/10.1016/j.chb.2021.106806

Google/Apple: Exposure notifications (2020). Accessed 31 Aug 2021. https://static.googleuse rcontent.com/media/www.google.com/en//covid19/exposurenotifications/pdfs/Exposure-Notification-FAQ-v1.2.pdf

Gürses, S., Troncoso, C., Díaz, C.: Engineering Privacy by Design. Conference on Computers, Privacy & Data Protection, Brussels (2016)

Hamed, A., Ben Ayed, H.K.: Privacy risk assessment and users' awareness for mobile apps permissions. In: 2016 IEEE/ACS 13th International Conference of Computer Systems and Applications (AICCSA), Agadir, Morocco (2016)

Hatamian, M., Serna, J., Rannenberg, K., Igler, B.: FAIR: fuzzy alarming index rule for privacy analysis in smartphone apps. In: Trust, Privacy and Security in Digital Business. LNCS, pp. 3–18. Springer (2017). Doi: https://doi.org/10.1007/978-3-319-64483-7_1

Hatamian, M., Wairimu, S., Momen, N., Fritsch, L.: A privacy and security analysis of early-deployed COVID-19 contact tracing Android apps. Empir. Softw. Eng. **26**(3), 1–51 (2021). https://doi.org/10.1007/s10664-020-09934-4

HSE: COVID Tracker app (2020). https://covidtracker.ie/?utm_source=covid_tracker&utm_med ium=app&utm_campaign=in_text%20. Accessed 31 Aug 2021

Kleinman, R.A., Merkel, C.: Digital contact tracing for COVID-19. Can. Med. Assoc. J. **192**(24), E653-656 (2020). https://doi.org/10.1503/cmaj.200922

Leith, D.J., Farrell, S.: Measurement-based evaluation of Google/Apple Exposure notification API for proximity detection in a light-rail tram. PLoS ONE **15**(9), 1–16 (2020). https://doi.org/10.1371/journal.pone.0239943

O'Callaghan, M.E., et al.: A national survey of attitudes to COVID-19 digital contact tracing in the Republic of Ireland. Irish J. Med. Sci. (1971 -) **190**(3), 863–887 (2020). https://doi.org/10.1007/s11845-020-02389-y

O'Leary, D.E.: Evolving information systems and technology research issues for COVID-19 and other pandemics. J. Organ. Comput. Electron. Commer. **30**(1), 1–8 (2020). https://doi.org/10.1080/10919392.2020.1755790

Rich, J.: How our outdated privacy laws doomed contact tracing apps. Brookings (2021). https://www.brookings.edu/blog/techtank/2021/01/28/how-our-outdated-privacy-laws-doomed-contact-tracing-apps/. Accessed 31 Aug 2021

Sein, M.K.: The serendipitous impact of COVID-19 pandemic: a rare opportunity for research and practice. Int. J. Inf. Manage. **55**, 1–3 (2020). https://doi.org/10.1016/j.ijinfomgt.2020.102164

Seto, E., Challa, P., Ware, P.: Adoption of COVID-19 contact tracing apps: a balance between privacy and effectiveness. J. Med. Internet Res. **23**(3) (2021). https://doi.org/10.2196/25726

Shubina, V., Holcer, S., Gould, M., Lohan, E.S.: Survey of decentralized solutions with mobile devices for user location tracking, proximity detection, and contact tracing in the COVID-19 era. Data **5**(4), 1–40 (2020). https://doi.org/10.3390/data5040087

Simko, L., Calo, R., Roesner, F., Kohno, T.: COVID-19 contact tracing and privacy: Studying opinion and preferences. arXiv e-prints, 2005.06056 (2020). https://arxiv.org/abs/2005.06056

Stanford Encyclopaedia of Philosophy: Privacy and information technology (2019). https://plato.stanford.edu/entries/it-privacy/. Accessed 31 Aug 2021

Vinuesa, R., Theodorou, A., Battaglini, M., Dignum, V.: A socio-technical framework for digital contact tracing. Results Eng. **8**, 1–4 (2020). https://doi.org/10.1016/j.rineng.2020.100163

WHO: Coronavirus disease (COVID-19): Contact tracing (2020). https://www.who.int/news-room/q-a-detail/coronavirus-disease-covid-19-contact-tracing. Accessed 31 Aug 2021

Zimmermann, B.M., Fiske, A., Prainsack, B., Hangel, N., McLennan, S., Buyx, A.: Early perceptions of COVID-19 contact tracing apps in German-speaking countries: Comparative mixed methods study. J. Med. Internet Res. **23**(2) (2021). https://doi.org/10.2196/25525

User Experience Design for Automatic Credibility Assessment of News Content About COVID-19

Konstantin Schulz[1]([✉])[iD], Jens Rauenbusch[2], Jan Fillies[2], Lisa Rutenburg[2], Dimitrios Karvelas[2], and Georg Rehm[1]

[1] German Research Center for Artificial Intelligence,
Alt-Moabit 91c, 10559 Berlin, Germany
{konstantin.schulz,georg.rehm@}dfki.de
[2] 3pc GmbH Neue Kommunikation, Prinzessinnenstraße 1, 10969 Berlin, Germany
{jfillies,dkarvelas}@3pc.de

Abstract. The increasingly rapid spread of information about COVID-19 on the web calls for automatic measures of credibility assessment [18]. If large parts of the population are expected to act responsibly during a pandemic, they need information that can be trusted [20].

In that context, we model the credibility of texts using 25 linguistic phenomena, such as spelling, sentiment and lexical diversity. We integrate these measures in a graphical interface and present two empirical studies to evaluate its usability for credibility assessment on COVID-19 news. Raw data for the studies, including all questions and responses, has been made available to the public using an open license: https://github.com/konstantinschulz/credible-covid-ux. The user interface prominently features three sub-scores and an aggregation for a quick overview. Besides, metadata about the concept, authorship and infrastructure of the underlying algorithm is provided explicitly.

Our working definition of credibility is operationalized through the terms of trustworthiness, understandability, transparency, and relevance. Each of them builds on well-established scientific notions [41,65,68] and is explained orally or through Likert scales.

In a moderated qualitative interview with six participants, we introduce information transparency for news about COVID-19 as the general goal of a prototypical platform, accessible through an interface in the form of a wireframe [43]. The participants' answers are transcribed in excerpts. Then, we triangulate inductive and deductive coding methods [19] to analyze their content. As a result, we identify rating scale, sub-criteria and algorithm authorship as important predictors of the usability.

In a subsequent quantitative online survey, we present a questionnaire with wireframes to 50 crowdworkers. The question formats include Likert scales, multiple choice and open-ended types. This way, we aim to strike a balance between the known strengths and weaknesses of open vs. closed questions [11]. The answers reveal a conflict between transparency and conciseness in the interface design: Users tend to ask for more information, but do not necessarily make explicit use of it when given. This

G. Meiselwitz et al. (Eds.): HCII 2022, LNCS 13517, pp. 142–165, 2022.
https://doi.org/10.1007/978-3-031-22131-6_11

discrepancy is influenced by capacity constraints of the human working memory [38]. Moreover, a perceived hierarchy of metadata becomes apparent: the authorship of a news text is more important than the authorship of the algorithm used to assess its credibility.

From the first to the second study, we notice an improved usability of the aggregated credibility score's scale. That change is due to the conceptual introduction before seeing the actual interface, as well as the simplified binary indicators with direct visual support. Sub-scores need to be handled similarly if they are supposed to contribute meaningfully to the overall credibility assessment.

By integrating detailed information about the employed algorithm, we are able to dissipate the users' doubts about its anonymity and possible hidden agendas. However, the overall transparency can only be increased if other more important factors, like the source of the news article, are provided as well. Knowledge about this interaction enables software designers to build useful prototypes with a strong focus on the most important elements of credibility: source of text and algorithm, as well as distribution and composition of algorithm.

All in all, the understandability of our interface was rated as acceptable (78% of responses being neutral or positive), while transparency (70%) and relevance (72%) still lag behind. This discrepancy is closely related to the missing article metadata and more meaningful visually supported explanations of credibility sub-scores.

The insights from our studies lead to a better understanding of the amount, sequence and relation of information that needs to be provided in interfaces for credibility assessment. In particular, our integration of software metadata contributes to the more holistic notion of credibility [47,72] that has become popular in recent years. Besides, it paves the way for a more thoroughly informed interaction between humans and machine-generated assessments, anticipating the users' doubts and concerns [39] in early stages of the software design process [37].

Finally, we make suggestions for future research, such as proactively documenting credibility-related metadata for Natural Language Processing and Language Technology services and establishing an explicit hierarchical taxonomy of usability predictors for automatic credibility assessment.

Keywords: Credibility · Usability · COVID-19

1   Introduction

This paper addresses user-centered software design criteria for the automatic assessment of credibility in the COVID-19 domain. We aim in particular to empower citizens in times of a global health crisis, by providing them with relevant, transparent and understandable information about the credibility of news content. Our focus is on the end-user perspective, which is why we will not address the comparison of different credibility measures or the theoretical distinction of closely related terms like misinformation, disinformation, fake news or trustworthiness. Instead, we seek to develop a design that builds a bridge between well-established research methods and the satisfaction of concrete information needs in the context of COVID-19, which is a known problem in the research community [57]. In other words, we are more interested in the usability, rather than the functionality, of automatic credibility assessment (ACA) [32]. As a consequence, one of our research questions will be the following: How do humans perceive an ACA expressed as a percentage and how does that influence their opinion of the text?

Such a formalized analysis in information systems has been on a steady rise since at least the year 2000, e. g., for news and official speeches [18]. However, it is a challenge for many people to distinguish reliably between trustworthy and fake news; they do not reflect critically on the relevant indicators: authorship, primary materials and state of evidence [40]. Instead, they are led astray by mere visual cues of presented content [71]. Their struggle intensifies even more when a distorting political bias in news texts is hidden behind seemingly innocuous category labels in publication organs [31], or when their own partisanship makes them prejudiced about information assessment [57]. Other groups of people, such as healthcare professionals, are more successful in that respect if topics belong to their domain of expertise, like COVID-19; even so, they usually do not make use of scientific arguments to explain their reasoning [3]. As a consequence, our society needs to make high-quality information about critical health issues like COVID-19 more readily available, and help people identify less trustworthy content more easily. Besides, the competent handling of fake news is desirable not only from the perspective of popular education: Expiring domains of fake news websites are often re-registered for criminal purposes, so people returning to their accustomed source of news content are being tricked into various kinds of fraud [9]. The situation gets even more precarious when the general lack of information literacy is combined with a global crisis like COVID-19, leading to an infodemic: rumors and misinformation spread like a disease, making it difficult for people to generate and share reliable knowledge about the existential threat [20]. In extreme cases, this exceptionally strong presence of misinformation can be lethal for many people [46]. There have been proposals for hindering the rapid spread of fake news by applying additional hurdles to the process of information sharing, but they often come at the price of a generally reduced willingness to interact on social platforms [26]. We, therefore, have to consider interventions on the receiving end, which usually do not prevent the curation of content.

In this paper, we first review related work on indicators of credibility, COVID-19 as a domain for credibility assessment and user experience design. We define key terms used in our experimental design, i.e., transparency, understandability, and relevance. Next, we introduce our methodology for ACA and evaluation of two graphical user interfaces. We then present each user interface and its evaluation in detail. Finally, we discuss our findings on automatic credibility assessment, algorithm transparency, understandability, and relevance, and reflect on the methodology.

2   Related Work

2.1   Indicators of Credibility

The perception of credibility is closely related to specific indicators that contribute to the overall impression. Various such signals have been proposed over the years. Some of them are rather universal, such as wording [18], political bias [15], emotional reaction [21] or overly frequent references to single persons, locations or institutions [30]. Others are more domain-specific, such as the cite-worthiness and adequate citation of external content [5]. Furthermore, the quantifications of each indicator range from simple binary values ('Fake or Real') to advanced multi-dimensional evaluation schemes [62]. This points to a lacking consensus about the definition of some credibility-related concepts, e. g., polarity or objectivity [14], leading to inconsistent implementations in practice, sometimes without proper documentation. One important reason for the fuzziness of these conceptualizations is the overlap with other constructs, such as political bias [1] or stance, e. g., with regard to vaccination against COVID-19 [15]. In most cases, this overlap is only partial, which makes many methods effective for assessing one, but not other concepts [18]. Such growing insight into the complexity of credibility assessment has lead to the application of distributed infrastructures [44,52] and entire frameworks like multi-criteria decision making [14,45] or ensemble models [13] to empower people in their daily struggle against unreliable news content. Furthermore, dedicated institutions like Media Bias Fact Check try to establish themselves as authorities to asses the credibility of online news content [18]. In many cases, authority is imposed by referring to a multitude of evidence, which can be expressed by a collection of statements or documents supporting a given claim [27,64], sometimes condensed into a short explanatory summary [4]. Other forms include the aggregation of multiple assessments from independent authorities [49,72]. This preference of holistic, widespread evidence seems to be in line with common detection patterns for disinformation campaigns (such as Astroturfing), focusing on social coordination instead of individual deviation from a given norm of information handling [34,67]. The specific challenge of integrating multiple aspects and measures of credibility in a single working environment [63] will be discussed further in Sect. 2.3.

2.2   COVID-19 as a Domain for Credibility Assessment

Depending on the domain, the broad collection of relevant documents has to be accompanied by a certain depth and specialization: If we want to help people recognize fake news about COVID-19, we need to take their information needs into account. What do they want to know? What do they have to know in order to judge a text's credibility reliably? This is the target of our studies. Previously, researchers have already made efforts to define relevant topics that contribute to a solid general understanding of COVID-19 [54]. This domain-specific approach to models of credibility and knowledge suggests itself because recipients of such content are known to be more critical towards user-generated texts if they refer to the medical domain [55]. Official documents from known authorities such as the government are held in higher esteem. The opposite is true in other domains like tourism: There, people gladly rely on personal experiences and reviews of others that are not tied to specific institutions. Thus, if we want to support individual judgments of content credibility in the COVID-19 domain, we need to provide relevant background information about origin and authorship of a text. As a rule of thumb, we may assume that content distributed through traditional media (newspaper, radio, television) is usually viewed as more credible than texts from the web [55]. The strong focus on this medical subdomain comes at a price: We lose the ability to create models that are robust and reliable in other domains, which has been noted as a general weakness of research on automated credibility assessment in recent years [62]. On the other hand, we face a more limited object of study, enabling us to build more expressive, more fine-grained representations of knowledge, for instance, in the form of ontologies [16,23] and datasets [53,59]. Besides, the reduced model complexity allows for easier automation, which is crucial in times of an ever-increasing distribution speed for newly created content [6]: If users can spread their texts in real time, they also need tools for maintaining credibility standards in real time, which is hard to achieve without a reasonable amount of computerization [47].

2.3 User Experience Design

When assessing a target group's attitudes towards machine-generated credibility scores, it is advisable to do so in the context of their direct interaction with an associated interface [7]. This approach, known as contextual inquiry, offers the benefit of uncovering thoughts that would have gone unnoticed otherwise. Such implicit attitudes are important for judging how well some individuals can satisfy their information needs using that specific interface, which should be seen as the main goal instead of just providing any frontend layer for a given credibility algorithm [22]. Ultimately, the outcome of such endeavors should be a service that is provided to the community, not just a software or its source code [28] as required by a number of theoretical user stories [10,33,61,69]. For end users to profit from such a service, it is imperative for them to be involved throughout the design process, thereby becoming software designers themselves [33]. As a side benefit, the early integration of their feedback and ideas enables the team to react to unforeseen challenges quickly and effectively [37]. The same goes for software developers: By participating in the design process from the very beginning, they contribute to a cross-functional team that considers problems from multiple perspectives [35], continuing the holistic approach to credibility research outlined in Sect. 2.1. However, the integration of user experience (UX) design and development work does not necessarily lead to a more streamlined process. Instead, research suggests that designers should usually be 'one sprint ahead' of other teams in an agile environment [35,48], enabling the early anticipation of possible challenges in user interaction. Accordingly, our backend development team used mock objects [58] to quickly provide Application Programming Interface (API) prototypes while the actual processing logic for ACA was not yet available. When evaluating a given prototype, the tasks and interactions of the chosen users should correspond closely to their everyday behavior, making the study's findings more generalizable [39]. We argue that this kind of environment is more closely emulated by our remote studies where participants use their own electronic devices (see Sect. 3), rather than in artificial laboratory settings.

2.4 Key Definitions

For a common understanding and evaluation of the results we are defining the key terms used in our experimental design. This lays the foundation for the evaluation of the responses. The definition of transparency has been evolving for many years [41]. In our understanding, we follow Michener and Bersch [41] who state that transparency is less a theoretical gathering point and rather a descriptive term focusing around state or quality of information. Furthermore, they define that when evaluating transparency, it is sufficient to consider two conditions: visibility and inferability [41]. Understandability can be defined in many ways [25]. We are following the definition of Tu, Tempero and Thomborson as the degree to which information can be comprehended with prior knowledge [66]. Relevance has no consensus for a general definition [29]. The underlying problem is that relevance is a temporal and fluid concept that is perceived at a specific moment by a specific user [29]. We are aware of this challenging definition process, but decided to follow Tu, Tempero and Thomborson and define the term within this study as the degree to which the information obtained by stakeholders answers their questions [66].

3   Methodology

Our algorithm for ACA, called Credibility Score Service, is based on the Credibility Signals[1] published by the W3C Credible Web Community Group[2]. It focuses on the content level and includes linguistic features such as orthography, vocabulary and syntax. Thus, the algorithm does not consider other aspects of credibility such as authorship or distribution platforms, which should be integrated in a separate step as part of future research. The single features are weighted differently and together form a single final score. These decisions are visible in the publicly released source code[3] and explained in the documentation[4], using open licenses for easy reuse. Additionally, we offer Docker images[5] for enhanced reproducibility and compatibility with various platforms. Finally, we integrated a running instance[6] of the software into the European Language

---

[1] https://credweb.org/signals-20191126.
[2] https://www.w3.org/community/credibility/.
[3] https://github.com/konstantinschulz/alpaca.
[4] https://alpaca-credibility.readthedocs.io/en/latest/credibility_signals.html.
[5] https://hub.docker.com/r/konstantinschulz/credibility-score-service.
[6] https://live.european-language-grid.eu/catalogue/tool-service/7348.

Grid[7] [50,51], a European platform for language technologies. This integration has multiple implications: First of all, it is open and free, which enables us to provide our backend software as a service to not just the design team, but anyone interested in ACA. Thus, the service stays available in a long-term infrastructure, even though the algorithm has originally been developed for the purposes of a time-limited research project, which is a notorious problem in the research community [24]. Second, the European Language Grid applies its own metadata management to each of its resources, thereby making them more findable in repositories and, as a consequence, more accessible to a broader public [36]. Finally, we hypothesize that the involvement of the European Language Grid influences the usability of our credibility service: the location of the servers and, accordingly, the applicability of European laws on data protection (such as General Data Protection Regulation, widely known as GDPR) can be important factors for some people when evaluating credibility-related software.

In a human-centered design approach, we developed two graphical user interfaces (GUIs) to visualize results of the Credibility Score Service and receive feedback from potential users. Due to our focus on UX, the limited time frames and budget constraints, we chose to conduct multiple small studies rather than a single larger one. Thus, we were able to evaluate the GUIs in two successive studies and simultaneously make adjustments to the designs. Therefore, the findings from the first survey had an immediate impact on the development of the second GUI. In the following, the design iterations will be referred to as GUI prototypes 1 and 2.

First, we performed a qualitative evaluation of the GUI prototype 1 by conducting a moderated UX study, which took place remotely with a small number of participants. The aim of this assessment was to gain broad understanding of users' expectations and preferences regarding an online platform aimed at providing information transparency in the context of COVID-19. The evaluation was performed as a formative usability study, i.e., it focused on identifying usability problems [60], as well as an overall assessment of the platform concept. Usability was assessed with regard to interaction design (e.g., conforming to GUI conventions), navigation (e.g., orientation), visual design (e.g., affordance of GUI elements), and wording (e.g., user interface copy). The qualitative study consisted of preliminary interviews during which participants are asked about their information-seeking behavior during the pandemic, of a clickable prototype with which the participants perform tasks given by a moderator, and of a short questionnaire they receive after interacting with the prototype. Using a moderated guidance is known to have a positive effect on the overall evaluation of design prototypes [43]. Throughout the study, participants were encouraged to think aloud. According to Nielsen (1994) [42], a small sample size of four to five participants is sufficient to discover the majority of usability issues in a thinking aloud test. Each of these moderated studies was also simultaneously observed and documented by a second researcher. A description of the prototype can be found in Sect. 4.

---

[7] https://www.european-language-grid.eu/.

GUI prototype 2 was created after interpreting the findings to address short-comings of the design, particularly in the realm of information credibility display and interaction. We conducted a remote non-moderated UX survey with a large group of participants to perform quantitative and qualitative evaluation of GUI prototype 2. The aim of the survey was to evaluate the design choices regarding the display of the Credibility Score and the users' interaction with it. There-fore, we decided to remove other typical sources of credibility assessment, such as textual authorship. We acknowledge that this leads to an incomplete under-standing of credibility; nevertheless, we wanted the users to focus specifically on the content-related elements that were covered by the Credibility Score.

The study was evaluated as a summative usability study, i.e., it focused on measurements via a survey [60], and overfulfilled the recommendations (see Budiu and Moran (2021) [8] following Sauro and Lewis (2016) [60]) of a general sample size of 40 participants for quantitative usability studies. To assess the design choices of the Credibility Score, two key aspects were identified accord-ing to the research literature: the origin (e.g., intellectual development) and the visual representation of the score (e.g., as a scale). The study consists of non-moderated qualitative and non-moderated quantitative parts. Firstly, an under-standing of the users' perspective is formed by assessing information-seeking behavior, followed by a short evaluation of the participants' general credibility requirements. After that, an enhanced GUI prototype is presented, along with questions to assess the identified key objectives. All stages use a mix of Likert scales, sliders, open-ended questions and multiple choice questions.

4   Experiments

4.1   Moderated Remote User Experience Study (GUI Prototype 1)

Experiment Setup and Overview of Participants. We performed a moder-ated remote UX study in July 2021 via video conferencing software and an inter-active, web-based prototyping tool. The study was facilitated by a moderator and documented by an observer, who created protocols containing observations and direct quotes from participants. Protocols[8] were anonymized and manually coded using a hybrid approach of inductive and deductive coding [19]. They will be referred to using a short form (e.g., P02, Pos. 61 for participant 2, protocol Sect. 61[9]). The study was conducted in German with six participants living in Germany, of various professional backgrounds (incl. consulting, education, IT, arts, professional services) and across a relatively broad age spectrum from 16 to 69 years (median: 29.5 years). Participants were briefly introduced to the GUI, which was described as a new digital platform for information transparency in

---

[8] https://github.com/konstantinschulz/credible-covid-ux/tree/main/1st-usability-study.

[9] See the file '210702_Panqura_Testdesign_P02.pdf' at https://github.com/konstantins chulz/credible-covid-ux/blob/main/1st-usability-study/210702_Panqura_Testdesign _P02.pdf.

times of crisis, particularly in the context of the COVID-19 pandemic. Users were asked to imagine searching for information on the subject of COVID-19 pandemic and vaccines, coming across this information platform which claims to contain up-to-date and transparent information about the subject. It should be noted that in an early stage of the project, the term *trustworthiness* (German: *Vertrauenswürdigkeit*) was used. It was chosen to qualify the relationship between the user and the platform. In prototype 2, it was changed to the broader term *credibility* (German: *Glaubwürdigkeit*) as the focus of the design was expanded to include aspects of authorship and responsibility. However, these terms are closely linked [3,68] and we believe that results from the first study can still be used to inform iterations of the GUI prototype.

 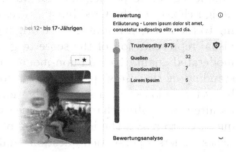

Fig. 1. Section of the landing page in the GUI for prototype 1.

Fig. 2. Section of the content view in the GUI for prototype 1.

  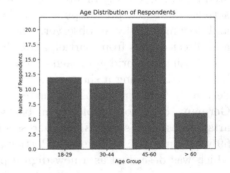

Fig. 3. Credibility score focused extract of GUI from prototype 2.

Fig. 4. Study 2: age distribution of respondents, aggregated to age groups.

Information-seeking Behavior During COVID-19. During preliminary interviews[10], most participants stated that they often seek information about the COVID-19 pandemic, i. e., daily or several times a day, and mostly do so using social networks, conversations with friends and family, digital news outlets, and public broadcasts (Fig. 5). Participants described these sources as informative, factual, critical, and transparent. They stated that relevant, factual information from transparent and reliable sources were either accessible or very accessible. Participants were mostly concerned with finding insights about current research on COVID-19, current general regulations, political issues, and travel information. Most participants stated that currentness and regionality of information are relevant or very relevant.

Description of GUI Prototype 1. Participants reviewed three screens, i. e., sections of the platform. The prototype enabled them to experience a common interaction flow from a landing page[11] (dashboard view, see Fig. 1) to a list of articles on a specific subject (search view) and a detailed display of one specific article (content view, see Fig. 2). The dashboard view showed a navigation area (containing the platform's logo and a menu) and three sections on COVID-19-related topics: vaccination, travel regulations, and restrictions in Germany. Each section contained several teasers of news articles which contained article data (image, headline, source, publication date) and additional, analytical information (vertical grey scale visualization indicating an article's trustworthiness, labels representing topics covered by the article). First, users were shown that they could click on the headlines' sections to see more content. Second, users could hover over the grey scale visualization to see a popup with a trustworthiness score, several sub-scores, and a verification icon. By clicking on the headline "COVID-19 Vaccination", participants entered the search view. It contained a prominent headline indicating the topic, a search bar above the headline to filter the results, and a list of search results including an option to change sorting order and a display of the total number of articles. The individual entries, i. e., search results, consisted of the same information as the teasers; however, they did not contain images or a trustworthiness score. The GUI also included a sidebar at the right edge of the screen containing various filters. By clicking on the first search result, participants entered the content view, where they could see the news article in full length, including a headline, subhead, an image, and metadata including source, author, and publication date. Additionally, a sidebar at the right edge of the screen displayed the trustworthiness score and sub-scores, an overview table containing metadata on the article, topics, named entities, and placeholders for further analyses. Within the article body itself, several sentences were highlighted in different colors as placeholder visualizations for further analyses.

---

[10] https://github.com/konstantinschulz/credible-covid-ux/blob/main/1st-usability-study/interview_data.csv.
[11] https://invis.io/WQ11VVW8A79S#/454763090_Landingpage.

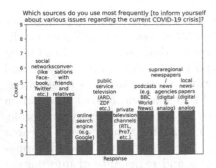

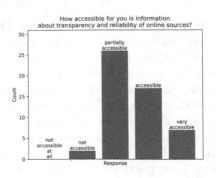

Fig. 5. Study 1: response options and counts for the sources used to inform oneself about COVID-19.

Fig. 6. Study 2: response options and counts for the accessibility of information about online sources.

Automatic Credibility Assessment. With regards to ACA, participants were mostly concerned about the source and the scale or interpretation of the credibility score (labeled as *trustworthiness*) while completing tasks regarding GUI prototype 1. Participants repeatedly questioned the source of the automatic assessment. For example, they asked: "Where does the trustworthiness score come from?" (P05, Pos. 61), "How did [the score] come about?" (P04, Pos. 14), and "Who says that this [news article] is trustworthy?" (P05, Pos. 14). Prior to learning more about the automatic assessment, one participant voiced the assumption that the team running the platform evaluates the news articles and performs fact-checking manually (P02, Pos. 61). After participants were told that an algorithm automatically assesses trustworthiness, they stated that this information should be made transparent (P03, Pos. 101) and that, nevertheless, they still do not understand how decisions are made by the system (P06, Pos. 78). Regarding the trustworthiness score itself (including sub-scores such as emotionality), most participants did not understand the scale or how to interpret it. They stated that "the scale is non-transparent" (P03, Pos. 80) and asked "What is emotionality?" (P06, Pos. 15) or "What does number 7 mean? [Is this the number of] parts which contain emotionality?" (P01, Pos. 63). However, some participants stated that they find the scale helpful (P05, Pos. 53) or that they would read an article with a low score plainly out of interest and curiosity (P06, Pos. 69). When asked whether a trustworthiness score would influence their own assessment of an article, participants' responses were mixed. Some expressed firm belief that such a score would not influence their opinion (P06, Pos. 70) and they would only trust it as much as they would understand it (P05, Pos. 62). Others expected that a score would indeed influence their opinion and assessment of an article (P01, Pos. 68; P02, Pos. 67). Participants frequently stumbled over the visualization of the trustworthiness score, for instance, asking whether they are supposed to click on the mark indicating the score along a grey scale visualization (P02, Pos. 15). Furthermore, the verification symbol was associated with verified accounts in popular social networks (P03, Pos. 26). The GUI led some participants to believe that the news article had been thoroughly checked for facts (P04, Pos. 54), while others stated that they would rather use their own knowledge of online sources to assess its trustworthiness (P06, Pos. 39).

Overall Evaluation of the Prototype. For an overall evaluation of the prototype, participants were asked to rate it in three dimensions using a Likert scale after completing the tasks. Responses were summarized and counted where applicable. The entire platform's **understandability** was rated as understandable to very understandable and its **relevance** was rated as relevant to very relevant. The platform's **transparency** was mostly found to be partly transparent (3x). Other participants rated it as non-transparent (1x), transparent (1x) or very transparent (1x; see the various PDF files).

4.2   Remote User Experience Survey (GUI Prototype 2)

Experiment Setup and Overview of Participants. We performed a summative usability study in October 2021. In order to generate, publish and find a fitting target group, we used the commercial online platform SurveyMonkey[12] and piloted our questionnaire internally. The provided data was anonymously collected. The target audience was compensated and clearly informed about the survey conditions (e. g., time frame, success criteria, context). The payment for the participants seemed to be higher than the legal minimum wage, but the exact amount was kept hidden by the survey platform. There was no possibility to interact with the participants during or after the survey. The survey itself was conducted in German. In total, 52 people living in Germany participated in the survey, 50 of which completed the questionnaire. Participants were recruited via the survey platform across all income levels and equally distributed across two genders (female: 25x; male: 25x; the platform did not allow screening for other genders). The rather high age of participants (see Fig. 4) may have induced significant demographic bias [56] regarding negative attitudes towards artificial intelligence and, thus, ACA [17]. No person below 18 years participated due to legal constraints by the platform.

Information-seeking Behavior During COVID-19. Participants were first asked about their information-seeking behavior during COVID-19. The findings are mostly in line with the qualitative study conducted earlier. Regarding sources of information on the COVID-19 pandemic, most of the participants stated that they use public television (which may also include consumption of this content via the internet), social networks and search engines. Similarly to the first study, participants described these sources as informative, factual, critical, and transparent (the less popular choices being: alternative, creative, inviting). One participant added "convenient"[13] as an answer. This illustrates that our curated

---

[12] https://www.surveymonkey.de.

[13] https://github.com/konstantinschulz/credible-covid-ux/blob/main/2nd-usability-study/survey_data.csv#L26.

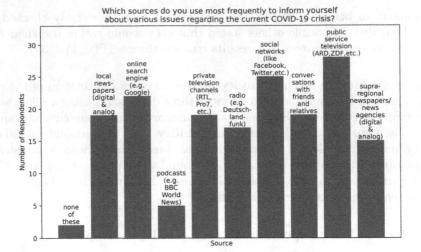

Fig. 7. Study 2: response options and counts for the sources used to inform oneself about COVID-19.

list of adjectives was successfully geared towards credibility and in line with our research focus. Participants were then asked how accessible they find information about transparency and reliability of online sources. While one half stated it to be only partly accessible, the other half opted for accessible or very accessible, with few exceptions (see Fig. 6). The answers are probably influenced by central tendency bias, i.e., a disproportionately high probability of choosing the medium value in surveys with scalar response options [12]. Nevertheless, there is still an indication that most people perceived the information as rather accessible.

Description of GUI Prototype 2. GUI prototype 2 (see Fig. 3) focused on the credibility score only, thus excluding other sections of the application. It contained an insinuated excerpt of a news article (allowing for larger display of the GUI) and a new section on the right-hand side entitled *Credibility Score*. The new GUI consisted of a fictitious overall score in percent, set to 83%, and a prominent binary display of credibility classification (credible/incredible), which was set to *credible*. We chose to work with a fictitious score rather than the real algorithm to present users with a potential dissonance between the article's content, which could be identified as fake news by some readers, and a relatively high credibility score to assess the effect of the score on the users. The news article will be introduced in the next section. Below the overall score, three exemplary credibility components (grammar, broad vocabulary, emotionality) were displayed with fictitious sub-scores in percentage terms, with the option to view the full list of components with their sub-scores. We chose these sub-scores with the expectation that they can be understood rather intuitively without additional information, as the static nature of the prototype did not allow users to interact with the help icon next to the scores. Furthermore, an overview of authors responsible for creating the score was added, separated into *infrastructure* ("European Language Grid (ELG), Location of Server: Europe"), *implementation* ("German Research Center for Artificial Intelligence (DFKI)"), and *conceptual framework* ("scientific community"). Additionally, the GUI contained elements which suggested that users could receive more information on the overall score and sub-scores. No further metadata about the text (such as author, source, publishing date) was added to the GUI. This choice was made to examine users' perception of the relationship between visual display of the ACA and article content, which the ACA is based on.

Credibility Assessment Criteria. Participants were introduced to a short news article (see Appendix A). Then, they were asked to rate the article's credibility and answer related questions. Our goal was to understand their approach to credibility assessment and introduce them to the topic. The article was an edited version of a longer news article by a German news paper[14]. It was chosen due to its content, which we expected might be considered fake news by some users. The article consisted of a headline, a subheading, a photo, and three paragraphs of text. No further information (such as author, source or date) was given, as motivated above. Participants rated the article's credibility on a scale from 0% (not credible at all) to 100% (completely credible). Ratings varied from 19.5% (1st quartile) to 66% (3rd quartile), the median was 49%, confirming our expectations that its credibility appeared mixed. Participants repeatedly mentioned that they mostly consider information about the source, the content itself, and the text's spelling or writing style. Similarly, participants stated that they require more information about the source or author to assess credibility.

Evaluation of the New Credibility Score GUI. To assess participants' understanding of the score scale (percentage), they were asked to select an interpretation they believed to be correct. Most participants stated that the credibility score (83%) should be interpreted as credible or very credible (43%). Almost equally many participants stated it should be interpreted as partly credible (40%), which may also be a result of the central tendency bias. Only 17% stated it should be interpreted as (very) incredible. We have to take into account that question 4^{15}, in which participants were asked to assess the article's credibility, had already introduced the scale and likely influenced its interpretation by the participants. Furthermore, to evaluate participants' understanding of the score's source, they were asked to state who they believed to be the originator of the credibility score. Some participants stated that they did not know who created the score. However, a pattern emerged in which most participants mentioned the three organizations shown in the lower section of the GUI, particularly the organization mentioned under the heading *implementation*, i.e.,

---

[14] See https://www.spiegel.de/wirtschaft/soziales/post-corona-programm-jugendliche-in-spanien-bekommen-kulturgutscheine-a-d768b360-22dc-473d-afbe-abde5a344482.

[15] See   https://github.com/konstantinschulz/credible-covid-ux/blob/main/2nd-usability-study/Data_All_211020-broad-audience.pdf, p. 5.

German Research Center for Artificial Intelligence. The question likely directed participants' attention towards the source, which they might not have noted otherwise. Participants were asked to rate GUI prototype 2 using a Likert scale in the same three dimensions used to assess prototype 1. However, the questions were phrased slightly differently in both studies. Besides, the second study was focused on the credibility score, whereas the first study contained the entire application, including sections which may not be directly related to credibility.

Table 1. How understandable (u.) is the prototype?

	Not u. at all	Not u.	Partially u.	Quite u.	Very u.
Responses	3	8	21	17	1

Table 2. How relevant (r.) is the prototype?

	Not r. at all	Not r.	Partially r.	Quite r.	Very r.
Responses	5	9	23	10	3

Table 3. How transparent (t.) is the prototype?

	Not t. at all	Not t.	Partially t.	Quite t.	Very t.
Responses	2	13	23	11	1

The new prototype was mostly perceived as partly **understandable**, with a tendency towards understandable (see Table 1). It was rated as neither extremely **relevant** nor irrelevant (see Table 2). Similarly, the new prototype was rated as partly **transparent** with a slight tendency towards non-transparent (see Table 3 and questions 7–9). When asked whether the credibility score (83%) influenced their own assessment of the news article's credibility (median of 49%), most participants claimed to be uninfluenced. Among the other answers, a slight tendency towards higher credibility (as opposed to lower credibility) was visible (see question 10). Finally, participants were asked to add any further comments or questions. Some participants stated that they still do not know how exactly the score was calculated ("there should be a better explanation for non-professionals how the score is calculated"). One participant stated regarding the sub-scores that "correct grammar does not reveal anything [about credibility]". Apart from this comment, sub-scores were not mentioned by the participants.

5   Results and Discussion

5.1   Automatic Credibility Assessment

Participants' understanding of the credibility score's scale apparently improved through design iterations. In the first study, participants had many questions about how to interpret the scale of the main score, while in the second study, there were few to no questions. Furthermore, participants' answers on how to interpret the scale in the second study showed a tendency towards our intended interpretation, even though there were still some deviations (besides the central tendency bias). Possible explanations include our improved indicators of whether a score should be interpreted as credible or incredible, using a binary display of these categories. Besides, participants in the second study rated the article's credibility before viewing the score, thereby being introduced to the scale. Furthermore, participants of the second study barely mentioned the sub-scores, whereas the first prototype raised many questions in this regard. This may be due to design improvements or changes in the experimental setup, or both. The sub-scores in the second prototype have more specific, understandable wording and consistent percentages, which may have caused less irritation among participants. At the same time, these changes did not improve the overall perceived transparency of our ACA. We infer that a simplified textual display of the score's meaning (i. e., a relationship between the percentage and terms credible/incredible) helps users comprehend the scale and should also be considered for other services which return a numerical value. Furthermore, manually completing the assessment once before interacting with ACA may help users understand (and critically reflect on) ACA. Future research may also specifically focus on perception and understanding of sub-scores, which play a crucial role in the conceptualization of the main score, and may be conducted via, e. g., eye tracking.

5.2   Algorithm Transparency, Understandability, and Relevance

In the first study, participants repeatedly asked about the source of the ACA (missing in the GUI). In response, the iterated prototype pointed participants of the second survey explicitly towards an elaborate display of the algorithm's source. Still, many participants stated that they did not know who created the score and the changes did not improve overall transparency, understandability, or relevance. Nevertheless, our qualitative analysis of free text comments reveals that participants were much more upset about the missing article source. This leads to the hypothesis that the source of content is more important than the source of ACA or that users are accustomed to interfaces in which text authorship is clearly indicated. Further research is needed concerning the effect of authorship information on users' perception of the text. In other words, there may be a stage-gate process of assessing credibility, where users first require several pieces of basic information (such as source and author of the content) before considering ACA. A significant share of participants, however, directly referred to the GUI for the source of the ACA. Among them, some participants stated all three organizations, while others only stated one or two or paraphrased the source. The organization responsible for algorithm implementation was mentioned more often than those responsible for infrastructure or conceptual foundations. Users seem to attribute the highest responsibility to the implementation, perhaps due to association of the term *implementation* with artificial intelligence, or computers in general. Or maybe all three terms (infrastructure, implementation, conceptual foundations) were too vague for users to make informed statements about the source, leading them to pick the entity which is perceived as the most scientific or authoritative. Overall, participants in both studies asked for more contextual information on both content and algorithm. This is a common theme in UX studies: Users request more written explanations in the GUI, for instance via help buttons and popup windows. However, field studies and eye tracking often reveal that users ignore additional information such as long UX copy. There is a general trade-off in the GUI between informativity or transparency on the one side, and conciseness, clarity, and ease of use on the other. A carefully constructed balance is needed to provide ACA to users effectively. Our findings are helpful, but strongly indicate that our designs have not yet achieved the desired trade-off.

5.3   Reflections on Methodology

We noticed a strong central tendency bias in many of the answers. This effect intensifies even more for questions with a high cognitive load [2], as was evident in our inquiries about understandability, relevance and transparency. Furthermore, participants' ratings of the GUI slightly worsened in the dimensions of understandability and relevance. While this may be attributed to changes in the design, there are several indicators that these declines are rather based on a change of methodology. First, the remote UX study was performed as a qualitative and moderated assessment in which participants engaged in face-to-face conversations with researchers. This may lead to more positive (or less harsh) responses due to social desirability bias [70]. Second, the subject of evaluation changed throughout the studies. In the first study, participants were asked to rate the overall prototype, including sections which were not related to ACA. In the second study, they were asked to specifically rate the credibility score GUI. As mentioned previously, this research took an iterative, agile approach in which several smaller studies with less preparation time and budget were conducted, as opposed to one larger study. Therefore, the design of both studies likely influenced the results in various ways that need to be considered when interpreting the findings. For example, viewing the rather high score of the ACA in the second study after manually assessing credibility of the article may have led some participants to state that the score increased their perceived credibility of the article. We did not evaluate whether a different order of questions or a lower score in the GUI (i. e., lower than 49%) would have reversed this effect.

In our experiments, we only used one COVID-19-related news article as an example, as opposed to multiple texts, in order to keep results comparable and the survey as short as possible, maximizing the number of participants obtainable for a fixed budget. Our findings are nevertheless valid, as described above.

6   Conclusion

All in all, participants of the second study seemed ambivalent about the article's credibility, which did not have any contextual information but could only be judged based on the content. Adding the ACA did not significantly change their perception. Since the score was generally interpreted according to our intentions, the assumption is that either users heavily rely on contextual information (metadata such as author, source, publishing date) to assess credibility and noted its absence in the GUI; or the score is lacking information which makes it transparent - or both. Regarding the latter, adding information about the creators of the score did not bring the desired effect of adding transparency and users still had questions. As a takeaway, more attention should be paid to providing metadata for the content, as well as general benchmarks for average credibility in the COVID-19 news domain. In some cases, participants admitted to being influenced by the given credibility score. Others denied it, criticizing the underlying criteria and questioning the authority of the people and institutions behind the algorithm. This shows that automatic assessments can provide helpful guidance for end users, but only if they agree with the conceptual basis of the measurements and if they trust the providers of the score. Unfortunately, authorship in terms of software as a service is a fuzzy concept for many people: Some cite the scientific community, others the software developers, still others refer to the server infrastructure while trying to attribute responsibility for a given calculated result. For most people, the source of an algorithm is less important than the authorship of the actual text when it comes to ultimately deciding on its credibility. This puts our efforts to make computational models more explainable into a different perspective: In the future, we should aim to establish a hierarchy of desirable information for assessing content credibility in the health domain.

Further, we want to adapt the Credibility Score Service according to our insights from the described studies. In particular, since the transparency and understandability of the score and its components did not reach a sufficient level, the API needs to be modified. Instead of just providing a label and a value for each component, it should also include short descriptions in its metadata (or in responses to invocations), briefly explaining the computation and meaning of each part of the score. Besides, due to the continuing demand for information about origin and authorship, the service should be associated with metadata about its development and infrastructure:

- Who invented the concept of ACA?
- Who implemented this particular credibility measure?
- Who runs this service and where are the servers located? Which data protection laws apply?

Finally, we are aiming to expand the basis of the Credibility Score Service by integrating and evaluating information about content authorship, dissemination platforms, coordination patterns and external fact-checking platforms.

Acknowledgements. The research presented in this paper is funded by the German Federal Ministry of Education and Research (BMBF) through the project PANQURA (http://qurator.ai/panqura; grant no. 03COV03E).

We are grateful to Yuewen Röder (3pc GmbH Neue Kommunikation, Germany) for assisting in the research; to León Viktor Avilés Podgurski for his research on and implementation of credibility signals.

A   Newspaper Article (Translation)

Spanish youths receive cultural vouchers

The culture industry around the world suffered from the corona pandemic. In Spain, young people now receive EUR 400 vouchers to take advantage of cultural offers - but one type of event is excluded.

To cushion the hardships of the corona pandemic, young people in Spain receive a cultural voucher . Everyone who will turn 18 next year should receive a voucher worth 400 euros from the government. But it cannot be used indefinitely: the recipients cannot buy tickets for bullfights with it.

The decision was one of the politically controversial measures the government included in the 2022 draft state budget. The vouchers are intended to help the country's culture and events industry recover from the loss of income during the corona lockdowns. According to the government, eligible teenagers can spend their 400 euros on cinema and theater tickets, books and concerts, for example.

The Ministry of Culture announced in a written communication to the state news agency Efe that "not everything that our legislation regards as culture will fall under this cultural support." Bullfighting is now rejected by a large part of Spanish society, especially young city dwellers.

B   Questions from the Online Survey (Study 2)

1. Which sources do you use most frequently to inform yourself about various issues regarding the current COVID-19 crisis?
2. Which 3 attributes describe your chosen sources best?
3. How accessible for you is information about transparency and reliability of online sources?
4. How credible is that article for you?
5. Which aspects do you consider most important when assessing credibility?
6. What further information would you like to obtain in order to better assess the article's credibility?
7. How understandable is the information on the right side?
8. How relevant is the information on the right side?
9. How transparent is the information on the right side?

10. Which influence does the information on the right side have on your assessment of the article?
11. How do you interpret the meaning of the percentage (83%)?
12. Who created the credibility score?
13. Which information do you lack with regard to the credibility score? Do you have any open questions or comments?

References

1. Aksenov, D., Bourgonje, P., Zaczynska, K., Ostendorff, M., Moreno-Schneider, J., Rehm, G.: Fine-grained classification of political bias in german news: a data set and initial experiments. In: Mostafazadeh Davani, A., Kiela, D., Lambert, M., Vidgen, B., Prabhakaran, V., Waseem, Z. (eds.) Proceedings of the 5th Workshop on Online Abuse and Harms (WOAH 2021), pp. 121–131. Association for Computational Linguistics (ACL), Bangkok, Thailand (8 2021), 1–6 Aug 2021, co-located with ACL-IJCNLP (2021)
2. Allred, S.R., Crawford, L.E., Duffy, S., Smith, J.: Working memory and spatial judgments: cognitive load increases the central tendency bias. Psychon. Bull. Rev. **23**(6), 1825–1831 (2016). https://doi.org/10.3758/s13423-016-1039-0
3. Amit Aharon, A., Ruban, A., Dubovi, I.: Knowledge and information credibility evaluation strategies regarding COVID-19: a cross-sectional study. Nurs. Outlook **69**(1), 22–31 (2021)
4. Atanasova, P., Simonsen, J.G., Lioma, C., Augenstein, I.: Generating fact checking explanations. In: Proceedings of the 58th Annual Meeting of the Association for Computational Linguistics, pp. 7352–7364. Association for Computational Linguistics (2020). https://doi.org/10.18653/v1/2020.acl-main.656
5. Augenstein, I.: Determining the credibility of science communication. In: Proceedings of the Second Workshop on Scholarly Document Processing, pp. 1–6. Association for Computational Linguistics (2021)
6. Bannon, L.J., Ehn, P.: Design matters in participatory design. In: Simonsen, J., Robertson, T. (eds.) Routledge International Handbook of Participatory Design, vol. 711, pp. 37–63. Routledge, London & New York (2013)
7. Berndt, E., Furniss, D., Blandford, A.: Learning Contextual Inquiry and Distributed Cognition: a case study on technology use in Anaesthesia. Cogn. Technol. Work **17**(3), 431–449 (2015)
8. Budiu, R., Moran, K.: How many participants for quantitative usability studies: a summary of sample-size recommendations (2021). www.nngroup.com/articles/summary-quant-sample-sizes/
9. Chen, Z., Freire, J.: Discovering and measuring malicious URL redirection campaigns from fake news domains. In: 2021 IEEE Security and Privacy Workshops (SPW), pp. 1–6. IEEE, San Francisco (2021)
10. Cohn, M.: succeeding with agile: software development using scrum. Pearson Education, Ann Arbor (2010)
11. Connor Desai, S., Reimers, S.: Comparing the use of open and closed questions for Web-based measures of the continued-influence effect. Behav. Res. Methods **51**(3), 1426–1440 (2018). https://doi.org/10.3758/s13428-018-1066-z
12. Crosetto, P., Filippin, A., Katuščák, P., Smith, J.: Central tendency bias in belief elicitation. J. Econ. Psychol. **78**, 102273 (2020)

13. Das, S.D., Basak, A., Dutta, S.: A heuristic-driven ensemble framework for COVID-19 fake news detection. In: Chakraborty, T., Shu, K., Bernard, H.R., Liu, H., Akhtar, M.S. (eds.) CONSTRAINT 2021. CCIS, vol. 1402, pp. 164–176. Springer, Cham (2021). https://doi.org/10.1007/978-3-030-73696-5_16
14. De Grandis, M., Pasi, G., Viviani, M.: Multi-criteria decision making and supervised learning for fake news detection in microblogging. In: Workshop on Reducing Online Misinformation Exposure, pp. 1–8. ACM, Paris, France (2019)
15. DeVerna, M.R., et al.: CoVaxxy: a collection of english-language Twitter posts about COVID-19 vaccines. In: Proceedings of the Fifteenth International AAAI Conference on Web and Social Media (ICWSM 2021), pp. 992–999. AAAI, Virtual (2021)
16. Dutta, B., DeBellis, M.: CODO: an ontology for collection and analysis of COVID-19 data. In: Proceedings of the 12th International Joint Conference on Knowledge Discovery, Knowledge Engineering and Knowledge Management, pp. 76–85. SCITEPRESS - Science and Technology Publications, Budapest, Hungary (2020). https://doi.org/10.5220/0010112500760085
17. Elias, S.M., Smith, W.L., Barney, C.E.: Age as a moderator of attitude towards technology in the workplace: work motivation and overall job satisfaction. Behav. Inf. Technol. **31**(5), 453–467 (2012)
18. Fairbanks, J., Fitch, N., Knauf, N., Briscoe, E.: Credibility assessment in the news: do we need to read? In: Proceedings of the MIS2 Workshop Held in Conjunction with 11th International Conference on Web Search and Data Mining, pp. 1–8. ACM, Marina Del Rey (2018)
19. Fereday, J., Muir-Cochrane, E.: Demonstrating rigor using thematic analysis: a hybrid approach of inductive and deductive coding and theme development. Int. J. Qual. Methods **5**(1), 80–92 (2006)
20. Gallotti, R., Valle, F., Castaldo, N., Sacco, P., De Domenico, M.: Assessing the risks of 'infodemics' in response to COVID-19 epidemics. Nat. Hum. Behav. **4**(12), 1285–1293 (2020)
21. Giachanou, A., Rosso, P., Crestani, F.: The impact of emotional signals on credibility assessment. J. Am. Soc. Inf. Sci. **72**(9), 1117–1132 (2021). https://doi.org/10.1002/asi.24480
22. Gothelf, J., Seiden, J.: Lean UX: designing great products with agile teams. O'Reilly Media Inc, Sebastopol (2016)
23. He, Y., et al.: CIDO, a community-based ontology for coronavirus disease knowledge and data integration, sharing, and analysis. Scientific Data **7**(1), 181 (2020)
24. Hettrick, S.: Research software sustainability: report on a knowledge exchange workshop. Tech. rep, The Software Sustainability Institute (2016)
25. Houy, C., Fettke, P., Loos, P.: Understanding understandability of conceptual models-what are we actually talking about? In: Atzeni, P., Cheung, D., Ram, S. (eds.) ER 2012. LNCS, vol. 7532, pp. 64–77. Springer, Heidelberg (2012). https://doi.org/10.1007/978-3-642-34002-4_5
26. Jahanbakhsh, F., Zhang, A.X., Berinsky, A.J., Pennycook, G., Rand, D.G., Karger, D.R.: Exploring lightweight interventions at posting time to reduce the sharing of misinformation on social media. In: Proceedings of the ACM on Human-Computer Interaction 5(CSCW1), pp. 1–42 (2021)
27. Jiang, Y., Bordia, S., Zhong, Z., Dognin, C., Singh, M., Bansal, M.: HoVer: a dataset for many-hop fact extraction and claim verification. In: Findings of the Association for Computational Linguistics: EMNLP 2020, pp. 3441–3460. Association for Computational Linguistics, Online (2020). https://doi.org/10.18653/v1/2020.findings-emnlp.309

28. Jureta, I.J., Herssens, C., Faulkner, S.: A comprehensive quality model for service-oriented systems. Software Qual. J. **17**(1), 65–98 (2009)
29. Kagolovsky, Y., Möhr, J.R.: A new approach to the concept of "relevance" in information retrieval (IR). In: MEDINFO 2001, pp. 348–352. IOS Press, Amsterdam (2001)
30. Kakol, M., Nielek, R., Wierzbicki, A.: Understanding and predicting Web content credibility using the Content Credibility Corpus. Inf. Process. Manage. **53**(5), 1043–1061 (2017)
31. Kang, H., Yang, J.: Quantifying perceived political bias of newspapers through a document classification technique. J. Quant. Linguist. Ahead-of-print (Ahead-of-print) **29**(2), 1–24 (2020)
32. Karray, F., Alemzadeh, M., Abou Saleh, J., Arab, M.N.: Human-computer interaction: overview on state of the art. Int. J. Smart Sens. Intell. Syst. **1**(1), 137–159 (2017)
33. Kautz, K.: Investigating the design process: participatory design in agile software development. Inf. Technol. People **24**(3), 217–235 (2011)
34. Keller, F.B., Schoch, D., Stier, S., Yang, J.: Political astroturfing on Twitter: how to coordinate a disinformation campaign. Polit. Commun. **37**(2), 256–280 (2020)
35. Kuusinen, K., Mikkonen, T., Pakarinen, S.: Agile user experience development in a large software organization: good expertise but limited impact. In: Winckler, M., Forbrig, P., Bernhaupt, R. (eds.) HCSE 2012. LNCS, vol. 7623, pp. 94–111. Springer, Heidelberg (2012). https://doi.org/10.1007/978-3-642-34347-6_6
36. Labropoulou, P., et al.: Making metadata fit for next generation language technology platforms: the metadata schema of the european language grid. In: Proceedings of the 12th Language Resources and Evaluation Conference, pp. 3428–3437. European Language Resources Association, Marseille, France (2020)
37. Lee, G., Xia, W.: Toward agile: an integrated analysis of quantitative and qualitative field data on software development agility. MIS Q. **34**(1), 87–114 (2010)
38. Ma, W.J., Husain, M., Bays, P.M.: Changing concepts of working memory. Nat. Neurosci. **17**(3), 347–356 (2014). https://doi.org/10.1038/nn.3655
39. MacKenzie, I.S.: Human-computer interaction: an empirical research perspective. Newnes, Waltham (2012)
40. McGrew, S., Breakstone, J., Ortega, T., Smith, M., Wineburg, S.: Can students evaluate online sources? learning from assessments of civic online reasoning. Theor. Res. Soc. Educ. **46**(2), 165–193 (2018)
41. Michener, G., Bersch, K.: Identifying transparency. Inf. Polity **18**(3), 233–242 (2013)
42. Nielsen, J.: Estimating the number of subjects needed for a thinking aloud test. Int. J. Hum Comput Stud. **41**(3), 385–397 (1994)
43. Ozenc, F.K., Kim, M., Zimmerman, J., Oney, S., Myers, B.: How to support designers in getting hold of the immaterial material of software. In: Proceedings of the SIGCHI Conference on Human Factors in Computing Systems, pp. 2513–2522. ACM, Atlanta (2010)
44. Pankovska, E., Schulz, K., Rehm, G.: Suspicious sentence detection and claim verification in the COVID-19 domain. In: Proceedings of the Workshop Reducing Online Misinformation through Credible Information Retrieval (ROMCIR 2022), CEUR-WS, Stavanger (2022)
45. Pasi, G., De Grandis, M., Viviani, M.: Decision making over multiple criteria to assess news credibility in microblogging sites. In: 2020 IEEE International Conference on Fuzzy Systems (FUZZ-IEEE), pp. 1–8. IEEE, Glasgow (2020)

46. Patwa, P., et al.: Fighting an Infodemic: COVID-19 fake news dataset. arXiv:2011.03327 (2021)
47. Przybyła, P., Soto, A.J.: When classification accuracy is not enough: explaining news credibility assessment. Inf. Process. Manage. **58**(5), 102653 (2021)
48. Raison, C., Schmidt, S.: Keeping user centred design (UCD) alive and well in your organisation: taking an agile approach. In: Marcus, A. (ed.) DUXU 2013. LNCS, vol. 8012, pp. 573–582. Springer, Heidelberg (2013). https://doi.org/10.1007/978-3-642-39229-0_61
49. Rehm, G.: An Infrastructure for Empowering Internet Users to Handle Fake News and Other Online Media Phenomena. In: Rehm, G., Declerck, T. (eds.) GSCL 2017. LNCS (LNAI), vol. 10713, pp. 216–231. Springer, Cham (2018). https://doi.org/10.1007/978-3-319-73706-5_19
50. Rehm, G., et al.: European language grid: an overview. In: Proceedings of the 12th Language Resources and Evaluation Conference, pp. 3366–3380. European Language Resources Association, Marseille, France (2020)
51. Rehm, G., et al.: European language grid: a joint platform for the european language technology community. In: Proceedings of the 16th Conference of the European Chapter of the Association for Computational Linguistics: System Demonstrations, pp. 221–230 (2021)
52. Rehm, G., Schneider, J.M., Bourgonje, P.: Automatic and manual web annotations in an infrastructure to handle fake news and other online media phenomena. In: Calzolari, N., et al. (eds.) Proceedings of the 11th Language Resources and Evaluation Conference (LREC 2018), pp. 2416–2422. European Language Resources Association (ELRA), Miyazaki, Japan (2018)
53. Rieger, J., von Nordheim, G.: Corona100d: german-language Twitter dataset of the first 100 days after Chancellor Merkel addressed the coronavirus outbreak on TV. Tech. rep., DoCMA Working Paper (2021)
54. Rieger, M.O., He-Ulbricht, Y.: German and Chinese dataset on attitudes regarding COVID-19 policies, perception of the crisis, and belief in conspiracy theories. Data Brief **33**, 106384 (2020)
55. Rieh, S.Y.: Credibility assessment of online information in context. J. Inf. Sci. Theory Pract. **2**(3), 6–17 (2014)
56. Rogers, A., Gardner, M., Augenstein, I.: QA dataset explosion: a taxonomy of NLP resources for question answering and reading comprehension. arXiv:2107.12708 (2021)
57. Saltz, E., Barari, S., Leibowicz, C., Wardle, C.: Misinformation interventions are common, divisive, and poorly understood. Harvard Kennedy School Misinf. Rev. **2**(5), 1–25 (2021). https://doi.org/10.37016/mr-2020-81
58. Samimi, H., Hicks, R., Fogel, A., Millstein, T.: Declarative mocking. In: Proceedings of the 2013 International Symposium on Software Testing and Analysis, pp. 246–256. ACM, New York, NY (2013)
59. Sass, J., et al.: The German Corona Consensus Dataset (GECCO): a standardized dataset for COVID-19 research in university medicine and beyond. BMC Med. Inform. Decis. Mak. **20**(1), 341 (2020)
60. Sauro, J., Lewis, J.R.: Quantifying the user experience: practical statistics for user research. Morgan Kaufmann, Cambridge, MA (2016)
61. Solis, C., Wang, X.: A study of the characteristics of behaviour driven development. In: Proceedings of the 37th EUROMICRO Conference on Software Engineering and Advanced Application, pp. 383–387. IEEE, Los Alamitos (2011)

62. Su, Q., Wan, M., Liu, X., Huang, C.R.: Motivations, methods and metrics of misinformation detection: an NLP perspective. Nat. Lang. Process. Res. **1**(1–2), 1–13 (2020)

63. Teyssou, D., et al.: The InVID plug-in: web video verification on the browser. In: Proceedings of the First International Workshop on Multimedia Verification, pp. 23–30. MuVer 2017, Association for Computing Machinery, New York, NY, USA (2017)

64. Thakur, N., Reimers, N., Rücklé, A., Srivastava, A., Gurevych, I.: BEIR: a Heterogeneous Benchmark for Zero-shot Evaluation of Information Retrieval Models. In: Thirty-Fifth Conference on Neural Information Processing Systems Datasets and Benchmarks Track (Round 2), pp. 1–16. NeurIPS, Virtual (2021)

65. Tu, Y.C.: Transparency in Software Engineering, Ph. D. thesis, The University of Auckland, Auckland (2014)

66. Tu, Y.C., Tempero, E., Thomborson, C.: An experiment on the impact of transparency on the effectiveness of requirements documents. Empir. Softw. Eng. **21**(3), 1035–1066 (2016)

67. Vargas, L., Emami, P., Traynor, P.: On the detection of disinformation campaign activity with network analysis. In: Proceedings of the 2020 ACM SIGSAC Conference on Cloud Computing Security Workshop, pp. 133–146. ACM, Virtual (2020)

68. Viviani, M., Pasi, G.: Credibility in social media: opinions, news, and health information–a survey. Wiley Interdisc. Rev. Data Min. Knowl. Discov. **7**(5), e1209 (2017)

69. Wautelet, Y., Heng, S., Kolp, M., Mirbel, I.: Unifying and extending user story models. In: Jarke, M., Jarke, M., et al. (eds.) CAiSE 2014. LNCS, vol. 8484, pp. 211–225. Springer, Cham (2014). https://doi.org/10.1007/978-3-319-07881-6_15

70. Williams, E.: Experimental comparisons of face-to-face and mediated communication: a review. Psychol. Bull. **84**(5), 963 (1977)

71. Wobbrock, J.O., Hattatoglu, L., Hsu, A.K., Burger, M.A., Magee, M.J.: The goldilocks zone: young adults' credibility perceptions of online news articles based on visual appearance. New Rev. Hypermedia and Multimedia **27**, 1–46 (2021)

72. Zhou, X., Mulay, A., Ferrara, E., Zafarani, R.: ReCOVery: a Multimodal Repository for COVID-19 News Credibility Research. In: Proceedings of the 29th ACM International Conference on Information & Knowledge Management, pp. 3205–3212. ACM, Virtual Event Ireland (2020)

Digital Traces of News Media Public on Facebook: Comparing Estonian and Latvian Russophone Publics

Anna Smoliarova[✉] [iD]

St. Petersburg University, St. Petersburg 199004, Russia
a.smolyarova@spbu.ru

Abstract. Digital traces that users leave in the course of everyday liking, commenting or sharing posts on Facebook pages allow the researchers to get a glimpse at least of their interpretative and productive activity [12]. This research aims to explore the interpretative and productive activity of followers of diasporic news media on Facebook. I focus on the geo-ethnic storytelling [9] assuming that diasporic media provide their audiences with access to both national public spheres, of the host and the home countries. To meet the informational needs of their audiences, they cover news agenda of the host country in the native language different from the language of mainstream media, possibly considering it from the angle of ethno-cultural or linguistic minority. Diasporic media also continue to include news from the home country, despite the fact that the mainstream media of this country can be accessible through Internet or in other ways. As other media, diasporic media create Facebook pages where users can easily interact with the news items published on these pages. Based on knowledge about connections between emotional responses and reactions provided by Facebook pages I assume that connection between geography of a news item and Facebook reactions on it reflect the user involvement into the public sphere of the host or home country. To explore this connection in detail, I compare the news user behavior on six Estonian and Latvian news media Facebook pages.

Keywords: News engagement · Russophone publics · Facebook reactions

1 Introduction

As shown by a comparative study of news user behavior in six countries, the number of users commenting and sharing news items in social media is higher than in the websites [7]. Still, the ongoing discussion tends to criticize the quality of discussions formed in the comment sections on a Facebook page even harder than for the news websites. This research aims to measure the level of the user engagement in the discussions that are formed through comments under FB posts published on the news media FB page. I focus on the media for migrants, since this group of Internet users tend to be excluded from the public sphere of the host country, but migrant media allow them to join the deliberation process.

© Springer Nature Switzerland AG 2022
G. Meiselwitz et al. (Eds.): HCII 2022, LNCS 13517, pp. 166–174, 2022.
https://doi.org/10.1007/978-3-031-22131-6_12

The Russian-speaking community in Baltic region constitutes a large ethno-linguistic minority (37% and 33% of the entire populations of Latvia and Estonia, respectively). 75% of the Russian-speaking community consider Estonia/ Latvia to be their homeland [6]. The media repertoires of the Baltic Russian-speakers include Russian-origin media, locally-produced Russian-language media and, to lesser extent, Western media [16]. Previous research on Russophone audiences in Baltic states have reported Facebook to be the most popular social networking site among them. "Baltic Russian-language social media should be treated as a rather distinctive, unique space where local-national information flows are blended with those originating in Russia and elsewhere" [6].

2 Theoretical Framework

2.1 News Engagement with Multiple National Public Spheres

The national model of the public sphere assumes that public communication is conducted on a national language of the state, while the existence of a common identity motivates citizens to participate in discussions on common issues. The Habermasian model states that the consensus articulated in the public sphere of the nation-state should be translated into laws binding on the citizens of the state. Thus, the language nature of the public sphere of the state and the predjudices of journalists working in the national mainstream media lead to the displacement of part of the members of the society outside the public discussion. Within such "national-oriented" media system, the media diet of the residents without citizenship of the host country might include mainstream media from the host country, or media produced in the country residents (or their parents) moved from, or media produced by and for migrants in the host country.

Mainstream news media in a modern state "still show a strong connection with their native audience, whose language they speak, whose opinion about political and other processes, world events they share or determine themselves, finally, many prejudices, ethnocentric worldviews and styles of foreign policy national interests" [3:729]. N. Fraser points out one of the reasons why in a modern multi-ethnic state the national public sphere cannot ensure the interaction of all social groups: the model of the public sphere proposed by J. Habermas suggests that "public communication is conducted in the national language and transmitted through the national media" [2: 11]. This ability of a dominant public sphere to exclude certain groups of the population from the potential participants in a public discussion leads to the dissatisfaction of minorities' communicative needs. Negativism in the coverage of immigrants in the mainstream media influences their news exposure.

F. Oji, S. Weber-Menges, A. Fleras and other researchers of ethnocultural, diaspora, immigrant media claimed that the exclusion of immigrants, ethnic minorities and indigenous peoples from the dominant public sphere, via underrepresentation or biased coverage of events leads to the creation of the alternative media institutions [1]. "The subjective feeling of those concerned that the information they produce, messages, news, etc. do not find their way into the mainstream media" [17: 96], or the real lack of reflection in the mainstream media of the experience of this social group leads to the creation of platforms for discussing and sharing marginalized experience. The editorial policy of the immigrant and diaspora media addresses the needs of their audiences. If the information needs of the audience differ from the requests of the media audience of the host society, the agenda of diaspora media differs. Thus, media outlets might pay more attention to the news form the country (countries) of origin or cover agenda of the host country in the native language(s) of their audiences. More sophisticated editorial policy includes alternative framing of the events in the host country and in the country (countries) of origin that reflects unique interests and opinions existing in the immigrant or diaspora publics.

There is a large volume of published studies describing the balance between covering news from the host and home countries in immigrant or diaspora media. The digital traces Facebook users leave while interacting with the news allow the examination of how decisions of the editors about news agenda meet the public's needs and interests.

2.2 Digital Traces of News Exposure on Facebook

Steensen, Ferrer-Conill, and Peters stressed the need of conceptualizing different types of engagement and interactionist behavior. In this paper I follow Sang and colleagues who defined news engagement as "news users' varying modes of interaction with news content and/or other users" [14: 468]. Following a Facebook page of a news outlet provides a user with one of the most convenient ways to engage with the news. The platform affordances even include the buttons for a rapid and spontaneous emotional sharing. "By curating one's news repertoire on Twitter or Instagram individual users are able to select and filter their own "newspaper edition", thereby becoming an editor or gatekeeper in their own right through practices of personal news curation" [11:1022] - the same words could be written about Facebook. Merten describes the news exposure on social media as incidental, non-exclusive and influenced by social contacts of a user [11]. The incidental character on the news exposure is partly designed by the algorithms of social media platforms. Digital traces a user might leave on a Facebook page of a news media influence the further structure of the individual Facebook feed.

A large and growing body of literature has investigated these digital traces. Much of the current literature on Facebook user reactions pays particular attention to the emotional nature of these small actions. Still, previous research findings remained contradictory. Heiss et. al. [5] have shown that positive emotions increased all three types of possible news user actions – shares, likes and comments. Among positive emotions, humoristic elements tend to be virally shared and commented [5], however, content inducing anger also induces users to share and to comment it [8]. Lischka & Messerli [10] argued that commenting a news item correlates with dissatisfaction of a news user. The regression analysis conducted by Tian and colleagues revealed that a significant predictive role for emotional, functional, communal, and overall social media engagement is played by warmth, and not by competence [15]. Guo and Sun studied Facebook pages of the local TV stations and found that political news attract more user comments than more consumer-oriented content. The latter tends to be shared more often, since Facebook users aim to be helpful and useful for their audiences. "News stories on crimes, entertainment, civic information, sports, transportation, environment/nature/animals significantly influenced at least two types of user engagement behaviors, while news posts on emergences, weather, health, education only affected one of three types of user interactions" [3: 748]. In this paper I adopt the methodological principles that were developed by Guo and Sun and explore which patterns of user behavior could be observed on Facebook pages of Russian-language media in Estonia and Latvia.

3 Methodology

For this study I selected six major news media in Estonia and Latvia. Posts from their official Facebook pages and their metadata for analysis were downloaded in January 2022 with Popsters, a Russian-based service for social media management. The general sample of posts published by six media outlets contains 41239 items published from 1st January 2018 to 31st December 2021. On average, a news outlet in the sample publishes 1700 posts during the year (MD = 1728, 5; and the difference in the Facebook posting policy between outlets has diminished in these four years: SD (2018) = 44,88, while SD (2021) = 17,92). Metadata for each post includes following: day and time the post was published; number of users' reactions (likes, shares and comments); multimedia attached to the post (link to the website, or photo, or video). Popsters also provides data about number of followers and engagement rates measured for each media outlet Facebook page (Table 1).

Table 1. General data about user engagement with the media outlets in the sample

Country	Media title	N of FB followers	General N of posts 2018–2021	ER per post	ER per day
Estonia	ETV +	32475	6785	0.513	2.383
Estonia	Delphi (Estonian branch; Russian language)	18104	6974	0.189	0.902
Estonia	Postimees	23108	6977	0.444	2.123
Latvia	LSM	43890	6789	0.586	2.721
Latvia	Mixnevs	72110	6740	0.070	0.324
Latvia	Delphi (Latvian branch; Russian language)	149471	6974	0.091	0.440

Since the number of posts per outlet is very similar, as well as the intensity of posting, for the dataset 100 hundred posts has been chosen for each outlet randomly. Text of each post was coded accordingly to the geography of news mentioned in the post, or in the title of the publication on the news website the link was leading to. The list of binary variables included mentions of 1) host country 2) Baltic region 3) Russia 4) other post-Soviet country (0 – not mentioned, 1 – mentioned).

4 Results

4.1 RQ1. News from Which Countries Are Covered on the FB Pages of Russian-Language News Media Outlets in Estonia and Latvia?

The majority of posts included into the randomized dataset were dedicated to the host country: Estonia or Latvia accordingly (Fig. 1). The international news website *Delphi* in both countries covered the events in the host country less often than other outlets, followed by Postimees (four out of five posts connected to the Estonian news) and the group of the last three outlets where only each tenth post did not mention the host country. Russia is mentioned on average 3 times more often than other Baltic countries. A possible explanation might be that the coverage of Russian news represents the political position of the outlet, while neighbourhood states from the tightly intertwined region could be easily consumed from other sources of information. Other post-Soviet countries can be covered even more often, first of all, in case of Ukraine and Belarus due to the importance of the Russian-Ukrainian conflict.

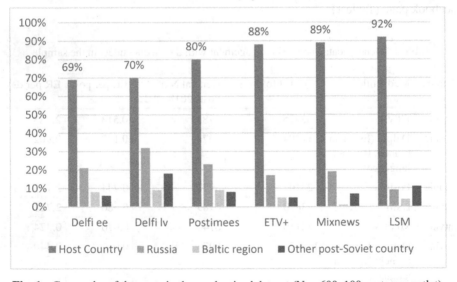

Fig. 1. Geography of the posts in the randomized dataset (N = 600, 100 posts per outlet).

4.2 Does the Context of the News Piece Correlate with the Data About the User Engagement on Facebook?

To analyze context of the news piece, I've chosen following criteria: host country where the media outlet is published; the media outlet itself; the number of followers on the Facebook official page of the media outlet; the community type of the page; year of the publication and the multimedia item included into the post.

As data in the Table X suggests, Estonian Facebook users tend slightly less to like posts of the media outlets, while Latvian Facebook users tend slightly more to repost news pieces to their own FB pages. The correlation with comments is statistically insignificant.

The media outlet is also slightly connected to the likes and reposts. The possible explanation might be the political position of a particular media outlet and its reputation that can influence the decision of public support and inclusion of the news piece into the digital representation of self on the Facebook page of a user. The inverse correlation between number of followers and likes per follower has been already shown in the existing literature on the user engagement, first of all, in the field of marketing research.

Community type of the Facebook page was coded accordingly the data in Table 2; Mixnews and Delphi (Latvian branch) are characterized as unengaged type: the biggest number of followers, the lowest engagement rate per post, the lowest engagement rate per day). Delphi (Estonian branch) could be described as a regular type: although the number of followers is the smallest in our sample, the engagement rate per day is twice more than on the pages of the unengaged type. The third type includes Postimees, ETV+ and LSM: they are characterized by the medium number of followers and the highest engagement rates. My results suggest that followers of the third type tend more to like posts on the Facebook page of a media outlet they follow (a moderate correlation) and slightly more to comment (a weak correlation) the posts.

Table 2. Spearman's rho: context and user engagement

	Likes per follower	Reposts per follower	Comments per follower
Country	**−0,20***	**0,18***	−0,08
Media outlet	**−0,23***	**0,21***	−0,10
N of followers	**−0,24***	0,08	−0,13
Community type	**0,38***	0,13	**0,15***
Year	**0,20***	0,001	**0,19***
Media 1	0,089	−0,004	−0,007
Media 2	−0,121	0,046	−0,013

(*Marked correlations are significant at p <,001).

Year of the post demonstrates the tendency of growing user engagement from 2018 to 2021. Of course, pandemic has increased the time of internet usage and people's involvement into discussions about news as well as the emotional intensity of their reactions. However, the correlation's strength is quite weak, and the absence of a statistically significant correlation between date of publication and reposts per follower could lead to even more fruitful discussion about the difference between these types of user behavior.

Finally, according to my data, the presence or absence of multimedia does not correlate with the user engagement: I did not reveal any statistically significant correlation between them. Only 1% of all posts did not contain any multimedia object; while the two thirds of the posts included into the dataset contained a link to the website of the media outlet (63%). Every fifth post included photo (19%), and in 17% of cases the video was the main item of the content or was attached to a textual part.

4.3 Do Users Tend to Repost Posts They Like More Than Comment on Them?

The six media outlets have not shown similar tendencies in the strength of association between types of Facebook reactions (see Table 3). At least for my dataset, such media as ETV+, Delphi (Estonian), and LSM support the consistent pattern revealed in the previous studies, namely, people tend more to repost pieces they liked and less to comment on them.

Table 3. Relations between different type of Facebook reactions

Media title	Likes & Comments	Likes & Reposts	Comments & Reposts
ETV+	0,54*	0,97*	0,55*
Delphi (Estonian)	0,35*	0,78*	0,33*
Postimees	0,62*	0,15	0,01
LSM	0,43*	0,84*	0,51*
Mixnews	0,58*	0,17	0,08
Delphi (Latvian)	0,72*	0,26*	0,06

(* Marked correlations are significant at p <,05).

The significant correlation between comments and reposts contradicts the previous results suggesting that people tend to comment on pieces to disagree and to argue with them, thus, commenting should be not strongly connected to reposts. This result needs further investigation. Based on the existing literature, one possible explanation might be that the polarized audience leaves digital traces demonstrating level of engagement but not a consensus in feelings and evaluations of the content.

The most surprising aspect of the data is the strong correlation between likes and comments in all news media in the studied dataset. Followers of Facebook pages of Delphi (Latvian), Postimees and Mixnews tend more to comment the posts they like rather than repost them. There is no significant correlation between likes and reposts in case of Postimees and Mixnews, and in case of Delphi (Latvian) the correlation between likes and reposts is tree times weaker than between likes and comments.

4.4 Do the Users of Media Outlets Differ in the Manner They Engage with the News About Their Host Country?

What stands out in the Table 4 is that the posts covering news about the host country slightly tend to engage users more than news about other states, including country (countries) of origin. Moreover, the news from the host country trigger the user behavior explicitly connected to the positive emotions and support (likes and reposts).

Table 4. User engagement with the news covering different countries

	Likes per follower	Reposts per follower	Comments per follower
Host country	**0,11***	**0,13***	0,075
Baltic region	−0,006	−0,007	−0,017
Russia	−0,048	−0,098	−0,034
Other post−Soviet country	−0,020	−0,029	0,045

(* Marked correlations are significant at p <,05000).

The patterns of followers' behavior differ for media outlets selected for analysis (Table 5(. The single most striking observation to emerge from the data comparison that followers of the Facebook page of Delphi (Latvian) tend to comment posts they like, while the data about the host country contradicts this tendency.

Table 5. News about host country and ...

Media title	... Likes	... Reposts	... Comments
ETV +	**0,34***	**0,41***	**0,25***
Delphi (Estonian)	nonsignificant	nonsignificant	nonsignificant
Postimees	nonsignificant	**0,30***	nonsignificant
LSM	nonsignificant	nonsignificant	nonsignificant
Mixnews	nonsignificant	nonsignificant	nonsignificant
Delphi (Latvian)	**0, 24***	**0,39***	nonsignificant

(* Marked correlations are significant at p <,05000).

While overall data about ETV+ page followers has shown that the more a post is liked the more it will be reposted, the data towards host country suggests that posts about host country tend to be slightly more reposted than liked. This result is somewhat counterintuitive, but comparing it with the high level of engagement of ETV+ followers I assume that publication of Estonian news even intensifies their involvement.

In summary, these results show that the geography of a news item does not play a one consistent and holistic role as a factor predicting user engagement with the diaspora media. This study has found that generally news from the host country inspire users to engage more actively in a supportive way via likes and reposts. The findings provided a deeper insight into the heterogenous nature of the diaspora/immigrant segments of media landscape of a modern state. Instead of general tendencies typical for the diaspora/immigrant media, the difference between media outlets and publics engaged on Facebook into the interaction with the news content seems to play a more important role.

Acknowledgments. This research has been supported in full by the project 'Center for International Media Research' of St. Petersburg State University, Russia, project #92564627.

References

1. Fleras, A.: Theorizing multicultural media as social capital: crossing borders, constructing buffers, creating bonds building bridges. Can. J. Commun. **34**, 725–729 (2009)
2. Fraser, N.: Transnational public sphere: transnationalizing the public sphere: on the legitimacy and efficacy of public opinion in a post-westphalian world. Theory Cult. Soc. **24**(4), 7–30 (2007)
3. Guo, M., Sun, F.S.: Like, comment, or share? exploring the effects of local television news facebook posts on news engagement. J. Broadcast. Electron. Media **64**(5), 736–755 (2020)
4. Hafez, K.: Zwischen Parallelgesellschaft, strategischer Ethnisierung und Transkultur. Die türkische Medienkultur in Deutschland. Blätter für deutsche und internationale Politik **25**(6), 728–736 (2000)
5. Heiss, R., Schmuck, D., Matthes, J.: What drives interaction in political actors' Facebook posts? profile and content predictors of user engagement and political actors' reactions. Inf. Commun. Soc. **22**, 1–17 (2018)
6. Juzefovičs, J., Vihalemm, T.: Digital humor against essentialization: strategies of baltic russian-speaking social media users. Polit. Geogr. **81**, 102204 (2020)
7. Kalogeropoulos, A., Negredo, S., Picone, I., Nielsen, R. K. Who shares and comments on news? a cross-national comparative analysis of online and social media participation. Social Media+ Soc. **3**(4), 2056305117735754. (2017)
8. Larsson, A.O.: Diversifying likes. J. Pract. **12**(3), 326–343 (2018). https://doi.org/10.1080/17512786.2017.1285244
9. Lin, W.Y., Song, H.: Geo-ethnic storytelling: an examination of ethnic media content in contemporary immigrant communities. Journalism **7**(3), 362–388 (2006)
10. Lischka, J.A., Messerli, M.: Examining the benefits of audience integration: does sharing of or commenting on online news enhance the loyalty of online readers? Digit. J. **4**(5), 597–620 (2016)
11. Merten, L.: Block, hide or follow—personal news curation practices on social media. Dig. J. **9**(8), 1018–1039 (2021)
12. Picone, I.: Grasping the digital news user: conceptual and methodological advances in news use studies. Dig. J. **4**(1), 125–141 (2016)
13. Sang, Y., Lee, J.Y., Park, S., Fisher, C., Fuller, G.: Signalling and expressive interaction: online news users' different modes of interaction on digital platforms. Dig. J. **8**(4), 467–485 (2020)
14. Steensen, S., Ferrer-Conill, R., Peters, C.: (Against a) theory of audience engagement with news. J. Stud. **21**(12), 1662–1680 (2020)
15. Tian, Y., Yang, J., Chuenterawong, P.: Share or not? effects of stereotypes on social media engagement using the stereotype content model. J. Pract., 1–27 (2021)
16. Vihalemm, T., Juzefovičs, J., Leppik, M.: Identity and media-use strategies of the Estonian and Latvian Russian-speaking populations amid political crisis. Eur. Asia Stud. **71**(1), 48–70 (2019)
17. Wimmer, J.: Counter-public spheres and the revival of the European public sphere. Javnost Public **12**(2), 93–109 (2005)

Servants, Friends, or Parents? the Impact of Different Social Roles in the Social Web of Things on User Experience

Jiayu Yin, Qinyan Dai, Xingyu Wang, Sinan Xie, Xinyue Kang,
and Pei-Luen Patrick Rau(✉)

Tsinghua University, Beijing 100084, China
rpl@mail.tsinghua.edu.cn

Abstract. The Social Web of Things (SWoT) is a paradigm comprising the social web and the Internet of Things (IoT), in which users can interact with IoT in the same way they use social network services. This study aims to investigate users' perceptions and preferences of the social roles of the SWoT agents in smart home scenarios. We designed three social roles of SWoT agents by different social status levels (low: servant, neutral: friend, high: parent). A three-day within-subject experiment was conducted on 15 participants in a Wizard-of-Oz manner, followed by questionnaires and in-depth interviews. Through descriptive analysis of questionnaire data and qualitative analysis of the interviews, we found that the friend role is the most favored because of emotional connection and effectiveness. Users are not comfortable with conversations that involve their private affairs. Furthermore, most users would want to buy SWoT appliances if their price is within 120% of traditional appliances. These findings can guide the future design of SWoT agents to provide a better user experience.

Keywords: Social Web of Things · Smart agent · Social role · Internet of Things

1 Introduction

The Social Web of Things (SWoT) is a paradigm considering social relationships between users and the Internet of Things (IoT). Smart objects are concerned as humans in a society in the SWoT, with their interconnections resembling social ties and communication resembling social interactions. Taking advantage of the SWoT, users can interact with IoT in the same way they use social network services [32–34]. Therefore, the SWoT is essential to build an interconnected network, which is helpful to create a scalable and user-centered interaction platform.

In order to enhance user experience while interacting with smart agents in SWoT systems, anthropomorphizing agents are widely adopted, such as Siri and Alexa [4]. Most of their anthropomorphic features are associated with general social categories, including personality, age, gender, or name. They imitate the nature of human-to-human communication [4–10, 16]. Additionally, the "social role" is another critical feature of anthropomorphism because it provides social expectations and determines proper

G. Meiselwitz et al. (Eds.): HCII 2022, LNCS 13517, pp. 175–186, 2022.
https://doi.org/10.1007/978-3-031-22131-6_13

behaviors for agents, and establishes social connections between users and agents in society [17]. For example, a friend-like agent is usually expected to provide emotional company, develop trust relationships, and increase users' life satisfaction [14]. Thus, the social role is functional for categorizing smart agents to a particular social position during social interaction. However few studies have been conducted on how different social roles can influence the user experience of SWoT-based environments.

The SWoT and smart home technology have become increasingly applied in our daily lives. Smart agents are embedded in some appliances, extending their functions for more using scenarios and better user experience. Nevertheless, the definition of the appliances becomes varied, which makes their roles in the smart home ambiguous. What roles should the appliances act like in the smart home remains an open question. Therefore, this study aims to investigate users' perceptions of different social roles of the SWoT agents and their preferences in the smart home by three social status levels. We used different address forms, tones, and emojis to alter the agents' perceived social roles by users. Servant agents are considerate, humble, respectful and address the users with 'master'; friend agents are relaxing cheerful, and address the users with their first name or nickname; parent agents are calm, dominant and address the users with a polite term used by an elder to refer to a junior. In addition, factors that potentially affect users' acceptance of appliances with smart agents can help us further understand users' preferences. Therefore, three research questions were addressed in this research seen as below:

RQ 1: Which social role of the smart agents do people prefer in the smart home, servant, friend, or parent?
RQ 2: How do people perceive the social role of smart agents?
RQ 3: What are factors that affect people's overall acceptance of smart agents in the smart home?

2   Literature Review

2.1   Anthropomorphic Interaction Style with Smart Agent

There are increasing numbers of anthropomorphic interactive products on the market, like Siri, Cortana, and Alexa. Nass & Brave (2005) proposed that humans tend to communicate with smart machines as they do with other humans [9]. Roy & Naidoo (2021) pointed out that anthropomorphic interactive products can lead to more effective consumer interaction and improve consumer experiences [4]. According to Wu et al. (2017), the interaction style impacts how audience receives and responds to the information received [1]. Users will depend heavily on the interaction style to shape their assessment when users interact with minimal understanding of the service [2]. Previous research demonstrates that the interaction style is a critical factor on a user's impression of an anthropomorphic smart agent [1–5]. And different interaction styles can be varied from different speech styles, personalities, and social roles [3, 5, 8, 16].

At present, there are many studies on the influence of the agents' personality and speech style of conversational agents on users [3, 16]. For example, Kim et al. (2013) discovered that people who chatted with a robot using a familiar speech style responded to the robot more actively than those who using an honorific speech style [3]. Wu et al. (2017) reported that the smart interaction with friendly and caring wording led to more positive brand warmth and brand attachment than the smart interaction with professional and indifferent wording [1]. Personality is another major attribute in the perception of embodied conversational agents (ECAs) [10–12]. According to Goetz et al. (2003), users anticipate an agent's personality to fit the task environment, e.g., a serious agent for a serious task [7]. In a study of personality traits of smart home agent, Mennicken et al. (2016) found that most participants prefer living with a conscientious, kind, and calm smart home agent, which demonstrated less proactivity. At the same time, an extroverted and cheerful smart home agent may be perceived as aggressive and too automated. Hence, the people's emotional reactions to human-like smart agents emphasize the significance of design for systems with human-like personality traits [13].

While interacting with a conversational agent, users may detect several social signs, such as gender or personality [16]. The social role of the conversational agent, on the other hand, has received little attention as a characteristic attributed to the agent [15]. Social role is important because it establishes expectations about how the agent will behave according to the social norms of the role and the social relationship with users [17]. Users perceived the smart agents they engaged with as "social actors" and applied some social roles as if they were interacting with human beings [19]. The social role assigned to the agent is a major indicator that triggers social reaction [15]. Currently, most conversational agents have the social role of a secretary or a personal assistant [18]. Also, Gao et al. (2018) discovered that many users characterize Amazon Echo (a voice intelligence agent) as a friend, a family member, or even a girlfriend in a large survey of Echo user reviews. The reviewers that personified Echo exhibited more favorable emotions than those that merely treated Echo as a product [14]. In a Chinese study on emotional voice interaction design, Sun et al. (2019) concluded that assistants and friends are the most anticipated relationships with smart voice agents, accounting for 51.3% and 48.7%, respectively, from a sample of 551 questionnaires [20]. Based on previous research, it can be concluded that the social role is a commonly assigned attribute to smart agents, which can be perceived by users and influence the user experience.

2.2 Roles of SWoT

Since the SWoT agents at homes are closely associated with users, determining the atmosphere in people's homes, inappropriate social roles of agents may lead to negative effects on user experience. The social roles of the SWoT agents and their social relationship with users are influential.

According to previous research, a conversational agent's social role can be identified by its verbal cues and speech styles, such as the address forms, tone of words, and agent proactivity [3, 15, 22–25]. This study used different address forms and tones to alter the SWoT agent's perceived social roles, creating three different social roles by different social status levels (low: servant, neutral: friend, high: parent, see Fig. 1).

The address forms can identify a conversational agent's relative social role. There are two types of address forms we usually use: honorific and familiar, which regulate social distance and often represent relative social roles. Honorific address is a prevalent address form used between strangers or superior subordinates. In contrast, familiar address is

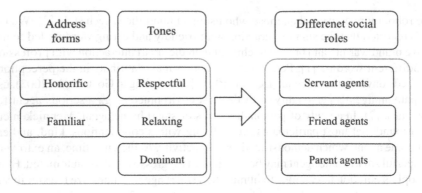

Fig. 1. Develop different social roles in SWoT agents

usually used when the addressee is younger than the speaker [25]. When a person calls another's name, the type of address is also influenced by the intimacy and relative social status between them [26]. If the addressee is intimate with the speaker such as a close friend, boy or girlfriend, or brother, the speaker shall call the addressee by the first name, such as "Hey, Lisa.". On the contrary, the speaker may use the title and last name, such as "Professor Smith,' "Mr. Zhang" if the addressee is above the speaker in age or social rank. This is especially prevalent in high-power distance societies like China. Accordingly, we applied "Master" to the servant agents' address to participants, the first name like "Lisa" to the friend agents' address to participants, and "Little + Last name" to the parent agents' address to participants.

Tones of words are broad in both spoken and written language. Tones usually express the author's attitude towards the audience and can be varied due to the subtle differences in the relationship between speaker and listener [28]. When someone is asked a question, the tone of their response may differ depending on who else is present in the conversation [21]. Thus, social roles can be differentiated by the tone of words used (e.g., tones of friendly, tones of respectful, and tones of dominant). In Rhee & Choi's (2020) study, the secretary-role conversational agent employed official, professional language and a formal tone, such as "would like to." Meanwhile, the friend-role agent often used words commonly in daily talks with close friends, such as "how about", and were utilized in a relaxed, informal style to create the impression of a more personal relationship [15]. Similarly, we applied a humble and respectful tone to the servant agents, an informal, relaxing, and cheerful tone to the friend agents, and a calm and dominant tone to the parent agents.

3   Methodology

3.1   Independent Variables and Dependent Variables

In this research, three SWoT agents named agents A, B, C were designed with different anthropomorphic social roles. Agents A was identified as servants, acting and communicating with participants like servants of users. Agents B was identified as friends. Agents

C was parent agents, acting like elder parents. Each specific difference of interactive styles among the three roles is shown in Table 1.

The only within-subject independent variable is the different social roles of SWoT agents when interacting with participants, including servant, friend, and parent. The information and services they provide are consistent.

The dependent variable includes participants' user experience of different SWoT agents' roles collected by the post-questionnaire (see Table 2). The questionnaire involves three dimensions, including personal preference, perceived usefulness, and satisfaction, which are designed and adapted based on the USE Questionnaire [30].

Table 1. Specific differences in language among three social roles

	Day 1: Agents A	Day 2: Agents B	Day 3: Agents C
Social Role	Servant	Friend	Parent
Address Form	Master	First name/Nickname (e.g., Lisa)	Little + Last name
Emoji	(˙ω˙)y, 9(>ﮩ)ﻭ	の: o(^▽^)o	None
Language Sample	"Master, how late you are coming home! I miss you so much! By the way, it's going to cool down these days. Please don't forget to wear thick clothes when you go out. The air conditioner has been adjusted to 26°C, waiting for you to go home. 9(>ﮩ)ﻭ If you need any adjustment, please tell me at any time ~(˙ω˙)y I'm glad to be at your service!"	"Hi! Lisa. Good evening~ Wel come back home~ o(^ ▽^)o It's going to cool down these days. Don't forget to wear thick clothes to go out of the office! I am freezing today (>﹏<). I have turned the temperature at home to 26°C, do you think it is OK?"	"Hey, little Lisa. Pretty late coming back home today, huh? It 's going to cool down these days. Remember to wear more clothes. The temperature in the house is set to 26°C. Maybe it 's suitable for you. If you're cold just tell me to turn it up."

Table 2. Content in post-questionnaire (Take Agents A for Example)

Measure	Questions	Score
Personal preference	1. I like the service from agents A the most among the agents A, B, and C 2. Reason (Fill in Blank)	1 Strongly Disagree 5 Strongly Agree

(continued)

Table 2. (*continued*)

Measure	Questions	Score
Perceived usefulness	1. Agents A help me be more productive 2. Agents A are beneficial to my life and work 3. Agents A can do everything I would expect it to do 4. Agents A make the things I want to accomplish easier to get done	1 Strongly Disagree 5 Strongly Agree
Satisfaction	1. It is fun to use agents A 2. I am satisfied with agents A 3. It is pleasant to use agents A 4. I am also willing to interact with them when I am in a bad mood	1 Strongly Disagree **5 Strongly Agree**

3.2 Participants

To test the influences of different anthropomorphic social roles of SWoT agents in smart home scenarios, this study targeted those who usually stayed at home in their free time, particularly the younger generation. Fifteen university students aged 20 to 30 were recruited for this study (see Table 3). Each participant had signed an informed consent form before the experiment to ensure voluntary participation.

Table 3. Overall background of participants

Criteria	Overall background
Gender	Male (3), female (12)
Age	19–22 (10), 23–26 (4), 27–30 (1)
Occupation	Computers and Internet (4), electronic engineering (2), consulting (2), finance (4), education (3)

3.3 Procedure

The whole procedure comprises three stages: experiment based on scenarios, post-questionnaire (see Table 2), and post-experiment interviews (see Table 4). The experiment was conducted in a Wizard-of-Oz manner for three days in smart home scenarios [29]. During the experiment, four experimenters respectively represented four "Social Web of Things" at home (air conditioner, refrigerator, washing machine, and microwave oven) to "chat" with participants. They completed conversations with participants in the WeChat group using different interaction styles.

Every "Thing" has two tasks performed by the experimenters in the experiment: "report work" and "ask for advice." Four experimenters took turns interacting with the participants, from reporting their housework to asking for participants' instruction. Each "Thing" can also interact with each other. All the interactions were limited to 15 min. Each participant interacted with one role of the SWoT agents per day. On the first day of the experiment, participants interacted and dialogued with the servant agents. On the second day, participants interacted with the friend agents. On the third day, participants interacted with the parent agents (see Table 1). Except the SWoT agents' role varied every day, the basic dialogue framework over the three days was consistent. To avoid the participants feeling more boring over time, the turn of four "things" for reporting work changed randomly (see Fig. 2).

Table 4. Interview questions

Q1	Briefly introduce yourself (e.g., personality and daily life)
Q2	Which is the most satisfactory agent among those three agents? Why satisfied?
Q3	Is there any agent you do not like? Why?
Q4	Were there any memorable conversations with the smart agents during the experiment? What are the reasons and feelings?
Q5	Have you ever felt inspired or reminded by some agents during the conversation?
Q6	Is there any touching moment during the communication?
Q7	Would you get bored if you had to communicate with them every day?
Q8	Willingness to buy
Q9	Would you prefer to have such agents at work or at home?
Q10	What do you want to say about the overall evaluation and suggestion of the experiment?

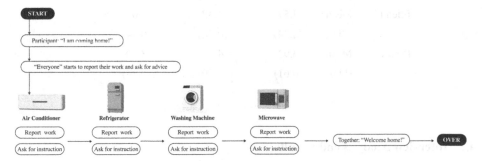

Fig. 2. Experiment flow chart

4 Results

This section conducted descriptive analysis of the post-questionnaire data and qualitative analysis of participants' interviews.

4.1 Descriptive Analysis

For the servant agents (A), friend agents (B), and parent agents (C), the mean and variance of their scores on the three indicators were calculated (see Table 5). The average satisfaction score of each role is above 4 out of 5, while the variance is low. The friend role's scores are higher on all three dimensions than the other two roles. Participants have a high acceptance of anthropomorphic SWoT, among which the friend role is the most popular. This finding was also supported by the comparative comments participants gave. For example, the word "enthusiastic" appeared most frequently in the comments of the servant agent (A). The servant agents received many complimentary words, such as "adorable," "like," "intelligent," "pleasant," and "considerate." Meanwhile, the servant agents also received some negative comments, such as "too enthusiastic," "distanced," and "unfamiliarity," which might explain why the servant agents' score is slightly lower than the friend agents'. As for the friend agents (B), many words of appreciation, such as "adorable," "interesting," "funny," and "closer," were mentioned by nine participants (out of 15). Thus, People's general impression of the friend agents was positive, which could explain participants scoring the highest to friend agents among the three dimensions. However, for the parent agents (C) with the lowest preference scores, some words expressing no emotion, like "somewhat," "kind of," or "not bad," frequently appeared in the comments, which indicated the participants might not have much positive emotion towards the parent agents.

Table 5. Mean and variance of descriptive scores

Role		Preference	Usefulness	Satisfaction
Servant	Mean	4.36	4.14	3.50
	(SD)	(0.28)	(0.34)	(0.82)
Friend	Mean	4.57	4.38	4.07
	(SD)	(0.24)	(0.38)	(0.64)
Parent	Mean	3.93	4.07	3.50
	(SD)	(0.61)	(0.49)	(0.34)

4.2 Interview Analysis and Results

Participants' personal preference differences towards different agents were further revealed in the interviews. In addition to further evidence that the most popular role of the SWoT agents was the friend role, many insights were found into the common qualities participants valued when interacting with SWoT agents and factors that potentially affected the acceptance of appliances with smart agents. They can be organized into three parts:

1 Reasons for user preference on the friend role agent.

2 Acceptability on premium in purchase decisions.
3 Keeping distance away from users' privacy.

Reasons for User Preference on Friend Role Agent

Based on the questionnaire and interview results, the friend role was the most popular one in this experiment. Most participants thought interacting with friend agents was like talking to their best friends, making them feel relaxed and comfortable. The common feeling towards the servant agents is not as amiable and intimate as the friend agent. And they think the third-day's interaction with the parent role is a little gossipy because they talked about their privacy. Additionally, female participants indicated that talking to the friend agents can release their fatigue, making them feel warm and cared for. *"I was touched when they told me what foods I can eat before I go home. It feels like I have such warm family or friends in my home."* said a participant. *"Those things (SWoT) always give me positive feedback and always care about me."* said another participant. To sum up, participants liked the friend role best because it is like their close friends and makes them relaxed and comfortable.

Acceptability on Premium in Purchase Decisions

Price premium is an important factor to be considered in a purchase decision. When asked about the purchase decision of SWoT appliances, most of the participants expressed that they would like to buy the whole set of SWoT "intelligent agents" if the price is less than 120% of traditional appliances at home. Only one male participant said he might buy one thing (the refrigerator or the washing machine) among the whole set of SWoT divides because he thought other items were not practical enough.

Keeping Distance Away From Users' Privacy

In the experiment, participants received a question from SWoT agents *"it seems that you always go back home late recently, are you in a relationship now/chuckle?"* And all the participants felt offended to different extents. *"I don't like being asked about my private business and my privacy by an electrical appliance, which makes me feel offended. I still want to keep my distance with an appliance,"* said one participant. Most of the participants held the same opinion like this. They don't want to share private business with SWoT, especially personal love stuff.

5 Discussion

The Social Web of Things (SWoT) concept was proposed to combine the social web and the Internet of Things (IoT) [2]. And the social roles of the SWoT agents and their social relationship with users are critical when measuring the user experience with the SWoT. This study explores users' perceptions and preferences of the social roles of the SWoT agents in smart home scenarios. The study results suggest that the SWoT is useful and satisfactory, while anthropomorphic interaction plays an important part in it. Among all three social roles (servant, friend, and parent), the friend role is the most popular because it is like users' friends and makes them relaxed and comfortable.

It is also worth mentioning that there are some differences between sexes regarding the smart agents' characteristics that users value. It turned out that male participants cared about efficiency most during the interaction with SWoT agents, while female participants cared more about emotional communication with them. One male participant indicated that the communication with SWoT agents should be short and practical because he needs spare time to accompany his family other than robots. *"In this experiment, I think I like refrigerators better because it doesn't talk too much, and it is pragmatic."* said a male participant. Pragmaticism is an important factor for this male participant. *"I even don't have enough time to spend with my family, let alone talk to those appliances,"* said another male participant. On the other hand, most female participants reported that emotional communication with SWoT could please them. All the female participants indicated that talking to the SWoT agents made them feel warm and cared for by someone. *"I was touched by the warmth of them every time they said 'welcome back,' 'we are waiting for you!' and things like that. They always give me positive feedback and always care about me."* said another female participant. They paid more attention to emotional communication with SWoT agents in smart homes.

When involved with the purchase decision of SWoT devices, most participants don't have much acceptance of extra expenses. It suggests that the price of a set of SWoT devices should not be much high. Besides, most participants don't want to be involved with some private topics with SWoT agents. They felt it offensive to some extent. This kind of concept may derive from the short time of interaction between them and those agents. It suggests that SWoT designers should keep a proper distance from users' private affairs.

This study remains some limitations. First of all, when participants were recruited, the sample size of the participants was small. It is difficult to obtain significant statistical results. Second, participants' freshness and curiosity vary over time. This factor of freshness may influence our preference results, which means the low score of the parent agents on the third day may be influenced by the decreased freshness of participants. Future studies should consider the sequence effect.

6   Conclusion

This study explores users' perceptions and preferences of three social roles (servant, friend, and parent) of the Social Web of Things (SWoT) agents and examines what roles should the SWoT agents act like in the smart home scenarios. The results suggest that the friend role of the SWoT agents is the most popular among all the three roles because of emotional connection and effectiveness. There are gender differences in how users value agents. Male participants value agents' efficiency more. Female participants focus more on the emotional connections with the agent. Factors such as price and privacy also influence people's acceptance of interacting with the SWoT. Future design of home SWoT agents could be endowed with a friend role in the home scenario, as users most favor the friend role. And the SWoT agents should be designed to keep a proper distance away from users' private businesses. Meanwhile, the price of new SWoT appliances on the market should not be higher than the price of traditional appliances too much.

References

1. Wu, J., Chen, J., Dou, W.: The Internet of Things and interaction style: the effect of smart interaction on brand attachment. J. Mark. Manag. **33**(1–2), 61–75 (2017)
2. Dion, P.A., Notarantonio, E.M.: Salesperson communication style: the neglected dimension in sales performance. J. Bus. Commun. **29**(1), 63–77 (1992)
3. Kim, Y., Kwak, S.S., Kim, M.S.: Am I acceptable to you? effect of a robot's verbal language forms on people's social distance from robots. Comput. Hum. Behav. **29**(3), 1091–1101 (2013)
4. Roy, R., Naidoo, V.: Enhancing chatbot effectiveness: the role of anthropomorphic conversational styles and time orientation. J. Bus. Res. **126**, 23–34 (2021)
5. Thomas, P., Czerwinski, M., McDuff, D., Craswell, N., Mark, G.: Style and alignment in information-seeking conversation. In: Proceedings of the 2018 Conference on Human Information Interaction & Retrieval, pp. 42–51. Association for Computing Machinery, New York (2018)
6. Li, J., Zhou, M. X., Yang, H., Mark, G.: Confiding in and listening to virtual agents: the effect of personality. In: Proceedings of the 22nd International Conference on Intelligent User Interfaces, pp. 275–286. Association for Computing Machinery, New York (2017)
7. Goetz, J., Kiesler, S., Powers, A.: Matching robot appearance and behavior to tasks to improve human-robot cooperation. In: The 12nd IEEE International Workshop on Robot and Human Interactive Communication, pp. 55–60. IEEE, New York (2003)
8. Metze, F., Black, A., Polzehl, T.: A review of personality in voice-based man machine interaction. In: Jacko, J.A. (ed.) HCI 2011. LNCS, vol. 6762, pp. 358–367. Springer, Heidelberg (2011). https://doi.org/10.1007/978-3-642-21605-3_40
9. Nass, C.I., Brave, S.: Wired for Speech: How Voice Activates and Advances the Human-Computer Relationship. MIT Press, Cambridge (2005)
10. Cassell, J.: Embodied conversational agents: representation and intelligence in user interfaces. AI Mag. **22**(4), 67 (2001)
11. Bickmore, T., Cassell, J.: Social dialongue with embodied conversational agents. In: Advances in Natural Multimodal Dialogue Systems, pp. 23–54. Springer, Dordrecht (2005). https://doi.org/10.1007/1-4020-3933-6_2
12. Catrambone, R., Stasko, J., Xiao, J.: Anthropomorphic agents as a user interface paradigm: experimental findings and a framework for research. In: Proceedings of the Twenty-Fourth Annual Conference of the Cognitive Science Society, pp. 166–171. Routledge, New York (2002)
13. Mennicken, S., Zihler, O., Juldaschewa, F., Molnar, V., Aggeler, D., Huang, E.M.: "It's like living with a friendly stranger" perceptions of personality traits in a smart home. In: Proceedings of the 2016 ACM International Joint Conference on Pervasive and Ubiquitous Computing, pp. 120–131. Association for Computing Machinery, New York (2016)
14. Gao, Y., Pan, Z., Wang, H., Chen, G.: Alexa, my love: analyzing reviews of ama-zon echo. In: 2018 IEEE SmartWorld, Ubiquitous Intelligence & Computing, Ad-vanced & Trusted Computing, Scalable Computing & Communications, Cloud & Big Data Computing, Internet of People and Smart City Innovation (Smart-World/SCALCOM/UIC/ATC/CBDCom/IOP/SCI), pp. 372–380. IEEE, New York (2018)
15. Rhee, C.E., Choi, J.: Effects of personalization and social role in voice shopping: an experimental study on product recommendation by a conversational voice agent. Comput. Hum. Behav. **109**, 106359 (2020)
16. Benbasat, I.: HCI research: future challenges and directions. AIS Trans. Hum. Comput. Interact. **2**(2), 16–21 (2010)
17. Biddle, B.J.: Recent developments in role theory. Ann. Rev. Sociol. **12**(1), 67–92 (1986)

18. Sinha, R.R., Swearingen, K.: Comparing recommendations made by online sys-tems and friends. In: Proceedings of the DELOS-NSF Workshop on Personalization and Recommender Systems in Digital Libraries (2001)
19. Reeves, B., Nass, C.: The Media Equation: How People Treat Computers, Television, and New Media like Real People and Places. Cambridge University Press, New York (1996)
20. Sun, Y., Li, S., Chen, X.: Emotional voice interaction design: human computer interaction research map and design case of baidu AI user experience department. Zhuangshi (11), 22–27 (2019)
21. Prendinger, H., Ishizuka, M.: Social role awareness in animated agents. In: Proceedings of the Fifth International Conference on Autonomous Agents, pp. 270–277. Association for Computing Machinery, New York (2001)
22. Tan, H., et al.: Relationship between social robot proactive behavior and the human perception of anthropomorphic attributes. Adv. Robot. 34(20), 1324–1336 (2020)
23. Chocarro, R., Cortiñas, M., Marcos-Matás, G.: Teachers' attitudes towards chat-bots in education: a technology acceptance model approach considering the effect of social language, bot proactiveness, and users' characteristics. Educ. Stud., 1–19 (2021)
24. Hu, T., et al.: Touch your heart: a tone-aware chatbot for customer care on social media. In: Proceedings of the 2018 CHI Conference on Human Factors in Computing Systems, pp. 1–12. Association for Computing Machinery, New York (2018)
25. Iksop, L., Ramsey, S.R.: The Korean language. J. Asian Stud. 60(4), 1212–1214 (2001)
26. Brown, R., Ford, M.: Address in American English. Psychol. Sci. Public Interest 62(2), 375–385 (1961)
27. Sung, Ja-Young., Guo, L., Grinter, R., Christensen, H.: "My Roomba is Rambo": intimate home appliances. In: Krumm, J., Abowd, G.D., Seneviratne, A., Strang, T. (eds.) UbiComp 2007. LNCS, vol. 4717, pp. 145–162. Springer, Heidelberg (2007). https://doi.org/10.1007/978-3-540-74853-3_9
28. Stoehr, T.: Tone and voice. Coll. Engl. 30(2), 150–161 (1968)
29. Bernsen, N.O., Dybkjær, H., Dybkjær, L.: Wizard of oz prototyping: how and when. In: Proceedings of CCI Working Papers Cognitiom Science/HCI, Roskilde, Denmark (1994)
30. Lund, A.M.: Measuring usability with the USE questionnaire. Usabil. User Exp. Newsl. STC Usabil. SIG 8(2), 3–6 (2001)
31. Gubbi, J., Buyya, R., Marusic, S., Palaniswami, M.: Internet of Things (IoT): a vision, architectural elements, and future directions. Futur. Gener. Comput. Syst. 29(7), 1645–1660 (2013)
32. Formo, J.: The internet of things in the eyes of the users. Ericsson Bus. Rev., 33–35 (2010)
33. Formo, J., Laaksolahti, J., Gårdman, M.: Internet of things marries social media. In: Proceedings of the 13th International Conference on Human Computer Interaction with Mobile Devices and Services, pp. 753–755. Association for Computing Machinery, New York (2011)
34. Rau, P.L.P., Huang, E., Mao, M., Gao, Q., Feng, C., Zhang, Y.: Exploring interactive style and user experience design for social web of things of Chinese users: a case study in Beijing. Int. J. Hum Comput Stud. 80, 24–35 (2015)
35. Moon, Y.: Similarity effects in human-computer interaction: effects of user personality, computer personality, and user control on attraction and attributions of responsibility, Unpublished doctorial dissertation, Stanford University, Stanford (1996)

Online and Adaptive Learning

Comparing the Effectiveness of Instructor-Led Versus Video-Based Learning Methods for Online Website Accessibility Training

Yvette Apatiga[✉] and Kim-Phuong L. Vu

California State University, Long Beach, CA 90840, USA
yvette.aa1@gmail.com, Kim.Vu@csulb.edu

Abstract. Past research has debated whether learning outcomes are dependent on the format of instruction and its design. More specifically, most have compared video-based learning with the traditional lecture environment. Although both possess advantages and disadvantages, certain factors can influence whether the instruction is effective or not. Cognitive load theory posits that three types of load (extraneous, intrinsic, and germane) can affect learning through the design of instructional materials. If not properly designed, instruction can hinder performance. Moreover, the usability of such materials can influence cognitive load and students' perception of the instruction. The present study examined if video-based and instructor-led online training showed differences in performance outcomes on website accessibility evaluation tasks. In addition, participants' ratings of usability, enjoyability, perceived usefulness, and intention to use were subjectively measured and compared. Participants completed a training session online by watching a set of videos or a live instruction and were asked to complete quizzes and an accessibility evaluation task on a website for four checkpoints. Results showed that participants performed significantly better on easy tasks than on more difficult ones; however, the type of instruction did not appear to impact learning outcomes. Instead, both video and lecture-based training were equally effective in teaching participants how to conduct evaluations, especially when the material is considered to be easy. We concluded that instructional design alone might not be enough to aid students in learning more difficult subjects. Instructors must consider other potential factors that may influence how well a student understands the material in an online learning environment. Limitations and future directions are discussed.

Keywords: Instructional videos · Cognitive load · Training · Online learning

1 Introduction and Literature Review

Video-based learning has continued to gain traction as a reliable tool for online courses over the past few decades [1, 2]. Although the use of videos as an alternative learning method is not new, the sudden shift from in-person to online operations resulting from the COVID-19 pandemic only further increased the need for effective online educational technologies [3]. Videos offer instructors the ability to present information in an

© Springer Nature Switzerland AG 2022
G. Meiselwitz et al. (Eds.): HCII 2022, LNCS 13517, pp. 189–206, 2022.
https://doi.org/10.1007/978-3-031-22131-6_14

audiovisual format. While this benefit has primarily helped instructors in an educational environment (i.e., teaching academic subjects), videos used for training purposes allow learners to watch demonstrations of the material instead of relying on text instructions, diagrams, or manuals [4, 5]. However, despite the prevalence of video-based learning, there is still much debate regarding the efficacy of their use when compared to an instructor-led lecture format.

While few studies have noted the benefits of online video-based learning over traditional instructor-led methods, most find that both produce similar outcomes [6–9]. For instance, Chotiyarnwong et al. [6] compared video versus lecture-based methods to educate patients on osteoporosis by evaluating their knowledge of the disease. Subjects in both groups showed similar test scores before and after the lesson, which led Chotiyarnwong et al. [6] to conclude that video-based training can teach patients about their health condition as effectively as the traditional, lecture-based approach. In other cases, video-based learning provides an advantage. Wong and Ng [10] found that engineering students completing an e-learning module on the fundamentals of operational amplifiers obtained higher test scores than those completing the same module in a lecture format. However, video-based learning does not always produce favorable outcomes. Roy and McMahon [11] found that participants reviewing a practice clinical case scenario to determine a patient's diagnosis did not exhibit sufficient critical thinking skills when using video-based materials compared to those exploring cases using text-based materials. The researchers alluded to potential distractions within the video as a reason for the difference in critical thinking processes between the two groups.

Aside from differences in performance, there are multiple advantages to adopting video-based learning versus instructor-led lectures and vice versa. Videos can be widely implemented online, allowing this educational tool to reach a broad range of students [12] easily. Additionally, learners completing video-based online instruction can progress through the learning material at their own pace [1]. In contrast, traditional methods allow students to ask questions in real-time during lectures and participate in facilitated discussions, impacting learning [13]. Attending lectures in person can also provide students with a more structured environment [14]. The format in which instruction is provided can result in varying learning outcomes. Therefore, when comparing video-based instruction versus online instructor-led lectures, it is crucial to consider the most effective design practices and methods for video development to aid learning.

1.1 Cognitive Load

Cognitive Load Theories. A major factor that influences learning outcomes is cognitive load. As one attends to new information, many mental resources are used to ensure later retrieval. A high cognitive load can make it difficult for one to hold information within working memory capacity, disrupting the learning process. A theoretical framework that describes cognitive load during learning is cognitive load theory (CLT). CLT posits that limited cognitive resources during the learning process can be depleted if the instruction is not well-designed to aid working memory [CLT; 15, 16]. To prevent high cognitive load, design guidelines for instructional materials must consider the contribution of the following components: intrinsic load, extrinsic load, and germane load. The first component, intrinsic load, involves the nature of the subject, as the more complex the information is, the more likely a person will experience cognitive load [17]. Generally, learning is placed on a spectrum as some information is easier to digest than others.

The second component, extraneous load, occurs when cognitive resources are consumed to process irrelevant activities instead of relevant ones needed for learning [17, 18]. For example, Chandler and Sweller [18] found that instructional materials that require students to seek information from two sources, split across two locations, can harm learning compared to when the same sources are integrated into a single location. Doing so aids with attention and prevents unnecessary cognitive load from being imposed on the learner. It is also essential for the design of instructional materials to omit nonessential explanatory information.

The third component, germane load, involves the cognitive effort needed to learn the material [16]. Improved outcomes occur when instructional materials are designed to increase germane load, as this allows students to integrate the information into schemas, a permanent storage of knowledge within memory [16]. In sum, Sweller et al. [16] emphasized that the goal of CLT design principles is to reduce extraneous load and enhance germane load. Additionally, high intrinsic load can harm learning if combined with high extraneous load.

An extension of CLT has been implemented for multimedia. The cognitive theory of multimedia learning posits that acquiring information from visual and auditory channels occurs through three types of cognitive processing [19, 20]. Essential processing allows learners to understand the information presented through the following cognitive tasks: selection, organization, and integration. Extraneous processing focuses on nonessential information within the instructional material. Generative processing is the effort needed to make sense of the information. Cognitive capacity can become overloaded during excessive extraneous or essential processing [21]. At the same time, minimal generative processing can result in the under-utilization of mental resources, which hinders learning [21].

Instructional Design and Format. As discussed, cognitive load can negatively influence learning if the instruction is poorly designed. The cognitive theory for multimedia learning presented here, in conjunction with CLT, promotes design principles that are catered to developing effective educational videos [21, 22]. When creating videos, the goal is to utilize principles to reduce the complexity of the information presented. For example, the signaling principle recommends highlighting critical information to reduce extraneous load by guiding a learner's attention towards elements they would otherwise need to search [23, 24]. This guideline is simple to implement with animation by adding color contrast changes to the selected area or arrows to point to the information. Mautone and Mayer [25] found that students learning about airplane mechanics showed better memory retention and understanding of the information when signaling was utilized. Other design principles focus on removing excess and distracting elements (i.e., coherence) or placing essential text next to graphics (spatial contiguity) [18, 21]. Instructors can utilize these recommendations when constructing videos to enhance student learning. Keeping the videos simple can be more beneficial for students.

In addition to reducing extraneous load, other aspects may influence how well an individual learns the material. For instance, the presence of the instructor may impact cognitive load. When students try to understand the material, germane load can benefit and optimize learning through the formation of schemas [16]. Support is essential as poor instructional design can hinder students' motivation to process the material. In a traditional classroom, the ability to ask questions for further clarification can foster cognitive processing, which can prove beneficial for more difficult topics. Generally, when instructors can effectively communicate the learning material, extraneous load is reduced, providing optimal learning [26]. Video-based learning can enhance germane load by allowing students to engage with others online [27].

Learning Environment. The format in which the instruction is presented may also affect cognitive load. It is also important to consider the environment in which the instruction occurs. A major concern to fully online teaching is distractions. Engaging in multitasking during video lectures can negatively impact performance [28, 29]. Distractions can interfere with learning by reducing the cognitive resources needed to process information, thereby increasing extraneous load. Students must actively regulate their behavior online to prevent any hindrance to their learning experience [30]. While online learners may or may not attempt to interact with multiple tasks at once, the physical environment, such as noise or the presence of others, itself may also pose issues to cognitive load [31]. To our knowledge, research has yet to focus on how online environments can differ when an instructor is moderating a session live or not. Current research has investigated whether establishing an instructor's presence online can influence the learning experience by providing supportive resources and feedback for asynchronous lecture formats [32]. Additionally, providing a recording of the lecturer in videos can prevent cognitive overload [33]. However, instructional designers need to remain mindful of how to properly integrate the instructor with the material [34, 35].

1.2 User Perceptions

Both instructor-led and video-based instructional methods have the potential to provide students with an enriching learning experience. However, the learners themselves may perceive one as being better than the other. Scott et al. [9] obtained learner preferences for the type of instructional material. They determined that most were satisfied with the online training, with minimal users stating they would have preferred attending the training sessions in person. However, the users in the same study reported that a major limitation of online learning is not having the option to ask questions or make comments about the material. A student's preference for a specific learning method can make it challenging to adopt a new one [36, 37].

Cognitive load is an essential factor that can influence how users rate their learning experiences. Huang [38] surveyed participants enrolled in a blended learning course that uses online and face-to-face lecture methods. The researcher found that students' subjective mental load and effort negatively impacted learning. Essentially, perceived difficulties in understanding the class material increased cognitive load and decreased motivation, satisfaction, and positive attitudes towards the course. Costley and Lange [39] found that germane load mediated the relationship between instructional design and future behavioral intentions to continue online learning. When courses provide an enriching experience that effectively prevents cognitive load from overwhelming the learner, the student will likely be satisfied. User satisfaction in online learning is an important factor for continued acceptance [40].

Additionally, the design of the videos, especially when implemented in an e-learning environment, can influence user perceptions. CLT and usability design principles possess related concepts [41, 42]. Poor usability can result in high extraneous load since users will need to manage their way around the interface [43]. On the other hand, Clarke, Schuetzler, Windle, Pachunka, and Fruhling [44] tested the design of an online health intake form and found that patients experienced high intrinsic load due to difficulty remembering information more so than extraneous load from the interface itself. Still, the researchers discuss the possibility of usability and cognitive load influencing a patient's intent to adopt the software. That is, intrinsic cognitive load may decrease if the interface follows the 'recognition not recall' heuristic [45]. As a result, usability has been considered for e-learning interface design to potentially aid student performance [46]. However, research has yet to consider usability metrics for video-based learning and how they may connect to CLT principles [47].

1.3 Current Study

It is necessary to consider how CLT can affect performance and the learning experience when designing instruction. Although most of the studies compared traditional face-to-face methods and online video-based learning, most did not mention cognitive load or implement CLT guidelines in the design. Thus, there is a lack of research on CLT and differences in lecture formats. Those who have studied CLT specifically evaluated extraneous load alone or in combination with intrinsic load [48]. There has also been little focus on how instructor-led or live online instruction can differ when comparing unmoderated video learning. Since the COVID-19 pandemic increased the need for students to attend lectures online via conferencing platforms, the study opted to recreate this type of format as one of the conditions. Lastly, the present study will investigate the relationship between instructional method and usability based on CLT design guidelines.

While prior research on learning includes a wide range of subjects, little has focused on website accessibility training. The World Wide Web Consortium (W3C) is an established international community that develops standards for websites to ensure all people, regardless of physical and cognitive abilities, can access the World Wide Web [49]. The current accessibility guidelines, Web Content Accessibility Guidelines (WCAG) 2.0, provide specific recommendations for web content authors and evaluators to determine if a website meets the standards for accessibility [50]. A website is considered accessible when it meets the following principles:

1. Perceivable
2. Operable
3. Understandable
4. Robust

Several guidelines are in place for each principle listed in WCAG 2.0 to assist evaluators. To determine if a guideline is met, the evaluator needs to test aspects of the site using a criterion, or checkpoints (i.e., items that need to be checked), for passing. For example, for a website to be considered operable, all content functionalities must be available for users to access with a keyboard. Thus, the process of conducting accessibility evaluations on websites is intensive. For some checkpoints, the material is simple and straightforward; however, most require more thinking as the answer may not be as clear-cut. As a result, the current study seeks to determine the effectiveness of different training methods for web accessibility that can prepare students to evaluate webpages based on WCAG 2.0 when CLT principles are utilized to design the instructional materials.

The purpose of this study was to examine which method, instructor-led lectures or videos, produced favorable learning outcomes, a more useable and enjoyable instructional format, better perceived usefulness, and higher continuance intent after participants completed a website accessibility training session. The following hypotheses were developed based on prior research:

1. Participants will show lower performance (i.e., lower scores) on quizzes and website evaluation for hard than easy checkpoints. This hypothesis is based on the fact that intrinsic load was manipulated through checkpoint difficulty. The higher the intrinsic load (i.e., the more difficult the material), the lower the performance.
2. Participants in the video-based training condition will show better performance (i.e., higher scores) on quizzes and evaluations than those in the online, instructor-led condition. This hypothesis is based on the idea that extraneous load should be lowered when the videos are implemented following best-practice design guidelines (i.e., the material presented was simple, and excess/unnecessary information was removed).
3. Participants in the video-based training condition and online, instructor-led condition will perform similarly on the easy checkpoints. However, differences will be seen for the hard checkpoints, such that participants in the video-training condition will show better performance on quizzes and evaluations. The predicted interaction is based on prior research on cognitive load, where lower extraneous load may prevent learning deficits when intrinsic load is present.
4. Participants in the video-based training condition will rate the instructional material higher in terms of usability, enjoyability, perceived usefulness, and intention to use compared to those in the online, instructor-led condition.

2   Methods

2.1 Participants

Forty seven participants were recruited through the California State University, Long Beach Psychology Department Subject Pool (SONA). One participant in the online, instructor-led condition was excluded due to missing quiz scores for one checkpoint. In the video condition, three participants were excluded due to spending less than fifteen minutes on the survey. Three others were excluded for spending significantly over the allotted estimated time, logging over 15 h to complete the 2-h training. In addition to the six, three participants were excluded for not completing the online survey. The remaining 37 participants were included in the final analysis. Participant ages ranged from 18 to 23 ($M_{age} = 18.86$, $SD = 1.42$). Most of the participants identified as female

(73%) compared to those who identified as male (24.3%), and one participant declined to respond (2.7%). When asked to disclose their familiarity with web accessibility, most participants said they were not familiar at all (43.2%), and most did not have any experience with accessibility software tools before (97.3%). Participants were also asked if they had prior experience with web development. Most were not familiar with web development (70.3%), nor did they have any coding experience with HTML (97.3%). Only one participant stated they had coding experience (2.7%), and two rated their HTML skill level as a novice (5.4%).

Table 1. Breakdown of age and gender by condition.

Condition	Age	Gender
Online, instructor-led (N = 17)	$M_{age} = 19.00$	$N_{male} = 6$ $N_{female} = 11$
Video-based (N = 20)	$M_{age} = 18.75$	$N_{male} = 3$ $N_{female} = 16$ $N_{omit} = 1$

2.2 Materials

Before the session, participants were provided a pre-study questionnaire to obtain demographic information and whether they had prior experience with web accessibility or development. Participants in both conditions reviewed the same content in two different formats. Video-based training included four videos that were developed using TechSmith Camtasia. Instructor-led lecture-based training included a moderator who taught each checkpoint using PowerPoint slides and website examples as provided. The instruction for all conditions followed a specific script to ensure that the training was similar for each participant. Participants were given their learning materials based on their assigned condition during the session. For each checkpoint covered, participants answered eight multiple-choice quiz questions on Qualtrics that tested their knowledge of the recently covered material. More than one attempt was allowed to ensure that participants were provided feedback to aid in the evaluation, however, comprehension scores for the analyses were based on the first attempt.

After each checkpoint, participants evaluated a website to determine if it passed or failed the criteria for a specified checkpoint. Findings were documented on the evaluation worksheet. Performance scores derived from the evaluation were based on the accuracy of the comment, which described the present error if applicable, and the rating, which labeled the website as either fail or pass based on the checkpoint criteria. Each checkpoint was worth two points, one for the comment and one for the rating. When evaluating participant responses, researchers provided a score based on the following point distribution: incorrect = 0; partially correct = 0.5; correct = 1. One checkpoint consisted of two tests instead of one, so scores were broken down to ensure that the comment and rating together resulted in a score of 2 (e.g., a comment for one test was worth 0.5 points).

The System Usability Scale (SUS) was used to determine the usability of the instructional materials provided during the training session. The questionnaire consisted of 10 items, each rated on a scale that ranged from 1 (strongly disagree) to 5 (strongly agree). The existing SUS items were altered to portray the content being rated by the participant. The word 'system' was changed to include 'training videos' for the video-based training conditions and 'instructional material' for the instructor-led condition. Scores greater than seventy indicate acceptable usability [51]. A post-study questionnaire that consisted of 9 items with a standard 5-point Likert scale was administered for participants to rate how much they enjoyed the training session (enjoyability), how useful or helpful was said session (perceived usefulness), and if they will continue to use the instructional material to continue training (intention to use).

2.3 Design

The study employed a 2 (instructional method) x 2 (checkpoint difficulty) mixed factorial design. The type of instruction provided for the training session was between-subjects. Participants were randomly assigned to one of the two training conditions: video-based training and instructor-led training. Checkpoint difficulty was within-subjects as all participants completed the same easy and hard checkpoints. The difficulty level was provided in a counterbalanced order, with some participants receiving the easy checkpoints first before the hard checkpoints and vice versa. The dependent variables included task performance, usability, enjoyability, perceived usefulness, and intention to use.

2.4 Procedure

Online Lecture. Participants received the instructor-led training in an online synchronous format. Each session took place over the Zoom videoconference platform. Before the lecture, participants were provided with a survey link to the pre-study questionnaire. They agreed to participate in the study by clicking on the forward button in the survey after reading the informed consent. The questionnaire inquired about demographic information, prior knowledge regarding web accessibility, and prior experience with web development. Once completed, participants began the training session with the order of the checkpoint difficulty varying due to counterbalancing. Participants were allowed to ask questions regarding the material during the lecture portion of the session. During the lecture, participants completed quizzes for each checkpoint over Qualtrics. Before starting the evaluation task, participants were taught how to use the software tools they would need to complete the test successfully. This only occurred after the first and third checkpoints. We included this general training into the session to ensure that performance was not affected due to participants' inability to navigate the software interface. After reviewing the checkpoint, participants were provided with a website and instructed to evaluate the site based on the criteria for the previously learned checkpoint. Using the remote-control function on Zoom, participants proactively completed the task in real-time using the necessary tools to find accessibility issues from the experimenter's computer. They typed their responses on an evaluation worksheet, where they provided a comment about the error if found or the rating (i.e., fail, pass, or not applicable). After completing the website evaluations, participants were asked to complete the SUS survey and post-study questionnaire. At the end of the session, participants were debriefed by the moderator and provided contact information for future reference.

Online Videos. Participants completed the video-based training session online through a Qualtrics survey. We chose this method to provide participants with an asynchronous instructional format that allowed them to complete the survey independently and at their own pace. The study was set up to be similar to the instructor-led condition. The presentation of the checkpoints was counterbalanced using the randomizer function. After consenting, participants watched a video for a checkpoint with interpolated quiz questions. When completed, participants were provided screenshots of a website and asked to evaluate the images to determine if the site passed or failed the checkpoint criteria. This process was repeated four times for all videos. After participants finished the training session, they completed the SUS survey and post-study questionnaire before being debriefed and compensated course credit for their time.

3 Results

3.1 Task Performance

Quizzes. Quiz scores were obtained for all checkpoints during the session. The percent accuracy was calculated using the following formula: number correct/total score * 100. One participant failed to answer one question for one of the provided quizzes. As a result, the percent accuracy was determined based on a total score of seven instead of eight. Results showed a main effect for checkpoint difficulty, such that participants completing Easy checkpoints ($M = 72.47\%$, $SD = 16.50\%$) scored higher than the Hard checkpoints ($M = 66.82\%$, $SD = 11.72\%$), $F(1, 35) = 5.38$, $p = .026$, $\eta^2 = .13$ (see Fig. 1). This finding coincides with the current prediction of CLT, where high intrinsic load (i.e., the difficulty of the subject) can lead to poorer performance, confirming our initial hypothesis. However, the format in which participants received the instructional materials did not affect their quiz scores, $F(1, 35) = .22$, $p = .621$. In essence, performance throughout all training sessions followed the same trend regardless of whether it was Instructor-led or Video. Additionally, the type of training session did not influence the outcome of quiz scores when difficulty was considered. Results showed no significant interaction between instructional method and checkpoint difficulty, $F(1, 35) < 1.0$. Thus, controlling for extraneous load did not prevent cognitive overload when participants underwent more difficult tasks.

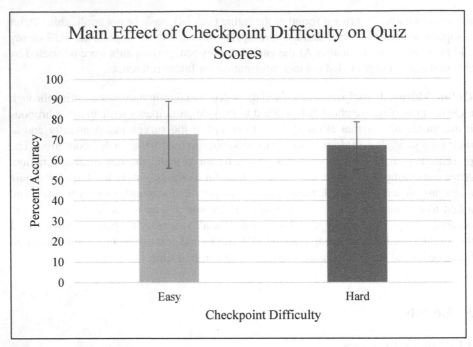

Fig. 1. Main effect of checkpoint difficulty on quiz scores. Higher percent accuracy is shown for easy checkpoints and lower for hard checkpoints. Error bars represent standard deviation.

Web Evaluation. Evaluation scores obtained for analysis were based on the comments and rating participants provided after checking the accessibility of an assigned website. Similar to the quiz scores, raw scores were transformed into percentages. As expected, the main effect for checkpoint difficulty was significant, $F(1, 35) = 105.98, p < .001$, $\eta^2 = .75$, with participants performing better for easy checkpoints ($M = 81.76\%, SD = 23.50\%$) than hard checkpoints ($M = 39.19\%, SD = 26.87\%$) (see Fig. 2). Thus, intrinsic load negatively influenced learning and subsequent ability to perform the task, following a similar trend with quiz scores.

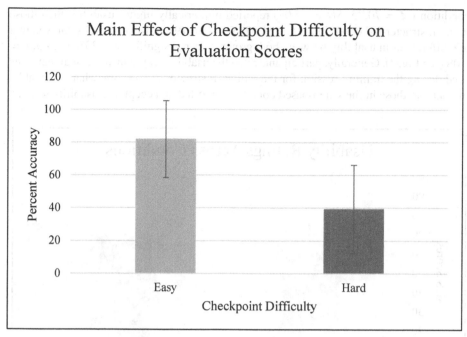

Fig. 2. Main effect of checkpoint difficulty on evaluation scores. Easy checkpoints resulted in higher percent accuracy than hard checkpoints. Error bars represent standard deviation.

Interestingly, the order in which the assigned checkpoints were presented had a significant main effect, $F(1, 35) = 4.12$, $p = .05$, $\eta^2 = .11$ (see Fig. 3). Within the easy condition, participants scored higher for the first checkpoint ($M = 85.14\%$, $SD = 25.32\%$) than the second ($M = 78.38\%$, $SD = 34.44\%$). The same trend was seen for the hard condition, with participants obtaining a higher score for the first checkpoint ($M = 43.92\%$, $SD = 24.58\%$) than the second ($M = 34.46\%$, $SD = 39.68\%$). These results indicate that participants did not perform better over time with practice. The type of training was not significant, $F(1, 35) < 1.0$, indicating that performance was not influenced by the format in which participants received the instruction. Additionally, the interaction between instructional method and checkpoint difficulty was not significant, $F(1, 35) = 2.96$, $p = .094$, as participants in the online, Instructor-led and Video-based training performed similarly in the Easy and Hard checkpoints. Consequently, the results did not support our hypothesis. Instead, performance scores showed that controlling for extraneous load did not prevent cognitive overload when completing difficult tasks.

3.2 Usability

SUS scores were obtained from participants across conditions. One participant did not fill in the Likert scale for one of the SUS items. As a result, the missing rating was replaced by the average rating from the other questions. An independent samples t-test was used to determine if differences in usability occurred among participants in each group. Interestingly, the average SUS scores showed that participants in the Video-based condition ($M = 70.75$, $SD = 17.09$) reported numerically higher usability than those in the Instructor-led condition ($M = 61.52$, $SD = 16.79$); however, results showed that the differences in usability between both groups was not significant, $t(35) = -1.65$, $p = .108$ (see Fig. 3). Generally, participants rated the usability of the instructional materials used during the training session for the online, Instructor-led as somewhat acceptable. In contrast, those in the video-based condition reported an acceptable usability score.

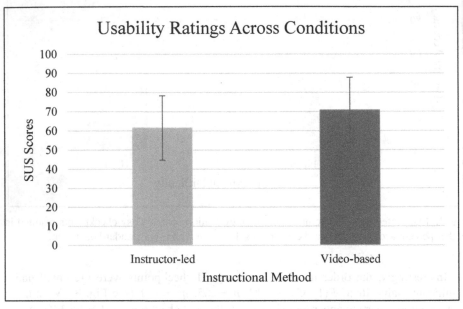

Fig. 3. Usability rating based on SUS scores for instructional method conditions. Video-based condition shows above-average usability compared to Instructor-led, which depicts a below-average rating. Error bars represent standard deviation.

3.3 Enjoyability, Perceived Usefulness, and Intention to Use

Participants rated the enjoyability, perceived usefulness, and intention to use items regarding their training session (see Table 1). Each construct was measured by obtaining the average scores across the relevant survey items. An independent t-test was utilized to determine differences between the aforementioned variables for both conditions. For enjoyability, participants in the online, Instructor-led ($M = 3.82$, $SD = .88$) and Video-based ($M = 3.45$, $SD = .87$) did not show significant differences, $t(35) = 1.30$, $p = .204$. Both instructional formats provided a similar experience, and the ratings show no potential trends favoring a specific method. For perceived usefulness, one participant did not rate a survey item, therefore, the missing rating was obtained based on the average. Overall, there were no significant differences for perceived usefulness, $t(35) = .97$, $p = .339$, between online, Instructor-led ($M = 4.21$, $SD = .79$) and Video-based ($M = 3.98$, $SD = .62$) training. Participants found their respective method useful for learning website accessibility evaluation. Lastly, online, Instructor-led ($M = 3.74$, $SD = 1.05$) and Video-based ($M = 3.85$, $SD = .76$) training did not show significant differences for intention to use, $t(35) = -.39$, $p = .703$. Participants rated both methods equally similar when asked if they would continue using the instructional format in the future.

A one-sample t-test was performed for enjoyability, perceived usefulness, and intention to use to determine if the scores obtained from the present sample are above or below the median rating (i.e., a rating of three on a 5-point Likert scale). Enjoyability score was significantly higher than the test value of 3.0, with a mean difference of .62, 95% CI [.33, .92], $t(36) = 4.29$, $p < .001$. Results for the perceived usefulness score had a mean difference of 1.09, 95% CI [.86, 1.32], where the score was significantly higher than the test value of 3.0, $t(36) = 9.43$, $p < .001$. Lastly, intention to use score also was significantly higher than the test value of 3.0, $t(36) = 5.43$, $p < .001$, and had a mean difference of .80, 95% CI [.50, 1.10].

To determine if enjoyability, perceived usefulness, and intention to use scores obtained from the present sample are significantly above or below a score of 4, which is labeled as above-average based on a 5-point Likert scale, a one-sample t-test was used. Enjoyability score was significantly lower than the test value of 4.0, with a mean difference of -.38, 95% CI [-.67, -.08], $t(36) = -2.61$, $p = .013$. Results for the perceived usefulness score and intention to use score were insignificant, with the former score slightly trending higher than a 4.0, with a mean difference of .09, and the latter trending lower, with a mean difference of -.20. Overall, while participants rated all variables as slightly above average, they did not view the training session as highly (i.e., far above-average) enjoyable, useful, or favorable for future use.

4 Discussion

The present study sought to determine if the instructional format can influence performance outcomes when cognitive load factors are considered. As predicted, the findings showed that participants performed worse for more difficult checkpoints than easier ones, indicating that harder tasks impose a more significant intrinsic load [17]. It was also hypothesized that participants in the video-based condition would exhibit better task performance than those in the online, instructor-led condition. Findings did not support the prediction, showing that both methods of instruction were equally effective during the training session. This result supports prior research showing no differences in learning outcomes when different instructional formats were tested [6–9]. Participants performed well for easy checkpoints, with average scores above 80% for website evaluation scores ($M = 81.76\%$, $SD = 23.50\%$). The training taught students how to assess websites for accessibility based on the criteria presented. However, for the hard checkpoints, participants in both conditions did not obtain high scores ($M = 39.19\%$, $SD = 26.87\%$). Compared to the easy checkpoints, the hard checkpoints required participants to analyze the content more thoroughly, using the accessibility software tools as a guide (since the errors were not explicitly shown), to determine if the content shown does not violate the specified criteria. Additionally, the hard checkpoints focused more on the HTML elements (e.g., headings and attributes) compared to the easy checkpoints. To improve these scores, participants may need more assistance from the instructor or instructional materials to understand how to assess a website. More examples and practice may be necessary to ensure that novices effectively learn the critical information needed for the more challenging tasks involved with web accessibility.

We predicted an interaction between variables, such that the video-based training condition would perform better in the hard checkpoints as the lowered extraneous load would prevent cognitive overload due to high intrinsic load. Results showed that our hypothesis was not supported, as participants in both conditions performed similarly for easy and hard checkpoints. There are a few possibilities for this finding. First, other confounding variables that we did not control for could have influenced performance. For instance, the learning environment was similar in both conditions since participants completed all sessions online at home, making it difficult to assume that no distractions were present [31]. To determine if distractions would change the performance of participants, we ran an additional group of 15 participants using the same video-based instruction but performed in a cubicle in our lab. As in the video training condition, this group of participants were taught website accessibility at their own pace without an instructor in a controlled laboratory setting. We found no significant differences in performance and participant ratings of usability, enjoyability, perceived usefulness, and intention to use) when the three groups were compared. Second, other internal factors, such as motivation, may better predict how well participants paid attention to the material [52]. Third, the design of instructional materials may not be enough to prevent cognitive overload during more challenging tasks. In contrast, the design practices implemented may have been too distracting for some videos than others [11].

We also hypothesized that usability ratings would be higher for video-based training than instructor-led; however, the findings do not fully support this hypothesis. No significant difference was found, but participants rated the training videos numerically higher in terms of usability ($M = 70.75$, $SD = 17.09$) compared to those in the online, instructor-led condition ($M = 61.52$, $SD = 16.79$) [51]. In essence, the participants found the videos easy and simple to use to complete the training. For enjoyability, perceived usefulness, and intention to use, we predicted that participants in the video-based training would rate each factor more favorably than those in the instructor-led sessions. However, this hypothesis was not supported. Participants in both conditions rated each variable similarly, with the average score being higher than the test score of 3.0, but not different or lower than 4.0.

There are a few limitations to consider. As mentioned earlier, participants completed all training sessions online, with the instructor-led condition taking place on the Zoom platform, and the video-based condition was embedded into a Qualtrics survey. Therefore, distractions within the environment were not controlled. Future research should consider this potential confounding variable in the experimental design. Although we examined one instance of this condition, the group was tested at the end of the semester, which made time a confounding factor. Due to COVID-19 restrictions, recruiting in-person participants was difficult, and we only recruited enough participants to fill one in-person condition at the end of the semester. Future research may consider evaluating how in-person lectures influence training performance compared to online lessons. Additionally, we could not account for any usability or technical issues experienced during the video-based training session. While the online, instructor-led condition can be argued as having ecological validity since the lecture was held in real-time and possessed a similar online learning environment to what is typically experienced by students in online courses, the video-based training, although fully online, was placed within a survey platform instead of an educational technology service (e.g., Khan Academy or a learning management system). Another limitation involves the use of self-report surveys to measure usability and user satisfaction. Surveys are subject to limitations, such as incomplete or demand characteristics.

5 Conclusion

The goal of the present study was to determine the effectiveness of different instructional methods on learning. We found that performance did not differ when the training instruction provided was in a video or lecture format in an online environment, showing that both methods produce similar, positive outcomes for easy material. Therefore, the findings from this study support the notion that videos and live lectures are equally effective for learning. When the topic of study is particularly challenging, instructors must consider other factors aside from the design of instructional materials to prevent performance deficits from occurring. Future research should consider what type of support or feedback has the most impact on student performance for complex subjects in an online environment.

Acknowledgment. We thank Jim Miles for constructive feedback on the content of the paper and to Vannessa Nguyen and Ryan Karp for their assistance in running participants.

References

1. Sablić, M., Mirosavljević, A., Škugor, A.: Video-based learning (VBL)—past, present and future: an overview of the research published from 2008 to 2019. Technol. Knowl. Learn. **26**(4), 1061–1077 (2020). https://doi.org/10.1007/s10758-020-09455-5
2. Yousef, A. M. F., Chatti, M. A., Schroeder, U.: Video-based learning: a critical analysis of the research published in 2003–2013 and future visions. In: eLmL 2014: The Sixth Int. Conference on Mobile, Hybrid, and On-line Learn, pp. 112–119 (2014)
3. Chick, R.C., et al.: Using technology to maintain the education of residents during the COVID-19 pandemic. J. Surg. Educ. **77**(4), 729–732 (2020). https://doi.org/10.1016/j.jsurg.2020.03.018
4. Surgenor, D., et al.: The impact of video technology on learning: a cooking skills experiment. Appetite **114**, 306–312 (2017). https://doi.org/10.1016/j.appet.2017.03.037
5. Xiao, Y., et al.: Video-based training increases sterile-technique compliance during central venous catheter insertion. Crit. Care Med. **35**(5), 1302–1306 (2007). https://doi.org/10.1097/01.CCM.0000263457.81998.27
6. Chotiyarnwong, P., Boonnasa, W., Chotiyarnwong, C., Unnanuntana, A.: Video-based learning versus traditional lecture-based learning for osteoporosis education: a randomized controlled trial. Aging Clin. Exp. Res. **33**(1), 125–131 (2020). https://doi.org/10.1007/s40520-020-01514-2
7. DuPaul, G.J., et al.: Face-to-face versus online behavioral parent training for young children at risk for ADHD: treatment engagement and outcomes. J. Clin. Child Adol. Psych. **47**, S369–S383 (2018). https://doi.org/10.1080/15374416.2017.1342544

8. Mallonee, S., Phillips, J., Holloway, K., Riggs, D.: Training providers in the use of evidence-based treatments: a comparison of in-person and online delivery modes. Psych. Learn. Tech. **17**(1), 61–72 (2018). https://doi.org/10.1177/1475725717744678
9. Scott, M., Feldman, B.N., Underwood, M.: Delivering professional development in suicide prevention: a comparison of online versus in-person training. Ped. Health Promot. **2**(4), 266–275 (2016). https://doi.org/10.1177/2373379916658667
10. Wong, W.K., Ng, P.K.: An empirical study on E-learning versus traditional learning among electronics engineering students. Am. J. Appl. Sci. **13**(6), 836–844 (2016). https://doi.org/10.3844/ajassp.2016.836.844
11. Roy, R.B., McMahon, G.T.: Video-based cases disrupt deep critical thinking in problem-based learning. Med. Educ. **46**(4), 426–435 (2012). https://doi.org/10.1111/j.1365-2923.2011.04197.x
12. Diwanji, P., Simon, B. P., Märki, M., Korkut, S., Dornberger, R.: Success factors of online learning videos. In: 2014 International Conference on Interactive Mobile Communication Technologies and Learning (IMCL 2014), pp. 125–132 (2014). https://doi.org/10.1109/IMCTL.2014.7011119
13. Chin, C., Osborne, J.: Students' questions: a potential resource for teaching and learning science. Stud. Sci. Educ. **44**(1), 1–39 (2008). https://doi.org/10.1080/03057260701828101
14. Jensen, S.A.: In-class versus online video lectures: similar learning outcomes, but a preference for in-class. Teach. Psych. **38**(4), 298–302 (2011). https://doi.org/10.1177/0098628311421336
15. Sweller, J.: Cognitive load during problem solving: effects on learning. Cog. Sci. **12**(2), 257–285 (1988). https://doi.org/10.1016/0364-0213(88)90023-7
16. Sweller, J., van Merrienboer, J.J.G., Paas, F.G.W.C.: Cognitive architecture and instructional design. Educ. Psych. Rev. **10**(3), 251–296 (1998). https://doi.org/10.1023/A:1022193728205
17. Sweller, J.: Cognitive load theory, learning difficulty, and instructional design. Learn. Instruct. **4**(4), 295–312 (1994). https://doi.org/10.1016/0959-4752(94)90003-5
18. Chandler, P., Sweller, J.: Cognitive load theory and the format of instruction. Cog. Instruct. **8**(4), 293–332 (1991). https://doi.org/10.1207/s1532690xci0804_2
19. Mayer, R.E.: Cognitive theory of multimedia learning. In: Mayer, R. E. (ed.) The Cambridge Handbook of Multimedia Learning, pp. 31–48. Cambridge University Press
20. Mayer, R.E., Moreno, R.: Nine ways to reduce cognitive load in multimedia learning. Educ. Psych. **38**(1), 43–52 (2003). https://doi.org/10.1207/S15326985EP3801_6
21. Mayer, R.E.: Evidence-based principles for how to design effective instructional videos. J. App. Res. Mem. Cog. **10**(2), 229–240 (2021). https://doi.org/10.1016/j.jarmac.2021.03.007
22. Brame, C.J.: Effective educational videos (2015). https://cft.vanderbilt.edu/guides-sub-pages/effective-educational-videos/
23. de Koning, B.B., Tabbers, H.K., Rikers, R.M.J.P., Paas, F.: Towards a framework for attention cueing in instructional animations: guidelines for research and design. Educ. Psych. Rev. **21**, 113–140 (2009). https://doi.org/10.1007/s10648-009-9098-7
24. van Merriënboer, J.J.G., Sweller, J.: Cognitive load theory in health professional education: Design principles and strategies. Med. Educ. **44**(1), 85–93 (2010). https://doi.org/10.1111/j.1365-2923.2009.03498.x
25. Mautone, P.D., Mayer, R.E.: Signaling as a cognitive guide in multimedia learning. J. of Educ. Psych. **93**(2), 377–389 (2001). https://doi.org/10.1037/0022-0663.93.2.377
26. Bolkan, S.: The importance of instructor clarity and its effect on student learning: facilitating elaboration by reducing cognitive load. Comm. Rep. **29**(3), 152–162 (2016). https://doi.org/10.1080/08934215.2015.1067708
27. Shadiev, R., Hwang, W-Y., Huang, Y-M., Liu, T-Y.: The impact of supported and annotated mobile learning on achievement and cognitive load. Educ. Tech. Soc. **18**(4), 53–69 (2015). http://www.jstor.org/stable/jeductechsoci.18.4.53

28. Blasiman, R.N., Larabee, D., Fabry, D.: Distracted students: a comparison of multiple types of distractions on learning in online lectures. Schol. Teach. Learn. Psych. **4**(4), 222–230 (2018). https://doi.org/10.1037/stl0000122

29. Song, K-S., Nam, S., Lim, H., Kim, J.: Analysis of youngers' media multitasking behaviors and effect on learning. Int. J. Multi. Ubiq. Eng. **8**(4), 191–198 (2013). http://citeseerx.ist.psu.edu/viewdoc/summary?doi=10.1.1.366.8581

30. Eitel, A., Endres, T., Renkl, A.: Self-management as a bridge between cognitive load and self-regulated learning: the illustrative case of seductive details. Educ. Psychol. Rev. **32**(4), 1073–1087 (2020). https://doi.org/10.1007/s10648-020-09559-5

31. Choi, H.-H., van Merriënboer, J.J.G., Paas, F.: Effects of the physical environment on cognitive load and learning: towards a new model of cognitive load. Educ. Psychol. Rev. **26**(2), 225–244 (2014). https://doi.org/10.1007/s10648-014-9262-6

32. Martin, F., Wang, C., Sadaf, A.: Student perception of helpfulness of facilitation strategies that enhance instructor presence, connectedness, engagement and learning in online courses. Int. High. Ed. **37**, 52–65 (2018). https://doi.org/10.1016/j.iheduc.2018.01.003

33. Wang, J., Antonenko, P., Dawson, K.: Does visual attention to the instructor in online video affect learning and learner perceptions? an eye-tracking analysis. Comp. Educ. **146**, 103779 (2020). https://doi.org/10.1016/j.compedu.2019.103779

34. Chen, C.-M., Wu, C.-H.: Effects of different video lecture types on sustained attention, emotion, cognitive load, and learning performance. Comp. Educ. **80**, 108–121 (2015). https://doi.org/10.1016/j.compedu.2014.08.015

35. Bai, X., Vu, K-P. L.: Online learning: Does integrated video lecture help you learn more efficienty? Hum. Aut. Int. (in press)

36. Newlon, J.L., Weber, Z.A., Isaacs, A.N., Plake, K.S.I., Zillich, A., Woodyard, J.L.: Pharmacy student perceptions and preferences of in-person versus video-recorded evaluations in skill-based courses. Amer. J. Pharm. Educ. **84**(11), 7976 (2020). https://doi.org/10.5688/ajpe7976

37. Pal, D., Patra, S.: University students' perception of video-based learning in times of COVID-19: A TAM/TTF perspective. Int. J. Hum. Comp. Interact. **37**(10), 903–921 (2020). https://doi.org/10.1080/10447318.2020.1848164

38. Huang, C-H.: The influence of self-efficacy, perceived usefulness, perceived ease of use, and cognitive load on students' learning motivation, learning attitude, and learning satisfaction in blended learning methods. In: ICETM 2020: 2020 3rd International Conference on Education and Techlogy Management, pp. 29–35. https://doi.org/10.1145/3446590.3446595

39. Costley, J., Lange, C.: The mediating effects of germane cognitive load on the relationship between instructional design and students' future behavioral intention. Elec. J. e-Learn. **15**(2), 174–187 (2017). https://academic-publishing.org/index.php/ejel/article/view/1830

40. Lee, M.-C.: Explaining and predicting users' continuance intention toward e-learning: an extension of the expectation-confirmation model. Comp. Educ. **54**(2), 506–516 (2010). https://doi.org/10.1016/j.compedu.2009.09.002

41. Feinberg, S., Murphy, M.: Applying cognitive load theory to the design of web-based instruction. In: 18th Annal Conference on Computer Documentation, pp. 353–360 (2000). https://doi.org/10.1109/IPCC.2000.887293

42. Hollender, N., Hofmann, C., Deneke, M., Schmitz, B.: Integrating cognitive load theory and concepts of human-computer interaction. Comp. Hum. Behav. **26**(6), 1278–1288 (2010). https://doi.org/10.1016/j.chb.2010.05.031

43. Davids, M.R., Halperin, M.L., Chikte, U.M.E.: Optimising cognitive load and usability to improve the impact of e-learning in medical education. Afr. J. Health Prof. Educ. **7**(2), 147–152 (2015). https://doi.org/10.7196/AJHPE.569

44. Clarke, M.A., Schuetzler, R.M., Windle, J.R., Pachunka, E., Fruhling, A.: Usability and cognitive load in the design of a personal health record. Health Pol. Tech. **9**(2), 218–224 (2020). https://doi.org/10.1016/j.hlpt.2019.10.002

45. Nielsen, J.: 10 usability heuristics for user interface design. Nielsen Norman Group (1994). https://www.nngroup.com/articles/ten-usability-heuristics/
46. Mohd Hashim, M.H., Tasir, Z.: An e-learning environment embedded with sign language videos: research into its usability and the academic performance and learning patterns of deaf students. Educ. Tech. Res. Dev. **68**(6), 2873–2911 (2020). https://doi.org/10.1007/s11423-020-09802-4
47. Granić, A.: Experience with usability evaluation of e-learning systems. Univ. Access Inf. Soc. **7**, 209 (2008). https://doi.org/10.1007/s10209-008-0118-z
48. Mutlu-Bayraktar, D., Cosgun, V., Altan, T.: Cognitive load in multimedia learning environments: a systematic review. Comp. Educ. **141**, 103618 (2019). https://doi.org/10.1016/j.compedu.2019.103618
49. World Wide Web Consortium (W3C). Accessibility (2018). https://www.w3.org/standards/webdesign/accessibility
50. Henry, S. L.: WCAG 2 overview. In: World Wide Web Consortium (W3C) (2022). https://www.w3.org/WAI/standards-guidelines/wcag/
51. Bangor, A., Kortum, P., Miller, J.: Determining what individual SUS scores mean: adding an adjective rating scale. J. Usabil. Stud. **4**(3), 114–123 (2009). https://uxpajournal.org/determining-what-individual-sus-scores-mean-adding-an-adjective-rating-scale/
52. Chen, K.-C., Jang, S.-J.: Motivation in online learning: testing a model of self-determination theory. Comp. Hum. Behav. **26**(4), 741–752 (2010). https://doi.org/10.1016/j.chb.2010.01.011

Impact of the Implementation of Resources with Augmented Reality in Education

Omar Cóndor-Herrera[1] and Carlos Ramos-Galarza[1,2]

[1] Centro de Investigación en Mecatrónica y Sistemas Interactivos MIST/Carrera de Psicología/Maestría en Educación Mención Innovación y Liderazgo Educativo, Universidad Tecnológica Indoamérica, Av. Machala y Sabanilla, Quito, Ecuador
{omarcondor,carlosramos}@uti.edu.ec
[2] Facultad de Psicología, Pontificia Universidad Católica del Ecuador, Av. 12 de Octubre y Roca, Quito, Ecuador
caramos@puce.edu.ec

Abstract. Augmented reality (AR) has shown positive effects in education. In the present investigation, the results of an educational intervention, which consisted in the implementation of AR resources in the teaching process, are presented. The research had as objectives A) to analyze students' perspectives on the implementation of AR in the educational field; B) to design resources with AR with the participants, as products of their projects; and C) to compare the performance of students doing projects with AR with their performance in a project done previously. The study was carried out with a population of 39 students between 12 and 16 years old who developed research projects on various topics in which they had to develop a product as the result of their research. The duration of the project was 6 weeks, for which the students worked in groups with the PBL methodology. To collect information about the learning experience, a survey was applied to the participants at the end of the intervention. Products, because of the project, were developed and presented by the students, and the grades obtained in the development of the project and qualifications obtained in previous projects were compared. Once the results were analyzed, it was evident that A) the vast majority of students surveyed gave answers in favor of the use of the technology to improve their motivation to learn, which significantly improved their willingness to carry out learning activities; B) the products developed were brochures and posters assembled with AR resources; and C) an increase of 2.24 points in the course average occurred in relation to the previous project.

Keywords: Augmented reality · Education · Innovation

1 Introduction

The educational context is currently going through a restructuring of its paradigms. It has gradually incorporated into its process different resources, methodologies, and tools linked largely to educational technology, which, during the COVID-19 pandemic, was

G. Meiselwitz et al. (Eds.): HCII 2022, LNCS 13517, pp. 207–220, 2022.
https://doi.org/10.1007/978-3-031-22131-6_15

accelerated because of educational activities in isolation migrating to virtual settings [1]. Various studies have suggested that the use of different technological tools improves the learning experience of students as well as their motivation and predisposition to learning [2, 3].

In the range of resources and platforms offered by technology, augmented reality (AR) is found. It has been implemented with positive results in various areas of education, such as anatomy teaching [4], literature, reading comprehension, immersive learning [5], preschool education, the creation of educational video games [6], and emotional intelligence [7] to cite some examples. Consequently, it can be mentioned that the use of this technology could facilitate the understanding of scientific concepts, since it complements the student's sensory perception of reality by incorporating computer-generated content into the environment. This offers a new form of interactivity between real and virtual worlds [8, 9], which, for the educational field, represents an innovative way for the teacher to present to students the contents to study [10] by combining them with methodologies such as gamification [11], PBL, or educational approaches such as STEAM education. At present, in the rise of digital technologies, technological tools can be considered powerful instruments at the service of education due to the ease and speed they offer to access information in different formats, as well as the various possibilities of immediate communication that they allow, the sharing of information online, etc., thus contributing to optimization of the teaching and learning process [12].

Next, the characteristics of AR platforms and applications to create resources are presented, as well as the benefits of the application of AR in learning. Later, the results found in the investigation are detailed.

1.1 Augmented Reality

AR can be defined as a technology that enables the combination of virtual objects and real objects in real time through technological devices [13]. AR all ows reality to be completed without replacing it, unlike virtual reality (VR), which immerses the individual in a non-real world in which one cannot see the world around [14]. Other authors define AR as the interaction of audio, graphics, text, and other virtual elements superimposed on reality, where objects can be displayed in real time. In reality, some AR applications use mobile devices such as smartphones and tablets to allow the user to interact with digital information integrated into physical space [15].

It is necessary to differentiate VR from AR, since the latter combines digital information with the real environment [16], unlike VR where the individual accesses information through an immersive, simulated environment.

1.2 AR Platforms and Applications

There are various platforms and applications that allow the development of resources with AR, among which we can mention mywebar.com as well as unitear.com [17], which are platforms that allow users to create resources with AR on triggers or activators created with QR codes, on images, on curved surfaces, or superimposed on real-life objects. The platform mywebar.com allows one to place images, text, audio, video, 3D models, and 360° images on the triggers or to create complete AR scenes, as shown in Fig. 1 [18].

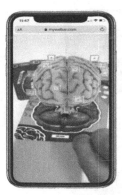

Fig. 1. AR resource platform mywebar.com

Mobile applications such as Quiver Vision [19] already present AR animations that can be used by the user. In the case of this application, the triggers are images of various themes such as cells, coloring drawings, and volcanoes, among others, as shown in Fig. 2. These AR animations can be used by students in the educational field.

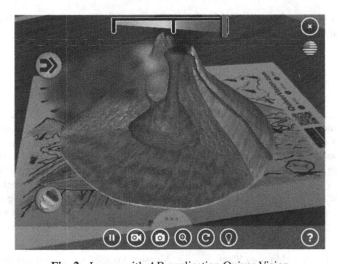

Fig. 2. Image with AR application Quiver Vision

Like this application, one can find many more that can be implemented without difficulty in different educational areas, depending on the content of the application. For example, the Animal 4D + application shows cards with AR animation of animals, and the AR application Cam 4D + is an AR camera application that allows one to create an AR environment anywhere and anytime. We also have the Humanoid 4D + application, which has AR resources on the human body (see Fig. 3). All these applications are from Octogon Studio [20]. In the case of Raap Chemistry, the application allows visualizing the anatomical structure of all the elements of the periodic table.

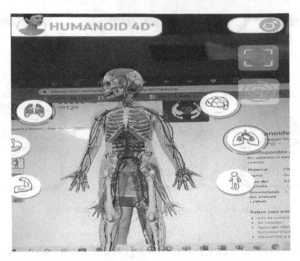

Fig. 3. Humanoid 4D +

1.3 Application of Augmented Reality in Education

In the table 1 the reader will find in detail the main findings in recent studies on the application of AR in education.

Table 1. Studies on the application of AR

Research title	authors	research	findings
Educational video games for girls and boys in preschool education using robotics and augmented reality	Méndez-Porras, Alfaro-Velasco, & Rojas-Guzmán, 2021 [6]	The objective of this work is to help preschool teachers strengthen STEM education in girls and boys through the use of a video game on topics from the didactic guide of public education	The first results show that functional video games can be developed using these technologies and following the didactic guide for preschool education
Augmented reality as a resource for training in higher education	Martínez Pérez, Fernández Bárbara, & Borroso, 2021 [13]	Measure knowledge students have about emerging technologies, specifically AR design; produce and apply digital objects in AR; assess the usefulness, potentialities, and limitations offered by the application of AR in higher education	AR can enhance collaborative group work creating inclusive scenarios and contexts

(continued)

Table 1. (*continued*)

Research title	authors	research	findings
Augmented reality system for teaching mathematics during COVID-19's times	Naranjo, Robalino-López, Alarcon-Ortiz, Peralvo, & Garcia, 2021 [21]	This article develops an AR system based on the Singapore method for teaching exact sciences	The students improved their academic average when using this type of tool
Comparing reading comprehension between children reading augmented reality and print storybooks	Delneshin, Hamid, Yazdan, & Hassan, 2020 [3]	Measures the reading comprehension of children reading an AR storybook and compares it to their counterparts reading the traditional print version of the same book	Children who experienced an augmented storybook were better at retelling and answering comprehension questions
Augmented reality as a support resource in the teaching-learning process	Hidalgo-Cajo, B., Hidalgo-Cajo, D., Montenegro-Chanalata, & Hidalgo-Cajo, I., 2021 [4]	The main objective of the research is to design, implement, and evaluate a didactic proposal based on AR; we worked with an intervention group and a control group	The control group obtained an average of 2.77 out of 10, while the experimental group obtained an average of 7.97 out of 10; The students considered that the AR resources aroused motivation in them
Literary education and reading promotion supported in immersive literary environments with augmented reality	del Rosario- Neira & del- Moral, 2021 [5]	To analyze 25 ILE created by future teachers aimed at promoting literary education and reading in preschool education; determine the level of satisfaction of future teachers at the end of the experience, through a survey	The innovative experience was very successful for pre-service teachers, who took advantage of AR opportunities to design activities for literary education and promote playful and multisensory learning
Innovation in the university classroom through augmented reality: Analysis from the perspective of Spanish and Latin American students	Cabero-Almenara et al., 2021 [22]	To analyze the experiences of university innovation with immersive technologies (AR) of various careers of the Pablo de Olavide University (Spain) and the Catholic University of Santiago de Guayaquil (Ecuador)	The advantages of AR perceived by students were the development of cognitive and digital skills

(*continued*)

Table 1. (*continued*)

Research title	authors	research	findings
Impact of augmented reality technology on academic achievement and motivation of students from public and private Mexican schools: A case study in a middle-school geometry course	Ibañez, Portillo, Cabada, & Barrón, 2020 [9]	Design of an AR application for students to practice the basic principles of geometry, and contrast it with an application implemented in a web-based learning environment	Students using the AR-based learning environments scored higher on the post-test than those using the web-based application
MantarayAR: Leveraging augmented reality to teach probability and sampling	Conley, Atkinson, Nguyen, & Nelson, 2020 [23]	The purpose of this study was to explore whether AR learning experiences can support learning for college-level students	Participants assigned to an AR experience condition reported a statistically significantly higher perception of engagement
EmoFindAR: Evaluation of a mobile multiplayer augmented reality game for primary school children	López & Jaen, 2020 [7]	The use of markerless mobile AR to improve the socialization, communication skills, and emotional intelligence of primary school children	The collaborative game version had a greater impact on the emotional affection, social interaction, and interest of the participants
Augmented songbook: an augmented reality educational application for raising music awareness	Rusiñol, Chazalon, & Diaz, 2017 [24]	Development of an AR mobile application that aims to sensitize young children to the abstract concepts of music	The application allowed the superimposition of increased content on pages of a songbook, which allowed obtaining positive results in the participants

1.4 Benefits

The field of AR has gained great relevance in recent years. Various investigations have found significant benefits with the application of AR in education, such as the study carried out at the Pablo de Olavide University of Seville (Spain) and the Catholic University of Santiago de Guayaquil (Ecuador) in which different AR applications were evaluated. The students indicated that they perceived the development of cognitive and digital skills as benefits of the application of AR in education [22]. Other studies have indicated that students considered that AR resources arouse in them the motivation to use them due to their ease of use and the interaction they experience between content and virtual objects, generating knowledge with entertainment [4].

1.5 Limitations for the Implementation of Augmented Reality

Among the limitations to successfully incorporating different AR resources in education are the digital skills of teachers in the use of technological tools. Thus, continuous training of teachers is inherently necessary because when they understand the application of technological resources as well as the management of teaching methodologies linked to a technology, better learning results can be expected when these resources are used [4, 6].

2 Investigation of Hypotheses

Base on the intervention carried out, it was projected that the students would benefit by the technological educational process, which would improve their average performance when comparing their measurements in the development of two projects, one with the incorporation of AR and the other worked in a traditional way. In the same way, it was expected that students would positively perceive the incorporation of AR resources in their learning process.

3 Methodology

Quantitative research was carried out in which a questionnaire was applied to identify aspects such as the educational benefit, motivation, and taste of students regarding the use of AR in their learning. The averages obtained by the students in the development of two projects, one without intervention with AR and one developed with an AR intervention, were compared.

There was a population of 39 students who consented to their voluntary participation in the intervention. The students were in a range between 12 and 16 years of age. All participants belonged to the E.U. Reply May 24 to the fiscal educational system of the city of Quito, Ecuador.

4 Results

Table 2 shows the response frequencies in the survey applied to the participants.

Figure 4 shows the percentages corresponding to the responses obtained in the survey.

Table 2. Results found in the applied questionnaire

Item	Answer frequency				
	Strongly agree	Somewhat agree	Neither agree nor disagree	Somewhat disagree	Strongly disagree
Q1. Have you had any previous experience using augmented reality activities in the classroom?	25	12	2	0	0
Q2. Do you think that the use of augmented reality resources encouraged your participation in the learning process?	25	12	2	0	0
Q3. Did you feel motivated working with the augmented reality resources?	21	13	5	0	0
Q4. Did you like the activities that could be carried out with the augmented reality resources?	25	8	6	0	0
Q5. Would you like to work on other projects with these resources?	21	12	3	1	2
Q6. Do you consider that you were able to learn the topics studied, with this way of working?	24	14	1	0	0

(continued)

Table 2. (*continued*)

Item	Answer frequency				
	Strongly agree	Somewhat agree	Neither agree nor disagree	Somewhat disagree	Strongly disagree
Q7. How would you rate this learning experience with augmented reality resources?	23	12	4	0	0
Q8. Did this learning methodology generate frustration?	0	0	4	12	23
Q9. Did this learning methodology generate motivation?	21	11	7	0	0
Q10. Does the application of these resources in education seem innovative to you?	27	9	3	0	0
Q11. Are you interested in learning how you could use this type of technology in other areas of study?	29	10	0	0	0

The vast majority of the students surveyed gave answers in favor of the use of the technology to improve their motivation to learn, which significantly improved their willingness to carry out learning activities.

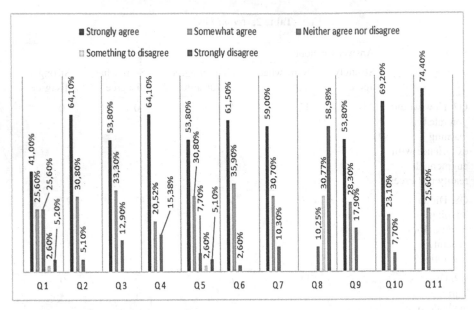

Fig. 4. Results found in the applied questionnaire

On the other hand, as products developed by the students, we find brochures, posters, buildables that incorporate ima ges, audio, text, video, and 360° images in triggers or activators in QR made with applications such as me-qr.com and mywebar.com. Figure 5 shows images of the work carried out.

Finally, we compared the averages obtained by the students in the development of the two projects: a project carried out before the intervention, which was worked in a normal way, and a second project developed incorporating AR resources.

In the development of the first project, the group obtained an average of 7.23 out of 10; in the second project, the group obtained an average of 9.47, increasing its performance by 2.24 points, which can be seen in Fig. 6.

Fig. 5. Works developed by the students

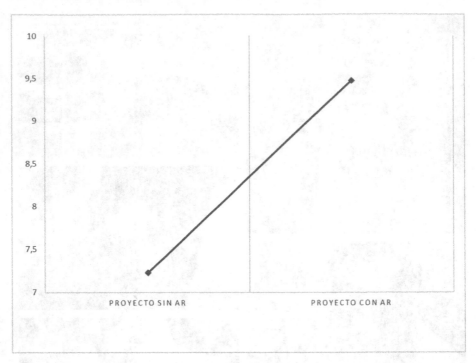

Fig. 6. Average obtained in project without AR intervention and average with AR intervention

5 Conclusions

In this article, we have reported the results of a research study that analyzed student perceptions of the use of AR resources in their learning process. The students were able to successfully develop resources with novel and useful AR elements for their training.

A high percentage of students expressed favorable responses regarding the use of AR in the teaching-learning process. The vast majority agreed that the use of AR improved their motivation to learn and increased their willingness to carry out learning activities. In general, they indicated that working with AR was a positive experience and that they would like to apply these resources in other areas of study.

The comparison between averages suggested the benefit of using these types of technological strategies in the teaching and learning process. These innovative practices generate a real challenge in the educational process since it is necessary, in the local context, for the migration of many traditional processes toward technological resources.

As future research, it is proposed to extend this type of intervention to other areas of knowledge and to a larger population; similarly, it is proposed to evaluate the usefulness of AR mobile applications for students.

References

1. Cóndor-Herrera, O.: Educar en tiempos de COVID-19. CIENCIAMERICA **9**(2), 31–37 (2020)
2. Cóndor-Herrera, O., Ramos-Galarza, C.: The impact of a technological intervention program on learning mathematical skills. Educ. Inf. Technol. **26**(2), 1423–1433 (2020). https://doi.org/10.1007/s10639-020-10308-y
3. Delneshin, D., Jamali, H., Mansourian, Y., Rastegarpour, H.: Comparing reading comprehension between children reading augmented reality and print storybooks. Comput. Educ. **153**, 1–24 (2020)
4. Hidalgo-Cajo, B., Hidalgo-Cajo, D., Montenegro-Chanalata, M., Hidalgo-Cajo, I.: Augmented reality as a support resource in the teaching-learning process. Revista Electronica Interuniversitaria de Formacion del Profesorado **24**(3), 43–55 (2021)
5. del Rosario-Neira, M., del-Moral, E.: Literary education and reading promotion supported in immersive literary environments with augmented reality. OCNOS **20**(3) (2021)
6. Méndez-Porras, A., Alfaro-Velasco, J., Rojas-Guzmán, R.: Educational video games for girls and boys in preschool education using robotics and augmented reality. RISTI - Revista Iberica de Sistemas e Tecnologias de Informacao **2021**(42), 472–485 (2021)
7. López, L., Jaen, J.: EmoFindAR: evaluation of a mobile multiplayer augmented reality game for primary school children. Comput. Educ. **149**, 1–42 (2020)
8. Kaur, N., Pathan, R., Khwaja, U., Sarkar, P., Rathod, B., Murthy, S.: GeoSolvAR: augmented reality based application for mental rotation. In: 2018 IEEE Tenth International Conference on Technology for Education, vol. T4E, pp. 45–52 (2018)
9. Ibañez, M., Delgado, C.: Augmented reality for STEM learning: a systematic review. Comput. Educ. **123**, 109–123 (2018)
10. Cóndor-Herrera, O., Acosta-Rodas, P., Ramos-Galarza, C.: Augmented reality teaching resources and its implementation in the teaching-learning process. In: Nazir, S., Ahram, T.Z., Karwowski, W. (eds.) AHFE 2021. LNNS, vol. 269, pp. 149–154. Springer, Cham (2021). https://doi.org/10.1007/978-3-030-80000-0_18
11. Cóndor-Herrera, O., Acosta-Rodas, P., Ramos-Galarza, C.: Gamification teaching for an active learning. In: Intelligent Human Systems Integration 2021. IHSI 2021. Advances in Intelligent Systems and Computing, vol. 1322 (2021)
12. García-Varcálcel, A., Gómez-Pablos, V.: Aprendizaje Basado en Proyectos (ABP): Evaluación desde la perspectiva de alumnos de. Revista de Investigación Educativa **35**(1), 113–131 (2017)
13. Martínez Pérez, S., Bárbara, F., Borroso, J.: La realidad aumentada como recursos para la formación en la educación superior. Campus Virtuales **10**(1), 9–19 (2021)
14. Azuma, R.: A survey of augmented reality. Teleoper. Virt. Environ. **6**(4), 355–385 (1997)
15. Dundeleavy, M., Dede, C.: Augmented reality teaching and learning. In: Handbook of Research on Educational Communications and Technology, pp. 735–745 (2014)
16. Liberati, N.: Augmented reality and ubiquitous computing: the hidden potentialities of augmented reality. AI Soc. **31**(1), 17–28 (2014). https://doi.org/10.1007/s00146-014-0543-x
17. UniteAR (2022). https://www.unitear.com/
18. mywebar.com (2021). https://mywebar.com/
19. QuiverVision (2022). https://quivervision.com/
20. octagon.studio (2022). https://octagon.studio/products-and-services/4d-flashcards/
21. Naranjo, J., Robalino-López, A., Alarcon-Ortiz, A., Peralvo, A., Garcia, M.: Augmented reality system for teaching mathematics during COVID-19's times. RISTI - Revista Iberica de Sistemas e Tecnologias de Informacao **2021**(42), 510–521 (2021)

22. Cabero-Almenara, J., Vásquez-Cano, E., Villota-Oyarvide, W., López-Meneses, E.: Innovation in the university classroom through augmented reality: analysis from the perspective of the Spanish and Latin American student. Revista Electronica Educare **25**(3), 1–17 (2021)

23. Conley, Q., Atkinson, R., Nguyen, F., Nelson, B.: MantarayAR: leveraging augmented reality to teach probability and sampling. Comput. Educ. **153**, 1–22 (2020)

24. Rusiñol, M., Chazalon, J., Diaz-Chito, K.: Augmented songbook: an augmented reality educational application for raising music awareness. Multimedia Tools Appl. **77**(11), 13773–13798 (2017). https://doi.org/10.1007/s11042-017-4991-4

Research on the Construction of Graphical Data Intelligence Education Driven by Digital Intelligence Integration

Yali Chen[1]([✉]), Zhenxi Gong[2], and Qiyan Xing[3]

[1] School of Design, South China University of Technology, Guangzhou 510641, China
chenyali@scut.edu.cn
[2] School of Architecture, Hunan University, Changsha 410082, China
[3] School of Design South, China University of Technology, Guangzhou 510006, People's Republic of China

Abstract. With the development and application of technologies such as 5G and big data artificial intelligence, humanity has entered the era of digital intelligence convergence (BD + AI), which has enabled the future of education and learning to move into a new era driven by graphical data. In the field of education, graphical data is intuitive, panoramic, interactive, intelligent, scalable and narrative, bringing effective experiential aspects to student learning, teacher teaching, learning assessment and teaching management. This paper discusses the application of digital intelligence to education and teaching with the help of its multi-technology fusion model, the research model of knowledge mapping, and the application of intelligent education as pictorial data that we can perceive and analyse, so that intelligent graphical data, data-driven, and data empowerment can provide better and more data experiences and services for teaching and learning in education.

Keywords: Digital intelligence integration · Data visualisation · Experience services

1 Introduction

The rapid development of technologies such as artificial intelligence, big data, AR/VR and 5G, especially the popular use of mobile terminals, has brought about tremendous impact and changes to classroom teaching, as well as unprecedented opportunities and possibilities for change and innovation in teaching.However, most of the current applications of intelligent technology in teaching are mainly characterised by intelligence, bringing more convenience and efficiency to teaching, while many deep-rooted problems in classroom teaching have not yet been well addressed. However, a glance at the current education system reveals that it still largely follows the traditional schooling model, i.e. classroom-based, large-scale and standardised training of talents [1]. This model, which was developed at the beginning of industrialised society, has become increasingly difficult to adapt to the development needs of human society in the smart age. Smart technology has become an interconnected and collaborative technological

© Springer Nature Switzerland AG 2022
G. Meiselwitz et al. (Eds.): HCII 2022, LNCS 13517, pp. 221–230, 2022.
https://doi.org/10.1007/978-3-031-22131-6_16

ecology. It is worth drawing the attention of the education community to gain insight into the future development of education and the realities faced in the process of change from the perspective of technology ecology. It is thus clear that in a future-oriented society, it has become a general consensus to use information technology to promote educational change. To this end, how to build an intelligent inquiry teaching model supported by intelligent technology and explore an intelligent inquiry teaching model that goes beyond traditional inquiry teaching, with a view to providing more reflections and references for inquiry teaching reform and innovative talents.

2   Literature Review

As media technologies continue to evolve, educational scenarios are expanding the boundaries of what they can do, i.e. they can combine the virtual with the actual, enabling real-time monitoring and simulation-reality interaction. The 'space' and 'presence' of education is redefined by the interconnectedness of the scenes. Digital intelligence technology has provided changes to professional practice and practical teaching, enhancing students' engineering practice and problem-solving abilities, in addition to paying more attention to innovative talent cultivation modes in the era of intelligent education. With the innovative application and integration of information technology in the field of education, virtual technology has gradually become popular in the teaching of engineering majors, continuously promoting the change of teaching mode.

Virtual experimental platforms are usually based on 2D or 3D modelling techniques to provide simulated and intuitive experimental apparatus and operating environments [2] to facilitate learners' understanding of relevant concepts and knowledge, and are now widely used in the teaching of secondary school science subjects. However, virtual technology only supports a shallow level of interaction between the learner and the learning environment and has significant limitations for the development of manipulative skills in laboratory teaching. While learners can compensate for some operational details through imaginative forms, the immersion experienced is relatively shallow. Virtual Reality (VR) technology creates immersive experiences for users by blending multiple information channels to create interactive 3D dynamic scenes and behavioural action simulations.Due to the advantages of depth of thought, richness of constructed scenarios and variety of sensory stimuli [3], virtual reality technology has great potential to improve learners' cognitive and motor skills by simulating realistic panoramic laboratory environments, dynamically modelling laboratory teaching methods and conditions, and providing posture-based behavioural interactions [4].

Internationally, scholars have applied VR technology to experiments in teaching or scientific knowledge exploration [5], and medical experimental studies [6], but most studies only focus on whether VR environments can improve learning outcomes and motivation, and do not delve into whether VR environments can facilitate the acquisition of cognitive transfer and motor skills. In China, there are also many scholars who are continuously exploring the potential of VR applications in education, but most of the research focuses on the application conceptualisation and system design development level [7]. In contrast, the presentation of information and sensory interaction in VR-based immersive laboratory teaching environments does not reflect an overwhelming feeling in the learners' experiential learning performance.

In smart education based on big data, cloud computing and other intelligent technologies, virtual simulation technology is used to create a smart curriculum that triggers the development of students' innovative abilities [8]; while smart management is based on a cloud platform for timely processing and accurate decision-making on external demands [9]. In addition to the inheritance and development of traditional classrooms, traditional curriculum and traditional management, smart education is also an important way to integrate smart technology for the development of teachers and students, so that both parties can have a better experience.

3 Research Method

Curriculum theorist H Taba suggests that the development of thinking requires the accumulation of thinking experience in the process of problem solving, and that a goal-oriented approach to teaching is likely to result in a lack of thinking experience for students [10]. In contrast to traditional teaching methods such as books and blackboards, resource tools integrated with information technology are becoming essential for the implementation of inquiry-based smart teaching. However, due to the imbalance between 'technical support and the need for enquiry', students' independent enquiry is generally under-performing [11]. This is coupled with the fact that students generally follow the instructions of the teacher and are severely lacking in the process of accumulating thinking experiences such as summarizing [12]. The traditional inquiry-based teaching model focuses more on delineating procedures for inquiry-based teaching activities, prompting students to focus on developing thinking experiences supported by intelligent technology [13]. For this reason, the construction of an intelligent inquiry-based teaching model supported by intelligent technology has certain theoretical and practical implications [14].

Firstly, a theoretical framework for an intelligent teaching model needs to be constructed to address the limitations of the traditional inquiry-based teaching model and to optimise the epistemological basis for the effectiveness of inquiry-based teaching practice [15]. The intelligent teaching model is achieved through the use of intelligent technology [16]. By setting up virtual simulation technologies such as XR, creating a variety of contexts to trigger the development of students' creative abilities, and relying on new generation intelligent technologies such as curriculum mapping and digital twins [17], students are motivated to actively construct scientific knowledge and develop higher-order thinking and scientific literacy.

Secondly, the key elements and structural features of the intelligent teaching model are constructed, focusing on the key elements of theoretical foundations, teaching objectives, conditions for achievement and teaching evaluation, and the evaluation structures of problem situations, learning paths, learning outcomes and the degree of integration with information technology, experience and cognition [18]. "5G + XR" creates scenarios that combine the digital simulation world with the real physical world. The graphical approach transforms traditional paper models to bring a richer immersive experience to students, bringing all of their senses into the interaction and even allowing them to perceive and touch the virtual world based on haptic technology [19]. "5G + XR" immersive simulations provide highly interactive, imaginative and immersive learning environments and experiences for intelligent teaching and learning, facilitating integrated learning of body perception, behavioural control and meaning construction.

4 Data Collection and Analysis

If the application of mathematical intelligence technology is based on a body of knowledge, it can provide an effective support tool for intelligent teaching and learning models, and then the process of learning practices oriented to the development of students' thinking becomes clear. To address this issue, in terms of theoretical basis and supporting technologies, problem-based subject knowledge mapping should be used as the core to facilitate the development and construction of thinking [20]. It is recommended that the structural model of subject knowledge mapping be constructed with the classification and ordering of subject problems as the core layer [21], and then the knowledge system should be retraced to achieve the transfer of students' knowledge to the development of competencies and to carry out educational practices based on the construction of thinking.

4.1 Expressive Teaching Objectives that Enhance the TEacher's Accurate Assessment of Learning and the Experience Gained

Students generally struggle to understand difficult knowledge, lack opportunities for integrated problem solving and do not receive real-time individual guidance from teachers that is tailored to their actual learning needs [22], which also makes it difficult for teachers to keep track of student learning and have a less accurate grasp of experience and a dynamic understanding of problems in teaching [23]. If big data can be used to create learner profiles, such as learners' knowledge structures, thinking styles and personality traits, then teachers can make accurate learning analysis of learner profiles, while setting objectives around core professional issues and specific content, and learners can avoid negative learning interests due to different levels of teaching, so that students at different levels can have a better sense of experience on their learning path [24]. The graphical technology clusters and analyses knowledge points, organises knowledge, methods and questions in an orderly manner with student characteristics as clues and student ability development as the goal, forming a targeted knowledge map [25]. Teachers are able to more accurately analyse and evaluate students' learning situations and characteristics, dissolving the absolute objectivity inherent in the characteristics of subject knowledge mapping and creating a relatively subjective sense of experience of students' ability levels, thus strengthening the intrinsic relevance of knowledge and ability.

4.2 Inspiring Problem Situations Give Learners Access to Authentic Problem Situations and Optimise the Sense of Authentic Experience of How Learners Think

The content of textbook knowledge learnt by learners is an indirect experience, and the internalisation of students' knowledge and the generation of their competences require the setting of certain conditions [26]. The graphical knowledge map uses the elements involved in the teaching process as entity nodes and the logical relationships between the teaching elements as edges, forming a semantic network to correspond to the numerous issues that arise in teaching [27]. The absolute objectivity of the intrinsic characteristics of the knowledge point structure of the subject knowledge map is dissolved, the relative subjectivity of the competence level is penetrated and attention begins to be paid to the intrinsic relevance of knowledge and competence, i.e. the construction of a bridge between the two through problems or tasks [28]. The integration of mathematics and intellectual technology is highly consistent with the overall requirement of knowledge transfer to competence development and then to quality education [29]. Through real-life situations generated by heuristic problems, the core problems of subject knowledge such as puzzles, combination problems and basic problems are stratified to sort out the methods, strategies and knowledge that learners should choose and use in solving various types of problems, using the problems as clues to link and reintegrate all relevant knowledge points. Through heuristic problem situations, students will improve their practical skills, problem-solving skills, systematic thinking skills, etc. Finally, the subject's knowledge map is no longer a single mind map model of knowledge points, but a visual experience built around the logical relationship of the subject's questions to the corresponding body of knowledge and competencies.

4.3 Dynamic Learning Paths, Constructing Learning Path Networks with Knowledge Mapping Intelligent Guidance Technology

Based on technologies such as big data, virtual reality and video recording, a network of learning paths is constructed based on students' learning patterns and real-time data analysis is conducted [30]. Through continuous iterative optimisation of the dynamic data, learners gain a better sense of experience in the dynamic pathway guidance [31]. With the aim of solving bottlenecks in classroom teaching, developing students' integrated problem-solving skills, systematic and innovative thinking [32], dynamically optimising teaching activities, allowing students to discover and initiate learning, personalising learning, following human-centred principles of logical learning [33], guiding students to better access and resource tools, and inspiring high-quality thinking patterns. At the same time, it enables teachers and students to have a more comprehensive and effective teaching and learning experience in a limited amount of time. The structure of the Dynamic Learning Pathway Network tests whether learners have achieved the learning objectives for the subject, considers the extent to which students have mastered knowledge and skills and, more importantly, allows students to experience that the subject knowledge system, the problem-solving skills system and the subject thinking system can be aligned [34]. Learners extract, combine and store knowledge in accordance with schemas when solving practical problems, linking independent experiences to find solutions, which are expressed in concrete practice as the transformation of learned knowledge into some kind of competent behaviour, a process of behavioural transformation known as the acquisition of learned insights of knowledge. The learner truly develops a mastery of the body of subject knowledge and solves problems in changing contexts, and the empirical nature of the subject's thinking representations becomes clearer and more systematic.

4.4 Along with Teaching and Learning Assessments, Teachers Have Access to a Variety of Rich Teaching and Learning Outcomes Through Digital Intelligence Technology, Making the Whole Assessment Experience More Objective and Accurate

Virtual reality technology enhances student practice in the classroom, allowing teachers to observe student performance and interactions to get an accurate picture of each student's learning status and trends [35], while helping teachers to accurately diagnose student learning problems and provide personalised interventions for emotional interaction and communication [36]. The development of learners' thinking is a process that moves from intuitive action to figurative thinking to abstract thinking. Students acquire various ways and means of solving problems with the help of digital intelligence technology [37], which to a certain extent reflects the mental models and cognitive processes of learners [38]. Students' sense of experience in different contexts is expressed in concrete learning processes. Effective learning practices take place in the context of authentic problems, situations and assessments [39]. On the basis of mastering a large amount of knowledge and methodological strategies, students use IT to practice problem solving, effectively developing learners' higher cognition and thinking, experiencing the knowledge learning process of identification, construction, internalisation and expansion and the thinking process of discovery, conceptualisation, induction and selection, and gaining authentic experience of creative problem solving.

4.5 Open-Ended Learning Outcomes Can Be a Two-Way Test of the Effectiveness of Digital Intelligence in the Teaching and Learning Process, Providing a Rich Outcome Experience for Teachers and Students

The open-ended learning outcomes are practical applications of the reasoning pathway and the integration of digital intelligence in a complex real-world context [40], allowing teachers to integrate digital intelligence into their instructional design while validating the practicality of the theory [41]. In turn, students can self-test whether the digital intelligence used in the classroom is deeply integrated with the subject content through the assessment objectives of the teaching outcomes, achieving the dual effect of experiential learning knowledge and thinking development [42]. Open-ended learning outcomes give students greater autonomy [43], but not all students are successful in achieving better learning experiences and better outputs. Teachers therefore support the open-ended production of learning outcomes by pre-designing various learning frameworks and embedding them into the learning process using digital intelligence. Learning frameworks take the form of paradigms, suggestions, diagrams [44], guides and questions. Paradigms are excellent works or typical cases that guide students in applying what they have learned and are suitable for learners who are interested in learning and have a strong capacity for independent learning [45]. Suggestions are less direct and inspiring statements of instructional problems and are suitable for learners with a weak foundation in experiential learning. Diagrams take the form of concept maps, flowcharts and other visuals to depict information, which help to activate students' intrinsic motivation and are suitable for learners with low interest in experiential learning. Guides focus on the overall ideas that produce results and are suitable for learners with a low level of systematic and logical thinking. Teachers therefore choose to design different forms of framework structures depending on the characteristics of the learner in order to provide effective support for the presentation of outcomes.

As shown in the diagram, digital intelligence is integrated into the building blocks of smart education Fig. 1.

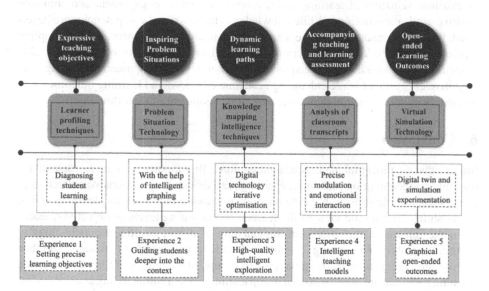

Fig. 1. Digital intelligence is integrated into the building blocks of smart education.

5 Discussion

5.1 The Hierarchy of Learning Objectives is Set Appropriately and Incorporates an Outcome-Oriented Framework Structure

Digital intelligence enhances students' interest in learning and their interest and experience in virtual scenarios is higher, but at the level of knowledge perception, the perceptual experience based on technological novelty is also accompanied by a decline in novelty and interest, and this superficial experience also leads to a lack of depth perception in knowledge acquisition. Low target levels lead to improved academic mood and performance of learners, so control the difficulty of the teaching task and design experiences to match the difficulty. At low target levels, a guided approach is used, while at high target levels, individual learner differences are taken into account and an outcomes-oriented framework is incorporated to improve learners' subjective evaluation of the value of the learning content, thus helping learners to have a positive emotional experience and better learning outcomes.

5.2 Infused with Experiential Perceptual Elements to Promote Learners' Emotional and Cognitive Engagement and Develop Higher Order Thinking

Digital intelligence is embedded in the design of learning content to enhance learning outcomes through the infiltration of experiential perceptual elements, such as the design of positive elements related to learning tasks, which enhance learners' intrinsic or extrinsic valuation of learning tasks, promote cognitive engagement and stimulate positive academic emotions. While knowledge is imparted and competencies are developed, the value connotations of the learning content are fully explored, positive implicit guidance is given to learners' experiences, so that learners make correct and valid value assessments of their knowledge acquisition and their own development, promoting their cognitive engagement while enhancing academic emotions and learning outcomes, and ultimately promoting the higher-order overall development of their thinking.

6 Conclusion

Smart Education's digital intelligence integration fully supports accurate assessment for teaching and learning optimisation, enabling real, dynamic and extensive collection of multi-scene, whole-process big data on student learning outcomes and learning styles, establishing a panoramic view of the learner. When setting teaching objectives, teachers make full use of the multiform implantation of digital intelligence technology to accurately analyse the learning of individual students and groups of students, and then understand the common learning patterns of groups of students and filter out common learning paths that are appropriate for group learning. When summarising student performance, based on a digital portrait of student learning, we can identify problems in student learning, provide targeted and personalised learning resources, arrange more appropriate experiential teaching and learning, help students to complete high-quality personalised learning and promote the development of higher-order thinking. TA more comprehensive and in-depth experiential study is conducted at three levels: teaching, learning and technology, focusing on the performance of students' knowledge acquisition results and more on how to effectively enhance students' cognitive structure, characteristics and learning process experience, in order to truly realise the technical and methodological design of digital intelligence and give full play to the educational value of integrating digital intelligence technology into the whole teaching process, ultimately realising the unification and Integration.

Acknowledgement. Thanks:
    The 13th Five-Year Plan for the Development of Philosophy and Social Sciences in Guangzhou, Project No. 2020GZGJ19.
    Central Universities Project, Project No. BSQD201910.

References

1. Jinxing, W., Zhengliang, Q., Ganzi, P.: A comparative study on the development strategies of agricultural vocational education in mid-industrialization. Educ. Dev. Res. **21**, 102–105 (2005)

2. Hongtao, Y., Xue, Y., Yanli, S.S.: Research on the teaching effect of desktop virtual experiment. Mod. Educ. Technol. (1), 115–118(2008)
3. Juhou, H., Rina, L., Xin, X., et al.: Design of learning evaluation index system based on immersive virtual reality system. Electrochem. Educ. Res. **39**(3), 75–81 (2018)
4. Burdea, G., Coiffet, P.: Virtual Reality Technology, 2nd edn. John Wiley & Sons, New York (2003)
5. Kim, P.: Effects of 3D virtual reality of plate tectonics on fifth grade students' achievement and attitude toward science. Interact. Learn. Environ. **14**(1), 25–34 (2006)
6. Smith, P.C., Hamilton, B.K.: The effects of virtual reality simulation as a teaching strategy for skills preparation in nursing students. Clin. Simul. Nurs. **11**(1), 52–58 (2015)
7. Juan, W., Yao, C.: A new form of resource construction:the connotation and design framework of virtual simulation resources. China's e-Learn. **12**, 91–96 (2016)
8. Li, Y., Wang, W., Shaochun, Z., Yuqing, F., Fan, F.: Research on wisdom-generating strategies in the smart classroom. Electrochem. Educ. Res. **38**(1), 108–114 (2017)
9. Rong, R., Xianmin, Y., Yaohua, C., Qiujin, Z.: New development of educational management informatization: towards intelligent management. China's Comput. Educ. (3), 30–37 (2014)
10. Chenglin, L.: Exploration of thinking teaching based on problem design-an example of information technology subject. Res. Electrochem. Educ. **35**(3), 111–115 (2014)
11. Chongde, L., Weiping, H.: The theory and practice of thinking classroom teaching. J. Beijing Normal Univ. (Soc. Sci. Ed.) (1), 29–36 (2010)
12. Rumi, L.: A discussion on some theoretical issues of teaching models. Curric.-Mater.-Teach. Methods (4), 25–29 (1996)
13. Goetz, T., Frenzel, A.C., Pekrun, R., et al.: The domain specificity of academic emotional experiences. J. Exp. Educ. **75**(1), 5–29 (2006)
14. Park, B., Knoerzer, L., Plass, J.L., et al.: Emotional design and positive emotions in multimedia learning: an eyetracking study on the use of anthropomorphisms. Comput. Educ. **86**(8), 30–42 (2015)
15. Shaochun, Z., Zhuo, Z., Jialong, F., Xuemei, Z., Lan, Y.: How intelligent technology supports the construction of new classroom teaching models. China's Electro-Chem. Educ. **421**(02) (2022)
16. Li, Z., Zhou, D.D., Wang, Y.: The educational knowledge graph from the perspective of "artificial intelligence+": connotation, technical framework and application research. J. Dist. Educ. **37**(4), 42–53 (2019)
17. Plass, J.L., Heidig, S., Hayward, E.O., et al.: Emotional design in multimedia learning: effects of shape and color on affect and learning. Learn. Inst. **29**, 128–140 (2014)
18. Zhuo, Z., Yewei, T., Shaochun, Z., et al.: Research on the construction of educational knowledge graph model supported by artificial intelligence, pp. 22–32 (2012)
19. AL-JARF R.: A model for enhancing EFL freshman students' vocabulary with mind-mapping software. Journal of teaching Englishfor specific and academic purposes,3(3):509–520(2016)
20. Juan, W.: Smart courses: conceptual content, structural model and design process. Modern Distance Education **3**, 25–33 (2017)
21. Zongkai,Y. Bie,W. Xudong,Z.: Education informatization 2.0: a critical historical leap in a new era of information technology transforming education. Educational Research, 39(4): 16–22(2018)
22. Webb, M.E.: Pedagogical reasoning:issues and solutions for the teaching and learning of ICT in secondary schools. Educ. Inf. Technol. **7**(3), 237–255 (2002)
23. Masschelein, J., Simons, M.: Education in times of fast learning: the future of the school. Ethics Educ. **10**(1), 84–95 (2015)
24. Brom, C., Starkova, T., D'Mello, S.K.: How effective is emotional design? a meta-analysis on facial anthropomorphisms and pleasant colors during multimedia learning. Educ. Res. Rev. **25**, 100–119 (2018)

25. Sepasgozar, S.M.E.: Digital twin and web-based virtual gaming technologies for online education: a case of construction management and engineering. Appl. Sci. **10**(13), 4678 (2020)
26. Sullivan, J.V.: Learning and embodied cognition: a review and proposal. Psychol. Learn. Teach. **17**(2), 128–143 (2018)
27. Burdea, G., Richard, P., Coiffet, P.: Multimodal virtual reality: input-output devices, system integration, and human factors. Int. J. Hum.-Comput. Interact. **8**(1), 5–24 (1996)
28. Diemer, J., Alpers, G.W., Peperkorn, H.M., et al.: The impact of perception and presence on emotional reactions: a review of research in virtual reality. Front. Psychol. (6), 26 (2015)
29. Fast-Berglund, Å., Gong, L., Li, D.: Testing and validating extended reality (xR) technologies in manufacturing. Procedia Manuf. **25**, 31–38 (2018)
30. Hoffman, E.S.: Beyond the flipped classroom: redesigning a research methods course for E3 instruction. Contemp. Issues Educ. Res. **7**(1), 51–59 (2014)
31. Huang, H.M., Rauch, U., Liaw, S.S.: investigating learners' attitudes toward virtual reality learning environments: based on a constructivist approach. Comput. Educ. **55**(3), 1171–1182 (2010)
32. Kim, C.M.: Using email to enable e3 (effective, efficient, and engaging) learning. Dist. Educ. **29**(2), 187–198 (2008)
33. Kim, S.Y.S., Prestopnik, N., Biocca, F.A.: Body in the interactive game: how interface embodiment affects physical activity and health behavior change. Comput. Hum. Behav. **36**, 376–384 (2014)
34. Stark, L., Malkmus, E., Stark, R., et al.: Learning-related emotions in multimedia learning: an application of control-value theory. Learn. Inst. **58**, 42–52 (2018)
35. Naeini, J., Duvall, E.: Dynamic assessment and the impact on English language learners' reading comprehension performance. Lang. Test. Asia **2**(2), 22–41 (2012)
36. Brom, C., Dechterenko, F., Frollova, N., et al.: Enjoyment or involvement? affective-motivational mediation during learning from a complex computerized simulation. Comput. Educ. **114**(11), 236–254 (2017)
37. Mayer, R.E., Estrella, G.: Benefits of emotional design in multimedia instruction. Learn. Instr. **33**, 12–18 (2014)
38. Hulleman, C.S., Godes, O., Hendricks, B.L., et al.: Enhancing interest and performance with a utility value intervention. J. Educ. Psychol. **102**(4), 880–895 (2010)
39. Mills, C., D'mello, S.K., Kopp, K.: The influence of consequence value and text difficulty on affect, attention, and learning while reading instructional texts. Learn. Inst. **40**, 9–20 (2015)
40. Stark, L., Malkmus, E., Stark, R., et al.: Learning -related emotions in multimedia learning: an application of control-valuetheory. Learn. Inst. **58**, 42–52 (2018)
41. Pekrun, R., Goetz, T., Daniels, L.M., et al.: Boredom in achievement settings: exploring control-value antecedents and performance outcomes of a neglected emotion. J. Educ. Psychol. **102**(3), 531–549 (2010)
42. Paas, F.G.: Training strategies for attaining transfer of problem-solving skill in statistics: a cognitive-load approach. J. Educ. Psychol. **84**(4), 429–434 (1992)
43. Park, B.Flowerday, T.& Brunken, R.: Cognitive and affective effects of seductive details in multimedia learning. Computersin human behavior,44:267–278(2015)
44. Chae, B., Zhu, R.: Environmental disorder leads to self-regulatory failure. J. Cons. Res. **40**(6), 1203–1218 (2014)
45. Repetto, C., Cipresso, P., Riva, G.: Virtual action and real action have different impacts on comprehen-sion of concrete verbs. Front. Psychol. **6**(176), 1–9 (2015)

Bibliometric Analysis of Existing Knowledge on Digital Transformation in Higher Education

Jorge Cruz-Cárdenas[1,2](✉) , Carlos Ramos-Galarza[3,4] ,
Jorge Guadalupe-Lanas[1,2] , Andrés Palacio-Fierro[2,5] ,
and Mercedes Galarraga-Carvajal[2]

[1] Research Center in Business, Society, and Technology, ESTec, Universidad Tecnológica Indoamérica, Quito, Ecuador
{jorgecruz,jorgeguadalupe}@uti.edu.ec
[2] School of Administrative and Economic Science, Universidad Tecnológica Indoamérica, Quito, Ecuador
{andrespalacio,mercedesgalarraga}@uti.edu.ec
[3] Facultad de Psicología, Universidad Católica del Ecuador, Quito, Ecuador
caramos@puce.edu.ec
[4] Centro de Investigación MIST, Universidad Tecnológica Indoamérica, Quito, Ecuador
[5] Programa Doctoral en Ciencias Jurídicas y Económicas, Universidad Camilo José Cela, Madrid, Spain

Abstract. Higher Education Institutions (HEIs) have been feeling great pressure to advance in digital transformation. This pressure has been intensified with the outbreak of the COVID-19 pandemic at the end of 2019. Because the digital transformation of HEIs has been attracting a growing number of publications, the present study sought to carry out a bibliometric analysis of such titles. For this purpose, 643 relevant documents were identified from the Scopus database in January 2022. The descriptive results show an accelerated growth of the relevant literature, with conference papers being the main form of publication, followed by articles, conference reviews, and book chapters. The areas with which the majority of documents were associated were computer science, followed by social science, engineering, and business and management. An analysis of the co-occurrence of terms based on the titles and abstracts enabled the identification of three thematic areas of interest: 1) digital transformation in teaching, particularly under the pressure exerted by COVID-19; 2) environmental influences on the digital transformation of HEIs; and 3) enabling technologies for digital transformation. A longitudinal analysis also based on titles and abstracts allows us to see how the primary focus shifted from the economic issue (in 2019) to the COVID issue (in 2021). This study concludes by discussing the theoretical and practical implications of the findings, demonstrating as a particularly interesting area for future research the study of the digital transformation of HEIs in a future post-COVID scenario.

Keywords: Digital transformation · Higher education · HEIs · Universities · COVID-19

G. Meiselwitz et al. (Eds.): HCII 2022, LNCS 13517, pp. 231–240, 2022.
https://doi.org/10.1007/978-3-031-22131-6_17

1 Introduction

Higher education institutions (HEIs) play a strategic role in all societies because they are central to research and innovation and the development of human capital [1]. Various factors, including the confluence of disruptive technologies and intensity of competition, have been putting pressure on HEIs to make strides towards digital transformation. This process implies the incorporation of digital technologies and, ultimately, a complete organizational change. Digital transformation efforts are particularly complex among HEIs, which have established organizational cultures that evolve slowly [1].

The pressure that HEIs had been experiencing amid their respective digital transformations has been raised by the effects of the COVID-19 pandemic. In a matter of weeks, these institutions were forced to adapt to new forms of work that used digital technologies intensively to provide online education and administrative services [2].

The great importance of the digital transformation of HEIs has meant that many academics have become attracted to investigating the topic, which in turn has become an area of exponential growth in research in recent years [3, 4]. However, among the problems associated with any rapidly growing research area is the potential division and lack of consolidation of the accumulating knowledge [5]. Although previous studies have focused their efforts on ordering and systematizing knowledge about the digital transformation of HEIs, their analysis efforts have covered only a few dozen studies. For this reason, this study seeks to contribute to the consolidation of existing knowledge concerning the digital transformation of HEIs using a broader focus than that of previous studies, and it aims to achieve the following objective:

- Establish through the use of bibliometric techniques the characteristics and structure of the existing body of knowledge on digital transformation in higher education institutions.

2 Digital Transformation in Heis

Digital transformation is a process of integrating technologies, and digital technology in particular, into an organization. This implies a deep organizational transformation across all areas [6]. HEIs began efforts towards digital transformation some years ago to improve their educational and administrative services and as a strategy to better compete in and serve new markets and society in general [1].

Before the COVID-19 pandemic, HEIs were rather conservative in their approach to digital transformation. They established an agenda that listed an order of priorities whereby teaching came first, followed by infrastructure, administration, research, business processes, and human resource management [4]. In addition, the use of digital technology in teaching processes—the first priority of HEIs—has focused on a limited number of technologies [7]. Additionally, the digital transformation efforts of HEIs have revolved around two actors: teachers and students [4].

This rather conservative process was changed by the emergence of the COVID-19 pandemic at the end of 2019. In response to government quarantine and social distancing measures, HEIs carried out rapid adoption of digital technologies to enable their activities to remain open. However, rapid and forced digital transformation also brings associated problems. Students and teachers reported experiencing anxiety, stress, and depression at levels that exceeded those observed before the pandemic [8, 9]. Specifically, the factors associated with these levels of stress and anxiety revolved around the players' lack of experience in using digital technologies, the enormous work required to adapt materials [10], delays in graduations, and the loss of job opportunities and internships [11].

Regarding past authors' attempts to order the existing literature, several previous publications were identified. However, these publications had different objectives than those of the present study: Aditya, Ferdina, and Kusumawardani [12] focused only on systematizing the barriers to digital transformation in HEIs. Alenezi [13] focused on reviewing the digital maturity models applicable to HEIs. Castro Benavides et al. [4] focused on a systematic review of the literature based on a few dozen articles.

3   Method

This research has followed the recommended stages for studies oriented to systematic literature reviews and bibliometric analyses [14, 15]. In this way, the present study is organized in three stages: 1) formulation of the objectives, 2) definition of the inclusion criteria and content search strategies, and 3) presentation of the results. Considering that the objectives of this study were already stated in the introductory section, this section focuses on detailing the inclusion criteria and the search strategies used. The following section will serve to detail the analysis carried out on the body of documents and the results obtained.

The objective of this study was the main guide for establishing content inclusion criteria. Thus, the documents included had to be relevant to the proposed objective (digital transformation in higher education institutions) and present an acceptable level of quality. In turn, these criteria guided the search strategies. Of the various academic–scientific information bases, Scopus was selected for its wide coverage, high level of quality, and built-in search and analysis tools [3]. As for the search terms, these were also guided by the objective of the research, and it was decided that two types of content would be present simultaneously: digital transformation and higher education. In this way, the following structure of search terms was used: ({digital transformation} AND ({higher education} OR universities OR university)).

An additional delimitation was to restrict the documents to the English language. No restrictions were adopted concerning the date or type of document. The search was carried out on January 24, 2022, and 643 documents were obtained.

4   Analysis and Results

A first approach to the body of documents analyzed was based on the evolution of the number of documents published over the years. As can be seen in Fig. 1, scientific and academic production on digital transformation and higher education was almost non-existent until 2015. A subsequent period, 2016–2018, showed moderate growth, and the 2019–2021 period showed explosive growth, which some authors have described as

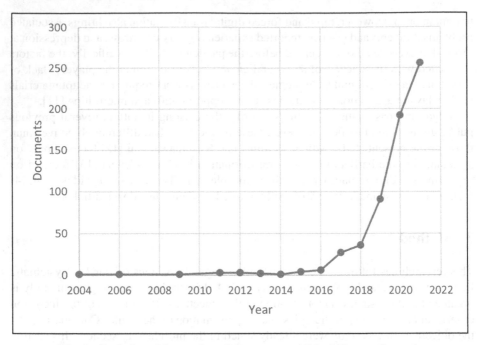

Fig. 1. Evolution of the number of documents published (Source: Scopus).

"exponential" [3, 4]. In 2021, the last full year analyzed, 256 documents were published on the topic under analysis.

Another descriptive analysis was carried out regarding the area of knowledge with which the publications were related (Table 1 presents the results). It is necessary to clarify in this regard that the same document could have been assigned to several areas.

Thus, most of the documents (n = 352; 54.7%) had Computer Science, followed by Social Science (232; 36.1%), Engineering (171; 26.6%), and Business and Management (112; 17.4%), among the related areas. These data reflect the multidisciplinary nature of digital transformation studies, in which both technologies and social and organizational issues are involved [16]. Another interesting aspect was the type of publication. Conference papers were the main form of publication, with 320 documents (49.8%), followed by articles (215; 33.4%). Other types of publication carried little weight.

Another important piece of information comes from the countries to which the authors are related, based on their institutional affiliation. In this regard, it should be considered that since the existence of several authors in the same document is very frequent, a document may be related to several institutions and countries at the same time. Thus, Russia stood out with 140 (21.8%) associated documents, followed by Germany (70; 10.9%), Spain (49; 7.6%), and the United States (34; 5.3%).

Regarding the authors' affiliated institutions, Table 2 presents the universities and institutions with more than five associated documents. As can be seen in the aforementioned table, 11 universities and institutions meet this requirement. Tecnológico de Monterrey of Mexico and Kazan Federal University of the Russian Federation lead

Table 1. Main areas of knowledge

Subject area	Documents	%
Computer Science	352	54.7%
Social Sciences	232	36.1%
Engineering	171	26.6%
Business, Management and Accounting	112	17.4%
Decision Sciences	94	14.6%
Environmental Science	61	9.5%
Mathematics	56	8.7%
Energy	44	6.8%
Earth and Planetary Sciences	30	4.7%
Economics, Econometrics and Finance	29	4.5%
Physics and Astronomy	21	3.3%
Psychology	20	3.1%

this group. It is also worth noting that the same document can be associated with several institutions; the same is possible for an author, who can be associated with several institutions.

Table 2. Main universities and institutions

University/Institution	Associated documents
Tecnologico de Monterrey	12
Kazan Federal University	11
Financial University under the Government of the Russian Federation	10
Peter the Great St. Petersburg Polytechnic University	9
Ural Federal University	9
International University of La Rioja	8
The State University of Management	7
Don State Technical University	7
Universidade de Aveiro	6
Telkom University	6
Centro de Estudos Organizacionais e Sociais do Politécnico do Porto	6

To analyze of the co-occurrence of terms, VOSviewer 1.6.15 software [17] was used, and an estimation was performed based on the titles and abstracts. The minimum number of occurrences of a term to be considered was set at 15, and 118 terms qualified. After cleaning the list of terms, which consisted of the elimination of very general terms and a grouping of terms of similar meaning, 107 terms qualified. The co-occurrence analysis generated three thematic clusters, which are presented in Fig. 2.

Cluster 1 (red; 41 items): This gathered the most elements. Terms such as "teaching," "COVID-19," "course," "teacher," "ability," "crisis," and "group" suggest that this thematic area focused on one of the applications of digital transformation—the one related to teaching—particularly under the pressure exerted by COVID-19.

Cluster 2 (green; 33 items): Among the terms that were part of this thematic area were "economy," "training," "labor market," "activity," "region," and "readiness." This composition of terms suggests an area focused on environmental influences in the digital transformation of HEIs.

Cluster 3 (blue; 33 items): Among the terms that were part of this cluster were "industry," "innovation," "artificial intelligence," "big data," "capability," "internet of

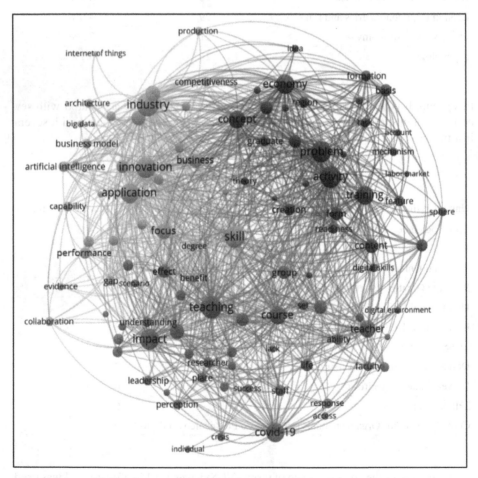

Fig. 2. Co-occurrence network of terms. (Color figure online)

things," "performance," and "application." This composition of terms suggests a thematic area focused on the enabling technologies of digital transformation and their applications.

An additional analysis carried out with the same VOSviewer 1.6.15 software was to overlay visualization of the existing terms in titles and abstracts. This tool makes it possible to visualize the currency of a term based on the average year of publication of the documents that mention it [17]. Figure 3 presents the results. The oldest terms appear in violet, the most current ones in yellow, and the intermediate ones in green.

As can be seen in Fig. 3, "COVID-19" was the most outstanding (largest node size) among the most topical terms in the digital transformation of universities. At the other extreme was "economy," which is a macro-environmental force and a term frequently mentioned by documents published in 2019.

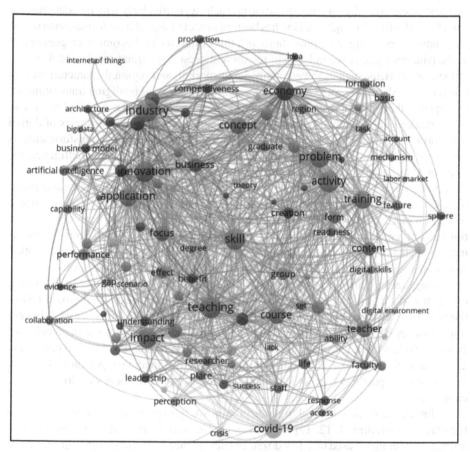

Fig. 3. Overlay visualization of terms. (Color figure online)

5 Discussion and Implications

The descriptive analysis of the body of documents on the digital transformation of HEIs reveals several characteristics. This area of research has in recent years shown growth characterized by a very steep curve. This trend coincides with the appreciation of various authors about the enormous interest that this research topic is arousing [3, 4]. As for the countries with which the authors and their affiliated institutions are related, Russia, Germany, Spain, and the United States—both developed and emerging countries (in the case of Russia)—stand out. In this regard, a recommendation for future research is to include other less studied scenarios such as developing countries.

One of the most important results of this study concerns the thematic areas of research on digital transformation and HEIs. Thus, three areas of interest could be established. The first is related to digital transformation in teaching, particularly with it under pressure from COVID-19. Although teaching has been an aspect of digital transformation to which HEIs have been giving more importance [4], this emphasis has become even greater due to the pandemic [2]. A second area of research interest is environmental or background influences on HEIs such as the economy, labor market, and regional characteristics. In this regard, it should be noted that HEIs were initially attracted by digital transformation to improve their products and services, improve competitiveness, and find more and better markets [1]. The final thematic area is related to enabling technologies of digital transformation. In this sense, it should be remembered that digital transformation is energized by the confluence of a series of technologies such as artificial intelligence, the internet of things, and big data [6].

Another very interesting aspect is given by the evolution over time of research priorities. Currently, COVID-19 is the factor with the greatest influence on the digital transformation of HEIs; however, the pandemic is following a very dynamic course [5]. For this reason, a recommendation for future studies is the investigation of digital transformation in HEIs in light of the evolution of the pandemic. For example, mass vaccination campaigns will mark new stages of behavior of governments and populations.

Going deeper into the subject of COVID-19, a topic of great interest for future research and for professional practice is the normalization process that would follow the massive vaccination campaigns and the decrease in cases. In this sense, it is very important for HEIs to maintain the digital capabilities developed during the pandemic. In short, do not think about a return to the same starting point as before the pandemic. Thus, the delivery of education through mixed or hybrid media (in person and online) in different proportions can contribute to the maintenance of these developed digital capacities.

A final issue is the relationship of the present study to previous attempts to organize the existing literature [4, 12, 13]. These studies focused on understanding and systematizing the literature based on a few dozen articles. Hence, a distinguishing characteristic of the present study is the quantity and variety of the studies considered. In total, this study included 643 documents of different formats, such as conference proceedings, articles, and book chapters. Therefore, a consequence for the theory is that the present study shows a more complete and broader (although not deeper) picture of the existing literature.

References

1. Branch, J.W., Burgos, D., Serna, M.D.A., Ortega, G.P.: Digital transformation in higher education institutions: between myth and reality. In: Burgos, D. (ed.) Radical Solutions and eLearning. LNET, pp. 41–50. Springer, Singapore (2020). https://doi.org/10.1007/978-981-15-4952-6_3
2. García-Morales, V.J., Garrido-Moreno, A., Martín-Rojas, R.: The transformation of higher education after the covid disruption: emerging challenges in an online learning scenario. Front. Psychol. **12**, 616059 (2021)
3. Abad-Segura, E., González-Zamar, M.-D., Infante-Moro, J.C., Ruipérez García, G.: Sustainable management of digital transformation in higher education: global research trends. Sustainability **12**(5), 2107 (2020)
4. Castro Benavides, L.M., Tamayo Arias, J.A., Arango Serna, M.D., Branch Bedoya, J.W., Burgos, D.: Digital transformation in higher education institutions: a systematic literature review. Sensors **20**(11), 3291 (2020)
5. Cruz-Cárdenas, J., Zabelina, E., Guadalupe-Lanas, J., Palacio-Fierro, A., Ramos-Galarza, C.: COVID-19, consumer behavior, technology, and society: a literature review and bibliometric analysis. Technol. Forecast. Soc. Change. **173**, 121179 (2021)
6. Neugebauer, R. (ed.): Digital Transformation. Springer, Heidelberg (2019). https://doi.org/10.1007/978-3-662-58134-6
7. Bond, M., Marín, V.L., Dolch, C., Bedenlier, S., Zawacki-Richter, O.: Digital transformation in german higher education: student and teacher perceptions and usage of digital media. Int. J. Educ. Technol. High. Educ. **15**(48), 1–20 (2018)
8. Li, Q., Miao, Y., Zeng, X., Tarimo, C.S., Wu, C., Wu, J.: Prevalence and factors for anxiety during the coronavirus disease 2019 (COVID-19) epidemic among the teachers in China. J. Affect. Disord. **277**, 153–158 (2020)
9. Rodríguez-Hidalgo, A.J., Pantaleón, Y., Dios, I., Falla, D.: Fear of COVID-19, stress, and anxiety in university undergraduate students: a predictive model for depression. Front. Psychol. **11**, 591797 (2020)
10. Johnson, N., Veletsianos, G., Seaman, J.: U.S. faculty and administrators' experiences and approaches in the early weeks of the COVID-19 pandemic. Online Learn. J. **24**(2), 6–21 (2020)
11. Aucejo, E.M., French, J., Ugalde Araya, M.P., Zafar, B.: The impact of COVID-19 on student experiences and expectations: evidence from a survey. J Public Econ. **191**, 104271 (2020)
12. Aditya, B.R., Ferdiana, R., Kusumawardani, S.S.: Categories for barriers to digital transformation in higher education: an analysis based on literature. Int. J. Inf. Educ. Technol. **11**(12), 658–664 (2021)
13. Alenazi, M.: Deep dive into digital transformation in higher education institutions. Educ. Sci. **11**(12), 770 (2021)
14. Osobajo, O.A., Moore, D.: Methodological choices in relationship quality (RQ) research 1987 to 2015: a systematic literature review. J. Relatsh. Mark. **16**(1), 40–81 (2017)
15. Cruz-Cárdenas, J., Arévalo-Chávez, P.: Consumer behavior in the disposal of products: forty years of research. J. Promot. Manag. **24**(5), 617–636 (2018)
16. Vaz, N.: Digital Business Transformation: How Established Companies Sustain Competitive Advantage from Now to Next. Wiley, Hoboken (2021)
17. Van Eck, N.J., Waltman, L.: Software survey: VOS viewer, a computer program for bibliometric mapping. Scientometrics **84**(2), 523–538 (2010)

How Design Helps STEM Education Curriculum Achieve Interdisciplinary Goals

Yufei Dong[1,2](✉)

[1] School of Future Design, Beijing Normal University, Zhuhai 519087, China
1449129140@qq.com
[2] School of Design, Guangxi Normal University, Guilin 541000, China

Abstract. In recent years, STEM education has received increasing attention in the design field [1]. Based on the knowledge structure, disciplinary development background and empirical research articles of foreign STEM product design research hotspots, and combined with children's cognitive psychology, we found that although many STEM products indicated that children's interdisciplinary ability should be improved, the final results were inconsistent with their goals. They still convey monodisciplinary knowledge. First, we discussed issues such as single STEM curriculum based on existing design cases. Second, we discussed the specific role of design in STEM education. Next, we found a new R&D path for STEM education product design to achieve the effect of interdisciplinary. Finally, we summarize the process of STEM curriculum development. It is hoped that this review will provide new ideas for the design of STEM educational products.

Keywords: STEM education · Product design · Child cognitive psychology

1 Introduction to STEM Education and Current Development

STEM stands for Science, Technology, Engineering, and Mathematics, which is a science-centered educational concept that organically integrates technology, engineering, and mathematics into real-life contexts [2]. Among them, science aims to build a way of thinking rather than scientific knowledge and mainly consists of observing, experimenting, asking questions, predicting, exploring how things work, and analyzing findings. Technology denotes a way of doing things and consists mainly of identifying problems, creating through tools, etc. [3] Engineering also indicates a way of doing things that includes solving problems, using different materials, designing and creating things that can be used in the workplace. Mathematics denotes a way of measuring, including classifying, counting, creating patterns, exploring shapes, volumes, sizes, etc. STEM educational concepts change traditional disciplinary thinking and reflect some typical characteristics, and since STEM is not a single field of study, they can be interpreted in many ways. Some researchers see STEM as a traditional set of separate disciplines, while others see STEM as somehow integrating specific disciplines, not necessarily branches within the four STEMs, so that STEM instruction can be understood as multidisciplinary or interdisciplinary.

© Springer Nature Switzerland AG 2022
G. Meiselwitz et al. (Eds.): HCII 2022, LNCS 13517, pp. 241–256, 2022.
https://doi.org/10.1007/978-3-031-22131-6_18

2 Data Sources and Research Methods

The researcher used CiteSpace software to draw a knowledge map to sort, analyze, and summarize the cognitive development trend and current situation of children from STEM education perspective in 2016–2021 to sort, analyze, and summarize the data from CNKI database with a total of 289 articles [4]. The frequency of keywords appears more than 10 times, the research heat is higher thus it can be seen that scholars pay more attention to STEM education subject area as shown in Fig. 1 high frequency keywords co-occur.

Piaget's theory of children's cognitive development states that all fruitful activities should be based on interest. Children will be governed by needs and interests, and children themselves are active. Children are intensely curious about what is around them and show a strong desire for knowledge. If their spontaneous enthusiasm for an activity is not stimulated, the impact of the activity will not be maximized. STEM education for younger children should start from the things and problems around children and guide them to analyze and solve problems by applying knowledge and principles of mathematics, science, engineering, and technology to stimulate their curiosity in using engineering and science, technology, and mathematics to solve problems and contribute to the harmonious development of STEM education in the future [5].

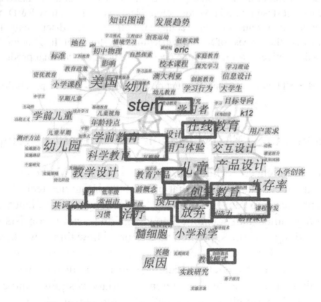

Fig. 1. High-frequency keyword co-occurrence

3 Current Status of Research

Although STEM education originated in the United States, it does not contradict the spirit of Chinese preschool programmatic documents. All indications are that the goals and requirements in the Guidelines for Learning and Development of Children Aged 3–6 are fundamentally aligned with the core values of the five major domains of STEM education. This model of educational practice is relevant for promoting language development, social development, scientific literacy, and enhancing the quality of children's learning. Nowadays, children's intellectual development has entered a completely new stage, and effective STEM education must follow the laws of children's cognitive development [6]. The rise of STEM education and children's cognition complement each other and have a strong impact on traditional educational concepts. Based on research on children's cognitive concept development, this paper finds that creativity, problem-solving skills, flexible thinking and responsibility in the design process are the keys to STEM education, and that only by combining STEM with design can we strengthen children's artistic and cultural enrichment and improve their overall quality and competitiveness. Here, Piaget's (Swiss psychologist) theory of children's cognitive development is combined with STEM education to discuss the education of younger children.

From the perspective of children's cognitive psychology, an attempt is made to construct a product-based STEM teaching model for children and to verify its feasibility through case studies. Therefore, the research content starts from the direction of children's cognition. The cognitive development of children can be divided into four stages: perceptual operation stage (0–2 years old), preoperational stage (3–6 years old), concrete operation stage (7–11 years old), and formal operation stage (11–15 years old), as shown in Fig. 2 The analysis chart of children's cognitive development. Among them, children aged 0–2 years should use touch, light, sound, graphic patterns, and color to develop their perceptual skills [7].

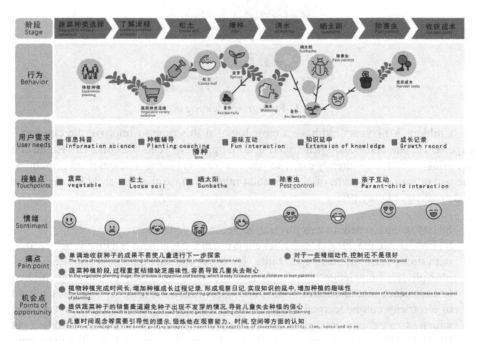

Fig. 2. User needs journey map

3.1 Different Age Characteristics and Product Analysis

Children aged 3–6 years old internalize appearance through their senses and have some thinking, subject to development to improve children's imagination or thinking ability of slightly older children. [8]From the perspective of classroom evaluation China's "3 to 6 years old children's learning and development guidelines" mentioned that in the process of children's learning, special attention should be paid to the quality of children's learning, to protect children's curiosity, develop good behavior, not afraid of difficulties, willing to imagine and create something.

1. Plant growth science toy. This science toy only requires planting a bean, using space for partitioning, setting up a maze for the direction of plant growth, and then allowing children to observe through this transparent pot at the same time through a magnifying glass to feel the biological secrets of plants and develop an interest in agroecology. Although these toys are rich in form, allowing children to improve their interest and initiative in the process of actual operation and observation, while improving children's scientific culture and providing a reference for children's product innovation and the development of science toys, the monitoring of children's scientific needs is still lacking. It cannot effectively expand children's knowledge (Fig. 3).

Fig. 3. Plant growth science toys

Children 7–11 years old have a clear logic, at this time to improve the children's experience, immersion in logical thinking training. 11–15 years old children assume that the thinking activities already exist, so you can combine some mathematical principles, the use of toys in the form of classification interaction, so that the child's imagination and creativity in play [9].

1. STEM science teaching aids physical experiment equipment
    STEM science teaching aids physics experimental equipment is a low-structure toys, with strong variability and operability. The experimental equipment simplifies complex physics knowledge into simple and interesting knowledge, allowing children to experience sound control, touch, and other functions [10]. The physics related to electricity can be learned while operating and piecing together the circuit parts, which saves experimental costs and reduces workload for the teacher. Children get immediate feedback and review their ideas by actually manipulating the manipulative aids under the guidance of the teacher, which stimulates children's interest in how circuits work from a sensory perspective.

2. ROVBLOCK is a remotely operated vehicle (ROV), a type of unmanned underwater vehicle (UUV), with a system composition that generally includes: power propulsion, remote electronic communication device, black and white or color camera, camera tilt head, user Peripheral sensor interface, real-time online display unit, navigation and positioning device, auxiliary lighting and Kevlar zero buoyancy towing cable and other unit components. With a variety of functions, ROVs are used to perform different tasks and are widely used in various fields such as military, coast guard, maritime, customs, nuclear power, water conservancy, hydropower, offshore oil, fisheries, offshore rescue, pipeline detection and marine scientific research, etc. Children can acquire multifaceted and multidisciplinary knowledge (Figs. 4 and 5).

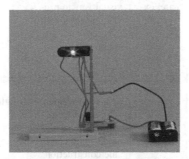

Fig. 4. STEM science teaching aids physical experiment equipment

Fig. 5. STEM science experiment traffic light teaching aids

From the point of view of user groups, science education products are based on children's cognitive development and product positioning is more targeted at children, which makes science education products more in line with children's use needs and more in line with children's STEM learning [11]. From the perspective of technology use, science education products will involve high-tech intelligent technology products, making the relevant technology easier to use and more operable, while the form of the product is improved for large technology products, both in terms of price or availability, which is more conducive to the popularization of the relevant technology in children's STEM education [1]. From the perspective of teachers' teaching, science education products are less difficult to get started and easy to integrate with existing teaching models, while the advantages of science education products in terms of difficulty and ability to measure help achieve teacher liberation.

The science education products applied to children's STEM teaching are organized and summarized in the following chart [12] (Table 1).

Table 1. Selection of science education products applied to children's STEM teaching.

Product name	Product type	Types of Technology in STEM Activities	Application function (purpose)	Application form	Advantages and disadvantages
1. Plant growth science toys	Entertainment	Communicate, express	Information collection and communication are carried out in a visual way to provide children with clearer and more intuitive data records.	Single	Advantages: rich learning content Disadvantages: The learning method is relatively simple
2. 3D printing pen for children	Education + Entertainment	Explore, build	It is convenient for children to construct complex models and enrich the construction and expression of children's creativity.	Single	Advantages: Inspires children's spatial thinking Disadvantage: single form
3. STEM science teaching aids physics experiment equipment				Single	Advantages: to develop children's brain development Disadvantages: Difficult for children, it is difficult for children to concentrate for a long time
4. ROVBLOCK			Based on AR, it converts 2D into 3D to help children establish an intuitive experience and enrich their cognitive experience.	Comprehensive	Advantages: Exercise children's hand-eye coordination ability Disadvantages: The market price is high, and it will be difficult for children to operate

3.2 Problems in the Current Development of STEM Education

STEM education in China has experienced an education boom in a short period of time, and driven by the government and the market, most primary and secondary schools have achieved relatively fruitful results in curriculum development, teaching implementation, and space construction, but it has also brought about problems such as formalization of project implementation, single subject, single message conveyed, fragmentation of curriculum development, slight loss of children's attention, and inability to exert subjective initiative on their own.

Formalized Project Implementation and Children's Inability to Take Initiative. STEM education requires the construction of "learning spaces" with basic equipment, facilities, and materials [13]. Current STEM education tends to focus too much on hardware construction, some schools set up luxurious facilities and equipment "learning space", the duplication of learning space construction makes STEM education into a 3D printing, laser cutting, robotics-based pile of materials movement failed to adapt to local conditions, the development and use of educational resources inside and outside the school [14]. The most significant problem is that these luxury facilities are closed most of the time and are only open to a few students at specific and limited times. This combats the rejection of STEM education by the majority of rural schools, weak schools, or children from economically disadvantaged families, and the popularity and inclusiveness of STEM education is low.

Single Subjects and Loss of Children's Attention. STEM programs focus on real-world, authentic problems, and program implementation revolves around solving real-life problems [16]. However, when some children learn in STEM programs, there are fewer problems with real solutions, more training of single skills, less going to explore their own problems and more solving others' problems instead. There are generally more problems solved with fixed answers and fewer open-ended problems. There are fewer problems involving comprehensive knowledge and more problems with single knowledge. Due to the lack of research and judgment on practical problems and needs of life and the lack of feedback on real user experience, students often end up designing and producing works that have no practical use and can only be used on paper for various competitions and exhibitions, and they fail to make full use of mathematical thinking, scientific principles, engineering techniques and technical tools to solve practical problems in life problems, and it is difficult to be truly creative and innovative [17].

Fragmentation of Curriculum Development by Conveying a Single Message. Currently, STEM curriculum development faces challenges such as single content, single format, single source, curriculum examples, IT discipline dominance, and education and business institution dominance [18]. Especially after the involvement of enterprises and commercial organizations, STEM school education has become to some extent an industry and market in the eyes of entrepreneurs, and the so-called new ecology of education by building a combination of industry, academia, and research has become the curriculum products they develop to sell to schools. Few STEM education resources are school-based and developed based on real-life scenarios, teacher resources, real-world and student needs issues [19]. In addition, STEM education in China faces many other problems and gaps, such as lack of high-level design at a national strategic level, lack of social liaison mechanisms, lack of integrated design across different school sectors, lack of standards and assessment mechanisms, lack of guidelines for teachers' professional development and corresponding teacher training, and lack of national model programs. Relationship Map.

Feature Analysis: Formalization of project implementation, single discipline, convey a single message, Fragmented curriculum development, single output	**Effects on children:** attention loss in children, Inability to exercise subjective initiative independently, more trained single	**In conclusion:** Inconsistent design goals and objectives Parents' requirements for children's learning skills cannot be more comprehensive

4 Solving Problems

4.1 Solving Real Problems

From the current common teaching tools in STEM education, there are two main types of tools: traditional toys and high-tech smart technologies [20]. However, traditional toys do not have intelligent educational functions, and the materials are scattered, high-tech intelligent technology is difficult to use, and the target group is not children. Science education products simply absorb the advantages of both, and after the toying of high-tech intelligent technology, the products suitable for children are products with specific and rich variety, and also meet the needs of children in different activity sessions of STEM [21]. For example, Makeblock Neuron Inventor Kit with the help of the kit's Bluetooth connection can even use the MakeBlock Neuron app to set up programming tasks from an iPhone or iPad using a very simple interface through which children can explore different functions on their own. Each module can be easily connected with the innovative use of different colored electronic modules wrapped in an elastic band, with the power and communication module in green, the input module in orange and the output module in blue, which children can easily distinguish. Another advantage of the elastic band is that it increases the friction of the parts, preventing young children from holding it and reducing noise when the modules are put together. The innovative neural design of the PogoPin magnetic interface is unique, so the modules and modules can be very closely connected together, and this connection greatly reduces the cost of trial and error in the creation process, making children more willing to try to create. The toy set is also accompanied by a wealth of video cases and tutorials, so beginners can quickly get started: step-by-step guidance for building and operating through constantly updated video cases; a wealth of hardware and software case cards and science experiment manuals and other tutorial resources, providing a systematic project-based learning program, allowing children to move from imitation to creation and constantly unlock new skills [22] (Fig. 6).

Fig. 6. Makeblock Neuron Inventor Kit

4.2 Student-Centered

STEM teaching emphasizes student-centeredness, starting with stimulating students' interest to inspire and motivate them [23]. Interest is the best teacher, and after stimulating interest students will have enough time to explore independently and explore the target knowledge according to the designed path with the guidance of the teacher. The images of bees that appear in cartoons and picture books in everyday life and in the curriculum are positive, with more cartoonish and cute shapes, which are very popular among young children [24]. However, in reality, beehives are difficult to obtain and since cities carry certain dangers to satisfy the curiosity of young children, a STEM activity based on the "build a beehive" project using science education products is planned to help children better understand the structural properties of beehives.

The core experience of the STEM activity "Building the Beehive" is the graphical characteristics and composition of a regular hexagon. The activities include activities related to recognizing and understanding regular hexagons and putting together regular hexagons, stimulating children's interest in the activity, and perceiving the abstract relationship between the composition and decomposition of shapes in Manipulation [7].

4.3 Focus on the Role that Design Thinking Plays

Design thinking is an innovative approach to solving complex problems that uses the designer's understanding and approach to match technical feasibility and business strategy with user needs, which translates into customer value and market opportunities. [26] As a way of thinking, it is generally processing-competent in nature, able to understand the context of a problem, able to generate ideas and solutions, and able to rationally analyze and find the most appropriate solution. In conjunction with STEM education, a key feature of STEM education is the integration of disciplinary knowledge through a small number of interdisciplinary concepts, encouraging children to explore the important principles of the content through practice and gradually developing children's understanding of the concepts. Specifically, it includes two main forms of horizontal integration and vertical integration (Table 2).

(i) Horizontal integration.
By horizontal integration, we mean the integration of horizontal curriculum across disciplines and fields [27]. For example, block building is an engineering-focused, problem-solving oriented activity that involves concepts from mathematics and science and uses

Table 2. .

Lesson plan	STEM Objectives of interdisciplinary activities	
Lesson 1. "Where Do Bees Live? Lesson content. Create a bee activity scenario. 2. Share pre-experience. 3. Ask: Where do bees live? 4. Children engage in free activities with the theme of bees and get involved in the activity situation. 	1. Teaching Objectives. 2. 1.S (Science): Know that the hive is where the bees live and store honey and pollen. 3. M (Math): Know the square hexagon	Instructional Preparation. For smart toys, 3D printing pens are provided as the primary tool for children to draw geometric diagrams with transparent pads. AR cognitive cards and supporting software on iPads are provided as tools for advanced activities for young children; as an optional tool for young children, early learning robots can be used as needed for activities. **Fig. 2.** Activity Tools
Lesson 2. Building a Beehive Lesson content. 1. Ask: What is the shape of a beehive? 2. guide children to observe that the material is hexagonal 3. give directional guidance 4. work in groups to determine a way to draw a design composed of positive hexagons as shown in Figure 7.	1. Teaching objectives. 2. 1.T (Technology): Draw the honeycomb structure using 3D printing pen. 3. 2.E (Engineering): Make a beehive structure according to the design. 4. M (Mathematics): Perceive the composition of a square hexagon.	 **Fig. 1.** Hexagonal
1. Lesson Three. 2. The Bees Go Home 3. Lesson Content. 4.Ask:What shapes are your regular hexagons made of?2. Compare different ways of composing regular hexagons?3. Use a child's camera to take notes.	1. Teaching Objectives. 2. T (Technology): Use children's camera science education products and equipment to record.	

technology. STEM instruction takes place in a project-based learning approach where children are required to think holistically, explore practices, and apply a variety of skills such as flattening, shelving, stacking, and enclosing. In block building, children need to maintain the balance of the buildings they construct and gradually develop an understanding of concepts such as symmetry and measurement as they explore and solve problems [28] (Table 3).

Table 3. Horizontal integration table.

Science and Engineering Clarify problems and tasks; discuss problems; conduct investigations; find relationships and solutions; work together to create models; test and improve models; present summaries		
Subject core concepts	Science	**Material Science**: Perceive the properties of objects and materials, the interaction of forces, the relationship between the speed of object motion and object properties, weight, distance, track slope, etc., and the relationship between changes in the direction of object motion and angles, etc.; **Earth and Cosmic Science**: Understanding Earth, Sun, Moon, and Human Activity
	Math	Perceive, understand basic quantitative relationships, number operations, geometric figures, spatial relationships, spatial measurements (size, area, etc.), spatial arrangement
	Project	Identify problems, find ideas, identify solutions, show and share
	Technology	Use a variety of commonly used technical tools and understand the practical application of science and technology in life
Interdisciplinary core concepts	Perceive causality, structure and performance (stability, weight, balance), stability and change	

(ii) Vertical integration.
The so-called vertical integration, which is based on the cognitive level of children at different stages, facilitates the integration of students' literacy with the extension of learning stages for coherent development [29]. In the process of learning, students continuously expand and deepen their understanding of the basic concepts of the subject. Vertical integration, which is essentially a gradual deepening and continuous development of understanding of basic concepts, can systematically help children learn the connotations of basic concepts and ultimately provide a solid foundation for students to understand them in a more comprehensive and systematic way. There is, of course, an interplay

between horizontal and vertical integration, which together contribute to the effective implementation of the curriculum [30] (Figs. 7, 8 and 9).

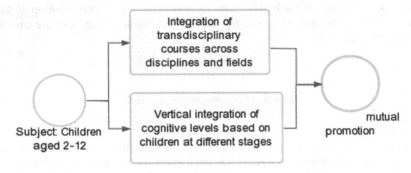

Fig. 7. Summary chart Summary

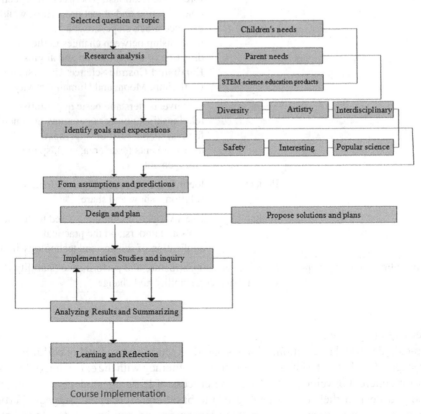

Fig. 8. Structure diagram

The basic method and process of STEM teaching - the nine-step method
Selected question or topic
Identify goals and expectations
Expand pre-learning and preparation
Form assumptions and predictions
Design and plan
Propose solutions and plans
Implementation Studies and inquiry
Analyzing Results and Summarizing
Extended Learning and Reflection

Fig. 9. Nine-step diagram.

5 Methodology

In short, STEM itself suggests that there are patterns to problem solving, and is in fact the epitome of what we call the scientific research method [31]. First, we use research and analysis to identify STEM educational offerings, children's and parents' needs, identify diverse, artistic, interdisciplinary, safe, fun, and scientific offerings, develop prior learning, formulate hypotheses and biases, design and plan, then propose our solutions and plans, conduct research and investigations, analyze the end results, and finally generalize, extend and reflect on them. Using this approach and process as a pedagogical method for students to imitate and solve problems based on the problem solving approach and process will gradually build basic ideas and habits to gradually gain the ability to solve unfamiliar problems in the future (Table 4).

Table 4. Vertical integration table

Grade	Year 2	Grade 5	Grade 8	Grade 12
Performance expectations and subject concepts	Divide the building blocks into two categories according to the different things, and be able to give more than 3 examples for each category	Perceive the properties of objects and materials, the interaction of forces, the relationship between the speed of object motion and object properties, weight, distance, track slope, etc., and the relationship between changes in the direction of object motion and angles, and give corresponding examples and evidence to support	Explain and understand basic quantitative relationships, operations with numbers, geometric figures,	Describe the process of using various commonly used technical tools and understanding the practical application of science and technology in life

6 Conclusion

In this literature, which examines the links between STEM education and design from 2000 to 2022, the results show that most assessments have focused on assessing single-disciplinary areas of learning and less on interdisciplinary learning and practice.

Therefore, this project takes children's cognitive psychology as the center of theoretical research, and takes the cognitive characteristics of psychology and children's behavior as the starting point to fully understand the cognitive behavior and characteristics of children at this stage, and carefully analyze, elaborate and summarize the product elements. Finally, the interdisciplinary research based on children's cognitive psychology, children's cognitive behaviors and characteristics, and the above-mentioned issues of exposing students to the real world greatly expand the breadth and depth of learning. Through these specific examples, we can appreciate the quality and value of classroom design based on "interdisciplinary literacy" and gain much experience and knowledge for classroom transformation. First, "interdisciplinary" is a subversion of the traditional "disciplinary view". Second, the purpose is to achieve higher efficiency, and "interdisciplinarity" implies a subversion of the traditional "disciplinary view". Both disciplinary and interdisciplinary teaching and learning are about developing students' knowledge and shaping their personality in interaction.

Research in STEM education has made great strides. However, there is still a long way to go. To help researchers and practitioners working in the field better calibrate their work, the nature of the disciplines involved and the mechanisms that link them should be clearly articulated in STEM education and teaching.

References

1. Zhang, B.: Research progress and enlightenment of international STEM education——based on the content analysis of the articles published in the SSCI journal "international STEM education journal". J. Math. Educ. **31**(02), 58–62+81 (2022)
2. Yang Kaicheng, F.: On why STEM education is special. China Distance Educ. **2022**(04), 48–54 (2022). https://doi.org/10.13541/j.cnki.chinade.2022.04.004
3. Min, H., Lei, B., Yingjie, H., Hua, X.: Comparison and enlightenment of the objectives, strategies and development models of stem education in china and the united states. Basic Educ. **17**(05), 34–46 (2020)
4. Yeping, L.: Research and development of STEM education: a rapidly growing international field. J. Math. Educ. **28**(03), 42–44 (2019)
5. National Science Foundation: Preparing the Next Generation of STEM Innovators: Identifying and Developing Our Nation's Human Capital, pp. 1–49. Arlington, Washington DC (2010)
6. Ronda, E., Adler, J.: Mining mathematics in textbook lessons. Int. J. Sci. Math. Educ. **15**(6), 1 097–1 114 (2017)
7. Fangyu, L., Le, Z.: Research on rural children's educational product design from the perspective of embodied cognition. Packag. Eng. **41**(16), 154–163 (2020). https://doi.org/10.19554/j.cnki.1001-3563.2020.16.023
8. Lu, Y., Liu, J., Zhang, Y., Wang, X.: Design of STEM education products based on smart classroom. Ind. Eng. Des. **3**(01), 19–25+31 (2021). https://doi.org/10.19798/j.cnki.2096-6946.2021.01.003

9. Ge, S., Jueqi, G.: Teachers' interdisciplinary literacy for integrated STEM: structural model and development path. Modern Distance Educ. Res. **34**(03), 58–66 (2022)
10. Denghun, L., Bingbing, B.: The integrated construction strategy of STEM curriculum under the control of the big concept: the practice and enlightenment of STEM Road Map. Global Educ. Prospects **51**(04), 101–111 (2022)
11. Feng, X., Zhu Zhigang, X., Wen.: Cultivation strategy of geographic practical ability based on STEM education concept——taking "longitude and latitude" as an example. Geogr. Educ. **05**, 50–53 (2022)
12. Li, X., Feng, L., Zhang, C., Wang, J., Wang, S., Hu, L.: Insulin-like growth factor binding proteins 7 prevents dental pulp-derived mesenchymal stem cell senescence via metabolic downregulation of p21[J/OL]. Sci. China Life Sci. 1–15 (2022). http://kns.cnki.net/kcms/det ail/11.5841.Q.20220525.1724.002.html
13. Zhang, W., Fang, X.X., Li, Q.C., Pi, W., Han, N.: Reduced graphene oxide-embedded nerve conduits loaded with bone marrow mesenchymal stem cell-derived extracellular vesicles promote peripheral nerve regeneration. Neural Regeneration Res. **18**(01), 200–206 (2023)
14. Tingbo, L.: Design of popular science toys for children aged 3–6 based on cognitive psychology. Shandong University (2020).https://doi.org/10.27272/d.cnki.gshdu.2020. 002783
15. Qian, L., Yong, J.: Children's concentration improvement and design of assembled toys. Design **35**(05), 146–148 (2022)
16. Juncheng, W.: The application of design psychology in the design of preschool children's toys. West. Leather **43**(22), 137–138 (2021)
17. Miaomiao, Z.: Research on the design of intelligent parent-child toys for preschool children. Design **34**(20), 120–123 (2021)
18. Zhiyan, W., Youxin, W., Yating, D., Yanjun, D.: Research on interactive design of children's intelligent toys guided by tactile experience. Packaging Eng. 1–9 (2022). http://kns.cnki.net/ kcms/detail/50.1094.TB.20210728.1635.002.html
19. Xingquan, Z., Wanrong, L.: Research on the design and application of teaching aids based on the concept of a-stem——taking the primary school science "sound" course as an example. Arts Sci. Navig. (Late) **06**, 18 (2021)
20. Xiaoyan, F.: Research on the blended teaching mode of off-campus STEM courses based on case analysis. Nanchang University (2021)
21. Yuqing, Z.: Research on the design of intelligent teaching aids based on STEAM education. Hubei University of Technology (2020). https://doi.org/10.27131/d.cnki.ghugc.2020.000187
22. Yi, Y.: Development of children's play with teaching aids based on STEM education. Wenzhou University (2019)
23. Mingyu, W.: Research on classroom design of STEM education in primary school. Southwest University (2018)
24. Huijing, Y., Xingxing, F.: Design strategy of online education products for primary school students based on user experience. Design **34**(23), 27–29 (2021)
25. Jinqin, Z.: User research and design and operation strategy research of children's online English education products. Beijing Institute of Graphic Printing (2019). https://doi.org/10. 26968/d.cnki.gbjyc.2019.000004
26. Kaidi, C.: Design and practice of innovative educational products for middle school students under the STEAM concept. Kunming University of Science and Technology (2019).https:// doi.org/10.27200/d.cnki.gkmlu.2019.001567
27. Xinyu, C.: Research on K12 online education product design based on developmental psychology. Yanshan University (2015)
28. Dandan, W., Li, X., Zikun, Y.: Visual analysis of domestic STEM education research.China Modern Educ. Equipment **2022**(06), 44–47 (2022). https://doi.org/10.13492/j.cnki.cmee. 2022.06.015

29. Pinghong, Z., Yukun, N., Kang, W., Yi, Z., Xing, L., Chaowang, S.: Teaching mode and application of STEM engineering design for computational thinking training. Modern Distance Educ. Res. **34**(01), 104–112 (2022)
30. Li Shijin, G., Xiaoqing.: Innovation-based AI-STEM integration new ecology: model construction and practical examples. Distance Educ. J. **39**(06), 30–38 (2021). https://doi.org/10.15881/j.cnki.cn33-1304/g4.2021.06.004
31. Guo Wei, X., Feifei, Z.Y.: Research on classroom teaching based on the concept of STEM integrated education. J. Jilin Provincial Inst. Educ. **37**(10), 43–48 (2021). https://doi.org/10.16083/j.cnki.1671-1580.2021.10.011
32. Ruirui, Z.: Research on the activity design of kindergarten science field based on the concept of STEM education. Northwest Normal University (2021)

Proposal of Sound-Color Sensory Discrimination Method Considering Periodic Fluctuation of Cerebral Blood Flow

Yuri Hamada$^{(\boxtimes)}$ ⓘ and Yosuke Kurihara ⓘ

Aoyama Gakuin University, 5-10-1 Fuchinobe, Chuo-ku, Sagamihara, Kanagawa 252-5258, Japan
hamada@ise.aoyama.ac.jp

Abstract. In the study of absolute pitch, there is a teaching method that links chords and colors using color- hearing synaesthesia. The aim of this method is to promote learning more effectively by using two senses. A method established to objectively confirm that students can recall sounds using both vision and hearing, can lead to teaching strategies and improve the motivation of learners. In this study, a method is proposed to measure cerebral blood flow during a task using near-infrared spectroscopy (NIRS) to discriminate whether a learner is recalling a sound using both senses or only one sense in color-hearing synaesthesia. In the proposed method, the features consider the periodicity of cerebral blood flow (CBF). Specifically, the measured cerebral blood flow rate is divided into intervals with an arbitrary number of points. Then, the CBF values of the subdivisions are calculated and the difference between CBF_{max} and CBF_{min} is used to define the feature value. The feature value thus calculated was used by the support vector machine (SVM) to determine whether sound recall is through both senses. The number of segmented intervals and the kernel function of the SVM were changed to compare the discrimination results. As a result, the maximum correct response rate of 0.972 was obtained when the number of segmented intervals was 3 or 5 and the kernel function was Gaussian process regression.

Keywords: NIRS · SVM · Synesthesia · CBF

1 Introduction

In recent years, learning methods based on synesthesia have been proposed in various fields. Synesthesia is the conscious experience of sensory attributes induced by particular conscious mental events, appearing in addition to sensations normally experienced by most people during such events [1, 2]. There are various types of synaesthesia, such as color-hearing synaesthesia, in which colors are perceived as sounds, chromatic synaesthesia, in which colors are perceived as letters, number synaesthesia, in which specific spatial arrangements in numbers are perceived, and mirror touch synaesthesia, in which a stimulus observed on another person's body is perceived as a stimulus in the same location in our own body. The stimulus that causes synesthesia is called the inducing

© Springer Nature Switzerland AG 2022
G. Meiselwitz et al. (Eds.): HCII 2022, LNCS 13517, pp. 257–265, 2022.
https://doi.org/10.1007/978-3-031-22131-6_19

stimulus, and the sensation caused as synesthesia is called the excitatory sensation [3]. In the case of color-hearing synesthesia, sound is the triggering stimulus and color is the excitatory sensation. In the case of color-letter synesthesia, letters are the triggering stimulus and colors are the excitation sensation. Thus, there are various combinations of triggering stimuli and excitation senses.

In the study of absolute pitch, a teaching method that uses color-hearing synaesthesia, in which sounds are perceived as colors, has been used to map chords to colors [3]. This method aims to promote learning more effectively by using two senses instead of a single sense. Establishing a method that can objectively confirm that students are recalling sounds using both senses can lead to the determination of teaching strategies and improve the learners' motivation. To determine the presence of true synaesthesia, a classifier is used to discriminate between tasks that use multiple senses versus a single sense. In this study, cerebral blood flow is measured using near-infrared spectroscopy to create a classifier to determine whether color-hearing synaesthesia is recalled using both senses of color and hearing, or whether it is recalled using only sound or only color.

2 Related Studies

There are many studies that use CBF to classify tasks. NIRS measures of CBF in the prefrontal cortex, have been used to classify many tasks, such as mental arithmetic [4–6], musical imagery [4, 6, 7], which are known to activate the prefrontal cortex.

There are many studies that calculate features from the cerebral blood flow measured by NIRS whereby the task is classified using the calculated features consisting of the average value [4, 8, 9], slope [10], variance [11], and amplitude [12] of CBF. Although most of these studies use basic statistics as features, they do not consider the periodic fluctuation of CBF. In this study, the proposed new features are used to capture the periodic fluctuation characteristics of CBF, whereby the proposed features are used to subdivide the measurement interval. In addition, the dynamic range of each subdivided segment is calculated and used as a feature value. This makes it possible to extract features based on the task cycle.

As classification methods, local density approximation (LDA) [13–15] and SVM [8, 16, 17] have been widely used and shown to be effective. In this study, SVM is used to classify whether the color-hearing synaesthesia is recalled using both senses or only one sense. In addition, the classification accuracy is compared for changing kernel functions.

3 Proposal Method

In the proposed method, CBF is measured by NIRS for stimulus discrimination, as illustrated in Fig. 1. Let S_A denote the event that stimulus A is presented, S_B denote the event that stimulus B is presented, and $S_{A, B}$ denote the events that the A and B are presented at the same time. The stimulus vector is $s = [S_A, S_B, S_{A, B}]$. Let $x(k)_{s,i}$ be the hemoglobin concentration in CBF measured by NIRS when each stimulus vector s is applied. Here, i is the area of cerebral blood flow measured where $i = 1, 2, 3 \ldots n_p$. The proposed method uses both oxidized and deoxidized hemoglobin concentrations, and applies signal processing to classify stimuli from $x(k)_{s,i}$. First, to capture localized changes in the measured CBF values $x(k)_{s,i}$, one interval of $x(k)_{s,i}$ is divided into ns intervals at M points to obtain $x(k)_{s,i,j}(j = 1, 2, \ldots, n_s)$. Next, to emphasize the change in cerebral blood flow, the difference in $x(k)_{s,i,j}$ is calculated for neighboring k's such that $x'(k)_{s,i,j} = x(k)_{s,i,j}(k) - x(k)_{s,i,j}(k-1)$. Furthermore, it is assumed that the component of CBF in response to the stimulus appears in the dynamic range of the difference $x'(k)_{s,i,j}$, and the difference between the maximum and minimum values of $x'(k)_{s,i,j}$ is determined as in Eq. (1) below.

$$D(k)_{s,i,j} = Max\left\{x'(k)_{s,i,j}\right\} - Min\left\{x'(k)_{s,i,j}\right\} \tag{1}$$

In this study, $D_{s,i,j}$ ($i = 1, 2, \ldots n_p$ and $j = 1, 2, \ldots n_s$) is used as a feature to discriminate the estimated stimulus $\hat{s} = [\hat{S}_A, \hat{S}_B, \hat{S}_{A,B}]$ by multi-class SVM.

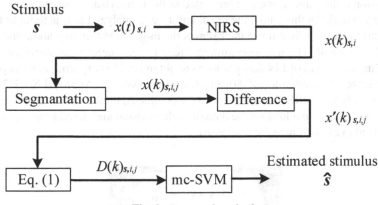

Fig. 1. Proposed method

4 Verification Experiment

4.1 Overview of the Experiment

In this experiment, HITACHI's NIRS (wearable optical topography) was used to measure the cerebral blood flow. The WOT-100 measuring device was used to measure the CBF in the prefrontal cortex corresponding to the frontopolar midline electrode (fpz) area of the international 10–20 method at a sampling frequency of 5 Hz at 10 points corresponding to 1 to 10 channels. ($n_p = 10$). The measurement area of this experiment is shown in Fig. 2. In this experiment, the oxidized hemoglobin concentration $x(k)_{s,i}^{oxy}$ and deoxidized hemoglobin concentration $x(k)_{s,i}^{deoxy}$ weremeasured.

In the chromatic synaesthesia experiment, it is assumed that stimulus A is chord recall and stimulus B is color recall. Therefore, the stimulus vector $s = [S_{sound}, S_{color}, S_{sound, color}]$. In this experiment, there are two stages: one is memorization, in which participants are asked to remember the presented stimuli, and the other is recall, in which participants are asked to answer what they remember. The flowchart of this experiment is shown in Fig. 3. In the memorization phase, the stimuli are presented for two seconds followed by a blank period for three seconds, repeated six times. In the recall phase, the stimulus is presented for two seconds three times. After that, in the memorization phase lasting 3 s, the participants are asked to answer which stimuli they remember. This process is repeated six times as one set. In the experiment of simultaneous presentation of chord and color stimuli ($S_{sound, color}$), participants memorize three combinations of chord and color. In the experiment with color stimuli (S_{color}), the subject memorizes three colors: red, yellow, and blue. In the chord stimulus (S_{sound}) experient, the subject remembers three types of chords in the middle range. Only one of the three stimuli presented in the recall session is the same as the one presented in the memorization session, and the rest are dummy stimuli. In this study, the recall ability was analyzed as it is thought that the participants in the experiment use their senses the most when thinking about the correct answer during recall. The memorization and recall experiments were conducted on 17 participants, and a total of 144 data points were obtained. This experiment was approved by the ethics review committee of Aoyama Gakuin University (Approval No. H21-004).

In this study, the NIRS measurements were conducted on the data of all 10 channels, that is, from 1 to 10. In addition, the data of both oxidized and deoxidized hemoglobin were utilized to discriminate the responses.

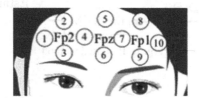

Fig. 2. Measurement area

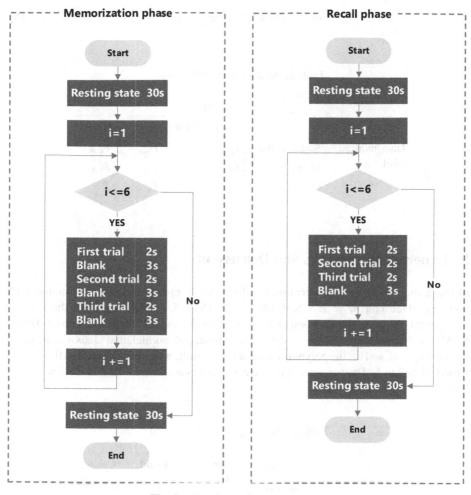

Fig. 3. Flowchart of the experiment

4.2 Evaluation Method

In the experiment, the classification accuracy of the task was evaluated using leave-one-out cross-validation. The classification results are tabulated in Table 1, and the overall correct response rate (accuracy) is calculated by Eq. (2). Similarly, the correct response rates of $S_{\text{sound, color}}$, S_{sound}, S_{color} ($accuracy_{sound,color}$, $accuracy_{sound}$, $accuracy_{color}$) are calculated by Eqs. (3)–(5).

$$accuracy = \frac{(T_{sc}+T_s+T_c)}{(T_{sc}+T_s+T_c+F_{s,sc}+F_{c,sc}+F_{sc,s}+F_{c,s}+F_{sc,c}+F_{s,c})} \tag{2}$$

$$accuracy_{sound,color} = \frac{T_{sc}}{(T_{sc}+F_{sc,s}+F_{sc,c})} \tag{3}$$

$$accuracy_{sound} = \frac{T_s}{(T_s+F_{s,sc}+F_{s,c})} \tag{4}$$

$$accuracy_{color} = \frac{T_c}{(T_c + F_{c,sc} + F_{c,s})} \qquad (5)$$

Table 1. Result classification table

		True label		
		Sound, Color	Sound	Color
Discriminated label	Sound, Color	T_{sc}	$F_{s,sc}$	$F_{c,sc}$
	Sound	$F_{sc,s}$	T_s	$F_{c,s}$
	Color	$F_{sc,c}$	$F_{s,c}$	T_c

5 Experimental Results and Discussion

In this experiment, the classification results were compared based on the number of divisions of the data ($M = 1, 3, 5, 9, 15 n_s = 45, 15, 9, 5, 3$). Note that when the number of segments $M = 1$, the segmented interval $n_s = 45$ and all the data are used. Using SVM, the different types of kernel functions (linear, polynomial, and Gaussian kernels) were compared, and for the polynomial kernel, the results were also checked as the degree varied from 2 to 5. The percentage of correct answers are summarized in Tables 2, 3, 4, 5, 6.

Table 2. Accuracy ($M = 1$ $n_s = 45$)

		All	Sound, Color	Sound	Color
Linear		0.646	0.563	0.542	0.833
Polynomial	2	0.646	0.583	0.542	0.813
	3	0.542	0.500	0.375	0.750
	4	0.243	0.292	0.229	0.208
	5	0.313	0.083	0.854	0.000
Gaussian		0.667	0.625	0.604	0.771

The overall correct response rate was 0.972 when the number of divisions corresponded to ($M = 9, n_s = 5$) or ($M = 15, n_s = 3$), using Gaussian process regression (Table 5, Table 6) as the kernel function. Table 4 shows that the maximum correct response rate was 0.917 for ($M = 5, n_s = 9$) and according to Table 3 it was 0.694 for ($M = 3, n_s = 15$). The correct response rate was 0.979 for the color and chord task, 0.938 for the sound-only task, and 1.000 for the color-only task for ($M = 15, n_s = 3$)

Table 3. Accuracy ($M = 3\ n_s = 15$)

		All	Sound, Color	Sound	Color
Linear		0.729	0.667	0.750	0.771
Polynomial	2	0.757	0.688	0.854	0.729
	3	0.694	0.667	0.771	0.646
	4	0.708	0.708	0.792	0.625
	5	0.674	0.667	0.771	0.583
Gaussian		0.694	0.896	0.542	0.646

Table 4. Accuracy ($M = 5\ n_s = 9$)

		All	Sound, Color	Sound	Color
Linear		0.854	0.813	0.938	0.813
Polynomial	2	0.917	0.938	0.938	0.875
	3	0.896	0.938	0.896	0.854
	4	0.854	0.896	0.896	0.771
	5	0.861	0.896	0.917	0.771
Gaussian		0.694	0.917	0.958	0.854

Table 5. Accuracy ($M = 9\ n_s = 5$)

		All	Sound, Color	Sound	Color
Linear		0.833	0.792	0.938	0.771
Polynomial	2	0.958	0.979	0.958	0.938
	3	0.944	0.979	0.917	0.938
	4	0.931	0.979	0.875	0.938
	5	0.882	0.917	0.854	0.875
Gaussian		0.694	0.972	0.958	0.958

(Table 6). The correct response rate for each task was 0.958 for the color and chord task, 0.958 for the sound-only task, and 1.000 for the color-only task when ($M = 9, n_s = 5$) (Table 5). The correct response rate was high for all tasks, especially for the color-only task, which could be discriminated completely. Table 1 also shows that the overall correct response rate without splitting was 0.667 ($M = 1, n_s = 45$), indicating the effectiveness

Table 6. Accuracy ($M = 15\ n_s = 3$)

		All	Sound, Color	Sound	Color
Linear		0.806	0.750	0.896	0.771
Polynomial	2	0.944	0.979	0.917	0.938
	3	0.938	0.979	0.875	0.958
	4	0.938	0.979	0.896	0.938
	5	0.944	0.979	0.917	0.938
Gaussian		0.694	0.972	0.979	0.938

of splitting. For $n_s = 3$, each interval was 3 s, and for $n_s = 5$, each interval was approximately 2 s. The data of recall used in this experiment showed that the duration of one stimulus presentation was 2 s and the duration of the response was 3 s, which was roughly the same as the number of seconds in one interval after data division. This suggests that the response in CBF in response to a single stimulus appears as the difference in feature values.

6 Conclusion

In this study, the cerebral blood flow measured by NIRS was used to determine whether color-hearing synesthesia is recalled using both senses of color/hearing or only sound or only color. In the proposed method, features that take into consideration the periodic fluctuation characteristics of cerebral blood flow are used. Task discrimination was performed by applying SVM to the calculated features, and the classification results were compared by the number of segmentation points and the type of kernel function. As a result, a maximum correct response rate of 0.972 was obtained when the number of segments M and the number of sections n_s were ($M = 9$, $n_s = 5$) or ($M = 15$, $n_s = 3$) with Gaussian process regression as the kernel function. The proposed method makes it possible to determine whether or not a sound is recalled using both senses in color-hearing synesthesia. In the future, the potential of the same method for color-letter synesthesia will be explored.

References

1. Alford, L.B.: A report on two cases of synesthesia. J. Abnorm. Psychol. **13**(1), 1–11 (1918)
2. Motluk, A.: Two synaesthetes talking colour. In Baron-Cohen, S., Harrison, J.E. (Eds.), Synaesthesia: Classic and Contemporary Readings, pp. 269–277. Blackwell Publishing. (1997)
3. Eguchi, T., Eguchi, A.: Changing piano lessons (3) new absolute tone program, Zen-On Music Co., Ltd. (2001). (in Japanese)
4. Hwang, H.-J., Lim, J.-H., Kim, D.-W., Im, C.-H. Evaluation of various mental task combinations for near-infrared spectroscopy-based brain-computer interfaces. J. Biomed. Opt.**19**(7), 077005 (2014)

5. Hong, K.-S., Naseer, N., Kim, Y.-H.: Classification of prefrontal and motor cortex signals for three-class fNIRS-BCI. Neurosci. Lett. **587**, 87–92 (2015)
6. Chan, J., Power, S., Chau, T.: Investigating the need for modeling temporal dependencies in a brain-computer interface with real-time feedback based on near infrared spectra. J. Near Infrared Spectrosc. **20**(1), 107–116 (2012)
7. Naito, M., Michioka, Y., Ozawa, K., Ito, Y., Kiguchi, M., Kanazawa, T.: A communication means for totally locked-in ALS patients based on changes in cerebral blood volume measured with near-infrared light. IEICE Trans. Inf. Syst. **90**(7), 1028–1037 (2007)
8. Fazli, S., Mehnert, J., Steinbrink, J., Curio, G., Villringer, A., Muller, K.R., et al.: Enhanced performance by a hybrid NIRS-EEG brain-computer interface. Neuroimage **59**, 519–529 (2012)
9. Faress, A., Chau, T.: Towards a multimodal brain-computer interface: combining fNIRS and fTCD measurements to enable higher classification accuracy. Neuroimage **77**, 186–194 (2013)
10. Hong, K.-S., Nguyen, H.-D.: State-space models of impulse hemodynamic responses over motor, somatosensory, and visual cortices. Biomed. Opt. Express **5**(6), 1778–1798 (2014)
11. Holper, L., Wolf, M.: Single-trial classification of motor imagery differing in task complexity: a functional near-infrared spectroscopy study. J. Neuroeng. Rehabil **8**(34), 1–13 (2011)
12. Stangl, M., Bauernfeind, G., Kurzmann, J., Scherer, R., Neuper, C.: A haemodynamic brain-computer interface based on real-time classification of near infrared spectroscopy signals during motor imagery and mental arithmetic. J. Near Infrared Spectrosc. **21**(3), 157–171 (2013)
13. Naseer, N., Hong, M.J., Hong, K.-S.: Online binary decision decoding using functional near-infrared spectroscopy for the development of brain-computer interface. Exp. Brain Res. **232**(2), 555–564 (2014)
14. Luu, S., Chau, T.: Decoding subjective preferences from single-trial near-infrared spectroscopy signals. *J. Neural Eng.* **6**(1), 016003 (2009)
15. Kaiser, V., Gauernfeind, G., Kreilinger, A., Kaufmann, T., Kubler, A., Neuper, C., et al.: Cortical effects of user training in a motor imagery based brain-computer interface measured by fNIRS and EEG. Neuroimage **85**, 432–444 (2014)
16. Sitaram, R., Zhang, H.H., Guan, C.T., Thulasidas, M., Hoshi, Y., Ishikawa, A., et al.: Temporal classification of multichannel near-infrared spectroscopy signals of motor imagery for developing a brain-computer interface. Neuroimage **34**, 1416–1427 (2007)
17. Tadanobu, M., Shinya, T., Tetsuya, S., Shigeki, H.: A brain–computer interface for motor assist by the prefrontal cortex. Electr. Commun. Japan **95**(10), 1–8 (2012)

Traditional Face-to-Face Educational Modality vs. Remote Face-to-Face: Its Impact on Academic Performance in the Context of the Covid 19 Pandemic

Irmina Hernández-Sánchez[1]([✉]), Samara Romero Caballero[1],
Mónica Acuña Rodríguez[1], Grace Rocha Herrera[1], Janiris Acuña Rodríguez[1],
and Javier Ramírez[2]

[1] Universidad de la Costa, 58 Street #55 66, Barranquilla, Colombia
ihernand8@cuc.edu.co
[2] Corporación Universitaria, Taller Cinco, Km 19, Chía, Colombia

Abstract. The purpose of this research proposal was aimed at analyzing the existence of a significantly differential academic performance depending on the class modality: traditional face-to-face vs. remote face-to-face, in students of the psychology program, who were studying the subject of fundamentals of measurement and psychological evaluation in a higher education institution in the city of Barranquilla/Colombia. To achieve this objective, a study framed in the postpositivist paradigm was developed, based on quantitative, non-experimental, correlational, cross-sectional and field research. The sample consisted of 37 students, divided into two groups: Group 1 traditional face-to-face modality: 20 students and Group 2 remote face-to-face modality with an N of 17. For the analysis of the data, the t-test was applied, for independent samples, using the SPSS version 18 statistical package. The results allowed to establish the existence of a significantly higher academic performance that favors the group that studied the subject under the traditional face-to-face modality. Elements that could explain this superior performance under the traditional education format, have to do with low level of adaptability of those involved to this new way of developing the teaching-learning process, alteration and emotional management in the face of this new learning atmosphere, low experience and little preparation of students and the teacher to digital management and connection platforms for the development of classes from face-to-face remote, not having the right tools to be able to work effectively lowers the remote connection.

Keywords: Face-to-face/remote educational modality · Higher education · covid19 · Quality of education

1 Introduction

The transformations of education in the last two years have demarcated an interesting analysis, in the face of the new demands that the pedagogical work and the dynamics,

© Springer Nature Switzerland AG 2022
G. Meiselwitz et al. (Eds.): HCII 2022, LNCS 13517, pp. 266–275, 2022.
https://doi.org/10.1007/978-3-031-22131-6_20

from the didactic, have implemented to respond to the current needs. That is why, for the history of humanity, covid 19 will undoubtedly imply a before and after in teaching and how to achieve knowledge.

The beginning of the pandemic generated alterations and changes in the different areas in which the human being develops; one of them was related to education and the way of teaching classes at the various levels of the formal education system. Faced with this situation, the Economic Commission for Latin America and the Caribbean [1] affirms that one of the decisions taken by educational institutions, both at the preschool, basic, middle and higher levels, was related to the implementation of distance learning modalities, either synchronously or asynchronously.

As indicated by Heimann Fernández et al., this measure led to the adaptation of face-to-face teaching to a non-face-to-face approach [2]. Students, teachers and the entire educational system in general, abruptly had to adjust their experiences to new trends, which although they were part of everyday life, did not have a high-latency closeness like the one that has recently been experienced, where the need to evaluate technological perceptions, the surrounding environment, digital skills intensified, the system of relationships from a primordial component, emotions [3].

It is important to recognize then, that the implementation of pedagogical actions from remote or remote work, invited as explained by Pulido and Ancheta, first, to recognize the tools that countries have, which would allow contextualizing the needs and possibilities of each scenario, thus reformulating the preparation of teachers in the system, locate concrete dialogical experiences, develop new guidelines for the evaluation and monitoring of pedagogical work based on feedback, dynamism and creativity [4].

In this line of thought, Capilla et al. argue in a report by the Organization of Ibero-American States for Education, Science and Culture (OEI) that if an optimal adjustment and development of online training activities is achieved, following a methodology and contents according to and teachers are trained in this type of educational modality the result in the performance of students does not it has to be different from those achieved in traditional face-to-face education. Therefore, the impact of COVID-19 on the university environment is a shared responsibility that must be assumed by teachers, students, authorities and society in general to promote education of excellence, science, culture and research [5].

Hodges et al. called the distance education modality implemented emergency remote teaching, given that they consider that it is a temporary change from the traditional face-to-face modality to an alternative modality to develop the teaching-learning process, product of the crisis generated by Covid 19 [6].

In this order of ideas, it is important to clarify that remote face-to-face education and traditional face-to-face education are not the same, but each of them has great importance because they have responded to a need and a historical moment; so one of the most important challenges in this new normal was to integrate and motivate students through technologies, although, most of them are familiar with digital platforms, there were those who did not even have the right tools to be able to work, however, over time each one adapted in the best way [7].

Thus, in the face of the pandemic situation, with the especially remote face-to-face classes which were not expected, a diversity of experiences has emerged, which for constructive purposes allow to cement the path towards the transformation of education. This, taking into account lessons of appropriation, roles, training and a cultural background more important than the technology itself.

Hernández Rangel et al. mention that the success in teaching-learning processes during the pandemic by covid 19 are products of [8]:

The optimal use of technologies, of training processes to use the technological resources that were created to respond to the accelerated transformation that takes place in the educational system.

The diversity of pedagogical strategies applied by university teachers to favor the achievement of the results of learning.

In this way, Paniagua-Valdebenito affirms that the institutions formulated the way to keep the educational process active, thus avoiding its fall and subsequent loss of the school year or semester, which has led the institutions to transform [9].

However, one of the elements that has generated resentment has to do with the quality of education, that is, if remote education maintains the quality that is presented under the modality of traditional face-to-face [10].

In this sense, Pérez-López et al. consider it essential to analyze the quality of remote teaching received, in such a way as to elaborate diagnoses based on precise evidence; which could favor the design of educational interventions and scenarios in the short and medium term, aimed at maintaining an educational quality from excellence and effectiveness [11].

Therefore, civil society organizations have worked together with governments to implement educational innovation programs, new technologies, teacher training and many others so that all students in the region can learn. Because in the two scenarios – basic and higher education – there were experiences, which were not expected, which managed to put the spotlight on issues that had not been identified before. And it's not just about connectivity issues, although access to both the connection and devices is a chapter that has drawn attention for years; in the emergency, the need to access the Internet to study and work was perceived.

In spite of everything, during the pandemic a variety of experiences have emerged, which for constructive purposes allow to cement the path towards the transformation of education. Educational roles changed, didactic strategies were transformed, technological tools emerged, and cultural background became more important than technology itself.

Although, at first, without a doubt, the attention was focused on socio-emotional aspects, as time progresses, the concern is focused on the learning of students and the slow progressive return to classrooms where numerous uncertainties still reign López [11]. That is why is collaborative work who is has become a primary tool that allows the teacher to assume the new demands of virtual, remote and hybrid work, otherwise which is invited to enhance the educational vision of competences that must sustain and guarantee teaching and learning.

From what has been developed throughout the previous paragraphs, a variable of interest to study, under this framework of face-to-face and remote educational modality, is academic performance; in this regard Pérez-López et al. express that students perceive greater dedication in the preparation of the subjects they take under remote modality than that destined in the face-to-face format. They also state that, although there is an increase in study time, students do not point out differences in academic performance [12].

Similarly, what is related to the academic performance of students in the face of the new modalities of studies, different from the face-to-face in the classroom, allow us to point out that without a doubt high-income countries have not been so affected in terms of the quality of their training and the results that are expected, while low-income countries not only weigh the immersion to the new demands of training, but the purposes of learning have been hindered, according to the barriers that diminish the effectiveness of work methodologies.

It is necessary to mention that the transformation of educational systems according to the evaluation of the performance of their students, the changes in roles and the assimilation of the technologies of the present and the future as inputs that require appropriation and adaptation in the lives of students, lead to rethink the goals of training quality, to the environments in which the student and the teacher are immersed, the possession and quality of the resources that will determine the scope of the academic objectives set [13].

An aspect to highlight with respect to this theme, is the perception of students about their digital skills, in this sense Ramírez García et al. report that students usually consider to have these abilities in a degree that goes from acceptable to very good; however, they consider that their level of interest and motivation towards the educational modality related to e-learning, that is, a training system, based mainly on a connection that is made through the internet or connected to the network; it is at ground level: this disinterest is caused by low quality of the internet signal, teaching methodologies not adapted to the modality, as well as negative experiences lived in previous learning situations [14].

Based on what has been said, it seems relevant to develop studies that allow comparing the academic performance achieved in subjects that are studied both in person and remotely and thus provide evidence that demonstrates whether there are statistically significant differences in said performance.

Thus, the research proposal developed had as a general objective to analyze, within the framework of the Covid19 pandemic, the possible difference in academic performance or performance, depending on the class modality (traditional and remote face-to-face witness) of a group of students of the psychology program, of a higher education institution in Barranquilla/Colombia; considering as a null hypothesis the non-existence of significant differences in the average of grades reached at the end of the first cut of the academic period 2021-1, between those students who took the subject of fundamentals of measurement and psychological evaluation in traditional face-to-face modality and those who developed learning in a remote face-to-face modality.

2 Material and Method

To achieve this purpose, a study based on the post-positivist paradigm was developed, based on a quantitative, field, cross-sectional, non-experimental, correlational investigation of mean differences. The variables of interest were (Fig. 1):

In addition to the variables indicated, it should be noted that the strange variable related to the teacher responsible for the subject was controlled, since it was the same

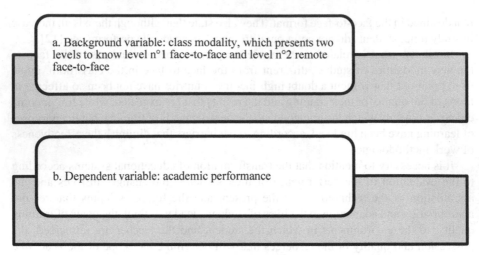

a. Background variable: class modality, which presents two levels to know level n°1 face-to-face and level n°2 remote face-to-face

b. Dependent variable: academic performance

Fig. 1. Variables of interest.

person who had under his responsibility the two groups. Likewise, the strange variable related to the evaluation strategies was also controlled, for the two groups the same strategies were used to evaluate the knowledge achieved in the subject.

The participating population was constituted by the students enrolled in the psychology program, in the subject fundamentals of measurement and psychological evaluation of the academic period 2021-1, of a higher education institution of Barranquilla-Colombia, in this sense the group that worked under the face-to-face modality was 20 students and the one that worked under the remote connection was 17 students.

To perform the statistical calculations that would allow to test the guiding hypothesis of this research, the SPSS version 18 program was used, specifically the mean analysis was applied for independent groups or t-test, given that the N of the groups is less than 30.

3   Results

In order to verify the hypothesis proposed, we proceeded to calculate the means and standard deviation of each group and then to perform the analysis of comparison of mean, by means of the t test; the results obtained are shown in the following tables (Table 1):

Table 1. Descriptive statistics

— Groups	— N	— Media	— Deviation
— Face-to-face AR	— 20	— 4.42	— 0.48
— Remote face-to-face AR	— 17	— 3.05	— 1.12
—	—	—	—

Table 2. Half-test analysis t

—	— Levene test for equality of variance						
—	— F	— Sign	— t	— df	— Sign. (two tails)	— 95% confidence interval	
						— inferior	— superior
— Equality of variance is assumed	— 7.04	— 0.12	— 4.99	— 35.00	— 0.000	— 0.82	— 1.94
— No se assumes equality of variance	—	—	— 4.71	— 20.97	— 0.000	— 0.77	— 1.99

The data of the mean analysis described in Table 2, show the existence of significant differences between the averages of academic performance obtained depending on the modality of class taken (face-to-face vs. remote face-to-face), which allows us to conclude that the null hypothesis raised is rejected and therefore the existence of a significantly differential academic performance is accepted depending on the modality in which the class is taken; showing a higher performance in the subject of fundamentals of measurement and psychological evaluation those students who studied the subject under a traditional face-to-face format.

What has been described so far supports that resentment that Vega Aponte pointed out when referring to the possibility that education under remote modality favored the development of quality learning and an educational process for students [10].

This significant difference in performance from the class modality studied could be explained from a set of variables, which would possibly be generating a negative effect on the development of classes in remote face-to-face format. One of these variables has to do with a low level of adaptability of those involved to this new way of developing the teaching-learning process, as pointed out by Heimann Fernández et al., who highlighted the need to make adaptations of the process in an assertive and effective way [2].

On the other hand, in addition to the ability to adapt, the element of alteration and emotional management before this new learning atmosphere, built from the synchronous connection of remote cut, by students and the teacher responsible for the subject of interest could also be acting negatively and generating a lower academic performance in the students who studied the subject under the remote face-to-face modality, highlights how this was an aspect pointed out by Villarroel et al. as of great relevance that had to be taken into account to achieve success in the learning obtained [3].

In addition to the above, the statistically significant difference between the means of academic performance according to face-to-face modality vs. remote face-to-face modality could be the product of low experience and little preparation of students and teacher to digital management and connection platforms for the development of classes from remote face-to-face, Note how Pulido and Ancheta and Sanz and Sainz highlight that the achievement of learning from the online/remote format is associated with an adequate preparation of teachers and students in what has to do with the management of the required digital tools [4, 5].

In this line of thought, this significant difference could be explained, as expressed by Ramírez García et al. (2021), by a level of interest and motivation towards the educational modality related to e-learning, classified as low, because the teaching-learning methodologies were not adapted to the modality, as well as to the negative experiences lived in learning situations that implied this approach through the remote/virtual connection [14].

One might also think that, as mentioned by Zetina, part of the students did not have the right tools to be able to work effectively and thus achieve optimal performance [7].

Finally, although students do not consider that there are differences in academic performance, as indicated by Camargo et al., the results achieved in this research exercise show that there is certainly a statistically significant difference in academic performance in favor of those students who took the subject under the traditional face-to-face modality [13].

4 Conclusions

The results obtained in this research experience, of quantitative, correlational nature and the possible reasons that could support these results that show a significantly higher academic performance in the students who took the subject of fundamentals of measurement and psychological evaluation in a format or modality of face-to-face class, over those who developed the experience of teaching learning from the remote face-to-face modality lead to the reflection on whether the implementation of remote education has met the basic parameters for it to be successful.

According to the approaches of the different authors treated in this research, it could be concluded that the success of achieving significant learning in a remote/online education under a synchronous modality rest on the aspects listed below:

- Attitude or disposition towards technology considered as positive and open, on the part of those involved in the teaching-learning process, such as students, teachers, managers and administrators of higher education institutions
- Level of digital skills and abilities, both of teachers and teachers, that guarantee the optimal use of technological platforms and tools
- An adequate level of emotional and motivational intelligence, which favors a positive approach to the remote/online learning experience
- Adaptation of the methodological, pedagogical and evaluation elements to the remote class modality, in such a way as to guarantee a learning result and assurance of the same that reflect the acquisition of the competences to be developed in each subject or subject of the curricular mesh of the academic programs of higher education.
- An attitude of openness towards the challenges and towards the change that education entails under an online/remote format.
- Have systems and devices that facilitate connectivity and access to remote cutting classes.
- To success of the development of the teaching-learning process under the remote modality it is necessary to have a systemic and ecological vision and understand that there must be a constant interaction between the microsystem, mesosystem, exosystem, macrosystem Next, this implies a link between the needs of society, public policies related to teaching-learning processes based on e-learning; the equipment required so that both students and teachers can develop the process in an optimal and assertive way and the willingness of those involved to assume education from this modality. In the following figure this vision is exemplified (Fig. 2):

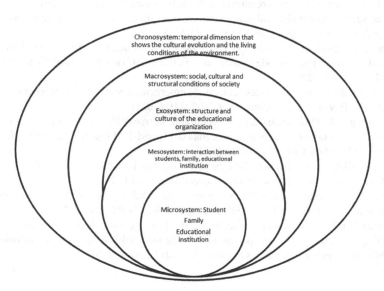

Fig. 2. Systemic interaction

Finally, it seems necessary for higher education institutions to always keep in mind what was stated by the United Nations Educational, Scientific and Cultural Organization (UNESCO) in 2009 regarding the opening and generation of new study modalities [15]: The growing demand for teaching superior cannot be satisfied only with the traditional activities of the face-to-face teaching. It will be necessary to use other strategies, such as open teaching and distance learning, and online learning, especially in areas such as education permanent adults and the formation of teachers. (p. 762–763).

References

1. Comisión Económica para América Latina y el Caribe (Cepal): La educación en tiempos de la pandemia de COVID-19. Organización de las Naciones Unidas para la Educación, la Ciencia y la Cultura, Santiago de Chile (2020)
2. Heimann Fernández, A., Ruiz Diaz Medina, A., Ayala Frasnelli, N.: dificultades en la aplicación de clases remotas durante la pandemia de covid-19 en la FACITEC. Saeta Digital Tecnología, Diseño e Innovación **6**(1) (2020)
3. Villarroel, V., Pérez, C., Rojas-Barahona, C., García, R.: Educación remota en contexto de pandemia: caracterización del proceso educativo en las universidades chilenas. Formación universitaria **14**(6), 65–76 (2021)
4. Pulido-Montes, C., Ancheta-Arrabal, A.: La educación remota tras el cierre de escuelas como respuesta internacional a la COVID-19. Revista Prisma Social **34**, 236–266 (2021)
5. Capilla, A., Sanz, I., Sainz, J.: Efectos de la crisis del coronavirus en Educación. España.: Organización de Estados Iberoamericanos para la Educación, la Ciencia y la Cultura (OEI) (2020)
6. Hodges, C., Moore, S., Lockee, B., Trust, T., Bond, A.: La diferencia entre la enseñanza remota de emergencia y el aprendizaje en línea. Educause Review **27** (2020)
7. Zetina, J.I.M.: From traditional education to remote education: challenges and opportunities within the health emergency. Educ. Quim. **31**(5), 88–91 (2020)
8. Hernández Rangel, M., Nieto Malpica, J., Bajonero Santillán, J.N.: Aprendizaje híbrido generado desde las Instituciones de Educación Superior en México. Revista de Ciencias Sociales (Ve) **22**(4), 49–61 (2021)
9. Paniagua-Valdebenito, L.: Clases remotas de emergencia, tensión y resistencia en espacios educativos. Revista Saberes Educativos **7**, 99–110 (2021)
10. Vega Aponte, J.: Dificultades detectadas durante la transición de clases presenciales a una modalidad remota en el marco de la pandemia del Covid-19. Programa de Ingeniería Civil en universidad pública, Caso de estudio (2020)
11. Pérez, E., Vázquez, A., Cambero, S.: Educación a distancia en tiempos de COVID-19: análisis desde la perspectiva de los estudiantes universitarios. RIED **24**(1), 331–350 (2020)
12. López, L.: Educación remota de emergencia, virtualidad y desigualdades: pedagogía en tiempos de pandemia. 593 Digital Publisher CEIT **5**(5–2), 98–107 (2020)
13. Ramírez García, A., Rodríguez Sauceda, E., Pirela Hernández, A., Castillo Escalante, I.C.: Habilidades digitales e interés por estudiar en la modalidad E-Learning en estudiantes de Bachillerato. Revista de Ciencias Sociales (Ve) **22**(4), 30–48 (2021)

14. Camargo-Velastegui, D., Velastegui-Montoya, A., Chang-Silva, R.: Emerging remote assessment in times of the COVID-19 pandemic: analysis of experience in higher education. In: 19th LACCEI International Multi-Conference for Engineering, Education Caribbean Conference for Engineering and Technology: Prospective and Trends in Technology and Skills for Sustainable Social Development and Leveraging Emerging Technologies to Construct the Future, LACCEI 2021 (2021)
15. Organización de las Naciones Unidas para la Educación, la Ciencia y la Cultura - UNESCO: Conferencia Mundial sobre la Educación Superior - 2009: La nueva dinámica de la educación superior y la investigación para el cambio social y el desarrollo (Sede de la UNESCO, París, 5–8 de julio de 2009). Avaliação: Revista de Avaliação de Educacão Superior (Campinas) **14**(3), 755–766 (2009)

Educational Quality in Virtuality During the Covid 19 Pandemic in Colombia

Henry Herrera[1]([⊠]), Alonso Barrera[1], Javier Ramírez[2], Marlene Ballestas[3], Ingrid Ballestas[4], and Sonia Ethel Duran[5]

[1] Universidad de la Costa, 58 Street #55 66, Barranquilla, Colombia
hherrera8@cuc.edu.co
[2] Corporación Universitaria Latinoamericana, 58 Street #55 66, Barranquilla, Colombia
[3] ITSA, 18 Street # ##39-100, Soledad, Colombia
[4] Universidad del Atlántico, 43 Street #50-53, Puerto Colombia, Colombia
[5] Universidad Libre de Colombia, Barranquilla, Colombia

Abstract. This study is developed in order to determine the educational quality in Colombia during the covid 19 pandemic from the perspective of the student experience. The methodology used is framed towards the quantitative field with a correlational level and a field-non-experimental design. For data collection, the database "Cuarentena COVID 19 Jóvenes" is taken as a reference, which is supplied by the mayor of Medellin. The sample under study consisted of a total of 2058 subjects to whom a questionnaire is applied with 12 questions related to their sociodemographic characteristics, access, and availability for classes in virtual modality, and their perception of the experience in the learning processes during virtuality. For the statistical processing of the information, a descriptive analysis of the data is developed in the first instance, based on the frequency and percentage statistics, to subsequently generate cross tables between the elements related educational quality in Colombia during the covid 19 pandemic from the perspective of the student experience, and finally an analysis of the correlations between the elements is presented through the Chi-squared test. The whole process is developed through the SPSS statistical software. The results allowed to identify in the first instance a high level of students who took classes in their virtual modality, which had access to the internet (74.9%) and an electronic device (78.6%) that allowed them to access these classes in virtual modality. In turn, students considered in a high level of proportion that virtual classes had impaired the learning experience by 69%.

Keywords: Covid 19 · Educational quality · Virtual education

1 Introduction

During the last two years the world has been immersed in a situation of uncertainty, product of the Covid 19 pandemic, a disease associated with a high trend of direct contagious respiratory infection, this health problem led to the establishment of radical quarantines, states of emergency, strong biosecurity measures and one socio-emotional

© Springer Nature Switzerland AG 2022
G. Meiselwitz et al. (Eds.): HCII 2022, LNCS 13517, pp. 276–285, 2022.
https://doi.org/10.1007/978-3-031-22131-6_21

conditioning that in the beginning of it affected a high percentage of the population. Since one of the initial processes was the closure of companies, health institutions and recreation, since there was no knowledge of what they were facing [1].

In 2020, in full emergency and confinement at home, the World Health Organization maintained that SARS-CoV-2 was not going to disappear and that survival strategies had to be created and faced, for Velásquez, this implied that humanity would have to prepare to face this reality prospectively, which further complicates the epidemiological situation of the different countries, because there were already situations that affected health and even high-risk social processes [2].

Undoubtedly, in the crisis that was being lived and in the uncertainty of how to face a pandemic and that the world did not collapse, the leaders of states began to generate strategy so that the economy did not die and look for alternatives for those sectors that could continue to function in virtuality. In this context, companies began to organize their actions and trends in service and customer service through digital systems [3, 4].

In this context, the education sector is involved, which in its purposes of keeping academic development and service management active, in a very fast and coordinated way activated virtuality as a strategic line to keep the sector active, where all its actors, Teachers, administrative staff, and workers they could continue to count on their work activities, receive their income to affront the crisis and the students could receive the required knowledge and not lose their academic activities [5].

For this, the universities were structured and organized using their technological platform or adapting a new trend, in the opinion of Rivera, Hernández, Duran and Garcia and Parra et al., technological education is a social need and must be oriented from the educational environments, to respond to the needs of the communities where the student is located [6, 7], which must respond to the pandemic.

In this order of ideas, it must be understood that the human being, in his intention to acquire more and better knowledge every day that allows him to configure his personal and or professional growth, to be in a position to develop his tasks before the complex and demanding world that he has had to live, needs and seeks alternative sources for his learning processes [8, 9], and this is a generalization that reinforced the pandemic from the year 2020.

In Colombia, the Ministry of Education authorized public and private academic entities to apply virtual education by emergency decree, this being a relief for students, since the uncertainty of the quarantine time put their studies and professionalization at risk. Within this framework, it was observed that the University management through technological platforms enhance learning in order to contribute efficiently to the development of Colombians and respond to the emergency situation created by covid 19 [10].

This was structured to respond to the challenges and needs generated and to be able to advance in a significant way, in education and in the levels of quality of life of citizens, as stated by Duran, Garcia and Parra [11]. Faced with this reality, the trend of virtual education is fostered by promoting the self-preparation of students through various didactic means, with the main idea of guiding the cognitive independence of the student's learning, strengthening their sense of freedom and autonomy and underpinned by the assistance of the teacher.

Undoubtedly, for this he had to prepare and train the teacher to be able to coordinate the academic actions, the strategies, the activities and also to be able to determine the learning results. Obviously, the trend of virtual education was already revolutionizing traditional university education, and this was like an opportunity that involved new challenges and commitments to the integral formation of the student.

In this order of ideas, virtuality, represents an innovative, creative process and profound changes, it was necessary in its practices to guarantee a humanistic, integral formation, which in the opinion of Parra and Duran [12], was able to achieve the harmonious integration of theoretical knowledge with practical knowledge, Knowing and doing consubstantiated in a synergistic and contextualized way.

Likewise, in Colombia, the line was channeled to promote more complex knowledge as a way towards transdisciplinarity, training by competences was integrated putting its scientific, technological and technical knowledge at the service of the community and in function of productivity and endogenous development in the social context.

In this context, it is necessary to emphasize that for the teacher, virtuality as a means of learning demanded significant changes, since it was necessary that it stop having the protagonism and develop functions as tutor, organizer of experiences, group leader and mediator of the learning process, committed to social development and with high interest in developing an academic work open to society of learning (form of social relationship derived from globalization), collaborative and at the same time protagonist.

What should generate in the student a participation, a constructivist tendency and development of shared meanings, but also the possibility of acquiring the required skills with self-learning. According to the above, the researchers focused on developing research that would allow them to determine the educational quality in Colombia during the Covid 19 pandemic from the perspective of the student experience.

2   Material and Method

The methodology used is framed towards the quantitative field with a correlational level and a field-non-experimental design. For data collection, the database "Cuarentena COVID 19 Jóvenes" is taken as a reference, which is supplied by the mayor of Medellin. The sample under study consisted of a total of 2058 subjects to whom a questionnaire is applied with 12 questions related to their socio-demographic characteristics, access, and availability for classes in virtual modality, and their perception of the experience in the learning processes during virtuality.

3   Results

The results of the field process carried out are presented below (Table 1):

Table 1. Age

		Frequency	Percentage	Valid percentage	Cumulative percentage
Valid	14	84	4,1	4,1	4,1
	15	103	5,0	5,0	9,1
	16	120	5,8	5,8	14,9
	17	138	6,7	6,7	21,6
	18	171	8,3	8,3	29,9
	19	134	6,5	6,5	36,4
	20	141	6,9	6,9	43,3
	21	142	6,9	6,9	50,2
	22	167	8,1	8,1	58,3
	23	163	7,9	7,9	66,2
	24	154	7,5	7,5	73,7
	25	139	6,8	6,8	80,5
	26	135	6,6	6,6	87,0
	27	124	6,0	6,0	93,1
	28	143	6,9	6,9	100,0
	Total	2058	100,0	100,0	

When reviewing the previous table it is possible to observe how the largest group of respondents belongs to the age range between 17 and 24, highlighting how the majority of subjects declare to be 22 years old with a percentage of 8.1%, 23 with 7.9% and 24 with 7.5% respectively. In turn, the ages with the lowest representation are in the range of 14 and 15 years with percentages of 4.1% and 5% (Table 2).

Table 2. Gender identity

		Frequency	Percentage	Valid percentage	Cumulative percentage
Válido	Man	750	36,4	36,4	36,4
	Woman	1302	63,3	63,3	99,7
	Other	6	,3	,3	100,0
	Total	2058	100,0	100,0	

With respect to the previous table, it is observed that in relation to the point of gender identity the vast majority of respondents identify as women with a frequency of 1302 and a percentage of 63.3%. Next, a percentage of 36.44% identified as male with a frequency of 750 respondents (Table 3).

Table 3. Ethnicity

		Frequency	Percentage	Valid percentage	Cumulative percentage
Válido	Indigenous	22	1,1	1,1	1,1
	NARP (Black, Afro, Raizal or Palenquero)	139	6,8	6,8	7,8
	Other	1893	92,0	92,0	99,8
	ROM-Gypsy	4	,2	,2	100,0
	Total	2058	100,0	100,0	

In relation to the previous table, it is observed how a total of 1893 subjects are identified within the ethnic group of 2otros with 92%, while 6.8% are recognized as Black, Afro, Raizal or Palenquero and finally, 4% identify as ROM-Gitano (Table 4).

Table 4. Civil status

		Frequency	Percentage	Valid percentage	Cumulative percentage
Valid	Married/Free Union	219	10,6	10,6	10,6
	Separated/Divorced/Widowed	4	,2	,2	10,8
	Bachelor	1795	87,2	87,2	98,1
	No data	40	1,9	1,9	100,0
	Total	2058	100,0	100,0	

The above table allows us to observe how the large number of subjects surveyed are in the marital status of singles with a frequency of 1795 subjects and a percentage of representation of 87.2%, then a total of 219 are married and in free union with 10.6%, 0.2% separated / divorced / widowed and 1.9% without data (Table 5).

Table 5. Highest educational level achieved

		Frequency	Percentage	Valid percentage	Cumulative percentage
Valid	Primary basic	28	1,4	1,4	1,4
	Secondary basic	262	12,7	12,7	14,1

(*continued*)

Table 5. (*continued*)

	Frequency	Percentage	Valid percentage	Cumulative percentage
Media	777	37,8	37,8	51,8
None	2	,1	,1	51,9
Don't know/Don't report	7	,3	,3	52,3
Postgraduate (Specialization, Master, Doctorate)	47	2,3	2,3	54,6
Preschool	2	,1	,1	54,7
Technical	356	17,3	17,3	72,0
Technological	196	9,5	9,5	81,5
University-undergraduate	381	18,5	18,5	100,0
Total	2058	100,0	100,0	

The results of the previous table allow us to observe how the vast majority of the subjects surveyed have completed secondary education with 37.8%, followed by the university level with 18%, technical training with 17.3%, secondary education with 12.7%, Technological with 9.5% (Table 6).

Table 6. Socioeconomic statum

		Frequency	Percentage	Valid percentage	Cumulative percentage
Valid	1	351	17,1	17,1	17,1
	2	828	40,2	40,2	57,3
	3	617	30,0	30,0	87,3
	4	144	7,0	7,0	94,3
	5	80	3,9	3,9	98,2
	6	26	1,3	1,3	99,4
	7	12	,6	,6	100,0
	Total	2058	100,0	100,0	

With respect to the socioeconomic stratum to which the surveyed subjects belong, it can be observed that the vast majority of these belong to stratum 2 with a frequency of 828 subjects and a percentage of 40.2%, followed by stratum 3 with 617 and a representation of 30%, stratum 1 with 351 people and a percentage of 17.1% and 4 with 7% (Table 7).

Table 7. Knowledge about the coronavirus hotlines

		Frequency	Percentage	Valid percentage	Cumulative percentage
Válido	Yes	1534	74,5	74,5	74,5
	No	524	25,5	25,5	100,0
	Total	2058	100,0	100,0	

With respect to the table shown above, it is observed that the vast majority of subjects, with a frequency of 1534 and a percentage of 74.5% if they know the lines of attention in Colombia for Covid 19, while 524 subjects and a percentage of 25.5% have no knowledge of these lines of care (Table 8).

Table 8. Are you currently enrolled in an educational institution?

		Frequency	Percentage	Valid percentage	Cumulative percentage
Valid	Yes	1371	66,6	66,6	66,6
	No	687	33,4	33,4	100,0
	Total	2058	100,0	100,0	

The results of the previous table allow us to observe that 66.6% of the respondents if they are currently linked to an educational institution at its various levels with a frequency of 1371 and 33.44% do not have active links with educational entities, being a total of 687 people (Table 9).

Table 9. Did the institution (School, College, or University) where you study continue to hold classes virtually?

		Frequency	Percentage	Valid percentage	Cumulative percentage
Valid	Yes	1014	49,3	49,3	49,3
	No	356	17,3	17,3	66,6
	Not aply	688	33,4	33,4	100,0
	Total	2058	100,0	100,0	

When inquiring about whether the institutions to which they are linked continued their activities virtually, it is observed that 49.3% with 1014 subjects declare that yes, while 17.3% with 356 subjects comment that no and 33.4% with 688 did not apply for such questioning (Table 10).

Table 10. Can you easily access the internet to carry out your academic activities?

		Frequency	Percentage	Valid percentage	Cumulative percentage
Valid	Yes	1024	49,8	49,8	49,8
	No	346	16,8	16,8	66,6
	Not aply	688	33,4	33,4	100,0
	Total	2058	100,0	100,0	

The table above shows the results of the questioning related to whether the respondents have had facilities to develop their academic activities virtually, where 49.8% declare that yes, while 16% allude to not having such access for their academic activities and 33.4% did not apply (Table 11).

Table 11. _Do you have any electronic device (computer or tablet) in your home that allows you to develop your virtual academic activities?

		Frequency	Percentage	Valid percentage	Cumulative percentage
Valid	Yes	1075	52,2	52,2	52,2
	No	295	14,3	14,3	66,6
	Not aply	688	33,4	33,4	100,0
	Total	2058	100,0	100,0	

When reviewing the results of the previous table, it is observed as 52.2% with a frequency of 1075 subjects if they have access to electronic devices in their home that allow them to develop their academic activities in virtual media, while 14.3% with 295 subjects do not have access to said dissipatives for their training in virtual environments (Table 12).

Table 12. How do you rate your experience with education from the virtual modality compared to the face-to-face?

		Frequency	Percentage	Valid percentage	Cumulative percentage
Valid	Very good	97	4,7	4,7	4,7
	Better	72	3,5	3,5	8,2

(continued)

Table 12. (*continued*)

	Frequency	Percentage	Valid percentage	Cumulative percentage
Equal	257	12,5	12,5	20,7
Worse	609	29,6	29,6	50,3
Much worse	335	16,3	16,3	66,6
Not applicable	688	33,4	33,4	100,0
Total	2058	100,0	100,0	

In the analysis of qualification of the experience between education in virtual media and in physical media, it is observed that the vast majority mention that the experience in virtual education has been worse with a total of 609 subjects and a percentage of 29.6%, 16.3% declare that it is much worse, 12.5% comment that it is the same and 3.5% and 4.7% as better and very good, respectively. These findings allow us to verify how the experience reported by the respondents has been mostly negative in comparison between virtual education and face-to-face education.

4   Discussion and Conclusions

The results of this study allow, in the first instance, to locate an important situation of need with respect to the access of the respondents to classes during the contingency period as a result of the covid 19 pandemic, since an important group could not continue with their activities. Academics during the mentioned period.

In turn, a large number of people who do not have access to the Internet to access their academic processes, as well as lack the necessary technological equipment for said activity, will be located. These results in a certain way can justify the low level of perception towards the quality of virtual classes during the pandemic, because the vast majority of respondents considered a deterioration in the quality of education during this mentioned period.

Certainly, the sociodemographic characterization makes it possible to locate that the surveyed population is largely belonging to groups with limited resources, who were certainly greatly impacted during the Covid 19 pandemic. The studies found in the present study certainly contrast with other investigations, which report a level of incidence in the difficulties of students to participate in classes virtually within the standards of educational quality.

It is essential that the public sector take a level of responsibility for the quality of the educational service towards groups with fewer resources, who have certainly been the most affected by the Covid 19 pandemic [13, 14].

References

1. Polo, J., Candezano, M.A., Núñez, L.N.: Dos enfoques matemáticos epidemiológicos para modelar el comportamiento de los decesos causados por el COVID-19. Invest. e Innovación en Ingenierías **8**(2), 75–86 (2020)
2. Velásquez, R.: La educación virtual en tiempos de Covid-19. Rev. Científica Int. **3**(1), 19–25 (2020)
3. Castillo-Esparcia, A., Fernández-Souto, A.B., Puentes-Rivera, I.: Comunicación política y Covid-19. Estrategias del gobierno de España. El profesional de la información (EPI), 29(4), (2020)
4. Lavander, S. M.: Comunicación para el cambio de comportamientos y estrategias sanitaria del gobierno peruano frente al COVID-19. Chasqui: Revista Latinoamericana de Comunicación, 1(145), 235–258, (2020)
5. García-Peñalvo, F.J., Corell, A., Abella-García, V., Grande-de-Prado, M.: Online assessment in higher education in the time of COVID-19. Educ. Knowl. Soc. **21**, 1–26 (2020)
6. Parra, M., Marambio, C., Ramírez, J., Suárez, D., Herrera, H.: Educational convergence with digital technology: integrating a global society. In: Stephanidis, C., Antona, M., Ntoa, S. (eds.) HCI International 2020 Late Breaking Posters. HCII 2020. Communications in Computer and Information Science, vol. 1294, pp. 303-310. Springer, Cham (2020).https://doi.org/10.1007/978-3-030-60703-6_39
7. Hernández, J.R., Hernández, M.M., Durán, S., Gulliany, J.G.: Educación en tecnología como paradigma didáctico, innovador e inclusivo en el marco del COVID-19. SUMMA Rev. Disciplinaria En Ciencias Económ. Y Soc. **2**, 195–215 (2020)
8. Lay, N., Ramírez, J., Parra, M.: Desarrollo de conductas ciudadanas en estudiantes del octavo grado de una institución educativa de Barranquilla. In: Memorias Del I Congreso Internacional En Educación E Innovación En Educación Superior. Caracas, Venezuela (2019)
9. Niebles, W., Martínez-Bustos, P., Niebles-Núñez, L.: Competencias matemáticas como factor de éxito en la prueba pro en universidades de Barranquilla. Colombia. Educ. y Humanismo **22**(38), 1–16 (2020)
10. Herrera, H., Barrera, A., Ballestas, M., Ballestas, I., Schnorr, C.: Virtual Classrooms for the Development of Practical Laboratories in a Colombian Higher Education Institution. In: Stephanidis, C., et al. (eds.) HCII 2021. LNCS, vol. 13096, pp. 417–425. Springer, Cham (2021). https://doi.org/10.1007/978-3-030-90328-2_27
11. Duran, S.E., Parra, M.A., Garcia, J.E., Marceles, V.S.: Dirección estratégica del talento humano para el fomento de valores en los cuerpos policiales venezolanos. Espacios 38(32), (2017)
12. Duran, S., Parra, M.: Diversidad Cultural para promover el desarrollo de habilidades sociales en educación superior. Cultura Educ. Y Soc. **5**(1), 55–67 (2014)
13. Choque, F.A.: Educación y pos pandemia: tormentas y retos después del Covid-19. Rev. Conrado **17**(83), 430–438 (2021)
14. Giannini, S.: Covid-19 y educación superior: De los efectos inmediatos al día después. Rev. Latinoa. de Educ. Comparada: RELEC **11**(17), 1–57 (2020)

The Content Improvement Service: An Adaptive System for Continuous Improvement at Scale

Bill Jerome, Rachel Van Campenhout(✉) ⓘ, Jeffrey S. Dittel, Richard Benton, Scott Greenberg, and Benny G. Johnson ⓘ

VitalSource Technologies, Pittsburgh, PA 15218, USA

{bill.jerome,rachel.vancampenhout}@vitalsource.com

Abstract. Advances in artificial intelligence and automatic question generation have made it possible to create millions of questions to apply an evidence-based learn by doing method to thousands of e-textbooks, an unprecedented scale. Yet the scaling of this learning method presents a new challenge: how to monitor the quality of these automatically generated questions and take action as needed when human review is not feasible. To address this issue, an adaptive system called the Content Improvement Service was developed to become an automated part of the platform architecture. Rather than adapting content or a learning path based on student mastery, this adaptive system uses student data to evaluate question quality to optimize the learning environment in real time. In this paper, we will address the theoretical context for a platform-level adaptive system, describe the methods by which the Content Improvement Service functions, and provide examples of questions identified and removed through these methods. Future research applications are also discussed.

Keywords: Content Improvement Service · Adaptive instructional systems · Iterative improvement · Grey-box systems · Artificial intelligence · Automatic question generation

1 Introduction

Adaptive instructional systems have varied widely in the past decades. Different technologies have focused on a range of adaptive strategies—including content level of difficulty, tutoring dialogues, self-correction, metacognitive prompts, etc.—with varying levels of effectiveness [2]. Systematic reviews have worked to make sense of a diverse field of research through categorizations and frameworks. Vandewaetere et al. [14] describes adaptive systems according to the source of adaptation (what determines adaptation), target of adaptation (what is being adapted), and pathway of adaptation (how it is adapted). Vandewaetere et al. identify the primary source of adaptation as learner characteristics that point to aptitude characteristics or a learner model. Martin et al. [8] expanded the adaptive source to include a content model and instructional model in addition to the learner model. Yet no matter the source of adaptation, we can see that these systems generally focus on an evolving relationship between the learner and the

© Springer Nature Switzerland AG 2022
G. Meiselwitz et al. (Eds.): HCII 2022, LNCS 13517, pp. 286–296, 2022.
https://doi.org/10.1007/978-3-031-22131-6_22

pedagogical path. What if the source and target of adaptation are one and the same? This paper will outline an adaptive instructional system which does not focus on an individual student as the source of adaptation, but rather focuses on individual question items to adaptively update the learning environment.

While Vandewaetere et al. [14] noted the increasing use of intelligent learning for adaptive systems, it was also still an evolving technology with unknown future impact. "Currently, Bayesian networks, fuzzy logic and neural networks are considered as new approaches to the development of learner models. However, based on our review, we can conclude that all of these newer techniques are still in the very early stage of development, and none of the techniques has been concretely implemented in an adaptive system," (p. 128). Artificial intelligence (AI) became part of Martin et al.'s [8] adaptive learning model framework, serving as part of the "adaptive engine" in their system (though notably this study did not address the use of AI in the literature it reviewed).

The adaptive system described herein was developed as a solution to a new challenge created by using AI for automatic question generation (AQG) on an enormous scale. Bookshelf CoachMe™ (BCM), a new learning feature of the Bookshelf e-reader platform from VitalSource Technologies, uses AQG to deliver formative practice questions alongside the e-textbook content so students can practice while they read. Millions of questions were generated using AI and released in over 4,500 e-textbooks as a free feature of the e-reader platform. The goal of these automatically generated (AG) formative questions is to help students become active participants in their learning process by practicing at the point of learning. This method of "learn by doing" has been shown to have six times the effect on learning outcomes compared to reading alone [6], and follow-up research has found that this method is causal to learning [6, 13]. As anyone who has created educational content is aware, no content is perfect. Historically, textbooks, courseware, and any learning content students see goes through review and QA prior to being released as well as after it's released, as it is inevitable that students find problems or errors. The AG questions described had extensive automated QA as well as targeted human QA prior to release. Research on questions generated through this AI process found that they performed equally as well with students as human-authored questions on several key metrics [11]. And still, as no human could write millions of perfect questions, neither will AI generate a perfect question set. So while AI has solved the problem of how to create formative practice for effective learning at scale, a new challenge presents itself in how to monitor and QA this enormous question set. The solution is an AI-driven adaptive system.

The Content Improvement Service (CIS) is an adaptive system not limited to a single instance of a course or learning environment, but rather is a platform-level system that monitors all questions delivered in all e-textbooks. The CIS uses all student responses to make decisions about the quality of the questions. In this way, the content is the source of adaptation as well as the target of adaptation. The CIS uses data at a micro level, as it is monitoring each individual question and every student answer. Yet at the same time, the CIS uses data at a macro level, as it is using millions of data points to make decisions for an entire platform.

We can begin to see the differentiation between an adaptive system that acts to move a student through a content path and one that adapts for the purpose of iterative improvement of the content itself. The concept of iterative improvement is one familiar to many fields, but is of particular importance to learning engineering. Learning engineering is a practice and process that uses human-centered engineering design and data-informed decision-making to support learners [4]. Iterative improvement is key to the process of learning engineering, both in the development of learning experiences, as well as the action following data analysis [5]. From previous case studies, we see examples of how this data-driven iterative improvement cycle can benefit students [10], yet often the data analysis is only done infrequently at specific points due to scarcity of expert human resourcing. The CIS uses real-time question responses and takes an action to adapt the learning environment for all students. This process is not one that happens at prescribed times (such as after a semester ends) but instead it occurs continuously. The CIS performs a continuous process of iterative improvement for the AG questions across the platform, thereby automating this key learning engineering cycle.

The goal of this paper is to examine the CIS as a tool for large-scale adaptation and iterative improvement. We will describe the architecture of this system, the technology driving its function, and examine examples of the improvements it identifies for AG questions. In this way, we hope to illuminate how combining learning science-based methods with adaptive instructional systems and scalable artificial intelligence technology can produce systems of great benefit to millions of learners worldwide.

2   Architecture of the CIS

As defined by Vandewaetere et al. [14], the Content Improvement Service is the pathway of adaptation, by monitoring question data, identifying problems, and carrying out decisions. Illustrated in Fig. 1, the CIS is the critical link between the live learning platform and the passive content management system (CMS). In many online learning environments, a manual feedback loop takes place after a course is delivered in order to improve the materials for the next semester. The CIS enables us to make changes as soon as enough data are available to demonstrate a need for a change instead of waiting, e.g., for an entire semester to go by. As students enroll and proceed at different rates through an e-textbook, we have the chance to improve practice for the next student to encounter it during the same semester without the semester (or more) lag.

The CIS has two essential types of input. The first is information about the questions and content available to students in the learning platform. Knowing some basic data—such as the question identifier, the textbook it belongs to, and the type of question (multiple choice, text entry, etc.)—provides the CIS with enough basic information do its analysis. Importantly, there is no domain knowledge required. The second type of input is data about student interactions with the content and questions, for example, correct and incorrect question attempts. Additionally, students are given the option to rate questions they answer and this feedback is also considered. No Personal Identifiable Information (PII) is tracked or needed within the CIS. The continuous stream of interactions is used to update a local database with summary statistics for each question being analyzed. Although the richness of both types of data may increase as new ideas are developed for automatically improving content, the two broad categories and pipelines ultimately remain the same.

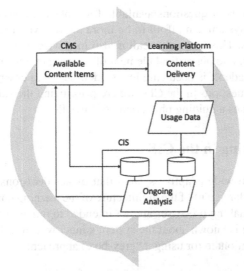

Fig. 1. An ongoing automatic cycle of content improvement based on usage data. Content is published from a CMS into a learning platform where students engage with the content. The data generated from that usage are monitored by the CIS coupled with basic information about the content it received during the publishing step. Should any rule apply to trigger content improvement, it messages the CMS with the relevant information allowing the CMS to publish the improvement to the live content in the learning platform.

In a continuous manner, the CIS updates the available summary data and determines what actions, if any, should be taken. For example, a decision rule may trigger that indicates a question is not performing acceptably and should be removed (or replaced if there is a replacement available). In response to this update from the CIS, the CMS automatically publishes an update to the live course and informs the CIS of the question removal and replacement (if any) and the cycle of automated iterative improvement continues.

3   Recall: The Guiding Philosophy of the CIS

An important design consideration for the tests of question quality is whether they should be oriented toward precision or recall. That is, is it more important to require a high degree of certainty that a question is unsatisfactory before removing it, or that as many unsatisfactory questions as possible are identified and removed? These two requirements are at odds with each other, and in general not possible to satisfy simultaneously (known as the "precision-recall tradeoff").

As a key goal of the CIS is to minimize the exposure of these questions to students, there is a need to identify them as quickly as reasonably possible. This means emphasizing recall over precision—erring on the side of caution rather than continuing to collect evidence in order to maximize confidence in the question's classification. The question generation process for BCM uses an overgenerate-and-rank approach [3] to ensure there is a surplus of questions available for replacing questions deemed unsatisfactory, and so the system can afford to be more aggressive in removing potentially problematic questions. This focus on recall is also in service to a student-centered approach of development, another critical element of learning engineering. In this context, the precision-recall tradeoff is occurring in a student learning environment so in maximizing the recall of questions in the CIS, we are prioritizing the student experience. In this way, recall becomes a guiding philosophy of the CIS.

4   Decision-Making in the CIS

The CIS is a platform-wide adaptive system that makes decisions about questions in real-time, making it a large part of the architecture of the learning environment. Because of this, the decision-making processes are not intended to remain part of a "black-box" system where nothing is known about the system's inner workings by its users. Sharma et al. [9] put forth a rationale for using a "grey-box" approach:

> ....where the input features can be informed from the context and the theory/relevant research, the data fusion is driven by the limitations of the resources and contexts (e.g., ubiquitous, low-cost, high precision, different experimental settings), and the [machine learning] method is chosen in an informed manner, rather than just as a way to obtain the optimal prediction/classification accuracy. In other words, this contribution aims to invite researchers to shift from the optimal ends (outputs) to the optimal means (paths), (p. 3007).

In the case of the CIS, the goal of the system is to make decisions about questions as quickly as possible, and so the learning science context is critical to determining the optimal means by which the CIS makes its decisions. Designed to address the challenge of continuously evaluating the performance of formative questions at scale, the CIS was developed with a recall philosophy and a learner-centered approach. The methods for its decision-making were derived from this context; incorporating research ranging from student perception to question psychometric properties shaped the methods by which the CIS operates.

This grey-box approach also fosters trust and accountability in the system through the transparency of its research base and methods. When decisions are being made in an automated fashion that impact student learning environments at scale, the ability to explain how those decisions are made is necessary. In this paper we outline several research-based optimal means that contribute to the optimal ends—the decisions of the CIS. It is also noteworthy that CIS uses the methods selected as tools, and that these tools can be modified, extended, added or removed based on evolving technological or theoretical breakthroughs. In this way, the CIS is itself a system that can be iterated upon based on data and research.

This grey-box approach of incorporating relevant theory and research into the methods of the CIS (or pathway of adaptation) is therefore also congruent with a learning engineering approach. Research is a critical input of the learning engineering process [10], and here it is also used to determine the methods of adaptation. The CIS was developed using the learning engineering approach, and to apply this domain expertise with the technical capacity to make research- and data-informed decisions at massive scale. It would be more difficult to trust a black-box system designed without regard for context or learning theory to make unsupervised determinations about content. Instead, a grey-box system designed by learning science experts to use research-based methods to achieve a student-centered outcome provides a responsible and accountable system.

4.1 Student Helpfulness Ratings

One simple and direct measure of question quality is student feedback, so the first method of the CIS we outline is the use of student helpfulness ratings. After answering a question in BCM, the student is given the opportunity to give it a simple thumbs up/thumbs down rating of helpfulness (Fig. 2). When a thumbs down rating is given, additional feedback can optionally be provided on why the student felt the question was not helpful.

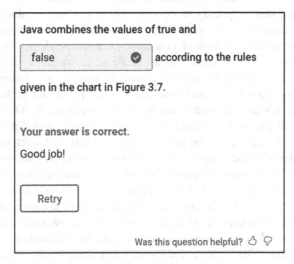

Fig. 2. Question helpfulness rating feature.

Analysis of a data set of BCM usage comprising 911,044 student-question interactions in 3,948 textbooks showed that students do not rate questions very often, only in 0.52% of rating opportunities, with a thumbs down rating 0.20% of the time.

A single thumbs down rating is generally not sufficient evidence that a question should be removed. Some students tend to challenge questions they answer incorrectly, and it is also well known that question rating agreement is often low even among trained reviewers [7], which can be common for subjective judgments. Determination of an appropriate decision rule or rules based on the number and context of thumbs down ratings requires calibration from data. However, an example from an economics textbook of a question with two thumbs down ratings shows that the additional information students can optionally provide can be helpful:

"The _____ of a new sports car doesn't just affect the person driving off the dealer's lot."

Answer: "sale"

Both students rating the question indicated that the question was not relevant to the subject matter, which increases the likelihood that it should be removed.

4.2 Bayesian Inference of Mean Score

The CIS also considers question quality as outlined by the literature as part of its methods. Of the psychometric properties relevant to question quality, perhaps the one of most interest is difficulty. For formative practice, for example, if questions are too easy or too difficult, it may risk diminishing student engagement and satisfaction. Therefore, it is necessary for the CIS to monitor difficulty so that questions not meeting the desired criteria can be removed. A common way to gauge a question's difficulty is by its mean score (sometimes called the difficulty index). If a question's mean score is not acceptable, our task is to learn this as quickly as possible from the observed data (to a specified confidence level) in order to minimize exposure of poorly performing questions.

Here, a simple approach is to model each question independently, treating students' answers to the question as Bernoulli trials. A Bernoulli random variable models an event with exactly two possible outcomes, such as success and failure (e.g., correct and incorrect), represented as 1 and 0, and has a single parameter p, the probability of success, which in this case represents the question's mean score. The Bernoulli trials model requires that the trials are independent, and that the probability of success or failure is the same for each trial. The first is reasonably satisfied (each trial is an answer by a different student) but the second is not, since this model approximates the probability of a correct answer as the same for all students (the mean score), when in fact it depends strongly on the individual student. While this assumption would be too restrictive for many analyses, it is entirely adequate here. While a more complex model like item response theory [1]—that takes student ability into account—would be more accurate, it would also require collecting much more data to make the assessment, which is at odds with our requirements. The higher accuracy afforded is not needed when we recognize that recall is more important than precision in identifying poorly performing questions; put another way, we are perfectly willing to sacrifice some acceptable questions in order to remove the unacceptable ones. Furthermore, when the mean score of an AG question is very low it is sometimes indicative of an error in the generation process that yielded a question that is not correctly answerable, making individual student abilities less relevant.

The need to assess a question's difficulty from a small sample of student data suggests a Bayesian approach. Bayesian methods provide a powerful and flexible approach to estimation of models from data. In particular, this enables probability distributions for a model's parameters to be learned from data rather than simply point estimates. The Bayesian approach combines prior knowledge or assumptions about the model parameter distributions with the likelihood of the observed data under the model to obtain the joint posterior distribution of the model parameters. A Bayesian approach can thus help us arrive at better-quality decisions more quickly by allowing us to incorporate what is known about question mean scores from prior experience. The total number of successes in a given number of Bernoulli trials has a binomial likelihood function, and for Bayesian inference it is common to use a beta distribution as the prior distribution of p since this has a closed-form solution for the posterior distribution, which is also a beta distribution.

The shape parameters α and β of the beta prior distribution can be determined by fitting the mean and variance of an empirically observed set of question mean scores. This gives a so-called "informed prior." A data set from a previous large-scale study on the difficulty of automatically generated and human-authored questions [11] was used to determine a prior in this manner. Figure 3 shows a histogram of mean scores of 809 AG questions and the beta distribution fit to it ($\alpha = 4.58$, $\beta = 1.82$).

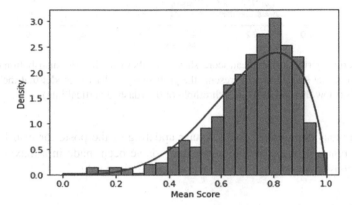

Fig. 3. Informed prior distribution for mean score obtained from AG question mean scores.

For the sake of illustration on a real example, suppose we wish to remove a question if it is at least 90% likely that its mean score is less than 0.5, i.e., more students will answer it incorrectly than correctly. A particular question in a human resources textbook had 4 correct and 16 incorrect answers in the first 20 students. Should it be removed? To decide, we must construct the posterior distribution of the question's mean score from the prior and observed data, and then evaluate the decision rule with it. The posterior is obtained by updating the prior's α and β values with the number of observed correct and incorrect answers, respectively, giving $\alpha = 8.58$, $\beta = 17.82$. The probability that the mean score is less than 0.5 is then simply the posterior's cumulative distribution function at 0.5, the shaded area in Fig. 4. Note that the posterior has been shifted significantly to the left of the prior based on the observed data. The shaded area is 0.968, or 96.8%, which is greater than the 90% threshold, so the question should be removed.

The question to be removed based on Bayesian inference on its mean score is:

"Employees want to work for employers that can provide them with a certain amount of _____ security."

Answer: "economic"

Among the incorrect answers students gave were "job," "employment," and "financial." Rather than corresponding to misconceptions, these responses are effectively synonymous with the expected answer, leading to the low mean score.

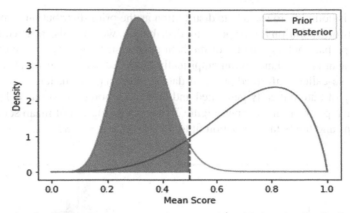

Fig. 4. Posterior distribution for mean score, shown together with the prior distribution from Fig. 3 for comparison. The shaded area represents the probability under the model that the question's mean score is below the decision rule's threshold of 0.5 (dashed vertical line).

In continuous deployment, with regular updating of the posterior distribution, the decision to remove the question could actually have been made in a maximum of 17 student responses (4 correct, 13 incorrect) using the given rule.

5   Conclusion

The use of artificial intelligence to scale effective learning methods is a significant milestone in the advance of educational technology as a whole. However, using automatic question generation at scale presents a new issue of scale: monitoring and taking action on questions. To do this for millions of questions is an impossible manual task in any scenario, so an automated system is a necessary solution. The Content Improvement Service was developed with a systems design perspective to work with the learning platform and the CMS to implement a feedback loop for continuous improvement. The CIS operates at enormous scale—across thousands of textbooks and millions of questions—and yet at the same time it operates at a micro scale—taking action at the individual question level. In the context of Vandewaetere et al.'s [14] adaptive model, the automatically generated questions are both the source and target of adaptation, with the CIS as the pathway to adaptation.

The CIS is a complex system that is a prime example of the technological advances Vandewaetere et al. [14] anticipated arising for the pathway of adaptation. A major objective of the CIS is to make decisions as quickly as possible in order to improve the learning experience for as many students as possible, so complex statistical models are employed to make these determinations efficiently. Yet the statistical methods of the CIS also need to be used in service to a student-centered purpose and in a research-based, grey-box approach. As seen in the examples previously outlined, the CIS uses student feedback as well as question performance data as methods for decision-making. If a question is underperforming, it should not wait to be identified until after potentially hundreds or even thousands of students have experienced it; that question should be removed and replaced the moment the CIS is confident in that decision. This goal is directly aligned with the student-centered approach of learning engineering. The CIS is the adaptive system that continuously works to optimize the learning resource for students. Furthermore, the CIS itself can adapt and undergo iterative improvement over time, as its methods of analysis are refined and learning science expertise continues to be added.

The CIS presents the opportunity to engage in large-scale data analytics that could reveal new insights in learning science. One clear avenue of future research is to study and improve the AQG process itself. As it is operating on the largest collection of automatically generated questions delivered for student use in natural learning contexts to date, the decisions made by the CIS will provide large, labeled data sets for question quality, which can be used for developing machine learning models to better detect suboptimal questions before they are released. The results of the CIS could also reveal interesting insights into the performance of these automatically generated questions across subject domains. Another avenue of future study is characterizing the timescales needed to optimize questions in the learning environment. Previously, data analysis to identify problematic human-authored questions occurred only after a semester or year of data had been collected, if even at all. In addition to the analysis itself, there is the need for expert review of the results and for any follow-up actions based on that review to be implemented manually. These practical requirements mean students may not receive the benefits of this improvement cycle for a year or longer. With the CIS, these analyses and decisions are improving the learning environment constantly, indicating that at a certain point, every question will have been optimized for students. Discovering this optimization point would be a valuable finding.

References

1. Baker, F.B.: The Basics of Item Response Theory (2nd ed.). ERIC Clearinghouse on Assessment and Evaluation (2001)
2. Durlach, P.J., Ray, J.M.: Designing adaptive instructional environments. Insights from empirical evidence (Technical report 1297). United States Army Research Institute For the Behavioral and Social Sciences (Arlington, VA) (2011). https://apps.dtic.mil/sti/pdfs/ADA552677.pdf
3. Heilman, M., Smith, N.A.: Question generation via overgenerating transformations and ranking (Technical report CMU-LTI-09–013). Carnegie Mellon University, Language Technologies Institute (Pittsburgh, PA) (2009). https://www.lti.cs.cmu.edu/sites/default/files/cmulti09013.pdf
4. IEEE ICICLE: What is Learning Engineering? (2020). https://sagroups.ieee.org/icicle/
5. Kessler, A.: Design SIG Colleagues. Learning Engineering Process Strong Person (2020). https://sagroups.ieee.org/icicle/learning-engineering-process/. Accessed
6. Koedinger, K., McLaughlin, E., Jia, J., Bier, N.: Is the doer effect a causal relationship? How can we tell and why it's important. In: Learning Analytics and Knowledge. Edinburgh, United Kingdom (2016). http://dx.doi.org/https://doi.org/10.1145/2883851.2883957
7. Kurdi, G., Leo, J., Parsia, B., Sattler, U., Al-Emari, S.: A systematic review of automatic question generation for educational purposes. Int. J. Artif. Intell. Educ. **30**(1), 121–204 (2019). https://doi.org/10.1007/s40593-019-00186-y

8. Martin, F., Chen, Y., Moore, R.L., Westine, C.D.: Systematic review of adaptive learning research designs, context, strategies, and technologies from 2009 to 2018. Educ. Tech. Res. Dev. **68**(4), 1903–1929 (2020). https://doi.org/10.1007/s11423-020-09793-2
9. Sharma, K., Papamitsiou, Z., Giannakos, M.: Building pipelines for educational data using AI and multimodal analytics: a "grey-box" approach. Br. J. Educ. Technol. **50**(6), 3004–3031 (2019). https://doi.org/10.1111/bjet.12854
10. Campenhout, R.: Learning engineering as an ethical framework. In: Sottilare, R.A., Schwarz, J. (eds.) HCII 2021. LNCS, vol. 12792, pp. 105–119. Springer, Cham (2021). https://doi.org/10.1007/978-3-030-77857-6_7
11. Van Campenhout, R., Dittel, J.S., Jerome, B., Johnson, B.G.: Transforming textbooks into learning by doing environments: an evaluation of textbook-based automatic question generation. In: Third Workshop on Intelligent Textbooks at the 22nd International Conference on Artificial Intelligence in Education. CEUR Workshop Proceedings, ISSN 1613–0073, pp. 1–12 (2021). http://ceur-ws.org/Vol-2895/paper06.pdf
12. Van Campenhout, R., Jerome, B., Johnson, B.G.: The impact of adaptive activities in acrobatiq courseware - investigating the efficacy of formative adaptive activities on learning estimates and summative assessment scores. In: Sottilare, R.A., Schwarz, J. (eds.) HCII 2020. LNCS, vol. 12214, pp. 543–554. Springer, Cham (2020). https://doi.org/10.1007/978-3-030-50788-6_40
13. Van Campenhout, R. Johnson, B.G., Olsen, J.A.: The doer effect: replicating findings that doing causes learning. In: Proceedings of eLmL 2021: The Thirteenth International Conference on Mobile, Hybrid, and On-line Learning, ISSN 2308–4367, pp. 1–6. https://www.thinkmind.org/index.php?view=article&articleid=elml_2021_1_10_58001
14. Vandewaetere, M., Desmet, P., Clarebout, G.: The contribution of learner characteristics in the development of computer-based adaptive learning environments. Comput. Hum. Behav. **27**(1), 118–130 (2011). https://doi.org/10.1016/j.chb.2010.07.038

What Makes Online-Merge-Offline (OMO) Education Succeed? A Holistic Success Model

JiuJiu Jiang, Lili Liu(✉), Peiping Zong, Fangting Tao, He Lai, Yaohao Chen, and Chuanmin Mi

College of Economics and Management, Nanjing University of Aeronautics and Astronautics, Nanjing, China

{llili85,Cmmi}@nuaa.edu.cn

Abstract. Universities all over the world have extensively adopt the OMO teaching method in the post epidemic era. This study aims to investigate what makes OMO education succeed. Based on Community of Inquiry framework, IS Success Model and Use and Gratifications Theory, we develop a holistic success model of OMO learning, intending to explore what affects students" learning satisfaction, and ultimately determine their academic performance. 395 valid responses were collected via a survey. SmartPLS 3 was used to verify the research model and hypotheses. The results show that: students" online learning satisfaction is positively affected by system quality, facilitating discourse and direct instruction, and offline learning satisfaction is positively affected by instructional design and organization, facilitating discourse and direct instruction. Online and offline learning satisfaction jointly affect academic performance. Theoretically, this study empirically explored the outcomes of OMO teaching method. Practically, our findings provided suggestions to improve the OMO teaching efficiency in colleges and universities.

Keywords: Online-Merge-Offline (OMO) · IS success model · Community of inquiry · Uses and gratifications theory · Academic performance

1 Introduction

Since 2020, the outbreak of the new crown epidemic has dramatically affected traditional offline teaching, and many universities have to switch from teaching offline to teaching online. According to the data released by UNESCO, as of April 16, 2020, the epidemic led to the suspension of classes in 192 countries worldwide, and 1.575 billion students were affected, covering 91.3% of the total number of students registered worldwide [20]. As a result, many colleges and universities have begun to change their teaching methods, opting for online teaching when the epidemic is severe and offline teaching when it is not. In other words, many universities have started to adopt the OMO (Online Merge Offline) teaching method.

The OMO was firstly proposed as a business model, then extended to education industry [13]. In Higher Education, OMO teaching method is an effective solution that

© Springer Nature Switzerland AG 2022

G. Meiselwitz et al. (Eds.): HCII 2022, LNCS 13517, pp. 297–308, 2022.

https://doi.org/10.1007/978-3-031-22131-6_23

meet the needs of students and teachers in the post-epidemic era. In practical application, OMO not only conforms to the policy of "stopping classes without stopping
school" issued and advocated by the Ministry of Education during epidemic, but also
solves the problem of cost pressure on the supply side of educational institutions and
the relative lack of educational resources on the demand side of students in third and
fourth-tier cities. OMO teaching is capable to maintain teaching efficiency and learners"
academic performance [13]. After continuous development in recent years, the OMO
model is gradually developing into an all-round integration of teaching process, business
process and management process, with the dual service characteristics of standardization, convenience of online education, as well as differentiation and refinement of offline
education.

In the meantime, the rapid development of technology provides new ideas and new
means to promote the deep integration of information technology and education, which
also promote the integration of online teaching and offline teaching. In the post epidemic
era, China"s education approach has begun to change to the OMO education approach,
and this will become a new trend in the future. However, OMO teaching has just been
applied to college education. We know little about students" attitude toward this method,
as well as the teaching output (e.g., students" academic performance). Therefore, this
study develops a holistic success research model to thoroughly investigate how OMO
teaching affect students" attitudes, which in turn determine their academic performance.

2 Theoretical Background

2.1 Community of Inquiry Framework (CoI)

Community of Inquiry was developed by Garrison, Anderson and Archer in 1999, and has
become the most influential theoretical framework in the field of blended teaching [23].
In particular, three core elements - cognitive presence, social presence and pedagogical
presence - interact to predict the learning outcomes. Or in other words, the community of
inquiry theoretical model refers to the process of creating deep and meaningful learning
experiences (educational experiences) through the development of three interdependent
elements (See Fig. 1) [23]. Past research has shown that blended teaching based on
Community of Inquiry helps to improve learning outcomes and creates a positive learning
experience for students [10], and the essence of teaching is reflected in its ability to ensure
desired learning outcomes by identifying needs and giving students timely information
and guidance [21].

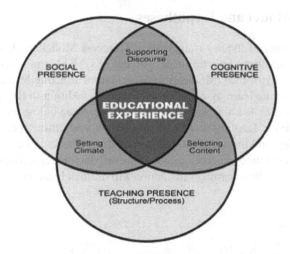

Fig. 1. Community of inquiry

2.2 IS Success Model (ISSM)

IS Success Model (ISSM) was firstly introduced by De Lone and Mc Lean in 1992, which is also known as D&M Model. In this model, there are six successful factors that inhibits IS Success, namely, information quality, system quality, use, satisfaction, individual impact and organizational impact [18, 22]. The model suggests that quality factors (system and information quality) directly influence user satisfaction and the use of IS. Additionally, satisfaction and use of system affect the individual impact and subsequently influence organizational impact [16].

On account of the appearance of end users, information systems need to supply services in addition to information products. In 2003, De Lone and Mc Lean added service quality as a new quality factor, in order to refine and update the original model [6]. The updated model has attracted scholars" attention in the field of IS, demonstrating that IS success can be evaluated via a set of quality factors (i.e., service quality, systems quality, and information quality). Subsequently, these factors influence user satisfaction and usage. ISSM theoretically indicates that a high-quality IS results in high user satisfaction and thus high levels of IS use and an increased perception of net benefits.

2.3 Use and Gratifications Theory (U&G)

Use and gratifications approach was developed by Blumler and Katz in 1974, which stood in the position of the audience and examined the psychological and behavioral utility of mass communication to human beings by analyzing the audience"s motivation to use the media and to satisfy needs [7]. In contrast to the traditional perspective on how messages influence audiences, it emphasizes audience activism and highlights the importance of the audience. The theory argues that audiences actively use medium to communicate, and states that the use of the medium is based solely on individual needs and desires. From the perspective of learning groups, analyzing the usage and needs of students can provide useful reference information for the educational institutions [5].

3   Research Model and Hypotheses

Based on Community of Inquiry framework, IS Success Model and Use and Gratifications Theory, we develop a holistic success model of OMO learning (shown in Fig. 2). Due to the specificity of the OMO learning, the factors affecting learners" satisfaction with online and offline learning could be different. In addition to the factors affecting both online and offline learning satisfaction, there is unique online teaching characteristics. We thus divide learning satisfaction as online and offline, i.e., system quality, instructional design and organization, facilitating discourse and direct instruction have different impacts on online satisfaction and offline satisfaction respectively. Online learning satisfaction and offline learning satisfaction will ultimately affect students" academic performance.

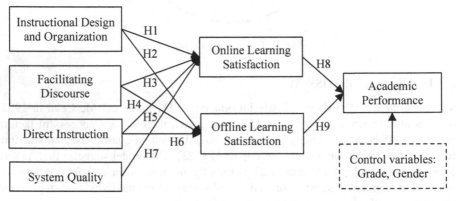

Fig. 2. Research model

3.1   Teaching Presence and Satisfaction

The community of inquiry framework has been widely adopted by educational research. We identify instructional design and organization, facilitating discourse and direct instruction as independent variables that affect students" satisfaction.

Instructional design and organization is defined as the planning and design of the structure, process, interaction and evaluation aspects of the online course. The design and organization has a direct impact on the content quality of courses, affecting students" learning experience. In terms of instructional design, there were findings related to a strong correlation between student achievement in the case study and the frequency of student teaching presence behaviors in the teacher"s course, suggesting a positive relationship between learning outcomes and online teaching effort [7]. We thus propose:

H1: Instructional design and organization has a positive effect on online learning satisfaction.
H2: Instructional design and organization has a positive effect on offline learning satisfaction.

Facilitating discourse is the means by which students are engaged in interacting about and building upon the information provided in the course instructional Materials, which enables students to participate in the interaction with the content of the course. It requires teachers to review and comment on students" dialogue, put forward relevant questions, observe the development of the dialogue towards the predetermined direction, and make the dialogue continue to advance effectively [21]. In OMO learning, especially when students learn online, interaction plays a significant role. Facilitating discourse plays an important role in stimulating learning results, thus we assume:

H3: Facilitating discourse has a positive effect on online learning satisfaction.
H4: Facilitating discourse has a positive effect on offline learning satisfaction.

Direct instruction is the instructor"s provision of intellectual and scholarly leadership, in part through sharing their subject matter knowledge with the students, including presenting content and issues, diagnosing misunderstandings, gathering discussion on issues, summarizing reflection and confirming understanding through evaluation and explanatory feedback, as well as solving technical problems [7]. The separation of time and space in OMO teaching method weakens the influence of teachers, so clear teaching instructions become more important. Therefore, we propose:

H5: Direct instruction has a positive effect on online learning satisfaction.
H6: Direct instruction has a positive effect on offline learning satisfaction.

3.2 System Quality and Satisfaction

OMO education cannot be operated without the support of technology, i.e. various information systems that support teaching and learning activities. Therefore, combing the perspective of IS success model, we identify an additional independent variable, system quality.

System quality refers to the quality of information processing system [14]. Bailey et al. evaluate system quality by convenience of access, flexibility, integration and response time [4]. Besides, Belardo et al. measure system quality by evaluating the reliability, response time, ease-of-use, and ease-of-learning [2]. In 2003, De Lone and Mc Lean summarized a decade of research that applied the IS Success Model, further verified the importance of system quality, which is measured by ease of use, functionality, reliability, and flexibility [3]. In an educational information system, learners acquire courses and other learning resources through the system. In this process, the system quality affects learners" access to learning resources, thus may affect their perceived satisfaction with the whole system. Thus, we hypothesize:

H7: System quality has a positive effect on online learning satisfaction.

3.3 Satisfaction and Academic Performance

Satisfaction is regarded as the intermediary variable that affects academic performance. Sun et al. find that university students" learning satisfaction is negatively related with students" pass rate [12], indicating that learning satisfaction has strong influence on university students" academic performance. Lin et al. argue that the higher the learning achievement of university students, the better their academic performance; the higher the students" satisfaction with course content and learning achievement, the stronger their learning initiative; the higher the satisfaction with course content and teaching equipment, the less likely they are to suffer from learning burnout [19]. Hence, we assume:

H8: Online learning satisfaction has a positive effect on academic performance.
H9: Offline learning satisfaction has a positive effect on academic performance.

4 Methodology

4.1 Data Collection

This study identified Chinese college students (undergraduates and postgraduates) as the research object. In the current situation, OMO teaching has been widely used in major cities in China. Students in these cities have rich online learning experience and can skillfully acquire knowledge through OMO learning. Therefore, our choice of research object is reasonable.

In late April 2022, an online survey was published on Sojump (the most popular Chinese online survey platform) to collect data from university students. When preparing the questionnaire, we adjusted the existing measurement scales [6, 10, 15] to fit the research background of the project, and used a Likert Five-level scale to measure all items, ranging from 1 (strongly disagree) to 5 (strongly agree). 395 valid samples were collected. SmartPLS 3.3.9 was used to test the research model and hypotheses. Table 1 shows an overview of the respondents. Among the 395 samples, female users accounted for 38.23% and male users accounted for 61.77%, which was in a reasonable range. The majority of student users were freshmen to graduate students, which ensureed the scope of users covered by this study. And the respondents covered multiple majors to ensure the reliability of the data.

Table 1. Respondents profile

Variable		Frequency	Percentage
Gender	Female	244	61.77%
	Male	151	38.23%
Grade	Freshman	42	10.63%
	Sophomore	116	29.37%
	Junior	143	36.20%

(*continued*)

Table 1. (*continued*)

Variable		Frequency	Percentage
	senior	44	11.14%
	postgraduate	47	11.90%
	Graduates	3	0.76%

In the questionnaire, the actual usage of OMO learning was investigated. Table 2 lists the proportion of time respondents spent on university courses with OMO method. In all samples, more than 50% of the students had studied through OMO for more than 6 months, implying that OMO learning has been widely applied to considerable university courses.

Table 2. Respondents OMO learning duration

Variable		Frequency	Percentage
Duration	Within 3 months	120	30.38%
	3 to 6 months	73	18.48%
	6 to 12 months	72	18.23%
	More than 12 months	130	32.91%

4.2 Measurement Model

Reliability was assessed by examining Cronbach"s alpha, composite reliability (CR), and average variance extracted (AVE) [1]. The threshold values used to evaluate these three indices were .70, .70, and .50, respectively [12]. As shown in Table 3, all item loadings were significant ($p < .001$) and ranged from 0.634 to 0.909, indicating adequate convergent validity [9].

Table 3. Reliability indicators

Construct	Item	Factor loadings	CR	Cronbach's alpha	AVE
System Quality	SQ1	0.79	0.87	0.81	0.63
	SQ2	0.82			
	SQ3	0.81			
	SQ4	0.77			

(*continued*)

Table 3. (*continued*)

Construct	Item	Factor loadings	CR	Cronbach's alpha	AVE
Instructional Design and Organization	IDAO1	0.81	0.86	0.76	0.67
	IDAO2	0.84			
	IDAO3	0.81			
Facilitating Discourse	FD1	0.78	0.89	0.83	0.66
	FD2	0.84			
	FD3	0.84			
	FD4	0.79			
Direct Instruction	DI1	0.91	0.91	0.80	0.83
	DI2	0.92			
Online Learning Satisfaction	ONLS1	0.83	0.91	0.86	0.71
	ONLS2	0.87			
	ONLS3	0.84			
Offline Learning Satisfaction	OFLS1	0.83	0.91	0.87	0.72
	OFLS2	0.85			
	OFLS3	0.86			
Academic Performance	AP1	0.86	0.90	0.86	0.70
	AP2	0.79			
	AP3	0.80			
	AP4	0.89			

Discriminant validity of the constructs could be verified by confirming the square root of the AVE to be higher than the inter-construct correlations [8]. The result in Table 4 shows that the square roots of the AVE of all the constructs were higher than all the correlations, suggesting good discriminant validity.

Table 4. Discriminant validity

	SQ	IDAO	FD	DI	ONLS	OFLS	AP
SQ	**0.80**						
IDAO	0.63	**0.82**					
FD	0.54	0.54	**0.81**				
DI	0.52	0.53	0.64	**0.91**			

(*continued*)

Table 4. (*continued*)

	SQ	IDAO	FD	DI	ONLS	OFLS	AP
ONLS	0.46	0.42	0.54	0.49	**0.84**		
OFLS	0.44	0.41	0.42	0.41	0.38	**0.85**	
AP	0.52	0.49	0.58	0.57	0.72	0.42	**0.84**

Notes: The diagonal elements depict the square root of the AVE SQ = System Quality; IDAO = Instructional design and organization; FD = Facilitating discourse; DI = Direct instruction; ONLS = Online learning satisfaction; OFLS = Offline learning satisfaction; AP = Academic performance.

4.3 Structural Model

The results of the structural model test were summarized in Fig. 3. As hypothesized, students" online learning satisfaction was positively affected by system quality, facilitating discourse and direct instruction, and offline learning satisfaction was positively affected by instructional design and organization, facilitating discourse and direct instruction. Independent variables jointly explained 34.9% variance of online learning satisfaction and 24.0% variance of offline learning satisfaction. H2, H3, H4, H5, H6, H7 were supported at significance levels of p < 0.05 or better. Furthermore, findings indicated that online and offline learning satisfaction significantly influenced academic performance, explaining 55.1% of its variance. H8 and H9 were supported at p < 0.01. Besides, two control variables (grade and gender) had significant impacts on academic performance (p < 0.05).

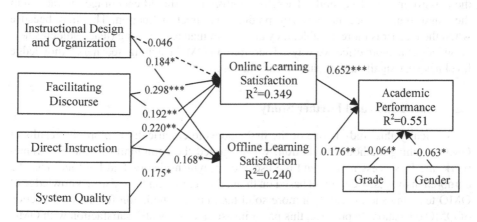

Fig. 3. Structural model

5 Discussion

5.1 Hypothesis Test

This study explores the impact of system quality, instructional design and organization, facilitating discourse and direct instruction on students" online and offline learning satisfaction. Online and offline learning satisfaction will further affect users" academic performance. Majority of our hypotheses have been confirmed.

In OMO teaching, online and offline content may partially overlap or complement each other. In any way, the teaching content will be regarded by students as the core of educational products. The design and organization of offline classes will also affect user satisfaction. And the better the design, the higher the satisfaction. As the main provider of teaching services, teachers should pay attention to service quality and improve professional ability. The impact of system quality on user satisfaction is also significant. With the rapid development of information technology, users are getting familiar with the information system, and they expect more from the information system (e.g., improved quality). Better system quality can ensure users" online learning experience, because it is the basis of online content and services. The results show that online and offline satisfaction will jointly affect students" academic performance. If users are satisfied with OMO learning, it means that this learning method is better than single online or offline learning, leading to improved performance. In the subsequent learning process, they will also tend to continue to use OMO learning.

From the structural model, it can be seen that facilitating discourse has the greatest impact on satisfaction. The reason is that facilitating discourse is a means for students to interact and construct based on the information provided in the course teaching materials. Compared with other variables, facilitating discourse can make students participate in the classroom more frequently. Therefore, universities should encourage interaction in the classroom. The second powerful predictor is direct instruction. This may because when the teacher is more capable, they are able to manage teaching (teach students new knowledge) in more effective ways. Therefore, in OMO teaching, teachers" knowledge level has very significant impact on satisfaction.

5.2 Contribution and Further Study

Theoretically, this study is one of the first studies to empirically explore the results of OMO teaching method. In addition, we integrated the community of inquiry framework, the IS success model, and the use and enjoyment theory, and built and tested a comprehensive research model based on them, thus enriching the existing knowledge of OMO teaching and providing a more solid theoretical foundation for the construction of OMO education. In practice, this paper investigates students" satisfaction with OMO learning and academic performance, and provides certain suggestions for universities to use OMO teaching and improve the way students are educated in the context of the epidemic era.

However, there are some limitations in our study. On one hand, OMO teaching in higher education is still in the early stage, thus the development model is immature and the theoretical background is not sufficient. On the other hand, the selected audience group is limited to college students, while the audience group of education is not only college students but also many junior and senior high school students, there are still some shortcomings in this aspect of data collection. We hope that in future discussions, the research of OMO education method can find more audience groups with different identities.

Acknowledgment. This study was supported by the Fundamental Research Funds for the Central Universities No. NR2021003 awarded to the second author.

References

1. Al-Adwan, A.S., Albelbisi, N.A., Hujra, O., Al-Rahmi, W.M., Alkhalifa, H.A.: Developing a holistic success model for sustainable e-learning: a structural equation modeling approach. Sustainability. **13**(16), 9453 (2021)
2. Bailey, J.E., Pearson, S.W.: Development of a tool for measuring and analyzing computer user satisfaction. Manage. Sci. **29**(5), 530–545 (1983)
3. Belardo, S., Karwan, K.R., William, A.W.: DSS component design through field experimentation: an application to emergency management. In: Proceeding of the Third International Conference on Information Systems, vol. 93, pp. 93–108 (1982)
4. Bhattacherjee, A.: An empirical analysis of the antecedents of electronic commerce service continuance. Decis. Support Syst. **32**(2), 201–214 (2001)
5. Blumler, J.G., Katz, E.: The uses of mass communications: current perspectives on gratifications research. In: Sage Annual Reviews of Communication Research Volume III (1974)
6. Delone, W.H., Mclean, E.R.: Information systems success: the quest for the dependent variable. Inf. Syst. Res. **3**(1), 60–95 (1992)
7. Delone, W.H., Mclean, E.R.: The Delone and Mclean model of information systems success: a ten-year update. J. Manage. Inf. Syst. **19**(4), 9–30 (2003). https://doi.org/10.1080/07421222.2003.11045748
8. Fornell, C., Larcker, D.F.: Structural equation models with unobservable variables and measurement error: algebra and statistics. J. Mark. Res. **18**(3), 382–388 (1981)
9. Garrison, D.R., Anderson, T., Archer, W.: Critical inquiry in a text-based environment: Computer conferencing in higher education. Internet High. Edu. **2**(2–3), 87–105 (1999)
10. Garrison, D.R., Arbaugh, J.B.: Researching the community of inquiry framework: review, issues, and future directions. Internet High. Edu. **10**(3), 157–172 (2007)
11. Haslwanter, T.: Multivariate data analysis. In: An Introduction to Statistics with Python. SC, pp. 221–225. Springer, Cham (2016). https://doi.org/10.1007/978-3-319-28316-6_12
12. Lan, G.S.: The community of inquiry theoretical model: a research paradigm for online and blended learning. Open Edu. Res. **24**(1), 29–40 (2018)
13. Li, K.F.: Rush to the OMO Era. Manager **2**, 4 (2018)
14. Li, X.: Exploring the use intention and effect of College Students" learning area at station B under the theory of use and satisfaction. Public Commun. Sci. Technol. **12**(22), 140–142149 (2020)
15. Lin, B., Yan, J.J., Mao, Y.F.: Researching the influence of college students" learning attitude and academic performance: from the perspective of learning satisfaction. Theory Res. **24**, 200–201 (2012)
16. Mason, R.O.: Measuring information output: a communication systems approach. Inf. Manage. **5**(1), 219–234 (1978)

17. Shea, P., Hayes, S., Vickers, J.: Online instructional effort measured through the lens of teaching presence in the community of inquiry framework: a re-examination of measures and approach. Int. Rev. Res. Open Dist. Learn.**11**(3) (2010)
18. Shannon, C.E., Weaver, W.: The Mathematical Theory of Communication, pp. 1–54. University of Illinois Press, Urbana IL (1949)
19. Sun, J.P., Zhu, Z.F., Lin, L.F.: An empirical analysis of College Students" academic performance. High. Agric. Edu. **S1**, 66–68 (2001)
20. UNICEF. Keeping the World"s Children Learning through COVID-19. https://www.unicef.org/coronavirus/keeping-worlds-children-learning-through-covid-19. Accessed 20 Apr 2020
21. Wang, L., Liao, B.Z.: The blended teaching based on community of inquiry in obstetrics and gynecology nursing. Chin. J. Nurs. Edu. **17**(6), 489–493 (2020)
22. Yang, J., Bai, X.M., Ma, H.L.: Review and prediction of research on the inquiry community of online learning. e-Edu. Res. **37**(7), 50–57 (2016)
23. Yang, X.: Some thoughts on Omo business model in the era of Internet economy. Contemp. Econ. **17**, 94–95 (2018)

Continuance Usage of Online-Merge-Offline (OMO) Educational Services: An Empirical Study

JiuJiu Jiang, Lili Liu[✉], Shanjiao Ren, Suting Yang, Peiping Zong, and He Lai

College of Economics and Management, Nanjing University of Aeronautics and Astronautics, Nanjing, China
{lilili85,joy9971}@nuaa.edu.cn

Abstract. OMO (Online Merge Offline), the combination of online and offline services, has attracted increasing attention in the education industry. This study aims to investigate the predictors of learners' continuance participation in OMO learning. Based on Expectation-Confirmation Theory, IS Success Model and Satisfaction-Loyalty Theory, we develop a research model to explore how online teaching quality (online content quality, online service quality and system quality) and offline teaching quality (offline content quality and offline service quality) jointly affect students' satisfaction and loyalty, and ultimately determine their continuance usage intention. 301 valid samples were collected via an online survey. SmartPLS 3 was used to verify the research model and hypotheses. Findings show that: (1) online content quality, online service quality, system quality, offline content quality and offline service quality positively affect satisfaction; (2) satisfaction positively influence loyalty and continuance intention; (3) continuance intention has positive impact on loyalty. Implications for theory and practice are discussed.

Keywords: Online merge Offline · Online teaching quality · Offline teaching quality · Satisfaction · Loyalty · Continuance intention

1 Introduction

The COVID-19 pandemic has posed great challenges to the field of education. In April 2020, the spread the COVID-19 pandemic across the globe compel a majority of countries to announce the temporary closure of schools, impacting more than 91% of students worldwide – approximately 1.6 billion children and young people [1]. By November 2020, the number had dropped to 572 million, still accounting for 33% of the enrolled students worldwide [2]. All these facts have revealed the need for new innovative methods to effectively maintain education in times of crisis and uncertainty. OMO (Online Merge Offline) learning approach, the combination of online and offline educational services, emerges as an effective solution that caters to the new needs of students and teachers in the post-COVID-19 era. OMO approach was firstly proposed by Kaifu Li in 2017, it has been demonstrated that OMO teaching practices could improve the efficiency of education, as well as learners' performance [3]. For instance, Xiao et al. argue that both

© Springer Nature Switzerland AG 2022
G. Meiselwitz et al. (Eds.): HCII 2022, LNCS 13517, pp. 309–319, 2022.
https://doi.org/10.1007/978-3-031-22131-6_24

teachers and school administrators recognize OMO teaching as an effective alternative of traditional offline or online teaching [4]. Reports imply that almost 60% of schools and educational institutions have applied OMO teaching approach in April 2021, where the epidemic has further promoted the occupation rate of OMO teaching.

The Chinese Government has awakened to the necessity of OMO learning. The document punished by Chinese Ministry of Education has clearly claimed that Online-merge-Offline should be regarded as one of the construction objectives in the field of educational informatization to create new supply and demand [5]. Chinese Ministry of Education has made great efforts to establish and improve Online-merge-Offline education. Firstly, 5118 first-class national undergraduate courses were selected and announced, including considerable Online-merge-Offline courses. Secondly, the application of e-learning space was getting further universal, contributing to the construction and normalization of an effective Online-merge-Offline teaching approach. Thirdly, in the exploration of every distinct, depending on online teaching platform, educational institutions need to promote the adaption of modern information technology, which enables interactions and integrations between online and offline, in and outside classroom, virtual and real space [6].

Despite the obviously increasing significance of OMO education approach, appeared as a new teaching method, OMO education is still in its primary stage, we have limited knowledge on students' assessment of their learning experiences. To fill the research gap, this study develops a research model to investigate the antecedents of learners' continuance participation in OMO learning.

2 Theoretical Background

2.1 Expectation Confirmation Model (ECM)

In marketing study, Oliver proposes a cognitive model, revealing the psychological mechanism governing consumers' repeated purchase of products [7]. That is, during a longer consumption cycle, consumers' decision process will go through the establishment and confirmation of expectations, which finally forms consumers' satisfaction and repurchase intention.

Similar to consumers repurchase decisions, the Expectation Confirmation Model (ECM) suggests that technology users make cognitive comparisons when considering continuance use decisions [8]. ECM is one of the most widely accepted theoretical models in information system sustainable use due to good prediction of users' continuance intention. A number of studies have adopted ECM to explain continuance usage of educational information systems, such as users' willingness to continue using online learning systems [9, 10], college students' willingness to continue using electronic library resources [11], and teachers' continuance usage of Blog teaching [12]. These scholars have improved the original ECM model and verified that the improved model can be applied to investigate the sustainable use factors of educational information system.

2.2 IS Success Model (ISSM)

IS Success Model (ISSM) was originally advanced by DeLone and McLean in 1992, also been regarded as D&M Model. In this model, six factors co-determine IS Success, namely, information quality, system quality, use, satisfaction, individual impact and organizational impact [13, 14]. The model suggests that quality factors (system and information quality) directly influence user satisfaction and the use of IS. Additionally, satisfaction and use of system affect the individual impact, and subsequently influence organizational impact [15].

In practice, information systems need to provide end users with services, in addition to information products. In 2003, DeLone and McLean incorporated service quality to refine and the initial IS Success Model [16]. The updated model has captured scholars' attention in the field of IS. Extensive studies have demonstrated that IS success can be assessed with a set of quality factors (i.e., service quality, systems quality, and information quality). Subsequently, these factors influence user satisfaction and use. ISSM theoretically indicates that a high-quality IS results in high user satisfaction and thus high levels of IS use and increased net benefits.

2.3 Satisfaction-Loyalty Theory

The correlation between customer's satisfaction and loyalty has been widely discussed since Olive proved the positive correlation between them [17]. Studies on mobile phone service market [18] and e-commerce [19] not only confirmed the positive correlation between satisfaction and loyalty, but also explored the mediators. Explorations have been executed in both online and offline environments. For instance, Jen points out that perceived service quality is the antecedent of loyalty, their relationship is partially mediated by satisfaction. [20]. The theory has been confirmed in many fields, including cultural tourism industry [21], cross-border e-commerce [22] and higher vocational colleges teaching [23].

3   Research Model and Hypotheses

Based on Expectation-Confirmation Theory, IS Success Model and Satisfaction-Loyalty Theory, we develop a model to investigate users' continuance use intention of OMO education service (shown in Fig. 1). Online teaching quality has been evaluated via online content quality, online service quality and system quality, while offline teaching quality has been measured via offline content quality and offline service quality. These antecedents jointly affect students' satisfaction and loyalty, and ultimately determine their continuance intention.

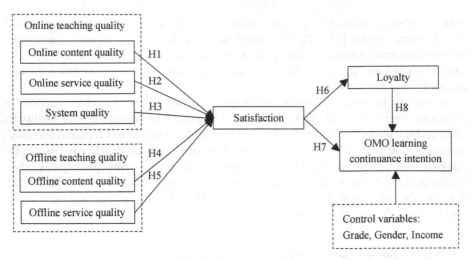

Fig. 1. Research model

3.1 Online Teaching Quality and Satisfaction

In the ISSM, information quality refers to the quality of the information produced by information system [8]. Numerous studies have shown that information quality is a critical factor affecting user satisfaction, this finding is applicable to different types of information systems [16]. In regard to educational information systems (EIS), information quality can be identified as content quality of lessons. Compared with other information systems, the intrinsic value of education system is more important, which can satisfy users' needs for learning [24]. Thus, we propose the following hypothesis:

H1: Online content quality has a positive effect on satisfaction.

Service quality originated in marketing and was later introduced into information system. Compared to the quality of goods or information, service quality is more difficult for consumers to evaluate [25]. SERVQUAL scale has been applied to many empirical studies of ISSM, validating its impact on satisfaction [16]. Online service quality is an important component of online teaching quality, the following hypothesis is thus proposed:

H2: Online service quality has a positive effect on satisfaction.

System quality refers to the quality of information processing systems [8]. In an EIS, learners acquire course materials and other learning resources through the system. In this process, the system quality affects learners' access to learning resources and may further affect their perceived satisfaction with the whole system. Thus we hypothesize that:

H3: System quality has a positive effect on satisfaction.

3.2   Offline Teaching Quality and Satisfaction

In OMO education, teaching process is composed of online and offline segments, which are closely related and integrated with each other. This study expands the ISSM, measuring offline teaching quality with two sub-dimensions: offline content quality and offline service quality. Similar to the content quality, we divide the service quality into online and offline parts. In the OMO education model, the providers of online and offline services might be different, and there are differences in services. For example, the offline service quality can be measured by the teaching equipment and environment, while the online service quality cannot. Therefore, we propose the following assumption:

H4: Offline content quality has a positive effect on satisfaction.
H5: Offline service quality has a positive effect on satisfaction.

3.3   Satisfaction, Loyalty and Continuance Intention

There are various definitions of satisfaction. Some scholars define it as the overall attitude of consumers towards the purchased products or services. Besides, based on Expectation Confirmation Theory, many scholars believe that satisfaction is the psychological state generated by the comparison between consumers' perceived performance of products or services and their expectations before use [27]. In marketing discipline, Cardozo prove that customer satisfaction has a positive impact on repurchase behavior [26]. The impact of satisfaction on continuous use intention has been empirically supported by some studies in the field of information system user behavior [28, 29]. We thus propose:

H6: Satisfaction has a positive effect on loyalty.
H7: Satisfaction has a positive effect on sustainable use intention.

Brown and Cunningham find that consumers continuously purchase different products from the same brand, which is recognized as brand loyalty [30, 31]. Many studies have shown that loyalty has long-term benefits for the sustainable development of enterprises, so it has always been the focus of enterprise marketing [32]. A large number of studies show that there is a significant positive correlation between satisfaction and loyalty. Therefore, we assume:

H8: Loyalty has a positive effect on continuance intention.

4   Data Collection and Analysis

4.1   Data Collection

Our research subjects are Chinese students in OMO educational institutions. We designed a survey on Sojump (the most popular survey website in China) to collect data. All of the measurement items were adapted from existing studies, and revised to fit the research context. After the preliminary design of questionnaires, we conducted a small-scale pre-survey (45 samples). The result showed good reliability and validity. In addition, most of respondents said that the questionnaire was easy to understand. 301 valid responses were collected. Table 1 shows respondents' profile. In 301 samples, female users accounted for 52.49% and male users accounted for 47.51%, which was in a reasonable range. Student users of all ages are distributed, which ensures the breadth of users covered in this study. The age distribution basically matches the grade of student users, which shows the reliability of the data.

Table 1. Demographics of respondents

Variable		Frequency	Percentage
Gender	Female	158	52.49%
	Male	143	47.51%
Grade	High school and below	138	45.85%
	Undergraduate	124	41.20%
	Postgraduate	19	6.31%
	Professional	20	6.64%
Age	Under 18	138	45.85%
	18–25	139	46.18%
	Above 25	24	7.97%

4.2 Data Analysis

Measurement Model. Reliability was assessed by examining Cronbach's alpha, composite reliability (CR), and average variance extracted (AVE) [33]. The threshold values used to evaluate these three indices were .70, .70, and .50, respectively [34]. As shown in Table 2, all item loadings were significant (p < .001) and ranged from 0.754 to 0.960, indicating adequate convergent validity [35].

Table 2. Reliability indicators

Construct	Item	Factor loadings	CR	Cronbach's alpha	AVE
Online Content Quality	ONCQ1	0.85	0.88	0.81	0.78
	ONCQ2	0.84			
	ONCQ3	0.75			
	ONCQ4	0.76			

(continued)

Table 2. (*continued*)

Construct	Item	Factor loadings	CR	Cronbach's alpha	AVE
Online Service Quality	ONSQ1	0.87	0.90	0.83	0.74
	ONSQ2	0.84			
	ONSQ3	0.88			
System Quality	SQ1	0.83	0.92	0.89	0.75
	SQ2	0.89			
	SQ3	0.89			
	SQ4	0.87			
Offline Content Quality	OFCQ1	0.90	0.94	0.92	0.80
	OFCQ2	0.92			
	OFCQ3	0.89			
	OFCQ4	0.87			
Offline Service Quality	OFSQ1	0.87	0.93	0.90	0.77
	OFSQ2	0.85			
	OFSQ3	0.89			
	OFSQ4	0.90			
Satisfaction	SAT1	0.91	0.94	0.91	0.85
	SAT2	0.92			
	SAT3	0.91			
	SAT4	0.94			
Loyalty	LOY1	0.94	0.97	0.95	0.90
	LOY2	0.95			
	LOY3	0.96			
Continuance Intention	CI1	0.94	0.94	0.91	0.85
	CI2	0.94			
	CI3	0.88			

Discriminant validity of the constructs can be verified by confirming the square root of the AVE to be higher than the inter-construct correlations [35]. The result in Table 3 showed that the square roots of the AVE of all the constructs were higher than all the correlations, suggesting good discriminant validity.

Structural Model. The results of the structural model test were summarized in Fig. 2. As hypothesized, OMO users' satisfaction was positively affected by online content quality, online service quality, system quality, offline content quality and offline service quality. Satisfaction had a positive effect on loyalty and continuance intention. There was also a positive correlation between continuance intention and loyalty. Factors in

Table 3. Discriminant validity

	LOY	CI	SAT	SQ	ONCQ	ONSQ	OFCQ	OFSQ
LOY	**0.95**							
CI	0.83	**0.92**						
SAT	0.76	0.74	**0.92**					
SQ	0.55	0.57	0.63	**0.87**				
ONCQ	0.61	0.64	0.68	0.62	**0.80**			
ONSQ	0.64	0.65	0.70	0.67	0.72	**0.86**		
OFCQ	0.54	0.57	0.68	0.53	0.59	0.62	**0.90**	
OFSQ	0.57	0.56	0.69	0.53	0.62	0.62	0.87	**0.88**

Notes: The diagonal elements depict the square root of the AVE; LOY = Loyalty; CI = Continuance intention; SAT = Satisfaction; SQ = System Quality; ONCQ = Online Content Quality; ONSQ = Online Service Quality; OFCQ = Offline Content Quality; OFSQ = Offline Service Quality

online and offline teaching quality jointly explain 64.1% of the variance of satisfaction. H1, H2, H3, H4, and H5 were supported at significance levels of $p < 0.05$ or better. Furthermore, findings indicated that satisfaction significantly influenced loyalty and continuance intention, explaining 58.1% and 71.5% of their variance respectively. H6, H7 and H8 were supported at $p < 0.001$.

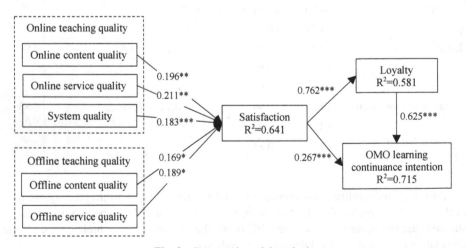

Fig. 2. Structural model analysis

5   Conclusions

This study explores the effect of online and offline teaching quality on students' user satisfaction in OMO teaching, which further affects users' loyalty and continuance intention. The results show that all the assumptions are supported. In OMO teaching, online and offline content may partially overlap, or complement each other. No matter online or offline, content will be considered as the core of educational products by students. Online and offline service quality also affect user satisfaction. The better the service quality, the higher students' satisfaction. Teachers should pay attention to service quality and improve their professional ability. The effect of system quality on user satisfaction is also significant. Better system quality can ensure users' online learning experience, since it is the basis of online content and services. According to the results, users' satisfaction positively affects loyalty and continuance intention. If users are satisfied with OMO learning, it means that this learning method is better than pure online or offline learning, resulting in higher loyalty. In the subsequent learning process, they will also tend to continuously attend OMO classes. The structural model shows that the most significant impact on satisfaction is the system quality. Therefore, OMO institutions should strengthen the construction of online learning system.

Theoretically, this paper suggests a continuous usage model of OMO education services that integrates the ECM, ISSM and SLT. Some crucial online and offline factors that determine users' continuance intention are identified and verified. Furthermore, in the IS Success Model, the content quality and service quality are applied to a situation combining online and offline settings, which expands the application background of the theory. This empirical study also extends our knowledge on user behavior in OMO educational services. Practically, this study investigates users' continuance intention in OMO education, which helps to maintain sustainable education in post-COVID-19 era. Our findings provide valuable advices for universities and education institutions which are seeking for OMO transformation on developing effective courses.

Finally, some limitations of this study are pointed out as a reference for the improvement of follow-up research: (1) We adopts the convenience sampling method in this study. Whether the selected users can represent all the current OMO could be verified by future studies; (2) data was collected from existing users of OMO educational institutions, ignoring users who terminate their use. Follow-up studies may collect data from these users to supplement this study.

Acknowledgment. This study was supported by the Fundamental Research Funds for the Central Universities No. NR2021003 awarded to the second author.

References

1. UNICEF. Keeping the World's Children Learning through COVID-19. https://www.unicef. org/coronavirus/keeping-worlds-children-learning-through-covid-19. Accessed 20 Apr 2020
2. UNICEF. UNICEF calls for averting a lost generation as COVID-19 threatens to cause irreversible harm to children's education, nutrition and well-being. https://www.unicef.org/ press-releases/unicef-calls-averting-lost-generation-covid-19-threatens-cause-irreversible-harm. Accessed 18 Nov 2020

3. Li, K.F.: Rush to the OMO Era. Manager **2**, 4 (2018)
4. Xiao, J., Sun-Lin, H.Z., Cheng, H.C.: A framework of online-merge-offline (OMO) classroom for open education: a preliminary study. Asian Assoc. Open Univ. J. **14**(2), 134–146 (2019)
5. Ministry of Education of P.R. China. Guiding opinions of six departments including the Ministry of education on promoting the construction of new educational infrastructure and building a high-quality education support system. http://www.moe.gov.cn/srcsite/A16/s3342/202107/t20210720_545783.html. Accessed 14 Oct 2021
6. Ministry of Education of P.R. China. Reply to proposal No. 4271 (Education No. 437) of the fourth session of the 13th National Committee of the Chinese people's Political Consultative Conference. http://www.moe.gov.cn/jyb_xxgk/xxgk_jyta/jyta_kjs/202111/t20211104_577687.html. Accessed 21 July 2021
7. Oliver, R.L.: A cognitive model of the antecedents and consequences of satisfaction decisions. J. Mark. Res. **17**(4), 460–469 (1980)
8. Bhattacherjee, A.: An empirical analysis of the antecedents of electronic commerce service continuance. Decis. Support Syst. **32**(2), 201–214 (2001)
9. Zhang, Z., Wang, Y.N., Chen, X.H., Gao, Y.: An empirical research on the factors affecting learners' continuous learning intention in MOOC: a modified expectation-confirmation model. e-Edu. Res. **22**(01), 100–111 (2016)
10. Yang, G.F.: Factors affecting the continued use of MOOC user behavior. Open Edu. Res. **22**(01), 100–111 (2016)
11. Yan, A., Yan, Y.L.: An empirical study of influential factors of the intention of continually using electronic resources in university library. Libr. Tribune **33**(03), 43–50+30 (2013)
12. Chen, C.P., Lai, H.M., Ho, C.Y.: Why do teachers continue to use teaching blogs? the roles of perceived voluntariness and habit. Comput. Educ. **82**, 236–249 (2015)
13. Shannon, C.E., Weaver, W.: The Mathematical Theory of Communication, pp. 1–54. University of Illinois Press, Urbana IL (1949)
14. Mason, R.O.: Measuring information output: a communication systems approach. Inf. Manage. **5**(1), 219–234 (1978)
15. Delone, W.H., Mclean, E.R.: Information systems success: the quest for the dependent variable. Inf. Syst. Res. **3**(1), 60–95 (1992)
16. Delone, W.H., Mclean, E.R.:. The Delone and Mclean model of information systems success: a ten-year update. J. Manage. Inf. Syst. **19**(4), 9–30 (2003)
17. Oliver, T.A., Oliver, R.L., Macmillan, I.C.: A Catastrophe model for developing service satisfaction strategies. J. Mark. 251–257 (1992)
18. Lee, J., Lee, J., Feick, L.: The impact of switching costs on the customer satisfaction-loyalty link: mobile phone service in France. J. Serv. Mark. **15**(1), 35–48 (2001)
19. Anderson, R.E., Srinivasan, S.S.: E-satisfaction and e-loyalty: a contingency framework. Psychol. Mark. **20**(2), 123–138 (2003). https://doi.org/10.1002/mar.10063
20. Jen, W., Tu, R., Lu, T.: Managing passenger behavioral intention: an integrated framework for service quality, satisfaction, perceived value, and switching barriers. Transportation **38**, 321–342 (2011)
21. Tian, C.Y., Pei, Z.B.: Study on the relationship between perceived value, satisfaction and loyalty of tourists in cultural heritage sites. J. Arid Land Resour. Environ. **35**(02), 203–208 (2021)
22. Yin, X.J., Xie, T.: Researching transformation path from consumer satisfaction to consumer loyalty of cross-border import e-commerce platform. J. Commercial Econo. **01**, 90–93 (2021)
23. Shi, M.: Investigating students' satisfaction and loyalty in Higher Vocational Colleges. Qingdao University (2020)
24. Huang, L., Pei, X.N., Zhu, Y.X.: A new study on the evaluation index system for content quality of online course: a perspective from learner experience and knowledge payment. J. Dist. Educ. **38**(01), 104–112 (2020)

25. Parasuraman, A., Zeithaml, V.A., Berry, L.L.: A conceptual model of service quality and its implication for future research (SERVQUAL). J. Mark. **49**(4), 41–50 (1985)
26. Cardozo, R.N.: An experimental study of customer effort, expectation, and satisfaction. J. Mark. Res. **2**(8) (1965)
27. Lee, M.C.: Explaining and predicting users' continuance intention toward e-learning: an extension of the expectation confirmation model. Comput. Educ. **54**(2), 506–516 (2010)
28. Inseong, L., Jaesoo, K., Jinwoo, K.: Use contexts for the mobile Internet: alongitudinal study monitoring actual use of mobile Internet services. Int. J. Human-Comput. Interact. **18**(3), 269–292 (2007)
29. Yang, G.F.: An empirical study on continuance intention of mobile reading service——to content aggregation APP as an example. J. Mod. Inf. **35**(03), 57–63 (2015)
30. Brown, G.: Brand loyalty-fact or fiction? Advert. Age **23**(1), 53–55 (1952)
31. Cunningham, R.M.: Brand loyalty-what, where, how much? Harv. Bus. Rev. **34**(1), 116–128 (1956)
32. Wang, C.X., Han, X.Y., Wen, B.Y.: An empirical study of the relationship between customer satisfaction and loyalty. Nankai Bus. Rev. **04**, 70–74 (2003)
33. Hair, J., Black, B., Babin, B., et al.: Multivariate Data Analysis (6ᵃ ed.) (2006)
34. Chin, W.W., Marcoulides, G.: The partial least squares approach to structural equation modeling. Adv. Hospitality Lsure **8**(2), 295–336 (1998)
35. Fornell, C., Larcker, D.F.: Structural equation models with unobservable variables and measurement error: algebra and statistics. J. Mark. Res. **18**(3), 382–388 (1981)

Digital Mediation in English for Specific Purposes Through the Use of Today's Favourite: Netflix

Elis Kakoulli Constantinou(✉) (iD)

Language Centre, Cyprus University of Technology, 30 Archbishop Kyprianos Str., 3036 Limassol, Cyprus
elis.constantinou@cut.ac.cy

Abstract. In English for Specific Purposes (ESP), an area which focuses on learners' acquisition of language used to carry out tasks in specific contexts, digital mediation proves invaluable, since, among other things, it allows learners' exposure to subject-specific terminology and genre. Netflix, a subscription-based streaming service that allows members to watch TV shows, movies and documentaries on internet-connected devices, has been gaining popularity among young audiences. Even though the use of videos in the ESP teaching and learning process is not new, research that describes the experience of using Netflix in ESP is limited. This paper presents an action research study, conducted during the COVID-19 pandemic, in the context of an English for Specific Academic Purposes (ESAP) course for first year students of Commerce, Finance and Shipping at the Cyprus University of Technology. The purpose of the study was to find a way in which students would be exposed to more authentic-like language related to their field of study and to increase motivation, amidst social distancing and online instruction; for this purpose, the course facilitator utilised Netflix. The participants in the study were 42 first year students of the Department of Commerce, Finance and Shipping. Data were collected through a mixed methods approach, an online questionnaire and student reflections. The results of the study showed students' overall satisfaction with the integration of Netflix in the learning process. Despite certain challenges they faced, students noted that generally the experience was beneficial in terms of language skills improvement as well as professional skills development, among others.

Keywords: Digital media · Netflix · ESP

1 Introduction

The advent of technology has brought with it many innovations including the integration of digital media in education. Digital media relates to the transmission of digital data, which involves digital cables or satellites sending binary signals to devices that translate them into audio, video, graphics, text, and more [1]. Digital media is used every time a device such as a computer, a tablet, a smartphone or an application is used. They

G. Meiselwitz et al. (Eds.): HCII 2022, LNCS 13517, pp. 320–330, 2022.
https://doi.org/10.1007/978-3-031-22131-6_25

may have the form of articles, videos, podcasts, advertisements, music, virtual reality, digital art, etc. This form of media, which is rapidly evolving as technology advances, has revolutionized the way educators in different areas of education operate. The fact that information can be transmitted through various devices and platforms in an array of forms has opened avenues for all fields including language education.

One of the most popular examples of digital media is Netflix, an American subscription streaming service and production company. Offering their customers the advantage of watching content on-demand and on any screen they wish, Netflix has become one of the most successful entertainment platforms nowadays [2].

This paper presents an action research study in which Netflix was used in an English for Specific Purposes (ESP) context at the Cyprus University of Technology during the COVID-19 pandemic, when education was disrupted and courses had to be delivered online. The purpose of the study was to find ways to maintain the same quality of language education by exposing learners to the target language while being confined at home.

2   Literature Review

2.1   Digital Media in Language Teaching: The Case of Netflix

In their book *Digital media for learning: Theories, processes, and solutions*, Martin and Betrus [3] use the term "digital media" as a synonym to the term "multimedia". According to their definition, digital media involves "digitized content that includes a variety of the media elements such as text, images, audio, video, animation" [3, p. 3]. This type of media, which are different from traditional ones such as newspapers, books, the radio or the TV, developed after the launch of the Internet and the advent of the digital era. Currently, digital media involve digital radio stations, podcasts, and audiobooks; streaming movie services, video sharing sites and simulators; social media; pop-ups and autoplay advertisements; literary websites, e-readers and online encyclopedias [2]. The affordances of digital media have been widely recorded in the language teaching literature. Research has shown that learning through a combination of language input and image can foster deeper learning in students, since understanding can be more easily achieved [4]. Multimedia presentation with graphics and video promotes vocabulary acquisition [5], and it improves student performance in grammatical accuracy, listening and writing [6].

Netflix, "a streaming service that offers a wide variety of award-winning TV shows, movies, anime, documentaries, and more on thousands of internet-connected devices" [7], is an example of a digital media service which is thriving nowadays. Upon creating a Netflix account, users can watch online from their personal computer or on any internet-connected device that offers the Netflix app, including smart TVs, smartphones, tablets, streaming media players and game consoles. Shows can even be downloaded so that users can watch them without an internet connection. This convenience and flexibility that Netflix provides to its users, and the fact that the users can watch what they like wherever and whenever they wish, are perhaps some of the main reasons why Netflix is so popular today. Some other reasons are the good quality of the shows and their originality as described in reviews of the platform, the variety of options, the ad-free content, the enhanced-user experience and the personalized experience of its users [2]. Due to its popularity among young people and its affordances, Netflix has the potential to facilitate the learning process in any educational context from medical [8] to language education [9].

Research in the use of Netflix in language teaching and learning is still very limited. Alm [9] describes a study conducted with 12 students of a B2 level of the Common European Framework for Languages (CEFR) German language course, in which students were encouraged to watch a German series of their own choice and write their reflections on a class blog. According to the results of the study, students used similar criteria to select the series to the criteria they used to choose a series in their mother tongue (L1). Students watched several episodes at once as entire seasons were released by Netflix at once. Another important finding of the study was that the students had the opportunity to watch the series they chose anytime anywhere; however, the time and students' concentration on the series affected their engagement with it. In other words, their reflections indicated that the quality of their learning experiences varied according to the chosen time and place of their viewings. Furthermore, the fact that they watched a series in which certain things were repeated, offered them the opportunity to understand the plot better. The possibility of adding subtitles to the series was another important aspect that facilitated language learning.

Another study investigated the extent to which English as a Foreign Language (EFL) learners use Netflix for second language (L2) learning and the means by which they access the service [10]. The participants in the study were nine Japanese English as a Foreign Language (EFL) students. According to this study, Netflix enhanced learning effectiveness, increased L2 motivation, provided better access to L2 knowledge, and hindered convenience. It was also found that learners watched primarily through mobile devices rather than their personal computers, and viewed more L2 titles than L1 programming.

In another context, Türkmen's [11] study investigated whether Netflix programmes are supportive in a second language environment. The study was conducted with 150 students from Zonguldak Bulent Ecevit University Çaycuma Vocational School Applied English and Translation Program. The results of the study showed that Netflix can be beneficial for listening, grammar, vocabulary and also writing competencies. Through Netflix, students may also learn the casual language usages such as slangs, cultural differences, vocabulary and grammar.

Apart from facilitating teaching and learning in general language teaching environments, the use of Netflix can be beneficial to more specific language contexts.

2.2 Using Netflix in English for Specific Purposes Contexts

ESP is yet another field that has been influenced by the use of digital media. According to the Encyclopedic Dictionary of Applied Linguistics [12, p.108], ESP is "a broad and diverse field of English language teaching" that relates to "language programmes designed for groups or individuals who are learning with an identifiable purpose and clearly specified needs". The main characteristics of this field, apart from the complicated role of the ESP practitioner, are its focus on needs analysis, the emphasis of course designers on the use of authentic material and real-life exposure to the lexis and the specific genre of a specific field of studies. According to Gilmore [13, p.98], authenticity has been given numerous explanations, therefore one could claim that "it can be situated in either the text itself, in the participants, in the social or cultural situation and purposes of the communicative act, or some combination of these". Being a tool that can easily provide students with exposure to language used in authentic or authentic-like ESP contexts, Netflix can be regarded as appropriate in language for specific purposes courses. Nevertheless, research in the use of Netflix in ESP is much more limited than in general language environments.

The beneficial use of Netflix in language teaching for specific purposes cannot only be proved by the studies in which Netflix is actually utilised in the language teaching and learning process, but it can also be implied from previous studies investigating the use of movies in teaching and learning languages in general [14–16]. Some of the benefits that have been reported in the literature are the fact that movies facilitate the acquisition of vocabulary since ESP learners are exposed to the specific discourse and the specific terminology related to the particular discipline, when the movies relate to their field of studies. Movies can also lead to the enhancement of oral skills, improvement of writing and development of fluency in general. They can also increase student motivation, since in most of the studies learners appear to enjoy watching the movies, which most of the times they find interesting since they relate to their area of expertise. Finally, movies may potentially cater for the needs of any type of learner, e.g. visual or auditory learners, since they combine audio, video and written text through the use of subtitles. The only major challenge mentioned in the literature that was examined was the fact that some students may face difficulties in understanding the discourse presented in the movie [16]. Literature on using movies and generally visuals in language teaching is quite extensive. For ESP courses in particular, the benefits that have been reported are more than the challenges that may be encountered.

3 The Background of the Study

This study was conducted in the context of an English for Specific Academic Purposes course (ESAP) for students of the Department of Commerce, Finance and Shipping at the Cyprus University of Technology. The main objective of the course was to enable students to communicate competently at a B2 level of the Common European Framework of Reference (CEFR) for Languages on academic issues as well as on issues related to their future professional careers. Until March 2020, the course was delivered through a blended approach with a combination of face-to-face and online instruction through the use of Google Workspace for Education. The course was based on a social constructivist approach to learning [17], in other words, it was based on the belief that knowledge is constructed when past experiences interact with new ideas and experiences learners come in contact with, in other words their social surroundings. This kind of approach is in favour of collaboration and engagement in problem-based, authentic-like activities. In order to achieve the learning objectives, in the context of this course, students were exposed to authentic language use, e.g. academic articles or extracts from academic books related to their field of studies. They also went for educational visits to companies, and they were provided with opportunities to attend presentations delivered by academics or professionals, watch videos related to their discipline in English, etc.

However, the COVID-19 pandemic and the disruption of education brought about many changes in the educational system in Cyprus in March 2020; one of those changes was the transfer of instruction to an online mode. Fortunately, in the case of this particular course, the transfer was not problematic, since the instructor had already been using technology in her classes, and students were familiar with tools that would be used in online instruction. The course continued as before the pandemic, based on the same approaches and teaching methodologies. However, because of the lockdown, the instructor faced the problem of having restricted sources of authentic or authentic-like communication in the target language, despite the fact that students had access to the internet and other technology tools. The instructor felt that she needed to come up with ideas on more resources that she could use with her students as well as ways in which she could keep them motivated and expose them in environments in which ESP was being used.

Talking to her students and realising that being confined at home they spent much of their free time watching series and movies on Netflix, the instructor thought that it would be a good idea if students used that for their own benefit. The vast majority of students had access to Netflix, either by owning a personal account or by sharing an account with a roommate. Having examined all the qualities and affordances of Netflix in relation to language teaching and learning and seeing how helpful it could be in ESP contexts, the instructor decided to assign her students to watch movies that related to their field of study. More specifically, the students were asked to watch three movies throughout the semester. The movies were *Moneyball, The Pursuit of Happyness* and *The Big Short*. They were all based on real life, and they all related to topics that had been discussed in class; leadership, strategy, marketing, and financial scandals. The students were requested to watch the movies with English subtitles on, in the hope that this would help them understand the language more easily, allow them to learn new vocabulary and perhaps improve their spelling. After watching the movies, they were asked to write summaries of the plot, and work on other activities such as taking quizzes, taking part in discussions on the movie and writing down their reflections on the movie and the tasks they were engaged in.

4   Research Methodology

4.1   The Purpose and Scope of the Study

This study falls under the umbrella of Action Research, which is "a form of action inquiry that employs recognised research techniques to inform the action taken to improve practice" [18, p. 446]. Action research develops in cycles of continuous improvement starting with the problem identification, the development of an intervention, moving on with its implementation and observation and finally reflection. These cycles go on and on until the researcher is satisfied with the results. The problematic situation that the instructor tried to provide a solution to in this case was the limited resources that were available at the time for learners' exposure to authentic or authentic-like language input, while they were confined at home. The instructor was also concerned that students might feel demotivated, due to the stressful situation created because of the pandemic and the imposition of social distancing. This paper reports on the results of the first cycle of the study.

4.2 Research Questions

The research questions that guided the study were the following:

1. Will watching the three movies on Netflix provide opportunities for students to be exposed to language related to their field of studies, and thus help them in practicing their English language skills in the specific discipline?
2. Will the use of Netflix keep students motivated in the time of the pandemic?

4.3 Participants

The participants in the study were 42 first-year students of Commerce, Finance and Shipping at the Cyprus University of Technology; 23 were female and 19 male. They were all native speakers of Greek having successfully completed an English for Academic Purposes (EAP) course in the first semester of their studies.

4.4 Collection and Analysis of Data

The tools that were utilised for collection of data were students' reflections which were written and stored in Google Drive during the semester as part of students' e-portfolios, and an evaluation questionnaire which was administered electronically using Google Forms after the completion of the course. As far as students' reflections were concerned, these were dedicated to the evaluation of the experience with the movies on Netflix. A total of 110 files were received, one file for each of the three movies per student. Regarding the questionnaire, its purpose was to evaluate the whole course, therefore some of the questions related to other aspects of the course apart from the Netflix project. The questionnaire consisted of 14 six-point Likert-scale questions, where 0 stood for "not at all" and 5 stood for "very much". It also included four open-ended questions. A total of 32 responses were received.

As far as data analysis was concerned, qualitative data were analysed using NVivo 12 and thematic analysis was conducted, while quantitative data were analysed in Microsoft Office Excel, and descriptive statistics were used to present them.

4.5 Results and Discussion

This section will report on the results obtained from both the students' reflections and the online questionnaire. Starting with the results of the analysis of students' reflections,

Table 1 summarises the major thematic categories and subcategories that resulted from thematic analysis (64 themes in total). As it is shown in the table, there were a lot of references on how students were benefitted from this project as well as elements that students liked. On the contrary, the challenges that were noted were few. Of course, there were some elements that students did not enjoy; those were related mainly with the plot of the movies.

Table 1. The thematic categories that resulted from students' reflections

Thematic categories	Files	References
Challenges	3	3
How students benefitted	98	314
Business English improvement	14	14
Familirisation with social life at the time	3	3
Grammar and syntax improvement	3	3
Knowledge about the financial crisis	1	1
Listening practice	11	11
Messages conveyed	46	155
Professional skills development	32	43
Pronunciation improvement	16	16
Speaking improvement	3	3
Spelling improvement	6	6
Vocabulary improvement	53	55
Writing improvement	3	3
Students were not benefitted	6	6
Suggestions for improvement	13	14
Characters	1	1
More movies	3	3
Music	1	1
Plot	8	8
The plot	65	65
What students did not like	31	40
Scenes from the movie	6	6
The characters	8	8
The length	1	1
The messages	1	1
The plot	19	22
Unknown terms	2	2
What students liked	68	118
Emotions created	8	8
Professional strategies displayed	7	9
Scenes from the movie	12	12

(*continued*)

Table 1. (*continued*)

Thematic categories	Files	References
The characters	21	21
The messages	15	18
The plot	32	35
The production	11	13
The task	1	1

Students expressed the view that through the project a lot of positive and inspirational messages were conveyed, such as "do not give up", "work hard", "pursue your goals", "love your family", "believe in yourself", etc. Moreover, this was an opportunity for them to improve their vocabulary and develop professional skills which related to the raise of awareness of the professional environment, critical thinking, awareness of hiring processes, awareness of ethical issues, knowledge of economics, etc. Some students also mentioned development of pronunciation and grammar and the four language skills. Some of these positive findings are also present in previous studies in the literature [11, 14–16]. With regards to the challenges faced, students referred to difficulties in understanding the movie and the pronunciation of words, challenges reported in other research studies [16]. They also said that there were a lot of facts to recall and a few of them expressed the view that the workload of the semester was heavy.

As far as the questionnaire is concerned, the first question focused on how much students had enjoyed the whole project during the semester (Fig. 1). The majority of students appeared to have enjoyed the project, even though there were students who did not enjoy it very much, and the main reason was the fact that the movies were complicated and the discourse was difficult to understand and also the semester workload was too much and this placed extra stress on the students. This was a challenge that was also noted in the literature by Kucukyilmaz et al. [16]. The results of the question appear in Fig. 1.

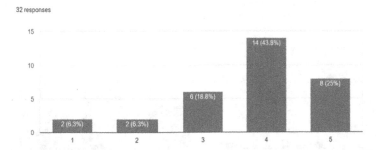

*0 = Not at all, 5= Very much

Fig. 1. How much students enjoyed the project

The words of one of the students, as taken from their reflections, briefly summon the results displayed in the graph:

"It was very enjoyable because first of all it was movies that I haven't seen them before so I saw them with more interest. Also, it was enjoyable because the topic of the movies concerned my field of study so from these movies I didn't only improve my English but I also learn many new things about my studies and my future profession."

The second question concentrated on the development of their English. The majority of the students responded that the project was helpful in the development of their English, while a small percentage of students responded that the project did not help much. These were advanced students who, as they explained, felt that the movies were a chance for them to be exposed to more language input, but were not actually responsible for improving their language performance (Fig. 2).

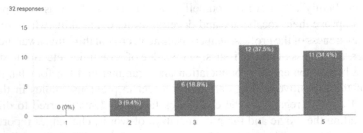

*0 = Not at all, 5= Very much

Fig. 2. How helpful the project was for the development of your English

Finally, Fig. 3 shows students' perceptions on how helpful the project was for their studies and professional careers. The majority of students regarded the project as helpful. This is in line with Gaglani and Haynes' [8] view on the value of digital media such as social media or Netflix in relation to the professional development of students of medicine. According to the researchers, digital media of this sort, which leverage data to make relevant recommendations to users about what to buy or watch, could serve well in connecting the curriculum with real life.

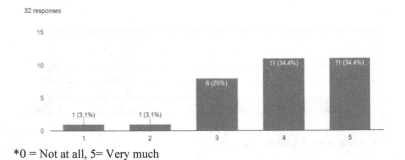

*0 = Not at all, 5= Very much

Fig. 3. How helpful the project was for the students' studies and professional careers

In general, in relation to the first research question, it can be claimed that Netflix created opportunities for students to experience language in authentic-like instances of communication pertaining to their field of studies. As aforementioned, students regarded their experience with the three movies as beneficial in their development of language, professional as well as other skills, despite the fact that certain challenges were faced in relation to the complicated plot of the movie or the difficult level of the language used. As far as the second research question is concerned, students appeared to enjoy the project with some of them being more excited than others. Nevertheless, a few students commented on the heavy workload of the curriculum.

The following comments of two of the students reflect the students' general view on the use of Netflix in the course:

"I enjoyed a lot this way of learning because it was more relaxed and chill way to learn things about our future sector of business."

"I got to see movies from a whole another perspective and also got to see movies I wouldn't choose to see on my own and I learned a lot of things for my future as a professional".

5 Conclusion

This paper reports on an action research study conducted at the Cyprus University of Technology during the COVID 19-pandemic in the context of an ESAP course for students of the Department of Commerce, Finance and Shipping. Even though this is a small-scale action research study, it may potentially carry implications for the integration of Netflix or similar digital media in similar ESP contexts. In this sense, it can prove useful to ESP course developers, practitioners, material designers, students or any other specialist in the field of language education.

References

1. Maryville University. What is digital media? All you need to know about this booming industry. https://online.maryville.edu/blog/what-is-digital-media/. Accessed 25 May 2022
2. The media lab. 7 key factors behind the success story of Netflix. https://www.themedialab.me/7-key-factors-behind-success-story-netflix/. Accessed25 May 2022
3. Martin, F., Betrus, A. K.: Digital media for learning: theories, processes, and solutions. In: Digital Media for Learning: Theories, Processes, and Solutions. Springer, Cham (2019). https://doi.org/10.1007/978-3-030-33120-7
4. Mayer, R.E.: The promise of multimedia learning: using the same instructional design methods across different media. Learn. Instr. **13**(2), 125–139 (2003). https://doi.org/10.1016/s0959-4752(02)00016-6
5. Kim, D., Gilman, D.A.: Effects of text, audio, and graphic aids in multimedia instruction for vocabulary learning. Educ. Technol. Soc. **11**(3), 114–126 (2008)
6. Li, L.: Integrating Technology in ESP: Pedagogical Principles and Practice. In: Muñoz-Luna, R., Taillefer, L. (eds.) Integrating Information and Communication Technologies in English for Specific Purposes. English Language Education, vol. 10, pp. 7–25. Springer, Cham (2018). https://doi.org/10.1007/978-3-319-68926-5_2
7. Netflix. Netflix. https://www.netflix.com/cy/. .Accessed 25 May 2022

8. Gaglani, S.M., Haynes, M.R.: What can medical education learn from Facebook and Netflix? Ann. Intern. Med. **160**(9), 640–641 (2014). https://doi.org/10.7326/M13-2286
9. Alm, A.: Language learning with Netflix: from extensive to intra-formal learning. EuroCALL Rev. **29**(1), 81–92 (2021). https://doi.org/10.4995/eurocall.2021.14276
10. Dizon, G.: Netflix and L2 learning: a case study. EuroCALL Rev. **26**(2), 30 (2018). https://doi.org/10.4995/eurocall.2018.9080
11. Türkmen, B.: Utilising digital media as a second language (L2) support: a case study on Netflix with translation applications. Interdiscip. Descr. Complex Syst. **18**(4), 459–470 (2020). https://doi.org/10.7906/indecs.18.4.6
12. Johnson, K., Johnson, H.: English for specific purposes (ESP). In: Encyclopedic Dictionary of Applied Linguistsics, pp. 105–110. Blackwell Publishers Ltd. (1998)
13. Gilmore, A.: Authentic materials and authenticity in foreign language learning. Lang. Teach. **40**(2), 97–118 (2007). https://doi.org/10.1017/S0261444807004144
14. Csomay, E., Petrović, M.: "Yes, your honor!": a corpus-based study of technical vocabulary in discipline-related movies and TV shows. System **40**(2), 305–315 (2012). https://doi.org/10.1016/j.system.2012.05.004
15. Ergenekon, B.: Using films for writing reaction-response essay: a class-room action research on Turkish ESP learners. Int. J. Lang. Lit. Linguist. **2**(2), 73–78 (2016). https://doi.org/10.18178/ijlll.2016.2.2.70
16. Kucukyilmaz, Y., Lokmacioglu, S., Balidede, F.: Military movies by hollywood: assisting ELT in ESP domain. Procedia. Soc. Behav. Sci. **199**, 81–84 (2015). https://doi.org/10.1016/j.sbspro.2015.07.490
17. Detel, W.: Social constructivism. In: International Encyclopedia of the Social & Behavioral Sciences, pp. 14264–14268. (2001). https://doi.org/10.1093/0199251614.003.0009
18. Tripp, D.: Action research: a methodological introduction. Educ. Pesqui. **31**(3), 443–466 (2005). https://doi.org/10.1049/ip-sen:20020540

Technology-Enhanced Instruction into Extensive L2 Academic Reading for Specific Purposes Within the ESP/ESAP Course for Postgraduate Language Pedagogy Students

Marina Kogan[1]($\boxtimes$) (ID), Maria Kopylovskaya[2] (ID), Anna Gavrilova[1] (ID),
and Elena Vdovina[1] (ID)

[1] St. Petersburg Polytechnic University, Polytechnicheskaya 29, 195251 St. Petersburg, Russia
kogan_ms@spbstu.ru
[2] Saint Petersburg State University, Universitetskaya Emb. 7/9, 199034 St. Petersburg, Russia

Abstract. Teaching and learning to read domain specific texts and research articles within the course of academic English for specific/academic purposes (ESAP) is often underestimated and outsourced to students' independent study with minimal instructors' intervention. Students often demonstrate inability to gain knowledge about basic conventions established in the international academic communities such as research article (RA) structure, style, rules of citation and referencing etc. while reading RAs. The study undertaken by researchers of Saint Petersburg State University (SPbSU) and Peter the Great Saint Petersburg Polytechnic University (SPbPU) showed that a specially designed extensive academic reading module (EARM) can help solve this problem. In the first part, the paper describes the underlying rationale for the development of the EARM, its syllabus, and its experimental approbation in the spring term of 2021–22 academic year with two academic groups of postgraduate language pedagogy students taking their master program at SPbSU and SPbPU. The second part of the paper focuses on the analysis of the data collected, namely two questionnaires completed by the experiment participants, their reports about extensive reading of RAs selected, and analysis of some structural and linguistic features of 36 RAs selected by the students which was conducted by the researchers. The role of technology in teaching the EARM is stressed. The positive attitude of students to the EARM and improvement of some their micro academic skills, e.g. pre-reading self-questioning, during the half-term experiment allow the authors to recommend including teaching academic reading module in ESAP course for postgraduate students on a regular basis. Further research steps are outlined.

Keywords: ESAP course · Extensive academic reading module · EARM · Structure of research articles · Title of research articles · Reference lists · Self-questioning · Padlet · VersaText

1 Introduction

Among all English teaching areas English for specific purposes is most tightly linked to the world of economics and business due to its targeting the language needed in the

© Springer Nature Switzerland AG 2022
G. Meiselwitz et al. (Eds.): HCII 2022, LNCS 13517, pp. 331–346, 2022.
https://doi.org/10.1007/978-3-031-22131-6_26

occupational or professional spheres. Rapid changes provoked predominantly by digital transformation of all spheres of people's life highlight the need for change in educational sphere [1, 2], which is recognized by a number of international and national goals-setting and standardizing documents (e.g., UNESCO Education 2030 Framework for Action, A New Skills Agenda for Europe, and Russian professional standards) [3, 4].

The dominant role of technologies in these changes determines the need for more complex skills in the more complex world. To be in line with these global changes ESP /ESAP whole course and /or its modules' design should be updated on a regular basis. On the other hand there is a clear trend in the Russian system of HE towards increase in the amount of independent master students studies in University electronic environment [5, 6] which has become especially important during the COVID- 19 pandemics [7].

Extensive reading (traditionally referred to as 'home reading' in the Russian specialist literature) usually falls into the category of students' independent work during the term while ESP instructors just control the results of this work. However, instruction on how to read academically specific texts and research articles within the course of English for specific academic purposes (ESAP) is often underestimated. According to Chmelíková, when studying a foreign language at university, the importance of developing skills in reading special texts is massively underestimated and delegated to students for 'outsourcing' [8]. Her study conducted in a number of universities in Slovakia shows that students of technical specialties read little, often superficially, and have too low level of linguistic knowledge to be able to understand domain-specific foreign language texts. In addition to background knowledge of the topic and linguistic knowledge of predicting, making connections, visualizing, inferring, questioning, and summarizing, the author suggested a number of prerequisites of more successful reading, such as knowledge of different reading models and strategies [8:65–66].

Leading Russian researcher in the sphere of academic writing Korotkina believes that any ESP course must be focusing on developing key academic skills: academic reading and writing that are more relevant for students studying in L1 linguistic environment than listening and speaking skills. It goes without saying that without processing enormous foreign language specialist literature any studies in a contemporary university are not viable. Processing authentic professionally oriented texts allows solving numerous problems predetermined by necessary writing skills as the one is conducive to interpreting research papers structure, style, rules of citation and referencing i.e. awareness of the basic conventions established in the international academic communities [9].

Doing a master degree nowadays presupposes an active involvement of the students into academic activities focusing on writing and publicizing the academic articles, written mostly in English and suggesting the opportunity to be published in reputable scholarly journals (according to leading Russian Universities requirements.). This means that the race *Publish or Perish* [10] begins at the stage of pre-service training of future professionals. This new reality highlights the importance of viewing reading research papers as a basis for development of writing research articles skills.

The connection between reading and writing is not so self-evident to language teachers as it might appear after reading and analyzing specialist literature. [e.g., 11 – 15]. For example, Hirvela admits that only after about ten years of teaching writing he discovered that 'some of the writing difficulties … were in fact reading difficulties' [15:10].

In our previous research we also investigated them separately: focusing on the analysis of problems related to formation of writing skills in undergraduate engineering students in the English class [16] and on fostering reading comprehension in English language learners with help of Internet resources during students' independent work [17].

The underestimated was the knowing of conventions of writing that helps read more efficiently understanding how to organize the search, 'what to look for and where to find it' [15:12]. Hirvela concludes that 'it makes more sense to include discussion of reading into writing class than to treat two skills separately' [15:12].

Meanwhile academic reading professionally-oriented authentic academic texts is a multifaceted complicated problem even for those who display C1 language skills and plan to work as the English language teachers in future. This is explained by a number of specific features of a research paper in English as a particular genre.

There is a number of differences between the international and Russian rhetorical and publishing conventions in social sciences and humanities, implying different approaches to formulating headlines [18], writing abstracts, structuring and organizing of an academic article, in-text references, bibliography items formatting etc., identified by the leading Russian researcher in the field Korotkina [19]. By the same token, Hyland emphasizes that a well-known Swalsian IMRD framework for the research article structure and CARS (Creating A Research Space) moves for the Introduction section are typical of RAs in hard fields with 'big journals, big names and big libraries within large discourse communities'. However, the investigation show that the authors of the articles from a number of other countries, e.g., Poland, Latin America, Malasia, Sweden, Russia, newly-independent states do not articulate research gap explicitly [20:317].

In the same article Hyland stipulates the principal difference between a textbook and a academic article. Textbooks are seen as repositories of 'codified knowledge', they serve as sources for the proven truths needed for students' basic training while 'advanced scholarship extends the theoretical envelope, [...] in journal articles' [20:.308–309]. Chapters in textbooks do not contain such parts as 'limitations" typical of any serious research papers, much less significance is ascribed to expressions of hedging and boosting, and other rhetorical devices used in research articles. Thus, reading textbooks does not lead to easy reading of RAs, which, among other things, requires developed critical thinking skills rather than 'blind trust' in textbooks students acquire through years [21].

Reading an academic article presupposes a well-prepared reader, familiar with prior texts and research in the field, as the authors often formulate their arguments in a highly standardized code [22], which might be quite challenging to most of novice researchers. By the same token, the authors might use a particular set of favored terms, sentence structures and logical syntax which is not easy for an outsider to comprehend and imitate [23:146].

The search of academic domain-specific articles in field of one's research interest published in reputable academic journals might be rather challenging for a novice researcher and require certain skills that they might lack even when the student continues the research started within the bachelor program though it is often the case that entering master studies program students initiate a completely new research on a newly-articulated theme.

Given all above-mentioned aspects we designed detailed instructions for an extensive academic reading module (EARM) aiming to improve skills of reading RAs. The EARM has been developed within the framework of RF Ministry of Education Regulations on the organization of students' self study work in country's universities [24]. The Document prescribes the stakeholders to allocate up to 25% total study load for independent work including supervised self-study work for all disciplines of the curriculum allowing University departments to organize and structure it according to the specificity of the discipline and students' preferences and needs. The Extensive Academic English module aims to shape and make more focused students' independent work with research articles to help them acquire and retain the RA's most salient features thus contributing to the progress in the ESAP course on the whole. The tasks of the module cover all problematic areas, i.e. the challenges of extensive academic reading of domain-specific periodicals while instructions to them intend to prepare students to overcome the problems and ease the process of self-study work. The major goals of the EARM are:

- To familiarize students with multiple problems they might face while selecting and reading research articles (RAs) relevant to their research interests;
- To teach them to extract maximum useful information from the RA meta-data;
- To draw their attention to a typical RA structure;
- To encourage them to stick to the stylistic language features(vocabulary chosen, syntactic structures, punctuation, etc.) using relevant digital tools (e.g., VersaText);
- To instigate cooperation and information exchange during the independent work using relevant digital tools (e.g., Padlet).

The main **Research questions** we are seeking to answer introducing this module to students are as follows:

- Have learners become more confident in searching for domain-specific research papers?
- Have learners become more effective readers of the research papers of their occupational/research interests?
- Which aspects of the EAR module have they found the most useful?

2   Description of the EAR Module

The Module was developed as a part of compulsory English for Specific and Academic Purposes course at Department of Foreign Languages and Linguodidactics Philology Faculty St. Petersburg State University and as a part of Academic writing course at department of Linguodidactics and Translation Studies Peter the Great St. Petersburg Polytechnic University. Students of both Departments are going to be foreign language teachers.The students have already completed their BA and have received training in teaching a foreign language at this level.

English for Specific Academic Purposes is central in the curriculum and embraces three terms out of four of complete Master program. It is subdivided into specific and academic purposes with two 90-min sessions a week, one of them focusing on academic writing. The course is to focus on ELT terminology studied within the integrated approach, which helps students use the terminology in professionally-oriented discourse. All in all, the materials are subdivided into six major themes: Module 1. Methods and Approaches, Module 2. Curriculum development and Syllabus Design, (1-st term). Module 3. Learning Language and Skills, Module 4. Learning Exercises and Activities (2-nd term), Module 5. Classroom Management, Module 6. Testing and Assessment (3-d term). The other 90 min sessions are devoted to academic writing focusing on grammar revision based on Advanced Learners' Grammar [25], writing academic English based on Writing Academic English textbook [26] with special focus on describing visuals.

During the course students are inclined to read the academic articles relevant to their research. Besides, twice a term students have a so- called "Home reading Class" as a part of their mid-term and final-term assessment. During the home reading classes the students present chapters from monographs (the first term), research articles on the studied theme (second and third terms) doing extensive reading of academic literature mainly independently outside the classroom. Noticing difficulties students face presenting the results of home reading in class stimulated us to develop an Extensive Academic Reading Module (EARM) for increasing efficiency of their independent work.

The EARM included three 45 min classroom sessions in addition to the mid-term class on home reading mentioned above (Table 1).

Table 1. The EARM syllabus

Class No./Term week	Class format	Topic	Assignment
1/1	Presentation. Completing Questionnaire 1	Meta-data of research papers. Basic principles of searching papers in e-databases	Search for a RA relevant to the field of research interests. Studying its meta-data. Sharing the lists of journals from Bibliography lists via Padlet
2/2	Presentation. Discussion based on students' selected article	IMRD structure of the RA	Reading the article, compiling a Glossary and critical summary for the 1-st article

(continued)

Table 1. (*continued*)

Class No./Term week	Class format	Topic	Assignment
3/4	Presentation Workshop	Using *VersaText*tools for analysis of language peculiarities of RA	Searching for another two RAs relevant to the research interests; formulating questions to the RA based on meta-data, sharing questions with the instructors; extensive reading and analysis according to the Plan. Preparing a Report on the Module
4/8	Discussion. Submitting Reports on the Module	Mid-term assessment	Completing Questionnaire 2. Preparing a research paper in English during the second half of the term

3 Procedure

3.1 Participants

The EARM was tested during the spring term (2-nd term of Master studies) of 2021/2022 academic year with two master groups (18 students in total) majoring in foreign language pedagogy at Saint Petersburg State University (8 female students, 1 male student) and at Peter the Great Saint Petersburg Polytechnic University (9 female students) simultaneously.

3.2 Data Collection

During the experiment three types of data were collected. They are the following.

The Two Questionnaires. They were made up in Russian in electronic format using Google Forms.

The First Questionnaire. It was completed at the beginning of the first class to establish how much prior knowledge students have on effective reading strategies; meta-data of the research articles (RAs); approaches they use searching for research articles relevant to subject of their Master thesis. All 18 participants in both groups completed it.

It consisted of 8 closed questions of a multiple-choice format with a single (5 questions) or several possible answers (3 questions) and 2 open-ended questions. The multiple-choice questions with a single answer dealt with meta-data of RA and here the students were asked whether they notice which institution(s) the authors are affiliated with, in which journal the RA was published.

The multiple-choice questions which assumed several answers concerned the sources of information about the article, memorization and comprehension techniques used by the students and techniques that help students overcome the difficulties they face reading original RAs. The items for reading memorization and comprehension techniques were adapted from questionnaires developed by other researchers in the field [27, 28].

The Second Questionnaire. It was filled out by the experiment participants after the 4-th Module session to elicit their reactions to the Module, its scope and content, as well as to its procedures. Only 16 students responded this time.

The questionnaire contained 8 questions. 5 out of them targeted the optimization of the academic search (finding the proper articles) and taking into account of the RA meta-data. The types of the questions included multiple choice format with a single (one question) or several possible answers (one question) and three open-ended questions with a numeric answer, in which the respondents were to indicate к how many new for them academic journals in line with their research they have found thanks to the Reference lists of the RAs they read, how many names of the researchers conducting their investigations in the same field they found and, and how many new academic journals they got to know thanks to the posts made by their group mates on the Padlet. Two questions were formulated with 5-point Likert scale. Open-ended question asked if the respondents found answers to these questions while reading their RA and if they undertook any steps to find answers to questions which remained unanswered by the author(s).

The Student's Reports. The participants had to submit reports on extensive reading of two RAs relevant to their research interests they found after the second-class session of the Module. The reports were carefully studied by the researchers to evaluate how students progressed in independent extensive reading of scientific papers. Reports were written according to a prescribed Plan developed by the researchers. It included the following rubrics:

- Analysis of the RA title;
- Info about the authors;
- Analysis of references;
- The list of journals they shared with their groupmates using Padlet;
- Analysis of vocabulary and grammar structures of Introduction section of the RAs using VersaText tool [29];
- Glossary of 30 preferably multi-unit vocabulary items with translation into Russian and explanations/definitions if necessary;
- Analysis of the structure of the RA in relation to the standard Swalsian IMRD structure;
- A critical review of the RAs.

The Analysis of Some Linguistic and Discourse Features of RAs. It was conducted by the researchers to verify conclusions about the structure of RAs in the field of Applied Linguistics.

4 Results and Discussion

4.1 Questionnaires 1 and 2

The analysis of students' replies to the question of the Questionnaire 1 concerning memorization and comprehension techniques they use demonstrated the most popular strategies were: making notes in the text, rereading of the unclear parts of the text, taking notes of the most outstanding ideas of the source.

At the same time only 11% chose the option "formulate the questions, answers to which can be given in the article". The analysis of the literature confirms that self-questioning techniques are most efficient for assisting better understanding of the text of RA [30]. However, it is not clear at which stage of reading (before, during, and after reading text) self-questioning is most beneficial. Under the conditions when the most important part of the work of reading the RAs is the students' independent work, formulating questions before full-fledged reading based on the title analysis and the analysis of the Abstract seems to be the most efficient as it allows teachers to coordinate students' reading in the distant mode.

Students had to submit their questions to their teachers together with the article for obtaining approval of the article from the teacher. As they were not sure whether or not the teacher approves of their choice of the RA they had hardly read the whole text before asking the questions. So, we can expect that the questions had been formulated before students read the RAs carefully. Thus, the self-formulated questions could be an additional stimulus to more focused reading of the RA seeking answers. Most of the respondents found answers to all questions they had asked. Only three students wrote that they did not find answer to one of the questions asked. To find the answers they read the articles in the similar academic fields and conducted a search on the Internet. The analysis of the pool of the students' questions let the researchers conclude, that they were mostly of factual type (e.g. *How long did the experiment last? Which software (apps) was used in the experiment?*), and the presence of the answer to them was well expected. This revealed that a micro-skill of formulating inferential questions should be trained on purpose.

The finalizing survey (Questionnaire 2) displayed 93,8% of respondents chose the option "completely agree" (75%) and "agree" (18,8%) with the statement "Formulating questions on the content of the article BEFORE reading it increases the efficiency if the academic reading". The same number of participants agreed with the statement that "EARM within the ESAP framework was useful" (62% choose "completely agree" option and 31,3% - the "agree" one).

Answers to the question about the ways of searching the research articles relevant to their own research interests in the Questionnaire 1 allowed us to conclude that the following ways are the most popular: search for the articles on the Internet (100%), following the recommendations of their scientific advisors (88.9%), and using Google Scholar (72.2%). Much less often they resort to the search in the specialized bibliographic database (Scopus, Web of Science) (16.7%), or address the web-sites of the relevant journals (22.2%) and use the references of the RA they have already read (33.3%).

The use of internationally-recognized bibliographic databases for the search of academic reading for the novice researchers is connected with access problems. Although major universities in Russia have the subscription to these databases they can be accessed only from the university campus. That is why we decided to make students pay more attention to Bibliography/Reference lists of RAs and the web-sites of the relevant journals within the EARM. Students were to analyze reference lists in RAs they had chosen. In the Report they were to:

- Indicate the number of the sources that the articles of their choice contained;
- Check up whether the reference list included the earlier works of the author/s of the RA, and
- Find out whether there were authors whose works they had read earlier;
- Select 3–5 journals publishing articles on the topics close to their academic interest and to share the list of these journals and find and present information about them (e.g. open acronyms of the name of the journal, if the article cited the contracted name (Applied Linguistic for Appl. Linguist, for example), URL of the journal's web-site, its impact-factor in Scopus. Students were also to visit the posts of their groupmates with brief information about journals on the Padlet app specially created for EARM for each group of students.

4.2 Students' Reports Analysis

We should admit that in some Reports (out of 18 submitted by the participants of the experiment) the table with the information about journals contained factual mistakes: the students put into it not only the journals, but also the conference proceedings, monographs and on some occasions even unpublished Master theses. This made it obvious that some students do not take into account the differences in the bibliography of different types that, besides, might be different in different journals. Regardless the disciplines that should have taught bibliography-related skills, this issue must be embraced by the EARM explicitly.

The replies to Questionnaire 2 on the ways of finding relevant RA within the EARM, which contained the same option that Questionnaire 1, clearly showed that the number of students who made use of reference lists from the first article and advice of their groupmates that those posted on the Padlet for finding the second and the third articles significantly increased: 68,8% of the learners addressed the professional journal web-sites and 56.3% used the reference list for the first article.

Totally, in their Reports students described 36 articles from 34 journals and 2 international conference materials. All the articles were open-access ones or were available through the University subscription. 11 journals and 2 conference materials were not registered in Scopus.

While reading the RA students were supposed to take note of the RA macro-structure, pointing out in their Reports subheadings of all parts of the RA structure (actual section heading) and compare it with the Swalsian IMRD structure. The level of variability among the rubrics appeared to be rather high. In all the articles except two there were found such rubrics as Introduction and References; in 3 articles Introduction sections contained from 2 to 6 subdivisions. In many RAs "the history of the issue" was presented in detail in the parts following the Introduction. It was presented under such headings as

Theoretical background or *Literature review*. The most detailed description in the articles based on experiments was the one of *Methods* which, as a rule, included 5–6 smaller parts. This is well in line with Swales and other researchers in the filed [31, 32], who maintained that in hard science the researchers tend to strictly comply with the prescribed standard methodology of conducting experiment and, thus, describe their experiments rather briefly, while in humanities the procedures of nearly every investigation has unique features and, thus, is described in all possible details, sometimes taking about 2 pages in a journal. The theoretically-focused articles may not possess the section *Research Methodology* at all.

The researchers have analyzed the structures of the articles that had been collected by the students participating in the EARM independently. The Results can be seen in the Table 2 presenting the headings found in the 36 articles more than once.

Table 2. Sections and Subsections distinguished by students in their RAs

Sections and Subsections	No. in RAs	Percentage in RAs
Introduction	34	94.4%
Conclusion	34	94.4%
Discussion	25	66.6%
Methodology	21	55.5%
Results	16	44.4%
Literature review	5	13.8%
Findings	4	8.3%
Research questions	4	8.3%
Background	2	5.5%

One may find that the results of our analysis of pedagogical RA's structure correlate with Anthony & Bowen's conclusions about the structure of mathematics papers which varies considerably from article to article following a less rigid format described in academic writing textbooks [33]. Interestingly, we noted that two RAs of our sample do not have heading Introduction, only one follows a typical IMRD pattern, and many papers break or drastically change this pattern. For example, RA *Contrasting Orthographically Similar Words Facilitates Adult Second Language Vocabulary Learning* [34] includes 4 headings of the 1-st level (Introduction – Experiment 1 – Experiment 2 – General discussion – Conclusion), 13 subheadings of level 2 (numbered e.g. 1.1., 2.3, etc.), and 23 subheadings of level 3 (numbered e.g., 1.1.1., 3.2.1, etc.).

This observation means the following: 1) taking into account the variety in structure of real research papers in Applied Linguistics field it can be recommended to draw students' attention to this fact, encourage them to contrast an IMRD pattern with a structure of RAs they read independently in the ESAP course and illustrate the variety of RAs' structures with particular examples during class discussion. 2) When teaching academic writing students must be trained to write short articles for the professionally-oriented conferences which seem to have a structure closest to IMRD pattern.

Formulating a title of the paper is another important thing. Although all style guides and journal requirements give recommendations how to formulate titles of RAs, many of them seem vague or contradictory for novice writers as Hyland and Zou noticed giving examples of such recommendations in their latest paper [35]. In their research they complied a corpus of 5070 RA titles from six domains, which exceeded all previous studies of titles. They discovered that RA titles in Applied Linguistics (App. Ling.) and Education (Educ.) tend to be quite long: over 12.5 words (over 75% of RA from these domains), most of them are indicative (not interrogative), compound, i.e. include two or more parts separated by punctuation, usually a colon (63.6% in App.Ling. and 70.7% in Educ.) thus allowing authors to extend the topic usually expressed with a noun group. Most of them are descriptive, that is, highlight only the subject of the article without details about the method used or results obtained though the detailed titles accounted for 28.2% in App. Ling. and 42.5% in Educ. We decided to check if RAs selected by the experiment participants can be described in these terms. Table 3 presents the results of our analysis.

Table 3. The features of RA titles

Pattern	No/%
Titles longer than 12 words	9/24
Titles with colon sign	10/27
Descriptive titles	24/67
Detailed titles	12/33

The results obtained show that 67% titles are of descriptive type and 33% are detailed ones, which is in a good agreement with Hyland and Zou findings. Thus, the task of analysing the form and structure of RA title should be included in the EARM. To get more experience students should be recommended to analyse not only the titles of RAs they have found but also those found by their classmates and shared via services such as Padlet.

Compiling a Glossary and Mastering VersaText. Compiling a Glossary is an important skill focusing key lexis while reading. It is also important in methodology as it allows teachers to check how attentive the student was in the reading. The EARM was to make students expand their keyword lists which are inalienable part of most of the RAs (33 out of 36 RA in our sample contained them). While the teachers were to invite students' attention to the fact that noun phrase prevail in the keyword lists the students' glossaries could include verb patterns as well on the condition that they were frequently met or important for the RA.

As a part of experiential learning they were to select collocations on the basis of frequency with the help of the VersaText tool. The said resource works with a single text as a corpus. After inserting the text in text format into a special frame the user gets the word cloud of most frequently met words of different colours that can be "formatted ' alongside with the following parameters the amount of frequently used words (from 10 to 100 with a step of 10), instead of the words one can form a cloud of lemmas, tags, indexes of parts of the speech (the 1-st group), including or excluding content words and function words (2-nd group). Unlike the first group of parameters where only one value is selected within the second group one can choose any combination. Clicking the word one can see it either in the view mode of Concordance where the target word is in the middle of a concordance line and can be sorted out by the left or right context, or in the context of a complete sentence or with the keyword missing (as a draft for a test).

The students were to get acquainted with the VersaTex studying the Introductions to the chosen RAs and to enjoy the usability of Concordance mode for the most frequently met nouns in the word cloud which was meant to help them find proper collocations. The benefits of applying this resource in compiling Glossaries was appreciated by the most of the students as they helped them in finding such combinations as *ESP courses, ESP teaching and learning, ESP program, ESP landscape, Objectives set, Core objectives, Learning objectives, Student's general objectives, EMI teaching faculty, EMI program, EMI experience, EMI environments, EMI implementation* etc. The majority of participants plan to use it in their further research and teaching activities.

Summary Writing. A number of researchers consider summary writing as an efficient tool for comprehension check-up [24]. The skills for writing summaries are being developed along with studying English within any course and ESAP also does it. Thus, we assumed that the 1-st year master students majoring in language pedagogy possess the skills of text paraphrasing, summarizing and evaluating. Students were to stick to the following structure of the summary. Their summaries were to start with a paraphrased abstract of a RA, in the second paragraph students supplemented it with details that they found most interesting, important, relevant, or striking during extensive reading of the RA (in particular, we asked them to pay special attention to the description of the experimental procedure if they chose to read an experimental RA). In the last paragraph students had to evaluate the RA in terms of relevance to the research interests, familiarity with the underlying theory or experimental procedure, comprehensibility, ability to repeat the experiment in their settings/with their students etc. The number of words in the summary equaled 500 words.

The summaries' scrutiny revealed that students were not very much successful in paraphrasing of the original abstracts as most of them opted to abridge the abstract, not trying to change syntactic structures of the sentences or find proper synonyms. Not all of them indulged in critical thinking as the last part presupposed that they would express their own opinion. In spite of the stipulated number of words assigned the length of the summaries varied from 224 to 732 words with the average length being 477.1 (*SD* 86.6).

5 Conclusions and Further Work

The above-described research indicated the expediency of including a module focusing on the coordination of the students doing their Master degree on extensive reading of research papers within the framework of an ESAP course.

The approbation displayed that students changed their learning behaviour towards RA meta-data, became more proficient in the use of reliable and verified sources in the search of the academic literature for their reading to write a qualification paper. They started more intensively use the academic journal's web-sites of journals in which their RA were published or RA from the reference lists to the RA of their choice. The exchange of information about relevant journals through modern Internet-services of sharing and cooperation, such as Padlet, for example, is beneficial for the purpose.

The experiment proved that formulating questions before reading based on the title and abstract analysis increases the efficiency of reading and motivates students to continue the search of the needed answers, if they are not present in the RA. It is possible to develop the habit and improve the quality of the questions before reading the RA if to insist on students' sending their questions together with the article to their instructors to get them approved. The analysis of the structure and the length of the title is important as a skill needed for formulating efficient titles of their own academic articles in future.

Glossaries and critical reviews are effective tools for checking reading comprehension. Such tool as VersaText Online allows users to find easily collocations of most frequently used nouns to be included in the RA Glossaries. Scrutinizing critical reviews revealed, that the skills of paraphrasing and the text analysis require further development within the ESAP course. The problem should be regarded as the one ascribed to Academic Writing class bearing in mind that unintended plagiarism among the novice authors writing in English is the reflection of their fear to make a mistake when attempting formulating an important statement put in their own words due to the lack of linguistic or subject competence. This explains why it is so important to introduce them to the best practices of the use of the reference lists when writing their own RA or other kinds of academic papers [36, 37].

The spotted within the experimental learning the diversity of structures among the RAs selected by the students for extensive reading allows teachers to propose specific research tasks focusing on the comparing and contrasting to well-known IMRD structure and invite students to writing short papers for the academic conferences where the structure would be the closest to the IMRD pattern.

The approbation of the EARM in the second term of studying the ESAP course showed that it is advisable to include this module into every term of an ESAP course. However, the priority for EARM in the 3-rd concluding term should be given to text comprehension strategies when reading different, sometimes conflicting RAs in the field of the academic interest (their Master theses) with the purpose of the following synthesis describing "the research field rather than independent sources" as Boulton once put it. The study although limited by a relatively small sample of participants clearly demonstrated the necessity of including teaching academic reading depending on the university provisions at least through EARM that can be a good addition to any postgraduate studies.

Acknowledgments. The research is partially funded by the Ministry of Science and Higher Education of the Russian Federation under the strategic academic leadership program 'Priority 2030' (Agreement 075-15-2021-1333 dated 30.09.2021).

References

1. Kopylovskaya, M.Y., Bajeva, G.A.: Hard-Core vs soft-core ESP in the light of education foresight. J. Teach. Eng. Spec. Acad. Purp. **5**(3), 589–602 (2017). https://doi.org/10.22190/JTESAP1703589K
2. Kopylovskaya, M.Y.: Tuning-in: Re-thinking an ESP methodology course in the digital age. In: Lazarević, N., Paunović,T., Marković, L. (eds.) Teaching Languages and Cultures: Developing Competencies, Re-thinking Practices, pp. 213–237 Cambridge Scholars, Newcastle upon Tyne (2018). http://www.cambridgescholars.com/teaching-languages-and-cultures
3. UNESCO Education 2030 Framework for Action. http://uis.unesco.org/sites/default/files/documents/education-2030-incheon-framework-for-action-implementation-of-sdg4-2016-en_2.pdf. Accessed 20 May 2022
4. A New Skills Agenda for Europe: Working together to strengthen human capital, employability and competitiveness (SWD 195. Communication From the Commission to the European Parliament, the Council, the European Economic and Social Committee and the Committee of the Regions (2016). https://eur-lex.europa.eu/legal-content/EN/TXT/?uri=CELEX%3A5 2016DC0381. Accessed 20 May 2022
5. Lvova, O.V., Kopylovskaya, M.Y., Shkapenko, T.M.: E-learning in Russian higher education: challenges and responses. In: Kryachkov, D.A., Yastrebova, E.B., Kravtsova, O.A. (eds.) The Magic of Innovation. New Techniques and Technologies in Teaching Foreign Languages. pp. 3–26. Cambridge Scholars, Newcastle upon Tyne (2015). http://www.cambridgescholars.com/the-magic-of-innovation
6. Kopylovskaya, M.Y., Linnik, Y.V., Sergaeva, Y.V.: Designing an online course for the 21st century learners of English.In: Kopylovskaya, M.Y., Kogan M.S. (eds.) Tradicionnoe i Novoe v Lingvistike i Lingvodidaktike: Mezhkul'turnaja Kommunikacija I Cifrovaja Kul'tura [The Traditional and new in linguistics and lingvodidactics] SPbSU Publishing House, Saint Petersburg (2019) (In Russian)
7. Windstein, E., Kogan, M.: Rapid response to the needs of ESL students of a technical university in the time of emergency Covid-19 transfer to online classes: ITMO university case study. In: Zaphiris, P., Ioannou, A. (eds.) Learning and Collaboration Technologies: New Challenges and Learning Experiences. Lecture Notes in Computer Science, vol. 12784, pp. 547–567. Springer, Cham (2021). https://doi.org/10.1007/978-3-030-77889-7_38
8. Chmelíková, G.: Possibilities of improving reading of subject-specific texts. J. Teach. Eng. Spec. Acad. Purp. **9**(1), 61–70 (2021). https://doi.org/10.22190/JTESAP2101061C
9. Korotkina, I.B.: Transdisciplinarnyj podhod k razrabotke kursa po akademicheskomu chteniju profil'nyh tekstov (na primere publichnoj politiki) [Transdisciplinary approach to the development of a course on academic reading of specialized texts on the example of public policy)]. In: Bagramova, N.V., Smirnova, N.V., Schemeleva, I.Yu. (eds.) Obuchenie chteniju na Inostrannom Jazyke v Sovremennom Universitete : Teorija i Praktika [Teaching reading in a foreign language at a modern university: theory and practice], pp. 123–142. Zlatoust, Saint Petersburg (2016) (in Russian)
10. Colpaert, J.: The "Publish and Perish" syndrome. Comput. Assist. Lang. Learn. **25**(5), 383–391 (2012). https://doi.org/10.1080/09588221.2012.735101
11. Tierney R.J., Pearson D.P.: Toward a composing model of reading. Language Arts. **60** (5), 568–580 (1983) Reading and Writing URL: http://www.jstor.org/stable/41961506
12. Stotsky, S.: Research on reading/writing relationships: a synthesis and suggested directions. Language Arts **60**, 627–642 (1983)
13. Tierney, R., Shanahan, T.: Research on the reading–writing relationship: Interactions, transactions, and outcomes. In: Barr, R., Kamil, M., Mosenthal, P., Pearson, D. (eds.) Handbook of reading research, vol. II, pp. 246–280. Lawrence Erlbaum, Mahwah, NJ (1991)

14. Parodi, G.: Reading–writing connections: Discourse-oriented research. Read. Writ. Interdiscip. J. **20**, 225–250 (2007). https://doi.org/10.1007/s11145-006-9029-7
15. Hirvela, A.: Connecting Reading and Writing in Second Language Writing Instruction, 2nd edn. University of Michigan Press, Ann Arbor, MI (2016)
16. Kogan, M.S., Gavrilova, A.V.: Continuity in formation of writing skills teaching a foreign language to engineering students: problems and possible solutions. St. Petersburg State Polytechn. Univ. J. Human. Soc. Sci. **10** (3), 100–112 (2019). https://doi.org/10.18721/JHSS. 10309. (In Russian)
17. Kogan, M.S., Gavrilova, A.V.: Didactic possibilities of using Internet resources in organizing students' independent work. Voprosy Metodiki Prepodavanija v Vuze [Issues of Teaching at University] **5** (19–1), 251–257 (2016). (In Russian)
18. Ryabtseva, N.: Academic paper titles and their dominating patterns: a Russian-english perspective Vestnik Volgogradskogo gosudarstvennogo universiteta. Seriya 2. Yazykoznanie [Sci. J. Volgograd State Univ. Linguist.] **17** (2), 33–43 (2018). (in Russian). https://doi. org/10.15688/jvolsu2.2018.2.4
19. Korotkina, I.B.: Russian scholarly publications in anglophone academic discourse: the clash of tyrannosaurs. Integratsiya obrazovaniya = Integr. Educ. **22**(2), 311–323 (2018). https:// doi.org/10.15507/1991-9468.091.022.201802.311-323
20. Hyland, K., Salager-Meyer, F.: Scientific writing. Ann. Rev. Inf. Sci. Technol. **42**(1), 297–338 (2008). https://doi.org//10.1002/aris.2008.1440420114
21. Paxton, R.J.: The influence of author visibility on high school students solving a historical problem. Cogn. Instr. **20**(2), 197–248 (2002). https://doi.org/10.1207/S1532690XCI2002_3
22. Hyland, K.: Applying a gloss: exemplifying and reformulating in academic discourse. Appl. Linguis. **28**(2), 266–285 (2007). https://doi.org/10.1093/applin/amm011
23. Hyland, K.: English for Academic Purposes. Routledge, London, New York (2006)
24. Pis'mo Minobrazovanija RF of 27 nojabrja 2002 g. N 14–55–996in/15 "Ob aktivizacii samostojatel'noj raboty studentov vysshih uchebnyh zavedenij" [Letter of the RF Ministry of Education of Nov.27, 2002. N 14–55–996in/15 "On the development of University students' self-study work"] (in Russian). https://cat.convdocs.org/docs/index-193224.html
25. Foley, M., Hall, D.: Advanced Learners' Grammar. Pearson Education Limited, London (2016)
26. Oshima, A., Hogue, A.: Writing Academic English. Pearson, White Plains (2012)
27. Taraban, R., Rynearson, K., Kerr, M.: (2000) College students' academic performance and self-reports of comprehension strategy use. Read. Psychol. **21**(4), 283–308 (2000). https:// doi.org/10.1080/027027100750061930
28. Denton, C.A., Wolters, C.A., York, M.J., Swanson, E., Kulesz, P.A., Francis, D.J.: Adolescents' use of reading comprehension strategies: Differences related to reading proficiency, grade level, and gender. Learn. Individ. Differ. **37**, 81–95 (2015). https://doi.org/10.1016/j.lin dif.2014.11.016
29. Thomas, J.: Two web-based tools for learning language from language (2020). https://www. versatile.pub/uploads/8/1/6/3/81634112/two_web-based_tools_for_learning_language_ from_language._thomas_2020_v2.pdf
30. Joseph, L.M., Alber-Morgan, S., Cullen, J., Rouse, C.: The effects of self-questioning on reading comprehension: A literature review. Read. Writ. Q. **32**(2), 152–173 (2016). https:// doi.org/10.1080/10573569.2014.891449
31. Swales, J., Feak, M.: Academic writing for graduate students (Ch. B). The University of Michigan Press, Michigan (2012)
32. Farnia, M., Baratizade, S.: Genre analysis of the method sections in applied linguistics research articles: a cross-linguistic study. Asian ESP J. **16** (6–1), 214 – 248 (2020). https://www.asian-esp-journal.com/volume-16-issue-6-1-december-2020/

33. Anthony, L., Bowen, M.: The language of mathematics: a corpus-based analysis of research article writing in a neglected field. Asian ESP J. **9**(2), 5–25 (2013)

34. Baxter, P., Bekkering, H., Dijkstra, T., Droop, M., van den Hurk, M., Leoné, F.: Contrasting orthographically similar words facilitates adult second language vocabulary learning. Learn. Instr. (2022). https://doi.org/10.1016/j.learninstruc.2022.101582

35. Hyland, K., Zou, H.: Titles in research articles. J. Eng. Acad. Purp. **56**. (2022). https://doi.org/10.1016/j.jeap.2022.101094

36. Liu, G.-Z., Lin, V., Kou, X., Wang, H.-Y.: Best practices in L2 English source use pedagogy: a thematic review and synthesis of empirical studies. Educ. Res. Rev. **19**, 36–57 (2016). https://doi.org/10.1016/j.edurev.2016.06.002

37. Davis, M.: The development of source use by international postgraduate students. J. Eng. Acad. Purp. **12**(2), 125–135 (2013). https://doi.org/10.1016/j.jeap.2012.11.008

Implementing Inquiry-Based and Online Mentoring in a Social Entrepreneurship Project

Anna Nicolaou(✉) ⓘ

Cyprus University of Technology, 3036 Limassol, Cyprus
anna.nicolaou@cut.ac.cy

Abstract. This paper presents the results of implementing an inquiry-based and online mentoring intervention in a project revolving around social entrepreneurship. The intervention was implemented in the context of an English for Specific Purposes (ESP) module at a higher institution and aimed at developing learners' 21st century skills, such as team work, problem-solving and communication as well as social entrepreneurial competence. Thirty-three ESP students majoring in Business Management at a higher institution participated in the intervention which was implemented within an online mentoring platform. The analysis of both quantitative and qualitative data yielded interesting results pertaining to the students' interaction and engagement activity on the mentoring platform, the learning gains, as well as their perceptions of the ways in which the online mentoring experience contributed towards the effective completion of their social entrepreneurship project. Emerging themes include the benefits of the intervention in building discipline-specific knowledge and social entrepreneurial competence, as well as in enhancing communication and team work skills. As for the challenges faced by the students during their online mentoring experience, these included difficulty in composing interesting and creative questions addressed to the mentors, lack of confidence in posting video questions on the platform, and delayed responses from the mentors.

Keywords: Inquiry-based learning · Online mentoring · Project-based learning

1 Introduction

1.1 Background

In light of the increasingly interconnected and highly competitive world we live in, many educational institutions have acknowledged the need to redirect their teaching and learning priorities and embrace new, purposeful learning experiences through the inclusion of 21st century competences in their curricula. Students going through education in the current era need to cultivate competences that go beyond the basic school subjects and skills of reading, writing, and arithmetic. Twenty-first century skills, such as creativity and innovation, critical thinking and problem solving, communication and collaboration [1] are now more important than ever for students in order to increase their opportunities to succeed in their academic and professional life, and to render them useful citizens in

© Springer Nature Switzerland AG 2022
G. Meiselwitz et al. (Eds.): HCII 2022, LNCS 13517, pp. 347–363, 2022.
https://doi.org/10.1007/978-3-031-22131-6_27

their contexts. The digital transformations that have shaped the world in the last decades, have made 21st skills even more essential but also more feasible to achieve.

With these realities in mind, different pedagogical approaches have been put in place, either by professional organizations or academic institutions, in order to facilitate the development of those skills. The present study is at the intersection of three such pedagogies, namely inquiry-based learning, mentoring, and project-based learning which were adopted when implementing a social entrepreneurship project, in an effort to foster 21st century skills in higher education language learning.

1.2 Literature Review

Inquiry-based learning (IBL), an approach that relates to self-directed learning [2], is "an umbrella term that encompasses a range of teaching approaches in which learning is stimulated by a question or issue, learning is based on constructing new knowledge and understanding, and the teacher's role is one of a facilitator" [3, p. 15]. IBL is characterized as a student-centred pedagogical approach [4] that can foster higher-order skills [5], workplace communication competence and collaborative mindset [6], while strengthening student motivation and engagement [7]. IBL has been defined in different terms including 'problem-based learning' (PBL) [5]. The classification of inquiry by Banchi and Bell [8, p. 27] identifies the following levels of inquiry on which IBL is based:

1. Confirmation Inquiry: Students confirm a principle through an activity when the results are known in advance.
2. Structured Inquiry: Students investigate a teacher-presented question through a prescribed procedure.
3. Guided Inquiry: Students investigate a teacher-presented question using student designed or selected procedures.
4. Open Inquiry: Students investigate questions that are student formulated through student designed or selected procedures.

The amount of scaffolding is central in the aforementioned levels of inquiry and so is the emphasis of learning – whether it is on existing knowledge or on building new knowledge. With this in mind, problem-based learning is defined as a subset of the broader term of inquiry-based learning, focusing on learning an existing body of knowledge [5]. Certainly, both problem-based learning and inquiry-based learning, despite being different, they have certain attributes in common: they are both student-centred and encourage active learning through investigation.

IBL places emphasis on the questions raised by the students during their investigations and during the process of solving problems. The importance of asking questions, and particularly good thinking questions, has been highlighted by many researchers as an integral part of inquiry. Students' questions can help them to "monitor their own learning, explore and scaffold their ideas, steer thinking in certain specific directions, and advance their understanding of scientific concepts and phenomena" [9, p. 34]. Therefore, teachers should place emphasis on developing their students' questioning skills and guide the process of inquiry. In the digital era we live in, teachers can create an educational environment to encourage students' questions through computer-supported inquiry learning [10]. This can be achieved by utilizing search engines, social media, and tools, such as community question answering (CQA) platforms [11].

"CQA sites have emerged as platforms designed specifically for the exchange of questions and answers among communities of users" [12, p. 631]. However, as Stokhof et al. [11] claim, during the process of progressive inquiry, having an increasing number of questions posted by students on CQA platforms is not adequate. What is important is the opportunity provided to learners to receive answers by experts who are not always easy to find. This often results in several problems, such as low participation rate of the users, long waiting time to receive answers and the low quality of answers [13]. Finding experts who are knowledgeable in the field would create the opportunities of providing quality mentoring to students and this could facilitate the inquiry process beyond the classroom's boundaries.

Mentoring programs have frequently been implemented in educational contexts as they facilitate learning by enhancing students' exploration of new perspectives within a supportive learning environment that builds their professionalism, identity and competence [14]. Online mentoring or e-mentoring programs have found a fertile ground lately not only due to remote teaching and learning, but also because of their advantages over face-to-face mentoring, such as flexibility in terms of time and space [15] and lack of stigmatizing mentees [16]. Regardless of being offered face-to-face or virtually, mentoring within CQA platforms can be promising in facilitating the inquiry processes during which students need to find the information they need in places beyond the textbooks and formal instruction [11] in order to complete a project. "Project-based learning (PBL) is an active student-centred form of instruction which is characterized by students' autonomy, constructive investigations, goal-setting, collaboration, communication and reflection within real-world practices" [17, p. 19]. Both project-based and inquiry-based learning activities can engage students in authentic discovery processes [18] beyond the classroom's four walls. The three aforementioned pedagogical approaches, inquiry-based learning, mentoring, and project-based learning, provided the theoretical background of the present study's intervention that will be outlined in the next section.

1.3 The Intervention

The intervention was implemented in the context of an English for Specific Purposes (ESP) module in Business Management at the Cyprus University of Technology. The specific module focuses on providing knowledge and training to students in the area of innovation and entrepreneurship as well as on building a social entrepreneurial mindset which seeks to provide business solutions to social problems in an ethical and sustainable way. The intervention spanned seven weeks of a 13-week semester and involved the completion of a collaborative project around social entrepreneurship. Students were tasked with a scenario-based activity which requested them to form small groups and follow the steps towards completion of the project. The first step included the familiarization with relevant processes of entrepreneurship, such as generation of an innovative idea, identifying a market, evaluation of opportunity, formation of a company, development of business plan, deciding on business model, planning of finances, seeking funding, pitching, investments, and launch of business. The familiarization with these processes was supported by relevant tasks and activities integrated in the specific curriculum. The following step required students to read the scenario below:

You own a successful company and you want to use your skills and experience to become a social entrepreneur and make a positive change in the world! You have decided to explore the needs in your region in order to identify an innovative solution to address a pandemic-related issue. You understand that this needs a lot of hard work, passion, inspiration and creativity, so you decide to join forces with your young and enthusiastic colleagues and come up with a feasible business idea to help the community. Your idea will be presented in a PowerPoint presentation and an elevator pitch to potential investors.

Having read the scenario, the students were involved in a brainstorming process within their groups in an effort to generate innovative ideas for business solutions to address the specific problem. The business solutions could take the form of a tangible product, a service, or an App. Students were required to think about market segmentation, their business model, design features and consumer benefits of the product, feasibility, competitive advantage, pricing strategy, branding, distribution, sales promotion, and funding opportunities. The project adopted a constructivist approach and the main expected outputs were the co-construction of four artifacts, namely a short business plan, a presentation, an elevator pitch, and an investor's report [See 19 for a more detailed description of the project in a different iteration]. The students were expected to adopt a social entrepreneurial mindset, understanding the social problem that they were tasked to solve, and being determined to design social initiatives in an ethical and responsible way.

The project was designed with specific learning outcomes in mind which included the development of students' ESP competences in the specific discipline, as well as the enhancement of students' 21st century competences, such as team work, problem-solving, critical thinking, and communication [1]. The project had a strong emphasis on entrepreneurship which has been highlighted by the Partnership for 21st Century Skills as a key theme of 21st century education [1] as well as a target competence in the Council of the European Union's recommendation on Key Competences for Lifelong Learning [20]. As the project was utterly challenging, the teacher provided continuous scaffolding, breaking up the project in phases, and providing resources and tools for each phase. Since the project was an open-ended task, the students were required to engage in a process of exploration and discovery in their groups in order to collect information from multiple sources. Considering that the specific students were digitally competent and studying at a university that has adequate technological infrastructure, the use of a CQA platform was integrated in the project to assist students in the process of inquiry. The platform that was utilized was 100mentors (www.100mentors.com).

100mentors is an educational technology CQA platform which follows a mentor-like approach. The platform can function with learners at different levels of education with secure registration upon the invitation of an educator. The educator initiates the discussion on the platform by creating a discussion topic under a specific thematic area whereby students post questions addressed to 'mentors' [11]. The mentors who are recruited on the platform to answer those questions are considered experts in the areas of the specific discussion topics and they provide answers drawing from their expertise and experience in their field. The platform has a web and mobile functionality and offers a space for a dialogic process between the students and their mentors through the cycle of question, answer, follow-up question and follow-up answer. The students can select to post their questions either in text or in a short video of no more than 10 s while the mentors provide answers in 100-s personalized videos. One question may receive answers from multiple mentors of diverse educational, professional, and cultural backgrounds. For the purposes of the specific project, the teacher created three topics under the main theme of Business Management in the duration of the 7-week project: social entrepreneurship, company finance and start-ups, and the elevator pitch. All students taking the specific module were invited to download the mobile application of the platform and register. Upon accessing the platform, the students were advised to navigate the space and familiarize themselves with the available themes and questions posted by students at different institutions. Then they were required to post questions under the specific topics either in text or video format in an effort to receive information and expert knowledge in relation to the different project tasks. With regard to the first topic which was created at the beginning of the project named 'social entrepreneurship', seven questions were posted by students and fifty responses were provided by mentors. As for the second topic created in the middle of the project named 'company finance and start-ups', seven questions were posted by students and thirty-nine answers were given by mentors. Finally, for the last topic which was created towards the end of the project named 'elevator pitch', five questions were posted, receiving forty-four answers from mentors.

1.4 Research Questions

The intervention aimed at encouraging inquiry beyond the classroom's boundaries by connecting the class with the outside real world and through engaging the students in a process of making interesting questions as part of the discovery process, acknowledging the importance of student questioning for constructivist learning [21]. Keeping the target competences in mind, the study seeks to answer the following research questions:

1. How do students use and engage in the CQA online mentoring platform?
2. What are the students' perceptions about the benefits and challenges of the CQA online mentoring platform for project-based learning and competence development?
3. What factors contribute to the effectiveness of the intervention?

2 Method

2.1 Participants and Settings

The study involved the participation of thirty-three first-year students at the Cyprus University of Technology, taking a required, degree-level English for Specific Purposes module in Business Management. Twenty-two (66.7%) of the students were female whereas eleven (33.3%) were male. The students had never used the specific CQA online mentoring platform before. All of them possessed mobile phones and were able to download and access the platform on their devices upon the teacher's invitation.

2.2 Measure and Procedure

The study employed a mixed-methods approach and included data collected by means of a survey as well as individual reflections shared in an online class community created in a Google Classroom environment. Data were collected upon completion of all the project's tasks. With regard to the survey, an online questionnaire was created using Google Forms and was administered to students. The questionnaire aimed at collecting data pertaining to the students' use of and engagement on the platform as well as their perceptions about the effectiveness of the platform in guiding them through their inquiry-based project on social entrepreneurship. The questionnaire included mostly multiple response and Likert-type questions. Informed consent was obtained from all students who were ensured that their participation in the survey was completely voluntary and there would be no penalty for not participating in terms of affecting their grade in the project. The students' reflections were collected at the end of the project. The prompt that initiated their reflections was the following: 'After posting your questions and watching the mentors' video responses, explain what you learned from this process and how it has helped you with your project". Quantitative data yielded from the survey (33 answers in the Google Form) were entered and analyzed in SPSS statistical software whereas qualitative data from students' reflections (24 reflective comments) were entered and analyzed in NVivo qualitative data analysis computer software package, following thematic analysis. In view of the study's objectives and research questions, the thematic analysis was performed in an inductive way with the following themes: learning gains, the mentors and their responses, challenges, and suggestions. Emerging codes pertaining to sub-themes were added in the codebook along the way.

3 Results

3.1 Activity and Engagement

The 33 participants seem to have been involved in different forms of activity and levels of engagement on the platform. The diverse forms of activity and levels of engagement are manifested in the extent to which they explored and exploited the platform's functionalities in order to advance their projects. In a multiple response question in the survey, participants were requested to select the types of activity and engagement on the platform. As indicated in Table 1, 29 students registered on the platform, 21 of them explored the platform by browsing its different pages, 18 familiarized themselves with the questioning approach by going through the questions of students at different schools and the mentors' responses, and 13 explored the mentors' profiles and expertise. The activity on the platform was defined in many cases by a team spirit as 24 of the participants collaborated with peers during the process. Sixteen students posted a question on the platform in one or more of the created topics. Even though the number seems low (half of the participants), these students were probably acting as representatives of their groups expressing the questions formulated in collaboration with their peers. A good number of students seems to have read or watched their peers' questions (27 students) and watched the mentors' responses (26 students).

Table 1. Activity and engagement on the online mentoring platform

Activity and engagement	Number of students	Percent of cases
Registered on the platform	29	87.9%
Browsed the platform	21	63.6%
Read/watched users' questions	18	54.5%
Posted a question	16	48.5%
Read/watched peers' questions	27	81.8%
Watched mentors' responses	25	75.8%
Browsed mentors' profiles	13	39.4%
Collaborated with peers	24	72.7%

A follow-up multiple response question requested students to indicate which of the activities they engaged in were most enjoyable for them. As shown in Fig. 1, students mostly enjoyed reading or watching their peers' questions, as well as watching the mentors' video responses. They equally enjoyed working in their groups to brainstorm questions, followed by using the mentors' responses in order to move forward with their social entrepreneurship project's tasks. What they seem to have liked least was to post a question in video format, compose an interesting question to be addressed to the mentors, and post a question in text format.

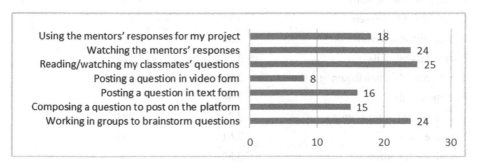

Fig. 1. Activities students liked most on the online mentoring platform.

3.2 Learning Gains

In the next part of the questionnaire, students were requested to mark their responses pertaining to the aspects of learning their activity and engagement in the online mentoring platform contributed to. Students were asked to respond to twenty items using a 5-point Likert scale with 1 meaning 'Not helpful at all' and 5 meaning 'Extremely helpful'. As demonstrated in Table 2, all the students' responses received a positive marking indicating above-average perceptions about the help they received through online mentoring in the various aspects of learning. The aspects of learning that seem to have benefited most are: acquire ESP knowledge (3.97), receive support for the social entrepreneurship project (3.94), become motivated (3.91), develop teamwork skills (3.91), communicate with peers (3.88), become creative (3.88), think critically when inquiring (3.82), and get advice that can be useful in future employment (3.82).

Table 2. Aspects of learning in which online mentoring has been helpful

Aspects	Mean	Std. deviation
Learn technical lexis /terms	3.73	.876
Learn basic concepts	3.79	.857
Learn new accents in English	3.79	.820
Make inquiries	3.67	.1.051
Make interesting questions	3.70	1.045
Acquire ESP knowledge	3.97	.883
Become motivated	3.91	1.071
Feel engaged	3.70	.847
Receive support for project	3.94	.864
Solve project's problem	3.85	1.004
Communicate with peers	3.88	1.166
Develop teamwork skills	3.91	1.071
Get insights from experts	3.73	.876
Feel confident interacting online	3.52	1.064
Improve social skills	3.73	1.126
Think critically when inquiring	3.82	.983
Become creative	3.88	.992
Use mobile Apps for learning	3.70	.984
Navigate tools	3.61	1.059
Get advice for future job	3.82	.950

The qualitative data analysis of the students' reflections corroborated the quantitative analysis with regard to the learning gains of the intervention and provided more in-depth insights. As in the survey, in their reflections the students highlighted several learning gains which include acquiring discipline-specific knowledge, understanding social entrepreneurship, developing a social entrepreneurial mindset, moving forward with the project, experiencing diverse perspectives, building social/personal skills, and acquiring insights that might be useful in a future job. The learning gains are summarized in Table 3 and are supported by students' verbatim quotes:

Table 3. Learning gains

Learning gains	Quotes
Discipline-specific knowledge	*I learned a lot of things mostly about a business, for example I learned that an important aspect in creating your own product the mentors mentioned, is to pay attention to the market trends and have a good strategy*
Understand social entrepreneurship	*100 mentors helped me to understand the meaning of social entrepreneurship as I had no idea about this before*
Develop a social entrepreneurial mindset	*They explained some of the most important things for a social entrepreneur which are: to have the ability to survive from all the difficulties, to be financially sustainable, to have emotional intelligence and to have good collaborations. Also, another mentor added that you need to have empathy, feel inspired, have passion, motivation and confidence about the things that you do. Finally, they said that it is crucial to have management skills, to have a strong team, to be bold, innovative and have accountability*
Move forward with the project	*This app helped us with our projects. Many people answered our questions by sending us a video and we learned and understood more. This made it easier for each team to complete our projects*
Experience diverse perspectives	*I reached the conclusion that every answer and approach from the mentors was different. Because each one of the mentors have their own story and their own way to resolve problems and this is a result of their own experience and their own way to achieve their goals. But in the end, all of their answers were helpful for me and my teammates to resolve our problems which we faced at the project*
Build social/personal skills	*100mentors helped in many ways. First of all, it helped me to not be shy to ask a question because a lot of people may wonder the same thing. Moreover, it improved my thoughts and expanded my horizons. It made me more active in my studies and made me search more about my interests in marketing. In addition, I learnt to use my creativity with more ease*
Future job	*I got practical advice that I may use in my future job*

A follow-up multiple response question, requested students to indicate the ways their activity and engagement on the platform helped them complete their social entrepreneurship project's tasks. As indicated in Table 4, the students' participation in the online mentoring platform was mostly conducive to understanding the concept and functions of social entrepreneurship, followed by creating their business plan which was one of the project's main outputs. In addition, the activity on the online mentoring platform seems to have helped students apply the necessary business knowledge to their entrepreneurial ideas and prepare their elevator pitches. Acquiring lexis related to the project and writing the investor's report were the tasks that were least selected by students. The investor's report was the final output of the project and no specific topic was created by the teacher on the platform in relation to this task.

Table 4. Online mentoring and social entrepreneurship project tasks

Project tasks	Number of students	Percent of cases
Understand social entrepreneurship	28	87.9%
Acquire lexis related to the project	12	36.4%
Create a business plan	19	57.6%
Apply business knowledge	18	54.5%
Prepare my elevator pitch	17	51.5%
Write investor's report	12	36.4%

The qualitative data indicate similar results with clear references to how the students' engagement with the platform contributed to the completion of their challenging project. In their reflections, students mentioned that the online mentoring experience helped them understand basic concepts in entrepreneurship, but also complete the various project's tasks, such as the development of a business plan: *The mentors' answers helped my business plan grow,* a student says.

3.3 The Mentors

On another part of the questionnaire, the participants were requested to indicate their views about the mentors who responded to their questions on the platform. The students had to mark their responses for twenty items using a 5-point Likert scale whereby 1 meant 'Strongly disagree' and 5 meant 'Strongly agree'. The 20 items pertained to the mentors' attitudes and ways of interaction. Some questions were included in the list of items for cross-checking purposes (paired positive and negative items indicating the same information). As shown in Table 5, the students' views about the mentors were overall positive, indicating above-average satisfaction with their attitude and responses. Students indicated that the mentors were willing to share their expert knowledge (4.39), they were inspiring (4.24), knowledgeable (4.21), had a positive attitude (4.15), provided clear answers to their questions (4.09), and were interesting to listen to (4.06). Negative views appear to be below average and mostly relate to the mentors speaking too fast

Table 5. Views about the mentors

Views	Mean	Std. deviation
Were knowledgeable	4.21	.820
Were inspiring	4.24	.614
Were impersonal	3.79	.927
Were willing to share knowledge	4.39	.788
Provided clear answers to questions	4.09	.765
Had a positive attitude	4.15	1.034
Were boring to listen to	2.39	1.248
Took a personal interest in answering	3.58	1.001
Had the relevant expertise	3.61	.966
Gave timely responses	3.70	.728
Had a negative attitude	2.03	1.185
Spoke too fast	2.91	1.156
Gave delayed responses	2.58	.936
Used advanced English	3.24	.969
Were interesting to listen to	4.06	.659
Were difficult to understand	2.58	1.001
Gave very long answers	2.85	1.004
Gave answers related to the project	3.88	.740
Gave short answers	3.30	.918
Gave irrelevant answers	2.30	1.185

(2.91), giving long responses (2.85), giving delayed responses (2.58), and being difficult to understand (2.58).

The qualitative data analysis corroborated the above findings. In their reflections, the students described the mentors as knowledgeable and their responses as *helpful, important for understanding the topic, specific,* and *to the point*. The students seem to have appreciated the fact that the mentors were experts and they found it *amazing how such good scientists listen to our questions and answer to us in such a specific way*. The students felt that the functionalities of the platform, but also the mentors' positive attitude made the mentors easy to reach: *if we had any questions, we could ask them directly and they would answer us directly too. They would answer us by sending us a video.*

3.4 Challenges, Suggestions, and Factors

As mentioned earlier, none of the students had previously experienced interacting on an education CQA online mentoring platform. Therefore, considering that this was a new experience for them, a multiple response question related to the challenges the participants faced was included. As indicated in Table 6, the greatest challenge was the lack of confidence in posting a video question. This is manifested in the fact that most questions uploaded on the platform were in text format. In addition, as the project was challenging and implied the completion of several tasks in its 7-week duration, the students identified the limited time to post questions as another challenge. This was coupled with difficulties in composing interesting wonderment questions that would intrigue mentors to respond. Finally, a challenge identified by students was their difficulty in understanding the mentors' accents in English. As already mentioned, the mentors who are recruited in the specific platform are of diverse cultural and linguistic backgrounds.

Table 6. Challenges

Challenges	Number of students	Percent of cases
Limited time to post questions	9	27.3
Lack of confidence in posting a text question	4	12.1
Lack of confidence in posting a video question	20	60.6
Difficulty in understanding the mentors' ideas	1	3.0%
Too many unknown words in the mentors' responses	2	6.1%
Difficulty in understanding the mentors' accents	6	18.2
Difficulty in composing an interesting question	8	24.2%
Problems in accessing the platform from my mobile phone	3	9.1%
Feeling burdened by participating in the platform	2	6.1%
Difficulty in connecting the mentors' responses to the project's tasks	1	3.0%

In their reflections, students described certain challenges that were also highlighted in questionnaire responses, such as difficulty in understanding the mentors' different accents in English and delayed responses which was also identified earlier in their views about the mentors. To curb those challenges, students put forward a few suggestions which are summarized in Table 7, supported by verbatim quotes:

Table 7. Suggestions

Suggestions	Quotes
Possibility to change the language of communication:	*There should exist the ability to select the country that you want to post, so some people who don't speak English can choose the language that they speak and understand*

(*continued*)

Table 7. (*continued*)

Suggestions	Quotes
Add subtitles to mentors' video responses	*They can also answer our question with some subtitles, whether any student have problem with the accent can read the subtitles*
Accelerate communication	*They can try to reply a little bit faster so we can use their advice on our tasks.* *To answer also the text questions as fast as the videos.* *Using online video calls to communicate*

3.5 Factors

The final part of the questionnaire requested participants to mark their responses in relation to the factors that contributed to the effectiveness of their online mentoring experience. Students had to respond to eight items using a 5-point Likert scale whereby 1 meant 'Not helpful at all' and 5 meant 'Extremely helpful'. Table 8 demonstrates the mean responses in the 8 items. As shown in the table, the factor that seems to have contributed most to the effectiveness of the online mentoring experience was the ubiquity of the platform as it could be accessed through their mobile devices any time any place (4.18). Because of this, the students' activity and engagement were possible not only in class through the web functionality, but also beyond the class hours through the mobile application. This way, students were able to browse the platform, upload questions, and view questions and responses without facing any space or time constraints. The second factor that seems to have been perceived as conducive to the effectiveness of the experience was the fact that the mentors provided their responses in video format rather than in text (4.15). Other factors relate to different forms of support provided by the teacher and peers. The teacher's provision of additional resources with regard to composing interesting questions (4.09), their collaboration with peers (4.09), as well as the fact that the teacher provided feedback on the students' questions (4.06) were perceived as conducive to the effectiveness of the online mentoring experience. The least important factors, but still above average, were the teacher's reminders (4.1) and receiving notifications on their mobile phones (3.73) when any form of an activity was taking place on the platform.

In their reflections, students also highlighted the fact that the process of question and answer was not affected by place or time constraints: *Anytime and anywhere you can make a specific question and some great professor can answer to you with also specific answers.* They also mentioned that they found the process of receiving an answer in a video format *very fun because via the video you are given the opportunity to meet new people.*

Table 8. Factors that contributed to the effectiveness of the online mentoring experience

Factors	Mean	Std. deviation
Teacher's support resources	4.09	.947
Notifications on my mobile phone	3.73	1.206
Teacher's reminders	4.1	.893
Working with peers	4.09	1.042
Teacher's feedback on questions	4.06	.899
Reflecting on my experience	3.88	.927
Ability to access any time any place	4.18	.769
Mentor's video responses	4.15	.906

4 Discussion

The intervention described in this manuscript yielded interesting results pertaining to the areas of investigation and in response to the research questions. With regard to the first research question, 'How do students use and engage in the CQA online mentoring platform', the analysis of the data demonstrates that the students interacted and engaged on the platform in diverse ways and at different levels. A good number of students made full exploitation of the functionalities of the platform, by exploring its content and actively participating through contributing their own questions either in text or video format. Several students were interested to view their peers' questions and the mentors' responses as these were considered to be useful for their project's tasks. The factors that contributed to the students' engagement include the ubiquitous nature of the platform allowing any time any place usage, as well as the responses of the mentors provided in video format which seems to have increased their interest, motivation, and understanding of the content. In addition, scaffolding activities by the teacher were critical in rendering the students' engagement more effective. Finally, students seem to have enjoyed interacting on the platform in their groups and adding their contributions following collaborative work. This is probably due to the fact that this was the first time students had interacted in an education CQA platform; therefore, they did not possess the required level of confidence in posting questions individually, particularly in video format.

With regard to the second research question, 'What are the students' perceptions about the benefits and challenges of the CQA online mentoring platform for project-based learning and competence development', students were able to highlight numerous learning gains. These include the development of discipline-specific knowledge. This process of 'discovery-oriented' inquiry-based learning in the form of question and answer seems to have been conducive to building disciplinary knowledge as Levy suggests [22]. Apart from subject-specific knowledge, the students highlighted the development of various 21st century competences, such as teamwork skills, communication with peers, creativity, critical thinking when making inquiries, and future employability skills. Being a self-directed pedagogy [2], inquiry-based learning contributes to a competence-based learning environment due to the students' engagement in an authentic scientific discovery process [18]. Stokhof et al. [21] have emphasized the important role of student questioning in increasing motivation and multiple skills such as critical reflection, autonomy, and the construction of knowledge. In this intervention, a constructivist inquiry-based learning approach was adopted, situated in a CQA online mentoring platform. The intersection of different pedagogies contributed to the construction of knowledge [9] which was manifested in the co-authoring of artifacts. The students' open investigations helped them complete their project work [9] while developing several 21st century competences. The process of inquiry was affected by certain challenges as highlighted by the participants and pertained mostly to the students' lack of confidence in composing an interesting question and posting it in a video format. The issue of limited confidence echoes Stokhof et al. [12] who emphasizes the need to guide effective student questioning from primary education. The authors posit that teachers should be trained to learn how to create a supportive classroom culture for question generation and they should also be guided when the process of questioning is visualized on a common platform. Another challenge underlined by the participants was difficulty in understanding the mentors' accents in English. Even though the mentors' diversified backgrounds were considered as one of the strengths of the platform as it afforded opportunities for getting insights from multiple perspectives, participants faced challenges in understanding the content of their responses. To curb this challenge, the students suggested having the possibility to interact in a different language or add subtitles to the mentors' video responses. A final challenge relates to the mentors' delayed responses. This may be due to the difficulty in finding expert mentors to respond in CQA platforms which results in long waiting time to receive answers [13]. Nevertheless, overall, students highlighted their satisfaction with the mentors' expert responses who were characterized as knowledgeable in the topic, an aspect which is crucial in CQA platforms [11].

As for the last research question 'What factors enhance the effectiveness of the intervention', the ubiquitous nature of the platform seems to have been critical in facilitating self-directed learning [23]. In addition, the collaborative aspect of project-based learning was deemed an important factor that increased the effectiveness of this intervention. Finally, the amount of support provided by the teacher was considered important in helping the students progress with their inquiries and complete the project, echoing the need for scaffolded inquiry activities [18].

5   Conclusion

This paper presented the results of implementing an inquiry-based and online mentoring intervention in a project revolving around social entrepreneurship in higher education ESP learning. Adopting the aforementioned pedagogies, the intervention aspired to develop students' 21st skills, such as team work, problem-solving and communication as well as social entrepreneurial competence. The study seems to have achieved the intended learning outcomes and it has succeeded in capturing the factors that contributed to the positive results of this intervention as well as the challenges involved. However, the study relies solely on the students' self-reported perceptions which can be limiting in drawing valid conclusions. To compensate for this limitation, the study attempted to triangulate the data through the collection of data from two different sources, namely survey results and reflections. Future research could involve the adoption of an experimental approach with pre- and post-intervention data in an effort to increase the reliability of the study.

References

1. Partnership for 21st Century Skills. http://www.battelleforkids.org/networks/p21 (2009). Accessed 15 May 2022
2. Lee, V. S.: Teaching and learning through inquiry: a guidebook for institutions and instructors. Stylus Pub LLC (2004)
3. Spronken-Smith, R., Walker, R., Batchelor, J., O'Steen, B., Angelo, T.: Enablers and constraints to the use of inquiry-based learning in undergraduate education. Teach. High. Educ. 16(1), 15–28 (2011)
4. Spronken-Smith, R., Walker, R.: Can inquiry-based learning strengthen the links between teaching and disciplinary research? Stud. High. Educ. 35(6), 723–740 (2010)
5. Spronken-Smith, R., Bullard, J.O., Ray, W., Roberts, C., Keiffer, A.: Where might sand dunes be on Mars? Engaging students through inquiry-based learning in geography. J. Geogr. High. Educ. 32(1), 71–86 (2008)
6. Chen, R.H.: Fostering students' workplace communicative competence and collaborative mindset through an inquiry-based learning design. Educ. Sci. 11(1), 17 (2021)
7. Buchanan, S.M.C., Harlan, M.A., Bruce, C., Edwards, S.: Inquiry based learning models, information literacy, and student engagement: a literature review. Sch. Libr. Worldw. 22(2), 23–39 (2016)
8. Banchi, H., Bell, R.: The many levels of inquiry. Sci. Child. 46(2), 26 (2008)
9. Chin, C., Osborne, J.: Students' questions: a potential resource for teaching and learning science. Stud. Sci. Educ. 44(1), 1–39 (2008)
10. Levy, P., Aiyegbayo, O., Little, S.: Designing for inquiry-based learning with the learning activity management system. J. Comput. Assist. Learn. 25(3), 238–251 (2009)
11. Stokhof, H., Meli, K., Lavidas, K., Grammenos, D.: Why answer this question? Experts' behaviors on educational community question-answering platforms. Electronic J. e-Learn. 20(2), 87–100 (2022)
12. Herrera, J., Parra, D., Poblete, B.: Social QA in non-CQA platforms. Futur. Gener. Comput. Syst. 105, 631–649 (2020)
13. Neshati, M., Fallahnejad, Z., Beigy, H.: On dynamicity of expert finding in community question answering. Inf. Process. Manage. 53(5), 1026–1042 (2017)
14. Crisp, G., Baker, V.L., Griffin, K.A., Lunsford, L.G., Pifer, M.J: Mentoring undergraduate students: ASHE higher education report, vol. 43, no. 1. John Wiley & Sons (2017)
15. Asgari, M.: Students' evaluation of success in an online mentoring program. Asian Assoc. Open Univ. J. 5, 1–9 (2010)
16. Shrestha, C.H., May, S., Edirisingha, P., Burke, L., Linsey, T.: From face-to-face to e-mentoring: Does the "e" add any value for mentors? Int. J. Teach. Learn. High. Educ. 20(2), 116–124 (2009)
17. Kokotsaki, D., Menzies, V., Wiggins, A.: Project-based learning: a review of the literature. Improv. Sch. 19(3), 267–277 (2016)
18. Pedaste, M., et al.: Phases of inquiry-based learning: Definitions and the inquiry cycle. Educ. Res. Rev. 14, 47–61 (2015)
19. Sevilla-Pavón, A., Nicolaou, A.: Artefact co-construction in virtual exchange: 'Youth Entrepreneurship for Society'. Computer Assisted Language Learning, pp. 1–26 (2020)

20. Council of the European Union, Proposal for a Council Recommendation on Key Competences for Lifelong Learning (2018). Accessed 10 Apr 2022
21. Stokhof, H.J., De Vries, B., Martens, R.L., Bastiaens, T.J.: How to guide effective student questioning: a review of teacher guidance in primary education. Rev. Educ. **5**(2), 123–165 (2017)
22. Levy, P.: Inquiry-based learning: a conceptual framework. Centre for Inquiry-based learning in the arts and social sciences. Unpublished Manuscript, University of Sheffield, Sheffield, UK. http://www.sheffield.ac.uk/content/1/c6/09/37/83/CILASS%20IBL%20Framework 20 (2009)
23. Jeong, K.O.: Facilitating sustainable self-directed learning experience with the use of mobile-assisted language learning. Sustainability **14**(5), 2894 (2022)

Developing a Checklist for Evaluating Virtual Learning Environments Through the Analysis of Evaluation Reports from an Educational Organization

Kennedy Nunes[1], Arthur Passos[1], João Santos[1], Yandson Costa[1,2],
José Durand[1], Mizraim Mesquita[1], Paola Trindade[1], Elza Bernardes[1],
Rayanne Silveira[1], Alana Oliveira[1,3], Davi Viana[1,2,3],
Ana Emilia Figueiredo de Oliveira[1], Mario Teixeira[1,2,3],
and Luis Rivero[1,2,3(✉)]

[1] Directorate of Technologies in Education – DTED/UNA-SUS, Federal University
of Maranhão (UFMA), Sao Luis, Brazil
{kennedy.anderson,arthur.passos,joao.davi,yandson.jesus,durand.jose,
mizraim.mesquita}@discente.ufma.br,
{paola.garcia,elza.bernardes}@ufma.br,
{rayanne.silveira,alana.oliveira,davi.viana,ana.figueiredo,
mario.meireles,luis.rivero}@ufma.br
[2] MSc Program in Computer Science – PPGCC, Federal University of Maranhão
(UFMA), Sao Luis, Brazil
[3] PhD Program in Computer Science – DCCMAPI, Federal University of Maranhão
(UFMA), Sao Luis, Brazil

Abstract. Virtual Learning Environments (VLEs) and online educational resources have emerged as proposals for popularizing and democratizing learning by promoting access and inclusion of all types of users. There are several approaches to evaluate the quality of VLEs and their contents. However, despite initiatives to provide evaluation methods for meeting usability criteria and end-user educational needs, most evaluation methods focus on identifying problems within VLEs and their resources after they have been deployed. In this paper, we present the proposal of a checklist considering quality attributes from an end-user and pedagogical perspective found in real evaluation reports from the Directorate of Technologies in Education at Federal University of Maranhão. In all, 19 reports were analyzed identifying 34 verification items for evaluating different quality attributes in VLEs and educational resources. The checklist can be used for evaluating educational resources and VLEs before validating the developed software with the pedagogical team and releasing the courses. We are currently employing the proposed checklist for internal evaluations gathering usage data.

Keywords: Chatbots · Requirements · Literature review · Quality assurance

G. Meiselwitz et al. (Eds.): HCII 2022, LNCS 13517, pp. 364–376, 2022.
https://doi.org/10.1007/978-3-031-22131-6_28

1   Introduction

As a result of technological advances, educational processes are being transformed [2]. Virtual learning environments (VLEs) and online educational resources have emerged as proposals for popularizing and democratizing learning by promoting access and inclusion of all types of users [3]. VLEs are tools aimed at providing learning opportunities through knowledge sharing and social interaction [4]. Among the features that VLEs provide, we can cite [8]: Dialogue and action (e.g. text chat, forum, shared whiteboard), Workspace awareness (e.g. use of realistic avatars, objects creation, role playing scenarios), Students' self-regulation/guidance (e.g. annotations), Teachers' assistance (e.g. log files) and others.

The literature presents a series of VLEs that are currently used by educational institutions, such as [11]: Moodle , Blackboard and Edmodo. At Federal University of Maranhão (UFMA) in Brazil, there is an education program from the Directorate of Technologies in Education (DTED) that uses Moodle as a VLE for teaching several courses in the field of health treatments and procedures. Within this education program, more than 50 online courses have been developed, including several online educational resources, such as: infographics, e-books, serious games, videos, interactive photograph and image panels, questionnaires, and others. Guaranteeing that these resources work properly and as expected is important to meet the educational needs and expectations of the students within the VLE.

Although there are several approaches to evaluate the quality of VLEs and their contents, most evaluation methods focus on identifying problems within VLEs and their resources after they have been deployed [10]. Therefore, there is a need for evaluation methods or artifacts that are applicable before the deployment phase of online courses within VLEs. By identifying problems from an end-user and pedagogical point of view before releasing VLEs and their resources, software development teams can improve the quality of the developed artifacts and reduce correction costs. To meet this gap, this paper presents the proposal of a checklist considering quality attributes from an end-user and pedagogical perspective. To develop the artifact, we analyzed the evaluation reports from the pedagogical team at Federal University of Maranhão from a software development perspective, obtaining 34 verification items for evaluating different quality attributes in VLEs and educational resources. The resulting evaluation checklist has been applied in the assessment of currently under development VLEs and educational resources.

The remainder of this paper is organized as follows. In Sect. 2, we present a background on VLEs and resources, while discussing work related with this research. In Sect. 3, we present our research methodology. Section 4 presents our results with a list of verification items for the evaluation of VLEs and educational resources. Finally, our conclusions and future work are described in Sect. 5.

2 Background

2.1 Virtual Learning Environments and Educational Resources

VLEs are tools aimed at providing learning opportunities through knowledge sharing and social interaction [4]. Virtual Learning Environment (VLE) and Learning Management System (LMS) are often used as synonyms describing a complex information technology system that integrates course management tools for the course administrators, online accessibility of learning materials and assignments; as well as a communication and collaboration platform for the students and lecturers [13]. Accordingly, it is understandable that the integration of new IT tools into the process of distance learning is outstandingly important. It is important to choose tools and interfaces that provide good communication are well maintainable and easy to use for both lecturers and students [9]. Therefore, it is necessary to guarantee the quality of both VLEs and online educational resources to meet the needs of students.

The quality and usability of a VLEs and their educational resources are the key features for their success by influencing user satisfaction and acceptance [13]. Usability is a complex discipline concerned with the activities, concepts and processes that promote and facilitate the design of human-computer interfaces that take the needs of users into consideration [5]. When evaluating the usability of VLEs and educational resources, one can focus on [6]: learnability, efficiency, memorability, error frequency and subjective satisfaction.

Considering the impact of VLEs and their resources in the context of online education, several studies have been conducted regarding the evaluation of e-learning users (distance learning) to measure the success of using distance learning systems [10]. Below, we present how these evaluations have been performed and their features.

2.2 Evaluation Methods for VLEs and Educational Resources

There are several approaches to evaluate the quality of VLEs and their contents. Mastan et al. (2022) carried out a systematic literature review and identified 38 publications describing approaches evaluating a range of quality criteria in VLEs, such as: usability, quality of service, learning performance, user satisfaction, technology adoption, and others. Within the context of usability and user experience evaluation, several approaches have been developed.

For instance, Harrati et al. 2016 proposed the use of the System Usability Scale (SUS) to gather data on the students' perception of VLEs. The authors inspect the usability of the e-learning Moodle platform, where usage metrics are computed automatically based on the recorded traces of all participants. The metrics include number of clicks, task duration, cursor distance and completion rate. Also, through the SUS analysis, the authors obtained information about the perception of the users towards the application. With the study, the authors managed to identify inconsistencies in the results of the real usage data and the perception of the users, since older people for the age group (50 – 65) reported similarly higher SUS score of 69.57% though the metrics obtained from their traces indicate poor performance during their interactivity.

Pal and Vanijja (2020) combined the System Usability Scale with the Technology Acceptance Model to evaluate online learning platforms. The authors state that although both instruments are popular in their respective domains, they have not been considered simultaneously in one work for the purpose of usability evaluation. By doing so, the authors attempt to streamline and unify the process of usability evaluation. The results from the experience from a large-scale survey of university students suggest the similarity and equivalency between the two methodologies, with the Perceived Ease of Use (PEOU) construct of TAM having greater similarity with SUS.

In another work, Priska et al. carried out a study to to consolidate the multi-dimensional aspects of e-learning evaluation by applying Balance Score-card (BSC) as a strategic measurement method. The goal was to seek an evaluation approach in which three equally important considerations must be balanced: organization, pedagogical, and technology. With the study, the authors concluded that the highest priority criteria in the learning and development perspective are the scalability of the e-learning system.

Despite initiatives to provide evaluation methods for meeting usability criteria and end-user educational needs, most evaluation methods identified by Mastan et al. (2022) focus on identifying problems within VLEs and their resources after they have been deployed. Furthermore, there are few methods that consider usability principals as well as pedagogical principals during the evaluation. To meet this gap, in the following section we describe how we carried out an analysis of the reports from a pedagogical evaluation team in order to identify quality criteria related to usability for VLEs and educational resources.

3   Research Methodology

The software development team from DTED/UFMA must meet internal quality standards to deploy the courses within the Moodle VLE. These standards include usability attributes, proper functioning of features and specificities related to pedagogical procedures. An internal evaluation is performed by the pedagogical team once all educational resources and the Moodle VLE are ready for deployment. Although the pedagogical team identifies several defects in the VLE and educational resources, there is no standard or artifact to guide the evaluation, thus allowing that problems remain unidentified, even if similar ones have already been corrected in previous educational resources or VLE instances of a course. Furthermore, the way in which the problems are described considers end-user language, which can make it difficult to understand what the problem is and what needs to be corrected.

To develop the checklist considering quality attributes from an end-user and pedagogical perspective, we analyzed 19 evaluation reports from the pedagogical team at DTED/UFMA from a software development perspective. Each report was verified by the development team, identifying for each described problem:

the location of the cause of the problem, the quality attribute, and possible solutions if described by the pedagogical team. When more than one problem within the reports referred to the same quality attribute, we merged them, trying to create the most accurate and thorough description of the attribute, so that the resulting verification item could be clearer for the development team, when using the final checklist in future evaluations.

Tables 1 and 2 shows examples of the analysis process. In these examples, we show two verification items: (a) "Only navigation and functionality icons in use must be displayed."; and (b) "The grades must appear on all pages in which the grades are shown. Also, they must be standardized to one decimal and show the correct value of scores after the evaluation activity.". For each verification item, note that we gathered data on where these problems occurred and how they were reported within the reports of the pedagogical team. We analyzed and extracted features or quality attributes from the reports and translated them into requirements using software engineering language (i.e. explaining the object to pay attention on and its features and/or how it should be implemented). Also, to support the development team in the implementation of the requirements within each verification item, we analyzed and grouped all the improvement suggestions within the reports and developed improvement suggestion instructions with the specificities of each item.

Table 1. Example of the development of verification item I23

Location	Verification item	Improvement suggestion	Problem reported within the evaluation report
Virtual Learning Environment - Functionalities OR Educational Resources – Functionalities	Only navigation and functionality icons in use must be displayed.	If a button or icon does not play a role in the system, it must be deleted from the screen.	This resource does not allow interaction. When clicking on the alternatives or arrows of the resource, without using the PDF stripe, the resource does not respond. And then the feedback is presented. Is that right?
			When clicking on the alternatives of the training activity, none can be selected - page 34;
			Feedback is already available on the next page; this button is not working nor necessary - page 35;
			This feature does not allow alternative selection and then the feedback is presented. Is that right?

Table 2. Example of the development of verification item I15

Location	Verification item	Improvement suggestion	Problem reported within the evaluation report
Virtual Learning Environment - Grades and Overall Course Status	The grades must appear on all pages in which the grades are shown. Also, they must be standardized to one decimal and show the correct value of scores after the evaluation activity.	Develop the correct calculation of grades. Show the grades according to the standard proposed by the pedagogical team. The final status of the evaluation of the course (pass or fail) should consider the calculation of the grades and evaluation rules from the pedagogical team.	The student's performance has a score of "zero" and one attempt was made and the score was 70.0. Please make correction for correct grade display.
			Standardize how the grade will be displayed so as not to confuse the student who expects a score of 100.0, while the system is showing other type of calculation.
			Check the description of the minimum grade as 70.0 and the questionnaire grade as 20.0 and the student has 100%, demonstrating here the need for correction of texts and presentation of the grade as previously stated.
			Check description of minimum grade as 70.0 and quiz grade as 60.0.
			There is a need for correcting the texts and presentation of the grades.
			Each question must be worth 10.0 points. The questionnaire shows 50.0 points and the final grade 100.0. In the performance menu, the student sees a failed status and a grade of 20.0 (not corresponding to the quiz grade).
			Failed status does not apply because the student has the course in progress and only Activities I and II were carried out. The grade status is incorrect.

4   Results

4.1   The Proposed Checklist

Table 3 shows the final version of our checklist. This checklist contains a total of 34 verification items identified within 19 evaluation reports from the pedagogical team at DTED/UFMA. All problems that were indicated by the pedagogical team had already been corrected in previous projects and by providing a complete list of recurrent problems in the form of verification items, we could avoid their appearance in future projects. In the final version of the checklist we also organized the items according to the location of the problem. We identified verification items for specific educational resources such as EBooks, Question-naires, Serious Games and Videos. Also, we identified generic items for the VLE or that applied to all the educational resources.

Table 3. Final version of the checklist for evaluating VLEs and Educational Resources

Code	Verification item
I01	EBook - The presentation of resources in pdf form in the eBook must be centralized and in such a way that the entire content of each page of the resource can be perfectly visualized.
I02	EBook and Questionnaire - The eBook questions must allow answers and editing after they have been answered.
I03	Questionnaire - Feedback must be present in the post test pages.
I04	Questionnaire - The system presents the edit and save option in the field for typing paragraphs (answer submission fields), in addition to allowing sending only if the field is not empty and editing immediately after sent, if necessary.
I05	Questionnaire - The wording and alternatives of the summative activities of the units must comply with the wording of the available alternatives.
I06	Serious Games - The Game page must have a screen return button.
I07	Serious Games - The Game page must save the chosen modality (medicine, nutrition, physiotherapy, etc.) and display a title with the name of the chosen modality.
I08	Videos - All videos intended to be displayed within the system must be working properly without interruptions nor distortion.
I09	VLE - After completion of the certification resource, it must generate the certificate as provided for in the planning, with the information of the course, student and workload.
I10	VLE - After logging in, the system must keep the student logged in on all pages accessed.
I01	VLE - Course progress must show 100% complete at the end of visiting all course pages.
I11	VLE - Courses must include the keyword on the course homepage as planned.
I12	VLE - If the Pre-Test feature is not finished, the other features must remain locked until it is finished.
I13	VLE - On the performance menu page there should be a column with the grade details, showing which score it refers to.
I14	VLE - Pages should load in time as predicted in the system execution planning or non-functional requirements table.
I15	VLE - The grades must appear on all pages in which the grades are shown. Also, they must be standardized to one decimal and show the correct value of scores after the evaluation activity.

(continued)

Table 3. (*continued*)

Code	Verification item
I16	VLE - The grades page should have a return to feedback button.
I17	VLE - The Notifications option should appear in the list of notifications sent to the student, such as messages, notices, alerts, etc. The number of notifications balloon must not cover the notifications title.
I18	VLE - The presentation of grades regarding the course and the student's performance should display the total grades.
I19	VLE - The system displays updated enrollment and certification dates in the schedule field on the course homepage.
I20	VLE - The system must present the expected page content as expected in the course.
I21	VLE and Overall Resources - All items must be reviewed and confirmed before being included on the course page, and then published.
I22	VLE and Overall Resources - If a resource is blocked for not having performed the resource assessment, it must remain blocked on all access links.
I23	VLE and Overall Resources - Only navigation and functionality icons in use must be displayed.
I24	VLE and Overall Resources - Resource links should open in another tab.
I25	VLE and Overall Resources - Resources must be present in all units of all courses, as foreseen in the current planning.
I26	VLE and Overall Resources - Resources must remain with "Soon" until its content is completed and reviewed. After confirmation, it must be updated as soon as possible.
I27	VLE and Overall Resources - The color of the items on the pages must have an adequate contrast and colors that follow a pattern that must be pre-established in a plan with the designer.
I28	VLE and Overall Resources - The content of the Pages must be displayed completely and clearly.
I29	VLE and Overall Resources - The hyperlink must redirect to the page defined in the planning.
I30	VLE and Overall Resources - The link that generates file downloads must direct to the predicted file, as planned.
I31	VLE and Overall Resources - The name of the buttons must correspond to their functionality and if in doubt, consult the pedagogical team.
I32	VLE and Overall Resources - The resources must be presented in the order they were indicated by the pedagogical team.
I33	VLE and Overall Resources - The text must be according to the current planning. Colors, fonts, size must match what is defined on each page.
I34	VLE and Overall Resources - The transcription download must be started only if the student wants, through the "Download" button.

4.2   An Evaluation Example

To provide a proof of concept of how the checklist could be applied, we evaluated an online course on "Health Care for the Elderly" from DTED/UFMA. Below, we present some problems that were identified using the checklist. Since the course was developed initially in Portuguese for Brazilian students, we will show print screens in Portuguese and an explanation in English.

Figure 1 shows an example of how item I01 was not followed, which indicates that: "The presentation of resources in pdf form in the eBook must be centralized and in such a way that the entire content of each page of the resource can be perfectly visualized.". This problem is related to an ebook which has not been properly resized, impairing visualization. To correct this problem, the development team must obtain the size of the current screen showing the resource and render it accordingly.

Fig. 1. Example of identified problem through verification item I01 of the proposed checklist.

Another example of a problem is shown in Fig. 2. In this example, item I24 indicates that "Resource links should open in another tab.". This item is valid for all resources and the VLE. In our example, since the VLE presents the educational resources internally, if external links are loaded within the VLE, the user can think that the content of the link is the resource, while it may be only additional information. Thus, it is important to separate the core content of the educational resource from external information.

Finally, another problem is shown in Fig. 3. In this example, item I32, which indicates that "The resources must be presented in the order they were indicated

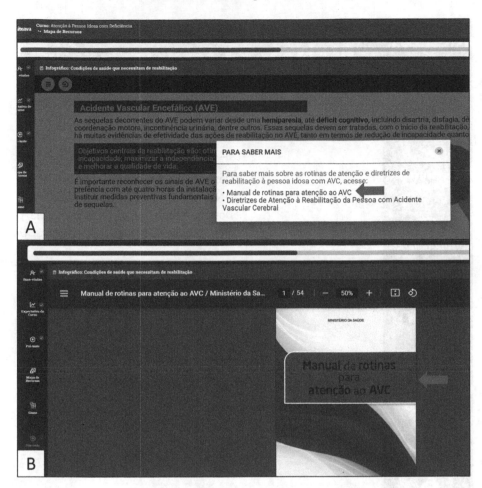

Fig. 2. Example of identified problem through verification item I24 of the proposed checklist. Part A shows a link to another content and part B shows an external content being loaded as if it was the current resource being viewed by the student.

by the pedagogical team.", has not been followed. In the course, an initial test to understand the current knowledge of the student must be taken by the student. This test is taken once and after that, later activities are unlocked. The evaluator of this course identified that although the initial test was taken, once the student reached a certain part of the course, (s)he could access the initial test and retake it, even if this was not the order in which the educational resources should be consumed. Therefore a problem was identified and marked as such through the checklist.

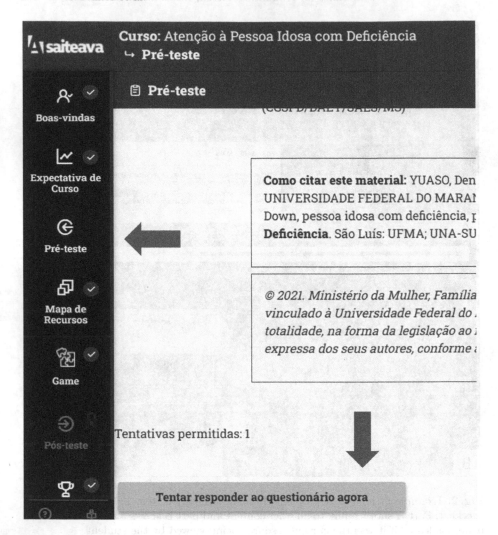

Fig. 3. Example of identified problem through verification item I32 of the proposed checklist.

With this proof of concept, we managed to obtain indicators that the inspection with this new checklist proposal could be promising to identify problems in VLEs and educational resources. In the following section, we present our conclusions and discuss future work.

5   Conclusions and Future Work

In order to support software development teams, this paper presented an initial version of an inspection checklist to assess the quality of VLEs and Educational Resources. The new checklist was generated from the analysis of attributes extracted from evaluation reports from the point of view of a pedagogical team at DTED/UFMA. We translated the contents into items considering the analysis of software engineers. As a preliminary result, a checklist was generated with 34 items in the form of statements, grouped according to the objects they evaluated.

The proof of concept indicated promising results regarding the use of the checklist to identify defects that would reveal future inconsistencies in VLEs and educational resources. Such results serve as support to identify improvement opportunities, thus making it possible to reduce the risk of releasing low quality VLEs and educational resources to the market.

We are currently employing the proposed checklist for internal evaluations gathering usage data. As the next steps of this work, we intend to carry out empirical studies to analyze its effectiveness, efficiency, and its overall acceptance from the point of view of the development team in real usage scenarios. In addition, we intend to apply the checklist in an industrial context, evaluating its applicability in the process of developing VLEs and educational environments. Through this research, we intend to provide a more reliable and robust checklist suitable for use by the software industry, as well as software engineers in the development of systems and online educational resources suited to high quality online education.

References

1. Agatha Priska, M., Aulia, D., Muslim, E., Marcelina, L.: Developing a framework to evaluate e-learning system at higher education in Indonesia. In: 2020 The 4th International Conference on Education and E-Learning, pp. 27–32 (2020)
2. Borba, M.C., Chiari, A.S.D.S., de Almeida, H.R.F.L.: Interactions in virtual learning environments: new roles for digital technology. Educ. Stud. Math. **98**(3), 269–286 (2018)
3. Brito, E., Dias, G.P.: LMS accessibility for students with disabilities: the experts' opinions. In: 2020 15th Iberian Conference on Information Systems and Technologies (CISTI), pp. 1–5. IEEE (2020)
4. Dillenbourg, P., et al.: Virtual learning environments. In: Proceedings of the 3rd Hellenic Conference Information & Communication Technologies in Education, pp. 3–18. Archive Ouverte HAL Rhodes, Greece (2002)
5. Figueroa, I., Jiménez, C., Allende-Cid, H., Leger, P.: Developing usability heuristics with prometheus: a case study in virtual learning environments. Comput. Stand. Interfaces **65**, 132–142 (2019)
6. Gunesekera, A.I., Bao, Y., Kibelloh, M.: The role of usability on e-learning user interactions and satisfaction: a literature review. J. Syst. Inf. Technol. 21(3), 368–394 (2019)

7. Harrati, N., Bouchrika, I., Tari, A., Ladjailia, A.: Exploring user satisfaction for e-learning systems via usage-based metrics and system usability scale analysis. Comput. Hum. Behav. **61**, 463–471 (2016)
8. Konstantinidis, A., Tsiatsos, T., Pomportsis, A.: Collaborative virtual learning environments: design and evaluation. Multimedia Tools Appl. **44**(2), 279–304 (2009)
9. Kristof, Z., Toth, K.: Developing and examining a virtual learning environment. Hung. Educ. Res. J. **9**(3), 511–526 (2019)
10. Mastan, I.A., Sensuse, D.I., Suryono, R.R., Kautsarina, K.: Evaluation of distance learning system (e-learning): a systematic literature review. J. Teknoinfo **16**(1), 132–137 (2022)
11. Mathew, I.R., Ebelelloanya, J.: Open and distance learning: benefits and challenges of technology usage for online teaching and learning in Africa (2016)
12. Pal, D., Vanijja, V.: Perceived usability evaluation of Microsoft teams as an online learning platform during COVID-19 using system usability scale and technology acceptance model in India. Child Youth Serv. Rev. **119**, 105535 (2020)
13. Vertesi, A., Dogan, H., Stefanidis, A.: Usability evaluation of virtual learning environments: a university case study. In: Isaias, P., Sampson, D.G., Ifenthaler, D. (eds.) Online Teaching and Learning in Higher Education. CELDA, pp. 161–183. Springer, Cham (2020). https://doi.org/10.1007/978-3-030-48190-2_9

AIS Adoption Challenges: The Role of Interactions Between Humans and Artificial Intelligence in Adoption of Adaptive Learning

Baran Osmanoglu[✉]

AIS Consortium, AEFA (Adaptive Education For All), 1 rue des Bauches, 75016 Paris, France
baran.osmanoglu@aefa.co.uk

Abstract. This paper investigates the development of new kinds of mutualistic relationships in the context of interaction and collaboration between human and artificial intelligence (AI), with the aim to address challenges in adoption of adaptive learning. The rise of adaptive learning appears as a step in the personalisation of education based on the development of new forms of AI trained with significant data and important computing capabilities. The future of adaptive learning promises a new era in education, while raising challenges. The findings of this paper suggest that the main challenges that arise with the adoption of adaptive learning can be classified as follows: i) ethical (privacy, trust and security risks related to data management); ii) changing educational process (changing role of teachers); iii) organisational and cultural (challenges related to implementation at scale of adaptive learning tools). This paper analyses how new forms of alliances between humans and technology can be defined in order to address these challenges. The methodology used for data collection was primarily semi-structured interviews, based on purposive sampling, further supported with literature review. The methodology used for data analysis was thematic analysis.

Keywords: Human-AI alliances · Adaptive learning · Educational process · Data privacy

1 Introduction

Adaptive learning has emerged as an important technological trend in the education technology (EdTech) sector. Global EdTech investments reached USD 18.66 billion in 2019 with a growing global market expected valued at USD 86.72 billion in 2020 (Emergen 2021).

Adaptive learning refers broadly to a learning process where the content taught or the way such content is presented changes, or "adapts", based on the responses of the individual learner (Oxman and Wong 2014). Adaptive learning systems, based on AI technologies, can be of various types, ranging from simple systems based on a preconceived set of rules to complex systems with self-learning algorithms. Adaptive learning is an adaptive instructional systems (AIS) approach developed with the application of AI techniques (Lee and Park 2007).

© Springer Nature Switzerland AG 2022
G. Meiselwitz et al. (Eds.): HCII 2022, LNCS 13517, pp. 377–389, 2022.
https://doi.org/10.1007/978-3-031-22131-6_29

The rise of adaptive learning appears as a step in the personalisation of education based on the development of new forms of AI. The recent advances in AI allow machines to sense, comprehend, act and learn, relying on algorithms trained with significant amount of data and important computing capabilities. My findings from interviews with practioners developing or using AI enabled tools suggest that technology-enabled adaptive or personalised learning is becoming more and more popular. In todays' context, adaptive learning tools are primarily used to support the teachers in the delivery of content.

The future of adaptive learning can make important contributions in education and improve student and teacher experiences, while raising challenges that can be formulated as impacts on human life, both at the individual and societal levels. The findings of this paper suggest that the main challenges that arise with the adoption of adaptive learning can be classified as follows: i) ethical (privacy, trust and security risks related to data management); ii) changing educational process (changing role of teachers); iii) organisational and cultural (challenges related to implementation at scale of adaptive learning tools). This paper investigates 1) what are the main challenges in the adoption of adaptive learning, and 2) why a participatory design involving students and teachers is required in the development of adaptive learning tools. The need to focus on human agency appears primordial to enhance the design of adaptive learning. A process that involves an embedded feedback system is proposed. The approach adopted is to extend research on Cybernetics theory and other research conducted on human-AI interactions to identify how to revise mutualistic relationship between humans and AI.

2 Methodology

The methodology used for data collection is primarily interviews conducted with different groups of AI enabled tools practioners (data scientists, software engineers, software vendors, and leaders within organisations, EdTech professionals). Specific open-ended questions were addressed to each group of interviewees located in various geographical locations (Europe, Middle East and United States). The interviews were conducted in person or remotely. Identification of interviewees and preparation of questions were based on purposive sampling method. Semi-structured interviews were chosen with the aim to generate in-depth understanding of the challenges and risks posed by the adoption of AI based systems. Interviews were best suited for the comprehensive understanding of the value of a multidisciplinary approach on "interaction and collaboration between human and artificial intelligence" as a way of addressing challenges for adoption of AI enabled tools. The interview questions not only allowed to have insights on challenges for adoption of AI based tools but also to open the discussion on how a potential collaboration between human and artificial intelligence-as feedback system-scan contribute to tackle these challenges. The methodology used for data analysis was thematic analysis. This study is further supported with extensive literature reviews on research conducted on cybernetics, education technology and adaptive learning, and analysis of case-studies of organisations in the process of adoption of adaptive learning systems.

3 Challenges in Adoption of Adaptive Learning

Research on the empirical impact of adaptive learning is still limited, mainly because adaptive learning systems are still in their infancy (Weber 2019). However, based on the findings provided by AI practioners, several challenges are involved with the adoption of adaptive learning tools.

Firstly, the usage of learning data arises as main concern in adoption of AI based systems. AI encompasses a range of technologies that learn over time as they are exposed to more data. AI includes speech recognition, natural language processing, semantic technology, biometrics, machine and deep learning, swarm intelligence, and chatbots or voice bots. An important amount of data is processed through these technologies. Learning technologies generate large volumes of educational data about learners and educators, their courses, technologies and activities, achievements, behaviours, choices learning strategies, and performance, from different sources (from synergetic confluence of several computing technologies, including high-speed networks, cloud and mobile computing technologies, and the Internet of Things). This data can be machine generated as well as contributed by teachers and students (Macfadyen 2017). The high volume of data that educational activities generate every day is growing exponentially as interaction with educational technologies increase (Macfadyen 2017). Organisations have argued that analytics (as learning analytics in educational context) should be used to optimise learning and learning environments. Learning analytics, is the use of analytic techniques to help target instructional, curricular, and support resources to support the achievement of specific learning goals (Gudivada 2017).

Secondly, even if more and more adaptive learning projects are initiated in organisations, the number of organisations having fully implemented adaptive learning tools remain relatively low. Leaders participated to interviews confirmed that following their investments on AI based technologies and algorithms, they experienced that scaling these tools require some new capabilities as well as changes in educational processes and organisation.

The findings of this paper suggest that the main challenges that arise with the adoption of adaptive learning include: i) how protection of personal data can be ensured considering the lack of framework on ethics, privacy, trust and security; ii) how existing learning processes and teaching practices should evolve when adaptive learning systems are implemented in organisations; iii) why implementation of adaptive learning tools at scale requires new methodologies, skills and resources and a change of organisations and culture.

4 Ethical Challenges (Privacy, Trust and Security Risks Related to Data Management)

Ethics, privacy, trust and security have always been important concerns in relation to technology, acquiring yet new dimensions in the context of intelligent environments. The use of learners' personal data to train AI algorithms for a personalised teaching and learning is central to usage of educational data (Koedinger and al Koedinger et al. 2015).

However, research has shown that there are significant concerns regarding the use of end-users' data (as students', teachers', organisational and administrative data) by adaptive learning tool, without their consent. Many AI based applications today are effectively "black boxes" lacking transparency, explainability and quality controls, increasing the risk of negative outcomes and leading to criticism regarding the balance between the benefits and the harms of this innovation. Most of interviewees and field experts on AI based tools mentioned that their biggest challenges were in the usage of personal data. For instance, as expressed by a data scientist interviewee, "using private information without learners' consent is not discussable, they should have the right to decide whether their information can be used or not, this is what a democracy requires; but, at the same time when the usage of this information serves to help the learner, the question then becomes how to proceed?" An additional observation was put forward by an AI consultant, "we observe many challenges; such as the use of data necessary to train the algorithms; in particular when it comes to students' school record, due to confidentiality and ethical reasons". A recent report published by The Digital Futures Commission highlights that "students in schools have no choice and control over the usage of their data by third parties, and their parents are often unaware of the extent or purposes of this data processing within or beyond the education system" (DFC 2021). Concerns have also been raised about how data is being tracked in online education spaces, particularly by major companies like Google engaging in the Educational Technology space. In fact, Google was sued in 2021 in the US by The State of New Mexico, for allegedly collecting student data through Google-Suite for Education (The New York Times, February 2020).

These findings provide evidence about the absence of frameworks, protocols and guidelines that would provide adequate privacy protection and security, ensuring that the collected data would not be exposed to third parties.

Studies conducted on privacy and data protection highlight that building frameworks for data protection requires regulations through laws and policies. Privacy policies are based on legal regulations, which are justified by political, cultural, economic and other kinds of discourses. Also, policies often are the purview of local authorities. When referring to educational technologies—as adaptive learning—it is referred to global solutions that have to align with all political and cultural climates, that requires to examine privacy and data protection in an international perspective, which raises the question of universal right to privacy (Hoel and Chen 2018).

Milberg et al. (1995) stated that it could be reasonably argued that protection of personal information privacy was a principle fundamental to human existence. However, the global ideological landscape does not invite to subscription of human rights ideas or other shared normative ethics principles to motivate regulatory consensus on data protection.

Privacy concerns can be conceptualised in different countries with different regulatory policies. Nevertheless, harmonisation of policies at the global level appears unlikely to occur due to the strength of ideological and cultural differences (Bygrave 2010).

Building a consensus about privacy and data protection policies not only from universal or individual rights perspectives, but also from an educational perspective appears also as a challenge. In some countries all learning activity data seem to be available for analysis (e.g. China), and in other countries whether learning analytics is legal is being questioned and their library data for analysis is restricted due to privacy issues (e.g. Norway) (Hoel and Chen 2018). This context does not support the ambition to develop a common policy.

Conversations about ethics for usage of educational AI among scholars are not recent (Aiken and Epstein 2000), and big-tech companies are forming their own oversight committees regarding ethical AI (Lee 2018). But AI enabled EdTech requires specific AI ethics for education. Similarly, privacy is a critical issue yet to be carefully addressed in educational AI. As expressed by Hagendroff (2020) a recent semi-systematic evaluation of 22 AI ethics guidelines has revealed that current guidelines have severe flaws and a range of AI ethics that are critical for AI research, development and implementation are actually missing or overlooked in such guidelines. The critical and urgent needs for educational AI ethics also call for collaborative efforts from all stakeholders, including educators, administrators, researchers, technology innovators and all societal members.

The landscape of education is fragmented-as it is addresses from young children at school to adults on lifelong learning, and diverse-as it can be local as well as global. This implies that the policies or regulations defined within systems should be addressing all stakeholders at local and global level. The ways in which educational organisations will use data and process the insights of analysis would require close dialogue/interaction with students, teachers and other education stakeholders, where openness and transparency are essential.

5 Changing Educational Process (Changing Role of Teachers)

The adoption of adaptive learning within organisations also poses challenges to the evolution of existing learning processes and teaching practices in the context of the implementation of adaptive learning tools in organisations. In fact, the changing role of teachers and students can have impacts, reduced course quality, leading to challenges in adoption.

According to studies, some educational (pedagogical) challenges related to the need of redesigning curriculum while adaptive learning technologies are being implemented (Educause 2019) and the role of faculty in the adoption process is particularly highlighted (Oxman and Wong 2014).

Introducing technology into teaching and learning activities requires to consider the values, policies and theories shaping educational systems, classroom environments and educational relationships. According to interviewees, "considering educational technology as a separated tool not integrated within the pedagogical process" is leading to resistance for adoption. Therefore, it is important that technologies used for instructional delivery are part of the components of instruction; and not detached from the educational process.

The relationship between technology in education and pedagogical decision-making is necessary to be acknowledge by teachers. According to Anderson and Borthwick (2002) research evidence shows that "participants whose technology instruction was integrated in their methods course reported more frequent use of technology for both teacher productivity and student projects during both on-campus courses and their first year of actual classroom teaching". There is no blueprint for technology integration, however, it is suggested that effort be made to link technology for instruction to all levels of pedagogical processes and activities as described next.

The role of technology in education can be determinant if teachers who use technology at the classroom level are involved during technology selection decision-making process. Teachers are in a better position to articulate their needs and identify their weaknesses, however they have minimal input in planning the technology they receive. Thus, technology integration becomes an identification of a software, which does not address specific learning problems nor pinpoint the way technology can be used to improve instruction (Okojie et al. 2005). Topper (2004) states that "for teachers to use technology in support of their teaching, and to see it as a pedagogically useful tool, they must be confident and competent with the technology they are planning to use. Unable to ignore such deeply permeating innovation, education authorities often succumb to societal pressure to adopt technology without having a thoughtful plan for implementation (Pierson 2001).

Currently, existing AI products include capabilities that can assist a certain learning process, but will not directly improve the quality and effect of teaching. Adaptive learning products can help to fundamentally improve the concept and way of learning only when AI technology penetrates into each core link and the whole process of teaching. This can only be achieved with the direct involvement of the teacher in impacting the algorithms used in adaptive learning tools.

Okojie and colleagues proposes that identifying learning objectives in a technology-based instruction requires teachers to select and/or adapt instructional technology to match the objectives based on the students' needs. This follows by proposing teachers to choose the methods that are relevant to the objectives, the technology selected, learning styles, modes and pace of learning. There is also a focus on evaluating technology-based instruction, designing follow-up activities, developing course enrichment materials, locating sources for additional instructional materials, as well as designing a dynamic classroom. Using technology requires teachers to provide opportunity for students to explore the course materials and to provide them with the opportunity to select and analyse course enrichment materials using technology in ways that broaden their problem-solving skills (Okojie and al. 2005).

The design of any learning system should respect the essence of education, since people have the unique characteristics of human beings, including emotions, thoughts, and specific teaching rules and methods. Human characteristics and educational rules should be fully considered in the study of adaptive learning. (Mirata and al. 2020) Adaptive learning products' development needs cross-boundary collaboration and joint exploration from multiple fields and disciplines, as teaching and research experience, pedagogy, psychology, computer, big data and artificial intelligence. In other words, educational processes as teaching and learning should be integrated within the technology and should not exist a discrete activity. Another important point to integrate as educational process within technologies is the accessible design that enables the equitable access of people with diverse educational needs (sight or hearing impairments, learning difficulties like dyslexia etc.).

Adaptive learning tools require a shift to adaptive teaching and learning, which involves redesigning instructional material and courses integrated within the technology.

6   Organisational and Cultural Changes

Like with many technological innovations, the implementation of adaptive learning occurs in stages. According to literature, available evidence from the current higher education landscape highlights that while learning analytic tools are being implemented and many may solve certain teaching and learning challenges, successful implementation at scale is rare and faces significant systemic challenges. And so, many organisations who acknowledge benefits of using AI based systems, that can benefit to their learning processes, are lacking capabilities as resources, structures, and/or capacity to being about complex system change.

The integration of adaptive learning technologies requires a complete review of the organisation and its processes as well as adapting to work differently. According to AI based tools practioners, "the projects of AI based tools implementation are usually successful from a technical perspective but the AI tool requires human intervention in various cases and this engendered difficulties that could not be overcome, that led to the decision of putting on hold the usage of the tool after a month of its introduction". As expressed by AI practitioners during the interviews, "we consider two important phases with AI based tools implementations; the first one is to design and implement these and the second one is to ensure the models remain consistent and meaningful over time, which requires an important degree of adaptation by the organisation to operate these AI based systems, since these tools are processing real time data". Thus, major organisational changes involve new skills that would allow people to interact with real time data (AI tools working principle) and to easily use complexity of adaptive systems. This can be related to existing roles being modified or new roles being defined. "Existing roles are evolving, and new role requirements are emerging, I don't know how this gap will be filled" as expressed by an interviewee from EdTech sector. "The key part is that we do not have multi-talented resources" as mentioned by a faculty manager, when referring to the challenges on having relevant results from a machine learning tool.

Impacts of adaptation also involve "change in people's attitude such as how to make decisions based on uncertainties while using AI based tools". "Also, some roles will constraint to a higher level of automatisation; leaving people to feel less useful in their jobs, leading to lack of motivation"; hence, "it is a challenge to accompany this movement of dramatic change". In particular, in the phase of piloting adaptive learning, faculties often struggle with the use of adaptive software for communicating with students and modifying learning content, because they have lack of experience with adaptive technologies or receive inadequate support (O'Sullivan 2018).

Some challenges discussed in the literature also relate to managerial issues. At higher education institutions, one commonly cited challenge is faculty engagement. When first exposed to the adaptive approach, faculties often show resistance towards using technology (Johnson and Zone 2018). In many cases, faculties express concerns about the benefits of adaptive learning, their diminishing role in a course design, loss of control over courses, and additional workload (Hall et al. 2016). Johnson and Zone (2018) argue, for example, that a successful adoption of adaptive learning can be achieved through faculty engagement, emphasising a faculty role in the adoption process and creating a faculty culture embracing technology use. The institutional commitment in the form of leadership appears as an important factor in the adoption process, involving the promotion of an innovation culture and allocation of necessary resources. In a survey on computing and information technology in higher education, Green (2018) found, for example, that a majority of higher educational leaders show a positive attitude toward adaptive learning and believe that it has great potential to improve student success. However, the same survey has found that just 8% of educational courses use adaptive learning technologies in praxis. According to surveys conducted 70 percent of the institutions see implementation of analytics systems and processes as a major priority. However, finding from interviews have confirmed that in spite of ambitious goals, the majority of organisations remain mired at pilot implementation level. Moving from evidence of good educational practice to effective action remains a challenge. A systems perspective is critical for successful implementation at scale of any educational innovation, including analytics.

Reflecting on the slow progress of its adoption, Weber (2019) concluded that the major challenge today is, an important investment in time, money, resources and vision, mainly due to the complexity of adaptive technology, high licensing fees and long-lasting scepticism of faculties towards its potential to disrupt education in general.

Despite the recognised benefits and growing interest in using adaptive learning in teaching, its broad implementation remains rather limited. The review of previous studies shows that organisations and higher education institutions face various barriers and challenges when testing or adopting adaptive learning concepts and implementing them at scale.

7   New Forms of Alliances Between Humans and Technology

In todays' context, adaptive learning tools are implemented to support teachers in the delivery of content and to provide students personalised learning, without necessary involving end users throughout the design and running phases of these tools. The findings indicate there is a need to focus on human agency and pedagogy to enhance the adoption of adaptive learning. This section investigates why a participatory design involving students and teachers is required in the development of adaptive learning tools. A process that involves an embedded feedback system is proposed. The approach adopted is to extend research on Cybernetics theory and other research on human-AI interactions to revise mutualistic relationship between humans and AI.

7.1   Cybernetics

Early studies on human-machine interactions are marked with the introduction, by Norbert Wiener, of the notion of cybernetics, defined as "the scientific study of control and communication in the animal and the machine" (Wiener 2019, 1961). The theory of cybernetics brings the idea to control entropy in a system through feedback. In other words, cybernetics is the science of feedback, information that travels from a system through its environment and back to the system (Wiener 1961). Cybernetics more broadly encompasses the study of how systems regulate themselves and act toward goals based on feedback from the environment. These systems are not just computational; they include biological (maintaining body temperature), mechanical (governing the speed of an engine), social (managing a large workforce), and economic (regulating a national economy) systems (Wiener 1961).

Feedback reports the difference between the current state and the goal, and the system acts to correct differences. This process helps ensure stability when disturbances threaten dynamic systems, such as machines, software, organisms, and organisations (Dubberly 2015). Learning and adapting to the needs of a system are the goals of both iterative design processes and cybernetics. Therefore, the theory of cybernetics can be used to propose a framework for interactions and collaborations between humans and AI-enabled tools, as for adaptive learning tools.

7.2 Interactive Machine Learning

An approach on how a feedback system can be envisioned where end users are interacting with AI enabled tools is referred in literature as "interactive machine learning". AI systems based on machine-learning techniques are more and more being used. Machine learning are transforming data into computational models that provide user-facing applications. However, potential users of these applications, who are often domain experts for the application, have limited involvement in the process of developing them. The stakeholders involved in machine-learning techniques are mainly skilled experts. In the traditional applied machine-learning workflow, these experts collect data, construct the model, and finally assess the quality of the model with an iterative approach. Any end-user involvement in this process is mediated by the practitioners and is limited to providing data, answering domain-related questions, or giving feedback about the learned model. This limits the end users' ability to directly affect the resulting models (Amershi et al. 2014). The question that arise is how end user's involvement can be embedded in AI enabled tools, eventually as AI subsystems that interact with people.

An approach was brought by Caruana and colleagues who developed learning algorithms that enable interactive exploration of the clustering space and incorporation of new clustering constraints (Caruana et al. 2006). In other words, creating a new cluster in the AI cluster that can allow interactions with end users. According to Amershi and colleagues, their approach is an example of interactive machine learning, that enable everyday users to interactively explore the model space and drive the system toward an intended behaviour, reducing the need for supervision by practitioners. They conclude that interactive machine learning can facilitate the democratisation of applied machine learning, empowering end users to create machine-learning-based systems for their own needs and purposes (Amershi et al. 2014).

7.3 HCI Design for AI Enabled Tools

As stated by Dubberly, learning and adapting to the needs of a system are the goals of both iterative design processes and cybernetics. Thus, cybernetics can provide a useful framework for augmenting designers in creating human-centred interactive AI-enabled products (Dubberly 2015). As these systems become more reliable and easier to work with, designers can embed them into tools-as AI subsystems-that can interact with people. This interaction can then support the AI subsystem to further learn and adapt to the user.

Many researches are conducted on design approaches for Interactive Machine Learning, all based on the principle that intelligent systems are designed to augment or enhance the human, serving as a tool to be wielded through human interaction. Researches conducted by Stanford University Human-Centered Artificial Intelligence Working group proposes focus on 'the human-in-the-loop approach' which they reframe it as a Human-Computer Interaction (HCI) design problem. The approach is based on the selective inclusion of human participation in the intelligent automation, the result of this input is defined as a process that measures the efficiency of intelligent automation while accommodating human feedback and remaining pertinent (Stanford HC AI). Each step that incorporates human interaction demands the system be designed to be understood by humans to take the next action, and human agency will be determining the critical steps. They state that this approach is expected to bring benefits in terms of transparency, while incorporating human judgment in effective ways. AI systems are built to help humans. The value of such systems lies not solely in efficiency or correctness, but also in human preference and agency (Stanford HC AI).

Cybernetics offers the language (both vocabulary and frameworks) that enable scientists (and designers and others) from different domains of knowledge and practice to communicate-to describe the structural similarities of systems and to recognise patterns in information flows. This shared language is especially useful in analysing, designing, and managing complex, adaptive systems, which are related with many of today's problems (Dubberly 2015).

Martelaro and Ju suggest that today's designers must consider how information flows through these systems, how data can make operations more efficient and user experiences more meaningful, and how feedback creates opportunities for learning. Knowledge of cybernetics can inform these processes (Martelaro and Ju 2018).

The necessity of involvement of human agency in participatory design is further enhanced by designers, as Medich, who states "We designed AI-like all tools-to extend a human ability: our ability to think. We created a cybernetic model with most of the onus on the human to maintain the system and encode the exchanged information into computer speak. The technological side of the cybernetic system has not spent a lot of time adapting and learning from the human side, except in this encoded translated format. The more fluent the human, in tech speak, the more powerful the things they can accomplish together" (Medich cited in Martelaro and Ju 2018).

Student and teacher agency appear as important at different stages of adaptive learning tools' lifecycle (design, development, set up and running). By providing constant feedback, students and teachers will help to contribute in increasing the capacity and effectiveness of adaptive learning tools, consequently the educational system. Adaptive learning tools are developed by humans, however within current systems students and teachers are not sufficiently involved. Through this new approach, more agency is delivered, to students and teachers. Contemporary regulatory approaches promote the creation of feedback platforms, aim to raise user by consulting stakeholders through these platforms.

Involving students, teachers and other stakeholders in self-managing their own data used for learning analytics, through a feedback system embedded within adaptive learning tools, ensuring compliance with regulations on privacy related to educational data can be a conceptual analysis that is also considering issues and concerns identified. Extensive interactions of students and teachers with the embedded feedback tools to adaptive learning systems can also bring an approach on integrating educational processes (pedagogy) into technologies, and these interactions can also contribute to solve skill gaps in operating AI based tools. Further research is required to analyse these hypotheses.

8   Conclusion and Future Work

The findings of this paper suggest that the main challenges that arise today with the adoption of adaptive learning today are classified as ethical (privacy, trust and security risks related to data management), changing educational process (changing role of teachers and students) and organisational (challenges with implementation at scale of adaptive learning tools).

In order to overcome challenges related to data ethics, harmonised policies or guidelines to provide an ethical framework at global level is unlikely to be defined in the near future, due to ideological and cultural differences between countries. Adaptive learning tools are today developed and operated by AI experts who consult teachers and students only as domain experts, which still constitutes a challenge for the integration of the educational (pedagogical) process within these tools. Deployment of AI based tools at scale require today some capabilities (as new skills for end users) that remain as gaps to be filled. This paper analysed whether an embedded feedback system in adaptive learning tools, based on participatory design, involving students and teachers would help to overcome these challenges related to the adoption of these tools. This paper has shown that there is a need to focus on human agency to enhance the design and setting up of adaptive learning, where students, teachers and other education stakeholders need to be actively involved.

This research will be further followed up with more empirical studies to investigate more details on how HCI design approaches, can address each of the identified challenge. The objective will be to further extend research on Cybernetics theory and other research on human-AI interactions to revise mutualistic relationship between humans and AI.

References

Aiken, R., Epstein, R.: Ethical guidelines for AI in education: starting a conversation. Int. J. Artif. Intell. Educ. **11**, 163–176 (2000)

Amershi, S., Cakmak, M., Knox, W.B., Kulesza T.: Power to the people: the role of humans in interactive. Mach. Learn. AI Mag. (2014)

Anderson, C.L. Borthwick, A.: Results of separate and integrated technology instruction in pre-service training. ERIC Reproduction Document # IR021919, p. 14 (2002)

Brinton, C.G., Rill, R., Ha, S., Chiang, M., Smith, R., Ju, W.: Individualization for education at scale: MIIC design and preliminary evaluation. IEEE Trans. Learn. Technol. **8**(1) (2015)

Brockman, J.: Possible Minds: 25 Ways of Looking at AI. Penguin Press, United States (2019)

Bygrave, L.A.: Privacy and data protection in an international perspective. Scandinavian Studies in Law (2010). http://www.scandinavianlaw.se/pdf/56-8.pdf. http://www.scandinavianlaw.se/pdf/56-8.pdf

Digital Futures Commission: Addressing the problems and realising the benefits of processing children's education data: report on an expert roundtable (2021). https://digitalfuturescommiss ion.org.uk/wp-content/uploads/2021/11/Roundtable-report-25112-final.pdf

Dubberly, H., Pangaro, P.: Cybernetics and design: conversations for action. Cybern. Hum. Know. **22**(é-3), 73–82 (2015)

EDUCAUSE Horizon Report: Adaptive learning: understanding its progress and poten- tial. In: EDUCAUSE Horizon Report 2019: Higher Education Edition, pp. 34– 35 (2019). https://library.educause.edu//media/files/library/2019/4/2019horizonreport.pdf?la= en&hash=C8E8D444AF372E705FA1BF9D4FF0DD4CC6F0FDD1

Emergen Research: Adaptive Learning Market Size (2021) https://www.emergenresearch.com/press-release/global-adaptive-learning-market

Glanville, R.: Researching design and designing research. Des. Issues **15**(2), 80–91 (1999)

Green, K.: Campus computing 2018: the 29th national survey of computing and information technology in American higher education (2018). https://www.campuscomputing.net/content/2018/10/31/the-2018-campus-computing-survey

Hagendorff, T.: The ethics of AI ethics: an evaluation of guidelines. Minds Mach., 99–120 (2020)

Hall Giesinger, C., Adams Becker, S., Davis, A., Shedd, L.: Scaling solutions to higher educa- tion's biggest challenges: an NMC Horizon project strategic brief, vol. 3.2. The New Media Consortium, Austin (2016). https://www.learntechlib.org/p/182095/

Hoel, T., Chen, W.: Privacy and data protection in learning analytics should be motivated by an educational maxim—towards a proposal. Res. Pract. Technol. Enhanc. Learn. **13**(1), 1–14 (2018). https://doi.org/10.1186/s41039-018-0086-8

Johnson, C., Zone, E.: Achieving a scaled implementation of adaptive learning through faculty engagement: a case study. Current Issues Emerg. ELearning **5**(1), 80–95 (2018). https://schola rworks.umb.edu/ciee/vol5/iss1/7

Kaplan, J.: Artificial intelligence: think again. Commun. ACM **60**(1), 36–38 (2016). https://doi. org/10.1145/2950039

Koedinger, K.R., D'Mello, S., McLaughlin, E.A., Pardos, Z.A., Rosé, C.: Data mining and education. Wires Cogn. Sci. (2015). https://doi.org/10.1002/wcs.1350

Lee, J., Park, O.C.: Adaptive instructional systems (2007). https://doi.org/10.4324/978020388 0869.CH37. Corpus ID: 415533 Published 22 December 2007

Lee, M.: Understanding perception of algorithmic decisions: fairness, trust, and emotion in response to algorithmic management. Big Data Soc. **5**(2018), 2053951718756684 (2018)

Macfadyen, L.P.: Overcoming barriers to educational analytics: how systems thinking and pragmatism can help. Educ. Technol. **57**(1), 31–39 (2017)

Martelaro, N., Ju, W.: Cybernetics and the design of the user experience of AI systems. Interactions **XXV**(6), 38 (2018). https://interactions.acm.org/

Milberg, S.J., Burke, S.J., Smith, H.J., Kallman, E.A.: Values, personal information privacy, and regulatory approaches. Commun. ACM **38**(12), 65–74 (1995). https://doi.org/10.1145/219663. 219683

Milberg, S.J., Smith, H.J., Burke, S.J.: Information privacy: corporate management and national regulation. Organ. Sci. **11**(1), 35–57 (2000). https://doi.org/10.1287/orsc.11.1.35.12567

Mirata, V., Hirt, F., Bergamin, P., van der Westhuizen, C.: Challenges and contexts in establishing adaptive learning in higher education: findings from a Delphi study. Int. J. Educ. Technol. High. Educ. **17**(1), 1–25 (2020). https://doi.org/10.1186/s41239-020-00209-y

Norman, D.: The Design of Future Things. Basic Books, New York (2007)

O'Sullivan, P.: APLU adaptive courseware grant, a case study: implementation at the University of Mississippi. Current Issues Emerg. ELearning **5**(1), 45–61 (2018)

Okojie, M.C.P.O., Olinzock, A.A., Okojie-Boulder, T.C.: Technology Training Dilemma: A Diagnostic Approach (2005). https://scholar.lib.vt.edu/ejournals/JOTS/v32/v32n2/okojie.html#Okojie

Oxman, S., Wong, W.: White paper: adaptive learning systems. Integrated Education Solutions, Snapwiz 1 (2014)

Peng, H., Ma, S., Spector, J.M.: Personalized adaptive learning: an emerging pedagogical approach enabled by a smart learning environment. Smart Learn. Environ. **6** (2019). Article number: 9

Pierson, M.: Technology integration practice as a function of pedagogical experts. J. Res. Comput. Educa. **33**(5) (2001)

The New York Times–New Mexico Sues Google Over Childeren's Privacy Violations, February 2020. https://www.nytimes.com/2020/02/20/technology/new-mexico-google-lawsuit.html

Topper, A.: How are we doing? Using self-assessment to measure changing teacher technology literacy within a graduate education technology program **12**(3), 303–317 (2004)

Venkat, N.G.: Cognitive analytics driven personalized learning. Educ. Technol. (2017)

Weber, N.: Adaptive learning: understanding its progress and potential. In: EDUCAUSE Horizon Report 2019: Higher Education Edition, pp. 34–35 (2019). https://library.educause.edu/-/media/files/library/2019/4/2019horizonreport.pdf?la=en&hash=C8E8D444AF372E705FA1BF9D4FF0DD4CC6F0FDD1

Wiener, N.: (reissue of the 1961 edition) Cybernetics or Control and Communication in the Animal and the Machine. The MIT Press, Cambridge (2019)

Wiener, N.: Cybernetics or Control and Communication in the Animal and Machine, vol. 25. MIT Press (1961)

Ya Ni, A.: Comparing the effectiveness of classroom and online learning: teaching research methods source. J. Public Affairs Educ. **19**(2), 199–215 (2013)

Yang, T.C, Hwang, G., Yang, S.: Development of an adaptive learning system with multiple perspectives based on students' learning styles and cognitive styles. Educ. Technol. Soc. **16**(4), 185–200 (2013)

Zhang, K., Aslan, B.: AI technologies for education: recent research & future directions, computers and education. Artif. Intell. **2**, 1000025 (2021)

Development and Evaluation of a Learning Analytics Dashboard for Moodle Learning Management System

Ivan Peraić[1](✉) and Ani Grubišić[2]

[1] Department of Information Sciences, University of Zadar, Zadar, Croatia
iperaic@unizd.hr
[2] Faculty of Science, University of Split, Split, Croatia
ani@pmfst.hr

Abstract. Learning analytics provides a potential for adapting learning, teaching and knowledge testing processes to individual needs. One of the ways of using learning analytics is a dashboard for providing feedback to students and teachers. This paper presents the development and evaluation of the learning analytics dashboard for students (LAD-S). The LAD-S displays three views: a look at student success, system activities and prediction based on machine learning algorithms. We have used LAD-S as a part of Moodle online courses, one during the second semester in the 2020/2021, and the other two during the first semester in the 2021/2022. A survey was designed to examine students' opinion about the LAD-S that included student's self-awareness, influence of the dashboard on learning effectiveness, satisfaction with the type of data collected, usefulness and ease-of-use, intention to use the learning analytics dashboard. Data from 33 undergraduate and graduate students were collected. The results have shown that students are satisfied with all examined aspects of the LAD-S above the average. Students express the greatest satisfaction for ease of use (M = 3.79), clarity of collected data (M = 3.6), usefulness (M = 3.6), SUS questionnaire (M = 3.6), behavioral intention (M = 3.4) and satisfaction with individual functions of LAD-S (M = 3.4). Lower, yet above-average satisfaction was obtained for the impact of the LAD-S on more effective learning (M = 3.2); intention to use (M = 3.3) and satisfaction with the possibility of behavioral changes (M = 3.1). To verify the reliability of the measures used, the Cronbach's alpha reliability coefficient was calculated for each scale. Satisfactory reliability of all measures used was obtained, with alpha coefficients ranging from 0.704 for the SUS questionnaire to 0.942 for the ease-of-use measure.

Keywords: Learning analytics · Learning analytics dashboard · Evaluation

1 Introduction

Teaching is a dynamic activity that needs to be constantly monitored and adapted to changes in the social context and needs of students in order to ensure high quality

G. Meiselwitz et al. (Eds.): HCII 2022, LNCS 13517, pp. 390–408, 2022.
https://doi.org/10.1007/978-3-031-22131-6_30

learning and teaching process [1]. As the use of online learning continues to increase, there is a need for effective strategies and tools to help learners achieve success in online environments [2]. During online learning, students leave a digital trail, which is appropriate for learning analytics. Learning analytics use the potential of increasing amounts of interaction, personal data, and achievement data [3]. According to the first international conference Learning Analytics and Knowledge (LAK), learning analytics (LA) is "measuring, collecting, analyzing and preparing reports on students and their context for the purpose of understanding and optimizing learning and the environment in which learning takes place" [4]. Suthers and Verbert [5] recognized the field of learning analytics as an "intermediate area" since it is at the intersection between technology and learning science. Moreover, the learning analytics should be seen as an educational approach guided by pedagogy rather than vice versa [6]. Online learning environments do not have the same support structure as traditional classrooms and many motivating social aspects are missing. One focus of research on learning analytics is empowering teachers and motivating students to make informed decisions about the learning process, mainly through visualizations of collected student data through dashboards [7]. Few [8] defines a learning analytics as an important information needed to achieve one or more objectives in one place. Teachers usually do not see how students communicate with the learning and teaching system; therefore, they need feedback to take appropriate actions. Feedback presented through Learning Analytics Dashboard (LAD) is used as a powerful metacognitive tool for students by encouraging them to think about learning activities and results [9] and enables teachers to create a real picture of students and teaching materials.

The following section analyses previous literature overviews regarding LADs. The third section describes development of a learning analytics dashboard for Moodle Learning Management System (LMS). The fourth section describes the methodology of the research. The fifth section presents the results of evaluation, the sixth chapter discuss the results and the seventh section gives future guidelines.

2 Research Background

2.1 Learning Analytics

Learning analytics is an emerging trend, particularly in higher education. The development of big data technologies and the widespread use of digital tools allow us to build up important data collections on student behavior [10]. We can now measure, collect, analyze and process this data in order to better understand learners and improve their learning levels [11]. The dashboard concept was defined by Few [8], stating that a dashboard is "a visual display of the most important information needed to achieve one or more objectives; consolidated and arranged on a single screen so the information can be monitored at a glance". The definition of the LAD usually refers to displays in a single view, but due to the space limitation, the concept has evolved from a single view to multiple views and purposes, supporting viewers to interact with different components to gain necessary context [12]. Schwendimann et al. [13] say that learning analytics dashboards still follow the traditional paradigm in which the teacher monitors the students. Main purpose of dashboards is to give feedback to students, teachers in order to improve the learning and teaching process. Feedback aims to improve students' self-awareness, which leads to improved academic performance as well as enhanced Self-Regulated Learning (SRL) [14]. Also, Matcha et al. [15] define SRL as an important role for achieving improved academic performance. LAD is undoubtedly an interesting tool because it visualizes a large number of information with which we can identify key problems in learning and teaching process. On the technical side, LAD is not a novelty, but it is still not completely clear how students accept online educational systems and how much these systems actually affect learning and teaching process. It has become a challenge for developers to design LAD that suits the needs in the educational domain to process the data generated by online learning activities [16]. Each analytics dashboard has features that do not necessarily fulfil every user's requirement [17].

A number of institutions developed systems for learning analytics and some of development objectives are monitoring and support [18–21], visualization [22–25] or prediction [26–29].

2.2 Support for Learning Analytics in Moodle

Moodle LMS (www.moodle.org) is a web-based system specifically developed to complement traditional learning methods. Moodle LMS is an open-source LMS developed using PHP programming language and was first released in 2002. With the increasing demand and usage of online learning, Moodle is one of the most used LMS [30]. Moodle LMS has a simple interface with drag-and-drop features and well-documented resources along with ongoing usability improvements. Moodle LMS has very high flexibility and scalability that can be customized to support the needs of both small classes and large organizations [31].

Moodle and other LMS systems collect extensive data on how staff and students are using the systems. The ability to track and store vast amount of data on students and instructional design is very helpful for educational institutions. Such tracking in Moodle is conducted through various tracking tools and reports and through different analytic graphs and dashboards. Moodle has a wide list of analytical tools and graphs such as Engagement Analytics, GISMO, Analytics Graphs, Heatmap, Analytics [32]. On the other hand, many authors are developing Moodle plug-ins to integrate analytics. Plug-ins give an overview of relevant metrics such as student engagement time and student interaction with specified activities. The most popular Moodle plug-ins are IntelliBoard, SmartKlass, My Feedback, Piwik Analytics, etc.

InteliBoard is a complete commercial implementation of the e-learning analysis frameworks in LMS [33]. In addition to the visual analysis through customizable dashboards, it defines a set of informed decision rules together with an Artificial Intelligence (AI) assistant called LISA. On the one hand, it integrates LMSs through web services and, on the other hand, an open-source plugin maintained by the company [34]. Admin reports, notifications, learner access rate, etc. are supplied from the analysis. The learner can use this for self-assessment by comparing their progress against course completion. Teachers and admins can track the course activities and acceptance among learners [35].

A free plug-in, SmartKLass is a dashboard for Learning Analytics that could be incorporated into the Moodle virtual learning platform to allow teachers monitor their students' behavior [36]. The technology analyzes the statements using machine learning algorithms and builds dashboard analysis with consolidated user information. It enables students to view their performances, see the evolution of the course, and receive or send alert messages [35].

My Feedback plug-in allows students to see an overview of all their grades and feedback on assignments [37]. It provides their visible grades and a link to their submission and any feedback that has been released to them. The report is intended to help students understand the variety of feedback they receive. Piwik Analytics provides reporting in the form of a comparative table. Data such as page views, bounce rate, and average generation time are recording to provide an overview for the user to understand their contents hit rate [31].

3 Learning Analytics Dashboard for Students (LAD-s)

The design specification of the analytics dashboard is influenced by the objective and the current design trend. Our Learning Analytics Dashboard (LAD-s) is created as a Moodle Block which may be added to any course in Moodle. Students access the LAD-s from the Moodle course page. There are three components (Activity Component, Success Component and Prediction Component) in the LAD-s system which generate feedback presented furthermore to the student in the Dashboard component. All the components are programmed in the PHP programming language. Prediction Component also use Python for integrated Machine Learning algorithms for prediction of student's success. In addition, HTML, CSS, and JavaScript are used for front-end development. The architecture of LAD-s is illustrated in Fig. 1.

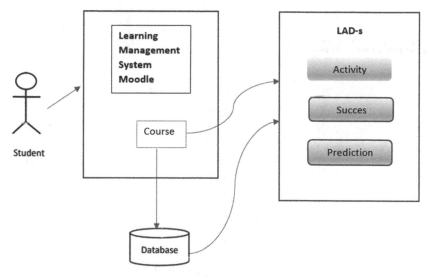

Fig. 1. LAD-s architecture

The LAD-s report for the student gives an overall view of each student's progress in the course.

3.1 Activity Component

Activity Component highlights student engagement levels based on students' logs. Activity Component has three different panels. The first panel shows the number of total logins and logins in last seven days (Fig. 2). This panel contains only descriptive analytics components and compares the learner's engagement versus that of the groups average, median, minimum and maximum.

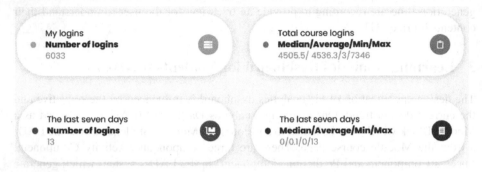

Fig. 2. Number of total logins and logins in last seven days

The other data visualization available in the Activity Component dashboard includes the bar chart. The bar charts show the individual logs of each student in terms of weeks. Figure 3 show the bar charts that are shown in the Activity Component.

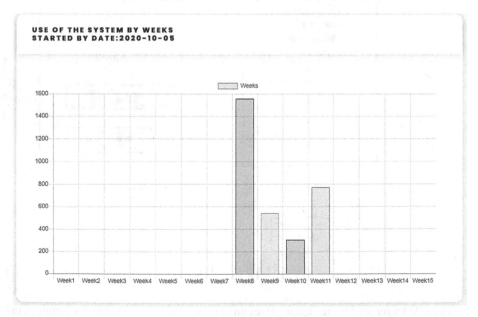

Fig. 3. Student's use of system

Besides data visualization, Activity Component also returns a message (Fig. 4). The message is visible to students as a system notification. The notifications are as follows:

1. "Your effort on the course is very low. Please try harder!"
2. "Your effort in college is low. Try harder please!"
3. "Your effort in college is average. Do your best please!"
4. "Your effort in college is high. Keep it up!"
5. "Your hard work in college is exceptional. Keep it up and you will surely succeed!"

SYSTEM NOTIFICATIONS:

Message based on processed data

Your hard work in college is exceptional. Keep it up and you will surely succeed!

Fig. 4. Notification based on student's logs

The aim of the Activity Component is to encourage students to see their engagement and, if they are not satisfied with their use of the system, which they can see from the previously described data, to approach the work more maturely and responsibly.

3.2 Success Component

Success Component gets information about their success and compare it with all colleagues keeping in mind the student's score, minimum grade, maximum grade, average

EXAM RESULTS

No.	Name	My grade	Details
1	Test Temeljni pojmovi iz programiranja	19	Show details
2	Test Elementi programskog jezika Python	23	Show details
3	Test Rad u Python IDLE okr datoteke, spremanje dato		

✕Test Elementi programskog jezika Python

My result : 23
Minimum result in class : 23
Maximum result in class : 23
Average result in class : 23
Median result in class : 22

Fig. 5. Exam results with details

grade and median grade. This Component has four panels. First panel (Fig. 5) displays the grades the student has achieved. Using this visualization student can compare his performance level with the class's best performance level, class's worst performance level, class's average performance level and class's median performance level by selecting Details. Student can create his/her own personalized learning environment to increase his performance level to the class best level. This visualization supports increasing the grades of the student.

The following overview (Fig. 6) allows the student an insight into the upcoming exams. Students can see how many exams they have till the end of semester, so they can do their best to make their performance better.

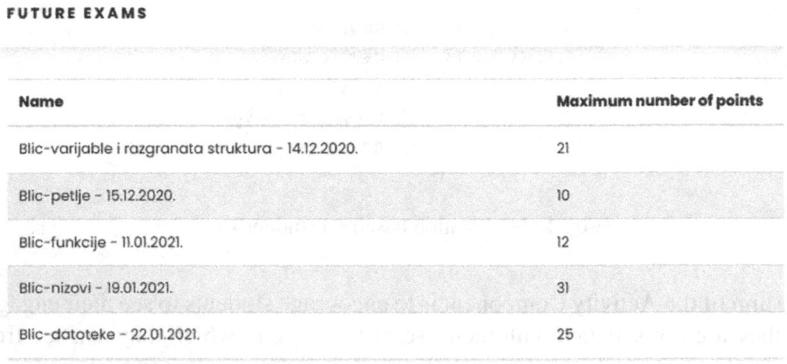

FUTURE EXAMS

Name	Maximum number of points
Blic-varijable i razgranata struktura - 14.12.2020.	21
Blic-petlje - 15.12.2020.	10
Blic-funkcije - 11.01.2021.	12
Blic-nizovi - 19.01.2021.	31
Blic-datoteke - 22.01.2021.	25

Fig. 6. Future exams

In order to show to students the activities they perform, students are shown a line graph. The graph shows the number of submitted materials, the number of resource views and the number of completed quizzes (Fig. 7). We believe that feedback on the student's success in the group is very important, because it can act as a trigger for the student to improve his results, so in the following graph we show the student his success. We singled out the success on all exams for student and compared it with average student success of all colleagues (Fig. 8).

3.3 Prediction Component

Data mining for educational purposes and learning analytics can be used to predict the success and possible giving up of students based on an assessment of their achievements, participation, engagement, assessment in the learning process, teaching and knowledge testing [38]. Data mining is used to define student behaviour and create learning patterns in order to create different profiles of students [39]. Based on our descriptive-analytic results, LAD-s generate predictive analytics. We wanted to predict a student's final results, our model will predict whether a given learner will be Poor, Average, or Good. Prediction Component use Decision Tree Algorithm, performance prediction is based on student's logs, score on first exam, activities on Moodle (number of submitted materials, the number of resource views and the number of completed quizzes) and time spent on

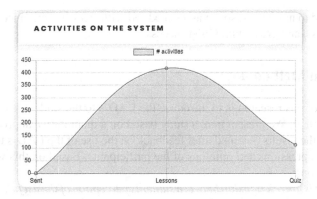

Fig. 7. Activities on the system

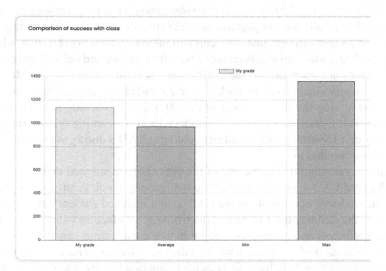

Fig. 8. Comparison of success

exam. In this case, idea is to see what student's think about Prediction Component, so the information is presented to students in the form of visualization (Fig. 9).

Fig. 9. Prediction component

We decided to use colors, so we associated red with Poor performance, yellow with Average success, and green with Good success.

4 Research Methodology

The objective of this research is to introduce the LAD-s to the student's and to see how students evaluate it. We present here a study based on a quantitative approach, with the aim to present the results obtained after feedback on the use of the LAD-s tool, and then to collect the impressions and opinions of the participants. Based on this we have three research questions:

RQ1: *What is the relationship between students perception of the usefulness of LAD-s, improvement suggestions, and comments on the use of LAD-s?*

RQ2: *How students accept LAD-s and their perception of the use in the future?*

RQ3: *Can the use of LAD-s affecct bihevioral changes during learning process?*

This study is conducted on a population of 228 student's (175 first year undergraduate students and 53 first year graduate students) all taking courses organized in a blended learning modality, which takes advantage of both face-to-face and online learning. Some course sections are done face-to-face, with some sections online on the Moodle 3.8 platform. Undergraduate students took a course entitled "Programming 1" over a 15-week period, during the first semester in the 2021/2022. Graduate students took two courses entitled "E-learning systems" (42 students) and "E-learning systems design" (11 students) over a 15-week period. Students could use LAD-s during the whole semester whenever they wanted to.

A survey was submitted at the end of the previously mentioned courses to the students who used LAD-s, in order to evaluate the presented tool. A survey was designed to examine students' opinion about the LAD-s, that included student's self-awareness, influence of the dashboard on learning effectiveness, satisfaction with the type of data collected, usefulness and ease-of-use, intention to use the learning analytics dashboard. The survey was adopted from recent work on the use of learning analytics dashboards as a decision support tool. Scheffel [40] presents evaluation framework for Learning Analytics. This framework has four dimensions (Data, Awareness, Reflection and Impact). Learning Analytics should stimulate the self-regulating skills of the learners [41] and foster awareness and reflection processes for learners and teachers. We adopted Self-awareness, Influence and Data from [40]. Kim, Jo and Park [21] indicate that students were not able to connect the dashboard information to their behavioral changes. We adopted Behavioral changes from [21] to see if LAD-s could have a better impact on changes during learning process.

Perceived usability affects greatly students learning effectiveness and overall learning experience. The System Usability Scale (SUS) is a well-researched and widely used questionnaire for perceived usability evaluation [42]. In order to research degree of learner's opinion on usability of LAD-s, SUS questionnaire was adopted from [43].

Using the principles of technology acceptance model (TAM) we explored students' acceptance of LAD-s. TAM model consist of four items Usefulness, Ease-of-use, Behavioral intention and Intention to use [44].

Participant's opinion and suggestions on LAD-s include questions to research what students thinks generally about LAD-s. Two open-ended questions are set to students to have the opportunity to offer something to add without currently being on the LAD-s and to give their suggestions for improvement in future.

The questions were translated to Croatian and adapted minimally to reflect the topic of the dashboard. As shown in Table 1, the survey consisted of 45 questions (43 questions using a five-point Likert scale and 2 open-ended questions). Thirty-three students completed a questionnaire, 6 of them enrolled in course "E-learning systems design", 8 in course "E-learning systems" and 19 in course "Programming 1".

Table 1. Summary of survey questionnaire

Part	Contents	Example	No. of questions
Student's self-awareness	Degree of conformity between learner's perceived online activity and real data	This dashboard makes me more aware of my current study situation	4
Influence	Degree of learner's influence of the dashboard on learning effectiveness	This dashboard stimulates me to study more effectively (as in: making sure to reach the target, in any way)	2
Data	Degree of learner's satisfaction with type of collected data	It is clear to me which data are being collected to assemble this dashboard	2
Usefulness	Degree of learner's usefulness with the LAD-s	LAD-s contains the feedback I want to know	3
Ease-of-use	Degree of learner's opinion on ease-of-use	The interaction with the LAD-s is clear and understandable	4
Bihevioral intention	Degree of learner's bihevioral intention to use LAD-s in future courses	It is important to use LAD-s during online teaching	3
Intention to use	Degree of learner's intention to use LAD-s in future	I will adopt the use the LAD-s system in the next semesters	2
Bihevioral changes	Degree of learner's bihevioral changes during use of LAD-s	I reflected on my learning behavior based on the info in LAD-s	6

(*continued*)

Table 1. (*continued*)

Part	Contents	Example	No. of questions
SUS questionnaire	Degree of learner's opinion on usability of LAD-s	I would imagine that most people would learn to use this dashboard very quickly	10
Participant's opinion and suggestions on LAD-s	Participant's opinion and suggestions on LAD-s	LAD-s shows your success over your peers. This feedback is of great importance for creating a sense of succss in course	9

5 Evaluation Results

The results will be given according to previously described parts.

5.1 Student's Self-awareness

The satisfaction with the way the LAD-s helps them raise their self-awareness and the way it encourages them to think about their own learning is generally above average among students. Regarding questions related to self-awareness and thinking in general, students express somewhat greater satisfaction with survey items such as "LAD-s helps me create awareness of my current learning situation" ($M = 3.39$, $SD = 1.27$), item "LAD-s encourages me to think about my learning behavior" ($M = 3.30$, $SD = 1.42$), and item "LAD-s stimulates me to change learning behavior or the way I study." ($M = 3.24$, $SD = 1.37$) and slightly lower satisfaction with the item "With the help of the LAD-s, I predict my possible learning situation" ($M = 3.09$, $SD = 1.33$). Individual differences were noted among students in terms of answering these questions, and individual answers ranged from 1 to 5.

5.2 Influence

The average satisfaction of the students with the way the LAD-s encourages them to learn more effectively (such as: "ensuring the achievement of the goal, in any way") is $M = 3.36$, $SD = 1.39$, while the average satisfaction with the way the learning analytics dashboard encourages them to learn more effectively (such as: "make sure you work the right way") $M = 3.12$, $SD = 1.34$.

5.3 Data

When considering the clarity for the students regarding the type of data to be collected and the clarity of the reasons for collecting the data presented on the LAD-s, medium to higher satisfaction was obtained. The average satisfaction with the item "I understand what data is collected for compiling and displaying the learning analytics dashboard" is M = 3.52, SD = 1.35 with about 2/3 of students giving a score of four or five. Satisfaction with the item "I understand why the data presented on the dashboard of learning analytics is collected" is M = 3.7, SD = 1.29 while again about 2/3 of students gave a score of four or five. There are individual differences among students.

5.4 Usefulness

Students thinks that the LAD-s contains useful feedback. Average satisfaction with the item "LAD-s contains useful feedback for me" is M = 3.55, SD = 1.27 with just over half of the students giving a score of four or five. Satisfaction with the item "LAD-s contains feedback I want to know" is also high M = 3.52, SD = 1.35 with more than half of the students rating this aspect at four or five. Satisfaction with the item "LAD-s improves online teaching system in the form of displaying feedback" is M = 3.64, SD = 1.17 with almost two thirds of students evaluating this aspect with a score of four or five.

5.5 Ease-of-Use

Students are very satisfied with the ease of use of the LAD-s, and almost two thirds of students rate this aspect with a score of four or five. The average satisfaction with the item "LAD-s is easy to use" is M = 3.85, SD = 1.18. "Using the LAD-s does not create difficulties" is M = 3.7, SD = 1.13; the item "Data presented by the LAD-s is clearly presented." M = 3.67, SD = 1.16 and the item "Interaction with the Learning Analytics Dashboard is clear and understandable" M = 3.94, SD = 1.06. It can be concluded that students perceive the LAD-s as easy to use, which does not create difficulties with clearly presented data and clear and understandable interaction.

5.6 Bihevioral Intention

Students would like to have the opportunity to use the LAD-s in the following semesters during online learning (M = 3.48, SD = 1.12) with almost half of them grading this aspect with a score of four or five. It is important for students to be able to use the LAD-s during online learning (M = 3.27, SD = 1.33), also about half of them rate this aspect with four or five. In addition, they would like to have access to the LAD-s in online courses at all times (M = 3.58, SD = 1.17).

5.7 Intention to Use

Item "LAD-s becomes a tool that I will add to every online course in the Moodle environment" has an average grade of M = 3.12, SD = 1.19 with almost half of respondents (42%) undecided whether to use this tool in each course, grading this aspect 3. In the question "I will use the dashboard of learning analytics in the next online courses", an average grade of M = 3.55, SD = 1.12 was obtained, indicating, a somewhat stronger intention to use, with about half (54%) of students rating this aspect 4 or 5.

5.8 Bihevioral Changes

In this research, we are also interested in the possible behavioral consequences of using this tool, e.g., whether there is a change in behavior in students. The answers obtained are quite widely scattered around the core values and it is difficult to draw any general conclusion as to whether the use of the tool has influenced behavioral changes. The average answers range mainly around the mean value, ranging from $M = 2.82$, $SD = 1.33$ for the benefit of the LAD-s in creating a learning plan to $M = 3.33$, $SD = 1.38$ for the positive impact of LAD-s on learning motivation.

5.9 SUS Questionnaire

The SUS questionnaire was used to measure the usability of this tool. The greatest satisfaction was obtained for the ease of use of the tool, as described by the item "I think this dashboard is easy to use" ($M = 3.7$, $SD = 1.07$), and the item "I guess most people would learn to use this dashboard very quickly" ($M = 3.9$, $SD = 1,01$). Approximately 2/3 of the students rate these aspects 4 or 5. On the other hand, approximately 2/3 of the students rate (grades 1 and 2) that they did not have to learn many things before they could start with this dashboard. An equal number of them estimate that they do not need help to be able to use LAD-s, nor do they think that LAD-s is too complex or inconvenient to use.

5.10 Participant's Opinion and Suggestions on LAD-s

When considering satisfaction with specific aspects of this tool, it is evident that students show the highest average satisfaction ($M = 3.91$, $SD = 1.16$) with a Success Component, among other things, upcoming exams give students a sense of course complexity by the end of the semester. Approximately 2/3 of students give this feature a score of 4 or 5. Students are also relatively satisfied ($M = 3.55$, $SD = 1.33$) with features such as minimum grade, maximum grade, grade point average and Median success on the exam that allow them to compare performance level with the class's performance. Slightly more than half of the students (60%) give this panel a score of 4 or 5. The average high grade (with about half of the respondents giving a grade of 4 or 5) was obtained, in addition, for the item "Minimum grade, maximum grade, average grade and Median success on the test allow me to create a vision of my knowledge in relation to colleagues".

Lower than the previously mentioned functions, but satisfactory average grades were also obtained for the remaining functions of the tool "LAD-s displays your login data compared to your colleagues. This presentation allows us to create a sense of effort and work on the course." $M = 3.3$, $SD = 1.41$; "LAD-s provides feedback in the form of a message that can be positive or negative. Example of a positive message: Your work is exceptional, Keep it up and you will surely succeed!" ($M = 3.3$, $SD = 1.47$); "The LAD-s uses a prediction algorithm to predict student success at the end of a course. I think that the presentation of the predicted situation in the course is very important" ($M = 3.3$, $SD = 1.41$) and "Mode, Median, Minimum and Maximum are functions that allow me to clearly compare my log data with my class logins" ($M = 3.06$, $SD = 1.20$).

Students also answered a question about three different views of the LAD-s. Students were able to choose from the three different views (Activity Component, Success Component and Predict Component) the one that they think is most important. The answer was offered by 25 students and 68% (17) think that the Success Component is the most important, 16% of them (4) think that the Activity Component is the most important, while the same number (16%) think that the Prediction Component is most important.

Students had the opportunity to offer something to add without currently being on the LAD-s. Four students gave their suggestions for improvement. One student's proposal is to add a part for independent enrollment, e.g. hours dedicated to the course (e-learning, memory), so that this is included in the amount of effort, because according to the student he personally learns more independently using the material than online with quizzes. He does not, however, see any need for the whole dashboard idea, for someone who is organized. He believes that this is a surplus of information that anyone can access on their own. Another student would not add anything, but he thinks that it would be good if the interface was not graphically simple, but that it was a little more graphically interesting to the eye. The third student suggests that it would be good to have more options, e.g. suggests a settings page where students can turn on or off whether they want to compare their data with others and that they can filter which data they compare (first test, total only…).

Another suggestion for improvement is to reduce the emphasis on certain activities, e.g. the number of logins to the system. This student feels that this does not reflect the real situation (e.g. some students have studied through the system so they have more logins compared to others who have downloaded materials to the computer).

6 Discussion

If we compare student's perception of the usefulness of LADs, improvement suggestions, and comments on the use of LADs, we come to the conclusion that LAD-s is dashboard that students are globally satisfied with. The guidelines in the more detailed report include more comparisons with their class, allowing for comparisons that students desire. Here we must be careful to define what and in what way it can be compared. Students acceptance level is also above average satisfaction. LAD-s is a tool that students would like to use in the future learning process. LAD-s is a tool that needs to be adapted to the needs of students. Teaching methods are changing, so we must always keep in mind a new ways to improve the learning process. Once LAD-s becomes a "must have" tool with online teaching, it will certainly need to adapt to the needs of students. Finally, behavioral changes is the most difficult to achieve. In this study, students expressed how LAD-s has a positive impact on learning motivation. However, the answers obtained are quite widely scattered around the core values and it is difficult to draw any general conclusion as to whether the use of the tool has influenced behavioral changes.

In order to compare individual dimensions that examined student satisfaction with LAD-s, the overall average results for each examined general aspect were formed. Based on individual questions within each appropriate measure from the survey, the overall results were formed. The total score on a particular measure was formed as the average score of each student on individual issues related to a particular measure. Before that, by calculating the Pearson correlation coefficient between individual items (questions), it was checked if all items within the same measure really belong to the same characteristic. If they refer to the same measure, it is expected to have a medium to high correlation between individual items. Medium to high correlations between items were obtained and it can be concluded that it is justified to construct total average results for each measure. When forming the total results, negative items were taken into account, which were recoded in the direction that the higher result on the particle represents the higher total result (4 items in total).

Table 2. Descriptive data of summary measures.

Part	M	C	D	Min	Max	SD
Student's self-awareness	3,26	3,25	3,00[a]	1,00	5,00	1,25
Influence	3,24	3,50	3,50	1,00	5,00	1,30
Data	3,61	3,50	5,00	1,00	5,00	1,22
Usefulness	3,57	3,67	4,00[a]	1,00	5,00	1,16
Ease-of-use	3,79	3,75	5,00	1,00	5,00	1,05
Behavioral intention	3,44	3,33	3,00	1,00	5,00	1,11
Intention to use	3,33	3,50	3,50	1,00	5,00	1,11
Behavioral changes	3,08	3,00	2,33[a]	1,00	5,00	1,09
SUS questionnaire	3,60	3,60	3,00	1,00	5,00	0,66
Participant's opinion and suggestions on LAD-s	3,42	3,71	3,71	1,00	5,00	1,02

From the summary results (Table 2), we conclude that students are above average satisfied with all examined aspects of the LAD-s. Students express the greatest satisfaction for Ease-of-use (M = 3.79, SD = 1.05), Data (M = 3.6, SD = 1.22), Usefulness (M = 3.6, SD = 1.16), Sus questionnaire (M = 3.6, SD = 0.66), Behavioral intention (M = 3.4, SD = 1.11) and satisfaction with individual functions of this tool (M = 3.4, SD = 1.02). Lower, yet above-average satisfaction was obtained for the Influence of the LAD-s on more effective learning (M = 3.2, SD = 1.30); Intention to use (M = 3.3, SD = 1.11) and satisfaction with the possibility of Behavioral changes (M = 3.1, SD = 1.09) (Table 3).

To verify the reliability of the measures used, the Cronbach's alpha reliability coefficient was calculated for each scale. The number of items by which each aspect of satisfaction is measured varies from at least 2 items to up to 10 items (Sus questionnaire). Satisfactory reliability of all measures used was obtained, with alpha coefficients ranging from 0.704 for the SUS questionnaire to 0.942 for the Ease-of-use measure. Despite the small number of items in some measures, all measures are considered reliable and appropriate.

Table 3. Reliability of measures

Part	α	No. of items
Student's self-awareness	0,941	4
Influence	0,898	2
Data	0,826	2
Usefulness	0,908	3
Ease-of-use	0,942	4
Bihevioral intention	0,902	3
Intention to use	0,911	2
Bihevioral changes	0,918	6
SUS questionnaire	0,889	10
Participant's opinion and suggestions on LAD-s	0,704	9

7 Conclusion

Learning analytics dashboards are becoming increasingly commonplace within the educational sector with the aims of improving the quality of the learning process. This study presents the development and evaluation process of our LAD-s dashboard. The LAD-s report for the student gives an overall view of each students progress in the course. This study found that students overall satisfaction on LAD-s is above average satisfied with all examined aspects. The greatest satisfaction is found for Ease-of-use. Data, Usefulness, Sus questionnaire, Behavioral intention and Satisfaction with individual functions of this tool. Lower, yet above-average satisfaction was obtained for the Influence of the LAD-s on more effective learning, Intention to use and satisfaction with the possibility of Behavioral changes. The impression remains that students will use LAD-s for the purpose of making better progress.

Comments from open-ended questions provided the direction for another point of view. For example, a student mentioned, "reduce the emphasis on certain activities, eg. The number of logins to the system". This student feels that this does not reflect the real situation. Another students mentioned, "it would be good to have more options, suggesting a settings page where students can turn on or off whether they want to compare their data with others and that they can filter which data they compare (first test, total only...)". These facts coincide with the choice of the Success Component as the most important view of the LAD-s. Students want different possibilities of comparison, but the question arises, where to draw the line.

As a further study, it is necessary to examine the impact of the LAD-s empirically in different contexts to prove its usefulness more precisely. The impact of LAD-s could be very different between a full online class and a blended learning class. LAD-s use a prediction of student success. As a further study it is important to research and implement the best prediction model. We believe that students would pay more attention to prediction if they are shown the way it works. Limitations of this study are working conditions due to the Covid-19 pandemic. On the one hand, it allowed students to track their successes and activities on the system, on the other hand, we feel that too many courses have moved unprepared to online learning, thus leaving negative consequences on online learning.

Acknowledgment. This work was supported by the Office of Naval Research grant, **N00014– 20-1–2066** "Enhancing Adaptive Courseware based on Natural Language Processing".

References

1. Dyckhoff, A.L., Lukarov, V., Muslim, A., Chatti, M.A., Schroeder, U.: Supporting action research with learning analytics. In: LAK 2013, 08–12 April, Leuven, Belgium (2013)
2. Bodily, R., Ikahihif, T.K., Mackley, B., Graham, C.R.: The design, development, and implementation of studentfacing learning analytics dashboards. J. Comput. High. Educ. **30**, 572–598 (2018)
3. Ferguson, R.: Learning analytics: drivers, developments and challenges. Int. J. Technol. Enhanced Learn. **4**(5–6), 304–317 (2012)
4. Siemens, G.: Learning analytics & knowledge. In: LAK 2011, Banff, Alberta (2011)
5. Suthers, D., Verbert, K.: Learning analytics as a middle space. In: Proceedings of the Third International Conference on Learning Analytics and Knowledge (2013)
6. Greller, W., Drachsler, H.: Translating learning into numbers: a generic framework for learning analytics. Educ. Technol. Soc. **15**(3), 42–57 (2012)
7. Durall, E., Gros, B.: Learning analytics as a metacognitive tool. In: 6th International Conference on Computer Supported Education, Barcelona, Spain (2014)
8. Few, S.: Information Dashboard Design: Displaying Data for At-a-Glance Monitoring. Analytics Press, Burlingame (2013)
9. Charleer, S., Klerkx, J., Duval, E., De Laet, T., Verbert, K.: Creating effective learning analytics dashboards: lessons learnt. In: European Conference on Technology Enhanced Learning, (2016)
10. Safsouf, Y., Mansouri, K., Poirier, F.: TaBAT: design and experimentation of a learning analysis dashboard for teachers and learners. J. Inf. Technol. Educ. Res. **20**, 331–350 (2021)
11. Siemens, G., Baker, R.S.J.D.: Learning analytics and educational data mining: towards communication and collaboration. In: Proceedings of the 2nd International Conference on Learning Analytics and Knowledge, pp. 252–254, April 2012
12. Sarikaya, A., Correll, M., Mela, L.B.: What do we talk about when we talk about dashboards? IEEE Trans. Visual Comput. Graph. **25**(1), 682–692 (2018)
13. Schwendimann, B.A., et al.: Perceiving learning at a glance: a systematic literature review of learning dashboard research. IEEE Trans. Learn. Technol. **10**(1) Siječanj-ožujak (2017)
14. Zimmerman, B.J., Moylan, A.R.: Self-regulation: where metacognition and motivation intersect. In: Hacker, D.J., Dunlosky, J., Graesser, A.C. (eds.) Handbook of Metacognition in Education, pp. 299–315 (2009)
15. Matcha, W., Gasevic, D., Ahmad Uzir, N., Pardo, A.: A systematic review of empirical studies on learning analytics dashboards: a self-regulated learning perspective. Trans. Learn. Technol. Svibanj (2019)
16. Aldowah, H., Al-Samarraie, H., Fauzy, W.M.: Educational data mining and learning analytics for 21st century higher education: a review and synthesis. Telematics Inform. **37**, 13–49 (2019)
17. Gasevic, D., Dawson, S., Rogers, T., Gasevic, D.: Learning analytics should not promote one size fits all: the effects of instructional conditions in predicting academic success. Internet High. Educ. **28**, 68–84 (2016)

18. Naranjo, D.M., Prieto, J.R., Moltó, G., Calatrava, A.: A visual dashboard to track learning analytics for educational cloud computing. Adv. Sens. Technol. Educ. **19**, 2952 (2019)
19. Ruiperez-Valiente, J.A., Munoz-Merino, P.J., Gascon-Pinedo, J.A., Kloss, C.D.: Scaling to massiveness with ANALYSE: a learning analytics tool for open edX. IEEE Trans. Hum.-Mach. Syst. **47**, 909–914 (2016)
20. Hussain, M., Hussain, S., Zhang, W.: Mining Moodle data to detect the inactive and low performance students during the Moodle course. In: ICBDR, 27–29 October 2018
21. Park, Y., Jo, I.-H.: Development of the learning analytics dashboard to support students' learning performance. J. Universal Comput. Sci. **21**(1) (2015)
22. Podgorelec, V., Kuhar, S.: Taking advantage of education data: advanced data analysis and reporting in virtual learning environments. Electron. Electri. Eng. **8**(114) (2011). ISSN 1392–1215
23. Aljohani, N.R., Daud, A., Abbasi, R.A., Alowibd, J.S., Basheri, M., Aslam, M.A.: An integrated framework for course adapted student learning analytics dashboard. Comput. Hum. Behav. (2018)
24. Azcona, D., Hsiao, I.-H., Smeaton, A.F.: Personalizing computer science education by leveraging multimodal learning analytics. IEEE (2018)
25. Shi, C., Fu, S., Chen, Q., Qu, H.: VisMOOC: visualizing video clickstream data from massive open online courses. In: IEEE Pacific Visualization Symposium, 14–17 April 2015
26. Akçapinar, G., Bayazit, A.: MoodleMiner: data mining analysis tool for moodle learning management system. Elementary Educ. Online, 406–415 (2019)
27. Tervakari, A., Kuosa, K., Koro, J., Paukkeri, J., Kailanto, M.: Teachers' learning analytics tools in a social media enhanced learning environment. In: International Conference on Interactive Collaborative Learning (ICL), 03–06 December 2014
28. Corrin, L., et al.: Loop: a learning analytics tool to provide teachers with useful data visualisations. In: Ascilite, Perth, Australia (2015)
29. Martinez-Maldonado, R., Pardo, A., Mirriahi, N., Yacef, K.: The LATUX workflow: designing and deploying awareness tools in technology-enabled learning settings. In: International Conference on Learning Analytics and Knowledge, At Poughkeepsie, NY, USA (2015)
30. Gamage, S.H.P.W., Ayres, J.R., Behrend, M.B.: A systematic review on trends in using Moodle for teaching and learning. Int. J. STEM Educ. (2022). Article number: 9
31. Xin, O.K., Singh, D.: Development of learning analytics dashboard based on moodle learning management system. Int. J. Adv. Comput. Sci. Appl. **12**(7) (2021)
32. Moodle docs, Moodle. https://docs.moodle.org/400/en/Analytics_plugins. Accessed 15 Apr 2022
33. Create better learning experiences. https://intelliboard.net/
34. Marticorena-Sánchez, R., López-Nozal, C., Ji, Y.P., Pardo-Aguilar, C., Arnaiz-González, Á.: UBUMonitor: an open-source desktop application for visual E-learning analysis with moodle. Open Source Softw. Learn. Environ. (2022)
35. Krishnan, R., et al.: Smart analysis of learners performance using learning analytics for improving academic progression: a case study model. Entrepreneurship Sustainability High. Educ. (2022)
36. SmartKlass™ learning analytics moodle. https://moodle.org/plugins/local_smart_klass
37. My Feedback. https://moodle.org/plugins/report_myfeedback. Accessed 15 Apr 2022
38. Parack, S., Zahid, Z., Merchant, F.: Application of data mining in educational databases for predicting academic trends and patterns. In: IEEE International Conference on Technology Enhanced Education (ICTEE), Kerala, 2012, pp. 1–4 (2012)
39. Tempelaar, D.T., Rienties, B., Giesbers, B.: In search for the most informative data for feedback generation: learning analytics in a data-rich context. Comput. Hum. Behav. **47**, 157–167 (2015)

40. Scheffel, M., Drachsler, H., Toisoul, C., Ternier, S., Specht, M.: The proof of the pudding: examining validity and reliability of the evaluation framework for learning analytics. In: Data Driven Approaches in Digital Education. EC-TEL 2017. Lecture Notes in Computer Science, vol. 10474. pp. 194–208. Springer, Cham (2017). https://doi.org/10.1007/978-3-319-66610-5_15
41. Persico, D., Pozzi, F.: Informing learning design with learning analytics to improve teacher inquiry. Br. J. Edu. Technol. **46**(2), 230–248 (2014)
42. Orfanou, K., Tselios, N., Katsanos, C.: Perceived usability evaluation of learning management systems: empirical evaluation of the system usability scale. Int. Rev. Res. Open Distance Learn. **16**(2), 227–246 (2015)
43. Celi, E.: Application of dashboards and scorecards for learning models IT risk management: a user experience. In: International Conference of Design, User Experience, and Usability (2015)
44. Ramirez-Anormaliza, R., Sabate, F.: Evaluating student acceptance level of e-learning systems. In: 8th International Conference of Education, Research and Innovation At: Sevilla Volume: ICERI2015 Proceedings (2015)

How Good is your Drawing? Quantifying Graphomotor Skill Using a Portable Platform

Dharma Rane[1] , Pragya Verma[1]([✉]) , and Uttama Lahiri[2]

[1] Electrical Engineering and Center for Cognitive and Brain Sciences (Joint First Authors), Indian Institute of Technology Gandhinagar, Gandhinagar, Gujarat, India
{parashuram_rane,verma_pragya}@iitgn.ac.in
[2] Electrical Engineering, Indian Institute of Technology Gandhinagar, Gandhinagar, India
uttamalahiri@iitgn.ac.in

Abstract. Graphomotor skill essential for completing various academic activities such as drawing of shapes or handwriting of text is conventionally judged based on observation in terms of graphic output's similarity with a reference and often tends to miss other aspects, like one's pen-tip velocity that can affect the quality of the graphic output. Thus, there exists a need to quantify one's graphomotor skills while incorporating both pen-tip velocity and the quality of the graphic output (in terms of similarity/dissimilarity with a reference template). Hence, we have developed a tablet-based platform to quantify one's graphomotor skill in terms of a Graphomotor Skill Index (a single numeric value obtained as a linear combination of pen-tip velocity and quality of graphic output). A feasibility study with eight pairs of typically developing children and those with Autism indicated that the Graphomotor Skill Index can capture heterogeneity in their graphomotor skills suggesting the potential of the platform for assessment of one's graphomotor skill.

Keywords: Graphomotor skill · Tablet · Autism

1 Introduction

One's ability to execute graphic tasks is often related with graphomotor skill [1]. Having adequate graphomotor skill is essential for drawing of shapes, handwriting of text, etc. that are frequently a part of a child's academic routine [1]. Thus, one's graphomotor skill can affect his/her academic performance which in turn has been shown to be related to one's self-esteem and confidence [2]. Some of the graphic tasks, such as writing of text or drawing of shapes on a sheet of paper placed horizontally on a table require one to primarily use his/her distal appendages (i.e., wrist and fingers) and proximal appendages (i.e., shoulder and forearm, to some extent) while operating in a limited workspace to execute the task (Distal Graphomotor Task (DGT henceforth)). Again, reorienting the writing or drawing surface, such as an upright canvas might need one to primarily use

---

D. Rane and P. Verma—Equally Contributed.

© Springer Nature Switzerland AG 2022
G. Meiselwitz et al. (Eds.): HCII 2022, LNCS 13517, pp. 409–422, 2022.
https://doi.org/10.1007/978-3-031-22131-6_31

his/her proximal appendages and distal appendages (to some extent) while operating in a larger workspace to execute the task (Proximal Graphomotor Task (PGT henceforth)). Literature shows that occupational therapists often emphasize the importance of practicing such Proximal Graphomotor Tasks for individuals demonstrating graphomotor skill deficits [3]. In addition, children are often expected to execute both Distal and Proximal Graphomotor Tasks as a part of their daily academic routine [3].

The quality of the graphic output resulting from such Distal and Proximal Graphomotor Tasks can be affected by one's graphic execution agility that can be reflected through the tip velocity of the drawing tool [4], such as a pen. For example, in the competitive era, completion of drawing/writing assignments, etc. within a specific time-bound often require one to demonstrate high writing speed that has relation to one's pen-tip velocity. Again, lack of control in regulating one's hand movement [5] during a Distal or Proximal Graphomotor Task might have implications on the movement of the writing/drawing tool causing variations in the pen-tip velocity, adversely affecting the quality of the imprint (i.e., graphic output) indicating a trade-off between pen-tip velocity and quality of graphic output [6]. The quality of a graphic output (that can be an important measure to understand the graphomotor skill of an individual performing the task) can be quantified in terms of similarity/dissimilarity of the created imprint with respect to a given reference template. While variation in graphomotor skills of children (irrespective of them being Typically Developing (TD) or with developmental disorders) have been reported in literature [7, 8], studies have also reported that children with Autism often have difficulty in graphic execution compared to their age-matched TD counterparts [9–11]. Specifically, researchers have shown that children with Autism often demonstrate higher writing speed than their TD counterparts [5] that in turn leads to the deterioration in the quality of the graphic output (quantified in terms of shape similarity), attributed to writing speed (affecting the pen-tip velocity) exceeding the comfortable speed limit [12]. Additionally, several researchers have used the graphic output to diagnose tremors in case of Parkinson patients [13] while performing a spiral drawing task (i.e., as a Distal Graphomotor Task). The focus of these studies had been to assess an underlying condition rather than quantification of graphomotor skill [13]. Again, many of the past studies do not consider both DGT and PGT. Further, past studies show that though researchers have considered aspects like pen-tip velocity (along with the quality of graphic output) [4, 13], however, none (to the best of our knowledge) evaluate one's graphomotor skill in terms of a single numeric value (computed using multiple aspects) for both DGT and PGT.

While quantifying the quality of a graphic output is important, it is also critical to assess the graphomotor skill of the individual creating the graphic output that might need to look at various aspects, such as the pen-tip velocity (used by the individual performing the task), the degree of similarity/dissimilarity of the graphic output with a given reference template, etc. Thus, there is a need for a platform that can quantify one's graphomotor skill in terms of an index that can consider such aspects and in turn provide a single numeric value estimation of one's graphomotor skill. Motivated by this, in our present research, we have come up with a novel tablet-based graphomotor skill assessment tool that can quantify one's graphomotor skill (during execution of Distal and Proximal Graphomotor Tasks) using a single numeric value (i.e., a Graphomotor Skill Index, computed while looking to the pen-tip velocity (used by the individual performing the task) and the degree of similarity/dissimilarity of the graphic output with a given reference template). For this, the tablet stylus was augmented with a position tracker and a switch button. The objectives of our current study were three-fold, namely to (i) develop a portable graphomotor skill assessment platform, (ii) propose a novel quality index (computed by incorporating stylus-tip velocity and similarity/dissimilarity of graphic output with a reference) to quantify one's graphomotor skill and (iii) understand the significance of Distal and Proximal Graphomotor Tasks with regard to one's graphomotor skills while characterizing Typically Developing children and those with Autism. The overall aim is to come up with a graphomotor skill assessment platform that can serve as a complementary tool in the hands of the teachers, therapists as well as caregivers. The rest of the paper is organized as follows. Section 2 describes our System Design. The Experiment and Methodology is in Sect. 3. An overview of the Results obtained is in Sect. 4 followed by Conclusion in Sect. 5.

2 System Design

Our portable tablet-based graphomotor skill assessment platform (GraMoSAP) consisted of three modules, namely (i) Task Display/Interface (ii) Data Acquisition and (iii) Feature Extractor and Analyzer. The Fig. 1 shows a Bird's Eye View of GraMoSAP. The Display/Interface Unit was used to present the stimulus and/or the interface for drawing in case of the Proximal and Distal Graphomotor Task, respectively. While one executed either of the tasks, data on stylus-tip position (with respect to the tablet screen coordinates) was acquired in real-time (along with time stamping) using the Data Acquisition (DAQ) module. This data in turn was passed to the Feature Extractor/Analyzer module. The extracted features were used to compute the Graphomotor Skill Index that in turn quantified one's graphomotor skill.

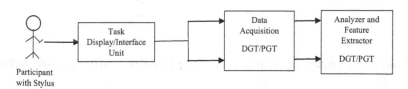

Fig. 1. Bird's eye view of GraMoSAP. Note: DGT refers to Distal Graphomotor Task; PGT refers to Proximal Graphomotor Task

2.1 Task Display/Interface Module

In this work, in our endeavor to understand the feasibility of developing a portable tablet-based graphomotor skill assessment platform, we have designed two different types of graphomotor tasks, namely, Distal Graphomotor Task (DGT) and Proximal Graphomotor Task (PGT). The idea was to explore the role of distal and proximal joint movements of the upper arm on one's overall graphomotor abilities. The tablet screen (i.e., monitor having 2736 × 1824 pixels) of the GraMoSAP was used as the task interface module for the Distal Graphomotor Task (DGT) and as the display/interface module for the Proximal Graphomotor Task (PGT).

Design of Distal Graphomotor Task. The DGT was designed so as to give a greater emphasis on the use of one's distal joints (of the wrist and fingers). The task required one to copy a curve (Fig. 2 (a)) having turns using a stylus while the portable tablet was kept horizontally on a table top. The execution of DGT required the participant to draw the shown curve on a 2D workspace comprising of the tablet screen of size 29.2 cm × 20.1 cm. This task was intended to replicate the natural day-to-day drawing/writing activities where children keep their drawing/writing surface horizontally on the table top and use any drawing/writing tool for the completion of the task.

Design of Proximal Graphomotor Task. The PGT was designed to give a greater emphasis on the use of one's proximal motor abilities. The task required one to trace a curve having turns as shown in Fig. 2 (b) on the portable tablet (using the stylus augmented with a tracker and switch; For details, please see Sect. 2.2) kept vertically on the table top. The tablet screen was mapped to a vertical workspace of 58.4 cm × 40.2 cm. This task required one to draw by flexing the upper arm at the shoulder joint against gravity that can be likened to using a vertical drawing canvas. We chose such a task since practicing drawing on vertical surfaces is often prescribed by occupational therapists for children facing difficulties in acquiring graphomotor skills [3].

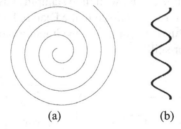

(a)   (b)

Fig. 2. Reference template for (a) Distal Graphomotor Task (DGT) and (b) Proximal Graphomotor Task (PGT)

2.2 Data Acquisition Module

While the participants executed each of the two graphomotor tasks, time-stamped screen (x, y) coordinate pair was acquired and stored at the backend of the tablet.

Data Acquisition for the Distal Graphomotor Task. For the Distal Graphomotor Task, the 2D workspace of the tablet screen was considered and the time-stamped (x, y) screen coordinate pair of the stylus-tip (touching the tablet surface) was recorded for subsequent analysis. This data was used to digitally recreate the trajectory drawn by the participant and extract the shape similarity/dissimilarity (quantifying the quality of graphic output with the given reference template; Sect. 2.3) and stylus-tip velocity (Sect. 2.3).

Data Acquisition for the Proximal Graphomotor Task. For the Proximal Graphomotor Task (PGT), a 3D workspace was used since we were interested in understanding the proximal motor ability (that needed flexion of the shoulder joint along with the upper arm against gravity). This required us to increase the size of the workspace beyond the tablet screen. While one executed the task, the time-stamped (x, y) screen coordinate pair of the projection of the stylus-tip on the tablet surface was recorded for subsequent analysis. For this, we augmented the stylus with (i) a position tracker to track the position of the stylus-tip in 3D space and (ii) a switch button (light-weight and toggle type) to simulate pen up action (OFF state) and pen down action (ON state) (Fig. 3). For pen down action, a trail of the stylus-tip was created on the tablet screen. To reduce any confounding effect due to the effort needed for toggling the switch, the switch button was chosen from a set of switches that can be operated by children after performing a pilot testing of the switch on a group of 5 children (age-matched with our participant pool). The light-weight tracker (mounted to the rear end of the Stylus to ensure easy grip of the stylus while tracing) was used to get the 3D coordinates of the stylus with the stylus-tip being mapped to the tracker position. Subsequently, projection of the Stylus-tip on the tablet screen was used to get the 3D to 2D conversion while offering the time-stamped 2D screen coordinates. To create a trail of the stylus-tip on the tablet screen (thereby offering visual feedback to the participant in real-time), the stylus-tip (in the physical space) was mapped to 2D projection in terms of (x, y) screen coordinate pair of a virtual object (a stylus-tip displayed on the tablet monitor). This data was used to extract the shape similarity/dissimilarity (quantifying the quality of graphic output with the given reference template; Sect. 2.3) and stylus-tip velocity (Sect. 2.3) for the PGT (Fig. 4).

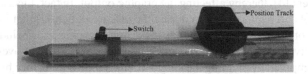

Fig. 3. Stylus augmented with position tracker and toggle switch

Fig. 4. Data acquisition module for proximal graphomotor task

2.3 Feature Extractor/Analyzer Module

For both the DGT and PGT, the trajectory drawn by an individual was used to extract different metrices, such as shape similarity/dissimilarity and average Stylus-tip velocity.

Computation of Shape Similarity/Dissimilarity. The ability to accurately copy/trace a curve has been shown to be an important indicator of one's graphomotor skill [14]. In order to remove any subjectivity associated with assessing the produced trace or drawing by human raters, we have used the Euclidean distance-based similarity measure as described by Perner et al. [15]. In accordance with the algorithm [15; (Fig. 5)], one's graphic output (i.e., trajectory drawn) by the participants was first aligned and scaled as per the given reference template. This was followed by calculation of pixel-based average Euclidean distance between the reference template and one's trajectory drawn during the DGT and PGT. The Shape Dissimilarity was thus measured in terms of error between the given reference template and one's graphic output. Further, we normalized the scores for Shape Dissimilarity on a 0–1 scale using Max Normalization [16]. Subsequently, the Normalized Shape Similarity was computed from (1 - Shape Dissimilarity) (Fig. 5).

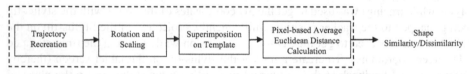

Fig. 5. Computation of shape similarity/dissimilarity

Computation of Average Stylus-Tip Velocity. It has been shown that the velocity of the pen-tip related to one's speed of graphic execution can impact the way he/she executes the pen movement [4], thereby affecting the graphic output. In fact, this can reflect one's ability to control and regulate the pen during the task execution [5] that in turn is useful in determining one's graphomotor output [5]. Thus, we chose to include the average stylus-tip velocity as a metric to quantify one's graphomotor skill. The average stylus-tip velocity was computed by dividing the length of one's drawn trajectory by the total time taken in drawing the trajectory. Finally, we used Max Normalization [16] to normalize the average stylus-tip velocity on a scale of 0 to 1.

Computation of Graphomotor Skill Index. Given that the quality of graphic output (quantified in terms of Shape Similarity/Dissimilarity with regard to a given reference template) can be affected by one's stylus-tip velocity and with both the quality of output and writer's stylus-tip velocity being related to his/her graphomotor skill (while executing DGT and PGT), it might be important to come up with a skill index that can provide a single numeric value estimate of one's graphomotor skill while taking into consideration the average stylus-tip velocity and the similarity/dissimilarity of the graphic output with a reference. Such a single value numeric estimation of one's graphomotor skill can have applicability in assessment, diagnostics and intervention outcome measure of one's graphomotor skill. With this motivation, we came up with a novel quality index, namely, Graphomotor Skill Index (GSI) as a linear combination of the effective average stylus-tip velocity (i.e., Stylus-tip Velocity$_{effective}$ defined as (1-normalized average stylus-tip velocity)) and Shape Similarity measures. Specifically, since literature suggests that there exists a trade-off between one's stylus-tip velocity and the quality of the graphic output [6], we propose to include effective average stylus-tip velocity while calculating one's GSI. Please note that here we have used linear combination of these measures as an initial approximation. We wanted a higher GSI score to reflect a better graphomotor skill than a lower GSI score. Hence, we computed the GSI using Eq. 1.

$$GSI = [axShapeSimilarity] + [(1 - a)xStylus - tipVelocity_{effective}] \tag{1}$$

where, "a" is a real coefficient. To understand the efficacy of GSI (on a scale of 0–1) given varying weightage of both the measures (i.e., Shape Similarity and Effective Stylus-tip Velocity), we considered candidate values of coefficient "a" set as 0.25, 0.5 and 0.75.

3 Experiment and Methodology

3.1 Participants

A total of 16 participants (8 children with ASD (Group$_{ASD}$ *henceforth*) and 8 age-matched (p-value > 0.05 using non-parametric Mann Whitney U Test [17] given a limited sample size) TD children (Group$_{TD}$ *henceforth*) took part in our study (Table 1). All participants belonging to Group$_{ASD}$ were recruited through local mental health institute based on therapist's recommendation. The participants belonging to the Group$_{TD}$ were recruited from the neighbouring school. We administered the Social Responsiveness Scale (SRS) [18] and Social Communication Questionnaire (SCQ) [19] to get an estimate of the participants' autism measure.

It can be observed that all the participants belonging to Group$_{ASD}$ were above the clinical cut-off level for SRS and/or SCQ. On the other hand, all the participants in Group$_{TD}$ were below the clinical threshold of SRS and SCQ measures. Since we were interested in exploring the graphomotor skill, we ensured that all the participants had manual dexterity using the 9-Hole Peg Test (9HPT) [20]. All the participants were able to complete 9HPT. Also, all the participants were right-handed and used their right hand for completing the graphomotor tasks.

Table 1. Participant characteristics

ID	Gender	Age (Yrs)	SRS (Cut off = 60)	SCQ (Cut off = 15)	9HPT (Seconds)
Group_{ASD}					
1	M	4	64	20	52.48
2	M	9	80	17	44.35
3	M	9	64	17	67.35
4	M	5	67	18	40.59
5	F	8	67	12	44.02
6	M	6	60	16	56.86
7	M	7	66	20	82.56
8	F	4	78	14	28.32
Mean (S.D)	–	6.5 (2.07)	68.25 (7.02)	16.75 (2.76)	52.06 (16.93)
Group_{TD}					
1	M	9	56	12	20.21
2	M	9	42	2	19.71
3	M	7	42	1	22.49
4	M	9	48	7	19.83
5	M	5	43	5	21.49
6	M	5	58	12	32.79
7	M	7	42	1	16.64
8	M	7	42	1	21.19
Mean (S.D)	–	7.25 (1.66)	46.62 (6.73)	5.12 (4.76)	21.79 (4.76)

3.2 Experimental Setup

The setup comprised of (i) a portable tablet, (ii) a stylus (that comes with the portable tablet augmented with a switch and tracker), (iii) a table and a height-adjustable chair. The tablet was placed horizontally on the table top for the DGT and upright for the PGT (Sect. 2.1, Fig. 6 (a) and (b) respectively).

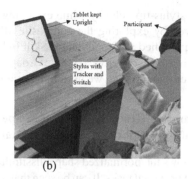

(a)   (b)

Fig. 6. Experimental setup for (a) DGT and (b) PGT. Note: DGT refers to Distal Graphomotor task; PGT refers to proximal graphomotor task

3.3 Tasks and Procedure

When a participant entered the study room, the experimenters introduced themselves and asked the participant to sit comfortably on a height-adjustable chair. Then one of the experimenters explained the tasks using a visual schedule. Also, the participant was given the stylus and told that he/she was free to draw (whatever they liked) on the screen of the tablet. The idea was to get them accustomed to using the stylus. Once they were ready to start the task, signing of the consent form was administered. Also, the participant was told that he/she was free to discontinue his/her participation in the study in case of any discomfort. In addition, the participant was told that he/she was free to ask for breaks during the task. For the Distal Graphomotor Task, a reference template (Fig. 2 (a)) was placed on the table in front of the participant. The task required the participant to draw the curve on the screen of the tablet (placed horizontally on the table top) using the stylus. For the Proximal Graphomotor Task, the participant was instructed not to rest his/her elbow on the table (during the task execution). The participant was expected to trace the curve displayed on the screen of the tablet (placed upright on the table top) by moving his/her stylus so that its tip moves in a vertical plane in his/her front (i.e., parallel to his/her sagittal plane) while closing the switch (i.e., ON state) with the GraMoSAP showing the traced trajectory (using the 3D (as sensed by the tracker) to 2D projection). The tasks (DGT and PGT) were presented to the participants in a randomized manner so as to avoid confound due to any ordering effect [21]. Completion of both the tasks required a commitment of ~15 min from each participant. The study was conducted following the Institute Ethics (IEC/UL/2021/001).

4 Results

We analyzed the data collected from Group$_{ASD}$ and Group$_{TD}$ using the GraMoSAP. The idea was to understand the feasibility of GraMoSAP to (i) quantify one's graphomotor skill using a single numeric value estimate and (ii) understand the significance of distal and proximal tasks with regard to one's graphomotor skill while characterizing both the Group$_{ASD}$ and Group$_{TD}$. For this, we extracted metrices such as, one's shape dissimilarity and average stylus-tip velocity while executing the Distal and Proximal Graphomotor Tasks followed by exploring the composite effect of the two metrices (with varying weightage) quantified as Graphomotor Skill Index (i.e., a single numeric value estimate computed using the two metrices) for the $Group_{ASD}$ and $Group_{TD}$. For statistical analysis, given a limited sample size, we used non-parametric Mann Whitney U Test [17].

4.1 Comparative Group Analysis of Shape Dissimilarity (Measured by GraMoSAP) for Distal and Proximal Graphomotor Tasks

The Fig. 7 shows the normalized shape dissimilarity for the $Group_{ASD}$ and $Group_{TD}$ for the distal and proximal tasks. It can be seen that the shape dissimilarity for $Group_{ASD}$ was statistically greater (p-value < 0.05) than that for $Group_{TD}$ irrespective of the type of task ($\Delta\% = 65.56\%$ and 60.62% for Distal and Proximal Graphomotor Tasks, respectively). Such an observation can be possibly attributed to most of the participants belonging to the $Group_{TD}$ being more cautious (so as to ensure accuracy of the output for each graphomotor task) during the task than the $Group_{ASD}$ (as reported by the experimenters) leading to better quality of graphic output of the $Group_{TD}$ than that of $Group_{ASD}$.

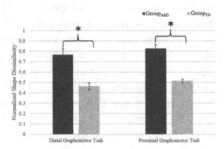

Fig. 7. Comparative group analysis for shape dissimilarity. Note: * indicates p-value < 0.05.

4.2 Comparative Group Analysis of Average Stylus-Tip Velocity (Measured by GraMoSAP) for Distal and Proximal Graphomotor Tasks

The Fig. 8 shows the normalized average Stylus-Tip velocity for the $Group_{ASD}$ and $Group_{TD}$ for the distal and proximal tasks. It can be observed that the velocity for $Group_{TD}$ was statistically lower (p-value < 0.05) than that of $Group_{ASD}$ irrespective of the type of task ($\Delta\% = 61.27\%$ and 72.29% for Distal and Proximal Graphomotor Tasks, respectively). Such an observation corroborates with the findings of a previous study [5] and can be possibly due to the difficulty faced by individuals with ASD in controlling their hand movement during a graphomotor execution [5] leading to poorer quality of graphic output of the $Group_{ASD}$ than that of $Group_{TD}$.

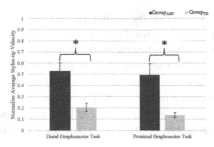

Fig. 8. Comparative group analysis of average stylus-tip velocity. Note: * indicates p-value < 0.05

4.3 Comparative Analysis of Graphomotor Skill Index (Computed by GraMoSAP)

The normalized group average Graphomotor Skill Index (GSI) scores for Group$_{ASD}$ and Group$_{TD}$ for the distal and proximal tasks were computed using Eq. (1) with coefficient "a" (weightage allocated to the shape similarity and the effective stylus-tip velocity) set as 0.25, 0.5 and 0.75, respectively (Sect. 2.3). The group average GSI score of Group$_{TD}$ was higher (p-value < 0.05) than that of the Group$_{ASD}$ irrespective of the type of task or the value of "a", inferring superior graphomotor skill of the Group$_{TD}$ than that of Group$_{ASD}$. In addition, we wanted to understand the relative implication of choosing various values of the coefficient "a" on the GSI scores for Group$_{ASD}$ and Group$_{TD}$ for the distal and proximal tasks.

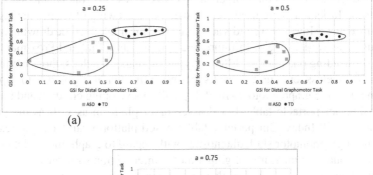

(a)

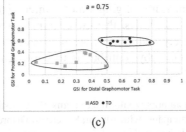

(c)

Fig. 9. Scatter Plot of normalized group average GSI for Group$_{ASD}$ and Group$_{TD}$ for distal and proximal graphomotor task for coefficient "a" set as (a) 0.25, (b) 0.5 and (c) 0.75

The Fig. 9 (a), (b) and (c) show the scatter plot of normalized group average GSI for Group$_{ASD}$ and Group$_{TD}$ for the distal and proximal tasks with coefficient "a" set as 0.25, 0.5 and 0.75, respectively. Irrespective of the value of "a", we can see a ceiling effect along with closely spaced values of Graphomotor Skill Index of the Group$_{TD}$ and heterogeneously distributed scores of Graphomotor Skill Index of the Group$_{ASD}$ that can be attributed to the spectrum nature of the graphomotor skill of children with Autism. Irrespective of the coefficient "a", we can see that the Graphomotor Skill Index during the distal and proximal tasks can be used to group the participants into two separate clusters.

5 Conclusion

In our present study, we have developed a portable tablet-based graphomotor skill assessment platform that can quantify one's graphomotor skill. Additionally, we have proposed a novel quality index, the Graphomotor Skill Index, that gives a quantitative estimate of one's graphomotor skill based on performance as measured by shape similarity and effective average stylus-tip velocity while executing Distal and Proximal Graphomotor Tasks. In our feasibility study, we observed that our developed system was able to capture the heterogeneity in the graphomotor skills of children with Autism and their age-matched typically developing counterparts that corroborates with the findings of previous studies [9–11]. Thus, the results obtained highlight the potential of the developed portable assessment platform as well as the proposed quality index to quantify one's graphomotor skill. Though the preliminary results are promising, our current study had certain limitations. The current study was carried out with a limited sample size of eight pairs of Typically Developing children and those with Autism. However, in future we plan to conduct the study with a larger sample size. Presently, the Distal and Proximal Graphomotor Tasks that were used were restricted to drawing of shapes having curves without any edges. However, a child's academic routine might include drawing of shapes having curves as well as edges. In future, we plan to add Distal and Proximal Graphomotor Tasks needing one to draw different types of shapes (such as, those having edges as well). Nonetheless, our current results are indicative that it is possible to capture the heterogeneity in the graphomotor skill of Typically Developing children and those with Autism using our portable tablet-based assessment platform as well as the proposed Graphomotor Skill Index. Our portable tablet-based platform can have applications in assessment of graphomotor skill, diagnostics with regard to graphomotor deficits along with offering outcome measures of graphomotor intervention strategies. Thus, this can find application in schools, clinics, therapy centers, homes, etc. This in turn will be helpful in providing timely and appropriate intervention strategies so as to improve one's graphomotor skills thereby contributing to improvement in one's self-esteem and confidence.

Acknowledgements. The authors would like to thank B.M. Institute of Mental Health, Ahmedabad for helping enroll participants with Autism Spectrum Disorder. The authors would also like to thank all the participants and their families for their participation in our study. The authors would also like to express their gratitude to TCS Research Scholar Program and Indian Institute of Technology (IIT) Gandhinagar for supporting this work.

References

1. Galaz, Z., Mucha, J., Zvoncak, V., et al.: Advanced parametrization of graphomotor difficulties in school-aged children. IEEE Access Pract. Innov. Open Solutions **8**, 112883–112897 (2020)
2. Feder, K.P., Majnemer, A.: Handwriting development, competency, and intervention. Dev. Med. Child Neurol. **49**(4), 312–317 (2007)
3. Portnoy, S., Rosenberg, L., Alazraki, T., Elyakim, E., Friedman, J.: Differences in muscle activity patterns and graphical product quality in children copying and tracing activities on horizontal or vertical surfaces. J. Electromyogr. Kinesiol. Official J. Int. Soc. Electrophysiol. Kinesiol. **25**(3), 540–547 (2015)
4. Chihi, I., Abdelkrim, A., Benrejeb, M.: Analysis of handwriting velocity to identify handwriting process from electromyographic signals. Am. J. Appl. Sci. **9**(10), 1742–1756 (2012)
5. Grace, N., Enticott, P.G., Johnson, B.P., Rinehart, N.J.: Do handwriting difficulties correlate with core symptomology, motor proficiency and attentional behaviours? J. Autism Dev. Disord. **47**(4), 1006–1017 (2017)
6. Jens Förster, E., Higgins, T., Bianco, A.T.: Speed/accuracy decisions in task performance: built-in trade-off or separate strategic concerns? Organ. Behav. Hum. Decis. Process. **90**(1), 148–164 (2003)
7. Cox, M., Eames, K.: Contrasting styles of drawing in gifted individuals with autism. Autism Int. J. Res. Pract. **3**(4), 397–409 (1999)
8. Martin, N.: Assessing portrait drawings created by children and adolescents with autism spectrum disorder. Art Therapy J. Am. Art Therapy Assoc. **25**(1), 15–23 (2008)
9. Kushki, A., Chau, T., Anagnostou, E.: Handwriting difficulties in children with autism spectrum disorders: a scoping review. J. Autism Dev. Disord. **41**(12), 1706–1716 (2011)
10. Fuentes, C.T., Mostofsky, S.H., Bastian, A.J.: Children with autism show specific handwriting impairments. Neurology **73**(19), 1532–1537 (2009)
11. Fuentes, C.T., Mostofsky, S.H., Bastian, A.J.: Perceptual reasoning predicts handwriting impairments in adolescents with autism. Neurology **75**(20), 1825–1829 (2010)
12. Harris, T.L., Lawrence Rarick, G.: The problem of pressure in handwriting. J. Exp. Educ. **26**(2), 151–178 (1957)
13. Kuosmanen, E., Kan, V., Visuri, A., Hosio, S., Ferreira, D.: Let's draw: detecting and measuring Parkinson's disease on smartphones. In: Proceedings of the 2020 CHI Conference on Human Factors in Computing Systems. ACM (2020)
14. Nan-Ying, Y., Chang, S.-H.: Kinematic analyses of graphomotor functions in individuals with Alzheimer's disease and amnestic mild cognitive impairment. J. Med. Biolog. Eng. **36**(3), 334–343 (2016)
15. Perner, P.: Determining the similarity between two arbitrary 2-D shapes and its application to biological objects. Int. J. Comput. Softw. Eng. **3**, 2 (2018)
16. Li, W., Liu, Z.: A method of SVM with normalization in intrusion detection. Procedia Environ. Sci. **11**, 256–262 (2011)
17. MacFarland, T.W., Yates, J.M.: Mann-Whitney U test. In: Introduction to Nonparametric Statistics for the Biological Sciences Using R, pp. 103–132. Springer International Publishing, Cham (2016)
18. Coon, H., Villalobos, M.E., Robison, R.J., et al.: Genome-wide linkage using the social responsiveness scale in Utah autism pedigrees. Mol. Autism **1**(1), 8 (2010)
19. Chandler, S., Charman, T., Baird, G., et al.: Validation of the social communication questionnaire in a population cohort of children with autism spectrum disorders. J. Am. Acad. Child Adolesc. Psychiatry **46**(10), 1324–1332 (2007)

20. Wang, Y.-C., Bohannon, R.W., Kapellusch, J., Garg, A., Gershon, R.C.: Dexterity as measured with the 9-Hole Peg Test (9-HPT) across the age span. J. Hand Therapy Official J. Am. Soc. Hand Therapists **28**(1), 53–9 (2015). Quiz 60
21. Durbach, I., Lloyd, G.: Eliminating order effects in association tasks without using randomisation. Int. J. Mark. Res. **57**(5), 759–776 (2015)

Evaluation of the Effect of Voice Technology in a Game Teaching E-Book on English Learning

Meng-Dar Shieh[1][(✉)], Chang-Chen Ho[1], Fang-Chen Hsu[2], and Chih-Chieh Yang[2]

[1] National Cheng Kung University, 1, University Ave, Tainan, Taiwan ROC
mdshieh@gmail.com
[2] Southern Taiwan University of Science and Technology, Yongkang City, Taiwan ROC

Abstract. The progress of modern technology has led to diversified teaching methods. Currently, many teaching tools are gradually being combined with technology to create interactive experiences that differ from those of the past. PlayTalk English Teaching E-book was developed in this study through the use of the Voice-flow platform. Teaching e-book for the fifth and sixth grades on an online education platform was used as a reference for the teaching contents. This study used Learning Motivation Scale and General Self-Efficacy Scale to evaluate students' learning effects under two of the above-mentioned different teaching methods. During the experiment process, the subjects were divided into two groups. In the experimental group, the subjects learned English by means of the PlayTalk English Teaching E-book, while in the control group, the subjects were taught by means of a web-based education platform e-book. All the subjects were tested by the Learning Motivation Scale and General Self-Efficacy Scale before and after teaching. The experimental results indicated that the average score of PlayTalk English Teaching E-book teaching on the Learning Motivation Scale was 4.396 (out of 5.0), which was higher than the average score (3.770) of the web-based education platform e-book. The conclusions of this study can be used as a reference for future educators who design e-books to improve school children's learning interest and to improve the existing learning platforms, as well as extend the application of new technologies in teaching so as to provide students with a higher quality teaching system.

Keywords: Voice technology · Interactive E-book · Game teaching · English learning

1 Introduction

1.1 Research and Application of Voice Technology

Since natural voice technology increasingly matures, many products bring users more convenience. The common voice virtual assistant and voice ordering system are successful instances of applying voice technology. Jung et al. (2020) created the interface for drivers by utilizing mature voice technology in combination with the sense of touch to come up with the concept of "Voice + Touch", an interactive interface. They designed the

G. Meiselwitz et al. (Eds.): HCII 2022, LNCS 13517, pp. 423–436, 2022.
https://doi.org/10.1007/978-3-031-22131-6_32

interaction of multiple voices + touch in each voice interaction interface stage, as well as four voice and touch interaction themes: status feedback, input AD adjustment, output control and fingerprint feedforward. During the study on driver users, voice + touch interaction showed higher efficiency and improved user experience without causing extra disturbance [1].

Jung et al. (2019) developed a set of voice interactive games named "TurtleTalk". With the help of voice interaction method coordination interface, children are able to learn programming in an easy, pleasant, and confident manner [2]. There are evident application instances of NLP technology in certain professional fields. For example, commodity trading behaviors have been replaced by chatting robots [3].

1.2 Children's Online Education Under the Influence of Covid-19 Pandemic

Recently, due to the global outbreak of Covid-10 pandemic, many countries have adopted measures like quarantine and travel prohibition in order to control the virus transmission and lower human contact to reduce infection. As a result, school courses are available through online distance teaching. The methods of online teaching have also been increasingly emphasized, but the challenge faced by educators has gone beyond expectation. Atiles et al. (2021) pointed out difficulties regarding children's online education, including inadequate preparation for distance teaching and training that are required to satisfy the requirements of children's distance education. Problems include a lack of preparation for transitioning from face-to-face teaching to distance teaching, and the necessity to inform nursing personnel when children are found physically unwell [4].

In March 2020, almost every school in the United States was shut down due to the pandemic, and school education was replaced by distance teaching and online learning. Online learning is an education process performed through networking, where the learning experience is provided for students online. The skills required in using these network teaching tools in distance teaching affect children's education, their motivation and learning. Kim (2020) reconsidered the teaching model from online teaching, and divided it into three phases: planning, implementation and reflection. Among these three phases, the reflection phase focuses on students' individual differences and development level. Since online teaching restricts the frequency of interactions with children, teachers have to maximize their language competence in order to establish a comfortable educational environment for each child, while targeting students' various learning styles, personality and interest [5].

2 Research Process

The main purpose of this study is to examine and evaluate the effects of applying voice technology in a game teaching e-book on English learning and develop the game teaching e-book in combination with voice technology for verification. In this section, the research steps are planned as two stages according to the research purpose.

Stage 1: It's the stage of design and development of the e-book with the application of voice technology. In terms of voice technology, VoiceFlow was adopted as the voice development platform, and Alexa Echo Show 10 smart speaker was used as the experimental device to present the pictures of PlayTalk English Teaching E-book and voice interactions required to complete Alexa voice system through the Alexa Echo Show 10 screen.

Stage 2: It is the main experiment process. In this study, subjects were divided into the experimental group and control group, and there were three stages in the experiment process: pre-test, the experiment and post-test. The pre-test includes the tests on Learning Motivation Scale, General Self-Efficacy Scale and Learning Achievement Scale. The experiment was carried out in the experimental group and control group after completion of the pre-test. After the experiment teaching parts were completed, the post-test was carried out for the two groups. Both the pre-test and post-test included the tests on learning motivation, self-efficacy and learning achievements. The subjects in both the experimental group and control group were a similar mix of students in the fifth and sixth grades of primary school, with ten students in each group without replication.

2.1 Voice Development Platform (Voiceflow)

Voiceflow, a company whose headquarters is located in San Francisco, specializes in producing software for voice application programs. Voiceflow develops software in the form of platforms, enabling both individuals and enterprises to build and develop voice application programs. Voice application programs can be applied in companies' chatbots or product voice development. Voiceflow is currently used in education, sales of electronic products, and marketing.

This platform can be used to design and produce prototypes and release voice application programs for Amazon Alexa and Google Assistant. Users can drag and drop "Block" in Voiceflow platforms to create user-defined voice application programs; the application programs created can also be tested on the platforms of Amazon Alexa and Google.

Teaching Flow and Game Design. This study aimed to examine and evaluate the effects of applying voice technology in game teaching e-books on English learning motivation, self-efficacy and learning achievements. The passive interaction in the part of introduction of vocabulary is changed, requiring users to read the designated vocabulary. After the introduction of vocabulary, the process of the game will begin, which changes the test to games (Fig. 1). Quiz games and comparison games are used as examples. The quiz games focus on the vocabulary introduced previously. Children have to decide which vocabulary item learned previously is the answer to the quiz game (Fig. 2). The comparison game compares the vocabulary of articles (Fig. 3). Children have to answer the vocabulary of articles related to the scenarios in real life (e.g., relative size or length of articles).

The flowchart of uploading to the experimental device Alexa Echo Show 10 is shown in Fig. 4. The teaching e-book is uploaded to the Alexa rear-end console through the Voiceflow platform, while logging in the Alexa user account. It requires logging in the same user account when starting Alexa Echo Show 10. Alexa Echo Show 10 will acquire instructions from the rear-end console, and be started on the screen of the device

Fig. 1. Picture of introduction of the vocabulary

Fig. 2. Picture of quiz game

Fig. 3. Picture of comparison game

Fig. 4. Flowchart of uploading to echo show 10

after receiving users' instruction to start the voice teaching e-book, while having direct dialogues with the device and carrying out the subsequent learning and game.

Planning the Experiment Flow. This study adopted the quasi-experimental research method. In this method of experimental design, researchers assign subjects and control experimental scenarios by random sampling in experimental scenarios and cannot do whatever they please. The research objects were the fifth and sixth grades (primarily

11–12 of age) in primary school. There were two groups (i.e., the experimental group and control group). The experimental group received the "PlayTalk English Teaching", while the control group received the "Web-based Education Platform English Teaching". The experimental design flow is shown in Table 1. The pre-tests (A1, A2) were carried out for both the experimental group and control group before English teaching. After completion of the pre-tests, English teaching of PlayTalk English Teaching E-book and web-based education platform (X1, X2) were performed for the experimental group and control group, respectively. The post-tests (B1, B2) of the experimental group and control group were carried out after completion of teaching.

Table 1. Explanatory table of experimental design

Group	Pre-test	Teaching	Post-test
Experimental group	A1	X1	B1
Control group	A2	X2	B2

A1 and A2: Pre-tests of Learning Motivation Scale, General Self-efficacy Scale and Learning Achievement Scale were carried out for the experimental group and control group.

X1: English teaching of PlayTalk English Teaching E-book.

X2: English teaching of web-based education platform.

B1 and B2: Post-tests of Learning Motivation Scale, General Self-efficacy Scale and Learning Achievement Scale were carried out for the experimental group and control group.

Variables in the Experiment. The variables in this study include independent variables, dependent variables and control variables according to the aforesaid experimental design. The variables of this study (Fig. 5) are described as follows.

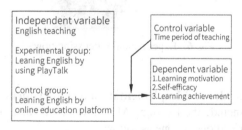

Fig. 5. Research variables

1. Independent variables: In this study, there were two groups (i.e., experimental group and control group) divided according to teaching methods. The experimental group received the teaching of PlayTalk English Teaching E-book, while the control group received that of the teaching e-book provided by web-based platform.

2. Dependent variables: Dependent variables are the experimental results of this study including learning motivation, self-efficacy and learning achievements.
3. Control variables: Control variables are the fixed variables set up in the study to lower the effects of other factors on the experimental teaching. Since no teacher was involved in teaching in this study, the main control variable of this study was teaching time.

2.2 Research Subjects and Experimental Flow

The subjects of this study were mainly the fifth and sixth grades in primary school. In the experimental teaching design, the experimental group (10 subjects) received the teaching of PlayTalk English Teaching E-book, and the control group (10 subjects) that of web-based education platform.

The experiment processing and implementation procedures of this study include three parts (i.e., pre-test, teaching intervention and post-test) as shown in Fig. 6. The students from the experimental group and control group received the pre-tests of learning motivation and self-efficacy first before implementation of teaching. After completion of pre-tests, the experimental group received the teaching of PlayTalk English Teaching E-book, while the control group that of web-based education platform. After completion of experimental teaching, the students in the experimental group and control group received the post-tests of learning motivation and self-efficacy.

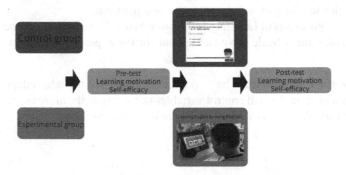

Fig. 6. Experimental processing flow

Design of Research Scales and Implementation of Experiment. The scales adopted in this study mainly include the Learning Motivation Scale and General Self-Efficacy Scale which are described one by one as follows:

1. Learning Motivation Scale: There are six questions in the Learning Motivation Scale used in this study, divided into two aspects (i.e., intrinsic and extrinsic motivation) (Table 2).
2. General Self-Efficacy Scale: There are seven questions in the General Self-Efficacy Scale used in this study. A Likert five-level scale was adopted as the scoring method: 1 point for "Strongly Disagree", and 5 points for "Strongly Agree" (Table 3).

Table 2. Questions of the learning motivation scale

No	Questions	Motivation type
1	After experiencing the courses of the voice interactive game e-book, I prefer using textbooks that are different from school because I can learn new knowledge	Intrinsic motivation
2	I prefer textbooks that could arouse my interest, even though the courses are more difficult	Intrinsic motivation
3	If there are related courses in the future, I will spontaneously choose the courses that I can get new knowledge from	Intrinsic motivation
4	It is very important for me to show excellent English skills in front of my family, friends, teachers or others	Extrinsic motivation
5	If it is possible, I hope I can get my highest score in the English test after learning the English courses of the voice interactive game e-book	Extrinsic motivation
6	It is the best thing for me to get good grades in the English course of the voice interactive game e-book	Extrinsic motivation

Table 3. Questions of the general self-efficacy scale

No	Questions
1	I believe that I can get excellent results in the English courses
2	I believe that I can understand the contents of the English courses taught on the voice interactive game e-book
3	I can understand the most difficult part of the English courses on the voice interactive game e-book
4	I am confident that I can finish the specified contents of the English courses well on the voice interactive game e-book
5	I am confident that I can understand the English courses on the voice interactive game e-book, including the basic concepts taught in the courses
6	I am confident that I can understand the English courses on the voice interactive game e-book, including the most difficult and complex units in the courses
7	I expect that I can get high scores in the following English courses

3   Experimental Results and Discussion

This section primarily examines whether the learning motivation and self-efficacy differed significantly between the experimental group and control group after two different kinds of experimental teaching activities. Analysis of Covariance (ANCOVA) was adopted in this study to analyze the pre-test and post-test data of learning motivation and self-efficacy questionnaires so as to understand whether voice technology in combination with game teaching interactive e-book affected the learning motivation and self-efficacy in the English teaching of the fifth and sixth grades in primary school. Two aspects in learning motivation (i.e., intrinsic motivation and extrinsic motivation), and the results of self-efficacy are discussed below.

Intrinsic Motivation. In order to test if the data on intrinsic motivation conforms to the basic hypothesis of ANCOVA in this study, regressive homogeneity verification of the scores of the pre- and post-tests of two groups has to be done before ANCOVA. If the regression coefficient in the group is homogeneous, subsequent ANCOVA should be carried out. In the "test of effect items among subjects" (Table 4), the value is 0.875 which is greater than 0.05, indicating that the data conform to the hypothesis of ANCOVA: The regression coefficient in the group was homogeneous, indicating that subsequent ANCOVA could be continued.

Table 4. Tests of effect items among subjects (intrinsic motivation)

Source	Sum of squares (Model III)	df	Mean square	F	Significant
Corrected mode	2.541[a]	3	0.847	1.455	.291
Intercept	5.122	1	5.122	8.801	.016
Group	.004	1	0.004	0.006	.940
Mean of intrinsic motivation	1.474	1	1.474	2.533	.146
Group * Mean of Intrinsic Motivation	0.015	1	0.015	0.026	.875
Error	5.237	9	0.582		
Total	215.778	13			
Corrected Total	7.778	12			

a. R square = .327 (Corrected R square = .102).

In the subsequent ANCOVA, "Levene's test for equality of variances," the probability was "0.264", which was greater than the significance level of 0.05 (Table 5), indicating no significant difference in the variation of dependent variables between the two groups. Therefore, they were homogeneous.

Table 5. Levene's test for equality of variances (intrinsic motivation)

F	df1	df2	Significant
1.389	1	11	.264

In the results of the "test of effect items among subjects", we can see the value of "probability" in the column of "Group" was "0.752", which was greater than 0.05, indicating no significant difference between the two groups (Table 6).

Table 6. Test of effect items among subjects (intrinsic motivation)

Source	Sum of squares (Model III)	df	Mean square	F	Significant	Net correlation eta square
Corrected mode	2.525[a]	2	1.263	2.404	.140	.325
Intercept	7.740	1	7.740	14.736	.003	.596
Mean of Intrinsic Motivation	2.381	1	2.381	4.533	.059	.312
Group	0.055	1	.055	0.105	.752	.010
Error	5.253	10	.525			
Total	215.778	13				
Corrected Total	7.778	12				

a. R square = .325 (Corrected R square = .190).

Finally, the results of "estimated marginal means" show the group means of post-tests after regression adjustment. The mean of Group 1 (i.e., the experimental group) was 3.911, while that of Group 2 (i.e., the control group) 4.056. It indicates that the post-test score of the control group after adjustment (4.056) was actually greater than that of the experimental group (3.911), which means the web-based platform education e-book had the greater effect on the students' intrinsic learning motivation. However, the mean of intrinsic motivation in the pre-test was 3.205 (Table 7), while the mean of the post-test of "PlayTalk English Teaching" (3.911) was still higher than that of the pre-test (3.205).

Table 7. Estimated marginal means (intrinsic motivation)

Group	Mean (Post-test)	Standard deviation	95% Confidence interval	
			Lower bound	Upper bound
1	3.911[a]	.341	3.152	4.670
2	4.056[a]	.264	3.467	4.645

a. Use the following values to estimate the covariates that appear in the model: Average value of pre-tested Intrinsic motivation = 3.20513.

Extrinsic Motivation. In order to test if the extrinsic motivation data conform to the basic hypothesis of ANCOVA in this study, a regressive homogeneity test of the scores of the pre-test and post-test between the two groups had to be done before ANCOVA. If regression coefficient in the group was homogeneous, subsequent analysis of covariance could be carried out. In the "test of effect items among subjects" (Table 8), the probability was 0.236, which was greater than 0.05, indicating that these data conform to the hypothesis of ANCOVA: The regression coefficient in the group was homogeneous. Therefore, the subsequent ANCOVA could be continued.

Table 8. Test of effect items among subjects (extrinsic motivation)

Source	Sum of squares (Model III)	df	Mean square	F	Significant
Corrected mode	1.726[a]	3	.575	2.179	.160
Intercept	2.260	1	2.260	8.559	.017
Group	.580	1	.580	2.195	.173
Mean of Extrinsic Motivation	1.642	1	1.642	6.219	.034
Group * Mean of Extrinsic Motivation	.427	1	.427	1.616	.236
Error	2.376	9	.264		
Total	245.333	13			
Corrected Total	4.103	12			

a. R square = .421 (Corrected R square = .228).

In the subsequent ANCOVA, the probability of "Levene's test for equality of variances" was "0.517", which was greater than the significance level of 0.05 (Table 9), indicating no significant difference in the variation of the dependent variables between the two groups. Therefore, they were homogeneous.

Table 9. Levene's test for equality of variances (extrinsic motivation)

F	df1	df2	Significant
0.447	1	11	.517

In the results of the "test of effect items among subjects", we can see the value of "probability" in the column of "Group" was "0.282" which was greater than 0.05, indicating no significant difference between the two groups (Table 10).

Table 10. Test of effect items among subjects (extrinsic motivation)

Source	Sum of squares (Model III)	df	Mean square	F	Significant	Net correlation eta square
Corrected mode	1.300[a]	2	.650	2.318	.149	.317
Intercept	8.007	1	8.007	28.569	.000	.741
Mean of Extrinsic Motivation	1.286	1	1.286	4.588	.058	.315
Group	.363	1	.363	1.295	.282	.115
Error	2.803	10	.280			
Total	245.333	13				
Corrected Total	4.103	12				

a. R square = .317 (Corrected R square = .180).

Finally, the results of "Estimated Marginal Average" show the group means of the post-test after regression adjustment. The mean of Group 1 (i.e., the experimental group) was 4.072, while that of Group 2 (i.e., the control group) was 4.455, indicating that the post-test score of the control group after adjustment (4.455) was actually greater than that of the experimental group (4.072), suggesting that web-based platform education e-books had the greater effect on the students' extrinsic learning motivation. However, the mean of intrinsic motivation of the pre-test was 3.256 (Table 11). The mean of the post-test of "PlayTalk English Teaching" (4.072) was still higher than that of the pre-test (3.256).

Table 11. Estimated marginal means (extrinsic motivation)

Group	Mean	Standard deviation	95% Confidence interval	
			Lower bound	Upper bound
1	4.072[a]	.254	3.508	4.637
2	4.455[a]	.196	4.019	4.890

a. Use the following values to estimate the covariates that appear in the model: Average value of pre-tested extrinsic motivation = 3.25641.

Self-efficacy. In order to test that the self-efficacy data conform to the basic hypothesis of ANCOVA in this study, regressive homogeneity tests of scores from the pre-test and post-test of two groups were carried out before ANCOVA. If regression coefficient in the group was homogeneous, the subsequent ANCOVA could be carried out. In the "test of effect items among subjects" (Table 12), the probability was 0.597, which was greater than 0.05, indicating that the data conform to the hypotheses of ANCOVA: The regression coefficient in the group was homogeneous. Therefore, subsequent ANCOVA could be continued.

Table 12. Test of effect items among subjects (self-efficacy)

Source	Sum of squares (Model III)	df	Mean square	F	Significant
Corrected mode	2.674[a]	3	.891	1.573	.263
Intercept	6.036	1	6.036	10.653	.010
Group	.016	1	.016	.027	.872
Mean of Self-efficacy	1.370	1	1.370	2.417	.154
Group * Mean of Self-efficacy	.171	1	.171	.301	.597
Error	5.100	9	.567		
Total	216.918	13			
Corrected Total	7.774	12			

a. R square = .344 (Corrected R square = .125).

During the subsequent ANCOVA, the probability of "Levene's test for equality of variances" was "0.139", which was greater than the significance level of 0.05 (Table 13), indicating no significant difference in the variation of dependent variables between these two groups. Therefore, they were homogeneous.

Table 13. Levene's test for equality of variances (self-efficacy)

F	df1	df2	Significant
2.542	1	11	.139

In the results of the "test of effect items among subjects", we can see the value of "probability" in the column of "Group" was "0.161", which was greater than 0.05, indicating no significant difference between the two groups (Table 14).

Table 14. Test of effect items among subjects (self-efficacy)

Source	Sum of squares (Model III)	df	Mean square	F	Significant	Net correlation eta square
Corrected mode	2.504[a]	2	1.252	2.375	.143	.322
Intercept	10.014	1	10.014	19.001	.001	.655
Mean of Self-efficacy	1.274	1	1.274	2.418	.151	.195
Group	1.206	1	1.206	2.288	.161	.186
Error	5.270	10	.527			
Total	216.918	13				
Corrected Total	7.774	12				

a. R square = .325 (Corrected R square = .190).

Finally, we can see the results of "estimated marginal means", which indicates the group means of the post-test after regression adjustment. The mean of Group 1 (i.e., the experimental group) was 4.396, while that of Group 2 (i.e., the control group) was 3.770 (Table 15), indicating that the post-test score of the experimental group after adjustment (4.396) was actually greater than that of the control group (3.770), suggesting that "teaching of PlayTalk English Teaching E-book" had the greater effect on students than teaching of web-based education platform in terms of self-efficacy.

Table 15. Estimated marginal means (self-efficacy)

Group	Mean	Standard deviation	95% Confidence interval	
			Lower bound	Upper bound
1	4.396[a]	.325	3.673	5.120
2	3.770[a]	.257	3.198	4.342

a. Use the following values to estimate the covariates that appear in the model: Average value of pre-tested Self-efficacy = 3.61538.

4   Conclusions and Future Work

During the subsequent experimental interviews with subjects, it can be found that the use status of the experimental devices by students in the experimental group could also affect their learning motivation and self-efficacy. Students who are unfamiliar with the experimental devices can easily experience the problem of obstruction of voice reception during use. As for fault tolerance, the device should be used by students with higher fault-tolerance. The students who had smoother interaction with teaching devices would give higher scores in learning motivation and self-efficacy.

In the teaching of the control group, the students were more impressed by the examination process of web-based education platform e-book, which also indicates that web-based education platform had the greater effect on students' extrinsic learning motivation. The students also replied that the course contents of the web-based education platform were similar to those of school teaching materials and classroom teaching contents, which the students considered boring and monotonous. Therefore, we can see why the scores of web-based education platform were low in the aspect of self-efficacy.

References

1. Jung, J., Lee, S., Hong, J., Youn, E., Lee, G.: Voice+Tactile: augmenting in-vehicle voice user interface with tactile touchpad interaction. In Proceedings of the 2020 CHI Conference on Human Factors in Computing Systems, pp. 1–12, April 2020
2. Jung, H., Kim, H.J., So, S., Kim, J., Oh, C.: TurtleTalk: an educational programming game for children with voice user interface. In: Extended Abstracts of the 2019 CHI Conference on Human Factors in Computing Systems, pp. 1–6, May 2019
3. Chung, M., Ko, E., Joung, H., Kim, S.J.: Chatbot e-service and customer satisfaction regarding luxury brands. J. Bus. Res. **117**, 587–595 (2020)
4. Atiles, J.T., Almodóvar, M., Chavarría Vargas, A., Dias, M.J., Zúñiga León, I.M.: International responses to COVID-19: challenges faced by early childhood professionals. Eur. Early Child. Educ. Res. J. **29**(1), 66–78 (2021)
5. Kim, J.: Learning and teaching online during Covid-19: experiences of student teachers in an early childhood education practicum. Int. J. Early Child. **52**(2), 145–158 (2020)

Culture-Centered ICT Guidelines for Southeast Asian Secondary Schools

V. Sithira Vadivel(✉) ⓘD, Insu Song, and Abhishek Singh Bhati

James Cook University, 149 Sims Drive, Singapore 387380, Singapore
{sithira.vadivel,insu.song,abhishek.bhati}@jcu.edu.au

Abstract. The adoption of Information and Communication Technology (ICT) in Southeast Asian (SEA) secondary schools is slow and is considered incompatible with cultural barriers, affecting students' learning outcomes, and teaching and learning experiences. To improve ICT adoption and compatibility in SEA schools, we propose culture-centered ICT guidelines and practices to support teachers and developers in designing, planning, and implementing ICT learning activities. The culture-centered ICT guidelines make use of cultural values and cultural motivational elements (CME) to enhance teaching and learning. The beneficiaries are ICT designers, developers, teachers, and students. The guidelines and practices were developed based on the success of innovative use of cultural activity metaphors, cultural theme metaphors, and proposition metaphors in Southeast Asian secondary schools, which improved learning outcomes and teaching and learning experiences. We propose four culture-centered ICT guidelines and practices. A new enhanced Human Computer Interaction (HCI) model is proposed for future ICT designs for Southeast Asian secondary schools.

Keywords: Culture-centered ICT · Cultural emotional metaphors · Cultural Activity metaphors · Cultural-theme metaphors

1 Introduction

1.1 Challenges in Southeast Asia

As ICT plays an important role in education in SEA, schools in SEA are now heavily reliant on mobile and internet technologies both inside and outside of the classroom. The ministries of education in the Philippines, Malaysia, Indonesia, and Brunei have supported the adoption of technology-assisted learning in secondary schools to assist teachers and students in improving classroom activities. However, the adoption of ICT in SEA has been slow. For example, the countries surrounding Singapore have especially shown inefficient and ineffective use of ICT, with poor learning outcomes and inadequate learning experiences. In this paper, we summarize the findings from a literature review, a comprehensive survey, focus groups, and two studies. Study 1 is a study on the impact of cultural themes and study 2 is a study evaluating the impact of cultural activity as the groundwork for the proposal of culture-centered ICT guidelines and practices that

© Springer Nature Switzerland AG 2022
G. Meiselwitz et al. (Eds.): HCII 2022, LNCS 13517, pp. 437–454, 2022.
https://doi.org/10.1007/978-3-031-22131-6_33

mitigate the slow ICT adoption in SEA. Table 1 shows the summary of the findings of the literature review, comprehensive survey, focus group, study 1, and study 2 that contribute to the four culture-centred ICT guidelines and practices. Below is a summary of what this paper is designed to address.

Summary of what this paper aims to achieve: Research   Question–Do   cultural related activities and design improve teaching and learning experiences and learning outcome?

Aims–Develop new ICT guidelines and framework for secondary schools that will accelerate the adoption of ICT solutions in Southeast Asia.

Hypothesis–Southeast Asian cultural values and activities can improve teaching and learning experiences.

1.2   Summary of Studies and Findings

In reviewing the literature, we identified that Southeast Asian schools have been affected by slow adoption of Information and Communication Technology (ICT) in teaching and learning domains. Several factors were identified causing slow ICT adoption, mainly cultural differences between Asian and Western students and minimal technology use among teachers in Southeast Asian secondary schools [13].

A comprehensive survey was proposed and carried out to investigate the slow ICT adoption in Southeast Asia. In the comprehensive survey, teachers and students' data were collected from secondary schools in SEA, namely Brunei, Indonesia, Malaysia, and the Philippines. 342 teachers and 978 students participated in a study identifying factors affecting the problem of slow ICT adoption in teaching and learning in Southeast Asia. Quantitative and qualitative methods were carried out for data collection. Teachers and students were recruited after approval from the Ministry of Education of the respective countries. Results from the comprehensive study show that there was resistance among teachers and students in the use of ICT in SEA secondary schools. Cultural barriers exist making ICT incompatible with teachers and students in Southeast Asia. These were the factors identified causing slow ICT adoption [14].

After holding several focus groups, we propose that cultural theme ICT be evaluated in Southeast Asian secondary schools. In Study 1, we evaluate the impact of Cultural Theme or Festive-themed ICT. Festive-themed ICT was designed to test whether cultural artifacts expressed as game themes (festive cultural themes) can improve learning outcomes and learning experiences of students in Indonesia. 17 teachers and 84 students from three schools in Indonesia participated in the evaluation study. Evaluation results show improved learning experiences and learning outcomes [11].

In Study 2, we evaluate the impact of Cultural Activities ICT, in which cultural activities (non-auspicious and auspicious activities) were used as cultural activity metaphors to evaluate students' learning outcomes and teaching and learning experiences. Culture prototypes with cultural activities as a new cultural metaphor for non-auspicious and auspicious activities were designed and evaluated in schools in Brunei and Indonesia. The evaluation is based on a case study evaluating three prototypes: traditional activity, cultural auspicious activity, and cultural non-auspicious activity, in Brunei and Indonesian high schools. The cultural activity prototypes were integrated with elements that symbolize actual and familiar propositions as metaphors. 20 science teachers and 150 students were recruited to participate in this study. The evaluation results show that ICT designed cultural activities (both auspicious and non-auspicious) promote silent emotions among students that result in higher learning achievements.

Summary of the literature review, comprehensive survey, focus groups, study 1, and study 2 findings that contribute to the proposed guidelines:

Table 1. Summary of findings.

Findings	Description
Finding 1.1	Southeast Asian (SEA) teachers use less educational technology in teaching than previously found, contradicting the findings of UNESCO's report in 2021. This demonstrates a clear need for new ICT solutions for education in SEA
Finding 1.2	The current educational technology is not culturally compatible for SEA teachers. It causes anxiety for SEA teachers. Teachers feel uncomfortable using ICT for teaching, which limits students' opportunities with technology
Finding 2.1	Students prefer teacher-centered learning over mobile-based learning, which identifies cultural orientation among Southeast Asian students
Finding 2.2	SEA students are less anxious when ICT (e.g., mobile learning, LMS, online videos) is used during technology-assisted learning and when technology-assisted learning is **guided** by teachers
Finding 2.3	SEA students are less anxious using ICT for learning than teachers in using ICT for teaching, which identifies cultural orientation among Southeast Asian students
Finding 3.1	A variety of cultural emotional states, such as anxiety (while using technology), excitement (at technology interaction), relaxation (when guided by teacher), and engagement (while interacting with classmates), are present among SEA students when using ICT
Finding 3.2	When SEA students are interacting with their classmates with ICT, they feel engaged and satisfied instead of anxious. They report better collaboration with classmates, better teamwork, and better topic comprehension when learning with different technologies, which identifies cultural orientation among Southeast Asian students
Finding 3.3	SEA students are more relaxed and excited in the classroom when they are guided by teachers and teachers are present during technology-assisted learning
Finding 4	SEA teachers are more anxious using educational technology for personal use and teaching than students are using educational technology for learning. This result had minimal impact on students' intention to use ICT; students reported looking forward to using ICT in the classroom
Finding 5	There are cultural barriers. Current ICT tools are incompatible with SEA teachers and students as per findings in literature review and focus groups

(*continued*)

Table 1. (*continued*)

Findings	Description
Finding 5.1	SEA values, including a strong focus on race, religion, and customs and practices, are incompatible with Western values and approaches, thus hindering adaptation to Western-influenced technology
Finding 5.2	Customs, such as traditional rites, music, arts (e.g., silk painting, batik, handicraft, kite flying) and festivals are incompatible with Western customs, styles, artifacts, and presentation
Finding 5.3	SEA practices, such as showing respect for their traditions, auspicious practices, emphasizing the importance of family, artistic traditions, using hands and chopsticks for eating, respect for elders and God, humble greetings & gestures of 'Namaste' in Hindu culture, offerings, and focus on auspicious events, conflict with Western practices, such as emphasizing individualism, placing less importance on the advice of elders, and less focus on auspicious events
Finding 5.4	The presence of cultural emotions during ICT use were discovered from the analysis of data on teachers' and students' perspectives
Finding 6.1	SEA students' learning outcomes improved significantly in the classroom and in mobile learning when "festive theme" activities were used
Finding 6.2	Cultural themes have a "silent positive impact" on SEA students' learning outcomes
Finding 7	Students reported an improved learning experience with mobile learning with minimal negative interactions. SEA students rated both "standard theme" activities and "festive theme" activities similarly, with both having minimal negative interactions
Finding 8	SEA teachers' cultural emotional states were higher when "festive theme" ICT with a local setting was used for teaching and learning
Finding 9	Cultural activities (auspicious and non-auspicious) improve students' learning outcomes
Finding 10	Cultural activities (auspicious and non-auspicious) improve teachers' and students' teaching and learning experiences, respectively

The following are the four culture-centered ICT guidelines for SEA proposed based on the findings:

Guideline 1: **Cultural interactive activities as learning activities**– Learning activities, including ICT activities, adapted for culture lower cultural barriers by integrating customs and cultural practices, as shown in Findings 3.1, 3.2, 4, 5.1, 5.2, 5.3, 5.4, 9 and 10 respectively. The use of ICT with cultural activities as delivery modes in learning increases students' comfort levels and stimulates discussions in class, thus resulting in improved learning outcomes and learning experiences.

Guideline 2: **Auspicious activities as learning activity** - Interaction between students and ICT based on designing an auspicious object lowers cultural barriers, as shown in Findings 3.1, 3.2, 3.3, 5.3, 9 and 10. The use of ICT that incorporates building auspicious objects stimulates discussions in class, thus resulting in improved learning outcomes and learning experiences.

Guideline 3: **Cultural offering (gift) as cultural emotional metaphors** - Teaching and learning activities, integrated with cultural gifts that symbolize actual and familiar objects used in cultural and traditional events as a form of wishing good luck and good fortune as metaphors, lower cultural barriers as shown in Findings 5.1, 5.2, 5.3, and 5.4.

Guideline 4: **Use of cultural themes as cultural emotional metaphors** - Learning activities, including ICT activities, based on cultural themes stimulate empathy and lower cultural barriers, as shown in Findings 6.1, 6.2, 7, and 8. These result in improved learning outcomes.

1.3   Proposed Summary of Practices for Culture-centered ICT Guidelines

The following are brief practices for the four proposed culture-centered ICT guidelines:

I)   Interactive cultural activities as learning activity.

E.g., The use of a gasing activity (an Asian toy top) or batik printing activity further amplifies the effect of connecting the user to the cultural experience (mood).

ii)   Cultural themes as new cultural emotional metaphors.

E.g., The use of festive cultural themes or other Asian festival themes is not just using cultural artifacts for familiarity, but also that the festive theme makes the user interaction more meaningful and connected, evoking a festive mood.

iii)   Cultural Gift as cultural emotional metaphors.

Cultural gift metaphors are cultural offerings that symbolize actual intentions in cultural activities and traditional events as a form of wishing good luck and good fortune, e.g., cultural gifts such as 'Ang Pow' (red packet) and ketupat (rice dumplings), as metaphors etc. The use of cultural gifts and symbols clearly symbolizes cultural beliefs and ideologies that can be used as cultural emotional metaphors that stimulate cultural pride (CP) and cultural motivation (CM). Cultural gift metaphors can be used as hints/advice, such as giving rice dumplings, 'Ang Pow' packets, and lighted lamps as positive advice, or hints during learning activities that provide emotional cultural familiarity to promote learning with emotional experiences (mood).

iv)   Auspicious activities as learning activity.

E.g., The use of auspicious objects in activities such as designing or building an auspicious object such as lanterns, oranges, dragons etc. evokes emotional cultural experiences that stimulate cultural pride (CP) and cultural motivation (CM).

1.4 The Missing Element in HCI Design

In the HCI context, the cultural artifacts used as metaphors do not amplify cultural emotions. The cultural artifacts are simply used to promote and stimulate user experiences. Cultural emotional metaphors are used to stimulate and provoke users' emotions when users are involved and participating in cultural activities. The auspicious and non-auspicious cultural activities as cultural activity metaphors are typical settings for cultural motivations that can promote deep cultural essence that triggers deep cultural emotions and excitement.

1.5 Cultural Motivational Elements

At this stage, from the list of proposed guidelines, I propose Cultural Motivational Elements (CME) as an extension to the existing Human Computer Interaction (HCI) model and as a broad category of cultural elements for simplicity of design execution. The CME incorporates three items:

i) New Cultural emotional metaphors.

• Cultural Themes

ii) New Cultural emotional metaphors.

• Cultural gifts used during festivals that can present actual intentions in festivals and cultural occasions that symbolize actual intentions in cultural activities and traditional events as a form of wishing good luck and good fortune.

iii) Cultural Activity Metaphors as new deep cultural emotional metaphors.

• Interactive Non-Auspicious Activities
• Interactive Auspicious Activities

Deep cultural emotional metaphors are interactive cultural activity metaphors that go beyond simple cultural artifacts (metaphors). These approaches emphasize making or building auspicious objects or playing cultural activities that exemplify cultural emotional moods of excitement and joy of participating in cultural activities with cultural pride and cultural motivation.

A further extension to the current HCI model is required to support this expansion. Thus, the HCI model on user experience and interaction design is extended with an additional element of Cultural Motivational Elements (CME).

The CME is composed of (i) Cultural Emotional Metaphor - Cultural Themes (e.g., festive themes) in which emotional attachments towards cultural identity are evoked with the presence of cultural emotional metaphors and cultural themes such as festive themes, traditional wedding themes, etc.; (ii) Cultural Gift Metaphors that evoke emotional attachment, e.g., gifts that symbolize actual propositions of good luck and fortune in cultural or traditional events; and (iii) Deep Emotional Metaphors - Cultural Activities, which are activities including non-auspicious activities in which users are encouraged to play a traditional cultural game activity and auspicious activities in which users are encouraged to design or build an auspicious object. In both, users take great pride in completing the ICT activities.

I propose the following metaphor model as an overall contribution towards the Human Computer Interaction (HCI) domain as illustrated in Fig. 1 and as an updated HCI model for designers and practitioners.

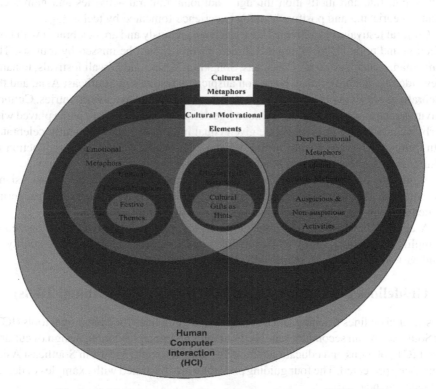

Fig. 1 CME (Cultural Motivational Elements) as part of HCI model

2 Culture-centered ICT Design

2.1 Definition of Culture-centered ICT

"Culture-Centered ICT with CME," encompasses any technology integrated with Cultural Motivational Elements (CME) that is used by teachers and students in the education setting and handles information that enhances and motivates teaching, aligning the learning experience with cultural interactive capacity and cultural values.

2.2 Culture-centered ICT Design with CME for Southeast Asia

A society that is rich in art and culture requires a varied educational design that aligns with its niche, diversified values. Southeast Asia, which comprises 11 countries, is a region with rich cultural and religious diversity. The primary religions are Islam, Christianity, Buddhism, and Hinduism. Despite the prevalence of multiple religions, races, and identities, Southeast Asia's cultural activities and festivals appear to unify the different religions and races [12]. The region's rich cultural diversity and values can be used to bridge the gaps that appear in technology-oriented learning. Encouraging students' excitement, fun, and motivation through traditional cultural activities and games can create an enriching and positive learning experience fomented by technology.

Cultural festivals and activities are treated auspiciously and are celebrated with both affection and pride [1, 8]. Many are attractions that cannot be missed by tourists. The Ramadhan, Lunar New Year, Christmas, Songkran, Vesak, and Diwali festivals, to name a few, identify the importance placed on auspicious festivals in Southeast Asia, and the celebrations are often observed as important events in their respective countries. Cultural activities such as wau bulan design (moon kite design), congkak (board game played with marbles), and gasing (a toy top) are given equal importance and frequently celebrated with cultural pride specifically in the villages. This demonstrates the conjunction of cultural events and activities in Southeast Asia.

Southeast Asia's cultural identity is rich and deeply rooted among Southeast Asians; consequently, this identity has great potential to be used as a motivator, triggering excitement, and promoting active learning along with the integration of ICT.

A cultural framework, with four guiding principles and practices, is proposed to exemplify the culture-based ICT guidelines and practices for ICT sustainability in Southeast Asian schools to shape individuals with culture-based ICT.

3   Guidelines for Culture-based ICT Design (Educational Tools)

This section outlines teaching and learning design guidelines for educational tools (ICT) for Southeast Asian secondary schools. Four guiding principles for the design of culture-based ICT solutions and educational tools for students aged 13 to 18 in Southeast Asian schools are presented. The four guiding principles are illustrated with examples of design and teaching practices.

The four guiding principles for the design of ICT solutions and educational tools in Southeast Asia cater to the requirements and preferences of educators, administrators, and students within the local context. Classroom teaching can be supplemented with ICT cultural activities. The four guiding principles highlight specific cultural elements that can be presented in ICT solutions and educational tools to stimulate cultural emotions to reduce cultural barriers. The sustainable use of ICT in the classroom will improve both the teaching and learning experiences. The guidelines can be incorporated individually or jointly, depending on the design of the ICT activity.

3.1 Guiding Principles

Guiding Principle 1: Interactive Cultural Activities as Learning Activities.
Learning activities based on cultural activities will lower cultural barriers by integrating

customs and cultural practices. Cultural activities that are commonly practiced in Southeast Asia can be identified as learning tools. The use of ICT with cultural activities and delivery modes stimulates cultural pride. Students will be keen to engage with others and will be spurred to complete the activity with excitement. The learning process will promote discussions that result in improved learning outcomes and learning experiences. The integration of cultural interactive activities in ICT learning boosts the use of ICT in the classroom.

Practices: Interactive cultural activities, such as designing a wau (kite), designing a batik (silk painting), and playing gasing (top), are common for Southeast Asians and are frequently seen in cultural events and sports. These are common activities that teachers and students understand how to play. Such activities can be integrated as metaphors and teaching activities to increase the comfort level between teachers and students. Furthermore, these activities relax teachers and students, helping them to actively enjoy the teaching and learning processes.

An interactive cultural activity can lower the anxiety level among teachers and students while using ICT for teaching and learning. The activity will be perceived as a game rather than a purely academic activity, which will promote cultural emotions and happiness among the students. Students learn the topic via a cultural activity through stimulating discussions with their peers and teachers. With a teacher's guidance, a smooth transition from teacher-centered learning to a more independent, ICT-based learning can result in the students becoming more resilient ICT users. Types of cultural interactive activities arc shown in Table 2. (Figs. 2,3 , 4 and 5).

Fig. 2 Gasing (spinning top)

Fig. 3 Congkak

Teachers can briefly illustrate the cultural activity before introducing the ICT activity. For example, teachers can post questions to students on the common cultural activities in which students have participated. Students can relate their knowledge of cultural events and activities, sharing their experiences with classmates and creating a comfortable interaction among teachers and students. Teachers can also draw or display images of the cultural activity to promote enthusiasm among students.

An interactive cultural activity encourages students to interact with the system by involving them in the activity in the form of 'doing.' The cultural activity can be presented as an animated object in an ICT activity that players can spin (gasing), kick

Fig. 4 Wau bulan (moon kite)

Fig. 5 Batik design (silk painting)

Fig. 6 Example 1: Ketupat used as hints

Fig. 7 Example 2: Oranges

Fig. 8 Example 3: Lantern

Fig. 9 Example 4: Ang Pow

(sepak takraw), collect (congkak), draw (batik/silk painting), or design (lantern). Students will enjoy the different animation aspects of a cultural activity while simultaneously completing the activity to achieve the desired learning outcome.

Guiding Principle 2: Cultural Offerings (Gift) Metaphors. Teaching and learning activities, integrated with cultural offerings (gifts) as metaphors that symbolize actual and familiar objects used in cultural and traditional events as a form of wishing good

Fig. 10 Lunar new year theme

Fig. 11 Ramadhan theme

Fig. 12 Example 1: Chlorophyll as christmas theme

Fig. 13 Example 2: Stomata as christmas theme

Table 2. Examples of cultural interactive activities in Southeast Asia gasing (a spinning top), wau bulan (moon kite), congkak, and batik design (silk painting).

Cultural interactive activity	Cultural interactive activity
See Fig. 2	See Fig. 3
See Fig. 4	See Fig. 5

Table 3. Examples of emotional metaphors; ketupat used as hints, Oranges, lantern, Ang Pow

Example of Emotional metaphors	Example of Emotional metaphors
See Fig. 6	See Fig. 7
See Fig. 8	See Fig.9

fortune, lower cultural barriers. These familiar gestures of receiving gifts evoke joy and happiness when received, which lowers cultural barriers. Elements that symbolize actual and familiar propositions as emotional metaphors improve teaching and learning experiences. The emotional metaphors amplify emotional experiences, which promotes teaching and learning.

Practices: Southeast Asian cultural icons can be used as deep emotional metaphors to present an idea cognitively and emotionally. Cultural gifts such as oranges, lamps, ketupat (rice dumplings), and ang pow (red packets) are often used during festive seasons as offerings. Cultural elements that symbolize actual propositions in cultural events or festivals can help students feel more engaged. There is a close association to Southeast Asians, which triggers cultural emotions of joy and happiness. The familiarity of cultural icons makes teaching and learning easier to assimilate and comprehend.

The use of cultural gifts as emotional metaphors strengthens cultural emotions and cultural pride among Southeast Asians. Students recognize the application of cultural icons more accurately. For example, the use of ketupat (rice dumplings) or ang pow (red packet) is perceived as a gift with good wishes during auspicious occasions. The icons can be used as hints or treats in learning activities. Positive advice with deep emotional metaphors encourages excitement and zeal towards the activity and students can revel in triumph. The positive vibes will increase the players' self-esteem and confidence, sustaining their interest in completing the activity. Players feel there is another chance to demonstrate their knowledge with guidance from the emotional metaphors. The positive and auspicious advice builds resiliency within students. Students feel inspired and motivated in completing the activity because the system presents positive and auspicious advice.

Positive advice can be integrated by using hints when incorrect choices are selected (e.g., providing keywords related to the correct answer, providing images to the correct answer, and offering more positive advice and interactions). Examples of emotional metaphors include ang pow (red packets) – clicked to obtain hints (Fig. 9); lanterns and lamps - lighted to obtain hints (Fig. 8); ketupat (rice dumplings) - clicked to obtain hints (Fig. 6); gesture as a form of greetings - blessings during festivals with oranges (Fig. 7); and Rangoli (patterns with colorful rice flour) - drawn to obtain hints.

Teachers can illustrate the cultural gifts before introducing the ICT cultural activity. Teachers can display images of cultural gifts to stimulate discussion among students about when they have received ang pow from their grandparents or have made ketupat (rice dumplings). Students can share their experiences with classmates.

Cultural gifts can be incorporated as metaphors in ICT solutions. The cultural gifts can be presented as hints (ang pow packets) or treats (ketupat) when a task is achieved. Cultural icons such as lanterns, dragons, and a wau bulan (moon kite) can also be used in decorating and designing activities. Additionally, these cultural gifts can be presented as deep emotional metaphors (animated objects) in activities.

Guiding Principle 3: Auspicious Learning Activity. Auspicious activities will lower cultural barriers and stimulate teaching and learning. The use of ICT with auspicious objects and CME in class will result in improved learning outcomes and learning experiences for students. Auspicious activities that require student to design or build an auspicious object with knowledge learned stimulates teaching and learning, thus reducing cultural barriers.

Practices: Students can design or build an auspicious object such as a lantern, red packet (ang pow), or lamp with objects or information learned. Auspicious activities promote the art of designing or building an auspicious object using ICT. The auspicious activity promotes emotional attachment as the students complete the task with ICT. Auspicious activities instill respect for tradition and culture, which promotes good habits.

Auspicious activities which include designing an auspicious object or building an auspicious object with knowledge gained can be integrated into ICT activities as tasks. Teachers can encourage students to create or design lanterns, lamps, a wau (kite), or dragons with knowledge acquired during lessons. This can be achieved by a designing, drawing, or building task focused on auspicious objects or activities. This promotes students to actively engage with what was taught during the lesson.

Guiding Principle 4: Cultural Theme for Educational Technology. Learning activities based on cultural themes with cultural motivational elements (CME) stimulate cultural pride and emotions that lower cultural barriers. ICT with cultural themes such as festive themes and traditional wedding themes can result in improved learning experiences and outcomes. Empathy towards cultural practices stimulates cultural emotions, thus fostering students' interest to fulfil the ICT activities and achieve the desired outcome or result.

Practices: ICT activities can be presented as cultural themes to stimulate empathy and respect for the cultural values and traditions. Presumably, teachers and students are familiar with the cultural theme, creating a close and comfortable bond with the ICT activity. Examples of cultural themes are ICT activities using festive themes (e.g., Lunar New Year; Fig. 10, Ramadhan; Fig. 11) as shown in Table 4.

Table 4. Examples of Lunar New Year theme and Ramadhan theme

Festive theme	Festive theme
See Fig. 10	See Fig. 11

Students learn better with empathy when the topic is presented in an ICT activity with a cultural theme. In this case, students feel more compassionate towards learning with ICT. Learning with empathy allows students to feel and share the emotions of other students. Hence, a cultural theme allows students to learn with the presence of cultural values and practices, which instils humility, the key enabler of empathy.

Empathy can be achieved with a cultural theme design (e.g., Ramadhan, Lunar New Year, Diwali, and traditional wedding themes). Indeed, empathy can achieve solace among students because they feel more connected with cultural values and traditions; as a result, learning becomes more meaningful. The smooth execution of ICT activities with cultural themes is possible, as students feel more culturally integrated and connected. A cultural theme can be integrated in ICT solutions as a cultural wedding theme, festive theme, New Year theme, water festival theme, or hungry ghost festival theme. Teachers can discuss with students the different types of cultural festivals in Southeast

Asia. Teachers can share pictures of festivals with students and discuss the significance of the festivals celebrated throughout Southeast Asia. Furthermore, teachers can encourage students to share their festival experiences with their peers. Festive themes can be integrated into ICT solutions as students share and become emotionally attached, creating a feeling of empathy while participating in the ICT activity. Examples of images used in Christmas festive theme as shown in Table 5. (Figs. 12 and 13).

Table 5. Examples of the Christmas festive theme for the topic photosynthesis.

Example of christmas theme images	Example of christmas theme images
See Fig. 12	See Fig. 13

4   Examples of Guiding Principles in ICT

Cultural ICT Guiding Principle 1. Cultural interactive activity (spinning the gasing) as shown in Fig. 14: guiding principle 1.

Fig. 14 Guiding principle 1

Cultural ICT Guiding Principle 2. Using cultural emotional metaphors as hints/advice during activity as shown in Fig. 15: guiding principle 2.

Fig. 15 Guiding principle 2

Cultural ICT Guiding Principle 3. Using Guiding Principle 3: Auspicious activities to stimulate teaching and learning as shown in Fig. 16: Guiding principle 3.

Fig. 16 Guiding principle 3

Cultural ICT Guiding Principle 4. Use of cultural themes for educational technology as shown in Fig. 17: Guiding principle 4.

Fig. 17 Guiding principle 4 (as video presentation)

Using the Guiding Principles to Plan Quality Learning Experiences. Teachers can stimulate and motivate students with cultural questions in discussions prior to ICT activities. Examples of questions to stimulate and motivate discussions include:

How many of you have played these games, when did you last play them, did you enjoy playing these games? Cultural discussion with students, as shown in Fig. 18. Students participate in culture-based activity as shown in Fig. 19.

Fig. 18 Students participate in cultural discussions via Zoom

Fig. 19 Students participate in culture-based activity

5 Conclusion

Culturally motivated elements are required to stimulate teaching and learning in Southeast Asia schools. Placing importance to cultural values in the design of educational tools will enhance teaching and learning experience. Cultural values have long lasting impressions to the local people despite the exposure of western approach in entertainment and media industry. These deep-rooted cultural practices and values can be triggered with the presence of cultural elements in the design and daily activities of which they have a sense of familiarity and belonging. The cultural values are the silent motivators and the key to rich teaching and learning experience for Southeast Asian schools to build an ICT resilient society.

References

1. Andaya, B.W.: The Future of Asia: Cross-cultural Conversations. SPAFA J. (1991–2013), **16**(1), (2006)
2. Ang Pow (red packet) image. https://www.fengshuimall.com/chinese-new-year-red-packets-hong-bao-with-fook
3. Batik image. https://jadibatek.com/batik/
4. Congkak image. http://traditionalgamescct.blogspot.com/2013/03/congkak.html
5. Gasing (top) image. https://www.carousell.sg/p/spinning-top-gasing-traditional-124890500/
6. Ketupat (rice cake) images. https://media.istockphoto.com/photos/ketupat-picture-id5443 26376?k=6&m=544326376&s=612x612&w=0&h=8oZqtWU697tL-8SI7-j_1Zva9PiYgL9-O1NPkOeYfDA
7. Lunar new year theme image. https://www.pre-kpages.com/newyear/
8. McLeod, M.W., Dieu, N.T., Nguyen, T.D.: Culture and customs of Vietnam. Greenwood Publishing Group (2001)
9. Orange image. https://www.shutterstock.com/image-photo/three-oranges-on-white-backgr ound-351518138
10. Ramadhan theme image. https://www.shutterstock.com/search/ramadhan+theme
11. Sithira Vadivel, V., Song, I., Bhati, A.S.: Culturally Themed Educational Tools for Enhancing Learning in Southeast Asian Secondary Schools. In: Arai, K., Kapoor, S., Bhatia, R. (eds.) FTC 2020. AISC, vol. 1288, pp. 950–968. Springer, Cham (2021). https://doi.org/10.1007/ 978-3-030-63128-4_71
12. Tong, X.: A cross-national investigation of an extended technology acceptance model in the online shopping context. Int. J. Retail Distrib. Manage. **38**(10), 742–759 (2010)
13. Vadivel, S., Song, I., Bhati, A.S.: Improving teaching and learning in Southeast Asian secondary schools with the use of culturally motivated web and mobile technology. In: Kim, K., Joukov, N. (eds.) ICISA 2017. LNEE, vol. 424, pp. 652–659. Springer, Singapore (2017). https://doi.org/10.1007/978-981-10-4154-9_75
14. Vadivel, V.S., Song, I., Bhati, A.S.: Cultural Emotion Games as Trajectory Learning in Southeast Asia. In: Baalsrud Hauge, J., C. S. Cardoso, J., Roque, L., Gonzalez-Calero, P.A. (eds.) ICEC 2021. LNCS, vol. 13056, pp. 62–74. Springer, Cham (2021). https://doi.org/10.1007/ 978-3-030-89394-1_5
15. Village image. https://www.istockphoto.com/photos/malaysia-kampung-house

Adaptive Instruction: A Case Study of Gamified Practice and Testing in a Large Introductory Psychology Course

Elizabeth S. Veinott(✉) 📵

Cognitive and Learning Sciences, Michigan Technological University, Houghton, MI, USA
eveinott@mtu.edu

Abstract. Understanding what methods are effective for learning in large lectures continues to be an important research goal and examining factors that support the use of adaptive systems in these large lectures is needed. In this case study, students from a large lecture class (n = 223) used an adaptive instructional system to cover 39 learning modules over 14 weeks. The weekly adaptive system gamified practice and ensured students distributed their studying before each exam. Using a mixed-methods approach in the context of the ICAP framework, student experience using the system was examined. Results indicated that the majority of students found the gamified activities useful for learning the material initially. The adaptive system helped students diagnose what concepts they knew and did not know, provided an additional way to review module topics, and provided additional testing of the material. However, the system did not help students know when they had studied enough. Overall students' exam performance in the course benefited from the addition of the active practice and gamified testing, and the strategies students used are important for future adaptive instructional system design.

Keywords: Adaptive instruction · Learning · Gamification

1 Introduction

An important goal of education is to increase the active and constructive learning that students engage in regularly [5, 9, 16, 46]. Large lectures have always been a challenge in higher education to support student cognitive engagement. Before the COVID pandemic, there were a variety of methods designed to increase the amount of active learning by incorporating different educational technologies into the large lectures. These methods include using class polls with clickers [10], social media such as Twitter [7], daily quizzes [3], word games [24, 26] and more recently learning dashboards and analytics [22, 35, 43, 47]. During the pandemic, the use of these types of methods has been even more important and pervasive as both instructors and learners engage in learning under a variety of different, and often new, environments (online, remote, hybrid). Students had to manage their own learning even more so than before the pandemic. Several studies found that while students preferred the flexibility of self-paced, online work, most students had extensive motivational challenges to do the work [2, 4, 32, 36]. Adaptive instructional

© Springer Nature Switzerland AG 2022
G. Meiselwitz et al. (Eds.): HCII 2022, LNCS 13517, pp. 455–467, 2022.
https://doi.org/10.1007/978-3-031-22131-6_34

(AIS) systems may have helped students manage their practice during the pandemic. The world's recent experience with the large-scale, ramp up of self-paced, online, remote, and hybrid learning during the pandemic only increases the importance of understanding how they are being used.

Recently Graesser et al., [16] point to several aspects of learning that adaptive systems can support from spacing practice to assessing how well students learn. For many years, we have known that active learning is more effective than passive learning [5, 16, 45], and adaptive instructional systems such as intelligent tutoring systems (ITS) have made important inroads in this area [2, 6, 13–16, 33–35, 37, 43, 44], but how to effectively incorporate computer-based instructional strategies into large lectures is an important, albeit a less examined area of research. Lectures provide a good opportunity to evaluate the impact of these systems on student learning experiences [17–19, 22, 34, 44]. However, not all strategies are effective. Recent studies suggest that students may not be best suited to assess their learning [2, 17, 37, 38, 44]. Karpicke [23] reported that students would stop their practice too soon, right after they initially learned the material.

2 Background Research

2.1 ICAP Knowledge Engagement Framework

Chi and Wylie's [9] ICAP (Interactive, Constructive, Active, Passive) is an empirically grounded framework [8, 9, 45] that provides four stages of cognitive engagement with predicted increasing levels of impact on learning. It provides not only strategies but expected measures for the transfer of learning [8]. These will be described with examples from a large introductory lecture class. Briefly, the first stage is *passive engagement*, such as reading the text, watching a video or a demonstration, or listening to a lecture with or without lecture notes. The next level is the *active engagement* or learning where information is manipulated by the student, which in many lecture classes would involve taking notes, answering questions in a tool (e.g., Kahoot or clickers) while listening to the lecture [10], or participating in a demonstration. *Constructive engagement* involves putting new knowledge into practice. Examples from a large psychology introductory course might include applying a basic psychological theory to solve a problem and writing about it, generating one's own test questions, and generating notes or links in a concept map of a topic. Finally, *interactive engagement* would be collaborating with others on a topic to generate new information, such as doing any of the constructive activities in a group [24].

Using the ICAP framework as a foundation, this paper describes the case of an adaptive instruction in a large introductory lecture course, focused on students' strategies using the AIS and their learning outcomes. This paper describes how the AIS was used from an instructional standpoint, as well as evaluations of student learning, and their personal experiences with the system. This paper contributes to a recent and growing body of work exploring learning outcomes in large lectures [4, 17, 19 32] and contributes to a call for more research on learning in psychology courses [18].

2.2 Ways Adaptive Instructional Systems Support Learning

While adaptive instructional systems (AIS) incorporate a broad range of tools, in this class the AIS focused on capturing what the learner knew, and what they needed to learn, and adjusting the quizzing content appropriately. If the learner did not master a topic, they received more items related to that topic. The adaptive instructional system was part of a larger mix of course material. The system focused on definitions and terms within each module. However, given that many find the science of psychology intuitive, not understanding or being able to use the terms correctly can be a barrier to student learning [24, 26].

The AIS can support learning: by improving engagement with the material, changing how students practice the material, and providing real-time feedback on that learning. These are all aspects that can be very useful in a large lecture course when there may be fewer options for individualized tutoring [36]. First, the AIS used in this course was designed to be engaging, because of the animation or variety of content to keep students engaged that might not otherwise be or motivate students to engage with the material longer. Second, it supported tailored learning as described above, with the idea that this is efficient for learning and may reduce boredom due to reviewing concepts the student has already mastered. Third, an AIS can change how students study, by increasing the time spent practicing, changing what they practice, or changing the way they practice. Each type of practice is critical for memory retention [11, 12, 25]. Next, an AIS can increase retrieval practice by implementing what has been called *the testing effect* through repeated and adaptive quizzing [3, 4, 12, 23, 30, 31]. Finally, an AIS can introduce dynamic content, provide worked examples [28, 44], and feedback making it particularly helpful in a large psychology lecture course to support new models of teaching [17–19].

2.3 Gamified Practice

Gamification in AIS systems is designed to increase time on task (studying) by gamifying the practice and reinforcing it with rewards (e.g., points or badges) [20, 29]. Similar to reviews of AIS research, meta-analyses of video games for learning (serious games) find mixed results in terms of learning effectiveness [42]. One positive learning example was a serious game, *Heuristica* [28], that examined a variety of AIS methods to improve decision learning outcomes after 8-weeks [4, 41, 44], in addition to increasing the cognitive fidelity of the tasks [40], or leaving hints for other players [39]. In the current study, the AIS used points, progress bars, and feedback for gamification [20, 47]. Because large lectures require students to be self-motivated to effectively learn, gamification may be very useful.

2.4 Teaching Large Introductory Psychology Courses

According to Gurung and Hackathorn [18], two areas for new research on teaching large introductory courses are identifying what methods are best for learning and determining what are key moderators that improve learning. Gurung [17] correlated student study methods and exam performance in a large introduction to psychology course without an adaptive tutoring system and found several statistically significant correlations. Controlling for students' ability using their ACT scores, the highest correlations with final exam scores came from memorizing one's notes ($r = .28$), testing one's knowledge ($r = .28$), generating examples ($r = .20$), and reviewing one's notes ($r = .18$). Interestingly, 75% of the students reported studying for each exam for fewer than 6 h. Interestingly, the total time studying for the final did not correlate with performance [17]. The current study contributes to this body of research by examining AIS use related to exam performance.

One challenge in teaching large introductory courses is the breadth of topics covered for a field and the level of detail for each topic. In psychology, students regularly feel the information is intuitive or obvious, which may lead students to falsely believe they have mastered the material before they have. Introduction to psychology is surprisingly hard for many students due to the breadth of topics. Some textbooks address this challenge by reducing chapters to manageable chunks or modules, other books reduce the content overall. An adaptive system, if designed properly, can help with this problem.

The goal of this mixed-methods study was to examine the gamified adaptive instructional system as one new method for learning that has been implemented in recent years. For gamification, the particular AIS in this class, which we will refer to as the PSYCH AIS, used points, progress bars, and feedback [20, 28]. Researchers have recently begun to examine the use of AISs to improve learning in psychology courses [4]. These classes provide excellent initial case studies of the integration of adaptive quizzing with gamification in a large lecture course. As summarized well in [16], an adaptive instructional system that complements learning is one that supports distributed and spaced practice over time[11, 25], provides worked examples [41, 42], helps students manage their studying [12, 22], includes interactive (visual and text) learning opportunities to support all learners [20, 37] and uses quizzing or the testing effect to support learning [23, 30, 31].

Research Questions. Given the exploratory nature of the research, the specific research questions were:

R1: Does the adaptive practice in the AIS improve learning outcomes?
R2: Does adaptive practice AIS support learning? If so, how?
R3: How are students using the AIS? What strategies are they adopting?
R4: How does the AIS fit within students' larger class context?

3   Methods

Two hundred and twenty-three students (70.4% male, 28% female, 1% not reporting) in a large introductory lecture course used an adaptive learning system weekly as a supplement to course lectures with demonstrations, research experience, lecture notes, key term sheets, and a textbook. It is important to note that most students in the course were non-majors. These data were evaluated to determine the effectiveness of the adaptive system for use in future classes. The study was IRB approved to analyze the archived de-identified data.

3.1 Class Format

The class format was typical for a large lecture and included short reading modules each week in the textbook, class lectures with notes, demonstrations of psychological phenomena, homework assignments, and exams. The course met for 14 weeks, and students interacted with the Psych AIS each week to complete a total of 39 modules (2–3 modules/week). Modules were due each Sunday, but students had the option to complete them any time during the week.

3.2 Class Adaptive Instructional System and Gamified Practice

The introduction to psychology course AIS, referred to as Psych AIS, was relatively new to the course and included the e-book, interactive exercises, and adaptive, gamified quizzing capabilities. In the introduction to psychology course, this scaffolding took the form of basic terminology, definitions, and examples with a focus on knowledge, not the application of that knowledge. The system used a depth-first strategy for each learning objective, meaning that students would get one topic or idea at a time and need to master that idea before moving to a new topic. Each module in the Psych AIS provided a more active experience than simply reading the module.

A key feature of AISs is the ability to automatically tailor instruction to fit the needs and skills of individual learners. Different systems use different methods. The Psych AIS did this through an initial assessment, followed by in-module exercises. Students were required to do at least one adaptive exercise per module. These exercises included several different activities. In addition, learning opportunities for each module were gamified in the adaptive system. Each week students needed to earn enough points (by answering questions and reviewing material) before they received assignment credit. This portion took students on average, at least 15 min per module. Students completed assessments or quizzes in the system and learning transfer was measured by their performance on the exams in the classroom. Exams included both short answer and multiple-choice questions focused on a mix of concepts and the application of psychological science.

3.3 Evaluating Adaptive System: Learning Measures and Student Reflection

One way to evaluate the effectiveness of the adaptive system was to compare the transfer of the learning to the exam scores. It should be noted that the exams would be considered more of a far transfer task in terms of learning because most of the items involved applications of concepts or integration of the ideas (out of a 50-item exam). Exam transfer is not a perfect measure, as there was no control group (who did not use the Psych AIS) nor was there a way to control for student effort or prior knowledge in this sample. Second, at the end of the term, students completed a short survey that asked them how they used the system. They also reflected on the PSYCH AIS tool to evaluate their metacognitive experiences with the system relative to other learning strategies. From this mixed-methods approach, we can identify student strategies for working with the adaptive system to learn the material and study for the exams.

4 Results

4.1 Student Learning Outcomes

R1: Does the adaptive practice in the AIS improve learning outcomes?

The first way this research question was evaluated was to analyze the partial correlations between the gamified practice time, quiz scores, and subsequent exam scores. The Psych AIS did not increase students' overall time studying for the class which was ultimately one of the things that supported students adopting the tool. However, self-reported time studying using the adaptive system each week and exam averages were positively correlated, (Pearson r = .155, p = .01). Studying longer improved exam scores. One interpretation might be that additional time on the gamified practice in the Psych AIS improved engagement, but because correlation does not indicate a causal association, one cannot rule out that higher achievers might have also studied more. While gamified practice time and exam scores were related, there was also a statistically significant positive correlation between exam scores and adaptive quiz scores (Pearson r = .299, p = .001). Doing better on the quizzes was associated with doing better on the exams.

Results from a one-way ANOVA indicated that using the Psych AIS improved performance for the first exam, $F(1,223) = 7.45$, $p = .007$. Based on a median split of weekly adaptive system time, students who used the system more (>45 min for two-three modules) scored higher on the exams than those who used the adaptive system less each week. Median scores on each exam were 79 to 80 percent and remained so over the term. The system improved learning for students struggling with particular content because they were either not spending enough time studying or doing the right type of studying (active, constructive). However, using the Psych AIS seemed to pull in the tail of the distribution, rather than shifting the entire distribution up as the exam median scores remained the same. This result is consistent with some other findings related to AIS tools [cf. 37, 43].

R2: Does adaptive practice support learning? If so, how?

Assigning the adaptive system each week forced distributed practice for the students without a lot of extra time. Students did not use the system to support distributed practice beyond the structure provided in the class. As can be seen in Fig. 1, 40%of the students used the adaptive system in one sitting, while 22% mixed it up between distributing the work across more than one sitting depending on the module and week.

The strength of the adaptive system was that it tailored their learning as it provided students with diagnostic information about what they understood and what they did not. It also provided them with more practice in areas and topics where they needed it. As discussed below a few students reported that they would use the Psych AIS to practice for exams on modules that they were weakest on and try to double or triple their points in the gamified portion of the tool.

R3: How were students using the adaptive instructional system? What strategies?

In trying to understand the usefulness of the system, students were asked about their strategies for using the quizzes specifically. Of the 223 students in the class, 31.8% reported not going back to the adaptive quizzes to review for the exams, 17.9% reported using them to diagnose where they needed additional information, 41.2% reported using

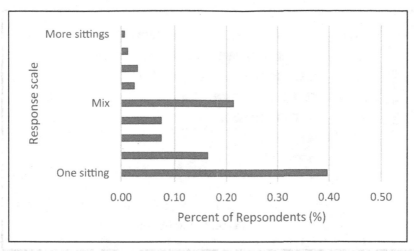

Fig. 1. Percentages of students using the adaptive instructional quizzing in one sitting, or more than one sitting.

them for review, and 8.9% reported only using the adaptive gamified content, not the quizzes. Being assigned each week, this adaptive strategy reinforced distributed practice between modules in a chapter. Following this learning, each student took a quiz. These quiz scores were compared for those reporting using the adaptive learning and quizzing system as a learning tool versus a studying tool.

Students realized that the Psych AIS was efficient. Most students completed a module in the adaptive instructional system in about 25 min per week, on average. While this may be less time than a student in their major might study per week, it is consistent with reporting from other introduction to psychology course case studies [17, 18]. What may be surprising to some is that 20-min per week using an adaptive system could support effective learning. If the practice is distributed and involves practice testing, it may be sufficiently effective for some students. Finally,t, students reflected on how the system fits into their study practices.

R4: How does the AIS fit within students' larger study context?
First, students reported that the Psych AIS was relevant for the material in the module most of the time (Fig. 2). When asked how they studied for the exams, 24.2% of the students reported using only more traditional methods (e.g., book, notes, lecture slides, key term sheets provided), while 34.1% reported using the adaptive system to master the material in the learning modules. Finally, 15.7% reported not using the adaptive system to study.

Finally, students were asked about how they studied for the exams. As can be seen in Fig. 3, the adaptive quizzes were not the most popular method for studying for the exams. Fifty-one percent of students reported using the key term sheet often, 40% reported using the lecture slides often, and 37% reported using the adaptive quizzes when studying for the exam. However, this may be due in part to the nature of the course exams, so may not be the case in other classes.

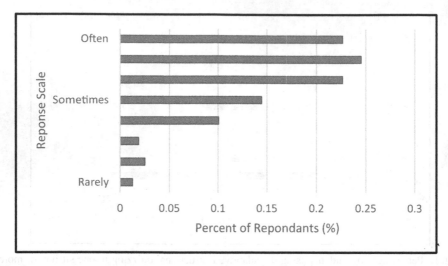

Fig. 2. Percentages of students saying the adaptive instructional quizzing was relevant to each module were more than 70 percent (sum of top three bars)

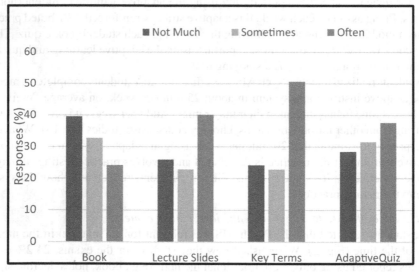

Fig. 3. Percentage of students reporting how much they used different information and tools for studying

4.2 Student Reflections

Finally, as mentioned earlier, students completed a brief evaluation of the system at the end of the course, in order to improve our Psych AIS use in the future. Students were asked two open-ended questions: *Were the module quizzes in the adaptive system useful for studying for the exams? If so, how?* and *What strategies did they use to study for the exams?*

Responses from 176 students who completed both questions were analyzed. Most students (64.8%) thought the quizzes were effective for diagnosing what they needed to study before the exam, for review, or for additional practice. The rest (35.2%) felt the quizzes were effective for initial learning, but not for studying for each exam. When asked how the quizzes in Psych AIS affected their studying, student comments highlighted some of the expected positive impacts of the Psych AIS.

- *I liked that there were the learning modules before the quizzes because it gave me extra practice that I might not have made time for otherwise and .... Taught me to probably make time [for them] in the future. [S172]*
- *I really appreciated the AIS and would like to see that in my future classes. It made it very easy to revisit pertinent information for the exam. It showed me how important it actually was to revisit the information [S201]*
- *I will likely be less reliant on memorizing vocabulary terms, and more likely to ensure links between concepts is more solid when I study [S165]*

Other students reported that using the Psych AIS replaced time they spent re-reading the textbook which would mean they were replacing passive learning with active learning. Others reported using it to replace taking notes in class, or reviewing class lectures, which would be replacing one type of active engagement with another. However, there is no suggestion that these are good replacements.

5 Conclusion

In this class, the adaptive learning tool provided opportunities to implement testing effect practices [3, 23, 30, 31] and spaced practice [11, 12], making it particularly helpful in a large lecture course and supporting new models of teaching introductory psychology [19]. Evaluating the use of this system in the context of a large class provided some data demonstrating an effective embedding of good practice strategies that improved learning. Interestingly, it did not increase the total amount of time or distributed practice across weeks.

This study contributes to research on socio-technical systems in education by showing that supporting new study habits for students that need to shift their habits can be effective and not intrusive. Interestingly, students completed their adaptive sessions in a single sitting and did not seem to spend more time studying. There were a few students who spent 1–2 h per module on the adaptive system early in the semester, but that was not the norm. However, the quality of that time was better spent. Students were not re-reading the book, a passive activity from the ICAP framework [8, 9].

The adaptive system embedded good habits by either augmenting what students already did or shifting their strategies and improving the efficiency of their studying. Most of the Psych AIS habits were active strategies in the ICAP framework, and a few were constructive, but none seemed to be interactive. Students did better when they used the Psych AIS more, but did not spend more time than they had previously. Therefore, it did not seem to increase engagement, but it made the student engagement efficient because the Psych AIS encouraged different types of studying as well. Despite being a large lecture, one of the limitations of this work is that it represents one class, a case study of students using the system.

Implications for Adaptive System Adoption and Future Research

The promise of adaptive instruction is there, but sometimes hard to achieve. Several aspects of the implementation seemed to help. An AIS needs to be embedded into the classroom or training strategically. In this psychology course, students did not want to use the system for the first few weeks, but setting it up to be easy to use by having it seamlessly embedded in the learning management system (e.g., no separate login) helped. Providing flexibility on when they did each module helped with adopting the AIS. Giving students choices on which activities to do in the AIS helped.

Future research should focus on the aspect of the adaptive experience that students want to control. For example, one of the questions in AIS has been whether and how to let students determine what they need to learn next [36]. At this conference previously, Whitaker et al. [41] reported on a study where trainees chose what they were going to learn next and found no differences in learning or transfer between those that chose and those that did not. The current case study was unable to test this in a large class, students did use the adaptive learning modules to review for the exams by focusing on what they knew and what they had trouble learning. While students may like the idea of choosing, it also may be demotivating at times [2, 43].

An IAS could manage more than students' knowledge [41, 42]. For example, it could manage their energy and motivation to support better practices in self-regulated learning [2]. One way this might work is if AIS systems leverage findings from research on making the AI [or AIS] explain itself [1, 21, 27]. Future research in AISs should focus on the constructive and interactive levels of the ICAP framework by studying how AISs support collaborative learning. This is one of the first studies examining introductory psychology courses from the perspective of the adaptive system (time, learner perceptions) and contributes to the research by generalizing some findings to a new domain. The pandemic allowed many people to become familiar with adaptive systems and practically tested some of the findings in this area. There is great promise in AISs to support lectures, but the way the systems are implemented and used matters.

References

1. Alam, L., Mueller, S.: Examining the effect of explanation on satisfaction and trust in AI diagnostic systems. BMC Med. Inform. Decis. Mak. **21**(1), 1–15 (2021)
2. Azevedo, R.: Using hypermedia as a metacognitive tool for enhancing student learning? The role of self-regulated learning. Educ. Psychol. **40**(4), 199–209 (2005)
3. Batsell, W.R., Perry, J.L., Hanley, E., Hostetter, A.B.: Ecological validity of the testing effect: the use of daily quizzes in introductory psychology. Teach. Psychol. **44**(1), 18–23 (2017)
4. Becker-Blease, K.A., Bostwick, K.C.: Adaptive quizzing in introductory psychology: evidence of limited effectiveness. Scholarsh. Teach. Learn. Psychol. **2**(1), 75 (2016)
5. Bell, B.S., Kozlowski, S.W.J.: Active learning: effects of core training design elements on self-regulatory processes, learning, and adaptability. J. Appl. Psychol. **93**, 296–316 (2008)
6. Biswas, G., et al.: Multilevel learner modeling in training environments for complex decision making. IEEE Trans. Learn. Technol. **13**(1), 172–185 (2019)

7. Chatterjee, S., Parra, J.: Undergraduate Students Engagement in Formal and Informal Learning: applying the Community of Inquiry Framework. J. Educ. Technol. Syst. **50**, 1–29 (2021)
8. Chi, M.T., et al.: Translating the ICAP theory of cognitive engagement into practice. Cogn. Sci. **42**(6), 1777–1832 (2018)
9. Chi, M.T., Wylie, R.: The ICAP framework: linking cognitive engagement to active learning outcomes. Educ. Psychol. **49**(4), 219–243 (2014)
10. Deslauriers, L., Schelew, E., Wieman, C.: Improved learning in a large-enrollment physics class. science, **332**(6031), 862–864 (2011)
11. Donovan, J.J., Radosevich, D.J.: A meta-analytic review of the distribution of practice effect: now you see it, now you don't. J. Appl. Psychol. **84**, 795–805 (1999)
12. Dunlosky, J., Rawson, K.A.: Practice tests, spaced practice, and successive relearning: tips for classroom use and for guiding students learning. Scholarsh. Teach. Learn. Psychol. **1**(1), 72 (2015)
13. Fahid, F.M., Rowe, J.P., Spain, R.D., Goldberg, B.S., Pokorny, R., Lester, J.: Adaptively scaffolding cognitive engagement with batch constrained deep Q-networks. In: Roll, I., McNamara, D., Sosnovsky, S., Luckin, R., Dimitrova, V. (eds.) Artificial Intelligence in Education. Lecture Notes in Computer Science (Lecture Notes in Artificial Intelligence), vol. 12748, pp. 113–124. Springer, Cham (2021). https://doi.org/10.1007/978-3-030-78292-4_10
14. Geden, M., Emerson, A., Carpenter, D., Rowe, J., Azevedo, R., Lester, J.: Predictive student modeling in game-based learning environments with word embedding representations of reflection. Int. J. Artif. Intell. Educ. **31**(1), 1–23 (2021)
15. Graesser, A., Hu, X., Sottilare, R.: Intelligent tutoring systems. In: the International handbook of the learning sciences, pp. 246–255. Routledge, NY (2018)
16. Graesser, A., Sabatini, J., Li, H.: Educational psychology is evolving to accommodate technology, multiple disciplines, and Twenty-First-Century skills. Annu. Rev. Psychol. **73**, 547–574 (2022)
17. Gurung, R.A.: How do students really study (and does it matter)? Education **39**, 238–240 (2005)
18. Gurung, R.A., Hackathorn, J.: Ramp it up: a call for more research in introductory psychology. Teach. Psychol. **45**(4), 30–311 (2018)
19. Gurung, R. A. R., Neufeld, G. (Eds.).: Transforming introductory psychology: expert advice on teacher training, course design, and student success. American Psychological Association (2022)
20. Hamari, J., Koivisto, J., Sarsa, H.: Does gamification work?--a literature review of empirical studies on gamification. In 2014 47th Hawaii international conference on system sciences, pp. 3025–3034. IEEE (2014)
21. Hoffman, R.R., Mueller, S.T., Klein, G.: Explaining explanation, part 2: Empirical foundations. IEEE Intell. Syst. **32**(4), 78–86 (2017)
22. Karaoglan Yilmaz, F.G., Yilmaz, R.: Learning analytics as a metacognitive tool to influence learner transactional distance and motivation in online learning environments. Innov. Educ. Teach. Int. **58**(5), 575–585 (2021)
23. Karpicke, J.D.: Metacognitive control and strategy selection: deciding to practice retrieval during learning. J. Exp. Psychol. Gen. **138**(4), 469–486 (2009)
24. Khaewratana, W., Veinott, E. S., Mueller, S. T.: Elaborating on Word Games for STEM: experimental Evidence. American Educational Research Association Annual Conference. San Diego, CA (2022)
25. Melton, A.W.: The situation concerning the spacing of repetitions and memory. J. Verbal Learn. Verbal Behav. **9**, 596–606 (1970)

26. Mueller, S.T., Veinott, E.S. Testing the effectiveness of crossword games on immediate and delayed memory for scientific vocabulary and concepts. In: Proceedings of the 2018 Cognitive Science Society Conference, pp. 2134–2139 New York, NY (2018)

27. Mueller, S.T., Veinott, E.S., Hoffman, R.R., Klein, G., Alam, L., Mamun, T., Clancey, W.J.: Principles of explanation in human-ai systems. arXiv preprint arXiv:2102.04972 (2021)

28. Mullinix, G., et al.: Heurisitca: Designing a serious game for training decision making. In: Games Innovation Conference (IGIC), 2013 IEEE International Games Innovation Conference, pp. 250–255. IEEE: Vancouver, BC (2013)

29. Nacke, L.E., Deterding, C.: The maturing of gamification research. Comput. Human Behav. **71**, 450–454 (2017)

30. Rivers, M.L.: Metacognition about practice testing: a review of learners beliefs, monitoring, and control of test-enhanced learning. Educ. Psychol. Rev. **33**(3), 823–862 (2021)

31. Roediger, H.L., III., Karpicke, J.D.: Test-enhanced learning: Taking memory tests improves long-term retention. Psychol. Sci. **17**(3), 249–255 (2006)

32. Ross, B., Chase, A.M., Robbie, D., Oates, G., Absalom, Y.: Adaptive quizzes to increase motivation, engagement, and learning outcomes in a first-year accounting unit. Int. J. Educ. Technol. High. Educ. **15**(1), 1–14 (2018)

33. Sottilare, R.A., Brawner, K.W., Sinatra, A.M., Johnston, J.H.: An updated concept for a Generalized Intelligent Framework for Tutoring (GIFT). In: GIFT tutoring, pp. 1–19 (2017)

34. Spain, R., Rowe, J., Goldberg, B., Pokorny, R., Lester, J., Rockville, M. D.: Enhancing learning outcomes through adaptive remediation with GIFT. In: Proceedings of the Interservice/Industry Training, Simulation and Education Conference, p. 19275 (2019)

35. Susnjak, T., Ramaswami, G.S., Mathrani, A.: Learning analytics dashboard: a tool for providing actionable insights to learners. Int. J. Educ. Technol. High. Educ. **19**(1), 1–23 (2022)

36. Tan, Y., Meadows, L., Meyer, M., Veinott, E.S.: Challenges for Learning and Lab (2020)

37. Work: Student and Faculty Perspectives from the COVID-19 Transition for a Mid-Sized STEM University. Presented at Learning @ Scale Conference. ACM

38. VanLehn, K.: Intelligent tutoring systems for continuous, embedded assessment. Future Assess. Shaping Teach. Learn. Chapter **6**, 113–138 (2008)

39. VanLehn, K.: The relative effectiveness of human tutoring, intelligent tutoring systems, and other tutoring systems. Educ. Psychol. **46**(4), 197–221 (2011)

40. Veinott, E.S., Whitaker, E.: Leaving Hints: Using Player In-Game Hints to Measure and Improve Learning. In: Stephanidis, C., Antona, M. (eds.) HCII 2019. CCIS, vol. 1088, pp. 222–230. Springer, Cham (2019). https://doi.org/10.1007/978-3-030-30712-7_29

41. Veinott, E.S., et al.: Is more information better? Examining the effects of visual and cognitive fidelity on learning in a serious video game. In: 2014 IEEE Games Media Entertainment. IEEE. 2014 IEEE International, pp. 1–6, IEEE. Toronto, ON (2014)

42. Veinott, E., et al.: The effect of camera perspective and session duration on training decision making in a serious video game. In: Games Innovation Conference (IGIC), 2013 IEEE International Games Innovation Conference (IGIC), pp. 256–262. IEEE. Vancouver (2013)

43. Vogel, J.J., Vogel, D.S., Cannon-Bowers, J., Bowers, C.A., Muse, K., Wright, M.: Computer gaming and interactive simulations for learning: a meta-analysis. J. Educ. Comput. Res. **34**, 229–243 (2006)

44. Whitaker, E., Trewhitt, E., Veinott, E.S.: Intelligent Tutoring Design Alternatives in a Serious Game. In: Sottilare, R.A., Schwarz, J. (eds.) HCII 2019. LNCS, vol. 11597, pp. 151–165. Springer, Cham (2019). https://doi.org/10.1007/978-3-030-22341-0_13

45. Whitaker, E. et al.: The effectiveness of intelligent tutoring on training in a video game. In: Games Innovation Conference (IGIC), 2013 IEEE International (pp. 267–274). IEEE. Vancouver, BC (2013)

46. Wiggins, B.L., Eddy, S.L., Grunspan, D.Z., Crowe, A.J.: The ICAP active learning framework predicts the learning gains observed in intensely active classroom experiences. AERA Open **3**(2), 2332858417708567 (2017)
47. Yannier, N., et al.: Active learning: hands-on meets minds-on. Science **374**(6563), 26–30 (2021)
48. Zamecnik, A., et al.: Team interactions with learning analytics dashboards. Comput. Educ. **185**, 104514 (2022)

SwaPS: A Method for Efficiently Relearning
Chinese Characters Just by Reading Documents Including Incorrectly Shaped Characters

Jianning Wei[✉], Kazushi Nishimoto, and Kentaro Takashima

Japan Advanced Institute of Science and Technology, Ishikawa 923-1211, Japan
jianning.wei@jaist.ac.jp

Abstract. Character amnesia is a recent phenomenon in which native Chinese or Japanese speakers forget how to write Chinese characters (*kanji* in Japanese), although they maintain the ability to read them. To solve this problem, we previously proposed a novel pronunciation-based input method called G-IM (Gestalt Imprinting Method), which is effective in preventing the loss of character shape memory. G-IM sometimes outputs GIM characters whose shapes are slightly incorrect, which forces users to pay close attention to character shapes and thus strengthens retention and recall. However, the task of finding and correcting such slight errors in writing documents is an originally high cognitive load act that is burdensome and discourages users from using G-IM. Therefore, in this work, we focus on the act of reading behaviors and propose a novel method for generating incorrect character shapes named SwaPS, which can effectively correct and strengthen the memory of character shapes by simply reading a document without increasing the user's workload. SwaPS generates incorrect characters named PS characters by using a deformation method that swaps the position of the semantic radicals and phonetic radicals of the phonogram characters, which account for 80% of all Chinese characters. By reading a document that includes PS characters, the user's attention is drawn to the character shapes, which is expected to correct and strengthen his or her memory of the character shapes. In the future, we aim to build an e-book reader that automatically generates and presents PS characters. In this paper, we conducted a basic investigation by printing manually created incorrect characters on paper and presenting them to users. The results of the user study confirmed that reading a document that includes PS characters significantly strengthens character shape memory compared to reading a document that contains only correct characters or slightly different incorrect characters used in the G-IM system. We also confirmed that reading a document that includes PS characters does not increase the user's load compared to reading a normal document that contains only correct characters.

Keywords: Character Amnesia · Incorrect character shapes · Phonogram characters · (Re)building retention and recall of character shapes · Relearning support

G. Meiselwitz et al. (Eds.): HCII 2022, LNCS 13517, pp. 468–482, 2022.
https://doi.org/10.1007/978-3-031-22131-6_35

1 Introduction

Character amnesia is a recent phenomenon manifested by the inability of native Chinese or Japanese speakers to recall how to write Chinese characters (*kanji* in Japanese), although they know these characters well and can still read them [1, 2]. It is generally believed that the constant use of computers and mobile phones equipped with pronunciation-based Chinese character input systems is the cause of character amnesia [3]. For example, if a Japanese person wants to get the character "歳" ("age"), he/she only needs to input its pronunciation "sai" in Japanese and checks that the character is not converted to a homophone, such as "再" ("re-") and "最" ("the most"). If the correct character "歳" is outputted, he/she just glances at it but does not check its detailed shape. As a result, the memory of the exact form of a Chinese character gradually fades, and he/she eventually falls into a state in which he/she can recognize the approximate form of the character but does not remember the exact form, that is, a state of character amnesia in which he/she can recognize the form of the character but cannot reproduce it. Thus, the existing pronunciation-based input methods are convenient tools, but they also have the characteristic of "harms of convenience" [4] in terms of weakening the memory of Chinese character shapes. We should avoid the intellectual loss of forgetting the knowledge of Chinese characters that we have acquired.

To solve this problem, we previously proposed a novel pronunciation-based input method called G-IM (This is an acronym of "Gestalt Imprinting Method", and, at the same time, "IM" is usually also an acronym of "Input Method" of Chinese characters), which is effective in preventing the loss of character shape memory. While the usual input methods of Chinese characters always output characters with correct shapes, G-IM sometimes outputs GIM characters whose shapes are slightly incorrect. By being made to forcibly correct the errors, users must pay close attention to the character shapes, which leads to strengthening retention and recall. User studies have demonstrated that G-IM significantly strengthens the retention and recall of character shapes compared to conventional input methods and writing by hand [5].

G-IM is a typical example of "intellectual activity support by interference" [6] promoted in our laboratory as well as of "the benefit of inconvenience" [4]: G-IM improves the user's intellectual ability through an obstructive function that outputs incorrect characters during the inputting process. However, the task of finding and correcting slight errors in writing documents that is an originally high cognitive load act is too burdensome and discourages users from using the system [5]. Therefore, a method that can support the correction and enhancement of character shape memory with a lighter (preferably negligible) load is required.

In this research, we propose an efficient and low-burden support method for correcting and reinforcing Chinese character shape memory just by reading documents. To this end, we propose a novel deforming method for Chinese characters based on the characteristics of Chinese character structures. Incorporating incorrectly shaped Chinese characters generated by the proposed deforming method into the document to be read can help achieve effective relearning of Chinese characters without increasing the workload. The final goal of our research is to build an e-book reader that automatically generates incorrect characters and incorporates them into documents. In this paper, as a basic investigation toward this final goal, we conducted a user study by using printed documents on paper that included manually created incorrect characters.

The rest of this paper is organized as follows. Section 2 reviews related studies on the learning and recognition of Chinese characters. Section 3 describes the proposed method. Section 4 shows preliminary experiments on the Chinese character amnesia problem for the types of Chinese characters handled by the proposed method (i.e., phonogram characters). Section 5 presents the results of the user studies, and Sect. 6 discusses the effectiveness of the proposed method. Section 7 concludes the paper.

2 Related Works

In recent years, many learning support systems for Chinese characters have been proposed. For example, a Chinese character learning system with the integrated use of a computer, projector, and camera

Gestalt Imprinting Method

Fig. 1. An example of the Sans Forgetica font (see the Sans Forgetica website: https://sansfo rgetica.rmit.edu.au/)

can aid learners in understanding the meaning, cultural background, and formation structure of Chinese characters using morphological and phonetic animation projection and handwriting instruction [7]. Ito et al. [8] generated a song for learning Chinese characters comprehensively that uses sounds to represent the formation structure of the character and lyrics that represent the meaning and usage. Fan et al. [9] proposed a Chinese character learning support system using augmented reality technology with learning cards. In these research cases, support functions that focus on the structure of Chinese characters and related information were adopted.

As the target of these conventional methods is basically "not yet learned" Chinese characters, they are not suitable for correcting and reinforcing the memory of "already learned" Chinese characters. Additionally, these systems require users to take time out of their busy schedules to use them, which leads to the problem of low utilization. To the best of our knowledge, there are no Chinese character learning support methods specializing in correcting and reinforcing already learned Chinese characters other than the G-IM system we developed [5].

Bjork pointed out that making the learning process harder for the learner results in better (long-term) retention than conventional learning, which is called "desirable difficulties" in cognitive psychology [10]. Based on the principle of desirable difficulties, RMIT University in Australia developed Sans Forgetica, a font that has the effect of retaining learning content in memory [11] (Fig. 1). This font was designed to make texts difficult to read, thus increasing the memorization effect of the written information. User studies have shown that information written in the Sans Forgetica font is more memorable than information written in normal fonts. G-IM [5] can also be regarded as a method for correcting and enhancing Chinese character shape memory based on the principle of desirable difficulties. However, as the characters used in G-IM were slightly incorrect, with only one or more strokes different from the correct ones, they were not easy to detect. In addition, because of the specification that the document file cannot be saved if even only one incorrect character is left unnoticed, the user was forced to check the shapes of all the output Chinese characters. Thus, G-IM imposes a high cognitive load on users. Therefore, the difficulties set by G-IM, although desirable, were considered somewhat excessive.

3   Proposal Method: SwaPS

In this research, we aimed to create a method for correcting and reinforcing character shape memory by introducing a "desirable and appropriate degree of difficulties". To this end, we propose an improved method called SwaPS for solving the character amnesia problem. In SwaPS, we modified two points based on the findings of the G-IM study [5].

Normal character   GIM character   PS character

Fig. 2. An example of a correctly shaped "蟀" (left), slightly incorrectly shaped character (middle) named the GIM character, and the proposed PS character (right).

The first point is that G-IM targets the act of "writing", while SwaPS targets the act of "reading". It is generally said that the problem of character amnesia has arisen because the act of writing characters by hand has been replaced by Chinese character input systems [3]. Therefore, in the G-IM study, we attempted to embed a way of solving the character amnesia problem in the act of "writing". However, writing documents is an originally high cognitive load action. G-IM embeds an additional high cognitive load task into another high-load task; this design concept violates UI design principles [12]. In this work, therefore, we focus on the act of "reading", which is generally less cognitively demanding than writing, and embed a means of solving the character amnesia problem within it. Furthermore, because the act of reading a document is an everyday activity that is more widely performed than the act of writing, it is expected to be able to solve the character amnesia problem for a wider range of people than G-IM.

The second point is the method of generating incorrect characters. Figure 2 shows an example of the correct form of a Chinese character (Normal), an example of an incorrect character used in G-IM (GIM), and an example of an incorrect character newly used in SwaPS (PS). The GIM characters are incorrect characters that contain only minor errors, such as the deletion or addition of one stroke from the normal characters (in the GIM character in Fig. 2, one stroke ["乀"] is missing). The reason for adopting such a slight error in G-IM is to make the reader pay more attention to the shape of the characters. However, such slight errors are likely to be easily overlooked in the act of "reading", and it is necessary to create conspicuous incorrect characters. At the same time, it is necessary to be able to provide all shape information about the correct form of the character, although it is incorrect. In the case of G-IM, when a user pointed out an incorrect character as "incorrect", it was immediately replaced with the correct form of the character. This function allowed G-IM users to know the correct form of the character, which was useful for correcting and reinforcing their memory of character shapes. Therefore, it is necessary for SwaPS to realize a method of generating incorrect characters that includes all the shape information to ascertain the correct character shapes, rather than wildly incorrect characters.

Thus, we focused on phonogram characters. A phonogram character is a combination of a semantic radical (meaning) and a phonetic radical (pronunciation). For example,

"雲" (it means "cloud" and is pronounced "un") is composed of the semantic radical "雨" ("rain") and the phonetic radical "云" ("un"). Phonogram characters account for a very high percentage of Chinese characters. Of the approximately 7,000 simplified Chinese characters used in the Chinese language, 81% are phonogram characters [13]. Of the approximately 3,500 Chinese characters in common use, 2,523 are phonogram characters, accounting for 72% of the total [14]. In addition, 91.1% of the phonogram characters in Chinese characters in common use have a structure in which the semantic radicals and phonetic radicals are aligned vertically or horizontally, such as in "雲" ("cloud") and "銅" ("copper") [14]. Focusing on these characteristics, we devised a method for generating incorrect characters by swapping the positions of the semantic radicals and the phonetic radicals of the phonogram characters with a structure in which the semantic radicals and the phonetic radicals are aligned vertically or horizontally. The incorrect characters generated in this way are named "PS characters" because they are generated by swapping Semantic radicals and Phonetic radicals. The PS characters shown in Fig. 2 were generated by swapping the "虫" (means "insect") and the "率" (is pronounced "ritsu") of the Chinese character "蟀" ("cricket"). Although the PS character is incorrect, it contains all the information regarding the correct shape. It can be converted to the correct character by switching the positions of the semantic radical and the phonetic radical.

By the way, even if we embed PS characters in a document, it will be meaningless if readers skip over them without noticing. A phenomenon called typoglycemia in which readers can comprehend text without any problem, even if the order of letters in the word is changed under certain conditions (e.g., "Document" to "Documnet") is known to exist in English [15]. The same phenomenon occurs in Japanese, especially in *hiragana*. It is possible that a similar phenomenon may also occur in Chinese characters when PS characters are used. Although the issue of the processing mechanism of the semantic radicals and the phonetic radicals in phonogram character recognition has long been a major concern of psycholinguists [16, 17], to the best of our knowledge, there are no studies on the recognition of characters with interchangeable semantic radicals and phonetic radicals. Therefore, it is necessary to verify the possibility of similar phenomena, such as typoglycemia, in PS characters.

4 Preliminary Experiment

A preliminary experiment was conducted to investigate the forgetting status of the shapes for phonogram characters.

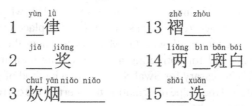

Fig. 3. Examples of the problems in the dictation test of the preliminary experiment.

Table 1. Results of the preliminary experiment in different point scales.

	All characters (points)		Characters in common use (points)		Characters in non-regular use (points)	
Perfect score	20	100	13	100	7	100
Average score	7.5	37.7	6.0	46.2	2.0	26.2

Table 2. Distribution of the dictation test results of the preliminary experiment.

Result (points)	All characters		Characters in common use		Characters in non-regular use	
	Number of people	Ratio	Number of people	Ratio	Number of people	Ratio
≥ 80	0	0	1	4.20%	0	0
79 - 60	2	8.30%	7	29.2%	0	0
< 60	22	91.7%	16	66.7%	24	100%

4.1 Procedure

A dictation test of the phonogram characters was administered to 24 Chinese students at our institution. The test was composed of 20 phonogram characters: 13 phonogram characters in common use selected from the list of frequently used characters in modern Chinese [18] and seven phonogram characters in non-regular use that are easy to misspell. Figure 3 shows part of the dictation test in the preliminary experiment. In the test, the participants were asked to refer to the pronunciation of the Chinese characters written in pinyin and to handwrite the underlined missing Chinese characters.

4.2 Results

The results of the experiment are shown in Table 1. The average score for the dictation test was 7.5 on the 20-point scale (37.7 on the 100-point scale). The average score for the phonogram characters in common use was 6.0 on the 13-point scale (46.2 on the 100-point scale), and the average score for the phonogram characters in non-regular use was 2.0 on the 7-point scale (26.2 on the 100-point scale). Table 2 shows the distribution of the number and percentage of each score band. Of the 24 participants, 91.7% received a score of less than 60 points on the 100-point scale for all characters, 66.7% for the characters in common use, and 100% in non-regular use characters. The results show that the percentage of students who did not memorize the correct shape of the characters was quite high, indicating that the problem of character amnesia still exists, even in the case of phonogram characters.

5 User Study

A user study was conducted to demonstrate the usefulness of the proposed SwaPS method.

5.1 Outline of the Experimental Procedure and Hypotheses

Twenty-four postgraduate Chinese students at our institution who did not participate in the preliminary experiments participated in the experiment. The experiment was conducted in three steps:

- Step 1. Pre-examination: A dictation test of 90 Chinese characters, including 40 target Chinese characters.
- Step 2. A task of reading material printed on paper that included target characters whose character is one of the three characters (PS character, GIM character, and Normal character) shown in Fig. 2.
- Step 3. Post-examination: A post-examination of the Chinese character dictation test (the same question as the pre-examination), reading comprehension questions, and ex post facto survey.

Based on the pre-examination results, we divided the participants into three groups (SwaPS group, GIM group, and Normal group) of eight to equalize the distribution of the pre-examination scores of the groups. Then, we evaluated the improvement in performance by comparing the score differences between the pre-examination and the post-examination for each of the three groups.

The hypothesis for this experiment was that the improvement in performance would be in the order of Normal $\leq$ GIM $<$ SwaPS. We assumed that the improvement in the GIM group would be greater than that in the Normal group because the recognition of incorrect characters in the GIM group would correct and strengthen the memory of the character shapes. However, as stated above, because GIM characters have only slight errors, there was a high possibility that the errors would not be noticed and would be skipped as Normal characters, in which case there would be no difference between the GIM group and the Normal group. Therefore, the overall improvement in the GIM group was expected to be slightly larger than or equal to that of the Normal group. However, as PS characters are more likely to be noticed as errors, the SwaPS group was expected to show the greatest improvement.

5.2 Details of the Experiment

In the pre-examination conducted in Step 1, we prepared 90 phonogram characters consisting of 60 characters in common use selected from the list of frequently used characters in modern Chinese [18] and 30 characters in non-regular use with a relatively large number of strokes. The experimental method was the same as that used in the preliminary experiment, as shown in Fig. 3.

Before Step 2, we divided the 24 participants into three eight-person groups (the SwaPS group, GIM group, and Normal group) based on the pre-examination results.

① the document including PS characters

天冷极了，下着雪，又快黑了。这是一年的最后一天——平安夜。在这又冷又黑的晚上，一个没戴帽子、没戴手套、也没穿鞋子的小女孩，在街上哆哆嗦嗦地走着。凛冽的寒风吹过她幼小的脸颊，她的衣服又旧又破，脚上穿着一双妈妈的大拖鞋在街上走着。她的口袋里装着许多盒火柴，一路上不住口地叫着："卖火柴呀，卖火柴呀！"人们都在买节日的食品和礼物，有谁会理她呢？

② the document including GIM characters

天冷极了，下着雪，又快黑了。这是一年的最后一天——平安夜。在这又冷又黑的晚上，一个没戴帽子、没戴手套、也没穿鞋子的小女孩，在街上哆哆嗦嗦地走着。凛冽的寒风吹过她幼小的脸颊，她的衣服又旧又破，脚上穿着一双妈妈的大拖鞋在街上走着。她的口袋里装着许多盒火柴，一路上不住口地叫着："卖火柴呀，卖火柴呀！"人们都在买节日的食品和礼物，有谁会理她呢？

③ the document including Normal characters

天冷极了，下着雪，又快黑了。这是一年的最后一天——平安夜。在这又冷又黑的晚上，一个没戴帽子、没戴手套、也没穿鞋子的小女孩，在街上哆哆嗦嗦地走着。凛冽的寒风吹过她幼小的脸颊，她的衣服又旧又破，脚上穿着一双妈妈的大拖鞋在街上走着。她的口袋里装着许多盒火柴，一路上不住口地叫着："卖火柴呀，卖火柴呀！"人们都在买节日的食品和礼物，有谁会理她呢？

Fig. 4. Part of a document, which included characters in three different types.

The participants were assigned so that the distribution of the pre-examination scores in each group would be even. To confirm this, we performed ANOVA at the one-factor, three-level with no correspondence. The analysis result showed that the main effect of the groups was not significant ($F (2, 21) = 0.002$, $p = 0.998 > 0.05$). There were no significant differences in the group assignments.

Next, we selected 40 target Chinese characters from the 60 characters in common use employed in the pre-examination in Step 1, transformed them into the PS or GIM character, and then embedded the PS or GIM character into the documents. Figure 4 shows part of each document: The SwaPS group was given a document embedded with the PS character of the target characters (① in Fig. 4), the GIM group was given a document embedded with the GIM character of the target characters (② in Fig. 4), and the Normal group was given a document consisting entirely of the Normal correct form of the target characters (③ in Fig. 4). All the materials were printed on paper, and the participants in each group were required to read the materials. In Fig. 4, the target characters embedded in the documents are shown in red for the convenience of readers, but the documents provided to the participants were in black.

The document used in the experiment was "The Little Match Girl" [19], which is a text from a Chinese textbook for third graders in elementary school. The total number of characters in the document was 2,233, and it contained all 60 characters in common use employed in the pre-examination in Step 1. The document used the SimSun font in 10.5 point, which is the standard character and character size for Chinese paper books. All incorrect characters were created by the first author of this paper using the Microsoft. private character editor on Windows 10.

The instructions given to the participants before the reading task in Step 2 were only to write down the start and end times on the provided paper. They were not allowed to ask any questions about the experiment during or after the task.

Table 3. Results of the pre-examination and the post-examination for the three groups.

Group	Step 1		Step 3		Step 3-Step 1	
	Average	StdDev	Average	StdDev	Average	StdDev
SwaPS	58.96	16.67	78.54	9.910	19.58	14.14
GIM	59.58	17.55	73.13	16.38	13.54	9.380
Normal	59.58	22.73	68.96	22.14	9.380	5.400

As all 40 target characters in Step 2 were included in the dictation test in Step 1, there was a possibility that the dictation test in Step 1 may have had some unexpected influence on the results for Step 2. To eliminate such effects as much as possible, Step 2 was conducted 15 days after Step 1. In addition, we mixed 20 other characters in common use (these 20 characters were also included in the Step 2 document) and 30 non-regular use characters (these 30 characters were not included in the Step 2 document) on the Step 1 dictation test.

Step 3 was conducted immediately after Step 2. After the reading materials were collected, participants were required to answer a reading comprehension test form (five questions), a dictation test form, and a questionnaire form in turn. The reading comprehension test was a single-choice question with four response options. The dictation test in Step 3 consisted of the same 60 characters in common use employed in the pre-examination in Step 1. The experimental method was the same as that used in the preliminary experiment. The questionnaire was administered only to the SwaPS and GIM group participants. The contents of the questionnaire were about the participants' impressions of the incorrect characters in the documents they read in Step 2.

5.3 Results

Dictation Test Results. Table 3 presents the average scores and standard deviations (stddevs) for the pre-examination and post-examination of only 60 characters in common use for each of the three groups with a perfect score of 100. the 60 characters were very basic characters included in the third-grade chinese textbook. in step 1, participants were also given a dictation test of 30 highly difficult characters in non-regular use, but the results shown in Table 3 do not include them. the "step 3-step 1" column in the table shows the average of the difference between the pre-examination and post-examination scores.

The average score for Step 1 was around 59, which is very low for a graduate student's performance on Chinese characters at the third-grade level of elementary school. This result indicated the existence of the character amnesia problem here as well as in the preliminary experiment in Sect. 4. For all participants, the results for Step 3 were higher than those for Step 1. A paired t-test was conducted on all participants' Step 1 and Step 3 scores, and the score difference was significant at the 1% level ($t(23) = 6.32, p = 0.00 < 0.01$). The post-examination scores were significantly better than the pre-examination scores.

The hypothesis of this experiment was that the improvement in performance would be in the order of Normal $\leq$ GIM $<$ SwaPS. The mean of the difference between Step 3 and Step 1 in Table 3 shows that the hypothesis was basically true. Based on the difference between Step 1 and Step 3 scores, we conducted William's test with the Normal group as the control group under the hypothesis above. The results were as follows:

The test statistic between the difference in the performance of the Normal group and the SwaPS group was *1.93*. Significant differences ($p < 0.05$) were found between the Normal group and the SwaPS group. The improvement in the SwaPS group was significantly greater than that of the Normal group.

The test statistic between the difference in the performance of the Normal group and the GIM group was *0.79*. No significant difference was found between the two groups. The improvement in the GIM group was not significantly greater than that in the Normal group.

Reading Time and Comprehension Performance.

In the case of English, it is known that sentences with transposed letters result in some cost in reading speed and comprehension [20]. Therefore, we verified whether inserting incorrect characters in a Chinese-language document affected reading speed and comprehension, as in the case of English.

Table 4. Average required time in minutes to read the document in Step 2 for the three groups.

Group	Average (min.)	StdDev
SwaPS	7.25	2.99
GIM	7.25	3.73
Normal	7.13	2.52

The average times taken to read the documents for the three groups are shown in Table 4, and the results of the reading comprehension for the three groups (20 points for one question, 100 points in total) are shown in Table 5. We performed ANOVA tests at the one-factor, three-level with no correspondence based on the results of Tables 4 and 5. The analysis results in Table 4 show that the main effect of the groups was not significant ($F(2, 21) = 0.316$, $p > 0.05$), and the analysis results in Table 5 also show that the main effect of the groups was not significant ($F(2, 21) = 0.452$, $p > 0.05$). Therefore, there were no significant differences in reading time and comprehension performances among the three groups.

Table 5. Results of the reading comprehension in Step 3 for the three groups.

Group	Average	StdDev
SwaPS	80.0	12.5
GIM	75.0	17.2
Normal	80.0	12.5

Questionnaire Results. The questionnaire about the participants' impressions of the incorrect characters in step 2 was administered only to the swaps and gim group participants. Table 6 shows the percentage of participants who noticed the incorrect characters in the documents, Table 7 shows the subjective impression of the participants who noticed the incorrect characters regarding how much the presence of incorrect characters in the documents affected the post-examination in step 3, and Table 8 shows the subjective impression of how much the presence of incorrect characters affected the comprehension and reading speed of the documents.

As shown in Table 6, all participants in the SwaPS group noticed the incorrect characters (PS characters) in the documents in Step 2. However, only half of the participants in the GIM group noticed incorrect characters (GIM characters). As shown in Table 7, all participants who noticed the incorrect characters indicated that their.

Table 6. Percentage of participants in the SwaPS group and the GIM group who reported noticing the presence of incorrect characters in the documents.

Group	Percentage
SwaPS	100%
GIM	50%

Table 7. Responses to the question about how much the presence of incorrect characters in the documents affected the post-examination.

Options	SwaPS group		GIM group	
	Number of people	Ratio	Number of people	Ratio
1.1.Very useful	5	63%	4	100%
2.2.Useful	3	37%	0	0
3.3.I can't say either	0	0	0	0
4.4.Not very useful	0	0	0	0
5.5.Useless	0	0	0	0

Table 8. Responses to the question about whether the incorrect characters in the documents in Step 2 affected participants' understanding of the documents or the reading time.

Options	SwaPS group		GIM group	
	Number of people	Ratio	Number of people	Ratio
1.1.It affected me a lot	0	0	0	0
2.2.It affected me to some extent	0	0	0	0
3.3.I can't say either	0	0	0	0
4.4.It didn't affect me very much	3	38%	2	50%
5.5.It didn't affect me	5	62%	2	50%

presence was helpful in the post-examination. As shown in Table 8, all participants who noticed the incorrect characters indicated that their presence did not affect the participants' comprehension of the content or their reading time.

6   Discussion

As shown in Sect. 5.3, the overall performance in the post-examination was significantly better than that in the pre-examination. This result indicates that reading documents has a beneficial effect on correcting and reinforcing the memory of character shape. In other words, reading materials such as books can improve the character amnesia problem to some extent.

This result also suggests that character amnesia is caused not only by the constant use of computers and mobile phones equipped with pronunciation-based Chinese character input systems but also by the decrease in opportunities to read documents. Alternatively, the quality of documents read daily may be declining due to the spread of social networking services. However, this explanation is only speculation. According to the results of a survey of elementary school children, a positive correlation between the amount of reading and vocabulary (which is different from Chinese character aptitude) was observed, but the correlation was not strong [21]. As far as we know, there are no studies on the relationship between the amount of reading and Chinese character aptitude among adults who have completed character learning, and further investigation is needed.

As stated above, reading documents was shown to be beneficial for solving the character amnesia problem, but the results shown in Sect. 5.3, that the improvement from pre-examination to post-examination was significantly larger in the SwaPS group than in the Normal group, illustrated that embedding PS characters in documents is more effective in solving the character amnesia problem. However, not just any incorrect characters can be used. In fact, the improvement in the GIM group using GIM characters was not significantly greater than that of the Normal group.

One possible reason is that it is difficult to notice embedded incorrectly shaped characters when GIM characters are used. Table 6 shows that all participants in the SwaPS group were aware of the existence of PS characters, while only half of the participants in the GIM group were aware of the GIM characters. In other words, a phenomenon similar to typoglycemia in English occurs in the case of GIM characters, but it is less likely to occur in the case of PS characters. The results shown in Table 7 indicate that all participants who noticed the incorrect characters found their presence useful in the post-examination (i.e., effective in correcting and reinforcing their character shape memory). If the incorrect characters were not noticed, the effect was equivalent only to that of the Normal group. Therefore, although the improvement in the GIM group was slightly larger than that of the Normal group (Table 3), it did not reach a level where a significant difference could be observed.

As described above, we found that the PS characters, which are incorrect characters created by swapping the position of the semantic radicals and phonetic radicals of the phonogram characters, are effective in making the reader aware of the presence of incorrect characters. Moreover, PS characters have all shape information about the correct form of the character. As a result, embedding PS characters in a document effectively corrects and strengthens character shape memory.

Although G-IM is effective in preventing the loss of character shape memory, users are reluctant to use it because of the excessive workload required to find and correct slightly different incorrect characters [5]. It is necessary to confirm whether a similar situation of avoiding the use of SwaPS occurred.

The results in Table 4 show the time taken to read the document in Step 2, and Table 5 shows the results of the reading comprehension in Step 3; no significant differences were found between the three groups. Table 8 shows the results regarding whether the presence of incorrect characters affected the comprehension and reading speed of the documents. There were no significant differences between the SwaPS and GIM groups.

These results indicate that embedded incorrect characters in either PS or GIM characters do not impede document reading: Users did not feel reluctant as they did when they used the G-IM system. Based on these results, the SwaPS method, which targets the task of reading a document and embeds PS characters, can be regarded as a kind of "desirably and appropriately difficult factor" [10] that works effectively to correct and strengthen the memory of character shapes. Note that the SwaPS method is a *relearning* method for those who have already mastered Chinese characters in their daily activities. People who are learning Chinese characters for the first time cannot determine whether the PS characters are correct or incorrect, and there is a risk that they will rather learn the PS characters as correct characters.

7 Conclusion

In this paper, we proposed a method called SwaPS, which can correct and strengthen the memory of character shapes just by reading documents that include incorrectly shaped characters called PS characters. The PS characters are generated by swapping the position of the semantic radicals and phonetic radicals of the phonogram characters with a structure in which the semantic radicals and phonetic radicals are aligned either vertically or horizontally.

To verify the effectiveness of the proposed SwaPS method in correcting and enhancing the memory of Chinese character shapes, we performed a user study under three conditions: reading a document that included the PS characters proposed in this study, reading a document that included the GIM characters with slight errors used in our previous study [5], and reading a document that included no incorrect characters. We compared and analyzed the score differences between the pre-examination and the post-examination for the three groups. A significant difference was found only between the PS group and the Normal group. For the GIM group and the Normal group, no significant difference could be found. We also checked whether the presence of incorrect characters affected reading time and comprehension. There were no significant differences in either reading time or the results of the comprehension questions. These results are consistent with the participants' subjective findings in the ex post facto survey. Therefore, the proposed SwaPS method using PS characters is an effective method for relearning character shapes for people who have already learned Chinese characters without placing an unnecessary burden on them.

We are currently developing an e-book reader system that automatically generates PS characters and embeds them in documents. As shown in this paper, the proposed method is effective for paper media. However, when considering its use in the real world there is concern, for example, that printing academic papers with embedded incorrect characters, such as PS characters, may have a negative impact on the quality evaluation of the papers. If an e-book reader that has a function for generating and replacing PS characters can be implemented, readers, not authors or publishers, can embed PS characters into documents at will. The previously described problems of usage scenarios can be solved. By embedding the PS characters into the reading materials, it would give the user a sense of "vujà dé", which makes the user feel as if he or she is seeing a character for the first time. This is expected to change the shallow cognitive act of recognizing well-known characters into a deeply cognitive act. In the future, we would like to verify the effectiveness of the proposed method on e-book readers. It has been reported that the degree of concentration and comprehension of content is lower when using electronic media, such as tablets, than when using paper media [22], and it will be necessary to verify whether the same effect can be observed in the proposed method. Furthermore, the same effect can be expected to be obtained by embedding PS characters into arbitrary visible text. For example, displaying the PS characters instead of the correct characters in the choice box of any existing pronunciation-based input method can make the user pay attention to the character shape. After the PS characters are selected, the correct character shape is displayed in the document. We would like to discuss such a different usage pattern in the future.

Acknowledgement. The authors sincerely thank all the research participants who willingly cooperated to our experiments. This work was supported by JST SPRING, Grant Number JPMJSP2102.

References

1. Character amnesia, Wikipedia. https://en.wikipedia.org/wiki/Character_amnesia Accessed May 2022
2. Hilburger, C.: Character Amnesia: an overview. Sino-Platonic Papers **264**, 51–70 (2016)
3. Kaiho, H., Atsuji, T.: Japanese who forgets Kanji (Chinese characters) – Psychology of Kanji forgetting and how to overcome it and Personal computer and Kanji forgetting, SINICA, vol. 14, Taishukan publishing, pp. 13–15 (2003)
4. Kawakami, H.: Toward System Design based on Benefit of Inconvenience. Journal of Human Interface Society : human interface **11**(1), 125–134 (2009)
5. Nishimoto, K., Wei, J.: G-IM: An Input Method of Chinese Characters for Character Amnesia Prevention, In: Proceedings of the Eighth International Conference on Advances in Computer-Human Interactions (ACHI2015), pp. 118–124 (2015)
6. Nishimoto, K., Yokoyama, Y.: Support by Obstruction -Let Me Improve Among The Deterioration (in other words)-, IPSJ SIG Technical Report, vol. 2014-HCI-159, No.10, pp. 1–8 (2014).
7. Yang, Y., Zhou, L., Li, R., Yao, H., Song, J., Ying, F.: Chinese Character Learning System. In: Extended Abstracts of the 2019 CHI Conference on Human Factors in Computing Systems (CHI EA '19), Paper No. LBW2218, pp. 1–5 (2019)
8. Ito, Y., Terada, T., Tsukamoto, M.: A system for memorizing Chinese Characters using a song based on strokes and structures of the character. In: Proceedings of the 17th International Conference on Information Integration and Web-based Applications & Services, Article No. 18, pp. 1–9 (2015)
9. Fan, M., Fan, J., Antle, A. N., Jin, S., Yin, D., Pasquier, P.: Character Alive: A Tangible Reading and Writing System for Chinese Children At-risk for Dyslexia. In: Extended Abstracts of the 2019 CHI Conference on Human Factors in Computing Systems (CHI EA '19), Paper No. LBW0113, pp. 1–6 (2019)

10. Robert A.: Bjork: Memory and Meta-memory Considerations in the Training of Human Beings, in Book "Metacognition: Knowing about knowing", pp.185–205, MIT Press, (1994)
11. Sans Forgetica. https://sansforgetica.rmit.edu.au/
12. Oviatt, S.: Human-Centered Design Meets Cognitive Load Theory: Designing Interfaces that Help People Think. In: Proc.eedings of the 14th ACM International Conference on Multimedia (MM '06), pp. 871–880 (2006)
13. Li, Y., Kang, J.S.: Analysis of phonetics of the ideophonetic characters in modern Chinese. In: Y. Chen (Ed.). Information analysis of usage of characters in modern Chinese, pp. 84–98 (1993)
14. Haiyan, Z.: An analysis on the frequently-used phonetic symbols and teaching of Chinese characters. The Study of Chinese Characters (2003)
15. Rawlinson, G.E.: The significance of letter position in word recognition, Ph.D. dissertation, Psychology Dept., Univ. Nottingham, Nottingham, U.K. (1976)
16. Wang Xieshun, W., Yan, Z.S., Chao, N.I., Ming, Z.: The effects of semantic radicals and phonetic radicals in Chinese phonogram recognition. Acta Psychol. Sin. **48**(2), 130–140 (2016)
17. Hui, C., Yan Guoli, X., Xiaolu, X.Y., Lei, C., Xuejun, B.: The effect of phonetic radicals on identification of chinese phonograms: evidence from eye movement. Acta Psychol. Sin. **46**(9), 1242–1260 (2014)
18. List of frequently used characters in Modern Chinese. https://lingua.mtsu.edu/chinese-computing/statistics/char/listchangyong.php
19. The Little Match Girl. https://www.thn21.com/xiao/liux/4484.html Accessed May 2022
20. Rayner, K., White, S.J., Johnson, R.L., Liversedge, S.P.: Raeding wrods with Jumbled lettres -There is a cost. Psychol. Sci. **17**(3), 192–193 (2006)
21. Inohara, K., Ueda, A., Shipya, K., Osanai, H.: Relation between multiple indices of reading amount and vocabulary and reading comprehension skills: a cross-sectional survey of japanese elementary school children. Jpn. J. Educ. Psychol. **63**, 254–266 (2015)
22. Kobayashim, R., Ikeuchi, A.: Effects on text understanding and memory by types of display media: comparison between e-book readers and papers, IPSJ SIG Technical Report, vol. 2012-HCI-147, No. 29,pp. 1–7 (2012)

Research on Innovative Design of STEAM Children's Educational Toys Based on Interaction Design

Ting Yang[✉], Ziwei Yang, and Liting Qin

Guangxi Normal University, Guilin 541006, China
673994417@qq.com

Abstract. At present, there is a lack of innovation in children's educational toys. The STEAM education concept is a comprehensive education concept that integrates technology, engineering, art, and mathematics. Based on the STEAM education concept, this paper focuses on the principles of innovative design of children's educational toys under the STEAM education concept, and designs a "little submarine" based on the principle of physical ups and downs experiments, and interacts with children through the screen. It is hoped that designers can better diverge design thinking, break through the design bottleneck, design highly educational, educational, interesting and interactive products, and promote the development of children's educational game toy design.

Keywords: Interactive design · Children's education · Augmented reality · AR recognition · Learning efficiency · Steam educational concept · Children · Educational toys · Interaction · Innovative design

1 Introduction

1.1 Background

With the rapid development of information technology in recent years, smart products have been used in various fields, and the scale of my country's children's smart toy industry has continued to expand. Since the 18th and 19th National Congress of the Communist Party of China established my country's comprehensive deployment of innovation-driven development strategy, "innovation" has become one of the keys to development, so it has had a great impact on traditional children's education. In order to alleviate the further impact of quality education reform on examination education, it is necessary to incorporate a large number of "innovative" elements into the design of teaching aids. However, in the current children's toy market, most of the children's toy teaching aids are still in a state of ideological solidification, less innovation and stagnant development. On this basis, we designed a children's educational game teaching aid that combines the STEAM concept with the physical principle, and added interaction to the design, so that children have better interaction with the product. It is conducive to product designers to better diverge design thinking, break through the design bottleneck, design highly educational, educational and interesting products, and promote the development of children's educational game toy design.

G. Meiselwitz et al. (Eds.): HCII 2022, LNCS 13517, pp. 483–490, 2022.
https://doi.org/10.1007/978-3-031-22131-6_36

1.2 Overview of STEAM Education Philosophy

STEAM is the abbreviation of Science, Technology, Engineering, Art, and Mathematics. STEAM education is a comprehensive education that integrates science, technology, engineering, art, and mathematics [1]. STEAM has evolved from the STEM education program. STEM is an educational program led by the U.S. government that aims to break the boundaries of disciplines, solve practical problems through the comprehensive application of disciplinary literacy, and cultivate comprehensive talents.

1.3 An Overview of the Principles of Interaction Design Interfaces

The interface principle is to give the described behavior and information timely and effective feedback to the users, that is, children, to carry out effective visual communication design of the interactive interface [2]. In order to help children have a better game experience and maximize the meaning of designing teaching aids, designers will spend a lot of effort to help users understand teaching aids. Connect the teaching aids with the user's behavior, and the design of the visual page just satisfies this connection. Including the color, shape, transmitted information, and constituent elements of the interface, etc., can vividly convey the use of teaching aids and game modes to users. Optimize the user experience of product users.

1.4 The Current Situation and Development Trend of Educational Aids for Children

In response to this paper, we have conducted extensive research on educational aids for children at home and abroad, and found that most educational aids for children on the market now focus on subject education, training of hands-on ability, and simple interaction. It is difficult to have children's educational teaching aids that integrate children's intelligence, exercise hands-on ability, interactive learning and interaction, and learning knowledge. There are very few toys designed based on the principle of physical "submersion and snorkeling", especially the users have fewer teaching aids for children. Most of them use its principle to move the submarine, which is extremely difficult and dangerous. Use on children. For children's educational aids, a good teaching aid is to teach children knowledge, and children need to learn and use knowledge through this teaching aid. The design of "little submarine" brings fun and simplicity to children. It increases children's interest in physical learning and makes teaching aids more attractive to them.

2 The Significance of Innovative Design of Children's Educational Toys Under STEAM Education

First of all, the science of STEAM education emphasizes the acquisition of knowledge. In the design of toys, we need to pay more attention to whether the toys can teach children relevant scientific knowledge, so that children can learn knowledge and acquire knowledge in the process of playing games. Pleasure. Secondly, through their own activities, children perceive, observe and operate the surrounding material world, discover problems and find answers. In this process, they gain extensive scientific experience, learn scientific methods, stimulate curiosity and develop intelligence, and feel their own abilities and success in the process of playing games, get a pleasant emotional experience, and generate interest in learning science And concern and love for nature. It is different from other science education, it avoids the misunderstanding of children's science education entering into scientific knowledge instillation and science education being elementary and adult, reflecting its particularity. Mr. Chen Heqin said that games are children's psychological characteristics, games are children's work, and games are children's lives. In a sense, children's various abilities are acquired in games. Games are the content of the curriculum, the background of curriculum implementation, and the way of curriculum implementation. It integrates scientific knowledge, scientific methods, and scientific spirit into children's life and games, and promotes children's overall and harmonious development.

3 Innovative Design Principles of Educational Toys for Children Under STEAM Education

3.1 Security Principles

Through data research, it is found that the focus of children's toy size research is the safety of children's size and specifications. Products suitable for children under the age of eight must not have edges. Any accessible parts of the toy or accessories, except for the sharp edges required for functional problems on the product, but there must be labels with instructions and warning words for children of sufficient maturity to read and understand these instructions, but this is not until the product There must not be any non-functional edge; in order to prevent children from swallowing, standards are formulated to limit the possibility of being swallowed by consumers and suffocating [3]; the structure is reasonable, strong and resistant to falling, and it is not easy to be broken and broken; in shape It should be easy to grasp, and there should be no sharp parts. It should be suitable for children to play without hurting other children. In the selection of toy materials, it should be non-toxic. In paints, color coatings, plastics, chemical fibers, electroplating Materials that are toxic and harmful, such as metals, require attention.

3.2 Educational Principles

What the STEAM education philosophy highlights is education. In traditional children's games, most of them are simple and easy-to-use ordinary children's toys without educational significance. It is difficult for children to learn and progress from them during use. However, the design of children's educational games uses the STEAM concept to make it easier for children to play The subtle learning in the process of the game improves children's thinking ability.

3.3 Fun Principle

The primary feature of children's game toys is that they must be interesting. Children will insist on playing if they are interested in games. Children's self-control and persistence are far less than adults. If a children's toy wants to attract children's attention, it must increase the fun of the game and the use of the game on the basis of scientific puzzles. Simplicity. In color and shape, it should be designed like a child's inclination.

3.4 Participatory Principleun Principle

In the living environment of children, the company of parents and the communication between friends are indispensable. Therefore, in the process of playing games, if there is the participation of playmates or the accompaniment of parents, it is an important part of the process for children to play games. If a children's game product only requires children to perform some simple operations, then children will definitely lose a part of the sense of participation and experience in the process of using the game product. If the toy can be designed to be simple to assemble and operate the game by yourself, the children will surely increase their interest in the game and greatly improve their hands-on ability. Appropriately adding parts that allow children to operate by themselves in the design of children's educational games can greatly increase the educational and scientific nature of children's games. It can also improve children's ability to cooperate and cooperate with teams.

4 Innovative Design Principles of Educational Toys for Children Under STEAM Education

4.1 Design Brief

"Little Diver" is an educational set game about physical ups and downs experiments. It uses the principles of physical ups and downs and gravity to apply to the existing small submarine toys on the market to upgrade the toy gameplay and is designed as a pipeline game mode. The combination of games and experiments can allow children to learn the knowledge of the principle of ups and downs. By setting a display screen under the base, the clearance game mode is fed back to the children. The image displayed on the screen is the clearance route. Among them, you can also work with parents to increase the sense of interaction between family members. The whole of the toy is a large submarine-shaped outer package, and the inside is the kit needed for the game. There are no sharp points on any part, ensuring the safety of children during use. The material of the toy is made of transparent PC + ABS material to ensure that children can see the inside of the pipe for easy operation (Fig. 1, 2).

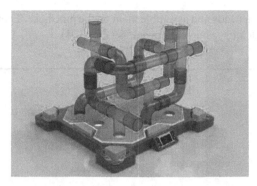

Fig. 1. Product overall renderings (Color figure online)

Fig. 2. Pipe material and submarine model (Color figure online)

4.2 Design Description

Pipe Assembly Gameplay. The game is composed of transparent pipes, pipe bases, small submarines, and game process cards (as shown in the figure). The transparent pipes can be assembled freely. Children can assemble them into different pipe forms

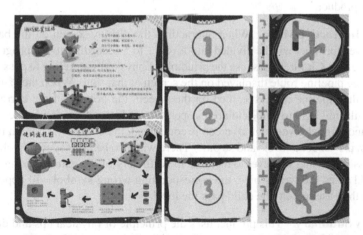

Fig. 3. Game accessories and use flow chart (Color figure online)

according to their own needs and assemble them on the pipe base. They can also assemble according to the matching game card prompts (Fig. 3, 4).

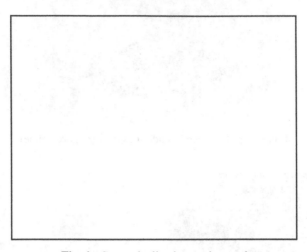

Fig. 4. Game pipeline instruction card

Mainly aimed at children aged 6–8, (as shown in the picture) assemble the pipe according to the instructions on the card, fill the pipe with water, put the small submarine toy and seal the cover, when the small submarine falls to a certain position, press and hold The button next to the pipe controls the movement of the small submarine. There are nine insertion ports on the base of the pipe. The pipe is made of transparent PC material with high visibility. There are four colors of watermelon red, vibrant orange, green apple green and crystal blue. The color matching of the small submarine toy is fresh and natural, which triggers children's ability to distinguish. Increase the intelligence and fun of the product.

Tangible Interactive Mode. When interacting, the display screen on the base of the "Little Diver" product will be divided into levels 1 to 5 according to the progress of the children's game. Children must use the principle of physical snorkeling to pass the "level 1" clearance pipeline route displayed on the screen at that time. When the "submarine" swims in the pipeline route specified on the screen, the bottom of the corresponding pipeline will emit light to guide children's operation and attract children's interest. When the clearance signal given by the screen is completed, the child can click on the screen to perform the "second level" and so on… There will also be corresponding obstacles in the process of passing the level to increase the difficulty of the game. During this time, if the child takes the wrong pipe, the corresponding wrong symbol will appear on the screen on the base to help the child pass the level.

Gameplay Summary. This product uses the principle of physical ups and downs and integrates the steam education concept. A pressing device acts under the gaming device. By pressing the button, the air in the pipe is applied to the small submarine above, making it go up, releasing the button, the air is drawn out, and it is diving. In different directions of the pipeline, there will be the same pressing device to carry out the up and down of the submarine. At the intersection of each pipeline, a blade that can be adjusted in direction is installed, and the blade is rotated by a hand-operated device to change the advancing direction of the small submarine. Children can replace different pipe sizes according to their own needs. Below the pipe, a product-related base is installed to insert the pipe and operate the button. The button is connected to the vacuum tube in the base for air outlet and suction. A water discharge port is also installed in the base, which is convenient for children to discharge water after playing games, and the operation is simple.

4.3 Aim of Design

The "Little Diver" ups and downs physics toy installation combines art, science and engineering.

It gives more artistic composition in appearance and shape. For example, the choice of color will be more in line with children's aesthetics. Since children are also more sensitive to changes in color [4], bright colors can attract children's attention., to improve children's aesthetic ability to shape and color.

In terms of science, "Little Diver" uses the principle of buoyancy experiment, and uses games to demonstrate the effect of buoyancy for children. It can arouse the curiosity of children, explore the origin of buoyancy, and achieve the effect of enlightenment.

In terms of interaction, children can operate according to the game clearance interface displayed on the screen. After turning on the clearance mode, they can "navigate" according to the corresponding clearance route that appears on the screen to pass the route and obstacles displayed on the screen. The game experience can increase children's freshness of teaching aids and improve children's learning interest.

In terms of engineering, the toy has a variety of ways to play and has strong flexibility. Children can diverge their thinking and assemble freely. The assembly method is like a shortened version of engineering splicing: the splicing between the base and the conduit, and the splicing between the conduit and the conduit all require children to discover the skills. Let the children experience the complete working procedure in the process of splicing, realize the role of each component in the project, and use each component to accomplish their own purposes [5]. Improve children's hands-on ability.

5 Summarize

Games can promote children's physical growth and development, improve children's exploration and imagination, improve cognitive ability, perception ability and thinking ability. Therefore, when designing this game, we are more inclined to better serve children in terms of shape, color, and component design. Users in "Little Diver" target children aged 6–8. Therefore, the design of the outer packaging and the main game equipment are also based on the submarines that children like at this stage. Since children like some natural elements and relatively refreshing tones [6], we also use the color design of the pipes. The colors of pink, blue, yellow and green that children generally like are used as the main colors. The transparent PC + ABS material is used as the material of the game pipeline to improve the transparency of the pipeline, better assist children to play games, and enhance the sense of experience. The built-in game instruction card and assembly instruction card scientifically assist children to play the game, and try to make the game rules as easy to understand as possible. To the greatest extent, it can meet the requirements of scientific puzzles, improve hands-on ability, strengthen parent-child relationship, etc., and give children a safe and interesting children's educational game.

References

1. Yongchang, Q.: Promoting deep learning with innovative experiments—taking the teaching of "Archimedes' Principle" as an example. Fujian Educ. **41**, 56–57 (2020)
2. Ying, D.: Research on the design method of cognitive toys for preschool children based on interaction design. Footwear Technol. Des. **1**(20), 115–118 (2021)
3. Yiting, L.: How to improve the teaching efficiency of early childhood science activities based on the STEAM concept. Questions Res. **34**, 105–106 (2020)
4. Yang, D.: Research on the Redesign of Chinese Folk Children's Toys. Jiangnan University, Wuxi (2004)
5. Xinfang, H.: The expression of color psychology in children's product design. Art Sc. Technol. **09**, 163–164 (2019)
6. Yudong, F., Lin, Y.: Design of educational furniture for preschool children based on transplant design method. Design **33**(21), 8–10 (2020)
7. Xiaoyu, Q.: Design of educational toys for children based on STEAM education [TS]. Furniture Inter. Decoration **08**, 80–82 (2020)

A Framework Design of Children's Educational APP Based on Metacognitive Theory

Qianfeng Yu and Jun Wang[✉]

School of Art Design and Media, East China University of Science and Technology, Xuhui District, No. 130, Meilong Road, Shanghai, People's Republic of China
2665943760@qq.com

Abstract. In the context of digitalization in the education industry, how to strengthen children's cognitive activity input in online educational APPs is an important research topic. Based on the cognitive development characteristics of preschool children, this paper introduces the design elements of language educational APP framework and constructs an educational APP framework suitable for preschool children, which provides designers with new design ideas to stimulate preschool children's interest in learning and improve their learning efficiency. Firstly, this paper adopts the literature analysis method and survey method to understand the problems of online educational APPs for preschool children; combined with the physiological, psychological and behavioral characteristics of preschool children, Three elements based on metacognitive theory: metacognitive knowledge, metacognitive experience, and metacognitive skills, respectively, and adopts design thinking to introduce the elements that promote preschool children to achieve self-learning, and reconstructs the suitable The educational APP framework for school-age children provides specific design references and suggestions for language-based game educational APPs, which helps have children plan, monitor and adjust their self-learning behaviors in an independent or chaperoned environment, thus improving learning efficiency.

Keywords: Children's education app · Metacognitive theory · Framework design

1 Introduction

With the advent of the digital era and the development of Internet technology at a younger age, mobile electronic devices such as tablets, cell phones and smart watches have become an integral part of children's lives. The Research Report on National Internet Usage of Minors in 2020 released by China Internet Network Information Center (CNNIC) shows that the number of minor Internet users in China reaches 183 million in 2020, and the Internet penetration rate is 94.9%. More than one-third of elementary school students start using the Internet before they are of school age, and the trend is increasing year by year, and the age at which children first touch the Internet is getting younger and younger [1]. With the opening of the three-child policy, in the future children will serve as the primary group of people cultivated in China, and early childhood

© Springer Nature Switzerland AG 2022
G. Meiselwitz et al. (Eds.): HCII 2022, LNCS 13517, pp. 491–503, 2022.
https://doi.org/10.1007/978-3-031-22131-6_37

education has become the focus of the national education system. Meanwhile, along with the outbreak of the COVID-19 in 2020, information technology is developing rapidly in the education industry, resulting in a wide range of online education APPs. Data shows that children's mobile applications in the App Store mainly focus on entertainment and education, online education APPs are story-based, entertaining, interactive and easy to use, often using a fun and educational teaching method, allowing children to The online educational app is story-based, entertaining, interactive and easy to use. Online education for preschoolers has a great impact on children's enlightenment, and it is crucial to improve the user experience of children's educational APPs for children's early education.

The literature search revealed that most scholars' research on educational mobile applications for children focused on the adoption of other external methods and technology development of educational apps to enhance children's learning interest through the entertainment of games. Based on entropy weighting method and eye-movement experiment, Xun Li et al. (2022), obtained the weights of eye-movement evaluation indexes from three dimensions of interest, salience and guidance to study the design evaluation method of role drawing method of educational mobile apps for preschool children [2]. Xin Wang et al. (2018), explored the emotional design methods used in actual APP cases from three aspects of the reflective layer of emotional design theory and product characteristic relationship, and proposed emotional design strategies for children's educational APPs, finding self-image, satisfying personalized needs and forming lasting memory and attention [3]. Rui Huang(2018) based on immersion theory, using the actual APP as a case, he proposes to explore the key elements affecting the design of the virtual learning environment system in terms of children's cognitive characteristics, ability limits, personality and psychology, and explores the optimized solution for the interaction design of children's educational APP [4]. Jung S (2016) uses smartphone APP to create animation for each Chinese character using stop-motion animation and blocks, mobile APP [5]. Fang et al. (2016), analyzed the current situation of interaction design for children's educational mobile apps at home and abroad, proposed the principles of interaction design for children's educational mobile apps from the physiological and psychological characteristics of preschool children, and initially verified the usability of the research results through cases [6]. The current research on children's educational apps generally adopts external techniques and methods to improve preschool children's participation through parental supervision, without considering the cognitive characteristics of preschool children and the influence of metacognition on self-planning, monitoring, and control. Therefore, based on the three elements of metacognitive theory: metacognitive knowledge, metacognitive experience, and metacognitive skills, this paper adopts design thinking to reconstruct a framework of educational APPs suitable for school-age children, providing parents and children with a better user experience and improving user retention and user stickiness.

2 Theoretical Research

2.1 Cognitive and Metacognitive Theory

The concept about cognition is often difficult to define. In a narrow sense, cognition is a purposeful activity, which is an individual's activity of acquiring and processing information about the objective world. Cognitive process is connected by self-monitoring process and monitoring system, so it can be said that it is a coupled process of monitoring and being monitored. For example, the formation of consciousness, knowledge, intelligence, ability, thinking, imagination, strategy and other activities such as reasoning, solving and classification belong to the normal human cognitive process. Learning is a special cognitive process, which is a functional system composed of sensory, perceptual, thinking, imagination, memory, judgment and other cognitive activities together.

In the 1970s, American psychologist Flavell first proposed the concept of "metacognition", pointing out that metacognition is the individual's cognition of self-cognitive activities, that is, the cognitive individual's knowledge of his or her own ability, mental state, task goals, activity strategies, etc. [7] At the same time, metacognition is the individual's self-awareness, self-regulation and self-monitoring of cognitive activities. It is also a dynamic process of self-awareness, self-regulation and self-monitoring. Metacognition is composed of three basic elements: metacognitive knowledge, metacognitive experience and metacognitive skills. Metacognitive knowledge is a component of the cognitive individual's knowledge system, which is the knowledge of one's own cognitive resources and learning situations, and is stable, expressible, and changing, and develops with age [8]. It can be subdivided into knowledge of intra-individual differences, inter-individual differences, and cognitive universals; metacognitive experience is the conscious cognitive and affective experience of the cognitive process, which exists throughout the process before, during, and after cognitive activities; metacognitive skills are the regulatory mechanisms used to attempt to achieve one's goals, including planning, monitoring, and adjustment; metacognitive skills are the core of metacognitive theory and can be directly monitoring of the subject. Metacognitive knowledge is a monitoring tool and strategy that provides knowledge support for cognitive activities. Metacognitive experience is the factor and main driving force that facilitates cognitive monitoring. These three elements are interrelated, mutually constrained, and interact with each other, and they have crucial roles in information communication, reading comprehension, language, attention, writing, memory, learning ability, and perception of things.

There are many studies on metacognitive theory in education and mobile applications at home and abroad, and all of them affirm the positive role of metacognition in educational apps. However, less research has been conducted on the special group of preschoolers, basically for students who already have basic cognitive ability and are in the stage of compulsory education and higher education. For preschoolers, who have low metacognitive ability and are still in the developmental stage, making full use of metacognitive theory can promote preschoolers to plan, test and adjust themselves, and effectively promote enlightenment education, meanwhile, the process of gamified learning is the process of children's metacognitive development, which can also effectively improve children's metacognitive level in the process of cognition and learning, which is a complementary and The relationship of mutual promotion is also conducive to exercising children's compulsory education afterwards, which is of great significance to the design of innovative educational APPs for preschool children.

2.2 Preschooler Characteristics

Preschoolers are children who have not yet reached the official school age, generally referring to children who are in kindergarten between the ages of 3 and 6, and the period before they officially start elementary school. Preschoolers are in the second stage of Piaget's cognitive development, namely the preoperational stage. Children in the preoperational stage develop language skills rapidly, have a rich desire to know, and are free from concrete actions, turn perceptual actions into representations, and appear to have symbolic functions, which can associate various things in real life based on representational symbols.

Psychological Characteristics of Preschoolers. Preschoolers tend to plateau in all aspects of development, have rich mental representations and more profound and diverse emotional expressions; they are often curious about novelty and inattentive; they are influenced by their emotions, which are usually variable and uncertain, and dominate their psychology and behavior; their language skills are in rapid growth, and they can use only a representational symbol (a word) to describe yesterday's They can describe things and events that happened yesterday or even the day before with just one representational symbol (a word); they perceive most things that are not alive or conscious as living beings with feelings; they develop a "wish psychology" and gradually tend to use wishes to explain their behavior and mental states [9].

Behavioral Characteristics of Preschoolers. Preschoolers from 3 to 6 years old have obvious physical changes compared to the previous ones, both body, bones and brain are gradually developing and maturing. They are active and like tactile and physical contact, and generally perceive the changing physical environment around them through tactile models; they like to imitate, and some of the things they cannot express are imitated by memory, which is an effective way to master skills; children at this stage can slowly grasp smaller objects, but at a slower speed, with a shorter grasp time, poor balance, and difficulty in holding them steadily, as reflected in their hand movements can hold a pencil to write, draw, use tools, etc.

Perceptual Characteristics of Preschoolers. In terms of vision: the eyes are the most sensitive of all organs in children, and 70% of brain information is derived from visual perception. At this stage of development, children's visual acuity and color vision gradually mature, and can see farther and clearer; at the same time, they have good color perception [10], can easily identify the four colors of "red, yellow, blue and green", and are often attracted to bright colors. In the auditory area: children's auditory ability is mature at the age of one week, and the auditory function has gradually stabilized from 3 to 6 years old, and can easily distinguish intensity, tone and timbre; preschoolers can feel different emotions according to different rhythms and rhymes, such as low-frequency sounds have a soothing effect on children, and can detect, discriminate and locate sounds.

In terms of touch: touch is an important means for children to understand the world. The main tactile organs of children are the mouth and hands, and information is transmitted to the tactile organs to trigger tactile responses; oral responses are the earliest tactile exploration of children, and newborn babies can perform sucking actions and explore the smell of milk through the mouth. Preschoolers are more likely to touch, slide, finger, point, pinch, and hold through their hands.

Preschoolers are characterized by fragmentation, variability, and instability. Their understanding and cognition are very limited, and they have relatively little monitoring of their own thinking, memory, understanding, and other cognitive activities, and are easily influenced by undesirable factors. They generally rely on their own senses and movements to know the world, their curiosity is strong and they are more willing to learn new things, but their attention is not focused and they lack sufficient self-cognition, planning and monitoring ability. Throughout, children's educational APPs do not take into account the influence of metacognition on children's learning, play and development. The following problems often exist: first, the dissonance between playfulness and education does not play a correct role in guiding and supervising learning, and children are easily addicted to games, disintegrating the essence of learning for the purpose of achieving personal knowledge appreciation; second, the content function does not take into account the cognitive developmental characteristics of children at all stages, which need to take into account entertainment, gamification, and educational content. Therefore, in order to achieve efficient independent learning and improve the quality of online education, children's educational APPs need to consider the role of metacognition in view of the unique cognitive development characteristics of children in this period.

3   Elements of Children's Educational App Under Preschool Children's Cognitive Characteristics and Metacognitive Theory

Education APP refers to the application software that uses Internet technology and uses cell phones, tablets and other electronic devices as the medium of learning for the purpose of learning and education, which has the characteristics of flexibility and portability, wide personality, various forms, efficiency and so on. [11] From the perspective of user experience, the process of product design can be distilled into five abstract levels, namely, the five elements of user experience, which are performance layer, framework layer, structure layer, scope layer and strategy layer. In this paper, in addition to following the general design principles of education APPs, when designing language game education APPs, we also extract the relevant design elements that constitute the framework layer and performance layer of mobile applications according to the cognitive characteristics of preschool children and metacognitive theory, which correspond to the three elements of metacognitive theory respectively, so as to propose a reasonable design architecture in terms of visual performance, interaction process and contextual experience. Taking language game education APP as an example, language education APP has six stages, namely, basic ability test, game fun, knowledge consolidation, teaching service, result acceptance and achievement socialization.

3.1 Metacognitive Knowledge Level

Preschool children need the guidance of metacognitive knowledge in the pre-preparation process and information comprehension process of using educational APPs for independent learning, and this process is also the process of growing metacognitive knowledge. In this paper, from the perspective of metacognitive knowledge, we put forward the following requirements for the design of language game educational APPs.

Enhance Parents' Perceptions of Their Children and Children's Perceptions of Themselves. Preschoolers are generally at a stage where they have never received systematic education before using educational apps, and the cultivation and development of their language skills come from the surrounding environment. Each child is an independent individual with certain differences in their intellectual factors, family, personality traits, and knowledge accumulation. Therefore, before the preschooler is taught online, both parents and children need to understand the child's willingness to learn, a priori knowledge, thinking skills, comprehension, mastery, and learning characteristics in order to choose the most effective way for the child to learn language. For example, in a language game education app, a basic knowledge test before formal learning can be used to understand the child's current language knowledge reserve and ranking among children of the same type, whether they are behind or above the average, so that parents can adopt a reasonable education method according to their language level; according to the child's a priori knowledge, an education mode that maximizes learning can be chosen. For children who already have a certain base of language knowledge, a lot of simple language learning is not effective in improving the ability to recognize, read, and write words, while for children who only have the ability to communicate on a daily basis, learning difficult patterns at the beginning, not being able to keep up with the pace of learning, and being frustrated, children will become bored with learning in the long run. In addition, basic information, style selection and game themes are included.

Therefore, in the language game education APP, it strengthens parents' cognition of their children and children's cognition of themselves to help children better identify themselves, which is conducive to choosing language learning methods and approaches suitable for children themselves and avoiding the result of blindly following teaching hotspots and online learning methods, which results in half-hearted efforts and causes anxiety in learning for parents and children. The framework of the education APP can introduce personal basic ability, title, studied courses, growth points and interactive information to help parents clarify their children's positioning and deepen their knowledge of them.

Enhancing Children's Perception of Audio-Visual Information at the Interface. Vision is an important part of the interactive interface and the main way to transfer information [6]. In view of the unique cognitive development characteristics of preschool children, their visual system is not fully developed and they cannot distinguish all colors, but they usually have a high discrimination of colors with high purity and brightness. For example, when learning Chinese characters or words related to "New Year", it is easier to mobilize children's learning enthusiasm by using a cool background with red decorative embellishments. Children's emotional ups and downs and arouse children's curiosity about learning. For example, soothing and relaxing music is used to help children think and remember during the learning process, so that they can immerse themselves in the learning atmosphere created; exciting sound effects can be used as encouragement when the course is successfully completed, so that children have a greater sense of achievement; when the course is not completed early, low and long sound effects can be used to encourage the children to learn.

The framework design of the language game app needs to strengthen children's cognition of the visual and auditory contents of the interface. Effective grasp of the interface visual and auditory content can help children understand the learning and game process and bring an immersive game experience. Therefore, we can introduce theme selection, so that users can choose the color style according to their preferences; introduce sound effects theme switching, providing users with rich and diverse music effects or voice effects of hot IPs, such as the voice effects of SpongeBob SquarePants, Mei Yang Yang, Patrick, and Crayola.

3.2 Metacognitive Experience Level

Metacognitive experience is the conscious emotional experience that accompanies cognitive activities [12]. It includes the whole process before, during and after the cognitive activity. In language game education APP, metacognitive experience includes activities such as language and text preparation stage before children learn, the process of gamified learning, interaction with parents and friends after learning, ranking of learning results, whether learning goals are achieved after learning, knowledge sharing and communication.

Enhance the immersive experience design of the game context. The meaning of gamification design is to let users gain knowledge in the game process in a relaxed and enjoyable way, [13] and an important measure of a good game is whether it can bring users an immersive experience. In the planning process of language education gamification, it should have both "playability" and "fun learning", and the planning process of language education gamification includes the whole story design, script design, character design, IP design, level design, game game mechanics, sound design, game art, etc. For the game's storytelling and character design to be suitable for preschoolers, anthropomorphization can be used to anthropomorphize things around preschoolers and create stories. Such as the anthropomorphization of plants and living objects. The metacognitive experience includes the experience of the background understanding of the language game, difficulty level, game classification, time required to complete a level, and whether the learning task can be completed; the experience of the learning mode, progress of the learning task, and interaction between parents and children during the game learning process; the experience of whether the result meets the learning goal, the ranking of learning results, achievement sharing, activities such as knowledge sharing and communication, rewards and punishments after the learning is completed The experience of the mechanism.

The framework design of the language game app needs to strengthen the immersive design of the game context. Therefore, elements such as game background introduction, novice tutorial and difficulty star can be introduced to help children understand the game play and choose the appropriate game difficulty mode according to their ability. The introduction of elements such as progress bar, points, milestones and medals helps children intuitively understand the learning status and feedback of learning results, helps users gain a higher sense of achievement, and enhances their interest and participation in game-based education; the introduction of elements such as ranking, social mapping, ranking and achievement sharing helps children understand their ranking in language learning after learning, and parents can share their parenting experience to Parents can share their parenting experience on social platforms such as friends and microblogs to promote the exchange and sharing of parenting knowledge; introduce interactive elements for parents and children, requiring them to find ways to break through the levels through cooperation with parents and providing small props for breaking through the levels when necessary.

3.3 Metacognitive Skill Level

In the process of learning, metacognitive skills are those that people use to continuously and consciously track and modify cognitive and learning behaviors to achieve desired learning goals using metacognitive knowledge. It has three kinds of basic skills: planning, monitoring and adjusting. In the language game educational APP, metacognitive knowledge is enhanced through gamified learning, in addition to facilitating the realization of metacognitive skills through the mastery of metacognitive knowledge and the metacognitive experiences that occur throughout the learning process for children. Meanwhile, the metacognitive experience helps to carry out the monitoring of metacognitive skills.

Plan. Planning is the goal of a cognitive activity and is the planning of the upcoming work. Before performing a cognitive activity, it further clarifies cognitive goals, identifies cognitive processes and sessions, anticipates cognitive outcomes, selects cognitive strategies and evaluates their effectiveness. In language based play education, planning includes setting learning goals, selecting targeted learning materials, generating questions for the learning content, developing game planning, identifying next tasks and analyzing how to efficiently accomplish the goals. Before children use the language-based game education app, they set learning goals together with their parents, plan the knowledge they will master after completing the gamified curriculum, and try to set them through quantitative methods, such as learning to recognize and write four thousand Chinese characters and five hundred words; select targeted learning materials according to children's metacognitive knowledge, and display the learning materials and game rules through interesting short stories. Children learn language knowledge and understand how to play the game while reading the story; during the game learning process, goals and tasks are set according to the progress and learning results, as a daily plan to be achieved urgently; at the same time, during the game learning process, parents also need to re-examine their children's language learning needs according to the progress and stage results, and plan for the next stage of learning activities to be adjusted so as to efficiently The parents also need to re-examine their child's language learning needs in light of the progress and milestones, and plan the next phase of learning activities so that they can efficiently accomplish their learning goals.

Therefore, in the design of language gamified education APP framework, parents and children need to be guided to make plans for learning activities through the setting plan function. When logging in for the first time each day, a daily goal pop-up window is introduced to help parents set the tasks to be completed today; in the gamification design, game length reminders are incorporated to remind children to pay attention to the control of entertainment time, coordinate the balance between learning and playing, and help children visualize their learning plans.

Monitor. Monitoring is the monitoring of the interactions and cause-effect relationships among influencing factors, environments, processes and elements in the cognitive process, and is a commonly used metacognitive strategy, which refers to constantly reflecting on and monitoring whether one's cognitive activities are proceeding in the right direction according to the cognitive goals, correctly estimating one's degree and level of achieving cognitive goals, and evaluating various cognitive actions, according to the validity criteria. The effectiveness of various cognitive actions and strategies is evaluated according to validity criteria. In the process of game-based language learning, in order to have high learning efficiency and improve concentration and attention during learning, it is necessary to monitor the progress of game-based language learning activities and understanding and thinking about the learning content, and to examine whether their learning path is in the same direction as their self-goals. For example, children usually become addicted to games in the process of game-based learning, and if the system detects that they have been in a purely game-based state for a certain period of time it will alert the child and parents to the control of playtime.

Therefore, in the process of language gamification learning, the feedback, main usage functions, time allocation and incentive mechanism of gamification are used to help parents monitor their children's learning status. The introduction of a daily clock element at the time of login motivates children to persist in language learning every day through rewards for each successful clock; the introduction of a question element in the gamified learning process helps parents understand their children's mastery of knowledge on the one hand, and urges children to study carefully and focus on the other. In the context of language gamification learning, users can use this real-time recording and timely feedback gamification system to break the limitations of linear thinking under the traditional learning model, which helps to identify cognitive biases, make timely adjustments or corrections, and provide opportunities for their own thinking and social interaction in the learning process.

Adjust. Adjustment is based on examining the results of cognitive activities, taking appropriate remedial measures if problems are found, difficulties are encountered, or goals are deviated from, and reflecting on and adjusting cognitive strategies in time to reap the best learning benefits. In the process of gamified language learning, moderation helps preschoolers to correct their learning behaviors and remediate learning deficits. For example, when learners find that they cannot comprehend the learning content of a level, they slow down their reading and comprehension, or go back to read, or read repeatedly; when they find that a pattern is more or less difficult and does not match their current knowledge of the language, they should promptly adjust the learning pattern and locate a more appropriate difficulty level; when they find that they do not have enough time during the level test, they skip the difficult questions and do the easy ones first. When parents find that their child's test scores for this stage of the course have been declining, consider whether there is some problem with the methodology or content.

Therefore, the process can be interrupted at any time during the language gamification learning process to make feedback and adjustments. Introducing scoring elements at the end of each game level, parents and children can score the overall situation, the fun of the game, and the coherence of the knowledge content; introducing learning progress display and feedback elements as a basis for parents and children to make adjustments; introducing today's knowledge mastery elements when children complete today's tasks to help parents and children judge the learning results and thus guide users to carry out adjustment measures.

4   Framework Design of Children's Educational App Under Metacognitive Theory

Based on the three basic elements of metacognitive theory and the cognitive developmental characteristics of preschool children, this paper constructs a three-layer structural

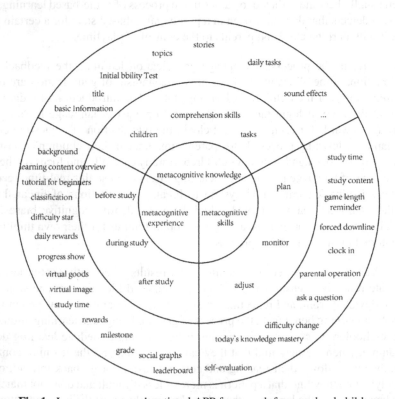

Fig. 1. Language game educational APP framework for preschool children

model of a language-based game educational APP for preschool children based on the above analysis.

The first layer is the core elements of children's educational APP, and also the three core starting points for building the framework design of language game educational APP. Based on the three elements of metacognitive theory, it cultivates children's metacognitive ability in the learning process. The second layer is the application elements guided by the core of metacognitive theory, through metacognitive knowledge, metacognitive experience, and metacognitive skills respectively, the specific design direction proposed for children's educational APPs. The third layer is the gamification framework elements, under the condition of meeting the needs of preschool children and parents, the cognitive ability is transformed into functional elements, which are integrated into each stage of the mobile application framework to form a complete framework structure. The elements and functions of children's gamified educational app under the three elements of metacognitive theory are shown in Table 1.

Table 1. Elements and functions of children's gamified educational app

Metacognitive elements	Definition	Related educational content	Element	Function
Metacognitive knowledge	Knowledge about the process of cognitive activity	Elements that affect the learning process in different ways	Basic information, initial ability test, theme selection, daily tasks	Used to help parents understand their child's own abilities, professional level, and clarify their perception of self
Metacognitive experience	Emotional experiences in cognitive processes	The environment and experience throughout the learning and playing process	Background introduction, learning content overview, newbie tutorial, difficulty stars, daily rewards, milestones, leaderboards, social graphs	Used to help enhance the user experience for children before, during and after gamified learning, providing immersive gamification scenarios that reinforce interest in learning

(*continued*)

Table 1. (*continued*)

Metacognitive elements	Definition	Related educational content	Element	Function
Metacognitive skills	Conditions for self-regulation in cognitive activity	Planning; checking; reflecting and revising	Learning time and content settings, game length reminders, forced disconnections, punch cards, self-evaluation, feedback	Used to help children set learning goals, aim to complete gamified learning tasks within a standard time frame, reflect on and revise learning activities

The framework is based on metacognitive strategies and cognitive development theories, which develop children's awareness of learning strategies while they are entertaining and learning, and help them to use their cognitive abilities autonomously in subsequent school learning, develop correct thinking about learning, and develop efficient learning methods.

5 Conclusion

Metacognitive theory is often applied in the field of pedagogy, and this paper proposes a framework of gamified educational APP for school-age children from different perspectives and special populations, combining educational and Internet mobile application fields. The paper combines the physiological, psychological and behavioral characteristics of preschool children and reconstructs an educational APP framework suitable for school-age children using design thinking based on metacognitive theory and three elements: metacognitive knowledge, metacognitive experience and metacognitive skills. Using a reasonable gamified learning framework to strengthen preschool children's metacognitive skills in the learning process facilitates children to plan, monitor and adjust their self-education behaviors in an independent or chaperoned environment, thus improving learning efficiency, providing parents and children with a better user experience, and enhancing user retention and user stickiness. However, this study is still at the stage of theoretical framework, and subsequent examples are needed to test and support it.

References

1. 2020 China Internet Network Information Center Report. 20 July 2021. http://www.cnnic.cn/hlwfzyj/hlwxzbg/qsnbg/202107/t20210720_71505.htm
2. Li, X., Zhang, B.C., Yang, Y.L., Gu, R.B., Wei, Y.Y., Yang.: A study on the evaluation of educational APP role mapping approach for preschool children based on entropy power method. Packaging Engineering 1–13. 17 May 2022
3. Wang, X., Wang, F.: A study on the emotional design of children's educational apps at the reflective level. Decoration **07**, 95–97 (2018)
4. Huang, R.: Interaction design of children's educational app based on immersion theory. Packag. Eng. **39**(10), 177–181 (2018)
5. Jung, S.: The Intelligence APP development for children's kanji character education using block and stop motion. Int. J. Adv. Smart Convergence **5**(2), 66–72 (2016)
6. Hao, F., Yanlin, Z., Tingting, Z., Mengpiao, X.: Research on the interaction design of educational APP for preschool children. Packag. Eng. **37**(20), 113–117 (2016)
7. Flavell, J.H.: Metacognition and cognitive monitoring: a new area of cognitive–developmental inquiry. Am. Psychol. **34**(10), 906–911 (1979)
8. Wu, Q., Zhang, Y.: A gamification framework design for social reading literacy cultivation under metacognitive theory. Intell. Theory Pract. **43**(04), 108–114+185 (2020)
9. Chen, C.: Research on the Design of Interactive Educational Products for Preschool Children Based on Cognitive Psychology. Southwest Jiaotong University, Chengdu (2015)
10. Hao, J.: Research on game APP interface design based on preschool children's cognitive psychology. China University of Mining and Technology, Beijing (2015)
11. Zhu, N.: Research on the Interactive Design of Children's Art Education App Interface. Guangxi Normal University, Guilin (2021)
12. Wumei, L., Xuefeng, W., Yan, Y.: Metacognitive experience: an important theoretical cornerstone of consumer behavior research. Foreign Econ. Manag. **41**(11), 86–98 (2019)
13. Yan, W.: The construction of flash educational game design model based on cognitive development theory. China Educ. **08**, 92–96 (2012)

Using Cooperative Multi-agent Systems to Support the Generation of Student Learning Profiles in the Deep Dive Land Bridge System

Chencheng Zhang[1], Sarah Saad[1], Thomas Palazzolo[1], Robert Reynolds[1(✉)],
John O'Shea[2], Cailen O'Shea[3], and Ashley Lemke[4]

[1] Wayne State University, Detroit, MI 48201, USA
robert.reynolds@wayne.edu
[2] University of Michigan, Ann Arbor, MI 48109, USA
[3] North Dakota State University, Fargo, ND 58102, USA
[4] University of Texas, Arlington, TX 76019, USA

Abstract. The goal of the project described here was to extend the immersive experience of the user in the Virtual Land Bridge. Such extensions would facilitate the use of the software system to contribute to the development of individual student learning plans over several different age categories. The principal strategy was to modify the multi-agent planning system to allow for the generation of local tactical behavior of the agents in the virtual world. This resulted in the addition of a new layer to the MAS planning system, producing a hybrid system that utilized global knowledge monolithically in the Pathfinder portion and local tactical knowledge in the VR layer. The resultant hybrid system was designed to produce improved caribou agent decision making and movement that could scale up to support large herds on the order of a hundred thousand and more. This new system is shown to increase user immersion that can contribute to the development of student learning profiles.

Keywords: Cooperative multi-agent systems · Student learner profiles · Embodied space · Virtual ethnography

1 Motivation

There are several reasons for modifying the HCI for an existing software system. They can include the following: improvements in supporting hardware technology; changes in supporting software; changes in required functionality; and shifting demographics and expectations. This paper represents a case study of a scenario in which the target functionality and demographics experiences a major shift over time. In this case there was shift from being a basic scientific tool for site prediction to one targeted towards developing critical thinking as part of a STEM educational program.

The Deep Dive Land Bridge simulation system was initially developed to aid underwater archaeologists in the discovery of ancient prehistoric sites located underwater in Lake Huron, one of the Great Lakes in the United States [1–3]. It utilized Artificial

© Springer Nature Switzerland AG 2022
G. Meiselwitz et al. (Eds.): HCII 2022, LNCS 13517, pp. 504–524, 2022.
https://doi.org/10.1007/978-3-031-22131-6_38

Intelligence and Virtual Reality to recreate the archaic semi-artic landscape and has facilitated the discovery of several ancient underwater sites [4]. The Land Bridge was above the Lake Huron water level for about 2,000 years from 10,000 B.P. to 8,000 B.P. Figure 1 shows the location of the Land Bridge relative to the State of Michigan in the USA and Canada. The two cells on the bridge represent areas that are the focus of current exploration. They were selected due to their location relative to the widest part of the Land Bridge. It was assumed that this would be the area of largest herd congregation if it was used as a migration route for caribou. While the system described here was developed to utilize the data relative to these locations, the framework is general enough for it to be used to support exploration in other geographical areas.

While the Land Bridge program was initially designed as an aid for the discovery of submerged prehistoric sites, the system's potential as a means for understanding traditional hunting practices, its use as an educational tool became rapidly apparent in two ways. First, it could be used to record hunters' observations about potential uses of the ancient landscape. Traditional Alaskan hunters were invited to enter the Virtual World and describe what they saw. By tracking the hunter's movements over the virtual landscape and by listening to their commentary, insight was gained into how traditional hunters view and conceptualize the landscape in general. In addition, their assessment of locations that might have served as sites for hunting structures and activities in the distant past were recorded [5].

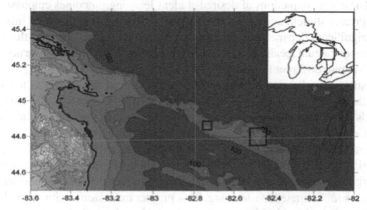

Fig. 1. The location of the Alpena Amberley Land Bridge. The explored areas are denoted as squares on the map.

Second, it could be used a vehicle for the development student problem solving skills. This idea was initially suggested by one of the traditional hunters who asked whether it would be possible to take other people with him in the Virtual World? He went on to explain that he wanted to teach his grandchildren how to hunt, but they only wanted to play video games. This idea was generalized to include the engagement of students more broadly. In part the hope is to engage students in the Virtual World itself, and to allow each to bring their own lived experiences with the outdoors and hunting to bear on the problem of finding caribou. At the same time, students would be encouraged to engage the students in the broader research process; predicting where hunting sites should be located on the submerged landscape, and then employing remote sensing technology (and direct siter examination) to test their predictions in the real world. The critical element for all these uses is the realism that is captured in the Land Bridge VW system. As we found with our pilot study with traditional hunters, aspects of the VW that did not 'ring true', be it the look of the landscape or the movement or composition of the herds, was potentially distracting and prevented the user from true immersion in the virtual world.

This new direction is intriguing as it works towards developing students around the 4 Cs of education (Critical thinking, Collaboration, Creativity, and Cross-communication). This is often the goal of many schools' district's "Portrait of a Graduate." Many school systems have responded to changing societal and economic contexts by creating learner profiles or profiles of a graduate.

A learner profile creates a wholistic profile of a student with a goal of building a student's self-awareness that facilitates their interaction with educators and families. Students can establish personal and academic goals and create action items designed to achieve these goals. A specific approach to creating such profiles is the International Baccalaureate Program (IB). It is the combination of three subsidiary programs: Primary Years (3–10); Middle Years (11–16); and Diploma Years (17–18). The ten aspirational qualities tracked across these programs are: Inquiring; knowledgeable; Thinking; Communicators; Principled; Open Mindedness; Caring; Risk Taking; Balanced; and Reflective [6]. These new depictions of desired student learning outcomes emphasize deeper learning, greater student agency, more authentic work, richer technology infusion, and often are significant departures from more traditional schooling practices that predominantly focus on factual recall and procedural regurgitation [7]. In turn, these new learning outcomes require different forms of teaching and learning.

With such considerations in mind, the current goal of the project is to extend the existing Land Bridge (Deep Dive) system and its interface for specific student audiences. This project is enticing as it attempts to reach students where they are and value their lived experiences. Current educational research has given an increased focused on culturally responsive schooling (see NYSE Culturally Responsive-Sustaining Education Framework) [8]. This work requires educators to look for ways not only to incorporate student culture into curriculum, but also encourage students to work collaboratively with their teachers to facilitate their learning. This project extension is vital as it allows student experiences to be valuable not only in the project, but also the learning of others. When students are given the opportunity to have "real-world" application and cross-communication with their peers across the globe then the learning the experience is not only engaging, but authentic in ways that were simply not possible before. With this, the audience is incredibly important as it requires knowledge of the present settings and contexts as well as and Indigenous Traditional Ecological Knowledge [9].

To extend the immersive functionality of the Deep Dive system one must first discuss the knowledge that is generated by the simulation that is critical to the VR experience, the generation of optimal caribou migration pathways. In other words, the model caribou are imbued with a basic intelligence provided by an optimal path planning algorithm. The algorithms plan is based upon environmental characteristics that include effort, risk, food consumption, and time to traverse. How the current simulation system generates that knowledge that is the basis for site prediction is discussed in Sect. 2. What additional path planning activities need to be added to the VR system to improve its immersive quality will be discussed in Sect. 3. Sect. 4 then describes how the Human Computer Interface needs to be adjusted to accommodate the new caribou agent behavior. Section 5 concludes with a discussion of how these extensions will support the generation of various aspects of a Learners Profile.

2 The Multi-agent Planning Framework for the Deep Dive Simulation Component

Figure 2 give an overview of the overall Deep Dive system. It has three basic components: The Pathfinder MAP Simulation system; the Graphical User Interface (GUI) for the simulation system; and The Virtual Reality system.

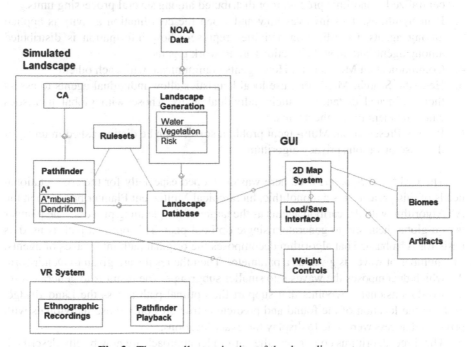

Fig. 2. The overall organization of the deep dive system.

The topographic data acquired from the National Oceanographic and Atmospheric database (*NOAA*) of the area was fed into the AI pipeline to *Generate* AI content via the Landscape. This created content includes the water level of various cells of the landscape to simulate which areas of the Land Bridge were above the current water level or not for a given year between 10,000 and 8,000 B.P. For a given year height map data for those portions of the landscape was calculated along with derived slope. Hydrologic information including the location ponds, swamps, and rivers that are present in the location at that time were then calculated. Given the location, water content, slope and sun angle the AI pipeline predicts the cells potential vegetation at each location on the Land Bridge. This information is stored in the *Landscape Database* for use by the *Pathfinder* system.

The basis for the simulation system is *Pathfinder*, a Cooperative Multi-Agent Planner (CMAPP). There are several deterministic general purpose MAP solvers available [9]. They include MAPR (MAP Planning by Reuse), CMAP (Cooperative MAP), mu-SATPLAN (Satisfiability based planning), among others. The different CMAP solvers can be classified by the mechanisms that they employ to address the planning process. The main features that can be used to characterize cooperative MAP solvers are:

1. Agent Distribution: The MAP process here involves multiple agents who are involved in the planning process either as active participants or as target for the planning process.
2. Computational Process: Whether the computational process is performed using a centralized monolithic processor or distributed among several processing units.
3. Plan Synthesis: This involves how and when the coordination activity is applied among agents. Coordination activities represent how information is distributed among agents and how their actions are to work together.
4. Communication Mechanism: How agents communicate with each other.
5. Heuristic Search: MAPs that use local heuristics allow individual agents to assess their estimated distance to their individual goals. Those with global heuristics calculate them for all the agents.
6. Privacy Preservation: Multi-agent problem solvers can be distinguished in terms of their use of various privacy algorithms.

The CMAP, *Pathfinder*, used here was developed especially for the computational needs of this project. It is a monolithic, hierarchical Multiagent Planner based upon the A* Algorithm with the caribou agents as the target of the planning process. The planner uses a global heuristic to generate a single optimal path. This optimal path is used as basis for A*mbush. That algorithm decomposes the original path into waves of agents. The number of waves is given as a parameter. Then the results are given to Dendriform A* which decomposes the waves into smaller subgroups. The result is to generate a set of two-dimensional waypoints that support the optimal path across the Land Bridge. To keep the location of the found and predicted structures only those individuals with privileged access were able to display the exact locations.

The three algorithms comprising the Pathfinder approach are now briefly described:

A*: A* is a popular search-based pathfinding algorithm that's an adaptation of Dijkstra's Algorithm. The difference being an additional heuristic allowing it to attribute cost to actual and estimated distance from the goal. Since the algorithm calculated point by point it allows the caribou agents to freely traverse the landscape while focusing on effort, risk, and nutrition.

A* Pseudocode
Add pathStart to openNodes
   Initialize pathStart scores
   While (openNodes count greater than 0)
   {
currentNode = openNodes [0]
   If (currentNode is goalNode)
   { assemblePath() and return true}
   Remove currentNode from openNodes
   Find currentNode's neighboringNodes.
   ForEach(neighboringNode) calculate f and g score
   If (neighborNode is not in openNodes) add to openNodes.
   Else {adjust neighborNode's position in the openList based on total score}
   }

Ambush: Also integrated into the system is A*mbush. A*mbush incorporates A* at its root. It uses the algorithm of A* but does so in separate waves instead of a single path. The waves are entered as a parameter, then the total herd size of Caribou is divided amongst the waves. The waves are then sent one after another with the nest wave entering the landscape as the last one completes its journey. Each wave consumes a certain proportion of available calories, leaving the remainder for the waves that follow.

Ambush Pseudocode:
for (generations=0; generations < ambushGenerations; generations++)
for (waypoint = waypoints-2; waypoint > 0; waypoint--)
{foundPath = AStar(waypoint, waypoint+1)
foreach(node in foundPath)
{Insert node in resultPath(generations) at index 0.}
} resultingHerd += calculateMigrationScore()
devourVegetation(foundPath)
}

Dendriform: Dendriform is the final algorithm used in the path planner portion on the Deep Dive system. It incorporates A* but also allows for branching during the exploration of the landscape. This means as the line of Caribou is traversing, they can divide on the spot allowing some of the herd to continue their path while the rest look for a separate path. This allows for more complex paths to be generated like the example in Fig. 3.

Dendriform Pseudocode:
Calculate optimal A* path
Add starting point and ending point to node list.
While node list has more than two nodes {
checkForNewDivergencePoints
select last two nodes in node list and A*mbush Devour path section.
Remove last node in node list.
If last node in node list is not starting point:
     Calculate optimal A* path to ending point.
}

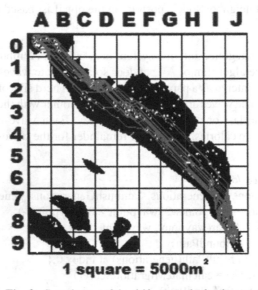

Fig. 3. Sample run of dendriform on the landscape.

Fig. 4. Current deep dive GUI.

The Simulation system then communicates with the simulation GUI in two basic ways. First, the user interface displays a series of tabs through which the user may navigate to a given data set or select an experiment to run as shown in Fig. 4. Maps can be viewed in a variety of data styles, such as biome data, topographical data, archaeological points of interest, ruleset hotspots, and so on. Pictured above, the user has selected to run six iterations of the A*mbush pathfinder, each wave being made up of 1000 caribou. The weight priority wheel on the bottom left allows the user to manually set the weights for Effort, Risk, Nutrition, and Time in the performance function. The priority weights control what will be important to the caribou in the current run. The green segment denoted by a "N" is the nutrition this will have caribou prioritize situations which will lead to an increase in calorie or food intake. The blue segment is effort ("E") increasing this priority will cause the caribou to avoid scenario which will lead to excess calories being spent for example going up a steep incline. The red segment is risk ("R") which influences caribou to avoid scenarios which would lead to a higher percentage of death. The last weight denoted by yellow is time, this prioritizes the amount of time it would take to cross the entirety of the portion of the land bridge simulated.

One of the factors impacting the relative weights of the performance function parameters is herd size. Simulation of the different levels of path planning using different levels of plan decomposition demonstrate that the land bridge can support herd sizes of several hundred thousand. Figure 5 compares the performance of Pathfinder when herds of

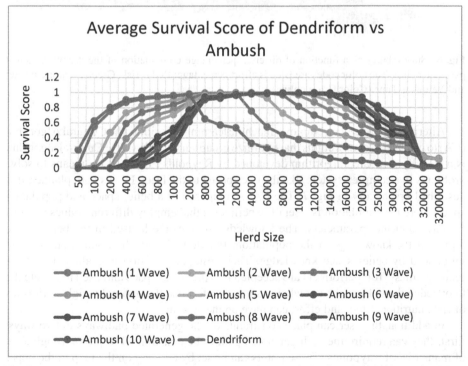

Fig. 5. Survival rates equalizing all weights using the A*, Ambush and dendriform algorithms across various herd sizes.

differing sizes are distributed via A*mbush with different waves and with Dendriform. Dendriform decomposes the waves into subgroups. For these experiments the weights of all four environmental parameters were set equal at 25%. Notice that the simulated environment can comfortably support herd sizes of 200,000 or more.

In addition, for any given herd size the optimization landscape can be very rugged. Finding the combination of weights that can produce optimal survivability for large herd sizes is a non-trivial task. Figure 6 provides a description of the set of all possible combinations of weights for a herd of size 40,000.

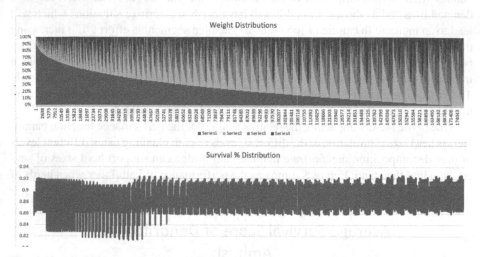

Fig. 6. Survivability as a function of different percentage combination of the 4 environmental parameter class. The color codes are Blue is effort percentage; Red is risk, Green is caloric intake; and Yellow is Time.(Color figure online)

Alternatively, users can employ a machine learning algorithm, the Cultural Algorithm (*CA*) to produce a set of weights that optimize group survivability. The Cultural algorithm is a socially motivated algorithm developed by Reynolds [9, 10]. It's a means to solve problems in a complex system like the ones posed to the Deep Dive's path planner. It is described graphically in Fig. 7. The CA is composed of a belief space and population space. Here the population is a set of experiments that employ different values weights for environmental parameters. The knowledge sources are housed in the belief space represent the knowledge of the population. Individuals from the population are then influenced by belief space knowledge. Their resultant decision is evaluated by their relative fitness. Top performers are accepted into the belief space and used to update the knowledge there. Here the knowledge sources determine the optimal weights priorities of risk, nutrition, time, and effort can have on the system.

In addition, the user can place constraints on the generated pathways in two ways. First, they can require the path generated path to be constrained to pass through a set of manually set waypoints. Those points can be set by clicking on the map in the upper left-hand corner of the screen. Also, users can select rules that constrain the regions within which the paths can be placed. The Rule Selection screen is shown in Fig. 8 below.

As shown in Fig. 3, the result of the Pathfinder simulation can be sent back to the GUI to be displayed in the manner discussed above. The results are two-dimensional sets of points that correspond to the generated pathways. These points are also sent to the Virtual Reality system for display. The VR can record the movements of individuals and their comments as they traverse the landscape. This affords the opportunity to record culturally meaningful insights of the users that relate the Land Bridge world with their experience in the real world. This is a feature that will be useful for use in the construction of Personal Learning Profiles.

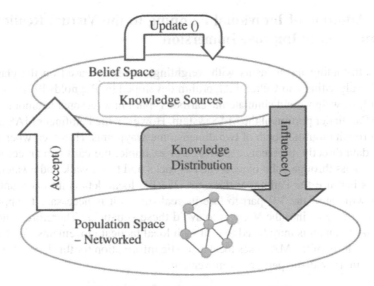

Fig. 7. Cultural algorithm representation.

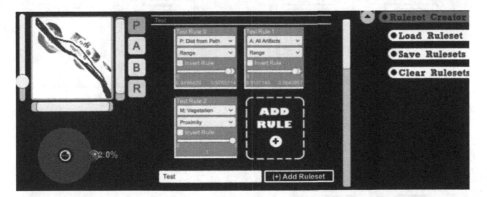

Fig. 8. The GUI screen used to display and modify heuristic constraints on generated paths.

The key is that these way points are two dimensional and do not take height into account. In addition, physical barriers such as rocks or swamps or collisions with other caribou are not considered. This is not so much of a problem if there are few obstacles and the herd sizes are small, but if one anticipates the simulation of large herd sizes as was suggested by the simulations above then the results could be very distracting. To remedy that, an additional level to the Path Planning activity was added at the VR level. While path planning in the Pathfinder was guided by global information, the individual agents need to modify their trajectories to reflect their local constraints. To do this another level of pathfinding was added to the VR to improve its immersive quality. This will be the topic of discussion in the next section.

3 The Addition of Individual Planning to the Virtual Reality Component to Improve Immersion

Several path-finding mechanisms with weighting strategies based on the classic A* pathfinding algorithm and Cultural Algorithm developed by Reynolds [9, 10] were utilized to adjust weights and simulate the caribous' path in a reasonable amount of time using the Pathfinder portion of the MAS system. However, the Pathfinder MAS can only provide a rough migration path of two-dimensional waypoints. However, when the part uses this data directly, problems can arise. For example, the caribou can collide with each other, pass through solid objects such as rocks and trees, walk underwater, and so on. This is because the Pathfinder does not take the local details into account. These problems will cause the VR part to lose its realism, so it is necessary to apply extra movement strategies into the VR part to avoid these situations. Therefore, a new path planning mechanism is introduced to deal with local tactical movements. As illustrated in Fig. 9 this level of the MAP uses local heuristic information for this level of sub herds to produce more realistic patterns of movement.

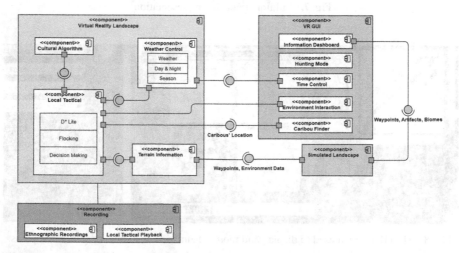

Fig. 9. Expanded VR component diagram with the local tactical component, D* Lite included.

In the Land Bridge system, the VR portion obtains the waypoints of the herd migration path generated by the weighted path-finding A* algorithm. To simulate the caribou's local tactics, we engaged the D* Lite algorithm by Koenig [11] to direct Caribou movement between every 2 waypoints along the path. The D* Lite algorithm combines the characteristics of the D* algorithm dynamic programming with the incremental search feature of LPA* algorithm which is very suitable for path planning in unknown terrain. A screenshot of a caribou herd in motion is provided in Fig. 10. Notice that caribou are moving around trees and are together as a herd with proper spacing and direction.

To allow caribou agents to realistically interact with their environment, it is necessary to introduce environment weighting mechanisms into the local path implementation rather than just simply converting the D* lite pathfinding algorithm from 2D to 3D. Not only do we need to consider gravity, but also individuals' flocking, decision making, and so on. Notice in the diagram the D*Lite component can be influenced by Weather conditions, terrain information, flocking preferences, and individual decision making.

Fig. 10. Caribou group movement along a path.

In the VR simulation, the terrain is complex and dynamic. First, the terrain is not flat, it has slopes on the ground, so the caribou expend more energy when they are going to uphill and vice versa. Then, as mentioned above, the height of the water surface changes over time: the walkable area is affected by the water level. Also, with changes in weather, the risk rate and movement speed along a path will also change. There are also many factors that affect a caribou's survival rating and movement strategies that need to be consider in the implementation.

Like for real world caribou agents, decision making also will be applied to inform caribous' local tactics. When they meet obstacles the D* lite algorithm will provide a detour path for the individual so they would behave as in the real world. Caribous will select to walk around or jump over the obstacles. For instance, when a herd of caribous is trying to cross the river, if the river is shallow, caribou will be able to cross the river directly while some of them will choose to take a detour. For obstacles like rocks or trees, some caribou will be able to select jump over the low obstacle, and while some of them will process collision avoidance and walk around. To make movement decisions, the following path cost formula is used.

$$C = D + \sum_i w_i T_i$$

where D is the distance of the Euclidean distance, w_i is the weighting factor for different tactics like steering, jump over, swimming, and T_i is the tactical quality, i is the number of tactics being supported [12]. Different tactics can be set up to avoid different object categories with weights based on the environment's static features such as terrain, and dynamic features such as group motion. We utilize DOTS in Unity 2020 to handle the simulation of several caribou in the virtual world.

Figure 11 shows the path produced for a caribou herd originally by A* in VR. The red lines are employed to represent the approximate route generated by the A* algorithm, and the blue lines represent the routes that are produced by local caribou tactics with D* Lite. It is not difficult to see that the red route provides a general direction of travel for the group, while the blue lines make corresponding route corrections according to the current terrain environment, providing more details.

Fig. 11. Local tactical pathways (blue) generated from the original A* path (red). (Color figure online)

Due to its incremental planning idea, the start node in D* Lite algorithm is always changing. It will set the current node as new start point and repeatedly calculating the path between the Goal point and the new Start point, thus D* Lite can achieve less replanning times and fewer re-planning influence nodes which can reduce the response time within a reasonable range and put more resources to work on VR graphics and effects quality. But when the state space is relatively large, that is, when the environment map is relatively large, the number of grid nodes that need to be maintained during the reverse search process of the adopted D* Lite path planning algorithm increases sharply. This increases the time complexity of the search. Therefore, we are using D* Lite in local environments to contribute local forward strategies between 2 waypoints. Moreover, we have carried out a more fine-grained rasterization of the local environment map to achieve a smooth and better path solution. In simulations for animation, or background effects in a game, fluid steering motion adds to the believability [12].

There is one more problem, how to deal with such many factors and huge number of caribou? In the future Cultural Algorithm (CA) will be applied to help optimize local tactics too. It can improve the knowledge of simulated caribou while refining their knowledge sources, making it more useful for complex situations composed of multiple factors [10]. Also, DOTS which is available in the Unity 2020 game engine will be used to handle the large number of simulated caribou in our virtual world. A listing of the D* Lite Pseudocode follows.

D*LITE PSEUDOCODE
Dictionary:
S: A set of waypoints.
Succ(s): Set of subsequent nodes of node s.
Pred(s): Predecessor node of node s
$g(s)$: The distance of node s to the goal.
s_{start}: The start position.
s_{goal}: The goal position.
$c(s, s')$: Cost between 2 nodes.
$rhs(s)$: For all adjacent nodes of s, find their distance to s plus the value of g of the adjacent node itself, and the smallest value is used as the rhs value of s
U: Queue, based on the Key value.
$h(s)$: Similar to A*, the estimated distance to the target node.
U.Top(): Returns a node with the smallest priority of all nodes in U.
U.TopKey(): Returns the smallest priority of all nodes in prior.
U.Pop: Pop the node with the smallest priority in U and returns this node.
U.Insert(): Inserts node into U with priority.
U.Update(): Changes the priority of node.

CalcKey(s)
[1] return $[\min(g(s), rhs(s)) + h(s_{start}, s) + k_m; \min(g(s), rhs(s))]$;

Initialize()
[1] $U = \emptyset$;
[2] $k_m = 0$;
[3] for all $s \in S$
    $rhs(s) = g(s) = \infty$;
[4] $rhs(s_{goal}) = 0$;
[5] U.Insert(s_{goal}, $[h(s_{start}, s_{goal}); 0]$);

UpdateVertex(u)

[1] if($g(u) \neq rhs(u)$ AND $u \in U$)

   U.Update(u, CalcKey(u));

[2] else if($g(u) \neq rhs(u)$ AND $u \notin U$)

   U.Insert(u, CalcKey(u));

[3] else if($g(u) = rhs(u)$ AND $u \in U$)

   U.Remove(u);

ComputeShorestPath()

[1] while(U.TopKey() < CalcKey(s_{start}) OR $rhs(s_{start}) > g(s_{start})$)

[2]   u = U.Top();

[3] k_{old} = U.TopKey();

[4] k_{new} = CalcKey(u);

[5]   if($k_{old} < k_{new}$)

[6]   U.Update(u, k_{new});

[7]   else if($g(u) > rhs(u)$)

[8] $g(u) = rhs(u)$;

[9]   U.Remove(u);

[10]   for all $s \in Pred(u)$

[11] $rhs(s) = \min\big(rhs(s), c(s,u) + g(u)\big)$;

[12]   UpdateVertex(s);

[13]   else

[14] $g_{old} = g(u)$;

[15] $g(u) = \infty$;

[16]   for all $s \in Pred(u) \cup \{u\}$

[17]   if($rhs(s) = c(s,u) + g_{old}$)

[18]   if$\big(s \neq s_{goal}\big) rhs(s) = \min_{s' \in Succ(s)}\big(c(s,s') + g(s')\big)$;

[19]   UpdateVertex(s);

Main()

[1] $s_{last} = s_{start}$;

[2] Initialize();

[3] ComputeShortestPath();

[4] while($s_{start} \neq s_{goal}$)

[5] s_{start} = arg $\min_{s' \in Succ(s_{start})}\big(c(s_{start}, s') + g(s')\big)$;

[6]   Move to s_{start};

[7]   Scan graph for changed edge costs;

[8]   if any edge costs changed

[9] $k_m = k_m + h(s_{last}, s_{start})$;

[10] $s_{last} = s_{start}$;

[11]   for all directed edges(u,v) with changed edge costs

[12] $c_{old} = c(u,v)$;

[13]   Update the edge cost c(u,v);

[14]   if($c_{old} > c(u,v)$)

[15] $rhs(u) = \min(rhs(u), c(u,v) + g(v));$
[16]   else if $(rhs(u) = c_{old} + g(v))$
[17]   if$(u \neq s_{goal})\ rhs(u) = \min_{s' \in Succ(u)}(c(u,s') + g(s'))$
[18]   UpdateVertex(u);
[19]   ComputeShorestPath();

A byproduct of allowing caribou agents fine grained interactions with their environment is that since users are also agents, one can take advantage of such enhanced capabilities to improve user immersion as well. This will facilitate more immersive interactions. How this will impact the VR GUI will be discussed in the next section.

4   Adding Depth to the User Experience Through the MAP

In the VR system the user can be viewed as an agent. The extension of the MAP system to support local tactical interaction between caribou agents also afforded users opportunities to interact with the environment in more immersive ways. This produced an opportunity to change the Virtual World interface substantially to involve the user more completely in the world. In this section the major changes are highlighted.

1. Improved Navigation: To begin, Fig. 12 gives a screenshot of the new dashboard. The dashboard provides the real coordinate of the player and caribou. Also, the user can select the "target" icon to pick up a location on the map and then directly teleport there. One of the biggest obstacles to user immersion was the inability of the user to efficiently navigate a relatively large area on the ground. It was not always easy to locate caribou or find areas of interest. The teleportation and navigation features are major improvement in that area.
2. Object Interaction and Manipulation. The user is now able to manipulate objects in the environment. Figure 13 give a brief set of instructions to a user about how to move around and manipulate objects in the virtual space. The addition of this feature facilitates the addition of tools and other objects into the virtual world.
3. Adding the feeling of Embodied Space: This allows the user to experience a feeling of physical presence in the environment. This feature will go a long way towards providing a notion of physical presence within the world. Figure 14 gives a screenshot of a user's hand interacting with the Virtual Interface.
4. Support Proactive Behavior: The tactical features can allow the user to be more proactive. Previously the user spent more time reacting to the environment rather than exploring it. Figure 13 illustrates the use of a wand to allow the user to transport to a point ahead of the herd. This allows the user to get a better handle on why the herd is moving in the direction and what a hunter might see if they were looking back at the herd moving towards them. This can provide useful information for hunting site selection.
5. Enabling more opportunities for information gathering: Now that the user can interact with objects in the world around them, adding detail to those objects can now provide opportunities for the users to make more detailed memories as well as better descriptions to others about their experience in the world. Figures 15 and 16 below

provide examples of how the ground and sky views can be enhanced to provide more opportunities for making memories and describing their experiences.

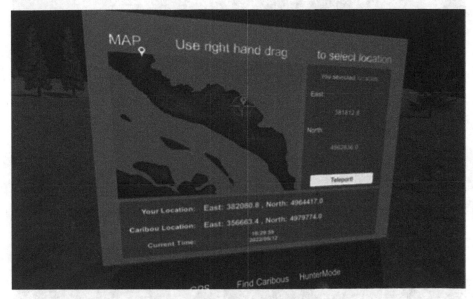

Fig. 12. Opening the option panel in VR.

Fig. 13. Instructions for object manipulation in the virtual world.

Fig. 14. The User's virtual hand interacting with the virtual reality GUI.

Fig. 15. Details of important landscape features can now use be to provide memories and recollections of individuals that will be useful in describing their experiences as recorded in the virtual ethnographies.

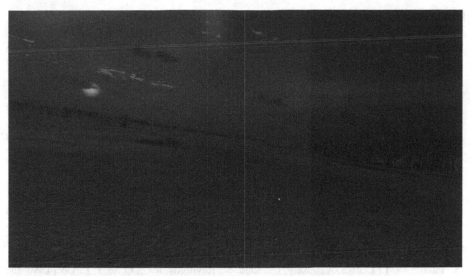

Fig. 16. Celestial information can provide information about navigation and orientation decisions. Previously respondents expressed a desire to have more celestial information for their decision making.

5   Enhancing the User Experience

The goal of the project described here was to extend the immersive experience of the user in the Virtual Land Bridge. Such extensions facilitate the use of the software system to contribute to the development of individual student learning plans over several different age categories. The principal strategy was to modify the multi-agent planning system to allow for the generation of local tactical behavior of the agents in the virtual world. This resulted in the addition of a new planning layer to the MAS planning system, producing a hybrid system that utilized global knowledge monolithically in the Pathfinder portion and local tactical knowledge in the VR layer. The resultant hybrid system was designed to produce improved caribou agent decision making and movement that could scale up to support large herds on the order of a hundred thousand or more.

In so doing the system was able to provide new opportunities for users to interact with the system in ways that can improve their immersive experience. This resulted in a major redux of the VR GUI to support more detailed user embodiment, immersion, and communication. All these features provide conduits that will support the expression of individual user behaviors in the virtual world, and their subsequence recording as part of their Personal Learner profiles.

Future work will investigate how the system can leverage the users experience in the Land Bridge virtual world as a means of addressing aspects of the Student Learner Profile. In other words, which of the attributes associated with Personal Learner profile can be enhanced through the Land Bridge immersive experience?

References

1. Reynolds, R.G., O'Shea, J., Che, Z., Gawasmeh, Y., Meadows, G., Fotouhi, F.: The agile design of reality game AI. In: Multi-Agent Applications with Evolutionary Computation and Biologically Inspired Technologies: Intelligent Techniques for Ubiquity and Optimization. IGI Global Press (2011)
2. Fogarty, J., Reynolds, R.G., Salamayeh, A., Palazzolo, T.: Serious game modeling of caribou behavior across lake huron using cultural algorithms and influence maps. In: O'Shea, J., Sonnenberg, E. (ed.) Archaeological, Ethnographic and Paleo-Environmental Perspectives on Caribou Hunting in the Great Lakes: Maps, Directions and Accommodations. University of Michigan Museum of Anthropology (2015)
3. Palazzolo, T., Reynolds, R.G., Stanley, S.: Exploring virtual worlds with cultural algorithms: ancient alpena-amberley land bridge. In: Cultural Algorithms: Tools for the Engineering of Social Intelligence into Complex Systems, pp. 203–271. IEEE Wiley Press, Hoboken (2020)
4. O'Shea, J, Lemke, A., Sonnenburg, E., Reynolds, R.G., Abbot, B.: A 9,000 year-old submerged caribou hunting structure in lake huron. In: Proceedings of the National Academy of Science (2014)
5. Palazzolo, T., Lemke, A., Zhang, C., Saad, S., Reynolds, R.G., O'Shea, J.: DeepDive: the use of virtual worlds to create an ethnography of an ancient civilization. In: Stephanidis, C., et al. (eds.) HCI International 2021 - Late Breaking Papers: Cognition, Inclusion, Learning, and Culture. Lecture Notes in Computer Science, vol. 13096, pp. 615–629. Springer, Cham (2021). https://doi.org/10.1007/978-3-030-90328-2_42
6. The IB Learner Profile. https://www.ibo.org/globalassets/publications/recognition/learnerprofile-en.pdf
7. McLeod, S., Shareski, D.: Different Schools for A Different World. Solution Tree Press, Bloomington (2017)
8. Culturally Responsive-Sustaining Education Framework. http://www.nysed.gov/crs/framework
9. Reynolds, R.G.: Culture on the Edge of Chaos: Cultural Algorithms and the Foundations of Social Intelligence, 1st edn. Springer International Publishing Basel, Switzerland (2018)
10. Reynolds, R.G.: Cultural Algorithms: Tools for the Engineering of Social Intelligence into Complex Cultural Systems. Wiley-IEEE Press, Hoboken (2021)
11. Koenig, S.: Fast replanning for navigation in unknown terrain. IEEE Trans. Rob. 21(3), 354–363 (2005)
12. Millington, I.: AI for Games, 3rd edn. CRC Press, Boca Raton (2019)

Transformer-Based Automated Content-Standards Alignment: A Pilot Study

Ziwei Zhou$^{(\boxtimes)}$ ⓘ and Korinn S. Ostrow ⓘ

Edmentum, Bloomington, MN 55437, USA
zzhou@edmentum.com

Abstract. The passage of the No Child Left Behind Act has increased an emphasis on developing K-12 curricula around existing and emergent state and national standards. The ever-growing volume of readily available K-12 digital content has increased the need for aligning learning and assessment content to relevant educational standards at scale. However, manual alignment is labor-intensive and time-consuming. Inspired by prior works on automated content alignment systems that leveraged recent advances in deep learning and NLP, this study explores a scalable solution for automatically aligning assessment items to multiple state and national standards. Results indicate the Transformer encoder-decoder model trained from scratch shows decent performance, reaching 34.3 BLEU score and 0.4 averaged ROUGE score on a holdout set. To investigate the limitation of the conventional evaluation metrics and gain deeper insights into the many-to-many relationships observed in the data, a series of metrics are utilized to evaluate the matches between the source and target sequences. In-depth error analysis identifies major error categories and explains the discrepancies in performances observed between the training and test set. Finally, this study discusses the potential for a production-level system and the future direction in extending the current approach to facilitate the development of a general skill taxonomy as a "crosswalk" for mapping educational content to standards.

Keywords: Educational standards · Assessment items · Transformer encoder-decoder model · Evaluation metrics · Error analysis

1 Background

1.1 Aligning Educational Standards

Educational standards describe what students are expected to know and should be able to do for a particular subject and a grade level [1]. By structuring and presenting learning content in a logical order, standards can be used to guide curriculum and assessment [2, 3]. The creation of measurable educational standards can be dated back to the 1983 report "A Nation at Risk" by the Commission on Excellence in Education [3–5]. The passage of the No Child Left Behind Act in 2001, which required states develop standards in core subject areas and held schools accountable for measuring students against those standards, has increased an emphasis on the design of K-12 curricula around existing and

© Springer Nature Switzerland AG 2022
G. Meiselwitz et al. (Eds.): HCII 2022, LNCS 13517, pp. 525–542, 2022.
https://doi.org/10.1007/978-3-031-22131-6_39

emergent state and national standards [6]. With the emphasis on assurance of learning and educational accountability, the Act has "led to increased standardization of educational goals and outcomes and a rapid growth in assessment of learning" [7].

Standard-based teaching and assessment implies an act of alignment, that is, matching standards with one or more educational or assessment resources [2]. This alignment enables "the tracking of student skill gaps, recommendation of remediative learning content, and mastery of discipline topics, skills, and cross cutting capabilities" [8]. However, with ever-growing volume of readily available K-12 digital content, aligning learning and assessment content with relevant educational standards at scale has been quite challenging.

Standard alignment is an onerous task because the body of educational standards is quite large. For example, the Achievement Standard Network (ASN), a publicly available database of K-12 standards, lists about 60,000 STEM standards in the U.S. alone [9, 10]. Different states have their own standards in the core subjects, and the standards are revised every five to seven years [6, 9]. National organizations, curriculum committees, and local districts also develop taxonomies of standards, and "each set of standards utilizes discrete language, differing grade bands, distinct organizational structures and different levels of specificity in the coverage of a particular standard" [6].

1.2 Automated Alignment

Challenges of manual alignment of these standards provide impetus for the development of automated alignment techniques [7, 11–13]. Several organizations and projects have developed databases for standards coupled with automated alignment services meant to address the "sheer massiveness and dynamism of the standards alignment problem" [14]. For example, the Achievement Standards Network (ASN) manages all U.S. K-12 standards in a Resource Description Framework (RDF) format [15]. The Curriculum Alignment Tool (CAT) and Standard Alignment Tool (SAT), made available by the Center for Natural Language Processing at Syracuse University [12], are Web services that provide "on-the-fly document-to-standard alignment (CAT) and standard-to-standard alignment (SAT)" [14].

According to [10], there are two main approaches for machine-based alignment. Whereas the direct approach is to build a machine learning classifier to find matches between an educational standard and associated content [7, 11], the transitive or "crosswalk" approach relies on semantic similarity from a taxonomy (e.g., other existing education standards or resources) to conduct alignment [10]. The standard assignment task is typically regarded as a text classification task where educational content is automatically assigned to one or more of the indices of the appropriate standards [12]. Automatic task classification in this problem considered information retrieval as well as statistical learning methods, such as naïve Bayes, decision tree, K-nearest neighbor, and support vector machine [12].

The automated alignment methods implemented in SAT or CAT are examples of the direct approach. SAT performs a multi-label text categorization task for aligning multiple state standards to the McRel standards based on an SVM model [16]. For CAT, Vector Space Model was built via TF-IDF (Term-Frequency-Inverse-Document-Frequency) matrix on the tokenized and POS-tagged from the textual content of educational resources and ASN standards. For a given educational resource's term vector, CAT scores all the standard's term vectors against it and assigns the highest-ranking standard(s) [7].

While standards tend to be high-level abstract statements about what a student is expected to do or know, the associated educational content is a "practical application of these theoretical constructs that require different vocabulary" [3]. The major challenge in automatically aligning educational content and standards is caused by the language and vocabulary issues inherent to the two sources; there may be little to no overlap between educational content and associated standards, and descriptors may present at different levels of granularity [3, 12]. While resolving such language and vocabulary issue involves "a conceptual match rather than straight vocabulary match" [12], an unwrapping process is recommended to unpack all the different concepts and skills encapsulated in a single standard [4, 17, 18].

NLP for Alignment. Natural Language Processing (NLP), which concerns equipping computers with the ability to understand, manipulate, and generate natural language data (including text and voice data), is a rapidly evolving field. The seminal paper "Attention is All You Need" from Google researchers [19] revolutionized the NLP industry by introducing the Transformer model architecture that effectively solved long-term dependency and parallel processing bottlenecks in the previously dominant neural network models, such as recurrent neural networks (RNN) and convolutional neural networks (CNN). The Transformer model has since become the state-of-the-art sequence-to-sequence (Seq2Seq) model architecture tackling several challenging NLP tasks, including machine translation, summarization, question-and-answer, natural language generation, etc. [20].

However, application of state-of-the-art NLP models in K-12 education settings to perform the standards alignment task has been quite limited, presumably due to the complexity of model architecture and technical details associated with the implementation. To the best of the authors' knowledge, [8] is the only application of a Transformer model to automatically tag educational content with the Next Generation Science Standards (NGSS) in developing an operational system called Catalog. The content tagging system performs semantic matching by the similarities between the educational content and NGSS standard vectors obtained via the pre-trained Transformer models. Compared with the semantic matching methods implemented in CAT or SAT that replied on keywords or search terms, the Transformer-based pre-trained language model approach "is built on a language modeling architecture that understands the deep semantic structure and relationship between concepts, topics, learning objectives and other attributes of content" [8]. However, their work focuses on aligning educational resources, such as reading passages, rather than assessment items, to a particular standard (which was limited to only 24 unique Biology NGSS PE standards), rather than multiple standards.

Similarly, [21] introduced their BERT-LSTM architecture that learns documentation representations (vector representation on the [CLS] token) from syllabi or job posts via the pre-trained BERT [22] and feeds the sentence vector through an LSTM [23] model sequentially to predict discrete skills. These recent alignment works that leveraged Transformer models mainly used the pre-trained models and cast the problem into a text categorization task, rather than neural machine translation (NMT) or abstractive summarization task, where the Transformer architecture is widely adopted [20].

To fill the avoid in automated alignment between assessment items and multiple state and national standards, this study explores a scalable solution by leveraging recent advances in deep learning and NLP, providing an initial feasibility analysis for a larger research effort in mapping content to a generalized skill taxonomy, which is mapped to different sets of standards rather than repeatedly mapping and remapping content separately to every set of standards.

2 Methods

2.1 Data

The data set consisted of 29,789 ELA (English/Language Arts) items for Grades 3–8 that were manually aligned to the Common Core State Standards [24] as well as various state standards, including Iowa, Indiana, Oklahoma, Ohio, and Pennsylvania. The manual alignment was conducted by a third-party vendor, where subject matter experts (SMEs) in the field went through rigorous training processes and applied the industry-standard alignment method [25, 26]. These items were developed and maintained by an educational technology company serving students primarily in the United States and used within either a personalized diagnostic assessment or a standard-based proficiency assessment. Raw text data for the items and standards were queried against the company's content management system. Item data consisted of item stems and/or content blocks. While the stem typically contained questions or instructions, the content block was displayed immediately after the stem and could contain interactive components (such as dropdowns).

Because the relationship between items and standards is many-to-many (i.e., an item is mapped to multiple national and state standards and a standard can be mapped to multiple items), there were 9,836 unique items and 822 unique standards in the data set. For example, the item that contained the question "Which sentence is punctuated correctly?" was mapped to 25 unique standards. Similarly, the standard "With guidance and support from peers and adults, develop and strengthen writing as needed by planning, revising, and editing" was mapped to as many as 269 unique items. Of all ELA items, 80% were partitioned into the training set and 20% into the test set via stratified sampling by grade, standard source, and product so that that the distributions of these variables were similar between the training and test sets.

Pre-processing. The pre-processing of the items and standards involved text data cleaning and tokenization. Data cleaning involved replacing or removing the special encodings and symbols, such as HTML tags, phonemic symbols, encodings of punctuations, etc., using regular expression rules. For example, all HTML tags were replaced by the "<HTML>" string and all image tags were replaced by the "<IMAGE>" string. As added tokens should be treated as a non-separable entity, they were added as special cases to customize Spacy tokenizer through its 'en_core_web_sm' model [27]. This process was used to standardize non-text elements to minimize noise for the model to better perform the alignment task.

2.2 Information Retrieval

Two information retrieval (IR) approaches were implemented. The TF-IDF approach concatenated the items and standards (to form the corpus) and calculated pairwise cosine similarities based on the TF-IDF matrix that consisted of n-grams of size one to five. For each item, the standard in the corpus that showed the highest cosine similarity score with the item was selected as the predicted standard. The second IR approach leveraged the pre-trained BERT model ('bert_based_uncased') from the "transformers" library [28]. Sequences from either items or standards were first pre-processed for the BERT model by adding '[CLS]' and '[SEP]' tokens, tokenized by the built in BertTokenizer, and converted to torch tensors. Then, input tensors were subjected to the pre-trained BERT model and the embeddings from the final layer were extracted and averaged over the tokens. For each item, its BERT embedding was compared against the BERT embeddings of all standards in the corpus. The standard that had the highest cosine similarity score with an item was selected as the item's predicted standard.

2.3 Model

Figure 1 shows the high-level model architecture, which maps a source sequence (an item) – for example, "Which of the following sentences should be placed between the second and third paragraphs?" – to the corresponding target sequence (a standard) – for example, "Provide a conclusion that follows from the narrated experiences or events." The encoder (in green) represents how the source sequence goes through the Transformer blocks into a contextual vector (denoted as "c"), which is then consumed by the decoder (in orange) that feeds the contextual representation into the Transformer blocks to predict the next token in the target sequence.

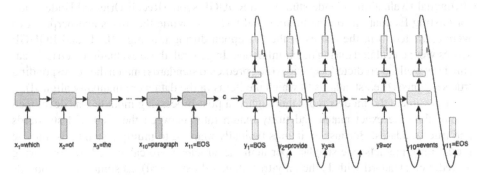

x_1=which x_2=of x_3=the x_{10}=paragraph x_{11}=EOS y_1=BOS y_2=provide y_3=a y_9=or y_{10}=events y_{11}=EOS

Fig. 1. Transformer encoder-decoder architecture. Note: original figure adapted from the work of Patrick Von Platen (Hugging Face), October 8, 2020; https://huggingface.com/blog/encoder-decoder). (Color figure online)

Model implementation followed [29] Github repo[1], which implemented a slightly modified version of the Transformer model from "Attention is All You Need" by [19].

---

[1] https://github.com/bentrevett/pytorch-seq2seq.

Modifications in the current implementation included: 1) learned positional encoding instead of static; 2) standard Adam optimizer with a static learning rate instead of one with warm-up and cool-down steps; and 3) a lack of label smoothing [29].

3 Analysis

3.1 Experimental Setup

Six Transformer models were tested. These models differed in terms of 1) whether all standards or only CCSS were used, and 2) whether pre-trained word embeddings, either GLOVE [30] or custom Word2Vec embeddings (trained via Gensim library [31]), were used in the model's embedding layer. All experiments were performed with fixed hyperparameters, including 20 epochs, gradient clipping by 1, hidden-dimension of 256, 3 Transformer blocks and 8 multi-head attention layers (for either the encoder or decoder stack), 512 dimensions for the point-wise feed-forward layer (with Relu activation function), a learning rate of 0.0005, and a dropout rate of 0.3^2.

The deep learning experiments were implemented using a Databricks notebook, where the Transformer models were built using the PyTorch framework (primarily leveraging torchtext library and torch.nn module). To enable GPU computation, 10.1 ML Databricks runtime was configured to use p3.2xlarge AWS EC2 instance (1 GPU and 128 GB memory) in the driver node and auto-scale 2–8 same instances on the worker node.

3.2 Evaluation Metrics

Model performance was evaluated by calculating the losses, perplexities, BLEU score (Bilingual Evaluation of Understudy), and ROUGE score (Recall-Oriented Understudy for Gisting Evaluation) on the training and test sets. While the losses and perplexities were extracted from the results of the last epoch during training, BLEU and ROUGE scores were calculated during batch-inference. In general, these evaluation metrics measure how well the predicted sequences (i.e., predicted standards) match the corresponding true sequences (i.e., standards to which the items in the data were manually aligned).

To evaluate the models more thoroughly, a post-processing module was developed to calculate the exact match and fuzzy match rates between the predicted standards and true standards. Because an item is typically mapped to multiple standards, but the model only predicts one standard per item, accuracies were calculated by comparing a predicted standard with 1) the only true standard (Standard), 2) some true standards (Standard-N), or 3) all true standards (Standard-All). In other words, a given predicted standard (associated with an item) was compared against either 1) one true standard in the test set (Standard), 2) all true standards in the test set (Standard-N), or 3) all true standards in the entire data set (Standard-All). Three versions of Levenshtein Distance were calculated in a similar manner. Figure 2 shows an example for the three versions of matches to calculate the accuracies.

---

[2] Slightly increased from the original 0.1 dropout rate to improve overfitting.

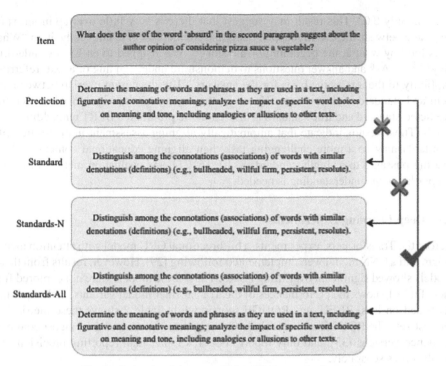

Fig. 2. Example of three versions of item-standard matches

In this example, the prediction does not match the true standard by the Standard or Standards-N criteria. For the given item, there is only one true standard in the test set. However, it is matched by the Standards-All criterion because there is another true standard from the training set, and the predicted standard matches with it.

For fuzzy match rates, IR approaches were adopted by calculating the cosine similarities between the predicted standard and true standards either via the TF-IDF matrix or the pre-trained Sentence-Transformer embeddings [32]. For comparisons that involved multiple true standards, only the optimal solution was reported. For example, in the scenario where multiple true standards were mapped to the same item, only the true standard with the lowest Levenshtein Distance or highest cosine similarity with the predicted standard was used in the calculation of fuzzy match rates.

4   Results

4.1   IR Experiments

Accuracies from implementing the IR approaches are generally poor. For example, the exact match rate between predicted and true standards (by the Standards-N criterion) is only 0.08 from the TF-IDF approach and 0.06 from pre-trained BERT embedding approach. For the TF-IDF approach, mean cosine similarity between the true and predicted standards (based on maximum cosine similarity from all standards with respect to a given item) is only 0.03. This result may suggest that there is very little overlap in terms of language between the text of mapped items and standards. For example, the item "What does the boy want at the beginning of the story?" was mapped to an Iowa standard in Grade 3 -- "Ask and answer questions to demonstrate understanding of a text, referring explicitly to the text as the basis for the answers". But the ngram overlap between the item and standard is almost none. However, the average cosine similarity between the predicted standard and true standard is 0.72 from the pre-trained BERT embedding app-roach. These results indicate that automatically aligning assessment items to multiple standards may be a more challenging task than aligning educational content such as reading passages to a single standard [8, 10, 16, 21], and evaluation metrics based on deeper language understanding is needed.

4.2 Deep Learning Experiments

Before the Transformers' experiments, a bi-directional GRU model with attention mech-anism and a CNN model were implemented following [29]. However, results from these models showed significant overfitting issues. Thus, these models were not explored fur-ther. Table 1 shows the performances of the Transformer model variants on the training set based on loss, BLEU, and ROUGE scores, while Table 2 shows these metrics on the test set. The ROUGE scores include the unigram, bigram and the longest common sequence versions [33], and only report f1-scores rather than reporting precision and recall scores separately.

In general, BLEU and ROUGE scores appear good against recent works in NMT and abstractive summarization [20]. However, these conventional metrics have major drawbacks. While BLEU score suffers from serious flaws in not considering meaning and sentence structure [34], ROUGE score only assesses content selection [20]. In the current study, these limitations manifest themselves when being compared with other evaluation metrics shown in Table 3 and 4. The models without the pre-trained GLOVE or custom Word2Vec embeddings performed better, with consistently lower losses and perplexities as well as higher ROUGE scores. This surprising finding warrants further investigation. [35] found that, for NMT tasks, the effect of pre-training embeddings can be associated with sample size and language similarity between the source and target sequences.

Table 1. Model evaluation metrics on training set

Evaluation criterion	All standards	CCSS	All standards GLOVE	CCSS GLOVE	All standards Word2Vec	CCSS Word2Vec
Loss	0.09	0.06	0.21	0.19	0.21	0.19
Perplexity	1.10	1.06	1.23	1.21	1.24	1.21
BLEU	45.20	66.73	24.68	32.77	26.47	32.27

(continued)

Table 1. (*continued*)

Evaluation criterion	All standards	CCSS	All standards GLOVE	CCSS GLOVE	All standards Word2Vec	CCSS Word2Vec
ROUGE-1	0.54	0.71	0.38	0.44	0.40	0.44
ROUGE-2	0.44	0.65	0.24	0.31	0.26	0.31
ROUGE-L	0.52	0.70	0.34	0.41	0.36	0.41

Table 2. Model evaluation metrics on test set

Evaluation criterion	All standards	CCSS	All standards GLOVE	CCSS GLOVE	All standards Word2Vec	CCSS Word2Vec
Loss	0.15	0.14	0.20	0.16	0.19	0.16
Perplexity	1.16	1.15	1.22	1.17	1.22	1.17
BLEU	34.30	39.85	24.01	29.80	25.57	29.80
ROUGE-1	0.45	0.49	0.38	0.42	0.39	0.41
ROUGE-2	0.33	0.38	0.24	0.28	0.25	0.28
ROUGE-L	0.42	0.46	0.34	0.38	0.35	0.38

Table 3. Exact and fuzzy matches from training set

Evaluation criterion	All standards	CCSS
Exact Match	0.35	0.60
Exact Match-N	0.69	0.87
Exact Match-All	0.71	0.88
Levenshtein Distance	74.87	47.45
Levenshtein Distance-N	29.71	11.03
Levenshtein Distance-All	27.49	8.95
Cosine Similarity (TF-IDF)	0.42	0.63
Cosine Similarity (S-BERT)	0.68	0.80
Cosine Similarity-N (S-BERT)	0.84	0.96
Cosine Similarity-All (S-BERT)	0.85	0.97

For the All Standards and CCSS models, though the final loss and perplexity values are lower in the training set, they are generally higher but decreased more rapidly in the training set from epoch to epoch during training. But the losses are quite similar

Table 4. Exact and fuzzy matches from test set

Evaluation criterion	All standards	CCSS
Exact Match	0.23	0.29
Exact Match -N	0.36	0.35
Exact Match -All	0.63	0.67
Levenshtein Distance	89.56	85.90
Levenshtein Distance-N	67.95	75.66
Levenshtein Distance-All	35.40	32.76
Cosine Similarity (TF-IDF)	0.30	0.35
Cosine Similarity (S-BERT)	0.62	0.63
Cosine Similarity-N (S-BERT)	0.69	0.68
Cosine Similarity-All (S-BERT)	0.84	0.86

during later epochs. As the cross-entropy loss is averaged over the batches, further investigations on the loss from batch to batch may be needed to get deeper insights. Also, performances from the CCSS model differ quite substantially between the training and test sets, presumably due to the overfitting issue as the CCSS is only a small subset of the data set that contained all standards. Despite the overfitting issue, CCSS model consistently performs better than the All Standards model. Presumably, as an item is only mapped to CCSS, the many-to-many issue is less severe for the CCSS model.

Table 3 shows the more granular model evaluation metrics (exact and fuzzy matches) for the All Standards model and the CCCS model based on the training set, while Table 4 shows these metrics on the test set. The "-N" suffix refers to the scenario where all standards in the test set that are mapped to the same item are referenced to calculate the match rates (i.e., Standards-N criterion) and "-All" refers to the scenario where all standards in the entire data set that are mapped to the same item are referenced to calculate the match rates (i.e., Standards-All criterion). For the distance and similarity metrics, mean values are shown.

When comparing the two models across the evaluation metrics, the CCSS model seems to suffer from more severe overfitting issues due to smaller sample size than the All Standards model. For the exact matches, there are increases in performance in terms of higher accuracies and lower Levenshtein distances when more true standards are used in the comparison (i.e., Standards-N and Standards-All criteria). The cosine similarity measures based on the S-BERT approach are much higher than those from the TF-IDF approach. This suggests that though there may be very little commonality on surface-level language and vocabulary features between the predicted and true standards, there may be deeper-level connections tapped by the embeddings from large pre-trained language models (i.e., S-BERT). For example, the predicted standard "Determine the main idea of a text; recount the key details and explain how they support the main idea." does not match exactly the true standard "Determine two or more main ideas of a text and explain how they are supported by key details; summarize the text" (moderate cosine similarity based on TF-IDF approach). However, the S-BERT similarity is 0.89, showing the deeper semantic connection between the two.

4.3 Error Analysis

Based on the error analysis for the All Standards model, the first error category can be attributed to the Exact Match-N scenario where a predicted standard mismatches with the true standard on the same row (of the prediction) but matches with a true standard in the test set. Table 5 shows some examples in this category.

In Example 1–3, the item ("Item" column) is mapped to both the true standard ("Standard" column) and the predicted standard ("Prediction" column) on the test set. In Example 1, there is also another highly similar standard in the test set mapped to the same item -- "Students will form and use verbs in the indicative, imperative, Interrogative, conditional, and subjunctive mood". Moreover, the predicted standard is mapped to a set of highly similar items from the same grade, product, and source of standard. For example, "Our healthcare may improve if everyone ate healthier. Which of these will make the sentence conditional in mood?".

Table 5. Example errors in standards-N category

No.	Item	Prediction	Standard
1	Your sister might even stay in school, if you lead by example. Which of these would make the sentence conditional in mood?	Use verbs in the active and passive voice and in the conditional and subjunctive mood to achieve particular effects (e.g., emphasizing the actor or the action; expressing uncertainty or describing a state contrary to fact)	Form and use verbs in the indicative, imperative, interrogative, conditional, and subjunctive mood
2	She picked up the pen and started her book report. The word pen means _____ in the sentence above	Use context to confirm or self-correct word recognition and understanding, rereading as necessary	Use sentence-level context as a clue to the meaning of a word or phrase
3	Which sentence has correct capitalization?	With guidance and support from peers and adults, develop and strengthen writing as needed by planning, revising, and editing	Capitalize appropriate words in titles

In Example 2, it turns out that while the true standard maps the item to an Iowa standard, the predicted standard maps the same item to the CCSS standard in the test set. In CCSS, the predicted standard in this example is mapped to a set of highly similar items within the same grade. For example, "Juan made a mark on his shirt with his pen and hopes it will wash out. The word mark means _____ in the sentence above." and "Michael did feel a bit sad that his mom was going to discontinue their meetings. What does the word discontinue most likely mean?".

In Example 3, the same item is mapped to 10 different standards, including both the true and predicted standards. Moreover, whereas there are only two examples for the item mapping to the true standard in the entire data set, the predicted standard is a very generic one that is associated with 162 unique items in the test set. This may have caused great confusion to the model and driven the prediction to be biased towards the majority.

The second error category can be attributed to the Exact Match-All scenario where a predicted standard mismatches with the true standard on the same row or the mapped standards in the test set but matches with a true standard in the training set. Table 6 shows some examples in this category.

In Example 1–3, the item is mapped to both the predicted standard and the true standard(s) in the training set. In Example 1, while the true standard mapped to this item is an Iowa standard, the predicted standard is an Oklahoma standard mapped to the same item. The predicted standard is also mapped to a highly similar item in the training set -- "The diagram shows the constellation Orion the Hunter. How does the diagram help the reader understand what constellations are?" Moreover, the true standard is mapped to a set of highly similar items within the same grade, product, and state standard source. For example, "How does the diagram help the reader understand the phases of the Moon?", "The diagram shows the constellation Orion the Hunter. How does the diagram help the reader understand what constellations are?", and "The purpose of the illustration is to". Besides, there exists a highly similar item-standard pair with Example 2, which may further perplex the model – the item "How does the diagram help the reader understand the piece better?" being mapped to the CCSS standard "Explain how specific images (e.g., a diagram showing how a machine works) contribute to and clarify a text".

Table 6. Example errors in standards-all category

No.	Item	Prediction	Standard
1	How does the diagram help the reader understand the passage?	Students will use graphic features including photos, illustrations, captions, titles, labels, headings, subheadings, italics, sidebars, charts, graphs, and legends to interpret a text	Interpret information presented visually, orally, or quantitatively (e.g., in charts, graphs, diagrams, time lines, animations, or interactive elements on Web pages) and explain how the information contributes to an understanding of the text in which it appears

(*continued*)

Table 6. (*continued*)

No.	Item	Prediction	Standard
2	How does sensory language in this passage help convey the plot to the reader?	Use precise words and phrases, relevant descriptive details, and sensory language to convey experiences and events	Produce clear and coherent writing in which the development, organization, and style are appropriate to task, purpose, and audience
3	Which of these, if any, is the clearest and most effective way to revise sentence 4?	With some guidance and support from peers and adults, develop and strengthen writing as needed by planning, revising, editing, rewriting, or trying a new approach, focusing on how well purpose and audience have been addressed	Students will edit and revise multiple drafts for organization, transitions to improve coherence and meaning, using a consistent point of view

In Example 2, the item is not only mapped to both the true and predicted standards, but there is also an additional mapped standard in the training set within the same grade, product, and standard source -- "Use narrative techniques, such as dialogue, pacing, and description, to develop experiences, events, and/or characters".

In Example 3, besides the predicted and true standards, the same item is mapped to a set of similar standards in the training set, such as "Place phrases and clauses within a sentence, recognizing and correcting misplaced and dangling modifiers", "Plan and develop; draft; revise using appropriate reference materials; rewrite; try a new approach; and edit to produce and strengthen writing that is clear and coherent, with some guidance and support from peers and adults", "Recognizing and correcting misplaced and dangling modifiers", etc. Similarly, the true standard is mapped to 145 unique items in the training set. The predicted standard, which is a generic one, is mapped to as many as 452 unique items in the training set.

The final error category can be attributed to the true errors where a given predicted standard does not match either the mapped standards in the test set nor the ones in the training set. This error category is the majority, accounting for 47.6% of total prediction errors from the All Standards model. Table 7 shows some examples in this category.

In Example 1, it turns out that there is only one such item-standard mapping in the entire data set. The predicted standard is mapped to a set of similar items, such as "What can the reader infer from the passage?", "What can the reader infer from this paragraph?", "Based on the events described in this story, the reader can infer that Ezra", etc. These nuances in wording in similar items and the paucity in training example for such pair may have caused the model to make the wrong prediction.

In Example 2, while there are only 17 unique items associated with the true standard, there are as many as 166 unique items associated with the predicted standard. The items associated with the predicted standard have greater variability than those associated with the true standard. In Example 3, the item is unique in the data set. With varied items, the unique number of mapped items for the true and predicted standards appears very similar in the data set.

Finally, there are examples of lengthy items (not displayed in the current study due to space limit), where there is a mix of HTML tags, images, phrases, and capital letters that appear in an announcement, followed by an item stem -- "The author wrote this section mostly likely to".

Table 7. Example errors in true error category

No.	Item	Prediction	Standard
1	Which of the following can be inferred from the passage above?	Cite several pieces of textual evidence to support analysis of what the text says explicitly as well as inferences drawn from the text	Cite the textual evidence that most strongly supports an analysis of what the text says explicitly as well as inferences drawn from the text
2	You _____ around the bases now. What goes in the blank?	Use context (e.g., the overall meaning of a sentence or paragraph; a word's position or function in a sentence) as a clue to the meaning of a word or phrase	Students will recognize verb tense to signify various times, sequences, states, and conditions in text
3	<HTML> Right after creating three equal isosceles triangles connected together, the reader should <HTML>	Refer to parts of stories, dramas, and poems when writing or speaking about a text, using terms such as chapter, scene, and stanza; describe how each successive part builds on earlier sections	Analyze in detail how a key individual, event, or idea is introduced, illustrated, and elaborated in a text (e.g., through examples or anecdotes)

Such item is mapped to the standard of "Determine an author's point of view or purpose in a text and analyze how the author acknowledges and responds to conflicting evidence or viewpoints." but predicted as "Determine the meaning of words and phrases as they are used in a text, including figurative, connotative, and technical meanings; analyze the impact of specific word choices on meaning and tone, including analogies or allusions to other texts". Conceivably, while the item stem appears to be most indicated of the mapped standard, the item length, coupled with the mix of non-text elements, which still appears messy after text-cleaning, may have caused tremendous confusion for the model.

5 Discussion

5.1 Conclusion

Leveraging the Transformer architecture, this study explores a solution for automated alignment between assessment items and educational standards. By evaluating the model performances through multiple metrics, the results demonstrate the limitations of conventional evaluation metrics (e.g., BLEU and ROUGE) as well as the challenges in handling the many-to-many relationship between the assessment items and the multiple national and state standards.

Though model performance shows discrepancy by evaluation metric, the ML solution is highly scalable by leveraging modern cloud computing platforms. For example, in training a Transformer model with 3,048,277 trainable parameters on a training data of 23,831 items-standard pairs, a single epoch only takes about 15 s. The powerful computation engine offered by modern cloud service, coupled with seamless integrations of MLOps workflows offered in the same platform (i.e., Lakehouse architecture for DataOps and MLFlow for model tracking, model registry, and model serving), there is great potential to develop the best-performing model into a production model serving an operational system.

5.2 Limitations

Due to the scope and time constraint, the current study explores feasibility in automated content-standards alignment focusing on only ELA items for Grade 3–8. Extending the current approach to math items requires special vectorization of the math formulas (currently encoded in Latex) and images (currently coded as HTML tags referencing the image source). These non-text elements typically convey relevant or complementary information to the textual elements in the items and would require special vectorization technique to concatenate them with the textual data.

As this study trains the Transformer encoder-decoder model from scratch, limited sample size may be related to the discrepancies in performance between the training and test set, which is indicative of overfitting. This study reveals that the challenges in automated alignment are largely related to the many-to-many relationships between the items and standards as well as the similarities among the items or standards. Better ways to structure either the items or the standards are needed.

5.3 Future Directions

One solution to the overfitting problem is to leverage the technique of warm-starting pre-trained Transformer encoder-decoder model to skip costly pre-training. [36] showed competitive results by warm-starting pre-trained encoder and/or decoder (e.g., BERT, GPT2) on multiple sequence-to-sequence tasks at a fraction of the training cost [37].

Moreover, model performance is expected to improve using more structured data. On the item side, incorporating structural tags that indicate the categories of content block or item stems and encode this information in the input layer can aim to make the model aware of the higher-level information in the item data. On the standards side, a transitive approach can be explored, where the encoder-decoder model can be trained to align the items to a general taxonomy of learning expectations developed by subject matter experts (SMEs), applying a higher level of abstraction across multiple state and national standards. Once the "crosswalk" is developed and validated by SMEs, it can serve as the target sequence to which either the assessment items or the standards can be mapped, establishing the link between the items and the standards.

References

1. Common Core State Standards Initiative. http://www.corestandards.org. Accessed 25 May 2022
2. Nelson, G.D.: AAAS Web page (1997). http://www.project2061.org/publications/articles/nelson/nelson1.htm. Accessed 25 May 2022
3. Diekema, A.R.: Implications and challenges of educational standards metadata. J. Libr. Metadata 9(3–4), 239–251 (2009). https://doi.org/10.1080/19386380903405157
4. Kendall, J.S.: The use of metadata for the identification and retrieval of resources for K–12 education. In: Proceedings of the 2003 International Conference on Dublin Core and Metadata Applications: Supporting Communities of Discourse and Practice—Metadata Research & Applications. Seattle, Washington (2003)
5. Purpose of this Work. http://www.mcrel.org/standards-benchmarks/docs/purpose.asp. Accessed 25 May 2022
6. Yilmazel, O., Ingersoll, G., Liddy, E.D.: Finding questions to your answers. In: IEEE 23rd International Conference on Data Engineering, pp. 755–759. IEEE, New York (2007)
7. Reitsma, R.F., Diekema, A.R.: Comparison of human and machine-based educational standard assignment networks. Int. J. Digit. Libr. 11, 209–223 (2010). https://doi.org/10.1007/s00799-011-0074-8
8. Khan, S.M., Rosaler, J., Hamer, J., Almeida, T.: Catalog: an educational content tagging system. In: Proceedings of the 14th International Conference on Educational Data Mining. Virtual (2021)
9. Jay, M., Longdon, D.: Death, taxes and correlations: a primer on the state of correlation in the K-12 education. Upgrade, SIIA, 20–21 (2003)
10. Reitsma, R., Marshall, B., Chart, T.: Can intermediary-based science standards crosswalking work? Some evidence from mining the standard alignment tool (SAT). J. Am. Soc. Inf. Sci. Technol. 63(9), 1843–1858 (2012)
11. Diekema, A.R., Yilmazel, O., Bailey, J., Harwell, S.C., Liddy, E.D.: Standards alignment for metadata assignment. In: Proceedings of the Joint Conference of Digital Libraries. Vancouver, BC (2007)
12. Diekema, A.R., Chen, J.: Experimenting with the automatic assignment of educational standards of digital library content. In: Proceedings of the 5th ACM/IEE-CS Joint Conference on Digital Libraries, pp. 223–224. Association for Computing Machinery, New York, NY (2005). https://doi.org/10.1145/1065385.1065436
13. Devaul, H., Diekema, A.R., Ostwald, J.: Computer-assisted assignment of educational standards using natural language processing. J. Am. Soc. Inf. Sci. Technol. 62, 395–405 (2011)
14. Reitsma, R., Marshall, B., Dalton, M., Cyr, M.: Exploring educational standard alignment: in search of 'relevance'. In: Proceedings of the 8th ACM/IEEE-CS Joint Conference on Digital libraries, pp. 57–65. Association for Computing Machinery New York, NY (2008). https://doi.org/10.1145/1378889.1378901

15. Sutton, S., Golder, D.: Achievement Standards Network (ASN): an application profile for mapping K–12 educational resources to achievement standards. In: Proceedings of the International Conference on Dublin Core and Metadata Applications. Berlin, Germany (2008)
16. Yilmazel, O., Balasubramanian, N., Harwell, S.C., Bailey, J., Diekema, A.R., Liddy, E.D.: Text categorization for aligning educational standards. In: Proceedings of the 40th Hawaii International Conference of Systems Sciences. IEEE, New York (2007)
17. Ainsworth, L.: "Unwrapping" the Standards: A Simple Process to Make Standards Manageable. Advanced Learning Press, Denver, CO (2003)
18. Sutton, S.A.: Metadata quality, utility and the Semantic Web: the case of learning resources and achievement standards. Cat. Classif. Q. **46**(1), 81–107 (2008)
19. Vaswani, A., et al.: Attention is all you need. In: Proceedings of the 31st Conference on Neural Information Processing Systems. Long Beach, CA (2017)
20. Ruder, S.: Tracking progress in natural language processing. NLP-progress (2022). http://nlp progress.com/
21. Yu, R., Das, S., Gurajada, S., Varshney, K., Raghavan, H., Lastra-Anadon, C.: A research framework for understanding education-occupation alignment with NLP techniques. In: Proceedings of the 1st Workshop on NLP for Positive Impact, pp. 100–106 (2021)
22. Devlin, J., Chang, M.W., Lee, K., Toutanova, K.: BERT: pre-training of deep bidirectional transformers for language understanding. arXiv preprint arXiv: 1810.04805 (2018)
23. Hochreiter, S., Schmidhuber, J.: Long short-term memory. Neural Comput. **9**(8), 1735–1780 (1997)
24. National Governors Association Center for Best Practices, Council of Chief State School Officers: Common Core State Standards for English Language Arts. National Governors Association Center for Best Practices, Council of Chief State School Officers, Washington, DC (2010)
25. Cizek, G.J., Kosh, A.E., Toutkoushian, E.: Gathering and evaluating validity evidence: the generalized assessment alignment tool. J. Educ. Meas. **55**(4), 477–512 (2018)
26. Martone, A., Sireci, S.: Evaluating alignment between curriculum, assessment, and instruction. Rev. Educ. Res. **79**(4), 1332–1361 (2009)
27. Honnibal, M., Montani, I.: spaCy 2: natural language understanding with Bloom embeddings, convolutional neural networks and incremental parsing (2017). https://spacy.io
28. Wolf, T., et al.: Transformers: state-of-the-art natural language processing. In: Proceedings of the 2020 Conference on Empirical Methods in Natural Language Processing: System Demonstrations, pp. 38–45 (2020)
29. Trevett, B.: pytorch-seq2seq [Source code] (2022). https://github.com/bentrevett/pytorch-seq 2seq
30. Pennington, J., Socher, R., Manning, C.D.: Glove: global vectors for word representation. In: Proceedings of the 2014 Conference on Empirical Methods in Natural Language Processing, pp. 1532–1543. A meeting of SIGDAT, a Special Interest Group of the ACL, Doha, Qatar (2014)
31. Rehurek, R., Sojka, P.: Gensim–Python framework for vector space modelling. NLP Centre, Faculty of Informatics, Masaryk University, Brno, Czech Republic **3**(2), 2 (2011)
32. Reimers, N., Gurevych, I.: Sentence-BERT: sentence embeddings using siamese BERT-networks. In: Proceedings of the 2019 Conference on Empirical Methods in Natural Language Processing and the 9th International Joint Conference on Natural Language Processing, pp. 3982–3992. Association for Computational Linguistics. Hong Kong, China (2019)
33. Lin, C.Y.: ROUGE: a package for automatic evaluation of summaries. In: Text summarization branches out, pp. 74–81 (2004)
34. Tatman, R.: Evaluating text output in NLP: BLEU at your own risk. Towards Data Science. (2019). https://towardsdatascience.com/evaluating-text-output-in-nlp-bleu-at-your-own-risk-e8609665a213

35. Qi, Y., Sachan, D.S., Felix, M., Padmanabhan, S.J., Neubig, G.: When and why are pre-trained word embeddings useful for neural machine translation? arXiv preprint arXiv: 1804.06323 (2018)
36. Rothe, S., Narayan, S., Severyn, A.: Leveraging pre-trained checkpoints for sequence generation tasks. Trans. Assoc. Comput. Linguist. **8**, 264–280 (2020)
37. Von Platten, P.: Leveraging re-trained language model checkpoints for encoder-decoder models. Hugging Face (2020). https://huggingface.co/blog/warm-starting-encoder-decoder

Games and Gamification

Servitization Through VR Serious Games: From Manufacturing to Consumer Electronics

Vassilis Charissis[1]([✉]) [iD], Mohammed Soheeb Khan[1], and David K. Harrison[2]

[1] Virtual Reality and Simulation Laboratory, School of Computing, Engineering and Built Environment, Glasgow Caledonian University, Glasgow, UK
`v.charissis@gmail.com`
[2] Department of Mechanical Engineering, School of Computing, Engineering and Built Environment, Glasgow Caledonian University, Glasgow, UK

Abstract. The provision of services instead of the actual products is becoming a major area of interest for the products provision companies involved in the manufacturing, electronics and construction industries amongst others. Current work in the dissemination of the benefits of this business strategy has highlighted significant issues particular in services that require complex planning and bespoke structure for each client. The provision of such services is gradually migrating from the manufacturing sector to fintech and consumer electronics. The latter is a key part of the automotive industry and the new emerging technologies adopted by the rising market of Electric Vehicles (EV). Based on previous work on gamification of fintech servitization, this work explores the use of gamification to promote and demystify new software services and technologies in the automotive sector. To gauge the impact of gamification for such complex servitization offers, this study employs a case study of a prototype Augmented Reality (AR) – Head-Up Display (HUD) system. The AR-HUD has been evaluated by 15 users in the Virtual Reality Driving Simulation Laboratory (VRDS Lab) aiming to identify user experience (UX) and educate the potential customers on the benefits of these technologies and the value of the relevant software upgrades.

Keywords: Consumer electronics · Car software · Servitization · Gamification · User experience · Augmented reality · Virtual reality · Head-up display · Simulation

1 Introduction

The current demand for sustainability for resources and products in manufacturing has led to a new business model termed servitization. In this model, the end-user receives the functionality of a product rather than the product itself [1]. Additional maintenance options and output improvements can be included to enhance the product's functionality and lifespan. This business strategy reduces waste and improves profits for the providing company [2]. Servitization has already been utilised in numerous industries with encouraging results [1, 2].

© Springer Nature Switzerland AG 2022
G. Meiselwitz et al. (Eds.): HCII 2022, LNCS 13517, pp. 545–555, 2022.
https://doi.org/10.1007/978-3-031-22131-6_40

Beyond the aforementioned benefits of this strategy, there are also a few drawbacks that could hinder the adaption of servitization offers. The most prominent is the customisation of the required product and services for each user and secondly the subsequent successful explanation of such offers to the customer. These offers can be challenging to comprehend for the majority of potential customers as they typically entail complex and diverse service structures and costings for customers and stakeholders. As a result, this could limit the customers' interest who cannot justify or reflect the services' value to their businesses.

To mitigate this issue various Digitally Enhanced Advanced Services (DEAS) technologies and schemes have been employed. Previous work has presented the use of emerging technologies such as Virtual/Augmented Reality (VR/AR), 3D, simulations and gamification that could better portray these complex offers. To this end, the use of serious games could entice potential customers to explore in a simple yet enjoyable manner the benefits of servitization offers [3].

The manufacturing arm of particular industries, such as automotive, heavily relies upon the inclusion of consumer electronics in modern vehicles [4–6]. The provision of consumer electronics (CE) and services play a major role in the users' experience (UX) and the decision-making process for the purchase of a vehicle and the subsequent services. This is becoming a major factor in electric vehicles (EVs) that primarily portray the provision of advanced technologies and comforts for the vehicle occupants [7, 8].

This paper will initially discuss the current manufacturing servitization process and the use of gamification to present the DEAS offers to the customer based on a real-life example from heavy industry [3–5]. In turn, it will present a prototype AR Head-Up Display (HUD) system that utilises gesture recognition for the interaction with the AR icons to control the vehicle's infotainment system safely [9–11]. As the majority of the future vehicles are expected to have VR/AR capabilities in the cabin, such applications could be downloaded and embedded into the main product/vehicle through a service offer/agreement. The provision of systems that enhance human responses and reduce collisions could further be linked to parametric insurance offers mirroring the selection of applications and systems that support safer driving. The explanation of the system and the related services are presented through a VR simulation serious game that enables the potential customers to experience the benefits of such a product and inform their decision regarding the acquisition of the relevant service.

The AR-HUD system has been evaluated by 15 users in the Virtual Reality Driving Simulation Laboratory (VRDS Lab). The latter is a scale 1–1, fully immersive VR driving simulator developed for the assessment of in-vehicle prototype systems. The results of the users' responses will be analysed and discussed in contrast to their initial appraisal of such systems before experiencing their functionality in the VR simulation.

2 Gamification and Servitization

2.1 Gamification for Servitization Offers

The majority of computer games produced are for entertainment; however, their application can be beneficial for various sectors and disciplines in conveying information, simulation and/ or education.

Businesses in various sectors that do not commonly engage with expertise beyond their specialism may not see the potential of this innovative technology as a solution to their problems. Current studies that utilise gamification for training purposes or to present complex ideas have produced encouraging results [12–15].

2.2   Servitization in Manufacturing, Fintech and Construction

The delivery of the aforementioned automotive servitization offers bears similarities to other servitization strategies, particularly in the fintech domain. Previous work on the latter presented significant difficulties in the explanation of such offers to the potential customers [3]. This was a result of the offers' complexity and bespoke structure which overcomplicated the potential choices. Such offers were met with reduced interest as the customers couldn't identify quickly and clearly the benefits of the offers or the potential risks of not acquiring them.

To alleviate this issue it was deemed essential to simplify the information and explain them through an unconventional conduit namely a serious game. The gamification of such complex information and its presentation through a relaxing and enjoyable channel presented a significant uptake by the potential customers as they experienced the different scenarios and the benefits of the offers through a playable simulation [3–5]. In the fintech project, several financial products were developed to customise the insurance offers for various construction projects.

These offers were designed to reflect different potential weather or construction issues that could hinder or in some cases stop completely the development of a building. The project embedded a complex set of weather data patterns based on previous recorded and analysed information. The above was used to predict potential weather issues that might negatively affect the construction as presented in Fig. 1 and 2.

Fig. 1. Screenshot of the 3D application which presents a construction progress overview.

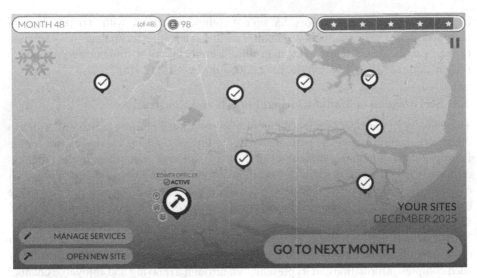

Fig. 2. Overview of the construction sites and weather predictions for each month.

3 Vehicular Consumer Electronics and Servitization

3.1 Current Consumer Electronics Trends

The servitization in the automotive industry currently appears through a two-fold approach. Firstly the automotive companies are experimenting with the monthly or yearly renting of vehicles through a subscription system. Through this avenue, the customer can use different vehicles of the same company or group of affiliated companies, for a period of time, by paying a monthly subscription that covers the use of the vehicle, services and other related expenses [6–8].

These offers vary per automotive company but this approach becomes gradually popular as enables the customer/user to experience different vehicles. The latter allows the customer to use vehicles for their different activities or requirements without committing to one particular type of car that might not be ideal for all situations. In addition, the companies are producing vehicles depending on the customer requirement trends and as such reducing waste both in materials and energy consumption.

The second type of servitization is focusing mainly on the consumer electronics embedded within the vehicles. Typically the hardware is preinstalled in these vehicles and the software can be activated remotely or through a quick visit to the authorized dealer depending on the customer's subscription. These subscriptions can enable various extra features related to infotainment, safety and automation of the vehicles and are becoming a major attraction point, particularly for the electric vehicles (EV). As electric motors have very specific capabilities and output the customization options of fossil fuel engines cannot be applied. As such EV manufacturers have redirected the customers' attention to consumer electronics that could offer additional interaction and user experience (UX) with the vehicle such as different User Interfaces (UI), live traffic visualization, karaoke, music and video streaming, internet browsing and different levels of autonomous capabilities [7, 8].

3.2 Vehicular Servitization

Based on the aforementioned fintech and manufacturing projects this work aimed to transfer the development experience and users' feedback to the automotive sector and particularly to the vehicular consumer electronics that employ emerging technologies such as VR/AR, and Artificial Intelligence [16–18].

As these technologies are not commonly available in the mainstream segment of the automotive market, their benefits are unknown to the everyday user and typically appear as another expensive gadget in a long list of add-on equipment in the vehicle's optional specifications. In addition, such devices could facilitate additional software add-ons and updates which could fall within the servitization business model. Yet, these software servitization offers are not typically selected as the hardware equipment is not selected and installed in the original vehicle specifications.

In order to present both hardware and software offers to the potential customers, we considered the gamification of the above through a driving simulator that could clarify the use and derived benefits of the equipment.

3.3 AR HUD Case Study

To test the above hypothesis, this work utilised a prototype AR HUD interface which assists the driver to filter and prioritise the incoming infotainment data. The particular interface presents three types of data related to navigation, mobile phone text messages and phone calls as illustrated in Fig. 3. The information is typically controlled and withheld by the software until is safe for the driver to read and interact with them. The interaction is enabled through a gesture-recognition interface that complements the visual User Interface (UI) [9]. This direct manipulation interaction method enables the user to operate the AR HUD without gazing away from the road [19, 20]. The latter advantage is in contrast to current Head-Down Display (HDD) and small screen HUD systems [21].

The benefits of the prototype system were documented through previous evaluation studies designed to compare existing Head-Down Displays and HUDs [10, 11, 20]. However, the demand for such systems is limited due to the inadequate clarification from the current servitization systems in place.

In addition, the potential customers have no prior user experience (UX) of even similar systems and this further contributed to the limited adoption. To identify the intention of the potential customers to use such a system and accept the servitization cost involved this work utilised the gamification option following closely the game design principles used for the fintech and manufacturing projects mentioned above. Nevertheless, the propagation of such systems and devices to newer vehicles is expected as the EV sales and servitization models gradually expand as a market segment against fossil fuel engine vehicles.

Fig. 3. Simulation screenshot of the AR HUD and gesture recognition for controlling infotainment sources.

4 Simulation

To evaluate the users' experience and acceptance of the prototype hardware, as well as the provision of different servitization, offers based on the software provision this work utilised a full-scale driving simulator based on a real-life vehicle (Mercedes A-Class 2003 model). The simulator immerses the user within a CAVE (Cave Automatic Virtual Environment) projection system. The immersion is further reinforced with the use of surround audio (5.1) and vibrotactile devices imitating road-surface irregularities [10].

5 Evaluation

5.1 Evaluation Method

For the evaluation of the system, this study employed 5-point Likert Scale Questions. The evaluation process involved a prequestionnaire of six questions which collected primarily the demographic information of the participants and previous knowledge of computing, computer games and driving habits.

In the second stage of the evaluation, the participants drove in a 28 miles Scottish motorway network between Glasgow, Edinburgh and Stirling. During the driving, a series of events (i.e. incoming text messages and navigation warnings) occurred aiming to distract the driver and increase the probability of rear collision with lead braking vehicles [10, 22, 23]. This scenario was repeated seamlessly with and without the HUD interface, following previous studies for HUD interfaces [10, 11, 24].

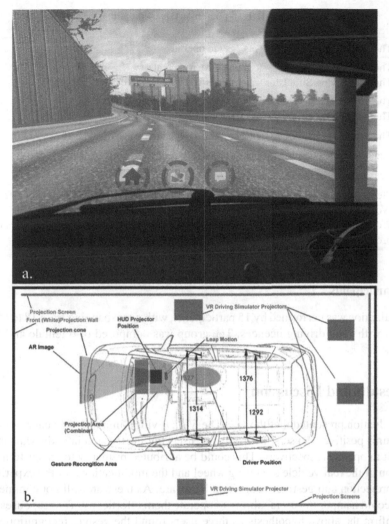

Fig. 4. (a) Driver's and gesture recognition version (b) Top view schematic of the Virtual Reality Driving Simulator laboratory (VRDS Lab)

After the simulation, the participants completed a post-questionnaire designed to acquire information related to their experience (UX), the simulation/serious game concept, and the embedded learning goals for the HUD system servitization offers as presented in Table 1. The questionnaire was based on similar studies that utilised Technology Acceptance Models to measure the user experience and identify the future purchasing tendencies for new products and services [25–29].

Table 1. 5 point likert questionnaire

Q7	The VR Driving Simulator was easy to operate
Q8	The gesture recognition system was easy to operate
Q9	The VR Driving Simulator was immersive and enjoyable
Q10	The AR HUD User Interface (UI), supported the driving experience
Q11	The AR HUD User Interface (UI), enhanced the driver's safety
Q12	The benefits of the AR HUD were clearly explained and experienced
Q13	I can clearly see the benefits of the AR HUD hardware
Q14	I can clearly see the benefits of the AR HUD software
Q15	Please rate your preference comparing the proposed AR HUD to the HDD interface
Q16	Would you purchase the AR HUD hardware for your vehicle?
Q17	Would you purchase additional software updates, subscriptions and service offers for this product?

5.2 Participants

The evaluation was performed by 15 participants, with ages spanning from 18 to 60 years old and with valid driving licences. The group was composed of 6 female and 9 male drivers.

6   Results and Discussion

The evaluation presented that the Q7 (The VR Driving Simulator was easy to operate) was mainly positive (10 users) with only two users finding the simulator difficult and very difficult to operate respectively. This could be attributed primarily to the custom reconstruction of the real vehicle's steering wheel and the modifications for the experimental HUD projection and gesture recognition hardware. As these are still not commercially ready, could hamper the users' ability to operate them effortlessly. The responses on the Q8 confirm the above hypothesis as three users found the gesture recognition system difficult to operate and two users were neutral. The results of Q9 were 100% positive (agree and strongly agree) on the statement "The VR Driving Simulator was immersive and enjoyable". This outcome highlights that the gamification method to present the functionality and benefits of additional software and servitization offers could entice the users through an enjoyable learning process.

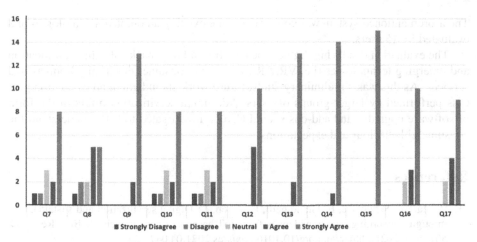

Fig. 5. Post questionnaire results of 15 users.

The HUD scored equally well on Q10 and Q11 proving again the point that the users experienced the product through this gamification avenue and understood the benefits of acquiring the relevant services that could improve their driving performance and reduce unnecessary distractions. In turn, Q12, Q13 and Q14 received high scores reinforcing further the above assumption.

The users' preference for the AR/ HUD interface (Q15) was 100% in contrast to the typical HDD highlighting a paradigm shift toward the typical vehicle instrumentation. This could be a result of the younger generations of drivers that are accustomed to advanced user interfaces that support smartphone/tablet interactions and gaming environments overall. Finally, the last two questions aimed to identify the intention to purchase the add-on equipment (Q16) and the software services (Q17) revealed that the users were keen to purchase (agree and strongly agree) both offers. Overall the results of the post-questionnaire illustrated an improved understanding of the software services and offers that could be provided with the use of an AR HUD system. This is in direct contrast to the pre-questionnaire where 100% of the users could not see the point of having a HUD device and the relevant software services. As such, before experiencing the system in the gamified version of the VR driving simulator, the users considered such devices and software applications as contemporary trends and gadgets with no particular value to the driving task. As shown by the post-simulation evaluation results their views on this matter changed significantly. This provides encouraging results for the future use of gamification for explaining complex services to potential customers.

7 Conclusions

The paper presented an overview of the servitization offers that currently advance in multiple domains such as manufacturing, finance and consumer electronics. In turn, the paper demonstrated the use of gamification through a VR driving simulator to convey and explain the benefits of emerging technologies and software upgrades in the vehicular environment. To demonstrate the above this work used an AR HUD interface case study.

The aforementioned system was contrasted to the existing automotive technologies and evaluated by 15 users.

The evaluation results highlighted the benefits and drawbacks of using gamification and emerging technologies (i.e. VR/AR) to present consumer electronic products and services. As this was a preliminary study, future work should entail an evaluation process performed by larger groups of users. Additional servitization offers in the form of software upgrades and add-ons should also be investigated to better understand the consumers' behaviour and expectations.

References

1. Paiola, M., Schiavone, F., Grandinetti, R., Chen, J.: Digital servitization and sustainability through networking: some evidences from IoT-based business models. J. Bus. Res. **132**, 507–516 (2021). https://doi.org/10.1016/j.jbusres.2021.04.047
2. Falcão, C.S., Soares, M.M.: Application of virtual reality technologies in consumer product usability. In: Marcus, A. (ed.) DUXU 2013. LNCS, vol. 8015, pp. 342–351. Springer, Heidelberg (2013). https://doi.org/10.1007/978-3-642-39253-5_37
3. Khan, M.S., et al.: Improving user experience and communication of digitally enhanced advanced services (DEAS) offers in manufacturing sector. Multimodal Technol. Interact. **6**, 21 (2022). https://doi.org/10.3390/mti6030021
4. Opazo-Basáez, M., Vendrell-Herrero, F., Bustinza, O.F.: Uncovering productivity gains of digital and green servitization: implications from the automotive industry. Sustainability **10**(5), 1524 (2018). https://doi.org/10.3390/su10051524
5. Schroeder, A., Naik, P., Ziaee Bigdeli, A., Baines, T.: Digitally enabled advanced services: a socio-technical perspective on the role of the internet of things (IoT). Int. J. Oper. Prod. Manag. **40**, 1243–1268 (2020)
6. Kjellberg, R., Lagerkvist, E.: Servitization in Car Industry: a case study of the concept Care by Volvo. Master's degree project in innovation and industrial management. School of Business, Economics and Law, University of Gothenburg (2018)
7. Tesla, Support: Full Self-Driving Capability Subscriptions (2022a). https://www.tesla.com/support/full-self-driving-subscriptions#pricing. Accessed 28 May 2022
8. Tesla, Support: Connectivity (2022b). https://www.tesla.com/en_GB/support/connectivity. Accessed 28 May 2022
9. Lagoo, R., Charissis, V., Harrison, D.K.: Mitigating driver's distraction: automotive head-up display and gesture recognition system. IEEE Consumer Electron. Magaz. **8**(5), 79–85 (2019). https://doi.org/10.1109/MCE.2019.2923896
10. Charissis, V., et al.: Employing Emerging technologies to develop and evaluate in-vehicle intelligent systems for driver support: infotainment AR HUD case study. Appl. Sci. **11**, 1397 (2021). https://doi.org/10.3390/app11041397
11. Wang, S., Charissis, V., Harrison, D., Augmented reality prototype HUD for passenger infotainment in a vehicular environment. Adv. Sci. Technol. Eng. Syst. J. 634–641 (2017)
12. Yang, Y., Asaad, Y., Dwivedi, Y.: Examining the impact of gamification on intention of engagement and brand attitude in the marketing context. Comput. Hum. Behav. **73**, 459–469 (2017)
13. García-Magro, C., Soriano-Pinar, I.: Design of services in servitized firms: gamification as an adequate tool. J. Bus. Indust. Market. **35**(3), 575–585 (2020). https://doi.org/10.1108/JBIM-12-2018-0413

14. Ciuchita, R., Heller, J., Köcher, S., et al.: It is really not a game: an integrative review of gamification for service research. J. Serv. Res. (2022). https://doi.org/10.1177/109467052 21076272

15. Falah J., et al.: Identifying the characteristics of virtual reality gamification for complex educational topics. Multimodal. Technol. Interact. **5**, 53 (2021). https://doi.org/10.3390/mti 5090053

16. Planing, P., Britzelmaier, B.: Understanding consumer acceptance of advanced driver assistance systems – a qualitative study on the german market. Int. J. Sales Retail. Market. 32–40 (2012)

17. Li, J., Cheng, H., Guo, H., Qiu, S.: Survey on artificial intelligence for vehicles. Autom. Innov. **1**(1), 2–14 (2018). https://doi.org/10.1007/s42154-018-0009-9

18. Frank, M., Drikakis, D., Charissis, V.: Machine-learning methods for computational science and engineering. Computation **8**, 15 (2020)

19. Tastan, H., Tuker, C., Tong, T.: Using handheld user interface and direct manipulation for architectural modeling in immersive virtual reality: An exploratory study. Comput. Appl. Eng. Educ. **30**, 415–434 (2022). https://doi.org/10.1002/cae.22463

20. Charissis, V., Naef, M., Papanastasiou, S., Patera, M.: Designing a direct manipulation HUD interface for in-vehicle infotainment. In: Jacko, J.A. (eds.) Human-Computer Interaction. Interaction Platforms and Techniques. HCI 2007. LNCS, vol 4551, pp. 551–559. Springer, Berlin, Heidelberg (2007). https://doi.org/10.1007/978-3-540-73107-8_62

21. Wang, Y., et al.: Inattentional blindness in augmented reality head-up displayassisted driving. Int. J. Hum. Comput. Interact. **38**, 9, 837–850 (2022). https://doi.org/10.1080/10447318.2021. 1970434

22. Young, K.L., Salmon, P.M.: Examining the relationship between driver distraction and driving errors: a discussion of theory, studies and methods. Safety Sci. **50**(2), 165–174 (2012) https://doi.org/10.1016/j.ssci.2011.07.008

23. Wang, J., Wang, W., Hansen, P., Li, Y., You, F.: The situation awareness and usability research of different HUD HMI design in driving while using adaptive cruise control. In: Stephanidis, C., Duffy, V.G., Streitz, N., Konomi, S., Krömker, H. (eds.) HCII 2020. LNCS, vol. 12429, pp. 236–248. Springer, Cham (2020). https://doi.org/10.1007/978-3-030-59987-4_17

24. Charissis, V., Papanastasiou, S., Mackenzie, L., Arafat, S.: Evaluation of collision avoidance prototype head-up display interface for older drivers. In: Jacko, J.A. (ed.) HCI 2011. LNCS, vol. 6763, pp. 367–375. Springer, Heidelberg (2011). https://doi.org/10.1007/978-3-642-21616-9_41

25. Andrae, A.S.G., Andersen, O.: Life cycle assessments of consumer electronics are they consistent? Int. J. Life Cycle Assess. **15**, 827–836 (2010). https://doi.org/10.1007/s11367-010-0206-1

26. Planing, P.: Innovation Acceptance: The Case of Advanced Driver-Assistance Systems, Springer Gabler (2014)

27. Marangunić, N., Granić, A.: Technology acceptance model: a literature review from 1986 to 2013. Univ. Access Inf. Soc. **14**(1), 81–95 (2014). https://doi.org/10.1007/s10209-014-0348-1

28. Altarteer, S., Charissis, V.: Technology acceptance model for 3d virtual reality system in luxury brands online stores. IEEE Access J. **7**, 64053–64062 (2019). https://doi.org/10.1109/ACCESS.2019.2916353

29. Kuo-Yi, L., Pei-I, Y., Pei-Chun, C., Chen-Fu, C.: User experience-based design of experiments for new product development of consumer electronics and an empirical study. J. Ind. Prod. Eng. **34**(7), 504–519 (2017). https://doi.org/10.1080/21681015.2017.1363089

The Moderator of Gamification of Physical Activities in Older Adults

Hsi-Jen Chen and Yao-Sheng Wu[✉]

Department of Industrial Design, National Cheng Kung University, Tainan, Taiwan R.O.C.
neilwu0906@gmail.com

Abstract. As the increase of age, many physical and psychological functions of aging and decline are derived. Through appropriate regular exercise, the impact of aging can be delayed. Based on the health problems of the elderly, this study attempts to understand the relationship between motivation and physical activity in older adults through gamification design strategies to help older adults stay healthy. Gamification design strategy is a design strategy that adds game elements in a non-game context, and to create a playing game-like experience to stimulates people's motivations and behaviors. Therefore, we conducted a questionnaire survey of 195 elderly people (over 50 years old) to analyzed the relationship between player motivation and gamification effects, further considering their individual differences such as gender, exercise frequency and game habits. The results shows the elderly people think that autonomy, sense of mission, and sense of accomplishment are all important; change is the least important. The elderly believe that major missions and calls, impact possibilities, development and achievement, social influence and empathy, and creativity and feedback are all important; scarcity and urgency, loss and avoidance are the least important. The elderly who play games agree that the sense of autonomy and accomplishment of the game is higher than that of the elderly who do not play games.

Keywords: Gamification · Player types · Physical activities · Older adults

1 Introduction

Many previous studies suggested that appropriate physical activities could reduce the impact of cognitive and physical senescence with aging (Clarkson-Smith and Hartley 1989; Hultsch et al. 1993; Penedo and Dahn 2005), and it is one of the important factors in healthy life (Pate et al. 1995; Chodzko-Zajko et al. 2009). Therefore, how to improve the amount of physical activity in older adults be an important issue in many fields research.

One of the most effective ways to promote physical activity in older adults is gamification (Consolvo et al. 2006; Shlomo et al. 2010), which uses game design elements, or game-like methods, to encourage older adults to increase their physical activity. Gamification design strategy is a design strategy that adds game elements in a non-game context, generating behavioral mechanisms similar to "playing a game" to motivate their target behavior(Hamari and Lehdonvirta 2010; Deterding et al. 2011; Chou 2016).Gamification

© Springer Nature Switzerland AG 2022
G. Meiselwitz et al. (Eds.): HCII 2022, LNCS 13517, pp. 556–566, 2022.
https://doi.org/10.1007/978-3-031-22131-6_41

design has been widely used for the purpose of promoting healthy living behaviors, improving sports performance (Consolvo et al. 2006; Shlomo et al. 2010), and can be effectively applied in the promotion of physical activity in the elderly (Ijsselsteijn et al. 2007; Kappen et al. 2016).

The effect of gamification on changing behavior can often be explained by the principles of self-determination theory (SDT) (Ryan and Deci 2000; Lamprinou and Paraskeva 2015; Landers et al. 2015), which suggests that gamification providing persuasive revelations and pleasant rewards (Fogg 2009 and 2002; Hamari et al. 2014) can increase extrinsic and/or intrinsic motivation more than the original context.

In recent years, research on gamification and player motivation has gradually shifted from exploring the motivation of the entire target group to considering the individual differences of the target group, so that gamification strategies can be driven more effectively and accurately. The factor including demographic variables (gender, Codish and Ravid 2017; age, Bittner and Shipper 2014), personalities (Sajanee 2010; Yuan 2016; Orji et al. 2017), player types (Tondello 2016).

As known from previous studies, gamification is driven by player's motivation that are affected by the factors of individual differences or player types. Therefore, the purpose of this study is to improve the physical activities of the older adults through gamification design, and to figure out the relationship between the effect of gamification to stimulate behavior changes and moderator in advance. The study expects to establish the predictive relationship between player motivations of the older adult and the effects of gamification, and add factors such as individual differences, exercise frequency, and game play habit to explore moderating variables.

1.1 Gamification Design Strategy

In the study, the key framework of Gamification Design Strategy is refer to Chou's (2016) book "Actionable Gamification: Beyond Points, Badges, and Leaderboards". Chou thinks gamification design is to extract interesting and fantastic elements from games and use them in real-world situations to improve users' engagement and motivation of target behaviors. According to Chou's book, eight core gamification strategies are proposed as a frameworks and strategy foundation for gamified design:

1. Epic Meaning & Calling (EC): this core strategy is to convince users that they are doing something meaningful and to feel a sense of adventure or competence.
2. Development & Accomplishment (DA): This core strategy is the most common in games. It lets users focus on growth, achieve specific goals and work hard, and in the process gain a sense of accomplishment such as player scores, badges, achievements, and milestones.
3. Empowerment of Creativity & Feedback (EF): this core strategy requires users to be creative and see immediate results. Diverse results are obtained through the infinite creativity in the game, so that users are deeply attracted.
4. Ownership & Possession (OP): this core strategy is closely related to ownership and possessiveness. Players can feel like they are doing something on their own terms - like developing a game, or earning their own virtual currency or collecting virtual treasures.

5. Social Influence & Relatedness (SR): this core strategy is derived from people's desire to socialize, in order to integrate into social groups, they often show behaviors that can be recognized by society to avoid social rejection. In games, such as the mentoring system, teamwork, and competition mechanisms.
6. Scarcity & Impatience (SI): This strategy is often used in business marketing. According to economics, scarcity occurs when demand exceeds a finite resource. Due to the scarcity of goods, users are fascinated by spending money and time queuing up to buy these goods.
7. Unpredictability & Curiosity (UC): People are curious about the unforeseen. This strategy uses the player's curiosity to drive the player. In Skinner Box, a famous behavioral experiment by psychologist Skinner (1990), it was found that unexpected positive reinforcement stimuli can increase the frequency of behavior more than expected or completely unrelated stimuli.
8. Loss & Avoidance (LA): This strategy comes from people's fear of losing things. The longest use of "health" in game characters is that there are many game designs. When the virtual character dies, the game journey must be restarted. Players feel that they have put in a lot of effort and time, and it would be quite frustrating to start over, so avoid this. In addition, Chou (2016) thinks that people are equally afraid of losing what they "already got" in addition to being afraid of losing what they "will get".

1.2 Gamification Design and Individual Differences

Discussions of individual differences in gamification research can be explored in terms of demographic variables, motivations, interests, personalities, habits, etc. As early as 1996, Bartle considered the relationship between different personality traits of gamers and game behavior, and proposed four types of gamers: achievers, socialites, explorers and killers. Each player type is attracted to different game elements, resulting in different behaviors and motivations. Yee (2006) further explores Bartle's (1996) player types and proposes three main components of player motivation: achievement (progress, mechanics, competition), social (social, relationships, teamwork), and immersion (discovery), role-playing, customization), out of reality). However, both Bartle and Yee's research materials are specific to the genre of games: massively multiplayer online role-playing games (MMORPGs), and application-level considerations are still open for research.

Later, as the concept of gamification was gradually applied, it was even discussed in academia. Marczewski (2015) formally proposed research on game player types, based on 4 intrinsic motivations and 2 extrinsic motivations defined by Self-Determination Theory (SDT). Marczewski's proposed a 24-item gamification player type test (user type test), which subscales 6 motivations (relatedness, autonomy, mastery, purpose, reward,change) and 12 player types for further comparison. Marczewsk's research makes gamification design develop from the game field to other non-game fields, laying an important foundation for gamification design research.

1.3 Physical Activity and Senior Health

Problems arising from the aging of the elderly, many studies in the past have pointed out that appropriate regular exercise can reduce the impact of cognitive and physiological decline in the elderly (Clarkson-Smith and Hartley 1989; Hultsch et al. 1993; Penedo and Dahn 2005), and even some studies suggest that proper and regular physical activity is one of the important factors affecting the healthy life of the elderly (Pate et al. 1995; Chodzko-Zajko et al. 2009). Numerous studies on aging have identified many of the health benefits of physical activity in older adults. In this study, the judging standard of the amount of physical activity, referring to the research method of Consolvo et al. (2006), took the amount of walking as its basic physical activity.

1.4 Purpose

Summarizing the above literature discussion, it can be inferred that gamification design has many factors affecting user behavior change, including intrinsic and extrinsic motivation, personal ability, difficulty of target behavior, personality and individual differences, behavior habits, etc. (Fogg et al. 2009; Marczewski et al. 2015). Therefore, this study focuses on the factors that influence the behavioral change of gamification design. Considering the user's motivational composition, behavioral habits and other factors, explore the interactive relationship between the benefits of gamification design strategies and behavioral motivations.

Different from the previous discussions on gamification design, which are mostly based on the perspective of analysis or design, this study will further explore the factors that affect the influence of multiple variables on gamification design strategies, and expect to establish a persuasive model for gamification design strategies. Through the setting of parameters (demographic variables, player types, behavioral habits, and the tendency of gamification design strategies), it is predicted that users will produce different degrees of behavioral change effects, which can be extended to subsequent habit establishment.

Explore the effects and moderating variables of the elderly on gamification strategies: from the existing research on gamification strategies, we compiled the main types of gamification strategies, and explored the effect of different gamification designs on the promotion of physical activity by the elderly through a questionnaire method. The degree of effect, as well as a comprehensive consideration of individual differences in the elderly, motivational preferences and player types, exercise habits, and game touchpoint habits. Then, through the analysis method of prediction model, the effect of gamification design on the elderly was clarified, and a quantitative model that could repeat the prediction was proposed.

2 Method

The purpose of this study is to explore the extent to which different motivations, behavioral habits, and frequency of exposure to games affect real behavior for each gamification design strategy. There are multiple factors interacting between behavior and motivation. The research focuses on using the player type scale as a tool to measure motivation, and formulating the corresponding questions of gamification design strategies as the basis for the influence of subjects on various gamification design strategies. Questionnaire items included demographic variables, the Marczewski (2015) Player Type Scale, and 9 gamified situational tests of everyday physical activity.

2.1 Material

The questionnaire method was used to conduct a questionnaire survey for middle-aged and elderly participants over 50 years old, and it is expected that at least 100 valid questionnaires can be collected. The questionnaire design consists of three parts:

1. The first part is a survey of demographic variables. It includes gender, age, whether you are retired, whether you have exercise habits and how often, the sports you do, exercise habits, average daily game frequency, and the name of the game you play.
2. The second part is the Marczewski Player Type Scale (2015). The scale consists of 24 items that can accurately describe the 6 motivations players prefer. Participants were asked to respond to the degree of agreement with the item statement. Items use a 7-point Likert scale ranging from "1: Strongly disagree" to "7: Strongly agree". In the study, the player type scale was translated into Chinese by an academic translation agency, and the final version was revised through a test study ($N = 20$, M of age $= 28.95$, $SD = 9.73$), as shown in Table 1.

Table 1. Test results of the translated version of the Marczewski Player Type Scale ($N = 20$)

Subscale	N of items	M	SD	Skewness	Kurtosis
Relatedness	4	4.69	1.33	0.37	−.535
Autonomy	4	5.70	0.93	−0.52	.082
Mastery	4	5.24	1.21	−0.22	−.330
Purpose	4	5.19	1.19	0.16	−.865
Reward	4	5.09	1.22	−0.38	−.270
Change	4	4.35	1.19	1.03	.452

3. The third part of the questionnaire is a 9-item gamification design situational test, as shown in Table 2. The main goal of gamification design is to enhance the physical activity of elderly people, so the content of the project will be driven by the 8 cores of the gamification design strategy by Chou's book (2016), corresponding to the content of 8 situational quizzes, and 1 question without gamification strategy (general statement). Participants were asked to judge the likelihood that the situation described by the item would affect their physical activity, using a 7-point Likert scale ranging from "1: very unlikely" to "7: very likely".

Table 2. Gamified situation items for the older adults' daily physical exercise.

No.	Statement of Gamified situations (English version)	Gamified strategy
1	The use of gamified design in daily life can encourage you to engage in more physical activity	(General statement)
2	There is a gamified design that let you feel you got an excellent talent, and born to be a star at daily walking	Epic meaning & calling
3	There is a gamified design that allows you to get corresponding scores, badges, achievements, milestones or continuous upgrades based on your daily walking steps	Development & accomplishment
4	There is a gamified design that allows you to activate your creativity and create everything you like, that based on the amount of daily walking steps	Empowerment of creativity & feedback
5	There is a gamified design that allows you to obtain virtual wealth or collect virtual treasures, that based on the amount of daily walking steps	Ownership & possession
6	There is a gamified design that allows you to take to cooperate or compete with your friends or players, that based on the amount of daily walking steps	Social influence & relatedness
7	There is a gamified design that gives you a chance to win precious and rare prizes, that based on the amount of daily walking steps	Scarcity & impatience
8	There is a gamified design that allows you to explore a novel things, and has a chance to get a unpredictable bonus, that based on the amount of daily walking steps	Unpredictability & curiosity
9	There is a gamified design that helps you to avoid virtual losses or penalties when you reach a goal of the amount of walking steps	Loss & avoidance

2.2 Participant

There are 195 participants who aged over 50 years old, including 47.7% of them are 50–59 years old, 46.2% of them are 60–69 years old and 6.1% of them are 70+ years old; there are 105 females adults (53.8%). Moreover, the most of them (91.8% are used to exercising regularly at least once a week; almost a half of the them (51.3%) are used to playing video games or mobile games.

3 Result

The all questionnaire data from 195 older adults (aged 50+ years old) were analysed by ANOVA. In order to figure out the influence and relationship between player types and gamification design preferences in older adults, the results show that their main effect and correlation with both two. Furthermore, to consider the difference of individual variables in older adults, such as their gender, exercise frequency and habits of playing games.

3.1 Main Effect

An analysis of variance (ANOVA) was calculated based on the participants' responses to the questionnaire. In the Table 3, the summary of the user type hexd scale shows that the within-subject test is significant, $F(3.87, 751.17) = 44.922, p < .05$ (the F-value should be adjected by Greenhouse-Geisser method, because the Mauchly's Test of Sphericitya is not significant, $p < .05$). Furthermore, through the LSD post hoc test, the result shows that there are significant differences between the subscales, summarizing: autonomy[2] = mastery[3] = purpose[4] > relatedness[1] = reward[5] > change[6].

Table 3. The ANOVA table of player types in the older adults.

Subscale	M	SD	ANOVA results	Post Hoc test
Relatedness [1]	4.73	1.51	$Df = 3.87, 751.17$	[1] > [6]
Autonomy [2]	5.12	1.29	F value = 44.922	[2] > [1], [5], [6]
Mastery [3]	5.03	1.28	p value = .000*	[3] > [1], [5], [6]
Purpose [4]	5.06	1.36		[4] > [1], [5], [6]
Rewards [5]	4.65	1.47		[5] > [6]
Change [6]	4.14	1.24		–

* significant at p = < .05.

The analysis of the situational test is shown in the Table 4, and the within-subject test is significant, $F(3.87, 751.17) = 44.922, p < .05$ (the Mauchly's Test of Sphericitya is not significant, too). And then, the result shows that there are significant differences between the subscales through the LSD post hoc test. The conclusion is: Epic Meaning & Calling [2] = Development & Accomplishment [3] = Social Influence & Relatedness [6] = Empowerment of Creativity & Feedback [4] > Ownership & Possession [5] = Unpredictability & Curiosity [8] > Unpredictability & Curiosity [8] > Loss & Avoidance [9].

The individual difference has been discussed frequently in the lots of the game or gamified research. In this research, discuss not only their motivations (that means user type hexad scale) but demographic variables and lifestyles to figure out the elaborate results for older adults.

Table 4. The ANOVA table of gamified strategies in the older adults.

Subscale	M	SD	ANOVA results	Post Hoc test
General statement [1]	5.10	1.61	$Df = 5.42, 1052.35$	(skip)
EC [2]	5.19	1.68	F value $= 11.529$	[2] > [5], [7], [8], [9]
DA [3]	5.07	1.73	p value $= .000*$	[3] > [5], [7], [8], [9]
EF [4]	5.03	1.64		[4] > [5], [7], [8], [9]
OP [5]	4.84	1.66		[5] > [7], [9]
SR [6]	5.04	1.67		[6] > [5], [7], [8], [9]
SI [7]	4.66	1.73		[7] > [9]
UC [8]	4.81	1.70		[8] > [7], [9]
LA [9]	4.43	1.740		–

* significant at p = < .05..

According to the participants' responses to the questionnaire, the one-way ANOVAs were calculated through 4 kinds of individual variables, including gender, retirement, exercise frequency and habits of playing games. The following Table 5 is composed of all the significance in the one-way ANOVA test, and the non-significant results were deleted to make sure the table is simplified and focused (Table 6).

Table 5. The ANOVA table of gamified strategies and player types in the older adults.

Variables		N	M	SD	ANOVA results	Post Hoc test
(Gamified Strategy × Gender)						
EC	Female	90	4.94	1.81	$F(1, 193) = 4.922$	Male > female
	Male	105	5.40	1.54	p value $= .028*$	
LA	Female	90	4.70	1.73	$F(1, 193) = 4.222$	Female > male
	Male	105	4.19	1.72	p value $= .041*$	
(Gamified Strategy × Exercise frequency)						
OP	Never or seldom [1]	16	4.31	1.08	$F(3, 191) = 2.903$	[3] > [2]
	Times monthly [2]	54	4.41	1.78	p value $= .036*$	[4] > [2]
	Times weekly [3]	67	5.03	1.60		
	Everyday [4]	58	5.17	1.67		
SR	never or seldom [1]	16	4.50	1.59	$F(3, 191) = 2.842$	[4] > [1], [2]
					p value $= .039*$	
	Times monthly [2]	54	4.67	1.77		

(*continued*)

Table 5. (*continued*)

Variables		N	M	SD	ANOVA results	Post Hoc test
	Times weekly [3]	67	5.10	1.62		
	Everyday [4]	58	5.47	1.56		
(Player types × Habits of playing games)						
Autonomy	Not playing games	100	4.91	1.38	F(1, 193) = 5.406	Play > no play
	Play games	95	5.33	1.15	p value = .021*	
Mastery	Not playing games	100	4.84	1.31	F(1, 193) = 4.844	Play > no play
	Play games	95	5.23	1.22	p value = .029*	

∗ Significant at p = < .05

Table 6. The correlation table of gamified strategies and player types in the older adults.

Gamified Strategy	Player Motivation					
	Relatedness	Autonomy	Mastery	Purpose	Reward	Change
(General statement)	.443*	.352*	.472*	.483*	.309*	.335*
EC	.494*	.399*	.443*	.533*	.362*	.322*
DA	.468*	.373*	.420*	.467*	.418*	.297*
EF	.513*	.366*	.444*	.469*	.410*	.299*
OP	.423*	.354*	.347*	.347*	.495*	.339*
SR	.544*	.414*	.446*	.501*	.465*	.283*
SI	.466*	.404*	.420*	.413*	.461*	.322*
UC	.520*	.416*	.454*	.509*	.439*	.299*
LA	.436*	.349*	.348*	.360*	.423*	.335*

* *Correlation is significant at the 0.01 level (2-tailed).*

4   Discussion

Elderly people (over 50 years old) think that autonomy, sense of mission, and sense of accomplishment are all important; change is the least important. The elderly believe that major missions and calls, impact possibilities, development and achievement, social influence and empathy, and creativity and feedback are all important; scarcity and urgency, loss and avoidance are the least important. The elderly who play games agree that the sense of autonomy and accomplishment of the game is higher than that of the elderly who do not play games. Elderly females believe that the game strategy of major missions and calls can more stimulate sports; the elderly male believe that the game strategies of loss and avoidance can more stimulate sports; elderly people who exercise more frequently think that game strategies of ownership and possessiveness, social influence and empathy are more capable of inspiring exercise.

References

Clarkson-Smith, L., Hartley, A.A.: Relationships between physical exercise and cognitive abilities in older adults. Psychol. Aging 4(2), 183 (1989)

Hultsch, D.F., Hammer, M., Small, B.J.: Age differences in cognitive performance in later life: relationships to self-reported health and activity life style. J. Gerontol. 48(1), P1–P11 (1993)

Penedo, F.J., Dahn, J.R.: Exercise and well-being: a review of mental and physical health benefits associated with physical activity. Curr. Opin. Psychiatry 18(2), 189–193 (2005)

Pate, R.R., et al.: Physical activity and public health: a recommendation from the Centers for Disease Control and Prevention and the American College of Sports Medicine. Jama 273(5), 402–407 (1995)

Chodzko-Zajko, W.J., et al.: Exercise and physical activity for older adults. Med. Sci. Sports Exerc. 41(7), 1510–1530 (2009)

Hamari, J., Lehdonvirta, V.: Game design as marketing: How game mechanics create demand for virtual goods. Int. J. Bus. Sci. Appl. Manage. 5(1), 14–29 (2010)

Deterding, S., Dixon, D., Khaled, R., Nacke, L.: From game design elements to gamefulness: defining "gamification". In: Proceedings of the 15th International Academic MindTrek Conference: Envisioning Future Media Environments, pp. 9–15 (2011)

Chou, Y.-K.: Actionable gamification: beyond points, badges, and leaderboards: Octalysis Group (2016)

Consolvo, S., Everitt, K., Smith, I., Landay, J.A.: Design requirements for technologies that encourage physical activity. Paper presented at the Proceedings of the SIGCHI conference on Human Factors in computing systems (2006)

Berkovsky, S., Coombe, M., Freyne, J., Bhandari, D., Baghaei, N.: Physical activity motivating games: virtual rewards for real activity. In: Proceedings of the International Conference on Human Factors in Computing Systems, pp. 243–252. ACM (2010)

Ryan, R.M., Deci, E.L.: Self-determination theory and the facilitation of intrinsic motivation, social development, and well-being. Am. Psychol. 55(1), 68 (2000)

Lamprinou, D., Paraskeva, F.: Gamification design framework based on SDT for student motivation. In: 2015 International Conference on Interactive Mobile Communication Technologies and Learning (IMCL), pp. 406–410. IEEE (2015)

Landers, R.N., Bauer, K.N., Callan, R.C., Armstrong, M.B.: Psychological theory and the gamification of learning. In: Reiners, T., Wood, L.C. (eds.) Gamification in Education and Business, pp. 165–186. Springer, Cham (2015). https://doi.org/10.1007/978-3-319-10208-5_9

Fogg, B.J.: Persuasive technology: using computers to change what we think and do. Ubiquity 2002(December), 2 (2002)

Fogg, B.J.: A behavior model for persuasive design. In: Proceedings of the 4th international Conference on Persuasive Technology, pp. 1–7 (2009)

Hamari, J., Koivisto, J., Sarsa, H.: Does gamification work?--a literature review of empirical studies on gamification. In: 2014 47th Hawaii International Conference on System Sciences, pp. 3025–3034. IEEE (2014)

Bittner, J.V., Shipper, J.: Motivational effects and age differences of gamification in product advertising. J. Consum. Market. 31, 391–400 (2014)

Codish, D., Ravid, G.: Gender moderation in gamification: does one size fit all (2017)

Halko, S., Kientz, J.A.: Personality and Persuasive Technology: An Exploratory Study on Healthpromoting Mobile Applications, pp. 150–161. Persuasive Technology, Springer (2010)

Jia, Y., Xu, B., Karanam, Y., Voida, S.: Personality, targeted/Gamification: a survey study on personality traits and motivational affordances. In: Proceedings of the SIGCHI Conference on Human Factors in Computing Systems (2016)

Orji, R., Nacke, L.E., Di Marco, C.: Towards personality-driven persuasive health games and gamified systems. In: Proceedings of the 2017 CHI Conference on Human Factors in Computing Systems, pp. 1015–1027 (2017)

Tondello, G.F., Wehbe, R.R., Diamond, L., Busch, M., Marczewski, A., Nacke, L.E.: The gamification user types hexad scale. In: Proceedings of the 2016 Annual Symposium on Computer-Human Interaction in Play, pp. 229–243 (2016)

Engaging Serious Games for Energy Efficiency

Emma Delemere(✉) ⓘ and Paul Liston ⓘ

Centre for Innovative Human Systems, Trinity College Dublin, Dublin, Ireland
delemere@tcd.ie

Abstract. Public engagement remains a challenge within energy behaviour change interventions, and serious games appear a promising mechanism to mitigate this. While social factors are commonly employed within such serious games, analysis of their specific impact is outstanding. This paper seeks to examine the social aspects of serious games and explore how they may be leveraged to support and incentivise energy related behaviour change. To demonstrate how social strategies may be used within a serious game to increase impact, the EVIDENT project is presented as a case study. Analysis of the literature suggests positive effects of social strategies within serious games, with peer comparison, collaboration, and competition commonly employed. However, as serious games often include multiple behaviour change strategies, both social and non-social, componential analysis is needed to determine the relative impacts of different approaches. As such, several social factors will be applied within the EVIDENT serious game including 1) stakeholder inclusion in design, 2) shared learning through social groups, 3) social inclusion, 4) social considerations to support maintenance of effects, and 5) social comparison. While positive effects for social factors within serious games are clear, this paper argues that additional analyses of how they may be best applied within serious games is needed.

Keywords: Serious games · Social factors · Energy · Energy efficiency · Behaviour change · Behavioural economics · Behavioural insights

1 Introduction

To mitigate the negative impacts of climate change, widespread behaviour change is needed [1]. One area in which behaviour change efforts have been directed is residential energy use [2]. While significant efforts to increase household energy efficiency have been made [2, 3], several barriers to success have been noted. Engagement of consumers within behaviour change interventions is one such challenge, with consumer ambivalence and reluctance often encountered [4]. This may be impacted by the often high temporal latencies between energy use and consequence [5], making behaviour change difficult due to the delayed consequence delivery negatively impacting the development of behavioural contingencies. Additionally, while household behaviour change requires significant effort, impacts on finances and energy use are often small [6]. As such, balancing the response costs of energy efficient behaviours with potential savings to support engagement poses a challenge.

© Springer Nature Switzerland AG 2022
G. Meiselwitz et al. (Eds.): HCII 2022, LNCS 13517, pp. 567–580, 2022.
https://doi.org/10.1007/978-3-031-22131-6_42

To address this engagement challenge within environmental initiatives, researchers have explored novel approaches to intervention delivery [7]. Serious games are one such approach, involving the application of gaming elements within non-traditional contexts with the goal of entertainment [8, 9]. Through serious games individuals can explore the impacts of their actions within a simulated environment, removed from real-life consequences [10]. Both simulation-oriented and education-oriented serious games have been effectively used to support energy-related goals, including consumption awareness, education and pro-environmental behaviour [11]. Importantly, serious games have been found to support user engagement [12] and facilitate discussion [13] due to increased emotional involvement [10], and a focus on learning through fun. As such, serious games appear a promising mechanism to enhance engagement within the delivery of environmental initiatives.

Exploring the use of serious games to support engagement in energy behaviour change is a key aspect of the European Union Horizon 2020 funded EVIDENT research project (www.evident-h2020.eu), which seeks to provide new insights into energy efficiency policy interventions. The overarching aim of this project is to devise and evaluate energy efficiency interventions which leverage technological advances, to reduce energy consumption and inform policy development. While there have been significant technological advances to support consumer reductions in energy consumption, such technologies are underutilised in practice. This "energy paradox" refers to the low adoption of energy efficient technologies despite the cost savings [14]. To combat this, an analysis of the factors impacting individual energy-related behaviour and decision making, inclusive of attitude, biases, and skills deficits, is needed. Through exploring the impacts of behaviour change interventions on energy consumption behaviours, the EVIDENT project seeks to establish how residential energy consumers may be best supported to make more efficient energy choices, minimising the energy efficiency gap. This will be accomplished through a series of experiments and quasi-experiments, including randomised control trials, big data analysis, surveys and qualitative analyses to explore the impacts of various energy behaviour change initiatives on consumption behaviours.

The EVIDENT project will also involve the development of a serious game to explore the impact of consumer financial literacy and behavioural biases on residential energy consumption and decisions to repair or replace household appliances. To ensure that this serious game effectively leverages social factors to support behaviour change, analysis of the current literature is needed. This paper seeks to examine the social aspects of serious games and explore how they may be used to support and incentivise energy related behaviour change. Based on this analysis, efforts can be made to ensure the EVIDENT serious game effectively employs social factors to enhance impact for consumers.

2 Social Factors Within Serious Games: What We Know

The efficacy of serious games has been demonstrated across many differing areas including, for example, healthcare monitoring [15] evacuation [16], way-finding in an emergency [17], industrial safety [18], and rehabilitation settings [19]. Serious games have been found to be particularly relevant in an safety-critical industries, due to the significant financial and time costs associated with safety drills [20], and low generalisation of safety behaviour to real-world contexts due to limited feedback on outcomes [21] and poor emotional investment [22]. Serious games are posited to address these challenges through increasing emotional engagement, aiding provision of feedback and facilitating drill completion through virtual environments, reducing cost and disruption [21]. As such, while serious games appear to effectively support behaviour change across varied industries, analysis of their impact in the context of energy behaviour is outstanding. To explore how social factors can be leveraged within serious games to increase energy efficient behaviour change, an overview of the current literature pertaining to the use of social factors in serious games is presented. Specifically, research exploring how serious games currently use social factors is described, in addition to an analysis of the impacts of such strategies on individual behaviour.

2.1 Social Aspects of Serious Games

Energy related social change presents a unique challenge due to its multifaceted, multi-component nature, involving daily decision making within a broader community context [23]. As climate change is a collective-risk social dilemma, social changes to address it require change on a global level [24]. For energy-related behaviour change to be relevant and measurable, communities, rather than individuals, must engage in behaviour change [23]. Broader engagement in turn can lead to peer modelling and comparison across community members, causing a chain reaction effect [23]. So, while behaviour change on an individual level is needed, it must occur in tandem with that of communities and groups, necessitating the use of social strategies.

Social factors have been harnessed within serious games to support behaviour change across a variety of domains from mapping complex systems to support community energy transitions [25], to increasing community awareness [18, 19]. Social interaction within serious games appears a key factor in supporting behaviour change [27], with positive effects of collaboration, peer support and competition within serious games noted [28]. While social factors support the efficacy of serious games [28], this relationship is bi-directional, with positive impacts on group problem solving, critical analysis, peer collaboration [29], and civic engagement obtained through collective learning [30]. This likely arises due to the safe simulated serious game environment, supporting experimentation in the absence of real consequences [31]. In the context of social groups and peer relations, this may allow users to engage in actions without concern for how this behaviour may reflect on them socially, thus affording users freedom to explore behaviours in the absence of social consequences. Different social factors are used across various gamification types to create impact. For example, in reflective gamification players receive points, levels, or rankings within a game, creating social visibility of achievements and peer recognition [32]. In comparison, social interaction gamification allows for collaboration and competition between peers. While serious games are often considered to be individual pursuits, group based serious games have also been developed in which players can interact with each other within the serious game. Co-located serious games, those in which group members play individually while in the same physical space, have also been associated with increased positive peer relations and knowledge sharing [33].

2.2 Limitations of Serious Games

While promising, several limitations to the use of serious games have been noted. Key concerns pertain to the absence of analysis of the mechanisms by which games have their effects [34]. While the importance of goal identification, nudges, feedback, and social interaction as key principles in serious games have been noted [27], analysis of the relative contributions of each is lacking [35]. While serious games often include social aspects, such as peer support or comparison, such strategies are often employed in collaboration with other behaviour change techniques [27]. Such an approach limits our understanding of the relative impacts of different social components of serious games on energy behaviour.

A further limitation pertains to user engagement and maintenance of serious game effects. Within simulation-oriented games specifically, issues pertaining to generalisability from simulated environments into, and across, real-world settings have been noted [28]. For example, within the EnerGAware simulation-based serious game, concerns pertaining to player attrition, engagement and maintenance of behaviour change were noted [26]. Concerns regarding generalisation of effects into real world settings were echoed by [36], who noted a need for objective data on energy use in real-life to be reflected within serious games to support generalisation efforts. A further key challenge is maintenance of effects over time. While behaviour change interventions have been found to have positive effects, research examining the extent to which these changes endure is limited [37]. This is thought to be due both to lack of long-term measurement and diminished effects over time [38].

2.3 Impact of Social Factors on Serious Game Outcomes

A number of European Union-funded projects have explored the use of social factors within serious games, commonly employing peer support, comparison and competition strategies [39–41]. Within the residential sector, several serious games have employed social factors to motivate energy related behaviour change. One such example is the Social MPower serious game [40], which explores the use of collective action within online communities to reduce the risk of blackout in a simulated environment. Within this serious game, players are tasked with working collaboratively to reduce energy use at peak times. Through establishing common shared knowledge and enabling shared actions, it was possible to create collective awareness. Peer-to-peer communication allowed group members to collaborate to reach shared goals. While reductions in energy consumption of 47% were found, analysis of the impacts of specific forms of social support (i.e. communication vs. feedback vs. group goal setting) in developing collective awareness was not explored.

While Social MPower leveraged collaboration between peers, other serious games have focused on competition to motivate energy behaviour change. Within the Energy Saving Game [42], peer comparison and social motivation were used to decrease energy consumption. Social motivation was slightly more effective when compared with financial motivation strategies. Of note, however, is the self-reported data from participants, who reported that social comparison had minimal effects on their energy saving behaviours. Additional analysis of the specific impacts of social comparison is needed to further explore this. A further serious game, the Powersaver Game [43], also used peer competition to motivate energy savings, with family teams competing against other family groups. Positive effects for peer competition on energy savings for residential users was found, with 8% more energy conserved by those in the competition condition in comparison to those in the control. However, as artificial social competition was used, rather than human competitors, caution is needed as such approaches may not capture fully real-life contingencies. Analysis of the relative effects of peer collaboration in comparison to competition was explored within the Green My Place serious game [41]. Within this game, players were assigned to a peer competition or peer collaboration condition, with an aim of reducing consumption. Both conditions were effective, with no significant difference found between the two approaches. This suggests the importance of any peer inclusion, rather than a specific form of social motivation, to support behaviour change.

Analysis of past serious games suggest the efficacy of peer comparison strategies in supporting energy efficiency behaviours, with peer collaboration, collective action and competition all having positive effects. However, additional analysis of the relative impacts of individual social strategies is needed, particularly comparing the impacts of peer competition versus collaboration, with mixed results observed to date. In addition, analysis of the effects of different peer groups, be they competitors or collaborators is needed to determine which peer groups may be most effective (i.e. self-selected peers, family, neighbours, strangers, etc.).

2.4 Overview of the EVIDENT Serious Game

The EVIDENT serious game is a simulation-type game which explores the factors which influence decisions to repair or replace a household appliance that has malfunctioned. This serious game will explore how different consumer types determine whether they should seek to repair or replace an appliance, and the impact of financial, environmental and energy literacy on this decision. The EVIDENT serious game also seeks to support consumers to make more effective decisions pertaining to household appliances by providing participants with advice on how best to approach these decisions while considering financial, environmental, and personal concerns. Users of the serious game will be given some simple tips they can then apply in real-life when making similar choices.

The EVIDENT serious game takes place within a simulated home environment which the player is required to maintain. Players must ensure that they remain comfortable (i.e. the temperature is at a habitable level and basic needs are met), minimise negative impact on the environment (i.e. through reducing energy consumed) and remain financially solvent (i.e. they spend within the budget imposed by the game). Participants will be assigned a role of either a landlord, tenant, or homeowner, determined by their role in real life. Participants can then move their avatar within their virtual home to engage with different home appliances, seeking to maintain their home and comfort. As players move through their virtual home and engage in activities such as cooking a meal or turning on the lights, the impacts on comfort, the environment and finances will be shown to them on indicative gauges. Participants final score upon completion of the game will be based upon their success in maintaining these gauges. Participants will be shown where they fall on a leaderboard, with performance relative to average performance shown.

Players will also be tasked with determining whether to repair or replace a faulty appliance within their virtual home. The player will be advised that an appliance has broken and that a repairperson should be contacted. The player will then enter into a discussion with the repairperson to decide if they would like to repair or replace the broken appliance. Following this, the player will negotiate the cost of their choice with the repairperson, to determine their willingness to pay for either the repair or replacement. To capture the circumstances of those who are tenants or landlords, an additional negotiation will occur. Tenants will be given the option to pay, and landlords given the option to receive, a fee from tenants in exchange for a better rated appliance. Once players have made their final choices they will be given feedback on their decision and its impacts, both financial and environmental. Simple suggestions and rules will be shared on how to determine between appliance repair and replacement. Users will then return to the task of maintaining their virtual home and will be presented additional decision points as more appliances break. Upon completion of the game, users will be given a final score and informed of where they fall on the leaderboard.

The serious game will be paired with a pre- and post-game survey which will seek to establish participant financial, energy and environmental literacy, environmental attitude and socio-demographic factors (see Fig. 1.). A follow-up survey will also be completed to explore generalisation of repair/replace behaviour in real-world settings. Finally, qualitative analyses will also be conducted using both individual interviews and focus groups following the serious game to further explore game impact and identify barriers or facilitators to energy decision making not captured within the serious game. Through this approach two primary questions will be addressed. Firstly, the impact of financial, energy and environmental literacy on decisions to repair or replace appliances across resident types will be established. Secondly the impact of providing additional information on how best to approach repair/replace decisions will be explored.

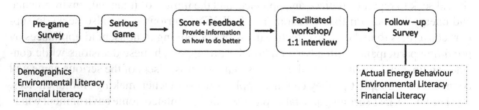

Fig. 1. Serious game research protocol overview

2.5 Leveraging the Social Aspects of Serious Games to Support Behavioural Change Within EVIDENT

To enhance the efficacy of the EVIDENT serious game, and to learn from the experiences of other serious games, it was important to consider how the social aspects of such games could be leveraged to increase behaviour change. To better understand and control for environmental and social impacts on participant serious game outcomes, several social factors were taken into consideration. These are 1) stakeholder inclusion in design, 2) shared learning through social groups, 3) social inclusion, 4) social considerations to support maintenance of effects, and 5) social comparison (see Fig. 2.).

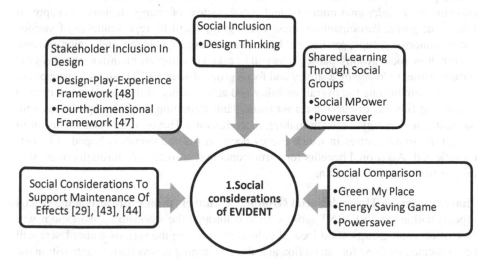

Fig. 2. Social factors leveraged within EVIDENT

Stakeholder Inclusion in Design. To ensure that serious games impact upon real-life behaviours and account for all relevant variables, it is crucial that real world contexts are reflected [29]. One means through which this can be achieved is co-design. Within co-design, different stakeholders share their knowledge, skills and experiences in an effort to support the development of a more reflective serious game [44]. The fourth-dimensional framework of serious game development outlines how such user input may be gathered [45]. This framework highlights the need to determine user requirements, define outcomes, support engagement, and reflect environments. The importance of co-design in enhancing player experience, gameplay, storytelling and learning is highlighted within the Design-Play-Experience framework of serious game development [46]. This supports the inclusion of relevant real-world variables within serious games through determining the environmental, individual and contextual factors that impact performance of the behaviour at present [29]. As such, meaningful cultural narratives, social rules and conflicts can be better represented within the serious game. This highlights the important role of social groups in learning, particularly pertaining to pro-environmental behaviour, and suggests an important role of the inclusion of users in co-design processes to support learning and enhance game quality.

As outlined above, user inclusion within serious game design offers several advantages. User co-design will be completed within the EVIDENT serious game through a series of focus groups, conducted across the development process. To date, initial user inclusion focus groups have been conducted to gather insight into the proposed serious game design, and to ensure important contextual factors are captured. Key concerns regarding duration and the complexity of serious games, and factors impacting energy investment decision making were raised. Input gathered highlighted additional considerations within the development of the EVIDENT serious game. User inclusion across prototype development will also take the form of focus groups, again with the aim of ensuring the broader environmental and social context of energy decisions is captured within the game. Participants in these focus groups will be representative of various socio-economic groups, particularly homeowners, renters, students and senior citizens. Within these focus groups, participants will be asked to complete an initial version of the serious game, followed by a survey and focus group discussion. These focus groups are hoped to demonstrate the overall usability and accessibility of the game, in addition to facilitating fulsome discussion across participants pertaining to their experiences with the game, and energy decision making more broadly. Through this user inclusion in design the social context in which energy decision making occurs is hoped to be better reflected. Additional benefits for participants may also emerge through co-learning arising from group discussion.

Shared Learning Through Social Groups. A further means of leveraging social aspects within the EVIDENT serious game is through the workshops. Workshops will consist of small groups of co-located individuals playing the serious game. Users will be co-located to allow for interaction and shared learning across participants within the group. Following this, group discussion will take place to allow individuals to share their in-game experiences, provide feedback and discuss their real-life experiences of making energy decisions. These groups will employ several social strategies to leverage their impact for participants. Firstly, through group discussion and reflection it is hoped that acquisition of learning from the game will be strengthened. In addition, group discussion is hoped to facilitate behaviour change through social support and peer-to-peer learning. The inclusion of groups is also hoped to support the EVIDENT serious game itself through highlighting key cultural and individual considerations which may need to be more effectively addressed within the serious game.

Social Inclusion. A key aspect of the EVIDENT serious game is to explore the energy investment decisions of groups who are often omitted within the literature, inclusive of the individuals from different cultures, socio-economic backgrounds, age groups, and interests. Efforts will be made to reflect the voices of a wide variety of individuals within serious game design. This will include the development of strategic relationships with stakeholder groups to support their inclusion in serious game design and implementation. Particular attention will be paid to stakeholder groups representing senior citizens, low-income households and other marginalised groups. To address this, design thinking approaches will be employed. Design thinking considers design as an ever evolving iterative process [47], with stakeholders at the centre. Inclusion of users in design allows for ongoing feedback [48], ensuring any omissions, assumptions or "blind-spots" can be identified and resolved early [49]. A similar user-centred design approach will be applied to the EVIDENT serious game development.

Social Considerations to Support Maintenance of Effects. A key challenge faced by serious games is maintenance of effects over time. The absence of longer-term analysis or follow-up measures within the research to date limits our understanding of whether the positive effects of serious games maintain [38]. A recent review of the literature highlighted a number of factors which impact maintenance of behaviour change, including motivation, habit, access to resources, and environmental and social variables [37]. As any form of behaviour change is difficult by nature, to support its maintenance this effort needs to be minimised. This can be achieved through developing habits, easing resource access, or manipulating environmental variables to support access to reinforcing contingencies. It is clear that there is a need to explore how the environmental choice architecture may be structured to facilitate ongoing behaviour change [37]. To address these factors in the context of the EVIDENT project, analysis of the broader environmental and social context in which energy decisions are made is needed.

One avenue which may offer insights into this broader context is qualitative analysis. An absence of qualitative methodologies within serious game [50, 51] and energy research [3] has been noted. Qualitative analysis may be particularly beneficial in this context however as it permits an in-depth analysis of the social and environmental factors encountered by individuals which may impact their decision making, which may not be captured using other methodologies.

To address the concerns regarding maintenance of behaviour change, and the absence of such analyses in the literature, the EVIDENT project will employ qualitative methods to explore individual experiences pertaining to energy investment decision making. Qualitative analyses will take the form of focus groups or individual interviews completed following the serious game. These discussions will explore both participants experiences within the game, and the environmental context, barriers and facilitators to decision making encountered in real-life. This qualitative data is intended to facilitate a deeper understanding of factors impacting consumers. For focus groups an additional advantage may be offered through social learning and support, arising from group discussion. Through open discussion of the factors impacting energy investment decisions, peers may learn from each other [52]. Debriefing in this manner within social groups may also facilitate learning through further contextualising and solidifying game experiences (e.g. [53]). As such additional exploration of the impact of social factors through group discussion on learning within energy related serious games will be considered within the EVIDENT project. This learning will be captured within a follow-up survey circulated between six to twelve months following the serious game, to determine if an opportunity to engage in repair/replace decision making occurred, and if behaviour change generalised from in-game to a real-world context.

Social Comparison. Social comparison has been successfully employed within energy serious game interventions [41, 42]. Facilitating comparison across peers appears an effective means of supporting behaviour change. This is consistent with the theory of social norms [54], which notes that individuals broadly seek to act in line with social expectations. Through increasing the salience of peer pro-environmental behaviour through direct comparison, peers may become more aware of their own behaviour and be motivated to better act in line with perceived social norms. As such, through facilitating social comparison increased interest in pro-environmental behaviour change may be observed at a community level. Social comparison will be addressed within the EVIDENT serious game through a leaderboard that will allow for users to compare their own performance to that of their peers. Social comparison across different peer types will be facilitated, with players advised of where they fall relative to the mean and within their neighbourhood. While leaderboard posting will be anonymous, players will be able to compare their performance within the game with peers through sharing their user name.

Social Comparison Through Social Media. Interactive social media such as real-time data visualisations and serious games have emerged to support reductions in energy consumption [55]. As social networks are increasingly used by consumers to support decision making when purchasing appliances, research has explored how these social networks may be leveraged to support energy related behaviour change [56, 57]. Use of social networks enhances engagement in behaviour change initiatives [58], which may also be of benefit in supporting uptake within communities. The benefits of social media, in terms of facilitating both social comparison and social learning, will be leveraged within the EVIDENT project. Players of the EVIDENT serious game will be able to share their overall score and place on the leaderboard to their social media. Sharing serious game scores on social media is hoped to facilitate comparison across peers, motivating further consideration of the serious game learnings and discussion to increase scores. Additionally, social learning may occur from peers sharing experiences and advice on the serious game in response to peer social media posts. While the overarching aim of facilitating social media sharing within the serious game is to draw peer attention towards the environmental and financial impacts of inefficient energy decisions, it also seeks to increase uptake of pro-environmental behaviour within communities through establishing social comparison across peers, motivating others to consider exploring their own energy decision making.

3   Conclusion

In order to support wide-spread pro-environmental behaviour change, community engagement in energy efficiency initiatives is needed. Serious games appear to be a promising means to address this, though additional analysis of how best to ensure social considerations are leveraged to increase the efficacy of such games is needed. The present manuscript highlights the effective use of social strategies within serious games thus far, with peer comparison, competition and collaboration commonly employed. While promising, the inclusion of multiple and overlapping elements within serious game interventions limits fulsome analysis of the relative contribution of individual social strategies. Additional analysis is needed to further explore the impacts of individual social strategies on energy behaviour to determine which may be most effective. Using learning from past research, the application of social strategies within serious games is demonstrated in the context of the EVIDENT project. To support external validity of the EVIDENT serious game, stakeholder inclusion in design will contribute to a complete analysis of cultural and community factors which should be reflected with the serious game. To support community-level engagement, focus groups, peer comparison and peer competition will be included. Through ensuring the EVIDENT serious game is reflective of the natural environment in which energy-engagement behaviour will be required to be exhibited, maintenance and generalisation of behaviour change is facilitated. As such, while social factors can be positively employed within serious games, additional analysis of the relative impact of different strategies over time is needed. The eventual roll-out and implementation of the EVIDENT serious game will contribute to knowledge to on this topic.

Acknowledgements. This research was conducted as part of the EVIDENT project, which has received funding from the European Union's Horizon 2020 research and innovation programme under grant agreement No 957117.

References

1. Whitmarsh, L., Poortinga, W., Capstick, S.: Behaviour change to address climate change. Curr. Opin. Psychol. **42**, 76–81 (2021). https://doi.org/10.1016/j.copsyc.2021.04.002
2. Seligman, C., Darley, J.M., Becker, L.J.: Behavioral approaches to residential energy conservation. Energy Build. **1**(3), 325–337 (1978). https://doi.org/10.1016/0378-7788(78)900 12-9
3. Doe, J., Francis, D.: What are we doing here? Analyzing fifteen years of energy scholarship and proposing a social science research agenda. Int. J. Soc. Stud. **1**(1) (2021)
4. Sovacool, B.K., Kivimaa, P., Hielscher, S., Jenkins, K.: Vulnerability and resistance in the United Kingdom's smart meter transition. Energy Policy **109**, 767–781 (2017). https://doi.org/10.1016/j.enpol.2017.07.037
5. Burgess, J., Nye, M.: Re-materialising energy use through transparent monitoring systems. Energy Policy **36**(12), 4454–4459 (2008). https://doi.org/10.1016/j.enpol.2008.09.039
6. DEWHA: Energy use in the Australian residential sector 1986–2020, Part 1 (2008). http://www.environment.gov.au/settlements/energyefficiency/buildings/index.html. Accessed 28 Jan 2022
7. Iweka, O., Liu, S., Shukla, A., Yan, D.: Energy and behaviour at home: a review of intervention methods and practices. Energy Res. Soc. Sci. **57**, 101238 (2019). https://doi.org/10.1016/j.erss.2019.101238
8. Göbel, S., Ma, M., Baalsrud Hauge, J., Oliveira, M.F., Wiemeyer, J., Wendel, V. (eds.): JCSG 2015. LNCS, vol. 9090. Springer, Cham (2015). https://doi.org/10.1007/978-3-319-19126-3
9. Detering, S., Dixon, D., Khaled, R., Lennart, P.: From game design elements to gamefulness: defining gamification. In: Proceedings of the 15th International Academic MindTrek Conference: Envisioning Future Media Environments (2011)
10. de la Torre, R., Onggo, B.S., Corlu, C.G., Nogal, M., Juan, A.A.: The role of simulation and serious games in teaching concepts on circular economy and sustainable energy. Energies **14**(4), 1138 (2021). https://doi.org/10.3390/en14041138
11. Morganti, L., Pallavicini, F., Cadel, E., Candelieri, A., Archetti, F., Mantovani, F.: Gaming for Earth: serious games and gamification to engage consumers in pro-environmental behaviours for energy efficiency. Energy Res. Soc. Sci. **29**, 95–102 (2017). https://doi.org/10.1016/j.erss.2017.05.001
12. Tilvawala, K., Sundaram, D., Myers, M.: Serious games for sustainable development: a decision-driven transformative approach. In: Proceedings of the Twenty-fifth Americas Conference on Information Systems (2019). https://researchspace.auckland.ac.nz/handle/2292/48993. Accessed 02 Apr 2021
13. Morschheuser, B., Riar, M., Hamari, J., Maedchea, A.: How games induce cooperation? A study on the relationship between game features and we-intentions in an augmented reality game. Comput. Hum. Behav. 169–183 (2017)
14. Jaffe, A.B., Stavins, R.N.: The energy-efficiency gap. Energy Policy **22**(10), 7 (1994)

15. De Maria, E., L'Yvonnet, T., Moisan, S., Rigault, J.-P.: Probabilistic activity recognition for serious games with applications in medicine. In: Hasan, O., Mallet, F. (eds.) FTSCS 2019. CCIS, vol. 1165, pp. 106–124. Springer, Cham (2020). https://doi.org/10.1007/978-3-030-46902-3_7

16. Ribeiro, J., Almeida, J.E., Rossetti, R.J.F., Coelho, A., Coelho, A.L.: Using serious games to train evacuation behaviour. In: 7th Iberian Conference on Information Systems and Technologies (CISTI 2012), pp. 1–6 (2012)

17. Almeida, J.E., Jacob, J.T.,P.N., Faria, B.M., Rossetti, R.J.F., Leça Coelho, A.: Serious games for the Elicitation of way-finding behaviours in emergency situations. In: 2014 9th Iberian Conference on Information Systems and Technologies (CISTI), pp. 1–7 (2014). https://doi.org/10.1109/CISTI.2014.6876951

18. Patriarca, R., Falegnami, A., De Nicola, A., Villani, M.L., Paltrinieri, N.: Serious games for industrial safety: an approach for developing resilience early warning indicators. Saf. Sci. **118**, 316–331 (2019). https://doi.org/10.1016/j.ssci.2019.05.031

19. Wiemeyer, J., Kliem, A.: Serious games in prevention and rehabilitation—a new panacea for elderly people? Euro. Rev. Aging Phys. Activity **9**(1), 41–50 (2011). https://doi.org/10.1007/s11556-011-0093-x

20. Gwynne, S.M.V., et al.: Enhancing egress drills: preparation and assessment of evacuee performance. Fire Materials **43**(6), 613–631 (2019). https://doi.org/10.1002/fam.2448

21. Feng, Z., González, V.A., Amor, R., Lovreglio, R., Cabrera-Guerrero, G.: Immersive virtual reality serious games for evacuation training and research: a systematic literature review. Comput. Educ. **127**, 252–266 (2018). https://doi.org/10.1016/j.compedu.2018.09.002

22. Chittaro, L., Buttussi, F., Zangrando, N.: Desktop virtual reality for emergency preparedness: user evaluation of an aircraft ditching experience under different fear arousal conditions. In: Proceedings of the 20th ACM Symposium on Virtual Reality Software and Technology, pp. 141–150 (2014)

23. Klimmt, C.: Serious Games and Social Change: Why They (Should) Work. In: Serious Games, Routledge (2009)

24. Milinski, M., Sommerfeld, R.D., Krambeck, H.-J., Reed, F.A., Marotzke, J.: The collective-risk social dilemma and the prevention of simulated dangerous climate change. PNAS **105**(7), 2291–2294 (2008). https://doi.org/10.1073/pnas.0709546105

25. Ouariachi, T., Wim, E.J.L.: Escape rooms as tools for climate change education: an exploration of initiatives. Environ. Educ. Res. **26**(8), 1193–1206 (2020). https://doi.org/10.1080/13504622.2020.1753659

26. Casals, M., Gangolells, M., Macarulla, M., Forcada, N., Fuertes, A., Jones, R.V.: Assessing the effectiveness of gamification in reducing domestic energy consumption: Lessons learned from the EnerGAware project. Energy Build. **210** (2020). https://doi.org/10.1016/j.enbuild.2019.109753

27. Krath, J., von Korflesch, F.O.: Designing gamification and persuasive systems: a systematic literature review. In: CEUR Workshop Proceedings, pp. 100–109 (2021). http://ceur-ws.org/Vol-2883/

28. Wu, X., Liu, S., Shukla, A.: Serious games as an engaging medium on building energy consumption: a review of trends, categories and approaches. Sustainability **12**(20), 8508 (2020). https://doi.org/10.3390/su12208508

29. Gugerell, K., Zuidema, C.: Gaming for the energy transition. Experimenting and learning in co-designing a serious game prototype. J. Clean. Prod. **169**, 105–116 (2017). https://doi.org/10.1016/j.jclepro.2017.04.142

30. Kuhk, A., Dehaene, M., Schreurs, J.: Collective learning experiences in planning: the potential of experimental living labs. Presented at the AESOP 2015 - Definite Space - Fuzzy Responsibility (2015). http://hdl.handle.net/1854/LU-8033544 Accessed 28 Jan 2022

31. Devisch, O., Poplin, A., Sofronie, S.: The gamification of civic participation: two experiments in improving the skills of citizens to reflect collectively on spatial issues. J. Urban Technol. **23**, 1–22 (2016). https://doi.org/10.1080/10630732.2015.1102419

32. Mekler, E.D., Brühlmann, F., Opwis, K., Tuch, A.N.: Disassembling gamification: the effects of points and meaning on user motivation and performance. In: CHI '13 Extended Abstracts on Human Factors in Computing Systems on - CHI EA 2013, p. 1137. Paris, France (2013). https://doi.org/10.1145/2468356.2468559

33. Fang, Y.-M., Chen, K.-M., Huang, Y.-J.: Emotional reactions of different interface formats: comparing digital and traditional board games (2016). https://doi.org/10.1177/168781401664 1902

34. Boehm, B.W.: A spiral model of software development and enhancement. Computer **21**(5), 61–72 (1988)

35. Beck, A., Chitalia, S., Rai, V.: Not so gameful: a critical review of gamification in mobile energy applications. Energy Res. Soc. Sci. **51**, 32–39 (2019)

36. Fijnheer, J.D.L., van Oostendorp, H.: Steps to design a household energy game. Int. J. Serious Games **3**, 12–22 (2016)

37. Kwasnicka, D., Dombrowski, S.U., White, M., Sniehotta, F.: Theoretical explanations for maintenance of behaviour change: a systematic review of behaviour theories. Health Psychol. Rev. **10**(3), 277–296 (2016). https://doi.org/10.1080/17437199.2016.1151372

38. Dombrowski, S.U., Avenell, A., Sniehott, F.F.: Behavioural interventions for obese adults with additional risk factors for morbidity: systematic review of effects on behaviour, weight and disease risk factors. Obes Facts **3**(6), 377–396 (2010). https://doi.org/10.1159/000323076

39. Wang, X., Liu, Z., Zhao, Z., Wang, J., Loughney, S., Wang, H.: Passengers' likely behaviour based on demographic difference during an emergency evacuation in a Ro-Ro passenger ship. Safety Sci. **129** (2020). https://doi.org/10.1016/j.ssci.2020.104803

40. Bourazeri, A., Pitt, J.: Social mpower: a serious game for self-organisation in socio-technical systems. In: 2014 IEEE Eighth International Conference on Self-Adaptive and Self-Organizing Systems, pp. 199–200. London, United Kingdom (2014). https://doi.org/10. 1109/SASO.2014.43

41. Cowley, B., Moutinho, J.L., Bateman, C., Oliveira, A.: Learning principles and interaction design for 'Green My Place': a massively multiplayer serious game. Entertain. Comput. **2**(2), 103–113 (2011). https://doi.org/10.1016/j.entcom.2011.01.001

42. Akasiadis, C., et al.: Incentives for rescheduling residential electricity consumption to promote renewable energy usage. In: 2015 SAI Intelligent Systems Conference (IntelliSys), pp. 328–337. London, United Kingdom (2015). https://doi.org/10.1109/IntelliSys.2015.7361163

43. Fijnheer, J., Oostendorp, H., Giezeman, G., Veltkamp, R.: Competition in a household energy conservation game. Sustainability **13**, 11991 (2021). https://doi.org/10.3390/su132111991

44. Visser, F.S., Stappers, P.J., van der Lugt, R., Sanders, E.B.-N.: Contextmapping: experiences from practice. CoDesign **1**(2), 119–149 (2005). https://doi.org/10.1080/15710880500135987

45. Oja, M., Riekki, J.: Ubiquitous framework for creating and evaluating persuasive applications and games. In: Rautiainen, M., et al. (eds.) GPC 2011. LNCS, vol. 7096, pp. 133–140. Springer, Heidelberg (2012). https://doi.org/10.1007/978-3-642-27916-4_15

46. Winn, B.: The design, play, and experience framework. Handbook of Research on Effective Electronic Gaming in Education (2008)

47. Brown, T., Wyatt, J.: Design Thinking for Social Innovation (2010). https://doi.org/10.1596/ 1020-797X_12_1_29

48. Lanezki, M., Siemer, C., Wehkamp, S.: Changing the game—neighbourhood': an energy transition board game, developed in a co-design process: a case study. Sustainability **12**(24), 10509 (2020). https://doi.org/10.3390/su122410509

49. Ampatzidou, C., Gugerell, K.: Mapping game mechanics for learning in a serious game for the energy transition. IJEPR **8**(2), 1–23 (2019). https://doi.org/10.4018/IJEPR.2019040101

50. Johnson, D., Horton, E., Mulcahy, R., Foth, M.: Gamification and serious games within the domain of domestic energy consumption: a systematic review. Renew. Sustain. Energy Rev. **73**, 249–264 (2017). https://doi.org/10.1016/j.rser.2017.01.134
51. McAndrew, R., Mulcahy, R., Gordon, R., Russell-Bennett, R.: Household energy efficiency interventions: a systematic literature review. Energy Policy **150**, 112136 (2021). https://doi.org/10.1016/j.enpol.2021.112136
52. Wolske, K.S., Gillingham, K.T., Schultz, P.W.: Peer influence on household energy behaviours. Nat. Energy **5**(3)(Art. no. 3) (2020). https://doi.org/10.1038/s41560-019-0541-9
53. Crookall, D.: Serious games, debriefing, and simulation/gaming as a discipline. Simul. Gaming **41**(6), 898–920 (2010). https://doi.org/10.1177/1046878110390784
54. Ehrhardt-Martinez, K.: Behavior, energy, and climate change: Policy directions, program innovations, and research paths (2008)
55. Liarakou, G., Sakka, E., Gavrilakis, C., Tsolakidis, C.: Evaluation of serious games, as a tool for education for sustainable development. Euro. J. Open Distance E-learn. **15**(2)(Art. no. 2) (2012). https://old.eurodl.org/?p=special&sp=articles&inum=4&article=546. Accessed 25 Jan 2022
56. Agha-Hossein, M.M., et al.: Providing persuasive feedback through interactive posters to motivate energy-saving behaviours. Intell. Build. Int. **7**(1), 16–35 (2015). https://doi.org/10.1080/17508975.2014.960357
57. Katsaliaki, K.: Serious games for sustainable development. J. Manag. Educ. **37**(6), 889–894 (2013). https://doi.org/10.1177/1052562913509219
58. García, Ó., Alonso, R., Prieto, J., Corchado, J.: Energy efficiency in public buildings through context-aware social computing. Sensors **17**(4), 826 (2017). https://doi.org/10.3390/s17040826

An Exploratory Study on Game Developer Needs and Game Studio Challenges

Nandhini Giri[1(✉)] and Erik Stolterman[2]

[1] Purdue University, West Lafayette, IN 47907, USA
girin@purdue.edu
[2] Indiana University, Bloomington, IN 47405, USA

Abstract. This paper studies professional game developers' experiences in the gaming industry to understand their professional needs and challenges of working in the industry. In this qualitative study we interviewed game developers and studio executives with the objective of learning more about their everyday workplace needs and challenges. The interviews highlighted major concerns in the areas of studio operations, game developer professional needs, game development processes, player research and game design scholarship comprising of theories, research, education. There are fundamental issues in the game development processes and studio operations that can benefit from a research scholarship for game design practices. The results from this study can lead to further research work that supports game developers in their professional design practices.

Keywords: Game developer needs · Game studio challenges · Game development process · Game design research

1 Introduction

This paper summarizes the results of a qualitative research study interviewing game developers and studio executives, to understand their major needs and challenges of working in the game industry. The study objective was to learn more about the everyday needs of game developers and the challenges faced by game professionals in the studio operations. An inquiry about gaming professionals' workplace challenges can provide deeper insights into their practice and lead to building theories that support professionals for effective practice. The interviews were open-ended enquiring gaming professionals about their professional and workplace challenges in the areas of studio operations, game developer professional needs, game development processes, player research and game design scholarship comprising of theories, research, education.

2 Related Research

Thomas Friedman in 'The World is Flat' [7] explains that the inadequacy of the leadership in high tech companies to adapt to disruptive and dislocating technological revolutions

© Springer Nature Switzerland AG 2022
G. Meiselwitz et al. (Eds.): HCII 2022, LNCS 13517, pp. 581–591, 2022.
https://doi.org/10.1007/978-3-031-22131-6_43

leads to their failure in navigating through rapid changes in the marketplace. There is a lack of flexibility and imagination and that it is not because the professionals are not smart or unaware, but because the speed of change is simply overwhelming. These changes are creating a new reality characterized by Volatility, Uncertainty, Complexity and Ambiguity [10]. The gaming industry is at the bleeding edge of technology and is constantly challenged by rapid advancement in technologies and market shifts. It is often difficult for studio executives and game developers to stay on top of this shifting technological landscape. Game design careers in a fast-paced environment with crucial deadlines and high-quality expectations can lead to very stressful experiences. Many gaming professionals have highlighted these high demanding workplace expectations in various conferences and formal talks. There is also a heightened sense of insecurity among gaming professionals due to the non-sustainable nature of studios.

Jason Schreier the author of 'Blood, Sweat and Pixels' [17] spoke with more than a hundred game developers and executives about their lives, jobs and why they sacrifice so much to make video games. The stories talk about games that were hampered by drastic technological changes, directorial shifts, or other wild factors beyond the developer's control. The solution is not about following industry standards or avoiding common pitfalls or making smarter decisions to surpass hardship, because according to Jason the alternative theory is that every single game is made under abnormal circumstances. A few possible reasons listed by the author as to why video game development is so hard, and challenging are because games are interactive. Video games do not move in a single linear direction and need to react to player's actions. Second, technology is constantly changing with new developments in software, graphics processing power, hardware devices, extended platforms, standards, and format. The tools are always different, and scheduling is almost impossible when it is not based on how long the tasks have taken in the past, but how to make this game more fun. Does adding another day in the schedule make the game more fun? It is also not possible to know how fun the game is until it is played and that even experienced game designers find it difficult to make educated guesses about the fun factor and outcome of the game compared to the level of effort that is put into the development phases.

The conclusions that can be drawn from this introductory discussion is that "there is no one prescribed method of designing games". This conclusion resonates with game developers and studio managers, who assume these abnormal circumstances as being part of their everyday workplace challenges. However, a deeper inquiry into these workplace challenges can provide common patterns and underlying principles to then develop solutions for professionals in their practices. In this context, it is important to look at previous academic research work and scholarly literature for well-researched theories that support designers in handling these real-time workplace complexities. Schon [15, 16] highlights the crisis of confidence in professional practice and sought for an epistemology of practice that explains how practitioners engage with their practice in dynamic real-life situations. Friedman and Cross [5, 6] suggest a systemic theory-driven approach to practice for a robust level of understanding that forms the foundation of effective practice. Nelson and Stolterman [14] propose that a solid philosophy of design should unify inquiry and action in diverse purposes and activities. These research literature reviews suggest that an inquiry into game professionals' everyday needs and challenges can lead to a design scholarship that supports their everyday practices. This research study is designed with this objective of supporting gaming professionals by understanding their everyday workplace needs and challenges.

3 Methodology

The main objective of this study was to understand the major challenges faced by game studios and investigate deeper into game developers' needs within game studios. Sixteen game development professionals were recruited and interviewed for this research study over a period of four months. Initially for the study recruitment, we made a list of potential interviewees based on attended conference talks, podcasts, women leaders in games top-listing and game development professional's recommendations. These professionals were contacted through Linkedin and interview sessions scheduled based on their interest in participation and availability. We also sent out a social media tweet looking for game developers to volunteer for this interview study, especially those who are outside United States. Interviewees in this research study held roles as game designers, consultants, researchers, studio executives, vice president, game developers (programming, AI, economy), game design professors, authors and advocates with experiences ranging from ten years to more than twenty years in the industry. Interviewees work for game studios (publisher, indie, self) or teach at universities in North America, Europe, and South America. For future studies, we'll also include questions to collection information related to the interviewee's demographics.

An approval for the study was obtained from the institutional review board to interview studio executives and game developers from various game studios. Initially, five pilot interview studies were conducted within a span of two days. Professionals from the gaming industry were first contacted through Linkedin and then the scheduling of the one-to-one meetings was done through email exchanges. Semi-structured interviews were conducted through Zoom sessions that lasted for 40–60 min. The online interviews were conducted from the researcher's apartment space and the interviewees joined in from their work or home office locations. The pilot study interview included the following open-ended questions on:

1. What are the challenges faced by game developers and studio executives in the video game industry?
2. What are some best practices and evaluation metrics used in the game industry?

After the initial pilot studies, we included more details in the introductory email about the scheduled interview session. The email format included a refined summary of the study objectives to understand the needs and challenges of game developers and studio executives. We also included the relevant areas of interest in this research study that include studio culture, development tools, processes and frameworks, player research, education & research. Hand-written notes and audio recordings from the interviews were then transcribed, coded, and interpreted. A thematic analysis was conducted to analyze the data from the interviews. After every interview, the data was analyzed and added to a document. The information obtained from the coding, analyzing and construct conceptualization process and the audio recordings were saved in a secure online location for storage and retrieval. This iterative process helped in familiarizing with the data and generate initial codes. Interview data was analyzed further to identify common patterns, reviewing, and categorizing the data into major themes. A grounded theory approach [1–4, 9, 12, 13] was used here for the analysis of the interview data.

The initial data analysis helped identify five key areas that summarize the major needs of game designers and challenges faced by game studios. These focus areas which form the major themes from the analysis include studio focus, game developer focus, game development focus, players focus and game design scholarship focus. Each of these key themes have subthemes that explain in detail the major challenges and key issues of game developers and studio executives in the gaming industry.

In the next section we go into the details of the insights from this research study. Also, in order to maintain the anonymity of the professionals, they are named interviewee #1, #2, #3... based on the order in which they were interviewed. All the quotes that appear in the following section of this chapter correspond to the actual interviewee from the study.

4   Insights from Interviews

The insights from the interviews led to five major themes that describe the needs of game developers and challenges faced by game studios. The following sub-sections elaborate on each of the five major themes.

4.1   Studio Focus

The interviews revealed several challenges that threaten the sustainability of studios and pointed at fundamental issues that slowdown everyday studio operations.

Leadership. "The game industry is very big on production in terms of tracking the project schedules, tracking budgets, doing scrum. Everybody has some sort of a production system...what really matters is fundamental leadership." (Interviewee #2) Studio executives and game industry veterans mentioned that the game industry lacks fundamental leadership and management training. A lot of operational issues arise due to the siloed nature of the game industry and the resistance of learning management science and apply its principles in game studio operations. People do not look outside to see what works in other industries. There is also an attitude that game industry is different "this amazing combination of creativity and technology...people are people, cultures are cultures..." (Interviewee #2).

Coherent Vision. "They don't have a shared clearly defined vision of what the game is and that is the cause of a lot of problems. Some people think it is a first-person shooter, some people think it is third person...survival, horror or exploration or whatever...so now you've got all these conflicting visions of games." (Interviewee #2). "What is the game you are working on and who is it for? Designers don't know the answer." (Interviewee #5). A surprising insight that came out of the interviews is that game developers do not fully understand the vision nor have a clear goal of what it is that they are developing. Often creative heads struggle with communicating their design decisions to the teams.

Studio Culture. "Build culture deliberately. Every game team I know of, or have worked on, generally thinks of culture as something that just "happens." Some game teams/studios have values statements/mission statements and use them in hiring, and that's good, but most could go much further in deliberately defining their culture and reinforcing their cultural values daily in a way that will maximize their odds of success". (Interviewee #2). Professionals expressed their concerns over the influence of toxic studio cultures in their productivity. They stressed the need for conscious culture building through everyday practices and incorporating conscious interventions in the game development process for better workplace experiences.

Team Building. "It's kind of strange the game designer role itself, every game studio knows that they need a game designer, however, they don't know exactly how to define that role, they don't know exactly how to test it, they don't know how to measure one over the other...let alone trying to figure out how they fit into their existing culture". (Interviewee #11). Executives spoke about hiring wrong people, not defining job descriptions clearly, failing to interview people properly and not having effective mechanisms to evaluate professionals leading to inefficient teams and a mismatch between project requirements and team skills.

4.2 Game Developer Focus

In this section, we focus on the insights that are related to game developers' professional development and frameworks that support their knowledge acquisition.

Communication. "Problems of communication, being the most common... multiple interpretations of briefs and documentation between team members." (Interviewee #12). "Games (industry) are just populated by a bunch of cowboys, and they are just flying by the seat of their pants in some respects...they feel that they don't need the backing up structure in clear communication." (Interviewee #11) All interviewees mentioned communication to be a major issue in studios. People have issues with interpersonal and organization level communications. Often, they do not care to enforce a structure for communication.

Tools, Models and Frameworks. "But what is missing is models, systems, and theories of change." (Interviewee #7). Game developers felt the need for frameworks especially in transformational games sector so that they can apply well-tested theories in game development, rather than following a trial-and-error method. Key performance metrics that explain design decisions to development teams and business stakeholders about the value of fun can be very helpful to developers. "How are you going to measure that you are getting closer to the goal...there are not many standardized practices." (Interviewee #12). Models and goal-oriented frameworks that help with scheduling can also improve production experiences.

Standardization of Roles and a Lack of Mentors. "We don't have a unified definition of roles...I was a lead designer when I was only three years in the industry...whereas if you are in 'xxxxx' (large studio) you have designer level 1, level 2... some of them are master level… I don't even know what that means." (Interviewee #1). A lack of standardization of roles across different game studios pose a major issue when developers work across multiple studios. A junior developer's career experience depends a lot on the first project and team that they work in. Developers also expressed a concern for the lack of mentorship and pairing beginner level professionals with seasoned mentors in the game studios.

Design Language. There was a consensus among interviewees that there is no universal design language on game development and that developers talk about design in terms of the previous games made in the studio. "So, you go to a studio, and they can hardly talk about game design. They can tell you like what games they like. They can tell you about what they have done on the current project, but they cannot actually talk about things more broadly… It is a huge stumbling block… For the most part, in my experience, they hire people…They always want somebody who is excellent in written and verbal communication skills. Everyone says that, but they also want someone who doesn't need to be told what to do to get work done. That they would be self-starters or whatever…All that is coded language to me that we are not going to teach you. We need you to make cool stuff and you are going to be solely responsible for it. So, we want to be able to take it from start to finish and then just fit it into the bigger picture. And the more and more applications I see like that I know exactly what kind of a studio you have." (Interviewee #11).

4.3   Game Development Focus

Again, this sub-section provides a list of areas that pose challenges to game developers in studios.

Business Metrics. "When I say game… I talk about the systems and the experience that makeup the core of what players are engaging with…and when I say product, I mean… the business design that encapsulates the game…there are all kinds of things that you have to deal with that are not part of the game design that go toward the success of the product. Product is the outer shell, Game is the inner shell…Without a game, you don't have a product, but you can certainly have a game that is not a good product." (Interviewee #10). A lot of game developers do not see the product in the game that they are developing leading to low visibility in the market when the game is released.

Content-Specific Metrics. "If you claim to respect your local customers, you need to reflect that in your content…culturalize it so that it meets local expectations…there is also local political expectations…legal requirements". (Interviewee #6). A lot of game studios are realizing the fact that they need to navigate through the maze of what the studio wants their players to see versus what the political and socio-economic context allows their people to see in games. Culturalization strategies help resolve these issues and also serve as policies for developing Artificial Intelligence (AI) algorithms that handle content creation and distribution across different regions of the world.

Pipeline-Specific Metrics. Interviewees expressed a lack of formalization of processes across studios that include documentation, libraries, tools building and pipeline specific processes. There is also a lack of understanding of how processes work - "I think Post-mortems help, but 95% of people don't know how to do it". (Interviewee #6). Another major issue is the ambiguity of pipeline processes in detecting issues earlier - "No design framework for early detection of problems. Often the problem that clients (game professionals as clients to a consultant) mention are not the actual problems". (Interviewee #5).

Value-Sensitive Metrics. Game professionals identified different business models and investments in the changing market trends. They had concerns about the current trends of game studios and the need for more value-sensitive products that respect the game development process. "A lot of studios are doing games as a service than a single one-off…games as a Netflix service is a bad idea. If you give people access to every single game on the planet at the push of a button that does not hold up. They start to play games less for their sort of interactive, experiential, and aesthetic quality and more for dislike… I want explosions… I want to feel good right now. I want instant gratification… That is a slippery slope. And when you combine that with a market that is like a race to the bottom at least for mobiles… Everything must be free and they are no longer charging for the game itself…charged to play the game more frequently or to take away ads. I feel like that's a sign of a weak game industry…trending in that direction toward you having an entire player base, that devalues the very thing that you're overly working through." (Interviewee #11).

4.4 Player Focus

UX Research. UX research is no longer an experimental activity and studios are realizing the need to invest in resources for UX teams and integration in the game development process. "We don't have a lot of formal language around that…we are pretty focused about UI/UX type thinking…we have a UI team that is massive…it is unbridged with systems design…is UX art or design…there is no consistent answer…sits squarely in design in a lot of companies". (Interviewee #10) The research interviews show a gap in terms of translating user experiences to design language for the development team to then work on the feedback. Professionals working in the mobile, casual and free to play games sector also mentioned the notion of motivation clusters that removes demographic binaries and focuses on the fluid motivational player profiles.

Player Dynamics and Community Research. UX research focuses on a single person's end to end experience and player dynamics focuses more on the emergence of experience through the interplay of players in the game system. Matchmaking based on player profiles is a major challenge in these communities. The interviews also provided insights on how game studios identify toxic behavior in online game communities. The less mature studios rely on punishing bad behavior, whereas the more mature studios rely on designing systems that build resilient communities that self organizes into a safe space for all players. The nature of gaming and the relationship between players and game developers is evolving - "On twitter you can follow your favorite developers down to the person working on the very thing you like, you can follow your favorite stream-ers…your favorite esports players…with twitch channel, youtube". (Interviewee #11). Game developers highlighted the fact that players can now use social media platforms to reach out to their developers and talk about design features. These changing dynamics require further research into the game development process and its interaction with the player base and the gaming community.

4.5 Game Design Scholarship Focus

Game Design Education. "A lot of students that I've talked to have a passion for games… that passion does not necessarily translate to studying them, writing about them, researching them, the less fun things". (Interviewee #11). The educators in the interview pool mentioned that students need accelerated experiences of the real-world game industry in order to decide early on whether this is the level of commitment they would like to make in their careers. Often times students join game design programs because they like playing games. The interviews also pointed out the lack of game design educators, programs that put together some 3D and programming courses that are not necessarily game design focused and the need for better educational design tools like paper/digital prototyping and documentation to teach game design courses.

Game Design Research. "On the creative end, from what I can tell, academic research doesn't address getting at the root of sort of design genres and creative sources of inspiration in the history of games… So a lot of times when trying to talk to developers and you want to engage them with their ideas, their ideas are so nebulous and kind of unstructured and difficult to articulate. It is really even hard to meet them where they are, to try to help them flesh out an idea. And if it is hard to do that within a company, that will be incredibly hard for any kind of academic research to sway them one way or another". (Interviewee #11). Game design professionals were skeptical about the application of game design research in everyday practice. There was some references to the flow theory and appreciation for how the theory can be applied in the game development process. The interviews also led to the fact that there are not adequate game design theories that support developers in their development process and everyday workplace issues.

5 Discussion

The insights from the interviews indicate fundamental issues in studio operations and red flags that require immediate attention in the game development process. The video game industry has been established for several decades now, but the industry faces some of the fundamental organizational, people, process management, and product design issues that have been studied and resolved across several software and management fields. These significant roadblocks and the siloed nature of how game studios operate lead to the challenges expressed by game developers and studio executives in these interviews. One approach to address these issues is to consider some of the standardized practices implemented in the software industry. Expertise development [11] through a set of structured levels and evaluation metrics can help assess the maturity levels of studios in the different focus areas that were discussed in the previous section. These assessments can inform studio executives to make decisions that can improve the overall expertise level of the studio and address game developer's everyday workplace concerns.

Figure 1 provides a summarizing view of the key insights from the interviews as a reference. The major themes identified in the interviews as game developer needs and studio challenges are organized as four key areas for further research and study through game design scholarship identified as an icon at the intersection of the four segments. Each key area comprised of the subthemes that provide a roadmap for gaming professionals and academic scholars for further research and continuous improvement.

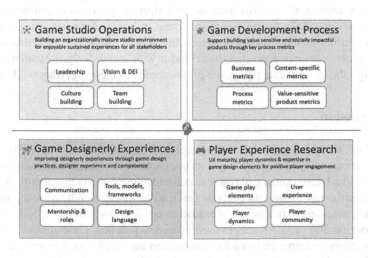

Fig. 1. Key areas of developer needs and studio challenges (Image reference from [8])

Some of the key concerns mentioned at a studio level indicate the need for more management theories that relate to the game development and game studio management concerns. Lack of management training is a key reason for leadership failures. Poor management leads to a failure in identifying issues proactively in the game development process. The concerns about studios not having a cohesive vision, negligence of culture building, and ad-hoc hiring policies indicate key areas of improvement within studio operations. Addressing some of the concerns at a studio level can lead to more enjoyable and sustainable workplace environments for game developers. Communication was one of the biggest concerns expressed by most of the interviewees. Creatives struggle communicating their design choices to the development team, which could be resolved by developing tools, frameworks, and models for better communication. A lack of a universal design language for games poses huge challenges for developers as they onboard into new projects at workplace. There is also a need for more mentors and better pipelines for students to transition from their academic training into entry level positions in the game industry.

Studios vary a lot in terms of the demographics they serve and the kind of games they develop. However, one thing that emerges from the interviews is that product thinking is the first step towards player-centric design. The earlier this mindset is implemented in the development process the more chances for the game product to succeed in the market. Identification of business metrics and using data-driven decisions for insights can improve the overall game product and player experience. This necessitates the development of frameworks and process-specific metrics. The interviews also provide insights on how studios have started realizing the importance of games user research. Allocation of resources and budget is a struggle in this area. Studios are nevertheless exploring better ways to conduct user research to build their brand and customized experiences for player communities.

A concluding discussion on the interview insights is about game design scholarship. Interviewees expressed concerns over game design programs not equipping students with the necessary skills to succeed in the game industry. A revisit into game design curriculum formation that is better aligned with industry job roles is recommended. The scholarship also requires a practice-based inquiry in game design research and build game design theories that support game professionals in their everyday workplace.

6   Conclusion

This research study has helped us build insights about game developer needs and challenges in various areas of the studio operations, game development process, game developer professional development, player research and game design scholarship. The themes derived from the interview data analysis can lead to theory building for a good understanding of game design practices and lead to an epistemology of game design practices that support gaming professionals in their everyday practice. Case-studies within each theme can provide deeper insights for comparison and application in production practices for better developer experiences in game studios. A body of design scholarship focused on everyday practice can help executives and developers deal with the volatility, uncertainty, complexity, and ambiguity of the gaming industry.

References

1. Charmaz, K.: Grounded theory as an emergent method. Handbook of Emergent Methods, vol. 155, p. 172 (2008)
2. Charmaz, K., Belgrave, L.: Qualitative interviewing and grounded theory analysis. The SAGE Handbook of Interview Research: The Complexity of the Craft, vol. 2, pp. 347–365 (2012)
3. Charmaz, K., Belgrave, L.L.: Grounded theory. The Blackwell encyclopedia of sociology (2007)
4. Creswell, J.W.: Qualitative Inquiry and Research Design: Choosing Among Five Approaches, 2nd edn. Sage Publications, Thousand Oaks (2007)
5. Cross, N.: Expertise in design: an overview. In: Design Studies, vol. 25, pp. 427–441 (2004)
6. Friedman, K.: Theory construction in design research. Common Ground, pp. 388–413 (2002)
7. Friedman, T.L.: The world is flat: the globalized world in the twenty-first century. Language, 8(600p), 22cm (2006)

8. Giri, N.: An Enjoyable Approach to Design Expertise in Gaming and Interactive Entertainment Industry Practices. Indiana University (2021)
9. Kvale, S., Brinkmann, S.: Interviews: Learning the Craft of Qualitative Research Interviewing, 2nd edn. Sage, Thousand Oaks, CA (2008)
10. Lawrence, K.: Developing leaders in a VUCA environment. UNC Executive Development, pp. 1–15 (2013)
11. Lawson, B., Dorst, K.: Acquiring design expertise. Computational and Cognitive Models of Creative Design VI. Key Centre of Design Computing and Cognition, pp. 213–229. University of Sydney, Sydney (2005)
12. Lazar, J., Feng, J. Heidi, Hochheiser, H.: Research methods in human-computer interaction. Chichester, vol. 134. Wiley, West Sussex, U.K. (2010)
13. Leavy, P.: The Oxford Handbook of Qualitative Research. Oxford University Press, Oxford (2014)
14. Nelson, H., Stolterman, E.: The Design Way – Intentional Change in an Unpredictable World, 2nd edn. MIT Press (2012)
15. Schön, D.A.: The Reflective Practitioner: How Professionals Think in Action. Basic Books, New York (1983)
16. Schön, D.A.: Educating the reflective practitioner (1987)
17. Schreier, J.: Blood, sweat, and pixels: the triumphant, turbulent stories behind how video games are made. Harper (2017)

Can Gamification Improve User Experience (UX) of Servitization in the Financial and Construction Sector?

Mohammed Soheeb Khan[1], Vassilis Charissis[1](✉) [id], and David K. Harrison[2]

[1] Virtual Reality and Simulation Laboratory, School of Computing, Engineering and Built Environment, Glasgow Caledonian University, Glasgow, UK
soheeb.khan@gcu.ac.uk, v.charissis@gmail.com
[2] Department of Mechanical Engineering, School of Computing, Engineering and Built Environment, Glasgow Caledonian University, Glasgow, UK

Abstract. The monetisation of the provision of consumer services rather than products is advantageous and leads to higher profit margins for the providing companies in comparison to the sole manufacturing of consumer products. This business model has gradually propagated in other areas that could offer customized services to their customers such as consumer electronics and fintech. However, the complexity of these offers could deter the potential customers as it could be difficult to understand and evaluate their benefits. Gamification of these offers is a newly adopted method with limited examples primarily in the manufacturing sector. This work presents the development of a serious game for the explanation of fintech servitization offers for the building construction industry. This work aims to identify the efficiency for improvement of user experience (UX) and behavioural intention of customers towards these offers. The project has been evaluated by ten users representing existing customers. The paper presents the evaluation results and concludes with suggestions for future applications and a tentative plan of work for enhancing the application.

Keywords: Servitization · Gamification · User experience · Fintech · Construction industry · 3D · Virtual reality · Simulation

1 Introduction

Servitization is a business model that is benefiting significantly the manufacturing sector as it provides services instead of manufactured products [1, 2]. This approach reduces significantly the development and manufacturing costs whilst the provision of services could utilise the existing products for multiple functions and/or clients, improving the profitability of the manufacturing company. This is achieved in a twofold method; primarily via a reduction in manufacturing and subsequently in energy and raw materials as well as via the acquisition of additional revenue.

A closely aligned sector offering similar servitization services is the financial sector. The overlapping area where the manufacturing and financial sectors interlink is a greatly unexplored domain of development.

© Springer Nature Switzerland AG 2022
G. Meiselwitz et al. (Eds.): HCII 2022, LNCS 13517, pp. 592–603, 2022.
https://doi.org/10.1007/978-3-031-22131-6_44

A major obstacle, however, to the expansion of this, lies in the complexity of the service offers. Such complexity potentially demotivates and reduces customer interest and final service offer uptake [3]. Communicating these service offers to the customer in an easy-to-comprehend and evaluate manner tends to be a challenging task for the staff of the provider company. Technological advancements have been employed to simplify and explain the offers to the customers. Digitally Enhanced Advanced Services (DEAS) have been utilised to clarify the process and include combinations of services offered to the final product [4, 5]. The above methods, however, are not ideal for optimising customer/user experience (UX), an area that suffers due to the aforementioned complexity issues.

The provision of DEAS from the finance sector in the manufacturing domain can further confound the potential customers. The adoption of new digital methods such as 3D Gamification was deemed an unorthodox, yet potentially useful method to convey such offers [6–8]. This paper presents the development of a 3D serious game that was designed in consultation with an industrial partner (EHAB) for the provision of parametric insurance for the buildings' construction customers. During the building process, the application suggests different insurance services that could prevent major financial issues under adverse weather conditions. The 3D game simulates different weather patterns based on a proprietary weather risk management system in a random pattern following the potential weather phenomena of the region and the month of the construction. The users are enabled to make their own decision regarding the insurance offers that they will use. When and if the building is completed a clear mapping of the different choices, costs and reputation performance is presented through analytical charts.

Firstly, the paper will present the current overlapping domain of financial services and construction. In turn, the paper will discuss the development of the 3D Serious Game and the evaluation results from 10 users aiming to identify their simulated learning experience (SLE). The results and their subjective feedback will be discussed in detail to form an initial appraisal of the suitability of using 3D gamification methods for explaining complex information such as DEAS. The paper will conclude with a tentative plan of future work which will entail the system evaluation with larger cohorts.

2   Construction Industry and Financial Products Servitization

Servitization provides the most fertile ground for the transformation of the manufacturing industry towards the provision of product services. The benefits of servitization have been highlighted in previous studies.

Yet the blend of financial technology and servitization with the construction industry can produce complex combinations of offers which include multiple variables per case for risk analysis. Consequently, these offers are challenging to explain to the potential customers irrelevantly to the significant benefits that they could yield if adopted.

Any type of construction has several risks involved, depending on the area and the topological conditions, which could further dictate logistical and localized weather issues. New services stemming from the use of emerging technologies such as Machine Learning (ML) could provide future insight on numerous risks related to the construction of buildings [9, 10]. These risks could be calculated by the analysis of historic and current data related to several factors such as environment temperature, types of ground and weather among others. The analysis of weather patterns could define potential issues and highlight risks and in response adapt to the projected financial risks and present the most appropriate insurance package that could alleviate the above issues.

This work was developed in collaboration with a fintech servitization company that is specialised in the provision of insurance deals for construction projects. To define better the provided offers the fintech company produced a Weather Ledger Platform (WLP) that combines Internet-of-Things (IoT) devices, distributed ledger technology (DLT), smart contracts, desktop tools and applications to reduce foreseen and unforeseen weather risks in the construction industry [11].

By using historic weather data in the pre-planning stages, construction managers can identify unknown risks. It further supports construction site teams to manage day-to-day weather risks. In situations where weather-related Compensation Events take place, it automates the overall claims and compensation processes. All these tools and services are designed with improving foresight, lowering the risk of impact, and facilitating better decisions in relation to risk management. The traditional way to predict the weather and potential construction issues was based on individual constructors' knowledge of the area without this being supported by any scientific methods. As such, detailed risk analysis and mitigation actions were not available and resulted in numerous damages and increased construction costs annually (Fig. 1).

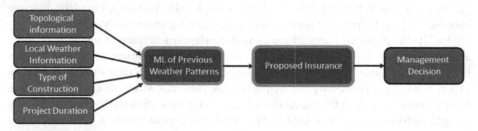

Fig. 1. Diagrammatic representation of the main process followed for a real-time proposed insurance package based on the main elements calculated by the ML.

3   Gamification of Fintech

3.1   Gamification in Various Domains

Serious Games/Gamification offers an innovative and creative way to communicate, engage and educate people. As well as bringing awareness and providing information, a serious game can potentially communicate complex information in a fun and simple manner. Notably, the vast majority of computer games are produced for entertainment purposes with a very small number of games targeting educational and training subjects for various domains and difficult subjects that require a different learning and understanding approach [12–17].

Although serious games have seen success in various other industries/education, only limited work has been carried out with DEAS [6, 14]. It was yet to be determined if such methods could be employed to enhance the communication, education and engagement of DEAS offers for the financial service providers.

To this end, this work was developed in conjunction with a fintech servitization company (EHAB) to design and produce a serious game focused on enhancing the understanding and education of their servitization offers.

3.2   Project Gamification Process

The proposed Serious Game was developed under the consultation of the fintech company to comply with all the relevant offers, and regulations and reflect the construction industry requirements and processes. As such the development team went through a training process to familiarise themselves with the services offered by EHAB, and to design an optimal solution for their challenges.

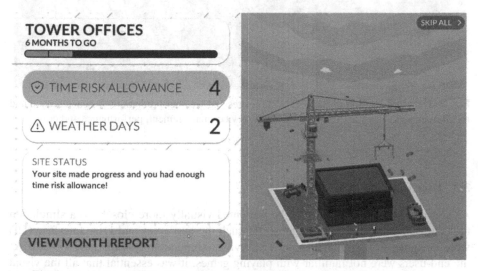

Fig. 2. Game Screenshot of 3D construction model progress and management menus.

The gamification of highly complicated and technical tools and services, supported by ML and designed as risk mitigation financial offers entailed several challenges and development issues.

During the training process, the fintech company highlighted the potential issue of the UI and visual cues of the game, which should follow a style acceptable to a simulation level rather than a game. If the UI appeared too imaginative or unconventional it might be rejected and not taken seriously by the end-users.

Furthermore, the construction simulation of any building should follow a specific development process and timelines reflecting the real-life scenarios. All the above should be transferred in the serious game whilst a 3D model of the actual building should be presented in one of the menus as illustrated in Fig. 2.

In addition, different types of buildings should be available for construction in the 3D environment, matching specific topographical information in different UK regions and the expected weather conditions and patterns of these areas as presented in Fig. 3 below.

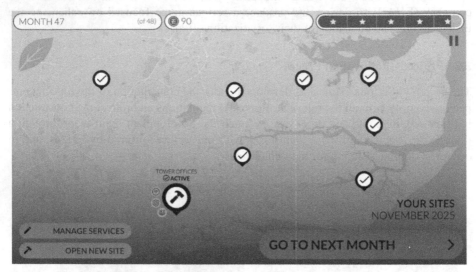

Fig. 3. Data visualisation of the construction sites and weather predictions for each season and month with supplementary information about services management, performance and cost

3.3 User Interface (UI)

As stated above, the game had to be presented visually more closely to a simulation tool rather than an entertaining game. As such the aesthetics and User Interface (UI) were designed in a similar manner to previous simulation systems [13, 18–20]. As the end-users were not familiar with playing games, it was essential that all the visual elements were clearly described and not abstracted to oversimplified or unknown icons. Any icons that were used followed a direct manipulation design concept in which any displayed objects of interest can be physically and incrementally manipulated by the users whilst they can reverse any of these actions and the effects of their actions can be directly noticeable on the screen [21–23]. As such the UI was designed in a minimalistic approach wherever possible, whilst descriptive menus have been maintained in visible positions to support the management of the site and investigate different insurance offers as shown in Figs. 2 and 3.

To entice the users to play the game and continue until their building is completed, it was deemed essential to add a scoring system as shown in Fig. 4 below.

Fig. 4. The scoring system presents a leaderboard that could be used for the comparison of different practices and decisions that affected the performance of a user.

This scoring system utilised proven game methods which entice the users to compete and learn from the best players on the leaderboard. In this leaderboard, the users could see analytical charts of their overall performance and contrast them with higher-scoring users. In this way, they could compare the different decisions and insurance choices that improved the completion rate of different constructions, and the cost-saving approaches. The overall profit and site completion number were counted towards the leaderboard place.

4 Evaluation

4.1 Evaluation Method

The evaluation of the serious game was performed by ten users specialising in the field and reflected the views of potential customers of the construction industry. The game application was evaluated to determine its effectiveness to support the dissemination of the fintech company information related to their offers. Secondly, as this type of system poses several issues for the evaluation and extrapolation of results in the larger population, this study employed a customized Technology Acceptance Model (TAM) that could offer valuable information regarding user acceptance and create a tool framework for future studies in the field of servitization and the use of serious games [25–27].

While the primary focus of the original project (Development of a Serious Game prototype to aid the education of smart contract policies) was to design, develop, and implement the serious game, this work aimed to explore and analyse the potential use of the game from a user experience (UX) point of view through a larger cohort.

This preliminary evaluation utilised a 7-point Likert Scale Questions (strongly disagree, disagree, somewhat disagree, neutral – neither agree nor disagree, somewhat agree, agree, strongly agree) referring to the custom TAM structure illustrated in Fig. 5 below.

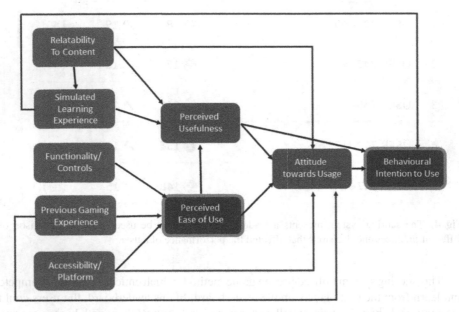

Fig. 5. Custom TAM structure for fintech servitization offers for the construction industry.

The ten users responded initially to a prequestionnaire which concerned with their demographic information and their computer literacy that could affect the outcome of this study.

In turn, the users played the serious game application and followed a typical construction process of a building for multiple months until completion. During the process, they could monitor their risk assessments, the predicted weather issues and their proposed insurance packages that could be implemented depending on the construction stage, development costs and overall performance.

After the game, the users completed a post-questionnaire following the custom TAM. This second questionnaire was designed to identify the user experience (UX), and the users' behavioural intention toward purchasing the fintech servitization offers.

This paper presents two of the most interesting sets of questions/statements that aim to reveal the users' Perceived Ease of Use (PEU) and their Behavioural Intention (BI) as presented in Table 1 [28–30].

Table 1. Perceived Ease of Use (PEU) and Behavioural Intention (BI) statements

PEU_1	I found the serious game easy to pick up and play
PEU_2	Learning to play this game was fairly simple
PEU_3	Interacting with the serious game did not require a lot of mental effort
BI_1	I would support the use of serious games to communicate complex servitisation offers
BI_2	If I had the opportunity I would participate in other simulation-based serious games
BI_3	I would like to see more of such serious games being utilised by manufacturing/ engineering companies to aid communication of their servitisation offers

5 Results and Discussion

The analysis of the TAM questionnaire provided some insight into the users' behaviour and their overall user experience. The three statements for the Perceived Ease of Use received positive responses from the users as illustrated in Fig. 6.

In particular, PEU1 scored 90% on the combined score of positive answers with only 10% neutral. This result was within the expected margins, yet additional changes on future versions will attempt to reduce this 10% further.

The PEU2 presented similar results showing that the users managed to learn to play this serious game fairly easily and quickly. This was identified during the development as a potential issue, as the majority of the target users don't play games. This concern was tackled by simplifying the game design and UI without losing through the detailed provision of servitization offers.

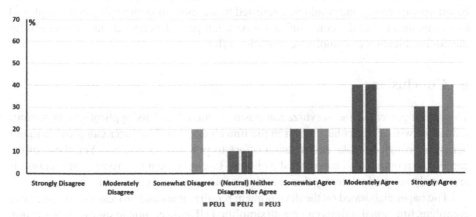

Fig. 6. Responses of 10 users in 3 statements describing their Perceived Ease of Use (PEU).

The PEU3 statement presented a slightly different output. Although 80% of the users appeared to be comfortable with the overall UI and the visual information as well as the menus and descriptions provided in the game design, 20% found it somewhat difficult and disagreed with the PEU3 statement (Table 1). This was a major concern that the fintech company highlighted during the consultation period at the early stages of the UI and the game development. However the concern was expressed as a potential complete refusal of the users to operate the game, so the 20% that found the interaction somewhat difficult was encouraging. To reduce this percentage this work will develop and experiment with new interface designs following the users' feedback and suggestions (Fig. 7).

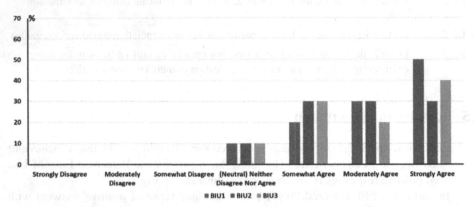

Fig. 7. Responses of 10 users in 3 statements describing their Behavioural Intention (BI).

The other three statements aimed to identify the users' behavioural intention (BI) towards the received overall positive results with only 10% responding neutrally. The users displayed comparable positive approaches and stated that they would be happy to use similar types of serious games to communicate and understand complex servitisation offers. They also responded that they would be keen to participate in other simulation-based serious games and would be interested to see more of such applications employed by companies to aid the communication between providers and clients, especially for the communication of complex servitisation offers.

6 Conclusions

This work presented the servitization business model and its applications in various industries with a particular interest in the fintech domain. The latter can provide major benefits through bespoke servitization offers to potential customers. Yet, these offers can be overcomplicated and deter the clients. To circumvent this issue, gamification is tentatively adopted to convey this complex information in an enjoyable manner.

The paper elaborated on the development requirements and process that resulted in a complete, functional serious game with simplified UI and a complete suite of servitization offers presented through the gameplay.

The final serious game was preliminarily evaluated by ten users, that are specialised in the construction and servitisation field. A custom TAM was developed to gauge users' acceptance of this type of technology. The paper presented the results of PEU and BI which were encouraging and supportive of the current serious game. The evaluation results emphasized the users' ability to understand and experience in a simulated 3D environment the benefits and drawbacks of the proposed insurance and other financial offers during the construction of a building. Furthermore, this initial testing highlighted the suitability of the gamification process to convey complex information for financial products.

Based on the users' feedback, additional UI elements and development will be required to improve the playability and acceptability for future similar 3D serious games and applications. In addition, a future plan will entail the evaluation of such game applications with larger and more diverse cohorts.

References

1. Kohtamäki, M., Parida, V., Patel, P.C., Gebauer, H.: The relationship between digitalization and servitization: the role of servitization in capturing the financial potential of digitalization. Technol. Forecast. Soc. Chang. **151**, 119804 (2020). https://doi.org/10.1016/j.techfore.2019.119804
2. Paiola, M., Schiavone, F., Grandinetti, R., Chen, J.: Digital servitization and sustainability through networking: some evidences from IoT-based business models. J. Bus. Res. **132**, 507–516 (2021). https://doi.org/10.1016/j.jbusres.2021.04.047
3. Wood, Z., Godsiff, P.: Establishing the core principles of servitisation for application outside manufacturing. Compet. Advant. Digit. Econ. 125–130. (2021). https://doi.org/10.1049/icp.2021.2425
4. Schroeder, A., Naik, P., Ziaee Bigdeli, A., Baines, T.: Digitally enabled advanced services: a socio-technical perspective on the role of the internet of things (IoT). Int. J. Oper. Prod. Manag. **40**, 1243–1268 (2020)
5. DEAS NetworkPlus: Digitally Enhanced Advanced Services EPSRC NetworkPlus Manufacturing Theme Research Agenda 2019; University of Westminster: London UK (2019). ISBN 978 185449 478 8. www.deas.ac.uk. Accessed 22 June 2022
6. Khan, M.S., et al.: Improving user experience and communication of Digitally Enhanced Advanced Services (DEAS) Offers in manufacturing sector. Multimodal Technol. Interact. **6**, 21 (2022). https://doi.org/10.3390/mti6030021
7. Romero-Rodriguez, L.M., Ramirez-Montoya, M.S., Gonzalez, J.R.V.: Gamification in MOOCs: engagement application test in energy sustainability courses. IEEE Access **7**, 32093–32101 (2019). https://doi.org/10.1109/access.2019.2903230
8. Falah, J., et al.: Identifying the characteristics of virtual reality gamification for complex educational topics. Multimodal. Technol. Interact. **5**, 53. (2021). https://doi.org/10.3390/mti5090053
9. Heinis, T.B., Loy, C.L., Meboldt, M.: Improving usage metrics for pay-per-use pricing with IoT technology and machine learning. Res. Technol. Manag. **61**(5), 32–40 (2018). https://doi.org/10.1080/08956308.2018.1495964
10. Frank, M., Drikakis, D., Charissis, V.: Machine-learning methods for computational science and engineering. Computation **8**, 15 (2020)
11. Bochenek, B., Ustrnul, Z.: Machine learning in weather prediction and climate analyses—applications and perspectives. Atmosphere **13**, 180 (2022). https://doi.org/10.3390/atmos13020180
12. Chung, C.H., Lin, Y.Y.: Online 3D gamification for teaching a human resource development course. J. Comput. Assist. Learn. **38**(3), 692–706 (2022). https://doi.org/10.1111/jcal.12641
13. Lagoo, R., Charissis, V., Harrison, D.K.: Mitigating driver's distraction: automotive head-up display and gesture recognition system. IEEE Consumer Electron. Magaz. **8**(5), 79–85 (2019). https://doi.org/10.1109/MCE.2019.2923896

14. Andrews, D., Dmitrijeva, J., Bigdeli, A.Z., Baines, T.: Snakes and ladders in servitization : using a game to capture inhibitors and enablers of transformation snakes and ladders in servitization using a game to capture inhibitors and enablers of transformation. Res. Technol. Manag. **61**, 1–12 (2018). https://doi.org/10.1080/08956308.2018.1516930

15. Ward, B.M., Charissis, V., Rowley, D., Anderson, P., Brady, L.: An evaluation of prototype VR medical training environment: applied surgical anatomy training for malignant breast disease. J. Stud. Health Technol. Inform. **132**(16), 500–505 (2008)

16. Alfalah, S., Harisson, D.K., Charissis, V., Evans, D.: Investigation of multimodal interaction and 3D simulation environment for prototype healthcare system. In: Mustafee N., Katsaliaki K. (eds.) Journal of Enterprise Information Management (JEIM), vol. 26, Iss: 1/2, pp.183–197 (2013). ISSN: 1741-0398

17. Pappas, G., Siegel, J., Vogiatzakis, I.N., Politopoulos, K.: Gamification and the internet of things in education. In: Ivanović, M., Klašnja-Milićević, A., Jain, L.C. (eds.) Handbook on Intelligent Techniques in the Educational Process. LAIS, vol. 29. Springer, Cham (2022). https://doi.org/10.1007/978-3-031-04662-9_15

18. Charissis, V., Papanastasiou, S., Mackenzie, L., Arafat, S.: Evaluation of collision avoidance prototype head-up display interface for older drivers. In: Jacko, J.A. (ed.) HCI 2011. LNCS, vol. 6763, pp. 367–375. Springer, Heidelberg (2011). https://doi.org/10.1007/978-3-642-21616-9_41

19. Altarteer, S., Charissis, V., Harrison D., Chan W.: Product customisation: virtual reality and new opportunities for luxury brands online trading. In: International Conference on 3D Web Technology/ACM SIGGRAPH, pp. 22–24 Anaheim, California, USA (2016)

20. Wang, S., Charissis, V., Harrison, D.: Augmented reality prototype HUD for passenger infotainment in a vehicular environment. Adv. Sci. Technol. Eng. Syst. J. **2**, 634–641 (2017)

21. Hutchins, E.L., Hollan, J.D., Norman, D.A.: Direct manipulation interfaces. Hum. Comput. Interact. **1**(4), 311–338 (1985). https://doi.org/10.1207/s15327051hci0104_2

22. Charissis, V., Naef, M., Papanastasiou, S., Patera, M.: Designing a direct manipulation HUD interface for in-vehicle infotainment. In: Jacko, J.A. (eds.) Human-Computer Interaction. Interaction Platforms and Techniques. HCI 2007. LNCS, vol. 4551. Springer, Berlin (2007). https://doi.org/10.1007/978-3-540-73107-8_62

23. Tastan, H., Tuker, C., Tong, T.: Using handheld user interface and direct manipulation for architectural modeling in immersive virtual reality: an exploratory study. Comput. Appl. Eng. Educ. **30**, 415–434 (2022). https://doi.org/10.1002/cae.22463

24. Ciuchita, R., Heller, J., Köcher, S., et al.: It is really not a game: an integrative review of gamification for service research. J. Serv. Res. (2022). https://doi.org/10.1177/109467052 21076272

25. Altarteer, S., Charissis, V.: Technology acceptance model for 3D virtual reality system in luxury brands online stores. IEEE Access J. **7**, 64053–64062 (2019). https://doi.org/10.1109/ ACCESS.2019.2916353

26. Marangunić, N., Granić, A.: Technology acceptance model: a literature review from 1986 to 2013. Univ. Access Inf. Soc. **14**(1), 81–95 (2014). https://doi.org/10.1007/s10209-014-0348-1

27. Vanduhe, V.Z., Nat, M., Hasan, H.F.: Continuance intentions to use gamification for training in higher education: integrating the Technology Acceptance Model (TAM), Social Motivation, and Task Technology Fit (TTF). IEEE Access **8**, 21473–21484 (2020). https://doi.org/10. 1109/ACCESS.2020.2966179

28. Yang, Y., Asaad, Y., Dwivedi, Y.: Examining the impact of gamification on intention of engagement and brand attitude in the marketing context. Comput. Hum. Behav. **73**, 459–469 (2017)

29. Kuo-Yi, L., Pei-I, Y., Pei-Chun, C., Chen-Fu, C.: User experience-based design of experiments for new product development of consumer electronics and an empirical study. J. Ind. Prod. Eng. **34**(7), 504–519 (2017). https://doi.org/10.1080/21681015.2017.1363089
30. García-Magro, C., Soriano-Pinar, I.: Design of services in servitized firms: gamification as an adequate tool. J. Bus. Indust. Market. **35**(3), 575–585 (2020). https://doi.org/10.1108/JBIM-12-2018-0413

Building the "Complete Game": An Overview Study of a Development Strategy for Geo AR Mobile Games

Hugh Xuechen Liu(✉) ⓘ

City University of Hong Kong, 83 Tat Chee Ave, Hong Kong SAR, China
Hugh.liu@my.cityu.edu.hk

Abstract. This paper presents a bibliometric analysis and literature review on the Geo AR mobile game, a new form of video game enabled by geolocation and augmented reality technology. The definition of the Geo AR mobile game, its development history and business status are identified and with the current research topics around it. It's noted that there is a prevailing problem of sustainable success among Geo AR mobile games, and it is little addressed in current academic conversations. Therefore, this paper proposes that Geo AR mobile games should be built as the "complete game" for sustainable success.

Keywords: Geo AR mobile games · Location-based augmented reality mobile games · Bibliometric analysis · Literature review · Overview study · Complete game

1 Introduction

Video games have become the most popular leisure information systems (IS) [1]. Over 60% of the online population plays video games [2]. Technology has empowered the development of video games in terms of general processing speed, graphics and way of playing. In recent years, cutting-edge technologies like geolocation systems (Geo) and augmented reality (AR) have received attention and have been expected to reshape the video game industry.

Geo and AR technology created a new genre of video games, namely a new category [3]. This new genre of video games is usually called "Geo AR mobile game," "pervasive augmented reality games," or "location-based augmented reality mobile games" among the public. For example, geolocation technology utilizes information about the geolocation of the player as a part of the gameplay, which creates a mapping and entanglement between the virtual game world and the real world the player resides. In recent years, geolocation games have mostly used augmented reality (AR) technology to enhance mapping and entanglement [4]. By capturing the real environment around, generating virtual objects and displaying them simultaneously on the screen of the game device, AR and geolocation technologies could create a strong feeling of copresence of real surroundings and virtual game objects [5]. As a result, Geo AR mobile games are expected

G. Meiselwitz et al. (Eds.): HCII 2022, LNCS 13517, pp. 604–622, 2022.
https://doi.org/10.1007/978-3-031-22131-6_45

to redefine how players engage with a game and disrupt the video game industry based on the media or analysts in 2016 [6, 7].

Although nearly six years have passed, Geo AR mobile games seem not pervasively successful or dominant in the mainstream game market as people used to expect. For example, in 2016, *Pokémon GO* reached over 20 million active users within two weeks, and daily usage was longer than *Facebook*, *Twitter*, and *Snapchat* combined [8]. *Pokémon GO* peaked at 100 million users worldwide and 45 million daily unique visitors, with 28.5 million in the U.S. alone. However, a third of its daily users vapored in merely one month [9]. Daily revenues fell from US$16m per day to US$2m (excluding the 30% app store fee), and daily downloads declined from a peak of 27 to 0.7 million [10]. A year later, *Pokémon GO* was almost forgotten. People thought *Pokémon GO* was already a dead game, as the usual scenarios of mobile games. Many reviews and critics say *Pokémon GO* failed [11, 12]. Although equipped with bleeding technology, Geo AR mobile games didn't become a rigorous and sustainable business.

Similarly, eight Geo AR mobile games were released in 2018 and 2019. Some of them, like *Harry Potter: Wizard Unite* and *Minecraft Earth*, came from famous and successful game series and became a success in the release weeks. However, when this paper was written, three of these eight games were discontinued, and those left seem to be rapidly losing active players and revenue [13–15]. If the success of Geo AR mobile games is pervasively unsustainable, it will threaten the business of Geo AR mobile game developers, further hinder the market's sustainable development and limit the general realization of Geo AR mobile games as an interface of the virtual-reality-mixed world.

Therefore, this research is conducted to perform an "environment scanning" of Geo AR mobile games as a start. Specifically, this paper wants to answer these questions:

Q1. Is there a commonly agreed definition of Geo AR mobile games?
Q2. Are there well-defined research directions within the overall Geo AR mobile games? If so, what are these topics?
Q3. Are there common business models among the Geo AR mobile games? If so, what are they?

The remained parts of this paper are arranged in the following order. Section 2 will describe the design of this research, including the methodology and methods of data collection and analysis. Section 3 presents the research results and answers the three research questions proposed. Section 4 discusses the findings for future Geo AR mobile game research. Finally, the paper will end with Sect. 5 providing a conclusion.

2 Design of the Review

2.1 Methodology

This paper presents an exploratory study. It aims to answer the three research questions proposed through a structured literature review. Following the guidelines of the structured literature review proposed by Kitchenham [16], the data is collected through documents and observations. The data would be analyzed through both bibliometric analysis and narrative analysis.

This study looks for information from objective records such as archives or update logs. Therefore, a structured literature review would be appropriate. It will be carried out in three consequential steps, namely (1) Planning the review, (2) Conducting the review and (3) Reporting the review [16]. Planning and conducting the review clarifies the data collection and analysis methods and will be discussed in the following. Reporting the review will be conducted in Sect. 3.

2.2 Methods

Rowley and Slack [17] suggested an excessive search on various materials and websites, such as academic research publications, archives of magazines and news chapters, and practitioner publications, to iteratively collect the first wave of keywords synonyms related to the topic. The chosen keywords and synonyms for inquiry included "Geo AR mobile games", "Geolocation AR mobile games", "Geo Augmented Reality mobile game"," location-based AR mobile games", "location-based augmented reality games", "augmented reality pervasive games", "augmented reality location aware mobile games", "augmented reality adaptronic mobile games." These keywords are inspired by previous studies [18].

First, data are collected from databases (e.g., *Web of Science, Scopus,* and *ProQuest).* These authoritative literature databases cover various subjects within multifarious disciplines [19]. Many literature review papers are based on the search results of these databases (e.g., Cheung and Thadani [20], Du, Ke [21], Suh and Prophet [22]). Second, however, websites like *Wiki* of the game or virtual communities like *Reddit* or *Discord* are also included as sources of information. Since the Geo AR mobile game topic is relatively new, screenshots, demos, or recordings on these websites are helpful for advancing the knowledge about Geo AR mobile games. These sources are collected called "other sources" in this paper. Third, games still available are downloaded and played by the author to gain first-hand information about the game.

This paper demonstrates a keyword-based search on these three databases with the identified keyword pool to extract relevant research papers by their titles, abstracts, and keywords (if any). Only articles in English are pulled out. In total, 369 articles are collected. After the automatic removing duplicates procedure through *Endnote,* 335 articles remained.

Next, these articles are screened and filtered by applying the inclusion and exclusion criteria (See Table 1 below). After manually filtering and removing duplicates, 207 articles are left for further analysis. Only 138 from *Scopus* are used for bibliometric analysis because of the restriction of the software used. But all 207 articles are read for narrative review, especially for identifying the games and business models. Among them, six articles gave definitions of Geo AR mobile games. So, they are used for the definition proposition. Figure 1 below summarizes the workflow of this research.

Table 1. Filtering criteria.

Criteria	No.	Description
Inclusion criteria	I1	The publication is an article with the empirical, technical, or theoretical focus
	I2	The publication covers all aspects of "geolocation," "augmented reality," and "mobile games"
Exclusion criteria	E1	The publication is a technical manual introducing detail of specific technology
	E2	The Geo AR mobile game is not relevant in the publication (say, "Geo AR mobile game" was just mentioned)

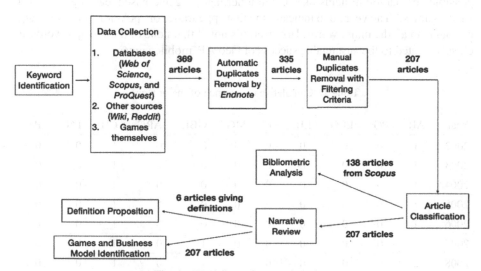

Fig. 1. Workflow of research design

Bibliometric analysis encapsulates the application of quantitative techniques on bibliometric data (e.g., units of publication and citation) [23]. It gained immense popularity for the advancement of bibliometric software, scientific databases and the diffusion of bibliometric methodology from information science to business research [24]. It is a structural way to review in a broad scope and therefore complements the traditional narrative literature review, mainly used for the specific scope of review. Generally, the bibliometric methodology primarily focuses on the constructs of publications [25]. Since this study wants to depict the general state of Geo AR mobile game research, bibliometric analysis is an appropriate methodology for us to start. As suggested by Linnenluecke, Marrone [25], the *Bibliometrix* package supported by the *R* programming language is used [26, 27]. *Bibliometrix* package is widely used in many publications [28, 29]. It is also friendly to researchers who don't want to code [30]. Although *Bibliometrix* only supports analyzing data from *Scopus*, this paper finds it acceptable since more than 60% of articles are from *Scopus*.

This paper also adopts a classic narrative literature review approach. All the 207 articles are screened to propose a definition of Geo AR mobile games and identify specific games and their business models.

3 Result

3.1 Bibliometric Analysis

Major Words. Among the 138 *Scopus* articles from 2002 to 2022, the top 11 frequently used keywords are identified as "major words" and their cumulative occurrence are shown in Table 2. Since 2002, early researchers have noticed the potential of technology like "augmented reality" and "location-based." These pioneers also noticed the possible application in fields like "cultural heritage," "game-based learning" and "pervasive games." The year 2016 indicates the first appearance of "pokmon Go" and a surge of counts in all the major words. However, it's noted that none of these major words are closely related to the sustainable success of Geo AR mobile games.

Table 2. Cumulative occurrence of major words.

Year	AR	PG	LBG	LB	G	MG	GBL	ARG	CH	PG2	PA
2002	1	0	0	0	0	0	0	0	1	0	0
2003	1	0	0	0	0	0	0	0	1	0	0
2004	1	0	0	0	0	0	0	0	1	0	0
2005	1	0	0	0	0	0	0	0	1	0	0
2006	1	0	0	0	0	0	0	0	1	0	0
2007	2	0	0	0	0	0	1	0	1	0	0
2008	2	0	0	0	0	0	1	0	1	0	0
2009	3	0	0	0	0	0	1	0	1	0	0
2010	3	0	0	0	0	0	1	0	1	0	0
2011	5	0	0	1	0	1	1	0	1	1	0
2012	7	0	0	2	0	1	1	0	1	1	0
2013	8	0	0	2	0	1	1	0	1	1	0
2014	9	0	0	3	0	1	1	0	1	1	0
2015	12	0	1	3	0	1	1	0	3	1	0
2016	19	1	3	4	0	3	2	0	3	3	0
2017	29	7	9	5	2	5	2	2	5	5	3
2018	37	11	9	7	2	5	3	4	5	5	4
2019	48	13	11	11	6	7	4	4	6	5	5

(*continued*)

Table 2. (*continued*)

Year	AR	PG	LBG	LB	G	MG	GBL	ARG	CH	PG2	PA
2020	56	19	15	12	8	10	7	7	7	7	6
2021	64	22	21	13	12	10	9	8	8	8	8
2022	65	22	21	13	12	10	9	8	8	8	8

Note: **AR**-Augmented Reality; **PG**-Pokmon Go; **LBG**-Location-Based Games; **LB**-Location-Based; **G**-Gamification; **MG**-Mobile Games; **GBL**-Game-Based Learning; **ARG**-Augmented Reality Games; **CH**-Cultural Heritage; **PG2** -Pervasive Games; **PA**-Physical Activity.

Co-occurrence Network Analysis. If two words appear in one paper's "Keyword" part, these two words have a co-occurrence relationship. A co-occurrence relationship is stronger if the related two words appear more often than others. Therefore, it is possible to pull out all the keywords in articles and find the existence and strength of the relationships between each pair of words. The words and relationships can be visualized as a "co-occurrence network." In this network, each word is called a "node" and each relationship is called an "edge." The frequency of a word and the strength of the relationship are accordingly visualized as the node's and edge's size. For each node, two typical indicators show its importance. Table 3 below explains these two indicators: Betweenness and Closeness [31]. The result of the co-occurrence network analysis on the 138 *Scopus* articles is shown in Table 4 and visualized in Fig. 2.

Table 3. Two indicators of co-occurrence network analysis.

Indicator	Definition	Meaning
Betweenness	It measures the number of times a node acts as a bridge along the shortest path between two other nodes	the importance of one node for the existence of the whole network
Closeness	1/(the sum of a node's distances to all other nodes)	the direct impact of one node on other nodes

Table 4. Co-occurrence analysis result.

Node	Cluster	Betweenness	Closeness
Augmented reality	1	506.385	0.022
Location-based	1	2.155	0.015
Gamification	1	2.339	0.015
Mobile games	1	0.000	0.014

(*continued*)

Table 4. (*continued*)

Node	Cluster	Betweenness	Closeness
Cultural heritage	1	0.000	0.013
Games	1	0.000	0.013
Mixed reality	1	0.000	0.013
User experience	1	0.000	0.013
Education	1	0.000	0.013
Location-based game	1	0.000	0.013
Pokemon go	1	0.000	0.013
Serious game	1	0.000	0.013
Higher education	1	0.000	0.013
Learning analytics	1	0.000	0.013
Location based	1	0.000	0.013
Location-based gaming	1	0.000	0.013
Locative media	1	0.000	0.013
Mobile applications	1	0.000	0.013
Pokmon go	2	142.521	0.017
Location-based games	2	97.273	0.017
Augmented reality games	2	0.000	0.012
Physical activity	2	0.000	0.011
Behavior change	2	0.000	0.012
Behavior change support system	2	0.000	0.012
Digital gaming	2	0.000	0.012
Exergames	2	0.000	0.012
Free-to-play	2	0.000	0.011
Injury	2	0.000	0.011
Game-based learning	3	35.000	0.014
Serious games	3	0.000	0.014
Mobile augmented reality	3	0.000	0.010
Pervasive games	4	1.326	0.014
Mobile gaming	4	0.000	0.013
Usability	5	0.000	0.013
Educational game design	5	0.000	0.013
Field of view	6	0.000	0.013
Line of sight	6	0.000	0.013

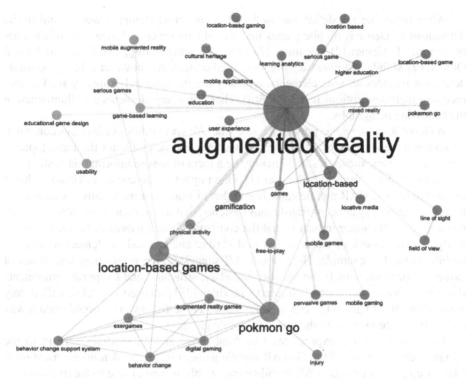

Fig. 2. Keyword co-occurrences of geo AR mobile game literature as a network plot.

The analysis shows that in current research on Geo AR mobile games, the dominant words are "augmented reality," "location-based games," and "pokmon go." They are the nodes that not only impact other nodes but are also crucial for the whole network. That indicates at least two points. First, the discussions are still focused on the trendy technological characteristics, namely AR and location-based technology. Even the game as a "mobile game" is hardly discussed. Second, the game *Pokémon GO* significantly increased the passion of researchers. *Pokémon GO* seems a synonym of Geo AR mobile games. However, the problem is still that sustainable success doesn't have a role in these academic conversations of Geo AR mobile games, let alone a central position. Even the sustainable success of *Pokémon GO* is hardly discussed.

3.2 Narrative Analysis

Definition of Geo AR Mobile Game. With the emergence of the conceptual, qualitative, and quantitative literature on Geo AR mobile games, a few definitions have been put forward across the various research fields like Geo games, AR mobile games and exergames [18, 32, 33]. To the best knowledge, the earliest academic definition appears in the work of Blum, Wetzel [34]. Subsequently, several definitions (e.g., Alha, Koskinen [35], Ku, Shang [36]) were proposed to capture new facets of this emerging phenomenon.

After reviewing the definitions in the literature, nine elements were found in the definitions of Geo AR mobile games that would capture core dimensions of the phenomenon: (1) Game; (2) Location; (3) Live; (4) Surrounding; (5) View; (6) Virtual Object; (7) Mobile; (8) Everyday life; (9) Collaborative. As shown in Table 5, no single definition includes all nine elements, typically highlighting only three or six key elements in their descriptions (e.g., [35, 36]). These nine key elements are illuminated in the following paragraphs.

A Geo AR mobile game must first be a Game. All six definitions cover this construct. Although there are tons of definitions of what a game is, that's not the main topic of this study. A game means it should mainly be a form of leisure information system (IS) and create hedonic values for the user [1]. One impact of the construct Game is that it differentiates a Geo AR mobile game from other utilitarian or informative systems, like tourist navigation systems or translations systems, that use similar geolocation and AR technologies. The other impact is that the construct Game enables us to use the given analytical framework of game design to describe, analyze and implement a Geo AR mobile game. For example, Holopainen [37] suggested one must cover four types of game components, namely the holistic, boundary, structural and temporal components if the game is to be understood. Similarly, Järvinen [38] proposed several so-called "key game elements" to grasp the essence of a game. These frameworks would open a way for further discussions with the Geo AR mobile game.

Live, including the expressions like "real-time" and "immediate," refers to the dynamic characteristic of the Geo AR mobile game. Five of six definitions mentioned Live. It emphasizes the Geo AR mobile game should be responsive to the dynamic situation where the player stays. This construct omits the possibility of presenting merely complete static content to meet the requirement.

Location (LOC), also commonly expressed with "position," meanings indisputably the geolocation position where the player (actually, the game device) sits. Four of six definitions mentioned it. Whether explicitly mentioning the Global Position System (GPS), Location in the definitions refers to the application of information about the absolute geolocation information. It could be used directly by displaying the concrete GPS coordinates or indirectly through the related information of landscape, weather condition and settings of roads and buildings.

Surrounding (SURR) brings the specific environment of the game and the player to the table. For example, GPS would provide information related to Location pointing out a statue in this district. But still, we know little about whether there are people around the statue at this moment of playing. In another word, the Surrounding is more context-based. Four of six definitions mentioned this construct.

Sensory (SEN) is a controversial one among the definition. Ramtohul and Khedo [39] proposed it as one of the components of their definition. But Ku, Shang [36] and Blum, Wetzel [34] limited the sensory aspect to be exactly sight ("view") or sight plus hearing ("live video stream"). However, these definitions share that Sensory is a vital construct to define Geo AR mobile game. And not only a single sensory capability be used, but multiple ones are also acceptable.

Virtual Information (VI) is mentioned by three of six definitions. The construct here means the information that doesn't exist in the direct physical world the player lives in but is generated and presented through the game device. Specifically, Blum, Wetzel [34] demands the virtual information must be a "virtual 3D object," while Ku, Shang [36] and SensorTower [40] include any virtual information or generated contents.

Surprisingly, only three of six definitions explicitly propose Mobile as one construct to define the Geo AR mobile game. Instead, Mobile is used as part of "mobile device" or "mobile game" in these three entries without further description. Therefore, Mobile should be understood commonly; the game terminal is small enough to hold and carry easily [41].

The last two constructs, Everyday Life (EL) and Collaboration (COLL) are mentioned in all the six definitions. On the one hand, Everyday Life means the routine activities of a player. Alha, Koskinen [35] argue the integration of gameplay into Everyday Life is a crucial characteristic of the Geo AR mobile game. On the other hand, Collaboration means the specific interaction between the Geo AR mobile game players. And it's one of the defining factors, as Ramtohul and Khedo [39].

These nine constructs convey unique defining aspects of Geo AR mobile games and are adequate. However, Everyday Life and Collaboration may be waived because each only has one mention in the six definitions. However, at least three of six definitions appear in the other seven constructs. Consequently, this paper proposes a definition of the Geo AR mobile game containing all seven constructs, namely:

The Geo AR mobile game refers to the location-aware mobile game that combines live surrounding-based experience with sensory virtual information.

Three points about the "sensory virtual information" in the definition are worth emphasis. First, the sensory information may usually be visual but not necessary. Second, utilizing multiple sensory information or just a single one is acceptable. Third, the virtual information may be presented as an illusion of a 3D virtual object on the display interface as seen these days, but it could be something else. Finally, the definition is expected to grasp the most significant and common parts of previous definitions and convey the essence of the Geo AR mobile game.

Table 5. Summary of the geo AR mobile game definitions.

GAME	LIVE	LOC	SURR	SEN	VI	MOBILE	EL	COLL	Source
✓	✓		✓	✓	✓	✓			[34]
✓	✓	✓	✓	✓		✓			[42]
✓			✓				✓		[35]
✓	✓	✓	✓	✓	✓				[36]
✓	✓	✓			✓				[40]
✓	✓	✓		✓		✓		✓	[39]
6	5	4	4	4	3	3	1	1	Counts

Note: **GAME**-Game; **LIVE**-Live; **LOC**-Location; **SURR**-Surrounding; **SEN**-Sensory; **VI**-Virtual Information; **MOBILE**-Mobile; **EL**-Everyday Life; **COLL**-Collaboration.

Games and Business Models. From the 207 articles collected, 29 games conform to the definition proposed previously. Therefore, it's not unreasonable to see these 29 games as "Geo AR mobile games." Limited to the length of this paper, readers are welcome to check the shared file[1] or request the author to see the full list.

A mobile game business model is a monetization strategy developers use to drive revenue for the app [43]. A mobile game will always adopt a one-time or freemium payment business model. A freemium business model is usually based on in-app purchases, ad monetization, or both. Based on the monetization level, Geo AR mobile games in history may be divided into three stages:

Stage I – Non-monetization Era (2000–2011). In this stage, the Geo AR mobile game was mainly developed as an experimental product by researchers in university labs or the league of geek designers. So there is little data about Geo AR mobile games in Stage I. But still, games at this stage little cared about the business model. And all these games were discontinued now.

Stage II – Early Monetization Era (2012–2015). This stage is marked by the game *eevoo*, developed by a startup company called *eelusion* in 2012. *Eevoo* is the first Geo AR mobile game demonstrating a clear freemium business model [44]. *Ingress*, developed by *Niantic Labs* in 2013, also adopted a freemium business model. But other games in this era either lack a clear business model or are unknown because of a lack of data. Another interesting point is that several games became vaporware. Namely, the projects were started but canceled later. For example, in Stage I, the prototypes may be usually completed for academic publications or communications between researchers. But in Stage II, the developers became agile and flexible to stop a project which was not promising. As a result, games at Stage II are either not released at all or discontinued at this moment.

Stage III – Broad Monetization Era (2016-present). This stage is symbolled by the launch of *Pokémon GO* in 2016. Since then, the Geo AR mobile game as a genre has gained immense attention from a mass audience [45]. Previously, location-based augmented reality games were mostly prototypes or games without significant commercial success [46]. Still, after the success of *Pokémon GO*, many location-based AR games are now entering the market [35]. Since then, all Geo AR mobile games have adopted a freemium business model. Table 6 shows the Geo AR mobile games in the broad monetization era.

---

[1] https://docs.google.com/document/d/1C9_pCUQ7ybFTJIz3nGTYuVCRAy4OckQU/edit?usp=sharing&ouid=103669851516348414625&rtpof=true&sd=true.

Table 6. Geo AR mobile games in broad monetization era.

Name	Developer	Year	Platform	Status	Business model	Source
Pokémon GO	*Niantic Labs*	2016	*iOS, Android*	Alive	Freemium (**Pr**)	**F:** [47] **S:** [45, 48]
Ingress Prime	*Niantic Labs*	2018	*iOS, Android*	Alive	Freemium(**Pr**)	**F:** [49] **S:** [48]
The Walking Dead: Our World	*Next Games*	2018	*iOS, Android*	Alive	Freemium(**Ad, Pr**)	**F:** [50] **S:** [48, 51]
Ghostbusters World	*NextAge*	2018	*iOS, Android*	**DC** since Aug 13, 2020	Freemium	**F:** [52]
Jurassic World: alive	*Ludia, NBCUniversal*	2018	*iOS, Android*	Alive	Freemium	**F:** [53] **S:** [54]
Dragon Quest Walk	*SQUARE ENIX CO., LTD., COLOPL*	2019	*iOS, Android*	Alive	Freemium	**F:** [55]
Harry Potter: Wizard Unite	*Niantic Labs*	2019	*iOS, Android*	**DC** since Jan 31, 2022	Freemium	**F:** [56]
Minecraft Earth	*Mojang Studios*	2019	*iOS, Android*	**DC** since Jun 30, 2021	Freemium	**F:** [57, 58]
Let's Hunt Monsters	*Tencent*	2019	*iOS, Android*	Alive	Freemium	**F:** [59, 60]
Arabian Nights: Genie's Treasures	*MENA Mobile*	2021	*iOS, Android*	Released on Apr 7, 2021; **DC** since May 17, 2021	**N/D**	**F:** [61]
The Witcher: Monster Slayer	*Spokko sp. Z o.o*	2021	*iOS, Android*	Alive	Freemium(**Pr**)	**F:** [62]
Pikmin Bloom	*Niantic Labs*	2021	*iOS, Android*	Alive	Freemium(**Pr**)	**F:** [63]

Note: **N/D**-No data; **N/A**-Not available; **F**-Firsthand source; **S**-Secondhand source; **Ad**-advertisement in-game; **Pr**-purchase in-game; **DC**-Discontinued.

4 Discussions

Table 7 below summarizes the findings of this study as responses to the research questions proposed. And the sustainable success problem of Geo AR mobile games doesn't receive enough attention from researchers. Besides the avalanche of *Pokémon GO*, among the eight Geo AR mobile games released in 2018 and 2019, three have been discontinued. Four alive games have only 1% of their peak Monthly Active User Numbers (MAU). There is only one alive game have 10%. In 2021, three Geo AR mobile games were released. One of them (i.e., *Arabian Nights: Genie's treasures*) was discontinued two months after its release. The other two games released in 2021, *The Witcher: Monster Slayer* and *Pikmin Bloom*, also have less than 10% of their peak MAU and seem to keep losing them without stopping. If the success and survival of Geo AR mobile games are not sustainable, the promising benefits in health promotions, cultural heritage or tourism will become invalid.

Table 7. Responses to the research questions.

Research questions	Responses
Q1. Is there a commonly agreed definition of Geo AR mobile games?	Yes. Although some agreements and disagreements, previous literature identifies that the Geo AR mobile game refers to the location-aware mobile game that combines live surrounding experience with sensory virtual information
Q2. Are there well-defined research directions within the overall Geo AR mobile games? If so, what are these topics?	Yes. As indicated by bibliometric analysis results, these topics are about technology and the application of Geo AR mobile games. Sustainable success is hardly addressed
Q3. Are there common business models among the Geo AR mobile games? If so, what are they?	No, and yes. Early Geo AR mobile games don't have a business model. Recent Geo AR mobile games, however, adopt a freemium business model

This paper suggests a development strategy from a perspective of technology components in Geo AR mobile games. First, Geo AR mobile games should enrich the game designs to make themselves "complete."

Geo AR mobile games may be decomposed into technology components that enable several significant and indispensable functions. Sasha [64] pointed out that there must be a "game engine" to realize the game design and balance. Kh. [65] provided a slimmer list of the components, including "a game engine," "location-awareness," "In-app purchase," and "notifications." Cubix [66] even shortlisted and proposed merely four components. Besides, an "AR engine" is necessary to produce mixed visual signals. Table 8 lists these technology components mentioned in the literature.

Currently, all these technology components have somehow saturated. For example, AR engines in early games (e.g., *eevoo* in 2012) were self-made. Later, software development toolkits (SDK) were developed specifically for AR. *Vuforia* is one example. After that, SDKs supported by operating systems came out. *ARCore* (supported by *Apple iOS*) and *ARKit* (supported by *Google Android*) enabled the better performance of AR and higher efficiency. Since 2017, all Geo AR mobile games have used either *ARCore* or

ARKit. It's reasonable to say the AR engine of Geo AR mobile games has saturated. Similarly, the most used Game Engine is *Unity*, and the Geolocation Engine is *Google Maps*. And it's the same situation with other technology components. It's hard to create sustainable success through innovating in the technology components of Geo AR mobile games.

However, the game design of Geo AR mobile games is instead a blue ocean. The lack of game features (e.g., players versus players, customization in the game, game seasons) bores the players. This lack has been seen in the failures of *Harry Potter: Wizard Unite*, *Minecraft Earth* and early *Pokémon GO* [12, 67, 68]. Also, the lack of updates, bug fixes and in-game support disappoint the players [69]. Based on that, this paper suggests that game developers actively update their Geo AR mobile games after the release to make their games "complete" gradually. In this way, the game would repetitively add new values to the players. For example, *Pokémon GO* added "Raid" in 2017. This game design encourages multiple players to fight one computer together. Compared with the previous version of *Pokémon GO*, "Raid" seems to bring in-game connections to the players. Also, in 2019, *Pokémon GO* added an "Extra Low Quality mode" to improve the game's compatibility. These updates are supposed to be connected with the resurgence of *Pokémon GO* [70, 71].

Table 8. Technology components of geo AR mobile game.

Technology components	Descriptions	Examples
AR Engine	The component matches the virtual sensory information, real surrounding-based experience and geolocation information (VRG) in organic and natural-looking ways. Therefore, to create the "AR" experience	*Vuforia, ARCore, ARKit, Wikitude SDK*
Map Service and Geolocation Tools	To acquire the information on map and geolocation for AR Engine	*Google API*; using the client's GPS data
Modules Dealing with Sensor Data	To acquire information like device orientation, acceleration speed and position for AR Engine	Using the client's sensor data
Game Engine (e.g., game balance, graphics and sounds)	The infrastructure builder of a general mobile game	*Unity, libGDX, Unreal*
Back-end Servers	To enable players' interaction and store data	Self-made servers; Cloud Servers like *Amazon Web Services (AWS), IBM Cloud*

(continued)

Table 8. (*continued*)

Technology components	Descriptions	Examples
In-game Purchase System	To monetize	*Google Play Billing Library, Google Player Developer API* for Android games; *StoreKit Framework* for *iOS* games
Notifications	To send a timely and important message regarding gameplay, promotion and updates to the players	*NotificationCompat API* for *Android* games; *PushKit Framework* for *iOS* games

5 Conclusion

This paper conducted an overview study of Geo AR mobile games. Through bibliometric analysis and narrative literature review, this paper extensively reveals the landscape of Geo AR mobile games from practical and scholarly perspectives. This study's two-fold contributions are hoped further to develop Geo AR mobile game research and industrial practices.

One intended contribution is to provide readers with a systematic knowledge background of Geo AR mobile games. As an emerging and rapidly developing area, the necessary background knowledge is essential for researchers and practitioners to capture the relevant phenomena of Geo AR mobile games well and truly. Therefore, this paper presented a comprehensive Geo AR mobile game definition. With element-highlighted definition and the systematic analysis of Geo AR mobile game academic and professional development, researchers would obtain a clear picture of the Geo AR mobile game phenomenon and distinguish Geo AR mobile game essence from other seemingly similar contexts.

Another intended contribution was creating an account of the existing literature via a systematic literature review of Geo AR mobile game research and practical publications. Such an "environmental scanning" is helpful for the start of further investigation and practice. This paper proposed a bibliometric analysis that illustrates the current Geo AR mobile game research. Three stages of the Geo AR mobile game development framework are proposed. Even if the framework is by no means exhaustive and the only understanding, it is believed that these suggested trends can assist us in understanding relevant Geo AR mobile game phenomena better and even shaping the future substantially.

This paper reveals that Geo AR mobile games' sustainable success is in danger, but little existing research is into it. Given other technology components of Geo AR mobile games have somehow saturated, making Geo AR mobile games complete through game design would be a reasonable approach.

This study is not without limitations. First, the literature included as data may not cover all those about Geo AR mobile games. Many early Geo AR mobile games hardly appeared on the Internet, but they are important for knowing the history of Geo AR mobile games. Second, the bibliometric analysis only considers articles from *Scopus* and may be biased. With better bibliometric analysis software, more diverse articles should be included for analysis. Third, the data of Geo AR mobile games are still insufficient. Games are scarce. And the business metrics of existing games are also scarce. Future researchers are encouraged to talk with game companies and developers to know what is happening in the industry and how practitioners see the sustainable success problem.

References

1. Hamari, J., Keronen, L.: Why do people play games? A meta-analysis. Int. J. Inf. Manag. **37**(3), 125–141 (2017)
2. Newzoo: Global games market report (2019). https://resources.newzoo.com/hubfs/Reports/2019_Free_Global_Game_Market_Report.pdf?__hstc. Accessed 23 Feb 2022
3. Apperley, T.H.: Genre and game studies: toward a critical approach to video game genres. Simul. Gaming **37**(1), 6–23 (2006)
4. Valentine, K.D., Jensen, L.J.: Mobile entanglements and communitas: the embodied nature of play in Pokémon Go. Educ. Technol. Res. Dev. **69**, 1955–1985 (2021). https://doi.org/10.1007/s11423-020-09930-x
5. Liu, L., Wagner, C., Suh, A.: Understanding the success of Pokémon Go: impact of immersion on players' continuance intention. In: Schmorrow, D.D., Fidopiastis, C.M. (eds.) AC 2017. LNCS (LNAI), vol. 10285, pp. 514–523. Springer, Cham (2017). https://doi.org/10.1007/978-3-319-58625-0_37
6. Landi, M.: Pokemon Go app named as the most popular game of 2016 on Google Play 17 July 2017. http://www.mirror.co.uk/tech/pokemon-go-app-named-most-9375173. Accessed 15 Dec 2016
7. Gupta, G.C.A.: Pokémon Go mania: an inflection point for augmented reality? Center for Air Power Studies **7** (2016)
8. Digital Stat. Hot game: Amazing Pokémon Go statistics (2016). http://expandedramblings.com/index.php/pokemon-go-statistics/. Accessed 28 Feb 2017
9. Kawa, L., Katz, L.: These Charts Show That Pokemon Go Is Already in Decline (2016). https://www.bloomberg.com/news/articles/2016-08-22/these-charts-show-that-pokemon-go-is-already-in-decline. Accessed 15 May 2020
10. Newzoo: Analysis of Pokémon GO: A Success Two Decades in the Making (2016). https://newzoo.com/insights/articles/analysis-pokemon-go/. Accessed 15 May 2020
11. Burns, C.: Pokemon GO failed us all (2018). https://www.slashgear.com/pokemon-go-failed-us-all-04513624/
12. Nelson, A.: Why do you think Pokemon GO failed? (2018). https://www.quora.com/Why-do-you-think-Pokemon-GO-failed
13. Silberling, A.: Harry Potter: Wizards Unite, Niantic's follow-up to Pokémon GO, is shutting down (2021). https://techcrunch.com/2021/11/02/harry-potter-wizards-unite-shut-down-niantic/. 23 Feb 2022
14. Staff: Minecraft earth coming to an end (2021). https://www.minecraft.net/en-us/article/minecraft-earth-coming-end. Accessed 23 Feb 2022
15. LuminousSpecter: Ghostbusters World Shutting Down (2020). https://www.gbworldhub.com/ghostbusters-world-shutting-down/. Accessed 23 Feb 2022
16. Kitchenham, B.: Procedures for performing systematic reviews, **33**, 1–26. Keele University, Keele, UK (2004)
17. Rowley, J., Slack, F.: Conducting a literature review. Manag. Res. News **27**(6), 31–39 (2004). https://doi.org/10.1108/01409170410784185
18. Ahlqvist, O., Schlieder, C.: Geogames and Geoplay. Springer, Cham (2018). https://doi.org/10.1007/978-3-319-22774-0

19. Meho, L.I., Yang, K.: Impact of data sources on citation counts and rankings of LIS faculty: Web of Science versus Scopus and Google Scholar. J. Am. Soc. Inform. Sci. Technol. **58**(13), 2105–2125 (2007)
20. Cheung, C.M., Thadani, D.R.: The impact of electronic word-of-mouth communication: a literature analysis and integrative model. Decis. Support Syst. **54**(1), 461–470 (2012)
21. Du, H.S., et al.: A bibliometric analysis of emergency management using information systems (2000–2016). Online Inf. Rev. **41**(4), 454–470 (2017)
22. Suh, A., Prophet, J.: The state of immersive technology research: a literature analysis. Comput. Hum. Behav. **86**, 77–90 (2018)
23. Broadus, R.N.: Early approaches to bibliometrics. J. Am. Soc. Inf. Sci. **38**(2), 127–129 (1987)
24. Donthu, N., et al.: How to conduct a bibliometric analysis: an overview and guidelines. J. Bus. Res. **133**, 285–296 (2021)
25. Linnenluecke, M.K., Marrone, M., Singh, A.K.: Conducting systematic literature reviews and bibliometric analyses. Aust. J. Manag. **45**(2), 175–194 (2020)
26. Aria, M., Cuccurullo, C.: bibliometrix: an R-tool for comprehensive science mapping analysis. J. Informet. **11**(4), 959–975 (2017)
27. Team, R.C., R: A language and environment for statistical computing. 2013
28. Addor, N., Melsen, L.: Legacy, rather than adequacy, drives the selection of hydrological models. Water Resour. Res. **55**(1), 378–390 (2019)
29. Lajeunesse, M.J.: Facilitating systematic reviews, data extraction and meta-analysis with the metagear package for R. Methods Ecol. Evol. **7**(3), 323–330 (2016)
30. Moral Muñoz, J.A., et al.: Software tools for conducting bibliometric analysis in science: an up-to-date review (2020)
31. Disney, A.: Social network analysis 101: centrality measures explained (2020). https://cambridge-intelligence.com/keylines-faqs-social-network-analysis/
32. Gutierrez, L., et al.: fAR-PLAY: a framework to develop augmented/alternate reality games. In: 2011 IEEE International Conference on Pervasive Computing and Communications Workshops (PERCOM Workshops) (2011)
33. Laine, T.H., Suk, H.J.: Designing mobile augmented reality exergames. Games Cult. **11**(5), 548–580 (2016)
34. Blum, L., et al.: The final TimeWarp: using form and content to support player experience and presence when designing location-aware mobile augmented reality games. In: Proceedings of the Designing Interactive Systems Conference (2012)
35. Alha, K., et al.: Why do people play location-based augmented reality games: a study on Pokémon GO. Comput. Hum. Behav. **93**, 114–122 (2019)
36. Ku, G.C.-M., Shang, I.-W., Li, M.-F.: How do location-based augmented reality games improve physical and mental health? Evaluating the meanings and values of Pokémon Go users' experiences through the means-end chain theory. In: Healthcare 2021. Multidisciplinary Digital Publishing Institute (2021)
37. Holopainen, J.: Foundations of gameplay. Blekinge Institute of Technology (2011)
38. Järvinen, A.: Games Without Frontiers: Theories and Methods for Game Studies and Design. Tampere University Press (2008)
39. Ramtohul, A., Khedo, K.K.: Location-based mobile augmented reality systems: a systematic review. In: Aurelia, S., Paiva, S. (eds.) Immersive Technology in Smart Cities. EICC, pp. 41–65. Springer, Cham (2022). https://doi.org/10.1007/978-3-030-66607-1_3
40. SensorTower: Game Taxonomy Definitions (2022). https://app.sensortower.com/docs/taxonomy. Accessed 22 Jan 2022
41. Wikipedia contributors: Mobile device (2022). https://en.wikipedia.org/w/index.php?title=Mobile_device&oldid=1067216894. Accessed 26 Jan 2022
42. Richardson, D.: Exploring the potential of a location based augmented reality game for language learning. Int. J. Game-Based Learn. (IJGBL) **6**(3), 34–49 (2016)

43. ironSource: Mobile game business models (2022). https://www.is.com/glossary/mobile-game-business-model/. Accessed 7 Jan 2022

44. David, K.: An eevoo-lutionary step forward for mobile gaming (2012). https://news.siliconallee.com/2012/07/11/an-eevoo-lutionary-step-forward-for-mobile-gaming/. Accessed 29 Jan 2022

45. Nick, W., Mike, I.: Pokémon Go Brings Augmented Reality to a Mass Audience (2016). https://www.nytimes.com/2016/07/12/technology/pokemon-go-brings-augmented-reality-to-a-mass-audience.html. Accessed 29 Jan 2022

46. Paavilainen, J., et al.: The Pokemon GO experience: a location-based augmented reality mobile game goes mainstream. In: Proceedings of the 2017 ACM SIGCHI Conference on Human Factors in Computing Systems (CHI 2017), pp. 2493–2498 (2017)

47. Pokémon GO: Pokémon GO - Get Up and Go! (2016). https://www.youtube.com/watch?v=SWtDeeXtMZM. Accessed 29 Jan 2022

48. DAS BOX: Encyclopedia of location based games (or GPS-games) (2016). https://dasbox.be/encyclopedia-of-location-based-games/. Accessed 26 Dec 2021

49. Wikipedia contributors: Ingress (video game) (2021). Accessed 29 Jan 2022

50. Ron Fox: How to play the walking dead our world (2018). https://www.youtube.com/watch?v=oZYNA8FtUX8. Accessed 29 Jan 2022

51. FandomContributors: The Walking Dead: Our World (2021). https://walkingdead.fandom.com/wiki/The_Walking_Dead:_Our_World. Accessed 7 Mar 2022

52. Souljuz, D.: Let's Play Ghostbusters World (2018). https://www.youtube.com/watch?v=myYX968_HWo. Accessed 29 Jan 2022

53. Jurassic World Alive (2022). https://www.jurassicworldalive.com. Accessed 7 Mar 2022

54. Takahashi, D.: Ludia unveils Jurassic World Alive mobile game (2018). https://venturebeat.com/2018/03/06/ludia-unveils-jurassic-world-alive-mobile-game/. Accessed 7 Mar 2022

55. Uptodown: Dragon Quest Walk Android Gameplay [1080p/60fps] (2019). https://www.youtube.com/watch?v=24HTjTMYkq8. Accessed 29 Jan 2022

56. Harry Potter: Wizards Unite: Gameplay Trailer (2019). https://www.youtube.com/watch?v=0pThkmngqJE. Accessed 29 Jan 2022

57. MrRetroGeek: Why Minecraft Earth Failed (2021). https://www.youtube.com/watch?v=7NX6XQmtOl0. Accessed 29 Jan 2022

58. Xbox: Minecraft Earth: Official Reveal Trailer (2019). https://www.youtube.com/watch?v=AQEizp-VrVU. Accessed 29 Jan 2022

59. Casual Gamers Online: Let's Hunt Monsters 一 起来捉妖 - Open Beta Gameplay Trailer Tencent AR Mobile Games 2019 (2019).https://www.youtube.com/watch?v=toxRSbMaWgU. Accessed 29 Jan 2022

60. Abacus News: Pokemon Go Clone App: China's Let's Hunt Monsters (2019). https://www.youtube.com/watch?v=fQ9MocKoKAs. Accessed 29 Jan 2022

61. @ArabianNightsAR: Arabian Nights: Genie's treasures (2022). https://www.facebook.com/ArabianNightsAR. Accessed 29 Jan 2022

62. Spokko sp. z o.o: The Witcher: Monster Slayer (2022). https://apps.apple.com/nz/app/the-witcher-monster-slayer/id1509704647. Accessed 30 Jan 2022

63. Nintendo: Pikmin Bloom - Game Overview Trailer (2021). https://www.youtube.com/watch?v=jp2StaIKZgk. Accessed 29 Jan 2022

64. Sasha: How much does it cost to develop an app like Pokémon GO (2016). https://stfalcon.com/en/blog/post/pokemon-go-clone-development-cost. Accessed 22 Feb 2022

65. Nataliya, Kh.: How Much Does It Cost to Create an App llike Pokemon Go (2021). https://www.cleveroad.com/blog/how-much-does-it-cost-to-create-an-app-like-pokemon-go. Accessed 22 Feb 2022

66. Cubix: How Much Does it Cost to Create a Game Like Pokémon Go (2018). https://med ium.com/@Cubix.Worldwide/how-much-does-it-cost-to-create-a-game-like-pokémon-go-ad5d10776277. Accessed 22 Feb 2022
67. mrtrevor3: Critique of Harry Potter: Wizards Unite (2019). https://www.reddit.com/r/harryp otterwu/comments/c7u1d9/critique_of_harry_potter_wizards_unite/. Accessed 25 May 2022
68. Twitch_Exicor: Minecraft Earth is boring (2019). https://www.reddit.com/r/MinecraftEarthG ame/comments/dpyq3d/minecraft_earth_is_boring/. Accessed 25 May 2022
69. LuminousSpecter: What went wrong with Ghostbusters World? (2020). https://www.gbworl dhub.com/what-went-wrong-with-ghostbusters-world/. Accessed 25 May 2022
70. Iqbal, M.: Pokémon GO Revenue and Usage (2021). https://www.businessofapps.com/data/pokemon-go-statistics/. Accessed 15 May 2020
71. Moreno, G.: Pokémon Go keeps going: data shows 2020 most profitable year (2021). https://www.valleycentral.com/news/pokemon-go-keeps-going-data-shows-2020-most-profitable-year/

User Awareness and Privacy Regarding Instant Games on Facebook

Stacy Nicholson[✉], Robert J. Hammell II, Joyram Chakraborty, and Aisha Ali-Gombe

Towson University, Towson, MD 21252, USA
{snicholson,rhammell,jchakraborty,aaligombe}@towson.edu

Abstract. On social networking sites (SSN) such as Facebook, users tend to share information and engage with third-party applications (apps). However, how knowledgeable, and aware, are users with regard to using a third-party service or app on Facebook? That is, do users really understand what information gets accessed, collected, and how Facebook shares their data with these integrated third-party apps/services? In this paper, Instant Games (IG), which are third-party apps on Facebook, were used to evaluate the user's understanding and awareness with respect to the following four core domains – data sharing, data collection, permission settings, and privacy policy. Findings showed that users, to a certain extent, understand that their personal information is been shared; however, they are not fully aware of the details regarding what information is being shared, accessed, and collected by the game apps. Furthermore, users are not fully aware with whom their data are being shared or who owns the game with which their social media profile and other personal data are being shared. An online survey was used to collect the data, and gameplay activity was done by the users using the Facebook mobile app. The contributions in this paper are a key step towards understanding the user's perception regarding data sharing, privacy policy, and privacy control options relating to IG. In addition, the research helps to uncover privacy concerns relating to IG that demonstrate a need for further study and research.

Keywords: Privacy · Data sharing · Instant games · Facebook · SNS · Awareness

1 Introduction

Over 350 million Facebook users each month engage in social gameplay via the instant gaming platform provided by Facebook [1]. Instant Games (IG) are a type of online third-party gaming app integrated on Facebook, including popular games such as 8 Ball Pool, Ludo Club, and Words with Friends, that are accessed through the user's Facebook account. These social games allow users to socialize and connect with friends both inside and outside of their friend's network. In this study, we define "Friend's network" as people who are a part of a user's friends list on Facebook. According to [2], in a social game, players can decide with whom to play a game. Online games have become popular as they encourage socialization and self-efficacy [3], and because they are "easy and convenient", "friendly and lively" and "socially interactive" [4]. One

© Springer Nature Switzerland AG 2022
G. Meiselwitz et al. (Eds.): HCII 2022, LNCS 13517, pp. 623–641, 2022.
https://doi.org/10.1007/978-3-031-22131-6_46

advantage of the third-party IG apps being on the Facebook gaming platform is that they have access to a wide range of users, and to Facebook's shared Data Application Programming Interface (API) [5]. For instance, once a user interacts with the game app on Facebook, that app can gain access to the username, profile photo, location, etc.

Prior studies noted some downside to Facebook data sharing practices; examples include user data harvested without their consent, user data being misused, intrusive access to users' personal data [6–8], and being vulnerable to cross-origin data sharing [9]. According to [10], user game activity and choices made during gameplay, when combined with other types of information, can be used to build a robust personal profile. The profile that these game apps can build has the potential to grow beyond what the user imagined or expected. This type of user profile building has the potential to lead to more targeted advertisement, tracking, privacy violations, and the like. Personality traits gathered during gameplay have the potential to affect the user's privacy and way of life. One disturbing example is that the introduction of the social credit system by the Chinese Government allows gathered data (such as the amount of video games played) to potentially result in a punishment [11, 12].

Previous research [9] "found that 86% of user's identifiable data (name, photo, and location) are shared with third-party domains." In addition, the study also stated that IG were accessing other Facebook user data in post-gameplay that was not mentioned to the user beforehand, which fosters additional privacy concerns. The study also exposed security flaws in the IG apps that can compromise the users' privacy. The work further pointed out the need for higher transparency relating to how user information is being shared with third-party game apps.

Users may also not know that their data are being misused by third-party apps on Facebook. In a study by [7], the authors uncovered instances where data shared with third-party apps led to incidents including ransomware, spam, and targeted advertising. The study further stated that the third-party terms of service (TOS) are not fully enforced by Facebook and several of the apps investigated did not honor data deletions requested by users or their data sharing practices.

Much research can be found in the literature related to privacy concerns associated with using Facebook. For example, work has shown that a significant user privacy concern on Facebook is the sharing of personal data with entities such as third-party apps [9, 13, 14]. The Cambridge Analytica privacy issue [6] demonstrated the vulnerability of user privacy when interacting with third-party apps. Other studies have focused mostly on user privacy concerns and knowledge of what data are being shared on Facebook [15], how user information is exchanged between Facebook and third-party apps [16], privacy threats associated with the use of third-party apps on Facebook [17], and user views regarding the lack of notification before data are collected [18]. The significant number of IG users and the lack of research relating to user perceptions and privacy concerns related to third-party apps on Facebook in general, and specifically related to IG third-party apps, motivates the need for this research.

This study investigates user perceptions of data sharing and privacy with Instant Games (IG) on Facebook by examining the users' level of understanding and awareness regarding who, where, and what types of personal information are being shared, accessed, and collected by the Instant Games app on Facebook. Four core areas were examined: data sharing, data collection, permission settings, and privacy policy.

Results show that the users' perceptions towards the privacy related domains vary from person to person and have the potential to change over time. Another key point is that, until the user understands how the sharing of their personal data with online entities can affect their privacy, they may continue to be at a disadvantage and at risk of having their data and privacy compromised.

Facebook is used as the subject area of focus as it allows third-party apps such as IG to gain access to the personal data of its users that engage in gameplay online. The term "Facebook" is used instead of the new name (Meta) since it is more known and is currently used in the literature. This paper details the data collection, analysis, and results from a study that evaluates the following domains: data sharing, data collection, permission settings, and privacy policy relating to Instant Games on Facebook from the user perspective of college students.

The following research questions (RQ) were used to guide the research focus of the study reported on in this paper:

- **RQ #1**- How knowledgeable are users about the types of personal data being accessed and what information they are sharing with IG apps?
- **RQ #2**- How aware are users about who their data are being shared with?
- **RQ #3**- Are users looking for privacy control options that give them more control over their data and its access by IG?
- **RQ #4**- How much attention are users paying to the IG privacy policy?

The remainder of this paper is organized as follows: A review of pertinent literature to help understand the issues and research is presented next. Section 3 explains the methodology used for the study. Then the essential analysis results are presented and discussed in Sect. 4. Finally in Sect. 5, discussion, conclusions, and future study directions are offered.

2 Related Work

The primary focus of this paper's research relates to privacy regarding data sharing and collection, third-party apps, privacy policy, privacy and security risk in online social networks, users' perceptions of Facebook online privacy and privacy control. Thus, pertinent introductory information from the current literature is presented in this section.

2.1 Privacy

Privacy is a user's right to have control over how their personal information is collected and used. The Cambridge dictionary, defines privacy as "someone's right to keep their personal matters and relationships secret" [19]. A prior study [20] infers that the user's privacy can be undermined due to various privacy threats on the web, perpetrated by third-party entities to unsuspecting users. Another study [21] claims that "if any adversary attack can be applied to learn any private and sensitive data, there is a privacy leakage".

In addition, parties should be limited by what they are able to learn from the data shared. This should include no more than insensitive information shared by other parties [21].

Prior research such as [22] found that the users Personally Identifiable Information (PII) data can be leaked to third-party servers via online social network. Hence, it's possible for third parties to link PII specific to a person causing the user to have their OSN identity linked with tracking cookies [22].

2.2 Data Sharing and Collection

Data sharing is necessary in today's digital environment to foster growth, connections, and collaboration between companies. It also provides users with enhanced features, better services, and so forth. On the other hand, data sharing with third-party apps on social sites such as Facebook can cause privacy risks to the user [6, 9]. According to [23], privacy risk is the likelihood of people having problems resulting from data processing, as well as the impact should they occur. Hence, user awareness, and understanding of how their data are being shared, accessed, and collected by apps will play a key role in safeguarding their personal data.

User data mining has grown tremendously over the years on the Facebook platform, to the point where user privacy has been comprised and placed at risk both online and offline. Research done by Pew Research Center [24] reported that 79% of U.S. adults are concerned with how their data are being used by companies that collect them; 40% of U.S. adults have concerns about the personal information that social media sites know about them; and 59% of U.S. adults stated that they have a lack of understanding when it comes to the use of the data collected.

2.3 Third-Party Apps

Third-party applications are external or non-native applications that have been integrated into an existing host system or social networking platform such as Facebook. These third-party apps are not owned by the hosting platform; however, they are able to access protected resources granted through an Application Program Interface (API) [25, 26]. Facebook offers third-party apps a diverse cross-platform environment where they can expand their services and products to a large pool of online users [1]. Third-party apps, such as Instant Games, that look to use and access Facebook resources such as user's names, locale, profile photos, etc., achieve this with the aid of APIs, and terms of services granted by Facebook [26].

2.4 Privacy Policy

A Privacy Policy (PP) is a legal document that states what information is collected about the user, device, application, etc. In addition, it describes how the data collected are used, stored and processed by an organization [27]. Prior work [28] has shown how privacy policy can affect the consumer privacy, trust online, and willingness to provide personal information. However, there are challenges/concerns in relying on PP to convey all the information to the users in a transparent and non-ambiguous manner [9].

Paying full attention or understanding what is stated in a privacy policy can be a daunting task. Research done by [29] examined university students' behavior and attention paid to online privacy policy (OPP) statements. The study revealed that university student's mindset towards reading privacy policy statements was influenced by privacy risks and privacy benefits. Another key point mentioned by the study was that the intent to read OPP statements was due to factors such as understanding the privacy policy, social norms, and "mainly by the willingness to spend time and effort reading the statements". Other research [30, 31] has also mentioned reasons such as length, understanding, time, and complexity. However, it is not clear whether this theory holds true for IG privacy policy as well.

2.5 Privacy and Security Risk in Online Social Networks (OSN)

Privacy and security aspects related to social networks (SN) are areas of concern that can have severe consequences. A prior study [32] has shown that online social network users are at risk when using social applications due to: 1) the potential of an application being malicious, 2) violation of the developer polices by app developers to control the user data, and 3) the potential and ability of third-party social apps to access data from OSN users regardless of need for the app operations. These are privacy risk factors that require the user to become more informed about what types of data are being shared with these third-party apps to enable them to take precautionary measures to protect their data and privacy online. Hence, in this study, one aim was to examine the users understanding of data sharing carried out by Facebook with third-party game apps.

2.6 Users' Perceptions of Facebook Online Privacy

The security of one's personal data and that of their friends and family raises concerns in social networking sites such as Facebook. A prior study [33] reveals that privacy concerns related to third-party access to users' data on Facebook are prevalent. The study also mentions that only one quarter of users trust Facebook. According to [33], users hold true to the fact that both Facebook and users have an equal obligation to protect users' information.

2.7 Privacy Control

Prior work [16] states that users do not have any control to limit third-party app's access to their personal information or "restrict the app's publishing practices". The authors [17] also stated that some categories of information can be edited by the users but only after the app is added. This shows the limitations in the privacy control option available on Facebook, preventing users from being able to decline or prevent access beforehand to their PII or other personal information from third-party app access. This may cause the user to wonder about their privacy even with their privacy setting is turned on.

According to [34] even though privacy control mechanisms have been implemented in popular online social networks (OSNs), the user's sensitive information can still be leaked even when privacy rules are configured properly. The authors findings stated that the existing "privacy control mechanisms do not protect the flow of personal information effectively", and that privacy exploits are still a concern. The leakage of Personally Identifiable Information (PII) via social networks is a consequence that continues to play a role in today's society. PII information are specific to an individual, that can be used to trace their identity with or without combining it with other linkable information specific to that user.

3 Methodology

An empirical investigation was conducted to answer the research questions posed, with two notable elements. Firstly, to evaluate users' level of awareness and understanding of the aforementioned four core areas, a test system was set up that allowed each participant to play an instant game on Facebook. This was done to protect the participants' privacy and to disallow third-party IG apps access to their personal data on Facebook (such as their name, profile photo, friends, contacts, and so on). This protection was added especially for users that only use Facebook for socialization and not for gameplay. Secondly, an online post-game-play survey instrument was used to gather and measure a mix of questions. Pertinent data were extracted and analyzed using both qualitative and quantitative analysis techniques. Past research that inspired this study used a survey method [24, 35]. In addition, [9, 17] influenced the investigation regarding the type of interface and data requirement presented to the user.

In the following subsection, the study design, recruitment process, experimental setup, data analysis approach, and the limitations of the study are discussed.

3.1 Study Design

The post-game-play survey was designed to investigate the users' level of awareness and understanding in four core areas: data sharing, data collection, privacy policy, and permission settings, and how they might be impacted by IG. The questions relate directly to these fours cores areas as they pertain to IG and the focus of this study.

The survey and the entire study protocol was approved by the Towson University Institutional Review Board (IRB), and consent was obtained from each study participant. After providing consent, demographic information such as age, social media sites use, area of study, etc. (seen in Tables 1 and 2) was collected using Qualtrics survey software. Each participant then signed-in to a scheduled online session to complete the main portion of the study, which consisted of playing an IG and then completing a post-game-play survey. After the participants played an IG on Facebook (see experimental setup), they were given the post-game-play survey questions to complete on their own personal device. The questions were focused around the RQs and the four core areas mentioned above. The questions, along with the analysis of participant answers, are presented in the Results section below.

3.2 Participants Recruitment

Participants were recruited from the Computer Information Science Department at Towson University through large group emails; this represents a simple random sampling method within the chosen participant pool of college students. College students in the computer science and information technology area were chosen as the target population as they align with the age group that mostly plays games online and to assess the role higher education plays in user knowledge and awareness. Participants were required to be experienced computer users familiar with social media and be 18 or older. Each participant had to sign a consent form before taking part in the study and then be given a random participant number. Table 1 shows some additional demographic characteristics and Table 2 indicates the popular social platforms used by the sample of respondents. Most users (41%) fall in the 18–22 age bracket and in the information technology field (89%). Participants who completed the study did not receive any monetary compensation. A total of 44 out of 50 participants complete the study in full.

3.3 Experimental Setup and Apps Selection

The experimental design was influenced by the study in [9]. A client machine running an Android emulator was set up and used to run the Facebook app. An Android mobile emulator was used to carry out the experiment without using the user's personal computing device. A generic user account was set up for data collection – this allowed the participants to feel more comfortable and take part in the study without compromising their Facebook user account, profile, and/or personal data; it also kept the users from exposing their friends and connections details to these third-party game apps. The gameplay was done via the Facebook app installed on an Android mobile emulator. The Android mobile emulator provided actual interaction with the Facebook app and IG on Facebook. Each student was allowed to choose any game to play and go through the gameplay stages as a user would using their own device and interacting with apps on Facebook. Note that all the games played had a homogenous default data requirement message presented to the user before gameplay as seen below (it was updated subsequent to the conduct of this study).

> *"Friends, connections, and other people that you play with will be able to see your game activity. The game will have access to your name, profile photo, locale/language, and the people you know who also play this game."*

3.4 Data Analysis Approach

To help analyze the qualitative data, thematic coding was done using NVivo software to code the opened questions responses. The Qualtrics survey data analysis tool and Excel were used to analyze the quantitative data items.

3.5 Study Limitation

The participant population was limited to college students in the computer and information program at Towson University. In addition to being readily available, this population was used for two main reasons" (1) it was expected that students in these areas would already have general knowledge, education, and exposure related to cybersecurity, and (2) most students fall in the range of age groups that typically play games online. However, the study findings may not necessarily be generalizable to the public.

4 Results

There is a critical need for IG users to understand how their data are being shared, and to understand the potential for data exposure and privacy risk. This section presents findings based on the study conducted to address the research questions outlined above. Out of 50 student participants, 44 completed all portions of the survey and gameplay testing; thus, the number of participants reported on is n = 44.

4.1 Social Media Usage

Results from the demographic survey showed that users in the age range 18–26 engage in multiple social media platforms more than those over the age of 26. Table 1 shows participant demographics; the majority (71%) fall in the age range from 18–26.

Table 2 shows the types of social media sites used by participants based on age group. For example, out of the 18 participants in the 18–22 age group, 11 use Facebook, 16 use Twitter, 15 use Snapchat, 15 use Instagram, and 1 does not use any social media. 32 out of 44 participants used Facebook as a social media outlet. Users in the 18–26 age ranges (first two rows of Table 2) use social media sites more than the other age groups.

4.2 Addressing RQ#1 and RQ#2

This section presents survey results regarding user level of understanding and awareness related to data sharing and data collection. The discussion is specifically associated with Research Question #1: *how knowledgeable are users about the types of personal data being accessed and what information they are sharing with IG apps?* and Research Question #2: *How aware are users about who their data are being shared with?* Findings from each of the survey questions pertaining to these RQ are presented below.

Was This Your First Time Playing an Instant Game on Facebook?
This question was posed to understand the participant's general level of interaction with IG on Facebook. Responses indicate it was the first time for 82% of them to play an IG on Facebook.

Table 1. Demographics of participants

	Range	Count	Percentage
Age Range	18-22	18	41%
	23-26	13	30%
	27-30	4	9%
	30-35	7	16%
	36-40	2	5%
Area of Study	Information Technology	39	89%
	Computer Science	5	11%
Computer Skill Level	Beginner	2	5%
	Moderate	20	45%
	Advance	18	41%
	Expert level	4	9%

Table 2. Types of social media sites used

	Social Media Sites Used by Age Group				
Participants	Facebook	Twitter	Snapchat	Instagram	None
18-22 (18 participants)	11	16	15	15	1
23-26 (13 participants)	8	9	11	12	0
Age Range 27-30 (4 participants)	4	4	3	4	0
30-35 (7 participants)	7	3	4	5	0
36-40 (2 participants)	2	1	0	2	0
TOTAL (of 44):	32	33	33	38	1

What User Information Do You Think was Collected by the Instant Game During Your Testing?

Results from the open-end analysis, regarding the types of data being collected, showed that the user's perceived knowledge and awareness were accurate to a certain point. However, the analysis reiterates the point that user's level of understanding regarding data collection is not high. Table 3 shows the types of data the users thought were being collected about them by the game app. For instance, 6 participants noted that their ads preference was collected and shared for marketing and advertisement purposes, while 26 out of 44 participants indicated that their game activity was collected during gameplay. 20 out of 44 participants stated that their age, name, profile photo, gender, etc. were collected by the game app. 16% of the participants stated that their location was being collected.

Table 3. User perception of the types of data collected by IG

User Perceived Data Collected/Accessed	Total Instances Noted by participants	Percentage (Out of 44 participants)
Ads Preference	6	13.5%
Device Details	1	2.3%
Friends' Information	2	4.5%
Game Activity (duration, moves, type, opponent details, score or results)	26	59%
IP address	4	9.1%
Location	7	16%
User Personal Data (age, date of birth, gender, name, profile picture, other personal data)	20	45.5%

Table 4. User perceived knowledge of with whom their data are being shared

User perceived knowledge of data sharing	Count	Percentage
Facebook	7	16%
Advertisers	4	9.1%
Third-party	3	6.8%
Friends, connections, and others	1	2.3%
Game developers	2	4.5%
Other websites	5	11.4%

Note that ALL of the data mentioned in the first column of Table 3 were collected from everyone [9, 36]. Participants also noted that cookies (4.5%) and email (2.3%) were possible personal data being collected. This analysis shows that users' awareness can affect their privacy and potentially place them at risk when they are not aware of what types of information are being accessed and collected by IG third-party apps on social media sites. This makes them vulnerable to data misuse, tracking, and potential data privacy and security exposure.

Apart from Facebook Do You Think Your Game Data Has Been Shared with Others?

To an extent, the participants had some knowledge of who their data may be shared with; however, they are not fully aware with respect to where, or with whom. The users perceived knowledge of who their data are being shared with is listed in Table 4. These include advertisers, third-party companies, etc. as entities with which Facebook shared their data.

Note that instances of the user data was shared with ALL of the entities listed in Table 4 as noted in prior research [9] and the default message shown in Sect. 3.3. The findings indicate that users do not really know the purpose for their game data, or the need for their Facebook user profile information and other personal data, to be shared with outside parties when playing games on Facebook. Individual user responses indicated that the users have some privacy concerns regarding the sharing of their data. Not all participants gave a response in this area, which hints that user may not be aware of with whom their data are being shared with.

All users should have an understanding that their game interest is shared with "Friends, connections, and other people that you play with will be able to see your game activity." as this was part of the default message presented to each user before gameplay, as shown in Sect. 3.3. However, only 1 out of 44 participants noted this. This may be due to the font size of the statement not being large enough to read or grab the user attention before clicking play. Another point to be made is that only 2 out of 44 participants understood that their personal data and game activity are shared with the game developers for each game that they play on Facebook using their social media account. 7 out 44 participants were aware that the IG that was played shared data with Facebook.

With respect to the number of users that have an awareness that their data are been shared with entities apart from Facebook, 37 out of 44 participants (84%) were aware that their data are being shared. The reasons for data sharing noted by the participants were classified in the following areas: marketing and advertisement, data purchasing, tracking, game preferences, software maintenance and upgrade.

Who Do You Think Owns the Instant Game that You Just Played?

Findings indicate that 30% of participants were not aware that the IG app is not owned by Facebook, and another 16% were "not sure"; just over half (54%) knew that the IG app was owned by a third-party game company. This further illustrates that millions of IG users may not be aware that they are sharing their data with a third-party company, thus, giving these companies access to their social user profile data, certain types of personal data, and information relating to their friends and family connections on Facebook.

It is clear that knowing who owns the IG would give the users better insight about with who their personal data are being shared. A recommendation that can be made here is for users to investigate who owns the game app on social media outlets before engaging in game play to protect their privacy, online social media user profile, and other personal data they do not wish to share.

Summary

In investigating RQ1 and RQ2, the findings show that the users' knowledge level is not yet at a place where they can fully understand the who, what and where when it comes to data sharing and collection with the IG apps. Slightly over half (59%) of the participants recognized that game activity details were being collected; about half (45.5%) understood that various user personal data were also collected. Taking on equal obligation to protecting their data when dealing with Facebook data sharing practices, will be a challenge for the users.

Regarding awareness of Facebook sharing their data, (84%) of participants understood this. However, considering RQ2, the awareness gap remains where less than 10% realized that their data are being shared with third parties, even though about half (54%) correctly identified that the IG app is not owned by Facebook. This also shows that almost half (46%) either thought the app was owned by Facebook or did not know who owned it. Another point is that the default data requirement message needs to be thoroughly examined and understood by users before clicking play, so they may explicitly consider whether playing the game is worth giving access to their personal data.

4.3 Addressing RQ#3

This results in this section pertain to Research Question #3- *Are users looking for privacy control options that give them more control over their data and its access by IG?* These findings relate to the user's awareness and use of the game permissions setting on Facebook. Secondly, the results explore the user's knowledge and need for more privacy control options to limit what information gets accessed and shared with the IG third-party game app and others on Facebook. Initially, Facebook allowed the IG apps to display the default message presented before gameplay, as shown in Sect. 3.3.

Note that this default data requirement statement was updated after the completion of this study. However, the changes were minimal. A potential contribution of this study is to help Facebook to see which areas are still a concern for its users and to further answer its users call for more privacy and permission control options with third-party apps. Another limitation users face with the Facebook prior permission settings control option is that it is only available AFTER the user plays the game.

Did You Know that You Could Review and Remove Your Instant Game Played on Facebook?

Findings showed that not all users are aware of and use the game permissions setting on Facebook. 64% of participants were not aware that they could review the permission settings and remove the IG game that they played on Facebook. Figure 1 shows the IG removal setting screen presented to users after gameplay. Based on viewing this removal notice, all users should have answered "Yes" to this question.

The results also shows that only a small percentage (36%) of users know where the game permission control options are on Facebook. In addition, the users may not know where to locate and view the game app permissions setting, since it is not actually inside the game app settings but rather under Facebook permission settings. Further, the users may be unaware that their personal and other user data previously shared and collected by the IG apps can still be accessed by each IG game played in the past.

It should be noted that Facebook has updated this notice (near the end of 2021), which was after the data in this survey were collected.

How Easy Would It Be to Delete the Information Shared with the Instant Game?
Privacy and permission settings play a key role in the user's ability to limit and remove the types of information that the user does not want to share with the IG third-party game app. 43% of participants correctly noted that it is not easy to delete information that was shared with the IG apps (difficult to very difficult). About the same number of participants (46%) were on the fence (neutral) regarding data deletion. One reason for this is that there are no adequate options for the user to do so from their Facebook account. As seen in Fig. 1 the user can delete the game but not the information shared previously.

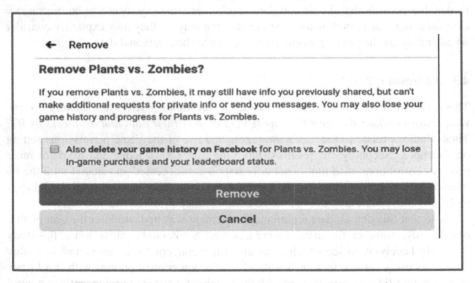

Fig. 1. IG removal setting screen presented to users after gameplay.

Another point to be made is that 11% of the participants stated that it was easy to extremely easy to delete their data. They are incorrect to assume this since, users would need to contact the developer or IG data operator to make a request to get their data deleted. This will depend on that company's policy for data retention. This shows that users may not be fully aware that removing the app from their user profile on Facebook does not remove the information previously shared with the game app. Hence, better control options need to be deployed by Facebook to allow users to delete, modify and limit third-party apps access to the user data without the hassle of having to contact these third-party apps companies to request deletion of their user personal data collected by the IG apps. Data deletion may not be possible, since now the user data is in another company's hands. Hence, we recommend the need to have these IG permissions to access personal data (such as name, profile photo, friends' connection, etc.) turned off by default, and then let the user choose which to allow.

Please Rate Your Ability to Delete Any Personal Information Collected by the Instant Game App
The finding shows that most users participating in the study consider their ability to be less than knowledgeable. Results showed that 27.27% identify as "beginners", 22.73% as "intermediate", and 31.82% of participants were in the middle, regarding data removal after collection by the IG. Only 18.18% were either "knowledgeable" (15.91%) or "expert" (2.27%). This may lead to users not wanting to play games on Facebook.

Before Playing an IG, Facebook Provides an Implied Statement (See Sect. 3.3) Showing Information that Will Be Collected by the Game App: Please Rate Your Level of Comfort with This Statement (1 = Uncomfortable and 5 = Comfortable)
The findings show that approximately 46% of participants (1 to 2 points on the scale) state that they were uncomfortable with the data requirement statement given before gameplay, whereas 27% of participants were in the middle. Likewise, 27% of participants (4 to 5 points) rated themselves as somewhat. Since the collection of these data, Facebook has updated the default gaming data requirement statement, which supports our projection that the users were uncomfortable about what was being collected and accessed by the game apps. The changes now specify who will be receiving the user data and provide the option to allow users to turn off access to their friend list. The changes also provide a global privacy setting for users to control who can see the type of IG game apps they play. However, the user control abilities are still limited regarding the types of personal and other user data to which they can prevent access to.

Instead of the Implied Statement (Shown with the Previous Question) Would You Prefer the Instant Game Request for Individual Permissions in a List Form Before Playing the Game?
The user preference as it relates to the privacy control option shows that 95% of users would rather be provided a permission list that they can use to modify what types of data and the amount of personal data being shared, accessed, and collected by the third-party game apps. They also hint that the types of user personal data requested may exceed the users comfort threshold. Thus, the desire for improved privacy control options when dealing with IG third-party applications needs to be addressed further.

Summary
What we learned from the analysis presented in this section relating to RQ3 is that users are starting to desire more privacy and permission controls, which allows them to protect their data from third-party apps on Facebook. 95% of users would prefer that Facebook employ more privacy control options towards IG gameplay. 43% of participants noted that it was not easy to delete information that was shared with the IG apps while 46% of the participants were in a neutral space regarding data deletion. More than 80% of the participants rated themselves as less than "knowledgeable" regarding their ability to remove data collected by an IG. A surprising finding was that 64% of the participants

were not aware that they could remove the game that they just played on Facebook. The user's awareness of the permission settings location and access to more control play a key role in protecting their privacy.

4.4 Addressing RQ#4

In this section, insights into the user's awareness and behavior towards the IG privacy policy are presented. The survey results discussed in this section relate to Research Question #4: *How much attention are users paying to the IG privacy policy?* Findings from each of the survey questions items are presented below.

Was a Privacy Policy Document or Link Shown?
When participants were asked whether a privacy policy (PP) document was presented to them, 54.55% stated that none was provided while 29.55% confirmed the existence of one. What is surprising is that 15.91% selected not applicable, even though a link was available.

This points to two key factors: The first being there is a visibility issue with the ways the IG privacy policy is being delivered to the users which may account for a lack of user awareness and readability of the PP. Secondly, the readability factor of the PP will also decline since users are not noticing the link to access the PP document.

Did You Read the Privacy Policy Provided?
The study showed that 79% (34 of 43 respondents) of participants did not read the privacy policy document. Out of the 43 participants that provided a response to this question, only 14% (N = 6) read the privacy policy documents, while 7% (N = 3) selected not applicable. Not reading the PP can affect the way users approach game play online; they may assume that Facebook owns the IG or that their data are only shared with Facebook and not with the third-party game app. Another point is that not reading may further reduce their awareness level regarding data collection, sharing, data retention etc., even if there is not a full understanding of the PP document content. The findings also show that users may not be willing to spend time and effort reading the PP statements which may lead them assuming rather than having some level of understanding.

Rate Your Familiarity with the Privacy Policy of the Instant Game that You Played?
The user's familiarity with the IG privacy policy illustrates that even at the college level, users of online games such as Instant Games can lack a true understanding of the privacy policy. Findings from the survey showed a low score in the familiarity factor, where 81% (36 of 44) of the participants stated that they were unfamiliar to very unfamiliar with the privacy policy.

When considering only the users that read the policy, the findings show that of the 6 participants who read the game privacy policy, 4 of them had somewhat of an understanding ("Neutral" in knowledge after reading) and 2 stated they still do not grasp it, even after going through the privacy policy document. It is noteworthy that NONE of the users that read the policy indicated a higher than neutral understanding of the policy.

This finding suggests that users' understanding of the IG privacy policy will fluctuate based on familiarity and reading of the privacy policy given, impacting the user's understanding of associated potential privacy threats and risk factors. Further, since the participants were all college students, the findings demonstrate that higher levels of education may not equate to a better understanding of privacy policies. Thus, there is a need for improved privacy control options that allow the user to fully control what information gets shared, collected, and accessed by third-party apps such as IG apps to better protect the user's privacy and safety.

Rate Your Confidence in the Instant Game Adherence to Their Privacy Policy?
The user's confidence in the IG adhering to their privacy policy showed that the user trust level is not high. Overall, 28 out of 44 (64%) participants were not confident to not at all confident, while only 9% (4 out of 44) were confident that the privacy policy would be upheld. 27% (12 out of 44) of the participants were in a neutral position regarding IG companies' adherence. Note that NONE of the participants indicated they were highly confident that the PP would be followed. User's trust in a company will play a role in whether they will continue to use their services or product.

Summary
RQ4 findings indicate users are not paying enough attention to the PP which contributes to their level of familiarity and understanding relating to the 4 core areas looked at in this study.

Insights into the user's awareness and behavior towards IG privacy policy (PP) showed that about half of the participants (54.55%) were not aware of a privacy policy document. Additionally, less than a third (29.55%) confirmed the existence of one. Readability of the IG privacy policy is a concern here since only 14% of the participants read the privacy policy document provided; 81% of the participants were unfamiliar to very unfamiliar with the privacy policy.

Another lesson learned from the analysis was that even after reading the PP, users still did not have a full understanding of it. 4 out of 6 participants that read the PP had somewhat of an understanding of what types of data are being shared, accessed, and collected by the IG. The user's confidence level trusting that the IG would adhere to their PP was at a low rate (9%), while 64% of participants show little to no confidence that the PP will be followed.

5 Discussion and Conclusions

This study differs in that it gives insight into a specific third-party product (Instant Games) on Facebook that has the potential to impact millions of users' privacy. The research questions investigated give preliminary high-value results that can lead to more in-depth future research. The contributions in this paper are a key step toward understanding user awareness regarding data sharing and collection, privacy policy, and permission control options relating to Instant Game (IG) third-party apps. The four core areas that were investigated (data sharing, data collection, permission settings, and privacy policy) relate to the data privacy and prior research looked at in this study have shown these areas to be of concern for users.

Findings showed some similarity with prior research [24], in that users are concerned with how their data are being shared. A significant difference uncovered in this study is that, while users care about how their personal data are being accessed and shared with the third-party IG apps on Facebook, there is a lack of understanding of how this is being done and with whom. Findings from Research Questions #1 and #2 showed that users may not fully understand or be aware of the implications of sharing or allowing third-party games apps access to their personal data and social media profile. In addition, their friends and connections information on Facebook can also be exposed to these third-party game apps. Hence, users need to carefully consider which IG games they play on Facebook and the types of data being accessed and collected. Secondly, the study showed that users do not really know who owns the IG apps, hence they may not be aware of where, or with who, Facebook is sharing their personal data with.

A prior study [33] indicated that users have an equal duty to protect their information. However, we differ here in that the user's awareness level and their control ability is limited with regards to protecting their data against third-party apps access based on the current data practice being employed by Facebook; this prevents them from having true equal obligation. What we can attest to is that users can attempt to increase their level of awareness regarding IG data requirements, access, and collection of personal data before game play, by looking at these key areas of the privacy policy document. This may allow users to understand what data are being collected about them, how it is being retained, and what data are also retrieved from their Facebook account. However, as stated by previous studies [9, 29] there are challenges in relying on the PP document to inform the user as illustrated by the RQ4 results; 54.55% of participants were not aware that a PP even existed. This may lead to the user not knowing that they are being tracked and their personal data shared whenever they play an IG on Facebook using their Facebook account.

Research question #3 provides insights into how much attention users are paying toward the permission settings. Results illustrate that users are looking for more control over the types of user data that are being accessed and collected by third-party IG apps. 95% of users would prefer that Facebook employ more permission control options towards IG gameplay. Findings also showed that users are not comfortable with the default data requirement statement given before gameplay. Prior research [34] stated that existing "privacy control mechanisms do not effectively protect the flow of personal information," and privacy exploits remain a concern. However, from the user perspective there is still a need for efficient control options to limit what gets access by third-party apps on Facebook. The users' perceptions towards the data privacy and awareness in the four core areas looked at in this study vary from person to person and has the potential to change over time. Awareness sets the stage for users to become knowledgeable about the who, what, and where, with respect to IG privacy.

The results of this study set the stage for further research that needs to probe deeper into data security and privacy concerns relating to IG on Facebook. This work can be applied to other target groups to gain further knowledge and areas for additional research. This result showcases a small number of questions to gain traction in the core areas of this study relating to IG data privacy and how it may impact the users playing IG games on Facebook. Further research can probe further into these areas with additional question sets to foster deeper awareness and understanding levels of IG privacy on Facebook.

Further, new, and existing users along with IG developers and Facebook, may benefit from this and additional future research directly relating to IG data privacy and its user impact. Another significant element that needs to be addressed in future research is to investigate mitigation measures that can be implemented.

References

1. Facebook: Best Practices - Games (2022). https://developers.facebook.com/docs/games/mon etization/best-practices/. Accessed 25 Apr 2022
2. Jackson, M.O., Watts, A.: Social games: matching and the play of finitely repeated games. Games Econ. Behav. **70**(1), 170–191, 2010. https://doi.org/10.1016/j.geb.2008.02.004. http://dx.doi.org/10.1016/j.geb.2008.02.004
3. Liu, C.-C.: Understanding player behavior in online games: the role of gender. Technol. Forecast. Soc. Change **111**, 265–274 (2016). https://doi.org/10.1016/j.techfore.2016.07.018. https://linkinghub.elsevier.com/retrieve/pii/S0040162516301627
4. Chen, K., Shen, K., Ma, M.: The functional and usable appeal of Facebook SNS games. Internet Res. **22**(4), 467–481 (2012). https://doi.org/10.1108/10662241211250999. https://www.emerald.com/insight/content/doi/10.1108/10662241211250999/full/html
5. Facebook: Instant Games SDK (2021). https://developers.facebook.com/docs/games/instant-games/sdk/fbinstant6.3. Accessed 05 Mar 2021
6. TIME: Facebook's Cambridge Analytica Controversy Could Be Big Trouble for the Social Network, 04 April 2018. https://time.com/5205314/facebook-cambridge-analytica-breach/
7. Farooqi, S., Musa, M., Shafiq, Z., Zaffar, F.: CanaryTrap: detecting data misuse by third-party apps on online social networks. Comput. Soc. **2020**(4), 336–354 (2020). https://doi.org/10.2478/popets-2020-0076. https://www.researchgate.net/publication/346937462_Can aryTrap_Detecting_Data_Misuse_by_Third-Party_Apps_on_Online_Social_Networks
8. Dance, G.J.X., LaForgia, M., Confessore, N.: As Facebook raised a privacy wall, it carved an opening for tech giants. New York Times, pp. 1–17 (2018). https://www.nytimes.com/2018/12/18/technology/facebook-privacy.html
9. Nicholson, S., Chakraborty, J., Ali-Gombe, A., Hammell, R.J., II: Data sharing and exposure: findings from descriptive and network analysis of instant games on Facebook (2021). https://proc.conisar.org/2021/pdf/5613.pdf. Accessed 14 Jan 2022
10. Polygon: The dangers of in-game data collection. https://www.polygon.com/features/2019/5/9/18522937/video-game-privacy-player-data-collection. Accessed 16 Apr 2022
11. INSIDER: China social credit system, punishments and rewards explained (2021). https://www.businessinsider.com/china-social-credit-system-punishments-and-rewards-explained-2018-4. Accessed 25 Apr 2022
12. ABC News: China's social credit system seeks to assign citizens scores, engineer social behaviour - ABC News (2018). https://www.abc.net.au/news/2018-03-31/chinas-social-cre dit-system-punishes-untrustworthy-citizens/9596204. Accessed 25 Apr 2022
13. Nyoni, P., Velempini, M.: Privacy and user awareness on Facebook. S. Afr. J. Sci. **114**(5/6), 27–32 (2018). https://doi.org/10.17159/sajs.2018/20170103. https://www.sajs.co.za/article/view/5165
14. The New York Times: Facebook's Suspension of 'Tens of Thousands' of Apps Reveals Wider Privacy Issues - The New York Times (2019). https://www.nytimes.com/2019/09/20/techno logy/facebook-data-privacy-suspension.html. Accessed 25 Apr 2022
15. Golbeck, J., Mauriello, M.L.: User perception of Facebook app data access: a comparison of methods and privacy concerns. Futur. Internet **8**(2), (2016). https://doi.org/10.3390/fi8020009. https://pdfs.semanticscholar.org/5732/7552d964d144a3c966c3a766aeabaa941903.pdf

16. Wang, N.: Third-party applications data practices on Facebook. In: Proceedings of the 2012 ACM Annual Conference Extended Abstracts on Human Factors in Computing Systems Extended Abstracts - CHI EA 2012, p. 1399 (2012). https://doi.org/10.1145/2212776.221 2462. http://dl.acm.org/citation.cfm?doid=2212776.2212462. Accessed 15 Oct 2019

17. Wang, N., Xu, H., Grossklags, J.: Third-party apps on Facebook: privacy and the illusion of control. In: Proceedings of the 5th ACM Symposium on Computer Human Interaction for Management of Information Technology - CHIMIT 2011, December 2011, pp. 1–10 (2011). https://doi.org/10.1145/2076444.2076448. http://dl.acm.org/citation.cfm?doid=207 6444.2076448

18. Symeonidis, I., Biczók, G., Shirazi, F., Pérez-Solà, C., Schroers, J., Preneel, B.: Collateral damage of Facebook third-party applications: a comprehensive study. Comput. Secur. **77**, 179–208 (2018). https://doi.org/10.1016/j.cose.2018.03.015. https://www.sciencedirect.com/science/article/pii/S016740481830302X. Accessed 15 Oct 2019

19. Dictionary.cambridge.org: Privacy (2021). https://dictionary.cambridge.org/us/dictionary/english/privacy. Accessed 23 Sept 2021

20. D Malandrino V Scarano 2013 Privacy leakage on the web: diffusion and countermeasures Comput. Networks 57 14 2833 2855 https://doi.org/10.1016/j.comnet.2013.06.013

21. Yang, C.C.: Privacy-preserving social network integration, analysis, and mining. In: Intelligent Systems for Security Informatics, pp. 51–67. Elsevier Inc. (2013). https://doi.org/10.1016/B978-0-12-404702-0.00003-3. Accessed 16 Sept 2021

22. Krishnamurthy, B., Wills, C.E.: On the leakage of personally identifiable information via online social networks. In: Proceedings of the 2nd ACM Workshop on Online Social Networks - WOSN 2009, p. 7 (2009). https://doi.org/10.1145/1592665.1592668. http://portal.acm.org/citation.cfm?doid=1592665.1592668

23. NIST: NIST Privacy Framework (2020). https://nvlpubs.nist.gov/nistpubs/CSWP/NIST.CSWP.01162020.pdf

24. Brooke, A., Lee, R., Monica, A., Andrew, P., Madhu, K., Erica, T.: Americans and privacy: concerned, confused and feeling lack of control over their personal information. Pew Research Center, 15 November 2019. https://www.pewresearch.org/internet/2019/11/15/ame ricans-and-privacy-concerned-confused-and-feeling-lack-of-control-over-their-personal-inf ormation/. Accessed 27 Sept 2021

25. Auth0.Inc.: First-party and third-party applications (2021). https://auth0.com/docs/applicati ons/first-party-and-third-party-applications#third-party-applications. Accessed 27 July 2021

26. Facebook: Facebook for developers (2022). https://developers.facebook.com/docs/games/ins tant-games

27. Costante, E., Sun, Y., Petković, M., den Hartog, J.: A machine learning solution to assess privacy policy completeness, pp. 91–96 (2012). https://dl-acm-org.proxy-tu.researchport.umd. edu/doi/pdf/10.1145/2381966.2381979

28. Wu, K., Yan, S., Yen, D.C., Popova, I.: Computers in human behavior the effect of online privacy policy on consumer privacy concern and trust. Comput. Hum. Behav. **28**(3), 889–897 (2012). https://doi.org/10.1016/j.chb.2011.12.008. http://dx.doi.org/10.1016/j.chb.2011. 12.008

29. Sigmund, T.: Attention paid to privacy policy statements. Information **12**(4), 144 (2021). https://doi.org/10.3390/info12040144. https://www.researchgate.net/publication/350 473200_Attention_Paid_to_Privacy_Policy_Statements

30. Obar, J.A., Oeldorf-Hirsch, A.: The biggest lie on the Internet: ignoring the privacy policies and terms of service policies of social networking services. Inf. Commun. Soc. **23**(1), 128–147 (2018). https://doi.org/10.1080/1369118X.2018.1486870. http://www.ssrn.com/abs tract=2757465

31. Fabian, B., Ermakova, T., Lentz, T.: Large-scale readability analysis of privacy policies. In: Proceedings of the 2017 IEEE/WIC/ACM International Conference on web intelligence, WI 2017, September 2017, pp. 18–25 (2017). https://doi.org/10.1145/3106426.310 6427. https://www.researchgate.net/publication/317400012_Large-Scale_Readability_Ana lysis_of_Privacy_Policies

32. I Kayes A Iamnitchi 2017 Privacy and security in online social networks: a survey Online Soc. Netw. Media 3–4 4 1 21 https://doi.org/10.1016/j.osnem.2017.09.001 Accessed 13 Jan 2022

33. O'Brien, D., Torres, A.M.: Social networking and online privacy: Facebook users' perceptions. In: An Introduction to Social Media Marketing, pp. 149–165 (2018). https://doi.org/10.4324/9780203727836-13

34. Li, Y., Li, Y., Yan, Q., Deng, R.H.: Privacy leakage analysis in online social networks. Comput. Secur. **49**, 239–254 (2015). https://doi.org/10.1016/j.cose.2014.10.012. http://dx.doi.org/10.1016/j.cose.2014.10.012

35. Van den Broeck, E., Poels, K., Walrave, M.: Older and wiser? Facebook use, privacy concern, and privacy protection in the life stages of emerging, young, and middle adulthood. Soc. Media Soc. **1**(2), 205630511561614 (2015). https://doi.org/10.1177/2056305115616149. http://journals.sagepub.com/doi/10.1177/2056305115616149

36. Facebook: What is public information on Facebook? Facebook Help Center (2021). https://www.facebook.com/help/203805466323736?ref=dp

The Roles of Instructional Agents in Human-Agent Interaction Within Serious Games

Mohammadamin Sanaei[✉], Stephen B. Gilbert, and Michael C. Dorneich

Iowa State University, Ames, IA 50010, USA
asanaei@iastate.edu

Abstract. Automated agent technology in video games is a form of artificial intelligence (AI) that interacts with humans, and thus can provide interactive skills training via human-agent interaction. Having a good framework for agent types could help industry agent designers make best use of agents' capabilities. This research extends the previously established Human-Agent Team Game Analysis Framework from traditional video games to serious games focused on learning by clarifying the instructional agent types based on characteristics from the literature. Using the characteristics of (1) interaction timing, (2) level of autonomy, and (3) memory, agents of type Planner, Advisor, Critic, Companion, Actor, and Player were analyzed across eight different serious games. The new clarification of agent types could help agent designers decide the best agent type appropriate for their applications.

Keywords: Human-agent interaction · Human-agent teaming · Video games · Serious games · Bots · Non-player characters

1 Introduction

Agents, sometimes called Bots, are character or non-character software-controlled entities capable of performing a task like humans. Early researchers defined distinct roles for agents in a wide variety of video games, including "tactical enemies, partners, support characters, story directors, strategic opponents, units and commentators" [1, p. 18]. The main roles of agents can be divided into two groups: competitive agents and cooperative agents [2]. Competitive agents combat or compete against humans or other agents during a game, while cooperative agents offer opportunities to help users perform various tasks.

To reduce the cost of real-world experiments, researchers can study video games capable of simulating the interaction between humans and agents similar to real-world scenarios. Video games have been used to simulate real-world scenarios such as Jellyfish for physical rehabilitation [3], Farmer's Tale for behavior change [4], Circuit Game for learning circuitry [5], and Operating Room for communication [6]. Agents are increasingly playing an important role in human-computer interaction within video games, and have serious applications for training and instruction.

© Springer Nature Switzerland AG 2022
G. Meiselwitz et al. (Eds.): HCII 2022, LNCS 13517, pp. 642–655, 2022.
https://doi.org/10.1007/978-3-031-22131-6_47

According to Bell & Sottilare [7], instructional technologies have been presented in many forms. Intelligent tutoring systems having a long history with instructional agents [8] helping the learners or with recommender systems instructing the users by suggesting actions [9]. But these systems are not typically embedded in serious games. The definition of instructional agent in this study focuses on cooperative agents within serious games in which humans and agents cooperate in order to improve human task performance with the help of agents' instructions. In real-world contexts, instructional agents have attracted attention in application domains such as piloting [10], educational services [11], and hospital room applications [12], among others.

Educational systems use agents in serious games to improve the quality of students' learning by measuring the learning outcomes [13], game-playing attitude [14], and students' interaction with games [15]. Games and agents applied to health systems have emerged as a motivational improvement of clinical performance by advising medical patients [16]. Effective military training sometimes requires a complete system of different kinds of agents to work alongside real humans [17]. Having an appropriate framework for agent types could help the mentioned systems to better understand what kind of agent is more efficient for their applications.

Serious games are different from traditional video games since they have additional goals beyond pure entertainment [18]. They try to be a serious application for acquiring knowledge and skills that is also entertaining. Compared to traditional video games, the increased training requirements of the serious games can lead to more complexity in an agent architecture. Given the complexity differences between traditional video games and serious games, it is worth examining whether it is possible to categorize agents in serious games using the same framework as traditional video games.

Previous work has proposed or developed frameworks for classifying human-agent teaming [19–22]. Tokadlı et al. [22] described a framework for the dimensions of human-autonomy teaming (HAT) interactions, but did not address the roles that agents play. Sepich et al. [21] enhanced the Human-Agent Game Analysis framework to include roles or "agent types" and analyzed three games using the framework. This paper intends to explore agent types and roles more deeply by 1) clarifying the agent types of Sepich et al. [21] for serious games, which often involve instruction, and 2) analyzing the role of agents in serious games examples in domains including management simulation, language learning, medical training, military training, and manufacturing safety.

2 Approach

The authors reviewed the literature using different keywords (i.e., [human-agent, autonomy] [interaction, teaming, teamwork, collaboration]; [role-playing, cooperative] agents in video games) to find out how the instructional agents in human-agent teaming within video games may differ from each other. During the search process, two criteria were used to include papers for this study: cooperative vs. competitive human-agent interaction and serious vs. traditional video games. The review focused on papers with cooperative games, in which the instructional agents and humans are on the same team and have the same goals. Also, the review focused on papers with serious games designed with goals such as better learning or more efficient teamwork in addition to entertainment.

Per the Human-Agent Team Analysis Framework [21], **agent types** are categorized into six groups: Companion, Actor, Player, Planner, Advisor, and Critic. Although this categorization is useful, few detailed characteristics were mentioned in the Framework paper about how these agent types were derived. This research found that HAT Analysis Framework used two characteristics implicitly without describing them: level of autonomy and interaction timing. Companion, Actor, and Player types differ in level of autonomy, and Planner, Advisor, and Critic differ based on the interaction timing. While these two characteristics were also considered independently of agent types as different elements of the HAT Analysis Framework, this study notes that adding one more characteristic enables the effective categorization of agent types. After (A) level of autonomy and (B) interaction timing, based on reviewing the literature, (C) memory is proposed as a third characteristic for categorization of agent types with video games or serious games.

Interaction timing is defined as when the humans and agents start their interaction together in each task process. This interaction could be **before** the task, when no action is taken yet, in **real-time** while the task is underway, or **after** the task when the action is already complete.

Agent *level of autonomy* (LoA) captures the way the instructional agents interact with humans. For agent type categorization, LoA could be either **deciding** some actions in human-agent interaction (high LoA, opt-out) or just **guiding** the humans without making any decision (low LoA, opt-in). This characteristic explains the decision-making authority of the agents and identifies whether they can make a decision without human permission. These two basic levels of autonomy (as opposed to six or more levels per other LoA theories [23] suffice for this analysis because they focus on the key aspect of whether the human must take initiative or not.

The characteristic of *memory* refers to whether the agents need to remember previous game actions. Memory levels include **retrospective**, in which gaming actions should be kept in agents' memory and **in-the-moment**, in which the agent acts based on the current game state, regardless of previous game actions. With the in-the-moment level, the agent's decision is based on inputs from a single moment in time at the current game state, in which the agent responds with an action based on previous training, while in the retrospective level, an agent's decision is based on both the current inputs and its memory of previous interactions of agents and the environment.

After reading the results of the literature search and extracting the mentioned characteristics for agent types, the authors discussed whether the agent types of the Human-Agent Team Analysis Framework worked for the agents found in serious games. Across the papers found in the literature search, eight sample video games were chosen that spanned enough information to cover a range of agent roles, and the characteristics of the agent was explored in each of them. These examples are presented to clarify agent types more explicitly.

3   Results

For each of the papers identified in the literature review, an analysis of the agents' behaviors in each paper was conducted. Table 1 shows the categorization of agent types based on the proposed characteristics. These results explore the details for each type and describe examples of each type in serious games.

Table 1. Agent type classification based on the proposed characteristics

	Interaction timing			Level of autonomy		Memory	
	Before	Real-Time	After	Deciding	Guiding	Retrospective	In-the-Moment
Planner	✔				✔	✔	
Advisor		✔			✔	✔	
Critic			✔		✔		✔
Companion		✔			✔		✔
Actor			✔	✔		✔	
Player	All			Both		Both	

The interaction timing for the Planner, Advisor, and Critic is based on the HAT Analysis Framework. This characteristic for the Companion and Actor were "real-time" and "after" per the presented definition for them (Companion cooperates with a human in real-time, and human can accept/reject the Actor's decision after the action). The Player agents are autonomous agents which are capable of performing as well as humans, so the authors decided not to restrict these characteristics to one level. The level of autonomy for all the types was "guiding" except for the Actor and Player, since they are the only types that can decide an action during the game without a human's intervention. In the Actor type, the teammates can accept/reject this decision, while in the Player type, the humans trust the agents completely. The memory characteristic level for each type was decided based on whether the agent has to remember previous game actions or not. For the Planner, Advisor, Actor, and Player types, the agents need to memorize previous interactions with human and environment, but for the Critic and Companion types, the agents can interact with the human based on information integrated within the agents' design without considering the previous actions. All mentioned characteristics were utilized to analyze one or two serious games for each type of agent, as described below.

3.1 Planner

The Planner is an instructional agent that **guides** the player by presenting the pros and cons of their actions **before** a player acts. In these games, the agents allow the players to make challenging decisions with the possibility of predicting the consequences of their actions by analyzing the considering the previous game actions (**retrospective**) (see Fig. 1).

Leemkuil and De Jong [24] used a critiquing advice agent in the form of an icon on top of the game screen to support players by giving warnings and hints. Previously, the same authors used a KM Quest game to improve the people's skill at knowledge management [25]. In this game, the player is a knowledge manager in a big company supposed to

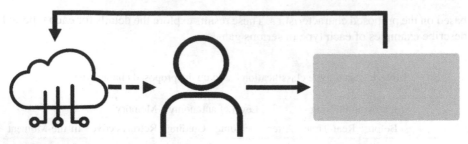

Fig. 1. Planner agent guides the human (dashed line), before action (the green box), and in a retrospective mode (the action noted by agent with straight line). (Color figure online)

improve the knowledge management process by optimizing the effective variables. When the player is not taking an appropriate direction in a knowledge management process, an icon above the screen (as an agent) starts blinking and warns the player of problems while presenting some hints about how to fix them.

Cooperation based on the tradeoff analysis by the Planner agents does not necessarily provide a specific solution for the teammates. Rather, the players are only aware of the pros and cons of their actions. Using this method is very useful in applications where the player challenges lead to the ultimate goal (for example, educational aspects that players can learn without having the final answer and by analyzing the available data). This method is not recommended for cases where an explicit answer is expected from the agent.

3.2 Advisor

This kind of agent tries to analyze the situation during the game (**retrospective**) and **guide** the players by evaluating if the player is in the right direction and then recommending the next human action (needs a **real-time** interaction with human). See Fig. 2. The main non-game use of these agents is to recommend products that a customer might want on the online store or make suggestions within other customer decision support systems [26]. However, the advisor has other applications in video games and virtual environments. For example, Rickel and Johnson [27] created the STEVE (Soar Training Expert for Virtual Environment) to offer the students individual coaching based on their previous actions within the domain of physical task. The studies related to MOBA (Multiplayer Online Battle Arena) games focused on character recommendation [28, 29] and item recommendation [30–32] so that players might choose the best team and best weapon items to succeed in battle. A good recommendation can not only help improve performance on a particular game but also smooth the learning curve [30].

Baker et al. [11] used an animated agent, Scooter the Tutor (designed from the Microsoft Office Assistant), to present a tutor that responded to a student's learning procedure by reacting to different scenarios with three different facial expressions. When the student is not gaming and focusing on learning, the agent looked happy, but the agent's behavior changed when the student is gaming without learning, even if they gave correct answers. Scooter presented two different unhappy face reactions to the distracted gaming conditions.

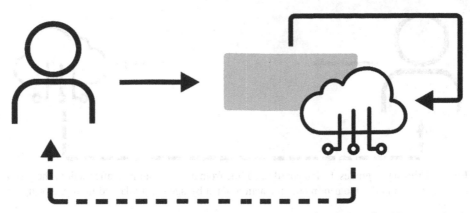

Fig. 2. Advisor agent guides the human (dashed line), in real-time interaction (the green box), and in a retrospective mode (the action noted by agent with straight line). (Color figure online)

There are multiple ways to train the advisor agents [33], but all these agents share the common functions of 1) evaluate the situation and then 2) make a recommendation. For evaluating the situation, an advisor agent needs to assess some previous actions (retrospective) while other in-the-moment agents just analyze the current state. This method is very similar to the real-world situation in which team members argue about the next action considering the previous history of actions rather than just focusing on the upcoming one. The downside of this approach is the time delay incurred by considering the previous actions. Therefore, the use of these agents is not recommended in cases where decision time plays a prominent role, such as co-piloting an airplane, in which a delayed error diagnosis could lead to unrecoverable consequences.

3.3 Critic

One of the widely used methods to **guide** humans in video games is by Critic agents. In this method, the player receives feedback about the action they have just taken. Feedback from an agent can have diverse forms such as text, speech, or sound effects. This type of agent does not need to follow the game process (**in-the-moment**); they wait for the player to act and then react appropriately (**after** the action) in different ways depending on its assessment of whether the player's action is right or wrong (see Fig. 3.). The type of Critic agents' reactions varies regarding multiple items. Assessment, audience, and privacy are three influential dimensions of feedback presented [34]. They consider that the feedback effectiveness would be changed according to being team vs. individual based, to whom the feedback is intended, and if the feedback is private or public. Johnson et al. [35] discussed critical characteristics that affect the efficacy of Critic agents for serious games and categorized them into three different groups: (1) whether the content of feedback messages is explanatory or true/false, (2) whether the modality in which feedback is presented is spoken or text, and (3) the timing of feedback presentation. The results of the studies showed that explanatory [5, 36], spoken [37, 38], and the sooner [39] form of feedback works better in serious games.

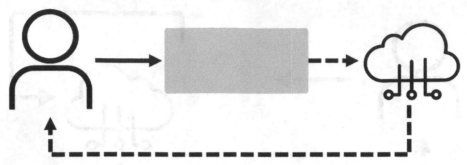

Fig. 3. Critic agent guides the human (dashed line from agent to human), after action (the green box), and in an in-the-moment mode (the action noted by agent with dashed line) (Color figure online)

Mayer and Johnson [5] used a Circuit Game to understand what type of feedback content works better in educational games. In this game, the players were supposed to choose which circuit has a higher current. After choosing the circuit by the player, an arrow and a text box near the correct answer would be displayed and explain why the previous choice is correct/incorrect. This is an example of Critic agents that interacts with players after the action, guide the players by presenting an explanation, and does not use any memory to evaluate tasks (in-the-moment).

Wik and Hjalmarsson [40] described the Ville platform and DEAL video game, containing an embodied conversational agent to improve student language. First, the student learned new words with the correct pronunciation by receiving guidance after pronouncing each new word in the Ville platform. Then, they were required to use new vocabulary to converse with an agent in a DEAL video game to prove they learned the new words.

Critic agents are instructional agents that interact with the human **after** the action. This type of interaction for applications such as education, in which the ultimate goal is teaching students and encouraging their reflection, can be very useful. However, like the advisor agent, the Critic agent is not suggested in special situations in which the interval between choosing a wrong action and failing a goal is short in time. For example, in a driving human-agent teaming context, if a human took an incorrect action, there might not be enough time for the agent to compensate for the error.

3.4 Companion

Companion agents are defined as software that interacts alongside the users in **real-time,** mostly through naturalistic cues, that is, cues that might appear in the real world (**guiding**). Nelson [41] considers this instructional method Reflective Guidance and defines it as providing tools to support the student's hypothesis generation and testing processes without necessarily offering direct answers or making judgments about particular student previous actions (**in-the-moment**) (see Fig. 4.). Since most of these agents use naturalistic cues to communicate with their teammates, the sense of real cooperation (human-to-human) is strong, but the agents do not perform any action without the human's permission. As technology enables agents attuned to more subtle communication cues, e.g., body language and gestures, Companion agents' guidance will likely expand beyond natural language.

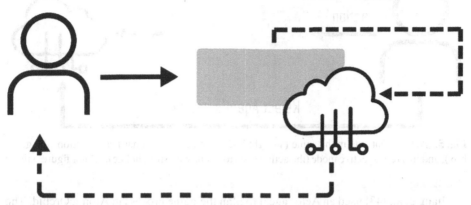

Fig. 4. Companion agent guides the human (dashed line from agent to human), in real time interaction action (the green box), and in an in-the-moment mode (the action noted by agent with dashed line). (Color figure online)

Van der Spek et al. [42] keep the player on the right learning path during a video game by using multiple cues. As an example, they used a Code Red Triage game in which the players learn how to prioritize the people who need medical attention. In this game, the agent provides naturalistic auditory cues like footsteps, snoring, fast breathing, and beating heart sounds to guide the player on which victim has what problems.

Companion and Advisor agents share many features. The Advisor agents analyze previous actions during the game and give real-time recommendations to their teammates. However, Companion agents report information about the games to the players, and there may be no recommendation for the player's action.

There are multiple ways to instruct players via companion agents, like changing color, adding text, verbal cues, and landmarks in different places of the games. The Companions agents may not be embodied. The rationale behind using this method is that sometimes the players may engage with irrelevant information or become overwhelmed with a large quantity of data [42]. In such cases, Companion agents can guide the player's attention to the relevant cues and required concepts and help the team members keep them in the right direction.

3.5 Actor

Actor agents work alongside the human and take actions without asking for the humans' permission in the game environment. Appropriate **deciding** comes from a good analysis of the game process, so the agents have to be aware of the game's process in the environment (**retrospective**). Though Actors have the higher LoA, other players usually do have the ability to veto the agent's decision, typically interacting **after** the action (see Fig. 5).

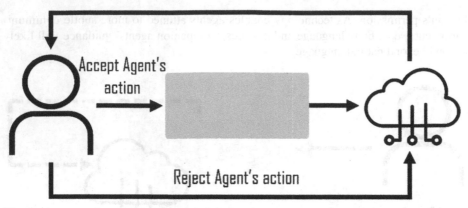

Fig. 5. Actor agent acts in the game (straight line from agent to human), after action (the green box), and in a retrospective mode (the action goes to agent with straight line). (Color figure online)

Jiang et al. [43] used an Actor agent to plan the game process in AtomicOrchid. The game's goal was rescuing the defined targets on the ground, and the agent's responsibility was to delegate different roles to the human players during the game. In the game there were multiple targets on the ground that should be rescued and taken to the drop-off zone before the clouds cover the game areas. In order to rescue every target, the agent receives the input information of the game (players' positions, the cloud cover's position, and other player's messages) and choose the players' roles for doing the task by sending messages to the players' in-game mobile application to optimize the number of rescue targets.

Goodman et al. [44] used the video game Space Navigator to understand the effect of automated task timing on the performance of a human-machine team in an air defense context. In this game, players connected spaceships to the appropriate planet by dragging lines. The role of the agents was to support the humans in drawing the most efficient lines.

Among the agent types described above, the Actor agent is the first type that can act (not just guide) in the game environment. The previous types could just guide their teammates, but the Actor agent instructs the human players by deciding actions which can be confirmed or rejected by the humans.

3.6 Player

The last categorization for instructional agents in serious games is reserved for agents that can emulate a player completely and have the power to perform all the actions that human players can. The intelligence of this kind of agent rises to the point where the agent decides independently based on its knowledge and operates in the game without human supervision. Due to the rapid rise in agents' technological capabilities, research efforts in the autonomous agent field have studied human-level communications between humans and agents. With a higher level of automation, agents might be play the role of the human's trusted teammate for real situations (**no restriction** for any of the characteristics) (see Fig. 6.).

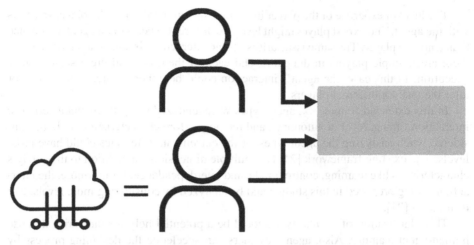

Fig. 6. Player agent and human are not different in doing the game tasks

McNeese et al. [45] experimented in an unmanned aerial context to make the autonomous agent a good teammate. In one of the conditions in this system, the role of the pilot was assigned to the virtual agent, which cooperated with two human teammates. Bishop et al. [46] used the Overcooked video game as a research platform to explore ways to improve human-autonomy teaming under chaotic conditions. The goal of this multi-player game is to complete as many food orders in a specific amount of time. The autonomous agent in this video game plays the role of one of the chefs in an instanced of a Wizard of Oz paradigm [47], in which a human experimenter control's the agent's behavior, another form of Player agent. Fully autonomous Player agents can be useful when task errors during teamwork can lead to life risks, when a teammate becomes unavailable, and when additional teammates might be useful.

4 Discussion and Conclusion

In this research, the authors extended the Human-Agent Game Analysis framework [21] by expanding the characteristics of agent types and applying them to serious instructional games. The results offered more detailed explanation for the categorization of agent types than previously described. For each agent type, one or two examples were provided, and the role of the agent was assessed in that game.

The Critic agent has a wide array of applications in different domains, especially in educational systems. Most educational technologies use a Critic agent as a virtual instructor in their application, possibly because of being more applicable to educational systems compared to the other types.

Player agents are the newest compared to the other types of agents. They are still evolving and under research [48] to optimize human-like characteristics such as reasoning, learning, planning, problem-solving, and perception. Player agents could be a good alternative for humans and offer lower costs in industry by reducing the cost of hiring human role players in training simulations.

The level of expertise of the player in a game may influence how the player interacts with the agent. The expert player might leverage different aspects of an agent's guidance than a novice player. The same issue arises for the interaction timing characteristic when there are multiple players in the game, and each of them is at different stage of task execution. In this case, the agent's interaction could be either before, in real-time, or after the task for different players.

In this extended framework, agent types were analyzed using three characteristics: interaction timing, level of autonomy, and memory. More characteristics could be considered when analyzing the agent types, or the current characteristics could have more levels. The existing framework [21] has multiple dimensions in addition to this study's characteristics like teaming, control mode, and interdependence. Furthermore, the interaction timing proposed in this study could be analyzed by considering more levels, like turn-based [21].

This clarification of agents' types could be a potential help for industries that use human-agent teaming. Also, agent designers can accelerate the designing process by getting familiar with the characteristics of every agent type (e.g., interaction timing, level of autonomy, memory). In future studies, analyzing the agents and validating the framework based on more characteristics can be considered.

Acknowledgements. Thanks to Harris Seabold for the creation of the figures in consultation with the authors.

References

1. Laird, J., VanLent, M.: Human-level AI's killer application: interactive computer games. AI Mag. **22**, 15 (2001). https://doi.org/10.1609/aimag.v22i2.1558
2. Ryu, H., Shin, H., Park, J.: Cooperative and competitive biases for multi-agent reinforcement learning. arXiv (2021). https://doi.org/10.48550/arXiv.2101.06890
3. Boulanger, C., et al.: Stroke rehabilitation with a sensing surface. In: Proceedings of the SIGCHI Conference on Human Factors in Computing Systems, New York, NY, USA, pp. 1243–1246. Association for Computing Machinery (2013). https://doi.org/10.1145/2470654.2466160
4. Jianqiang, D.S., Ma, X., Zhao, S., Khoo, J.T., Bay, S.L., Jiang, Z.: Farmer's tale: a facebook game to promote volunteerism. In: Proceedings of the SIGCHI Conference on Human Factors in Computing Systems, Vancouver, BC, Canada, pp. 581–584. ACM (2011). https://doi.org/10.1145/1978942.1979024
5. Mayer, R.E., Johnson, C.I.: Adding instructional features that promote learning in a game-like environment. J. Educ. Comput. Res. **42**, 241–265 (2010). https://doi.org/10.2190/EC.42.3.a
6. Lelardeux, C.P., Galaup, M., Panzoli, D., Lagarrigue, P., Jessel, J.-P.: A method to design a multi-player educational scenario to make interdisciplinary teams experiment risk management situation in a digital collaborative learning game: a case of study in healthcare. Int. J. Eng. Pedagogy **8**, 88–100 (2018)
7. Bell, B., Sottilare, R.: Adaptation vectors for instructional agents. In: Sottilare, R.A., Schwarz, J. (eds.) HCII 2019. LNCS, vol. 11597, pp. 3–14. Springer, Cham (2019). https://doi.org/10.1007/978-3-030-22341-0_1
8. Tutors, C.: Anderson, J.R., Corbett, A.T., Koedinger, K.R., Pelletier, Ray. Lessons Learned. J. Learn. Sci. **4**, 167–207 (1995). https://doi.org/10.1207/s15327809jls0402_2

9. Baylor, A.: Beyond butlers: intelligent agents as mentors. J. Educ. Comput. Res. **22**, 373–382 (2000)
10. Yang, X., Deng, L., Wei, P.: Multi-agent autonomous on-demand free flight operations in urban air mobility. In: AIAA Aviation 2019 Forum. American Institute of Aeronautics and Astronautics, Dallas, Texas (2019). https://doi.org/10.2514/6.2019-3520
11. Baker, R., et al.: Adapting to when students game an intelligent tutoring system. In: Ikeda, Mitsuru, Ashley, Kevin D., Chan, Tak-Wai. (eds.) ITS 2006. LNCS, vol. 4053, pp. 392–401. Springer, Heidelberg (2006). https://doi.org/10.1007/11774303_39
12. Chiou, E.K., Lee, J.D., Su, T.: Negotiated and reciprocal exchange structures in human-agent cooperation. Comput. Hum. Behav. **90**, 288–297 (2019). https://doi.org/10.1016/j.chb.2018. 08.012
13. Gee, J.P.: Good Video Games+ Good Learning: Collected Essays on Video Games, Learning, and Literacy. Peter Lang, New York (2007)
14. Hainey, T., et al.: Students' attitudes toward playing games and using games in education: comparing Scotland and the Netherlands. Comput. Educ. **69**, 474–484 (2013). https://doi.org/ 10.1016/j.compedu.2013.07.023
15. Tüzün, H., Yılmaz-Soylu, M., Karakuş, T., İnal, Y., Kızılkaya, G.: The effects of computer games on primary school students' achievement and motivation in geography learning. Comput. Educ. **52**, 68–77 (2009). https://doi.org/10.1016/j.compedu.2008.06.008
16. Bickmore, T.W., Pfeifer, L.M., Jack, B.W.: Taking the time to care: empowering low health literacy hospital patients with virtual nurse agents. In: Proceedings of the SIGCHI Conference on Human Factors in Computing Systems, New York, NY, USA, pp. 1265–1274. Association for Computing Machinery (2009). https://doi.org/10.1145/1518701.1518891
17. Chen, J.Y.C., Barnes, M.J.: Human-agent teaming for multirobot control: a review of human factors issues. IEEE Trans. Hum. Mach. Syst. **44**, 13–29 (2014). https://doi.org/10.1109/ THMS.2013.2293535
18. Susi, T., Johannesson, M., Backlund, P.: Serious games: an overview (2007)
19. Klien, G., Woods, D.D., Bradshaw, J.M., Hoffman, R.R., Feltovich, P.J.: Ten challenges for making automation a "team player" in joint human-agent activity. IEEE Intell. Syst. **19**, 91–95 (2004). https://doi.org/10.1109/MIS.2004.74
20. Neerincx, M.A., van der Waa, J., Kaptein, F., van Diggelen, J.: Using perceptual and cognitive explanations for enhanced human-agent team performance. In: Harris, D. (ed.) EPCE 2018. LNCS (LNAI), vol. 10906, pp. 204–214. Springer, Cham (2018). https://doi.org/10.1007/ 978-3-319-91122-9_18
21. Sepich, N., Dorneich, M.C., Gilbert, S.: Human-agent team game analysis framework: case studies. In: Proceedings of the Human Factors and Ergonomics Society Annual Meeting, vol. 65, pp. 1146–1150 (2021). https://doi.org/10.1177/1071181321651188
22. Tokadlı, G., Ouverson, K., Meusel, C., Garcia, A., Gilbert, S.B., Dorneich, M.C.: An analysis of video games using the dimensions of human-agent interaction. In: Proceedings of the Human Factors and Ergonomics Society Annual Meeting, pp. 716–720. SAGE Publications, Los Angeles (2018)
23. Vagia, M., Transeth, A.A., Fjerdingen, S.A.: A literature review on the levels of automation during the years. What are the different taxonomies that have been proposed? Appl. Ergon. **53**, 190–202 (2016). https://doi.org/10.1016/j.apergo.2015.09.013
24. Leemkuil, H., De Jong, T.O.N.: Adaptive advice in learning with a computer-based knowledge management simulation game. Acad. Manag. Learn. Educ. **11**, 653–665 (2012)
25. Leemkuil, H., De Jong, T., De Hoog, R., Christoph, N.: KM QUEST: a collaborative Internet-based simulation game. Simul. Gaming **34**, 89–111 (2003)
26. Komiak, S., Benbasat, I.: Abstract comparing persuasiveness of different recommendation agents as customer decision support systems in electronic commerce (2004)

27. Rickel, J., Johnson, W.L.: Animated agents for procedural training in virtual reality: perception, cognition, and motor control. Appl. Artif. Intell. **13**, 343–382 (1999)
28. Chen, Z., Amato, C., Nguyen, T.-H.D., Cooper, S., Sun, Y., El-Nasr, M.S.: Q-DeckRec: a fast deck recommendation system for collectible card games. In: 2018 IEEE Conference on Computational Intelligence and Games (CIG), pp. 1–8. IEEE (2018)
29. Hanke, L., Chaimowicz, L.: A recommender system for hero line-ups in MOBA games. In: Thirteenth Artificial Intelligence and Interactive Digital Entertainment Conference (2017)
30. Araujo, V., Rios, F., Parra, D.: Data mining for item recommendation in MOBA games. In: Proceedings of the 13th ACM Conference on Recommender Systems, pp. 393–397 (2019)
31. Looi, W., Dhaliwal, M., Alhajj, R., Rokne, J.: Recommender system for items in Dota 2. IEEE Trans. Games **11**, 396–404 (2018)
32. Villa, A., Araujo, V., Cattan, F., Parra, D.: Interpretable contextual team-aware item recommendation: application in multiplayer online battle arena games. In: Fourteenth ACM Conference on Recommender Systems, pp. 503–508 (2020)
33. Cheuque, G., Guzmán, J., Parra, D.: Recommender systems for online video game platforms: the case of steam. In: Companion Proceedings of the 2019 World Wide Web Conference, pp. 763–771 (2019)
34. Walton, J., Gilbert, S.B.: Evaluating the effect of displaying team vs. individual metrics on team performance. Int. J. Hum. Comput. Stud. **160**, 102759 (2022). https://doi.org/10.1016/j.ijhcs.2021.102759
35. Johnson, C.I., Bailey, S.K.T., Van Buskirk, W.L.: Designing effective feedback messages in serious games and simulations: a research review. In: Wouters, P., van Oostendorp, H. (eds.) Instructional Techniques to Facilitate Learning and Motivation of Serious Games. AGL, pp. 119–140. Springer, Cham (2017). https://doi.org/10.1007/978-3-319-39298-1_7
36. Moreno, R.: Decreasing cognitive load for novice students: effects of explanatory versus corrective feedback in discovery-based multimedia. Instr. Sci. **32**, 99–113 (2004)
37. Moreno, R., Mayer, R.E., Spires, H.A., Lester, J.C.: The case for social agency in computer-based teaching: do students learn more deeply when they interact with animated pedagogical agents? Cogn. Instr. **19**, 177–213 (2001). https://doi.org/10.1207/S1532690XCI1902_02
38. Fiorella, L., Vogel-Walcutt, J.J., Schatz, S.: Applying the modality principle to real-time feedback and the acquisition of higher-order cognitive skills. Educ. Technol. Res. Dev. **60**, 223–238 (2012). https://doi.org/10.1007/s11423-011-9218-1
39. Johnson, C.I., Priest, H.A., Glerum, D.R., Serge, S.R.: Timing of feedback delivery in game-based training. In: Proceedings of the Interservice/Industry Training, Simulation & Education Conference (2013)
40. Wik, P., Hjalmarsson, A.: Embodied conversational agents in computer assisted language learning. Speech Commun. **51**, 1024–1037 (2009)
41. Nelson, B.C.: Exploring the use of individualized, reflective guidance in an educational multi-user virtual environment. J. Sci. Educ. Technol. **16**, 83–97 (2007)
42. van der Spek, E.D., van Oostendorp, H., Wouters, P., Aarnoudse, L.: Attentional cueing in serious games. In: 2010 Second International Conference on Games and Virtual Worlds for Serious Applications, pp. 119–125 (2010). https://doi.org/10.1109/VS-GAMES.2010.8
43. Jiang, W., et al.: Social implications of agent-based planning support for human teams. In: 2014 International Conference on Collaboration Technologies and Systems (CTS), pp. 310–317. IEEE (2014)
44. Goodman, T., Miller, M.E., Rusnock, C.F., Bindewald, J.: Timing within human-agent interaction and its effects on team performance and human behavior. In: 2016 IEEE International Multi-disciplinary Conference on Cognitive Methods in Situation Awareness and Decision Support (CogSIMA), pp. 35–41. IEEE (2016)
45. McNeese, N.J., Demir, M., Cooke, N.J., Myers, C.: Teaming with a synthetic teammate: insights into human-autonomy teaming. Hum. Factors **60**, 262–273 (2018)

46. Bishop, J., et al.: CHAOPT: a testbed for evaluating human-autonomy team collaboration using the video game overcooked! 2. In: 2020 Systems and Information Engineering Design Symposium (SIEDS), pp. 1–6. IEEE (2020)
47. Kelley, J.F.: An empirical methodology for writing user-friendly natural language computer applications. In: Proceedings of the SIGCHI Conference on Human Factors in Computing Systems, New York, NY, USA, pp. 193–196. Association for Computing Machinery (1983). https://doi.org/10.1145/800045.801609
48. Rieth, M., Hagemann, V.: Automation as an equal team player for humans? – A view into the field and implications for research and practice. Appl. Ergon. **98**, 103552 (2022). https://doi.org/10.1016/j.apergo.2021.103552

Persona Finetuning for Online Gaming Using Personalisation Techniques

Dimitris Spiliotopoulos[1]([mail]) [iD], Dionisis Margaris[2] [iD], Kostas N. Koutrakis[2] [iD],
Panos I. Philippopoulos[2] [iD], and Costas Vassilakis[3] [iD]

[1] Department of Management Science and Technology, University of the Peloponnese, Tripoli,
Greece
dspiliot@uop.gr
[2] Department of Digital Systems, University of the Peloponnese, Sparta, Greece
{margaris,koutrakis,p.filippopoulos}@uop.gr
[3] Department of Informatics and Telecommunications, University of the Peloponnese, Tripoli,
Greece
costas@uop.gr

Abstract. Automatic persona generation has been shown to have specific measurable benefits for application creators and users. In most situations, personas
are adequately descriptive and diversified to achieve user type accuracy and coverage. For specific market segments, such as online gaming, using personas may
accurately describe existing user base but not changing habit and need that are
introduced by the fluidity of the offerings and the delivery methods. Changes in the
ways that applications are marketed, such as new payment methods, for example,
subscription models, pay-to-play and pay-to-win, payment-driven-gamification,
seriously affect user needs and result in direct impact on user acceptance. This
work utilises structured user needs from online gaming players to augment
personas using personalisation techniques. The personas are finetuned and de-
diversified to result in concise personas, based on user needs that successfully
convey information for creators and users alike.

Keywords: Persona · Online gaming · Diversification · Personalisation ·
Data-driven methods · Collaborative filtering · User study · Usability evaluation

1 Introduction

Data-driven automatic persona generation leverages data analysis and human insight and
can be used for digital marketing personalisation [1]. Digital marketing user segments are
constantly evolving, based on several factors, ranging from pandemics or other extreme
non marketing related events, to the introduction and adoption of disruptive technologies,
leading to innovative offerings, such as online music or the metaverse [2]. An illustrative
example is online gaming, a domain that hosts thousands of users, applications/games,
teams, and communities [3]. The complexity of the types of users in online gaming
depends on several dimensions that include behavioural and psychographic variables
[4].

© Springer Nature Switzerland AG 2022
G. Meiselwitz et al. (Eds.): HCII 2022, LNCS 13517, pp. 656–668, 2022.
https://doi.org/10.1007/978-3-031-22131-6_48

Online games can be clearly categorised according to genre, based on single or multiple parameters that represent aspects of gaming, as formulated by the designers. Social interaction is a major dimension that is used to classify online games, such as Massively-Multiplayer Online Role-Playing Games (MMORPGs) [5]. Effectively, online games may refer to multiple genres. However, they are commonly identified by a major genre and supplementally by one or two additional secondary genres. The genres are constructed on the basis of gaming dimensions that include technical factors such as achievement, social and immersion [6].

Depending on the dimensions, online games attract several types of players. The goal is to trigger and sustain the players' purchase motivation, which can depend on social interaction (I and my friends or co-players buy content to play together or in teams), unobstructed play (buy time or barrier lifts and progress through paywalls), and economical (investing in an entertaining activity, when pricing is judged to be reasonable) benefit [7].

Personas are user archetypes that are used to describe the user base for application, services and products [8]. In the era of big data, data-driven persona development utilised statistical analysis of data to create personas as a fast and accurate that corresponded to the quantified data [9]. Through the years, persona research shifted from data-driven quantification to digitalisation that uses a multitude of methods to model behavioural characteristics and interactivity into the personas [10].

Data-driven persona generation may accurately capture aspects that can be technically assessed at a point in time [11]. However, they may fail to sustain faithful descriptors due to inherent shortcomings, such as the persona diversification techniques [12]. A critical issue for online gaming, and online apps in general, are the new or shifting categories of applications that target multiple personas on specific aspects that cannot be quantified, such as the "respect of the user's time" and "pay once and play", which can also have specific effects on users [13].

The emerging categories refer to user needs or meta game genres that can be found in game reviews. Those are created by gamers and reviewers. For example, the term "gacha" refers to games that are designed to induce players to spend in-game currency to gain a relatively small chance to acquire game items. The need for a dedicated category name for gacha games was due to the fact that the nature of the game monetisation was an overarching descriptive factor that included several genres or other categories. This has also resulted in the formulation of other relevant categories, such as the "no in-app purchases", that describe the opposite game category. This is the result of expressing direct user needs that encompass other game preferences or needs, traditionally described by personas.

All the above indicate that personas may be descriptive enough to account for traditional user types, however emerging needs may require persona finetuning or even clustering to overarching personas, to accurately present the user types for online gaming.

This work explores how personas can be finetuned by users using real user needs that are pivotal to persona generation, such as gacha methods or no-ads preferences. The first research hypothesis (RH1) is that personalisation techniques can be used to create non-diversified personas that would potentially be used to mark seemingly minor user needs as important, through aggregation or collaborative filtering [14–16]. The second research hypothesis (RH2) is that users may successfully identify candidate personas and finetune them based on the marked user needs that would have been hidden, otherwise.

The rest of this paper is structured as follows: Sect. 2 introduces the related work in personas for online gaming, while Sect. 3 overviews the fundamental personalisation methods that are appropriate for this work. Section 4 describes the user study, that is the study setup and the experimental results. Finally, Sect. 5 concludes the paper and outlines the future work.

2 Personas in Online Gaming

Personas are used in user-centred game design to establish user narratives and marketing strategies during the design and development of games to model user behaviour [17]. Moreover, personas are useful for the monitoring and evaluation of user behavioural patterns during the experience with the games [18]. Personas have been an important tool for traditional marketing analysis experts and it has become even more crucial to business data analytics personalisation [19].

Surveys on game preference can be deployed to adequate numbers of players to collect data that can be used to generate player personas [20]. Surveys collect both standard user demographic information, as well as personal preferences and needs. Apart from the qualitative methods, quantitative and mixed methods are used to create or enhance personas, each to their own merit [21].

Personas can be matched to game types for targeted marketing and monetisation decisions [22]. Personas are the amalgamation of user needs and games characteristics, requiring user behaviour research and quantitative analysis or the collected user data [23]. However, depending on the game type, certain aspect of the user base may be biased or under-represented [24].

Data-driven personas can be constructed fast and with relative accuracy, since they utilise existing data from application stores, such as user standard demographic data and user entered reviews [25]. Automatic persona generation from large datasets can lead to a very high number of personas, depending on the generation method that is applied. Accordingly, this requires appropriate techniques to reduce the number of personas [26]. For instance, hierarchical clustering can be applied to the generated non-final personas to create a manageable number of representative personas [27].

By design, data-driven personas may include a lot of information that is hard to formally evaluate through users, since the templates provide the structured means to create the persona but do not offer a trustworthy method to assess and evaluate the data [28]. Therefore, data-driven personas would not be easy to curate for user experience evaluation of real-time applications using standard usability metrics [29]. Evaluation becomes more complex in situations where personas are generated from both standard data and high level user interaction information [30].

The above become more apparent when the data that are collected for persona construction is unstructured and informally collected, as in the case of social media [31]. Social media data aggregation for persona generation is a method that requires collection, analysis and processing of social media data, creating a real time representation of the user population [32]. It can be used to create and update personas as the pool of data can be augmented by additional sources or additional data at a future time [33]. Persona analytics is key to modelling personas by understanding how users interact with personas, thereby founding a basis on which to evaluate the complexity and accuracy to real life user types of personas [34].

Personas can be further enriched by automatically or semi-automatically selecting trivial information to eject and impactful information to insert to the generated personas [35]. Persona enrichment with non-standard descriptors may be very useful for marketing products that require user behaviour descriptions [36]. Social media contains implicit information regarding user behaviours as well as explicit user needs as expressed by user opinions, reviews and comments [37]. Social media data can be used to process standard demographics and segment customer types based on product parameters and market analysis [38]. In this case, persona evaluation becomes a study in complexity, since the human evaluator is faced with a mix of artificially generated data, such as pictures [39], automatically collected standard user demographic data, and post-processed information from various sources of user interaction from linguistically rich environments [40].

3 Personalisation

Personalisation is a research field that has attracted numerous research works over the last years. Rhee and Choi [41] explore the product recommendation persuasion mechanism produced by a conversational agent and examine the importance of types of social roles to the shopping of items using voice. They design an experimental study to test the effects of friends' role of a voice agent with low and high item involvement, as well as personalised content that reflected the users' preferences for item characteristics. The results show an important interaction effect for the social involvement and role. Xiao et al. [42] introduce a personalization model that explores higher-order friends in a social media to support recommendation of content. In the exploration and model designs, they consider the effects for both consumers and content creators in the social network platform. As a result, the platform can be benefited to encourage additional interactions between clients and creators, as well as attract more innovative content creators. Park et al. [43] introduce a personalised social learning companion system which modulates children's engagement and maximize their long-term learning gains, by using nonverbal and verbal affective cues. They present a reinforcement learning method which, for each student during an educational activity, trains a personalised policy. Aivazoglou et al. [44] introduce a social ecosystems fine-grained recommender system, which recommends media content (online clips, music videos, etc.) published by friends of the users. The design was based on the findings of a qualitative user study, which investigate both the requirements and the value of a recommendation component within a social media. The core idea of the recommender system is to create interest profiles, to calculate similarity scores between social media users at a fine-grained level. Metz et al. [45] explore both the consequences and use of self-personalisation on the Facebook social media platform. A content analysis of posts from politicians reveals that they often use self-personalisation, as a communication style, which is often presented in visual communication. They show that the use of a more private and emotional style benefits impression management. Furthermore, by suggesting the demands of the audiences for more emotional and intimate impressions of public figures, positive effects on audience engagement are achieved.

User classification and user clustering are important aspects of personalisation. Ferrari et al. [46] define a validation model to assess the performance of machine learning personalisation algorithms. They also assess the public datasets of a personalisation model, taking into account both the aspect of the physical similarity between people (height, weight, age, etc.) and the activity-based similarity aspect (based on the signals produced by people when performing). Last, they develop a personalisation model that takes into account both the aforementioned similarities.

Rajawat et al. [47] present a personalisation model for user preference, based on the Semi Supervised Support Vector Machines (S3VM) concept and apply it to online newspaper information, targeting at classification and recommendation improvement. They achieve an increase of the behaviour prediction performance and information classification, when compared with techniques using traditional machine learning algorithms. Margaris et al. [48] introduce a personalisation algorithm with clustering for recommending web services, to realise tailoring of business process execution. To produce recommendations, their algorithm takes into account the QoS values and functionality of the services, QoS weights and limits defined by the users, and the business processes past the execution history. Furthermore, they use a similarity metric in their collaborative filtering process, which extends the ones used in related works by considering both the QoS attributes' closeness and functionality resemblance. Last, the presented algorithm employs a clustering scheme that achieves both to improve recommendation time and leverage scalability.

Shamrat et al. [49] introduce a system which, out of all people registered, presents the suitable ones for a job. It helps job seekers, relate to the notification, and find jobs efficiently. More specifically, only the candidates that match the job title, expected experience and salary, based on their profile, get an email notification for the job. The system uses a decision tree which checks the data through a set of conditions, where their fulfilment determines whether a candidate is suitable for a job or not. Vijayalakshmi and Jena [49] present a web search approach based on the individual clustering and classification method. Their approach classifies the cluster data using multilevel association rules for recurring relationship and frequent pattern mining, and cluster the web usage using hierarchical methods with the personalisation user interest and navigating site. Furthermore, that approach supports real time personalisation and maximises the personalisation resource cost reduction.

Online gaming personalisation is a field that has attracted considerable research attention over the recent years. Naudet et al. [50] present and analyse experimental results obtained towards museum visit personalisation using a personal mobile guide, as well as an approach based on social networks gaming, user cognitive style and recommendations. The presented personalisation system is based on a Facebook game to infer the users' visiting and cognitive styles and interests, and a recommendation algorithm offering sequences of points of interests for a visitor to visit. Harteveld and Sutherland [51] present and analyse the need to personalise gamified research environments in order to motivate participation, by illustrating a playful platform, which allows users to create behavioural and social studies. Their work both contributes to theory-informed approaches to gamified personalisation technologies, as well as contributes to existing theories on player motivation. Raptis et al. [52] explore the interplay among cultural heritage gaming activities and human cognitive differences, towards visual behaviour and player performance. They conduct user studies under the field dependence/independence theory, which underpin cognitive differences in handling contextual of information and visual perception. Their findings provide useful insights for both researchers and practitioners, aiming at designing playful cultural activities based on the users' cognitive preferences. Jamil et al. [53] discuss the influence of the age and gender factors on user performance in gaming environments. They investigate the user performance on commonly used tasks (typing, pointing and clicking) using a gaming prototype, in controlled laboratory experiments. The user performance is analysed using multiple statistical methods. Significant differences between male and female participants are observed during interaction with the computer, similar to the ones found in the spectrum of age groups.

4 User Study

4.1 Experiment Setup

This paper reports on the user study of 44 computer science literate participants (68% male and 32% female) that are adept to online/mobile gaming. All participants were recruited from the university undergraduate and postgraduate course, though a departmental open call. The participant selection was based on the online gaming self-reported engagement. The participants that were recruited reported to have been engaging in online games (mobile or other) for at least five hours per week during the last three months, on average.

The facilitators collected the participants' player information. The player information included user and gaming data. Gaming data were collected through lists that the users submitted in their application. The user information included standard user data, as well as structured user needs. The user needs were collected through questionnaires that the users were asked to complete within seven days. The users were asked to fill in information regarding their experience with online games, their needs and fulfilment level, and their desired characteristics for their future gaming endeavours.

The participants were asked to validate automatically generated personas for the twenty most used games, as aggregated from the lists that the users provided as part of the experiment setup. No other artificially generated data regarding persona enrichment, such as pictures and gender categories, were used.

Collaborative filtering and user aggregation [54–57] were used to create user near neighbours, based on both data and needs. Two user representations were constructed, one using the standard user data as primary category points and one using the user needs as primary points. The participants were presented with the generated personas in a random order and were asked to evaluate them in terms of congruency (the level of correspondence to the users), transparency (the level of understandability of the information) and usefulness [58]. The participants could accept-as-is, accept-and-finetune (using either user representation data or both), or reject the personas. The accepted and finetuned personas were then aggregated, to merge duplicates or very similar personas, calculating the quantified percentage of information from the user needs and the standard user data between the finetuned and the accepted/rejected personas.

4.2 Results

The users reported a high number of persona rejection due to missing information on user needs, rendering the personas ineffective. On average, only 7% of the automatically generated personas were accepted without the need for augmentation by the majority of the participants (>50% of the participants). On the other hand, 27% of the personas were rejected by the majority of the participants (>50% of the participants).

Figure 1 depicts the evaluation results on the acceptance of the personas by the participants, based on four factors: congruency, transparency, usefulness, and overall acceptance. The participants rated each persona using the Likert scale 1 to 7 (low-high). The user representation sources were hidden from the participants to ensure unbiased evaluation.

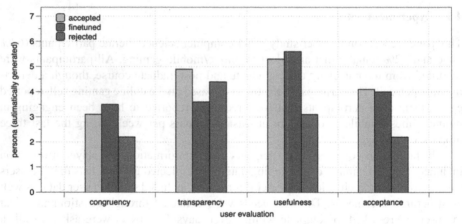

Fig. 1. User evaluation of automatically generated personas. Personas were either accepted as they were, accepted as candidate for finetuning, or rejected.

The users were then asked to finetune at least three personas of their choice, each, out of the pool of the personas deemed appropriate for finetuning. Peer review was used for the re-evaluation of the finetuned personas. Two random users (excluding the users that finetuned the persona) were asked to evaluate the finetuned personas.

Figure 2 depicts the user evaluation outcome of the personas finetuned by the users using the information collected from the user needs against the originally accepted-as-is personas from the first evaluation round. The participants reported that the finetuned personas rated higher than the accept-as-is personas. Especially for congruency, the evaluation result average for the finetunes personas was significantly higher. This may be partially explained by the overall low rating (3.1 on the scale) average of the accepted personas.

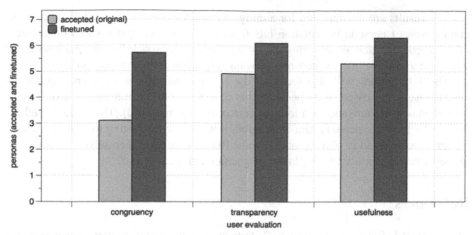

Fig. 2. User evaluation of the finetuned personas using the proposed method against the originally accepted automatically generated personas.

RH 1 was found true to a significant extent. The users reported to have successful and very positive results in finetuning using the data from the user needs representation (78% of the users). Additionally, user data were useful for validation and transparency verification, when used in conjunction with the user needs (49% of the finetuned personas).

RH2 was found to be true. The 11 personas finetuned by the users were aggregated to 5 (automatically) and down to 4 (collectively, by the users). The users reported that this was an equivalent approach to de-diversification based on explainable user need information, present in the finetuned personas.

Achieving representative personas that directly respond to user needs would be very beneficial to providers to understand potentially business and user base harming practices and decide on mitigation actions [59].

5 Conclusion and Future Work

This work reported on a user study that examined the level of which automatically generated personas based on user needs and standard user information are complete and fully accepted by real users. It also examined whether personas can be manually finetuned with low labour cost, when potentially important content can be recommended to users for use in the finetuning process.

The information that was presented to the participants was aggregated using personalisation methods. This method of content recommendation was also useful for persona aggregation, enabling the participants to aggregate personas based on important information, ensuring the sustainment of critical descriptors during the manual process.

The results from this study indicate that automatically generated personas can be contextually analysed for enhancement. Essentially, persona descriptors can be checked against information highlighted through personalisation methods to allow potential enhancement.

The results are encouraging for aiming to research toward a model for automatic comparison of persona information bits from recommender systems and other data-driven methods, such as clustering. A semi-automatic approach for persona finetuning would be useful for fast and accurate persona validation and enhancement.

The future work will also focus on the longitudinal effects of online gaming to specific user types based on the personas that describe them. The ultimate marketing use of personas is monetisation via long-term user engagement [60]. Therefore, based on the results from the persona data correlation, it would be interesting to examine which personas correspond to players that are most likely to commit themselves to long term money spending, or even be exploited by gacha mechanics [61, 62].

References

1. Jansen, B.J., Salminen, J.O., Jung, S.-G.: Data-driven personas for enhanced user understanding: combining empathy with rationality for better insights to analytics. Data Inf. Manage. **4**, 1–17 (2020). https://doi.org/10.2478/dim-2020-0005
2. Xu, Y., Lee, M.J.: Identifying personas in online shopping communities. MTI. **4**, 19 (2020). https://doi.org/10.3390/mti4020019
3. Goodman, W., McFerran, E., Purves, R., Redpath, I., Beeken, R.J.: The untapped potential of the gaming community: narrative review. JMIR Serious Game. **6**, e10161 (2018). https://doi.org/10.2196/10161
4. Hamari, J., Tuunanen, J.: Player types: a meta-synthesis. ToDIGRA. 1 (2014). https://doi.org/10.26503/todigra.v1i2.13
5. Granic, I., Lobel, A., Engels, R.C.M.E.: The benefits of playing video games. Am. Psychol. **69**, 66–78 (2014). https://doi.org/10.1037/a0034857
6. Yee, N.: Motivations for play in online games. Cyberpsychol. Behav. **9**, 772–775 (2006). https://doi.org/10.1089/cpb.2006.9.772
7. Hamari, J., Alha, K., Järvelä, S., Kivikangas, J.M., Koivisto, J., Paavilainen, J.: Why do players buy in-game content? An empirical study on concrete purchase motivations. Comput. Hum. Behav. **68**, 538–546 (2017). https://doi.org/10.1016/j.chb.2016.11.045
8. Nielsen, L, Nielsen, K.S., Stage, J., Billestrup, J.: Going Global with Personas In: Kotzé, P., Marsden, G., Lindgaard, G., Wesson, J., Winckler, M. (eds.) Human-Computer Interaction – INTERACT 2013. Lecture Notes in Computer Science, vol. 8120, pp. 123–133. Springer, Heidelberg (2019).https://doi.org/10.1007/978-1-4471-7427-1_7
9. McGinn, J., Kotamraju, N.: Data-driven persona development. In: Proceeding of the Twenty-Sixth Annual CHI Conference on Human Factors In Computing Systems - CHI 2008, p. 1521. ACM Press, Florence, Italy (2008). https://doi.org/10.1145/1357054.1357292
10. Salminen, J., Guan, K., Jung, S.-G., Jansen, B.J.: A survey of 15 years of data-driven persona development. Int. J. Hum.-Comput. Interact. **37**, 1685–1708 (2021). https://doi.org/10.1080/10447318.2021.1908670
11. Salminen, J.O., Jung, S., Jansen, B.J.: Are data-driven personas considered harmful?: Diversifying user understandings with more than algorithms. Pers. Stud. **7**, 48–63 (2021). https://doi.org/10.21153/psj2021vol7no1art1236
12. Salminen, J., Jansen, B.J., An, J., Kwak, H., Jung, S.-G.: Automatic persona generation for online content creators: conceptual rationale and a research agenda. In: Personas - User Focused Design. Human–Computer Interaction Series, pp. 135–160. Springer London (2019).https://doi.org/10.1007/978-1-4471-7427-1_8

13. Shibuya, A., Teramoto, M., Shoun, A., Akiyama, K.: Long-term effects of in-game purchases and event game mechanics on young mobile social game players in Japan. Simul. Gaming **50**, 76–92 (2019). https://doi.org/10.1177/1046878118819677

14. Xu, Z., Dukes, A.: Personalization from customer data aggregation using list price. Manage. Sci. **68**, 960–980 (2022). https://doi.org/10.1287/mnsc.2021.3977

15. Margaris, D., Spiliotopoulos, D., Vassilakis, C.: Social relations versus near neighbours: reliable recommenders in limited information social network collaborative filtering for online advertising. In: Proceedings of the 2019 IEEE/ACM International Conference on Advances in Social Networks Analysis and Mining, pp. 1160–1167. ACM, Vancouver British Columbia Canada (2019). https://doi.org/10.1145/3341161.3345620

16. Kluver, D., Ekstrand, M.D., Konstan, J.A.: Rating-Based Collaborative Filtering: Algorithms and Evaluation. In: Brusilovsky, P., He, D. (eds.) Social Information Access. LNCS, vol. 10100, pp. 344–390. Springer, Cham (2018). https://doi.org/10.1007/978-3-319-90092-6_10

17. Tychsen, A., Canossa, A.: Defining personas in games using metrics. In: Proceedings of the 2008 Conference on Future Play Research, Play, Share - Future Play 2008, p. 73. ACM Press, Toronto, Ontario, Canada (2008). https://doi.org/10.1145/1496984.1496997

18. Canossa, A., Drachen, A.: Play-Personas: Behaviours and Belief Systems in User-Centred Game Design. In: Gross, T., et al. (eds.) INTERACT 2009. LNCS, vol. 5727, pp. 510–523. Springer, Heidelberg (2009). https://doi.org/10.1007/978-3-642-03658-3_55

19. Amyrotos, C., Andreou, P., Germanakos, P.: Human-centred persona driven personalization in business data analytics. In: Adjunct Proceedings of the 29th ACM Conference on User Modeling, Adaptation and Personalization, pp. 175–180. ACM, Utrecht Netherlands (2021). https://doi.org/10.1145/3450614.3462241

20. Salminen, J., Vahlo, J., Koponen, A., Jung, S.-G., Chowdhury, S.A., Jansen, B.J.: Designing prototype player personas from a game preference survey. In: Extended Abstracts of the 2020 CHI Conference on Human Factors in Computing Systems, pp. 1–8. ACM, Honolulu HI USA (2020). https://doi.org/10.1145/3334480.3382785

21. Jansen, B.J., Jung, S.-G., Salminen, J., Guan, K.W., Nielsen, L.: Strengths and weaknesses of persona creation methods: guidelines and opportunities for digital innovations. In: Presented at the Hawaii International Conference on System Sciences (2021). https://doi.org/10.24251/HICSS.2021.604

22. Vahlo, J., Koponen, A.: Player personas and game choice. In: Lee, N. (ed.) Encyclopedia of Computer Graphics and Games, pp. 1–6. Springer, Cham (2018). https://doi.org/10.1007/978-3-319-08234-9_149-1

23. Zhang, X., Jia, Z., Jia, S.: User research and persona building method in mobile games. J. Phys.: Conf. Ser. **1168**, 032043 (2019). https://doi.org/10.1088/1742-6596/1168/3/032043

24. Rogstad, E.T.: Gender in eSports research: a literature review. Eur. J. Sport Soc. **19**, 1–19 (2021). https://doi.org/10.1080/16138171.2021.1930941

25. Park, D., Kang, J.: Constructing data-driven personas through an analysis of mobile application store data. Appl. Sci. **12**, 2869 (2022). https://doi.org/10.3390/app12062869

26. Jansen, B.J., Jung, S., Salminen, J.: Creating manageable persona sets from large user populations. In: Extended Abstracts of the 2019 CHI Conference on Human Factors in Computing Systems, pp. 1–6. ACM, Glasgow Scotland UK (2019). https://doi.org/10.1145/3290607.3313006

27. Zhang, X., Brown, H.-F., Shankar, A.: Data-driven personas: constructing archetypal users with clickstreams and user telemetry. In: Proceedings of the 2016 CHI Conference on Human Factors in Computing Systems, pp. 5350–5359. ACM, San Jose California USA (2016). https://doi.org/10.1145/2858036.2858523

28. Salminen, J., Guan, K., Nielsen, L., Jung, S.-G., Jansen, B.J.: A Template for Data-Driven Personas: Analyzing 31 Quantitatively Oriented Persona Profiles. In: Yamamoto, S., Mori,

H. (eds.) HCII 2020. LNCS, vol. 12184, pp. 125–144. Springer, Cham (2020). https://doi.org/10.1007/978-3-030-50020-7_8

29. Kouroupetroglou, G., Spiliotopoulos, D.: Usability methodologies for real-life voice user interfaces: Int. J. Inf. Technol. Web Eng. **4**, 78–94 (2009).https://doi.org/10.4018/jitwe.2009100105

30. Zhang, G.: Creating Enhanced User Experience Through Persona and Interactive Design: A Case of Designing a Motion Sensing Game. In: Marcus, A., Wang, W. (eds.) HCII 2019. LNCS, vol. 11583, pp. 382–394. Springer, Cham (2019). https://doi.org/10.1007/978-3-030-23570-3_28

31. An, J., Cho, H., Kwak, H., Hassen, M.Z., Jansen, B.J.: Towards automatic persona generation using social media. In: 2016 IEEE 4th International Conference on Future Internet of Things and Cloud Workshops (FiCloudW), pp. 206–211. IEEE, Vienna, Austria (2016). https://doi.org/10.1109/W-FiCloud.2016.51

32. Jung, S.-G., An, J., Kwak, H., Ahmad, M., Nielsen, L., Jansen, B.J.: Persona generation from aggregated social media data. In: Proceedings of the 2017 CHI Conference Extended Abstracts on Human Factors in Computing Systems, pp. 1748–1755. ACM, Denver Colorado USA (2017). https://doi.org/10.1145/3027063.3053120

33. Salminen, J., Jung, S., Jansen, B.: The future of data-driven personas: a marriage of online analytics numbers and human attributes: In: Proceedings of the 21st International Conference on Enterprise Information Systems, pp. 608–615. SCITEPRESS - Science and Technology Publications, Heraklion, Crete, Greece (2019). https://doi.org/10.5220/0007744706080615

34. Salminen, J., Jung, S.-G., Jansen, B.: Developing persona analytics towards persona science. In: 27th International Conference on Intelligent User Interfaces, pp. 323–344. ACM, Helsinki Finland (2022). https://doi.org/10.1145/3490099.3511144

35. Spiliotopoulos, D., Margaris, D., Vassilakis, C.: Data-assisted persona construction using social media data. BDCC. **4**, 21 (2020). https://doi.org/10.3390/bdcc4030021

36. Watanabe, Y., et al.: Retrospective based on data-driven persona significance in B-to-B software development. In: Proceedings of the 40th International Conference on Software Engineering: New Ideas and Emerging Results, pp. 89–92. ACM, Gothenburg Sweden (2018). https://doi.org/10.1145/3183399.3183410

37. An, J., Kwak, H., Jung, S., Salminen, J., Admad, M., Jansen, B.: Imaginary people representing real numbers: generating personas from online social media data. ACM Trans. Web. **12**, 1–26 (2018). https://doi.org/10.1145/3265986

38. An, J., Kwak, H., Jansen, B.J.: Validating social media data for automatic persona generation. In: 2016 IEEE/ACS 13th International Conference of Computer Systems and Applications (AICCSA), pp. 1–6. IEEE, Agadir, Morocco (2016). https://doi.org/10.1109/AICCSA.2016.7945816

39. Salminen, J., Jung, S., Kamel, A.M.S., Santos, J.M., Jansen, B.J.: Using artificially generated pictures in customer-facing systems: an evaluation study with data-driven personas. Behav. Inf. Technol. **41**, 905–921 (2022). https://doi.org/10.1080/0144929X.2020.1838610

40. Xydas, G., Spiliotopoulos, D., Kouroupetroglou, G.: Modeling Prosodic Structures in Linguistically Enriched Environments. In: Sojka, P., Kopeček, I., Pala, K. (eds.) TSD 2004. LNCS (LNAI), vol. 3206, pp. 521–528. Springer, Heidelberg (2004). https://doi.org/10.1007/978-3-540-30120-2_66

41. Rhee, C.E., Choi, J.: Effects of personalization and social role in voice shopping: an experimental study on product recommendation by a conversational voice agent. Comput. Hum. Behav. **109**, 106359 (2020). https://doi.org/10.1016/j.chb.2020.106359

42. Xiao, W., Zhao, H., Pan, H., Song, Y., Zheng, V.W., Yang, Q.: Beyond personalization: social content recommendation for creator equality and consumer satisfaction. In: Proceedings of the 25th ACM SIGKDD International Conference on Knowledge Discovery & Data Mining, pp. 235–245. ACM, Anchorage AK USA (2019). https://doi.org/10.1145/3292500.3330965

43. Park, H.W., Grover, I., Spaulding, S., Gomez, L., Breazeal, C.: A model-free affective rein-forcement learning approach to personalization of an autonomous social robot companion for early literacy education. AAAI. **33**, 687–694 (2019). https://doi.org/10.1609/aaai.v33i01.330 1687

44. Aivazoglou, M., et al.: A fine-grained social network recommender system. Soc. Netw. Anal. Min. **10**(1), 1–18 (2019). https://doi.org/10.1007/s13278-019-0621-7

45. Metz, M., Kruikemeier, S., Lecheler, S.: Personalization of politics on Facebook: examin-ing the content and effects of professional, emotional and private self-personalization. Inf. Commun. Soc. **23**, 1481–1498 (2020). https://doi.org/10.1080/1369118X.2019.1581244

46. Ferrari, A., Micucci, D., Mobilio, M., Napoletano, P.: On the personalization of classification models for human activity recognition. IEEE Access. **8**, 32066–32079 (2020). https://doi.org/10.1109/ACCESS.2020.2973425

47. Rajawat, A.S., Upadhyay, A.R.: Web personalization model using modified S3VM algorithm for developing recommendation process. In: 2nd International Conference on Data, Engineer-ing and Applications (IDEA). pp. 1–6. IEEE, Bhopal, India (2020). https://doi.org/10.1109/IDEA49133.2020.9170701

48. Margaris, D., Georgiadis, P., Vassilakis, C.: A collaborative filtering algorithm with clustering for personalized web service selection in business processes. In: 2015 IEEE 9th International Conference on Research Challenges in Information Science (RCIS), pp. 169–180. IEEE, Athens, Greece (2015). https://doi.org/10.1109/RCIS.2015.7128877

49. Javed Mehedi Shamrat, F.M., Tasnim, Z., Ghosh, P., Majumder, A., Hasan, Md.Z.: Personal-ization of job circular announcement to applicants using decision tree classification algorithm. In: 2020 IEEE International Conference for Innovation in Technology (INOCON), pp. 1–5. IEEE, Bangluru, India (2020). https://doi.org/10.1109/INOCON50539.2020.9298253

50. Naudet, Y., Antoniou, A., Lykourentzou, I., Tobias, E., Rompa, J., Lepouras, G.: Museum personalization based on gaming and cognitive styles: the BLUE experiment. Int. J. Virtual Communities Soc. Networking. **7**, 1–30 (2015). https://doi.org/10.4018/IJVCSN.2015040101

51. Harteveld, C., Sutherland, S.C.: Personalized gaming for motivating social and behavioral science participation. In: Proceedings of the 2017 ACM Workshop on Theory-Informed User Modeling for Tailoring and Personalizing Interfaces, pp. 31–38. ACM, Limassol Cyprus (2017). https://doi.org/10.1145/3039677.3039681

52. Raptis, G.E., Fidas, C., Avouris, N.: Cultural heritage gaming: effects of human cognitive styles on players' performance and visual behavior. In: Adjunct Publication of the 25th Con-ference on User Modeling, Adaptation and Personalization, pp. 343–346. ACM, Bratislava Slovakia (2017). https://doi.org/10.1145/3099023.3099090

53. Jamil, A., Nadeem Faisal, C.M., Habib, M.A., Jabbar, S., Ahmad, H.: Analyzing the Impact of Age and Gender on User Interaction in Gaming Environment. In: Khanna, A., Gupta, D., Bhattacharyya, S., Snasel, V., Platos, J., Hassanien, A.E. (eds.) International Conference on Innovative Computing and Communications. AISC, vol. 1087, pp. 721–729. Springer, Singapore (2020). https://doi.org/10.1007/978-981-15-1286-5_64

54. Barbiero, A., Blasi, S., Schwidtal, J.M.: The Impact of End-User Aggregation on the Electric-ity Business Ecosystem: Evidence from Europe. In: Sedita, S.R., Blasi, S. (eds.) Rethinking Clusters. SDGS, pp. 213–226. Springer, Cham (2021). https://doi.org/10.1007/978-3-030-61923-7_15

55. Shi, L., Song, G., Cheng, G., Liu, X.: A user-based aggregation topic model for understanding user's preference and intention in social network. Neurocomputing **413**, 1–13 (2020). https://doi.org/10.1016/j.neucom.2020.06.099

56. Margaris, D., Kobusinska, A., Spiliotopoulos, D., Vassilakis, C.: An adaptive social network-aware collaborative filtering algorithm for improved rating prediction accuracy. IEEE Access. **8**, 68301–68310 (2020). https://doi.org/10.1109/ACCESS.2020.2981567

57. Cui, Z., et al.: Personalized recommendation system based on collaborative filtering for IoT scenarios. IEEE Trans. Serv. Comput. **13**, 685–695 (2020). https://doi.org/10.1109/TSC.2020.2964552

58. Salminen, J., Santos, J.M., Jung, S.-G., Eslami, M., Jansen, B.J.: Persona transparency: analyzing the impact of explanations on perceptions of data-driven personas. Int. J. Hum.-Comput. Interact. **36**, 788–800 (2020). https://doi.org/10.1080/10447318.2019.1688946

59. Salminen, J., Jung, S.-G., Chowdhury, S., Robillos, D.R., Jansen, B.: The ability of personas: an empirical evaluation of altering incorrect preconceptions about users. Int. J. Hum Comput Stud. **153**, 102645 (2021). https://doi.org/10.1016/j.ijhcs.2021.102645

60. Petrovskaya, E., Zendle, D.: Predatory monetisation? A categorisation of unfair, misleading and aggressive monetisation techniques in digital games from the player perspective. J Bus Ethics.1–17 (2021).https://doi.org/10.1007/s10551-021-04970-6

61. King, D.L., Delfabbro, P.H., Gainsbury, S.M., Dreier, M., Greer, N., Billieux, J.: Unfair play? Video games as exploitative monetized services: an examination of game patents from a consumer protection perspective. Comput. Hum. Behav. **101**, 131–143 (2019). https://doi.org/10.1016/j.chb.2019.07.017

62. Close, J., Spicer, S.G., Nicklin, L.L., Uther, M., Lloyd, J., Lloyd, H.: Secondary analysis of loot box data: are high-spending "whales" wealthy gamers or problem gamblers? Addict. Behav. **117**, 106851 (2021). https://doi.org/10.1016/j.addbeh.2021.106851